REA's Test Prep B̶o̶o̶k̶s̶ ...!

(a sample of the <u>hundreds of letters</u> REA receives each year)

(more on next page)

(continued from front page)

" I just wanted to thank you for helping me get a great score
on the AP U.S. History exam... Thank you for making great test preps! "
Student, Los Angeles, CA

" Your *Fundamentals of Engineering Exam* book was the absolute best
preparation I could have had for the exam, and it is one of the major
reasons I did so well and passed the FE on my first try. "
Student, Sweetwater, TN

" I used your book to prepare for the test and found that the advice and the
sample tests were highly relevant... Without using any other material, I earned
very high scores and will be going to the graduate school of my choice. "
Student, New Orleans, LA

" What I found in your book was a wealth of information sufficient to shore up
my basic skills in math and verbal... The section on analytical ability was
excellent. The practice tests were challenging and the answer explanations most
helpful. It certainly is the *Best Test Prep for the GRE*! "
Student, Pullman, WA

" I really appreciate the help from your excellent book. Please keep up
the great work. "
Student, Albuquerque, NM

" I am writing to thank you for your test preparation... your book helped me
immeasurably and I have nothing but praise for your *GRE* preparation."
Student, Benton Harbor, MI

GRE® PSYCHOLOGY TEST

 TestWare® Edition

Robert T. Kellogg, Ph.D.
Chair and Professor of Psychology
Saint Louis University, St. Louis, MO

Richard Pisacreta, Ph.D.
Professor of Psychology
Ferris Sate University, Big Rapids, MI

Research & Education Association
Visit our website: www.rea.com
GRE Test Updates: www.rea.com/GRE

Research & Education Association

61 Ethel Road West
Piscataway, New Jersey 08854
E-mail: info@rea.com

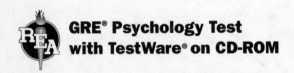

GRE® Psychology Test
with TestWare® on CD-ROM

Printed in the United States of America

Library of Congress Control Number: 2010920084

ISBN 13: 978-0-7386-0839-6
ISBN 10: 0-7386-0839-4

CONTENTS

GRE PSYCHOLOGY PRACTICE TESTS

ABOUT THIS BOOK AND TestWare®

This book and our accompanying GRE Psychology TestWare® software have been developed to effectively prepare you for the GRE Psychology Test. Included are six complete practice tests based on the most recent test administrations. Each test is 2 hours and 50 minutes in length, with every type of question you can expect to encounter on the GRE Psychology Test.

The book's Practice Tests 4, 5, and 6 are also on CD-ROM as part of REA's exclusive interactive GRE Psychology TestWare® package. The software provides timed conditions and instantaneous, accurate scoring, which makes it all the easier to pinpoint your strenghts and weaknesses. For your convenience, our interactive GRE Psychology TestWare® has been provided in Windows format. Our program calculates both raw and scaled scores fo reach test and subscore area, and detailed explanations are provided for every question. Instructions on how to install our software can be found on page 580.

By completing all six tests and studying the explanations that follow, you will put yourself in the best possible position to master the GRE Psychology Test.

ABOUT THE TEST

The GRE Psychology Test is given three times a year by Educational Testing Service under policies set by the Graduate Record Examinations Board, an independent board affiliated with the Association of Graduate Schools and the Council of Graduate Schools. Graduate school applicants submit GRE test results together with their undergraduate records as part of a highly competitive admissions.

The questions for the test are written by a committee of specialists who are selected from various undergraduate and graduate faculties. The test consists of *approximately* 205 multiple-choice questions that are designed to measure a student's knowledge and understanding of principles, theories, and concepts in the broad field of psychology. The questions are taken from the courses of study most commonly offered in an undergraduate psychology curriculum.

The content of the test is divided into three areas. **Social- or social science-oriented** (about 43% of the test) questions are concerned with developmental, personality, abnormal, clinical, and social psychology. **Experimental or natural-science-oriented** (about 40% of the test) questions are concerned with sensation, physiology, learning, cognition, and perception. **General** (about 17% of the test) questions draw on your knowledge of historical applied psychology as well as measurement, statistics, and research designs.

There are three separate scores:
- A total score based on all questions.
- A subscore* for social psychology questions only.
- A subscore* for experimental psychology questions only.

*The questions from which the subscores are calculated are not labeled separately and are distributed throughout the entire test.

GRE PSYCHOLOGY PRO STUDY PLAN

Making the Most of REA's 12-Week Pro Study Plan

As a busy student or professional, you may be wondering how you will find time to work, have a social life, take care of family obligations, and prepare for the GRE Psychology Subject Test. But don't worry, our GRE Pro Study Plan gives you a complete road map from now until test day. This flexible schedule allows you to work at your own pace and shows you how to prepare for the GRE Psychology Test as efficiently as possible. You'll get organized, stay on track, and make the most of your valuable study time.

You will need to make time *every day* to study for the GRE Psychology Test. How and when you study is up to you, but consistency is the key to completing your GRE preparation. Make studying a priority and consider it a "job" until you take the GRE exam.

Keep in mind that a high score on the GRE doesn't just help you get into a better grad school; it helps move your career forward. Therefore, a solid commitment to daily study is worth every minute of your time. The results will pay off in the long run!

This study schedule will help you become thoroughly prepared for the GRE Psychology. Although the schedule is designed as a 6-week study program, it can be compressed into a 3-week plan by combining two weeks of study into one. If you choose the 6-week schedule, you should plan to study for *at least* one hour a day. GRE examinees who are following a 3-week program need to set aside *at least* two hours for studying every day.

Find a study routine that works for you and stick to it! Some people like to get up early and study for an hour or two before going to work. Others might choose to study while commuting, on their lunch hour, at the library, or at home after work. Whatever schedule you choose, make a commitment to study every day – even on weekends. Remember, daily focused concentration on the GRE subject matter will help you retain more information, fully grasp the material tested, and improve your overall GRE score.

This GRE test prep with TestWare® offers you additional practice and reinforcement. We've included six practice tests in the book, and three of these practice tests appear on our interactive, easy-to-use CD. The TestWare® CD offers diagnostic feedback, on-screen detailed answer explanations, and timed testing conditions, so you can "practice for real" and know what to expect on the GRE Psychology before exam day.

The CD comes with step-by-step installation instructions and a tutorial that explains how to answer the practice test questions. No matter what your technological skill level, you will benefit from taking our exams on CD. It's a great way for you to practice your test-taking skills while mastering the GRE subject matter.

Week	Activity
1	Read our introduction to the GRE Psychology Subject Test. Be sure you understand the format and know exactly what is tested on the exam. Start your study routine by taking Practice Test 4 on CD to determine your strengths and weaknesses and to become familiar with the format of the test. Give yourself at least several hours after work, on a weekend, or at another convenient time to take the exam. You will need to concentrate, so take the practice test at a time and place where you will not be disturbed. After you have finished the test, record your scores. This will help you track your progress as you study. Later in the week, study the detailed explanations for the questions you answered incorrectly. In the cases where you erred, find out why. Take notes and pay attention to sections where you missed a lot of questions.
2	Make a firm commitment to study for at least an hour a day, every day for the next few weeks. It may seem hard to find time in your busy schedule, but remember: the more you study, the better prepared you will be for the GRE Psychology. Take Practice Test 1 in the book. Record your score and see how well you did. Study the detailed explanations of answers for any questions you answered incorrectly. Later this week, read through our glossary of 2,000 Psychology terms. Master this comprehensive list of must-know vocabulary, and you'll boost your score! Read a few sections of the glossary each day and take note of any phrases or definitions that are unfamiliar to you. If you find yourself in need of clarification on a topic, you may want to consult your textbook or ask a classmate or professor for additional help.
3	Congratulations! You've reached the halfway point! Success is just around the corner, but keep going, there's more work to be done. It's time to take Practice Test 2. By now you should be familiar with the format and content of the GRE Psychology, so take your time and read each question carefully before you choose your answer. Grade your practice test and see how well you did. Later this week, study the detailed explanations of answers for any questions you answered incorrectly. Make sure you understand why you answered the question wrong, so you can improve your test-taking skills. Continue quizzing yourself on the vocabulary terms throughout the week for added study.
4	Your hard work is paying off! By the time you've finished studying for the GRE Psychology, you'll have an excellent understanding of the material tested on the exam – and that will help you get a high score. This week, take Practice Test 3 in the book. As with the previous practice tests, record your score and note any areas in which you missed a lot of questions. Study the answer explanations to these questions and make sure you understand the material. Now would be the perfect time to review any questions you answered incorrectly on the previous practice tests. If you feel you need extra GRE vocabulary practice, why not study the glossary during your lunch hour or on your commute?

Week	Activity
5	Are you ready for even more practice? It's time to take Practice Test 5. After a day or two of additional study to reinforce any areas of weakness, take Practice Test 5 on CD. Allow yourself several hours to take the test in a quiet location. Remember what you've learned and answer every question to the best of your ability. After the test, thoroughly review all the explanations for the question you answered incorrectly. Remember, your primary goal right now is to get a high score on the GRE, so keep working!
6	You have just about reached your goal! After a day or two of additional study to reinforce any areas of weakness, take Practice Test 6 on CD. Remember what you've learned and answer every question to the best of your ability. How much has your score improved since you took the first practice exam? Study the detailed answer explanations for any questions you got wrong. In a few days, review your notes and test yourself on the vocabulary terms in our glossary. Now is a great time to retake the practice tests to help you boost your skills. Take Practice Test 4 again on CD again. After you've completed the exam, compare your two scores and see how much you've improved in just a matter of weeks!

**Congratulations! You've worked hard and you're ready
for the GRE Psychology Subject Test!**

How to score your practice tests

Obtain your total score by adding all your correct answers and
then deducting one-quarter of a point for every incorrect answer.
This gives you your total raw score. Use our score conversion
table on page 581 to figure your total scaled score.

IMPORTANT GRE PSYCHOLOGY REVIEW TOPICS

Here are the key subject areas covered on the GRE Psychology Test. Items on the test are pegged at the same level of difficulty as one would find in at typical undergraduate psychology course.

GENERAL
History
Industrial-Organizational
Educational

MEASUREMENT AND METHODOLOGY
Psychometrics, Test Construction,
 Reliability, Validity
Research Designs
Statistical Method and the Evaluation
 of Evidence
Ethics
Analysis and Interpretation of Findings

LEARNING
Classical Conditioning
Instrumental Conditioning
Observational Learning, Modeling
Theories, Applications, and Issues

THINKING
Representation (Catagorization, Imagery,
 Schemas, Scripts)
Problem Solving
Judgment, Decision-Making Processes
Planning, Metacognition
Intelligence
Theories, Applications, and Issues

SENSATION AND PERCEPTION
Psychophysics, Signal Detection
Attention
Perception Organization
Vision
Audition
Gustation
Olfaction
Somatosenses
Theories, Applications, and Issues

MEMORY
Working Memory
Long-Term Memory
Types of Memory
Memory Systems and Processes
Theories, Applications, and Issues

LANGUAGE
Units (phonemes, morphemes, phrases)
Syntax
Meaning
Speech Perception and Processing
Reading Processes
Verbal and Nonverbal Communication
Bilingualism
Theories, Applications, and Issues

PHYSIOLOGICAL
Neurons
Sensory Structures and Processes
Motor Structures and Functions

Central Structures and Processes
Motivational, Arousal, Emotion
States of Consciousness
Neuromodulators and Drugs
Hormonal Factors
Comparative and Ethology
Theories, Applications, and Issues

CLINICAL AND ABNORMAL
Stress, Conflict, and Coping
Diagnostic Systems
Causes and Development of Disorders
Neurophysiological Factors
Treatment of Disorders
Epidemiology
Prevention
Health Psychology
Cultural or Gender Issues
Theories, Applications, and Issues

LIFESPAN DEVELOPMENT
Nature-Nurture
Perception, Cognition, Memory, Social Cognition
Language
Learning, Intelligence
Social, Personality
Emotion
Socialization, Family and Cultural Influences
Theories, Applications, and Issues

PERSONALITY
Theories
Structure
Assessment
Personality and Behavior
Applications and Issues

SOCIAL
Social Perception, Cognition, Attribution, Beliefs
Attitudes and Behavior
Social Comparison, Self
Emotion and Affect
Influence and Persuasion
Interpersonal Attraction and Close Relationships
Group and Intergroup Processes
Cultural or Gender Influences
Evolutionary Psychology, Altruism, and Aggression
Theories, Applications, and Issues

Further information on the GRE Psychology Test is available by contacting:

GRE-ETS
P.O. Box 6000
Princeton, NJ 08541-6000
Phone: (866) 473-4373 or (609)771-7670
TTY: (609) 771-7714
Website: *www.ets.org*

The Graduate Record Examination in

PSYCHOLOGY

Test 1

THE GRADUATE RECORD EXAMINATION
PSYCHOLOGY TEST 1
ANSWER SHEET

1. Ⓐ Ⓑ Ⓒ Ⓓ Ⓔ
2. Ⓐ Ⓑ Ⓒ Ⓓ Ⓔ
3. Ⓐ Ⓑ Ⓒ Ⓓ Ⓔ
4. Ⓐ Ⓑ Ⓒ Ⓓ Ⓔ
5. Ⓐ Ⓑ Ⓒ Ⓓ Ⓔ
6. Ⓐ Ⓑ Ⓒ Ⓓ Ⓔ
7. Ⓐ Ⓑ Ⓒ Ⓓ Ⓔ
8. Ⓐ Ⓑ Ⓒ Ⓓ Ⓔ
9. Ⓐ Ⓑ Ⓒ Ⓓ Ⓔ
10. Ⓐ Ⓑ Ⓒ Ⓓ Ⓔ
11. Ⓐ Ⓑ Ⓒ Ⓓ Ⓔ
12. Ⓐ Ⓑ Ⓒ Ⓓ Ⓔ
13. Ⓐ Ⓑ Ⓒ Ⓓ Ⓔ
14. Ⓐ Ⓑ Ⓒ Ⓓ Ⓔ
15. Ⓐ Ⓑ Ⓒ Ⓓ Ⓔ
16. Ⓐ Ⓑ Ⓒ Ⓓ Ⓔ
17. Ⓐ Ⓑ Ⓒ Ⓓ Ⓔ
18. Ⓐ Ⓑ Ⓒ Ⓓ Ⓔ
19. Ⓐ Ⓑ Ⓒ Ⓓ Ⓔ
20. Ⓐ Ⓑ Ⓒ Ⓓ Ⓔ
21. Ⓐ Ⓑ Ⓒ Ⓓ Ⓔ
22. Ⓐ Ⓑ Ⓒ Ⓓ Ⓔ
23. Ⓐ Ⓑ Ⓒ Ⓓ Ⓔ
24. Ⓐ Ⓑ Ⓒ Ⓓ Ⓔ
25. Ⓐ Ⓑ Ⓒ Ⓓ Ⓔ
26. Ⓐ Ⓑ Ⓒ Ⓓ Ⓔ
27. Ⓐ Ⓑ Ⓒ Ⓓ Ⓔ
28. Ⓐ Ⓑ Ⓒ Ⓓ Ⓔ
29. Ⓐ Ⓑ Ⓒ Ⓓ Ⓔ
30. Ⓐ Ⓑ Ⓒ Ⓓ Ⓔ
31. Ⓐ Ⓑ Ⓒ Ⓓ Ⓔ
32. Ⓐ Ⓑ Ⓒ Ⓓ Ⓔ
33. Ⓐ Ⓑ Ⓒ Ⓓ Ⓔ

34. Ⓐ Ⓑ Ⓒ Ⓓ Ⓔ
35. Ⓐ Ⓑ Ⓒ Ⓓ Ⓔ
36. Ⓐ Ⓑ Ⓒ Ⓓ Ⓔ
37. Ⓐ Ⓑ Ⓒ Ⓓ Ⓔ
38. Ⓐ Ⓑ Ⓒ Ⓓ Ⓔ
39. Ⓐ Ⓑ Ⓒ Ⓓ Ⓔ
40. Ⓐ Ⓑ Ⓒ Ⓓ Ⓔ
41. Ⓐ Ⓑ Ⓒ Ⓓ Ⓔ
42. Ⓐ Ⓑ Ⓒ Ⓓ Ⓔ
43. Ⓐ Ⓑ Ⓒ Ⓓ Ⓔ
44. Ⓐ Ⓑ Ⓒ Ⓓ Ⓔ
45. Ⓐ Ⓑ Ⓒ Ⓓ Ⓔ
46. Ⓐ Ⓑ Ⓒ Ⓓ Ⓔ
47. Ⓐ Ⓑ Ⓒ Ⓓ Ⓔ
48. Ⓐ Ⓑ Ⓒ Ⓓ Ⓔ
49. Ⓐ Ⓑ Ⓒ Ⓓ Ⓔ
50. Ⓐ Ⓑ Ⓒ Ⓓ Ⓔ
51. Ⓐ Ⓑ Ⓒ Ⓓ Ⓔ
52. Ⓐ Ⓑ Ⓒ Ⓓ Ⓔ
53. Ⓐ Ⓑ Ⓒ Ⓓ Ⓔ
54. Ⓐ Ⓑ Ⓒ Ⓓ Ⓔ
55. Ⓐ Ⓑ Ⓒ Ⓓ Ⓔ
56. Ⓐ Ⓑ Ⓒ Ⓓ Ⓔ
57. Ⓐ Ⓑ Ⓒ Ⓓ Ⓔ
58. Ⓐ Ⓑ Ⓒ Ⓓ Ⓔ
59. Ⓐ Ⓑ Ⓒ Ⓓ Ⓔ
60. Ⓐ Ⓑ Ⓒ Ⓓ Ⓔ
61. Ⓐ Ⓑ Ⓒ Ⓓ Ⓔ
62. Ⓐ Ⓑ Ⓒ Ⓓ Ⓔ
63. Ⓐ Ⓑ Ⓒ Ⓓ Ⓔ
64. Ⓐ Ⓑ Ⓒ Ⓓ Ⓔ
65. Ⓐ Ⓑ Ⓒ Ⓓ Ⓔ
66. Ⓐ Ⓑ Ⓒ Ⓓ Ⓔ

67. Ⓐ Ⓑ Ⓒ Ⓓ Ⓔ
68. Ⓐ Ⓑ Ⓒ Ⓓ Ⓔ
69. Ⓐ Ⓑ Ⓒ Ⓓ Ⓔ
70. Ⓐ Ⓑ Ⓒ Ⓓ Ⓔ
71. Ⓐ Ⓑ Ⓒ Ⓓ Ⓔ
72. Ⓐ Ⓑ Ⓒ Ⓓ Ⓔ
73. Ⓐ Ⓑ Ⓒ Ⓓ Ⓔ
74. Ⓐ Ⓑ Ⓒ Ⓓ Ⓔ
75. Ⓐ Ⓑ Ⓒ Ⓓ Ⓔ
76. Ⓐ Ⓑ Ⓒ Ⓓ Ⓔ
77. Ⓐ Ⓑ Ⓒ Ⓓ Ⓔ
78. Ⓐ Ⓑ Ⓒ Ⓓ Ⓔ
79. Ⓐ Ⓑ Ⓒ Ⓓ Ⓔ
80. Ⓐ Ⓑ Ⓒ Ⓓ Ⓔ
81. Ⓐ Ⓑ Ⓒ Ⓓ Ⓔ
82. Ⓐ Ⓑ Ⓒ Ⓓ Ⓔ
83. Ⓐ Ⓑ Ⓒ Ⓓ Ⓔ
84. Ⓐ Ⓑ Ⓒ Ⓓ Ⓔ
85. Ⓐ Ⓑ Ⓒ Ⓓ Ⓔ
86. Ⓐ Ⓑ Ⓒ Ⓓ Ⓔ
87. Ⓐ Ⓑ Ⓒ Ⓓ Ⓔ
88. Ⓐ Ⓑ Ⓒ Ⓓ Ⓔ
89. Ⓐ Ⓑ Ⓒ Ⓓ Ⓔ
90. Ⓐ Ⓑ Ⓒ Ⓓ Ⓔ
91. Ⓐ Ⓑ Ⓒ Ⓓ Ⓔ
92. Ⓐ Ⓑ Ⓒ Ⓓ Ⓔ
93. Ⓐ Ⓑ Ⓒ Ⓓ Ⓔ
94. Ⓐ Ⓑ Ⓒ Ⓓ Ⓔ
95. Ⓐ Ⓑ Ⓒ Ⓓ Ⓔ
96. Ⓐ Ⓑ Ⓒ Ⓓ Ⓔ
97. Ⓐ Ⓑ Ⓒ Ⓓ Ⓔ
98. Ⓐ Ⓑ Ⓒ Ⓓ Ⓔ
99. Ⓐ Ⓑ Ⓒ Ⓓ Ⓔ

100. Ⓐ Ⓑ Ⓒ Ⓓ Ⓔ	140. Ⓐ Ⓑ Ⓒ Ⓓ Ⓔ	180. Ⓐ Ⓑ Ⓒ Ⓓ Ⓔ
101. Ⓐ Ⓑ Ⓒ Ⓓ Ⓔ	141. Ⓐ Ⓑ Ⓒ Ⓓ Ⓔ	181. Ⓐ Ⓑ Ⓒ Ⓓ Ⓔ
102. Ⓐ Ⓑ Ⓒ Ⓓ Ⓔ	142. Ⓐ Ⓑ Ⓒ Ⓓ Ⓔ	182. Ⓐ Ⓑ Ⓒ Ⓓ Ⓔ
103. Ⓐ Ⓑ Ⓒ Ⓓ Ⓔ	143. Ⓐ Ⓑ Ⓒ Ⓓ Ⓔ	183. Ⓐ Ⓑ Ⓒ Ⓓ Ⓔ
104. Ⓐ Ⓑ Ⓒ Ⓓ Ⓔ	144. Ⓐ Ⓑ Ⓒ Ⓓ Ⓔ	184. Ⓐ Ⓑ Ⓒ Ⓓ Ⓔ
105. Ⓐ Ⓑ Ⓒ Ⓓ Ⓔ	145. Ⓐ Ⓑ Ⓒ Ⓓ Ⓔ	185. Ⓐ Ⓑ Ⓒ Ⓓ Ⓔ
106. Ⓐ Ⓑ Ⓒ Ⓓ Ⓔ	146. Ⓐ Ⓑ Ⓒ Ⓓ Ⓔ	186. Ⓐ Ⓑ Ⓒ Ⓓ Ⓔ
107. Ⓐ Ⓑ Ⓒ Ⓓ Ⓔ	147. Ⓐ Ⓑ Ⓒ Ⓓ Ⓔ	187. Ⓐ Ⓑ Ⓒ Ⓓ Ⓔ
108. Ⓐ Ⓑ Ⓒ Ⓓ Ⓔ	148. Ⓐ Ⓑ Ⓒ Ⓓ Ⓔ	188. Ⓐ Ⓑ Ⓒ Ⓓ Ⓔ
109. Ⓐ Ⓑ Ⓒ Ⓓ Ⓔ	149. Ⓐ Ⓑ Ⓒ Ⓓ Ⓔ	189. Ⓐ Ⓑ Ⓒ Ⓓ Ⓔ
110. Ⓐ Ⓑ Ⓒ Ⓓ Ⓔ	150. Ⓐ Ⓑ Ⓒ Ⓓ Ⓔ	190. Ⓐ Ⓑ Ⓒ Ⓓ Ⓔ
111. Ⓐ Ⓑ Ⓒ Ⓓ Ⓔ	151. Ⓐ Ⓑ Ⓒ Ⓓ Ⓔ	191. Ⓐ Ⓑ Ⓒ Ⓓ Ⓔ
112. Ⓐ Ⓑ Ⓒ Ⓓ Ⓔ	152. Ⓐ Ⓑ Ⓒ Ⓓ Ⓔ	192. Ⓐ Ⓑ Ⓒ Ⓓ Ⓔ
113. Ⓐ Ⓑ Ⓒ Ⓓ Ⓔ	153. Ⓐ Ⓑ Ⓒ Ⓓ Ⓔ	193. Ⓐ Ⓑ Ⓒ Ⓓ Ⓔ
114. Ⓐ Ⓑ Ⓒ Ⓓ Ⓔ	154. Ⓐ Ⓑ Ⓒ Ⓓ Ⓔ	194. Ⓐ Ⓑ Ⓒ Ⓓ Ⓔ
115. Ⓐ Ⓑ Ⓒ Ⓓ Ⓔ	155. Ⓐ Ⓑ Ⓒ Ⓓ Ⓔ	195. Ⓐ Ⓑ Ⓒ Ⓓ Ⓔ
116. Ⓐ Ⓑ Ⓒ Ⓓ Ⓔ	156. Ⓐ Ⓑ Ⓒ Ⓓ Ⓔ	196. Ⓐ Ⓑ Ⓒ Ⓓ Ⓔ
117. Ⓐ Ⓑ Ⓒ Ⓓ Ⓔ	157. Ⓐ Ⓑ Ⓒ Ⓓ Ⓔ	197. Ⓐ Ⓑ Ⓒ Ⓓ Ⓔ
118. Ⓐ Ⓑ Ⓒ Ⓓ Ⓔ	158. Ⓐ Ⓑ Ⓒ Ⓓ Ⓔ	198. Ⓐ Ⓑ Ⓒ Ⓓ Ⓔ
119. Ⓐ Ⓑ Ⓒ Ⓓ Ⓔ	159. Ⓐ Ⓑ Ⓒ Ⓓ Ⓔ	199. Ⓐ Ⓑ Ⓒ Ⓓ Ⓔ
120. Ⓐ Ⓑ Ⓒ Ⓓ Ⓔ	160. Ⓐ Ⓑ Ⓒ Ⓓ Ⓔ	200. Ⓐ Ⓑ Ⓒ Ⓓ Ⓔ
121. Ⓐ Ⓑ Ⓒ Ⓓ Ⓔ	161. Ⓐ Ⓑ Ⓒ Ⓓ Ⓔ	201. Ⓐ Ⓑ Ⓒ Ⓓ Ⓔ
122. Ⓐ Ⓑ Ⓒ Ⓓ Ⓔ	162. Ⓐ Ⓑ Ⓒ Ⓓ Ⓔ	202. Ⓐ Ⓑ Ⓒ Ⓓ Ⓔ
123. Ⓐ Ⓑ Ⓒ Ⓓ Ⓔ	163. Ⓐ Ⓑ Ⓒ Ⓓ Ⓔ	203. Ⓐ Ⓑ Ⓒ Ⓓ Ⓔ
124. Ⓐ Ⓑ Ⓒ Ⓓ Ⓔ	164. Ⓐ Ⓑ Ⓒ Ⓓ Ⓔ	204. Ⓐ Ⓑ Ⓒ Ⓓ Ⓔ
125. Ⓐ Ⓑ Ⓒ Ⓓ Ⓔ	165. Ⓐ Ⓑ Ⓒ Ⓓ Ⓔ	205. Ⓐ Ⓑ Ⓒ Ⓓ Ⓔ
126. Ⓐ Ⓑ Ⓒ Ⓓ Ⓔ	166. Ⓐ Ⓑ Ⓒ Ⓓ Ⓔ	206. Ⓐ Ⓑ Ⓒ Ⓓ Ⓔ
127. Ⓐ Ⓑ Ⓒ Ⓓ Ⓔ	167. Ⓐ Ⓑ Ⓒ Ⓓ Ⓔ	207. Ⓐ Ⓑ Ⓒ Ⓓ Ⓔ
128. Ⓐ Ⓑ Ⓒ Ⓓ Ⓔ	168. Ⓐ Ⓑ Ⓒ Ⓓ Ⓔ	208. Ⓐ Ⓑ Ⓒ Ⓓ Ⓔ
129. Ⓐ Ⓑ Ⓒ Ⓓ Ⓔ	169. Ⓐ Ⓑ Ⓒ Ⓓ Ⓔ	209. Ⓐ Ⓑ Ⓒ Ⓓ Ⓔ
130. Ⓐ Ⓑ Ⓒ Ⓓ Ⓔ	170. Ⓐ Ⓑ Ⓒ Ⓓ Ⓔ	210. Ⓐ Ⓑ Ⓒ Ⓓ Ⓔ
131. Ⓐ Ⓑ Ⓒ Ⓓ Ⓔ	171. Ⓐ Ⓑ Ⓒ Ⓓ Ⓔ	211. Ⓐ Ⓑ Ⓒ Ⓓ Ⓔ
132. Ⓐ Ⓑ Ⓒ Ⓓ Ⓔ	172. Ⓐ Ⓑ Ⓒ Ⓓ Ⓔ	212. Ⓐ Ⓑ Ⓒ Ⓓ Ⓔ
133. Ⓐ Ⓑ Ⓒ Ⓓ Ⓔ	173. Ⓐ Ⓑ Ⓒ Ⓓ Ⓔ	213. Ⓐ Ⓑ Ⓒ Ⓓ Ⓔ
134. Ⓐ Ⓑ Ⓒ Ⓓ Ⓔ	174. Ⓐ Ⓑ Ⓒ Ⓓ Ⓔ	214. Ⓐ Ⓑ Ⓒ Ⓓ Ⓔ
135. Ⓐ Ⓑ Ⓒ Ⓓ Ⓔ	175. Ⓐ Ⓑ Ⓒ Ⓓ Ⓔ	215. Ⓐ Ⓑ Ⓒ Ⓓ Ⓔ
136. Ⓐ Ⓑ Ⓒ Ⓓ Ⓔ	176. Ⓐ Ⓑ Ⓒ Ⓓ Ⓔ	216. Ⓐ Ⓑ Ⓒ Ⓓ Ⓔ
137. Ⓐ Ⓑ Ⓒ Ⓓ Ⓔ	177. Ⓐ Ⓑ Ⓒ Ⓓ Ⓔ	217. Ⓐ Ⓑ Ⓒ Ⓓ Ⓔ
138. Ⓐ Ⓑ Ⓒ Ⓓ Ⓔ	178. Ⓐ Ⓑ Ⓒ Ⓓ Ⓔ	
139. Ⓐ Ⓑ Ⓒ Ⓓ Ⓔ	179. Ⓐ Ⓑ Ⓒ Ⓓ Ⓔ	

GRE

PSYCHOLOGY TEST 1

TIME: 170 Minutes
217 Questions

DIRECTIONS: Choose the best answer for each question and mark the letter of your selection on the corresponding answer sheet.

---

1. In the visual system, sensory transduction

    (A) accounts for the sum of activity in the receptor cells.

    (B) is the chain of sensory reception, including the cornea, pupil, lens, and retina.

    (C) translates physical information from our environment into electrical information for the brain processes.

    (D) conducts energy from the cone receptor cells to the rod receptor cells.

    (E) none of the above

2. The retina

    (A) is the round opening in the center of the eye through which light passes.

    (B) is the photosensitive curtain of nerve cells located at the back of the eye.

    (C) bends and focuses light rays.

    (D) protects the internal parts of the eye.

    (E) is the muscle holding the pupil in place.

3. In a test situation, the examiner wants there to be only one independent variable — the individual being tested. To ensure this, the examiner administers a (an)

    (A) item analysis.   (B) factor analysis.

    (C) standardized test.   (D) normal test.

    (E) individual test.

4. Which of the following is the most widely accepted significance level for demonstrating significance in experimental results?

   (A) .5   (B) .05

   (C) .55   (D) 5.0

   (E) .10

5. In auditory sensation, pitch

   (A) is the only variable by which we distinguish sounds.

   (B) is closely related to the loudness of sound.

   (C) is closely related to the frequency of sound.

   (D) is closely related to the intensity of sound.

   (E) is measured in decibels.

6. In the auditory system, the cochlear branch

   (A) is located in the middle ear next to the tympanic membrane.

   (B) is responsible for balance.

   (C) connects the ear canal with the throat.

   (D) is composed of three fluid filled canals, located in the inner ear.

   (E) both (B) and (D)

7. Children learning the alphabet is a common form of

   (A) serial learning.   (B) repetition.

   (C) pairing.   (D) rehearsal.

   (E) mediation.

8. The basic types of verbal learning are

   (A) serial learning and serial anticipation learning.

   (B) paired-associate learning and free recall learning.

   (C) serial learning and free recall learning.

   (D) paired-associate learning and serial learning.

   (E) all of the above

9. The law of effect was first formulated by

   (A) E.L. Thorndike.   (B) B.F. Skinner.

(C) H. Rachlin.   (D) W. Wundt.

(E) A. Bandura.

10.   If we determine the heights and weights of a group of college men, the data generated is

    (A) random.   (B) discrete.

    (C) continuous.   (D) normal.

    (E) modal.

11.   Ivan P. Pavlov is famous for his research on

    (A) teaching machines.   (B) perceptual learning.

    (C) forward conditioning. (D) classical conditioning.

    (E) backward conditioning.

12.   A stimulus that elicits a response before the experimental manipulation is a (an)

    (A) response stimulus (RS).

    (B) unconditioned stimulus (UCS).

    (C) generalized stimulus (GS).

    (D) conditioned stimulus (CS).

    (E) specific stimulus (SS).

13.   The probability that the null hypothesis (H_0) will be rejected when it is in fact true is called a (an)

    (A) type II error.   (B) type I error.

    (C) two-tailed test.   (D) experimental error.

    (E) false validity.

14.   According to association theory, behavior

    (A) is a function of reinforcement.

    (B) is a function of motivation and performance.

    (C) can be attributed to modeling.

    (D) consists of associations made between responses and stimuli.

    (E) consists of associations between responses and reinforcements.

15. The ruling-dominant (choleric) and getting-leaning (phlegmatic) personality types were proposed by

    (A) C. Rogers.   (B) E. Fromm.

    (C) H. Eysenck.   (D) A. Adler.

    (E) W. Kohler.

16. Erikson proposed that trust or mistrust develops during the

    (A) muscular-anal stage.

    (B) locomotor-genital stage.

    (C) latency stage.

    (D) oral-sensory stage.

    (E) maturity stage.

17. The id draws its psychic energy from

    (A) outer reality.   (B) bodily instincts.

    (C) the ego.   (D) the superego.

    (E) the collective unconscious.

18. When an individual thinks and acts in a fashion directly opposite to the unconscious impulse (e.g., a person threatened by his own fascination with pornography may become a strong advocate of censorship), he is employing which defense mechanism?

    (A) reaction-formation   (B) displacement

    (C) sublimation   (D) compensation

    (E) projection

19. H. Harlow is most famous for his studies of

    (A) the effect of frustration on play behavior.

    (B) single parent families.

    (C) the effect of maternal deprivation on infant development.

    (D) language acquisition in young children.

    (E) aggression modeling in children.

20. Human factors engineering is concerned with

(A)   providing therapy using physical methods.

(B)   the design of equipment and the tasks performed with the operation of equipment.

(C)   the application of computers and scientific measurement to the betterment of human society.

(D)   automated instruction methods.

(E)   human perceptions of the machines they operate.

21.   One effect of anxiety on learning is

(A)   the removal of mental blocks.

(B)   a reduction in performance on difficult tasks.

(C)   a reduction in the ability to discriminate clearly.

(D)   more interference with familiar material than with new material.

(E)   reduction in the ability to perform any task.

22.   A young child tries to recite the alphabet. He begins "A, B, C, D" and ends with "X, Y, Z" but the middle is a scrambled assortment of letters. This is a common example of

(A)   the associate learning effect.

(B)   the conceptual learning effect.

(C)   the rehearsal effect.

(D)   the serial-position effect.

(E)   the dyslexic effect.

23.   All of the following are characteristics of verbal materials that influence how effectively we learn them EXCEPT

(A)   list length.   (B)   item position.

(C)   word length.   (D)   similarity.

(E)   meaningfulness.

24.   The type of learning that is unique for humans is

(A)   classical conditioning.   (B)   operant conditioning.

(C)   verbal learning.   (D)   discrimination learning.

(E)   motor task learning.

25. According to Carl Jung's personality theory, the terms "anima" and "animus" refer to

    (A) the collective unconscious.

    (B) the personal unconscious.

    (C) feminine and masculine archetypes.

    (D) the shadow archetypes.

    (E) the animal instincts in man's unconscious.

26. Intelligence tests are not considered reliable

    (A) at any age.   (B) before seven years of age.

    (C) before puberty.   (D) before twenty years of age.

    (E) none of the above

27. Physiologically, emotional responses take place

    (A) in the brain.

    (B) in the autonomic nervous system (ANS).

    (C) in the muscles and internal organs.

    (D) in the sympathetic nervous system.

    (E) in all of the above

28. A "lie detector," or polygraph, is often used to ascertain an individual's guilt in a crime. It does this by measuring

    (A) brain waves and heart rate.

    (B) heart rate, respiration and galvanic skin response.

    (C) brain waves and eye movement.

    (D) the truthfulness of an individual.

    (E) the tone, or pitch, of the voice.

29. A "positively skewed" distribution is

    (A) a distribution that has a few extremely high values.

    (B) a distribution that has a few extremely low values.

    (C) a flat distribution, with a wide dispersion of values.

    (D) a distribution that is very peaked and leptokurtic.

(E) a distribution that is both flat and leptokurtic.

30. A few extreme scores in a distribution will affect

(A) the value of the median more than that of the mean.

(B) the value of the mean more than that of the median.

(C) the values of the mean and median equally.

(D) the value of the mode more than that of the median.

(E) neither the value of the mean nor the median.

31. Which of the following is no longer considered a scientific method appropriate for psychology?

(A) non-parametric statistics   (B) introspection

(C) field research   (D) parametric statistics

(E) hypothesizing

32. A psychologist wants to observe language development. He studies five children over a ten-year period. This psychologist is performing a

(A) longitudinal study.   (B) case study.

(C) factor analysis.   (D) laboratory study.

(E) durational study.

33. By obtaining two scores for one subject with just one test, a researcher achieves

(A) test-retest reliability.   (B) alternate reliability.

(C) split-half reliability.   (D) parallel reliability.

(E) scorer reliability.

34. Which is an advantage of group testing?

(A) reduction of cost   (B) more reliable norms

(C) more objective scoring   (D) both (A) and (B)

(E) all of the above

35. Weber's Law, well established in perceptual research, states that

(A) a stimulus must be increased by equal value to be just noticeably different.

(B)   a stimulus must be increased by twice its amount to be just noticeably different.

(C)   a stimulus must be increased by a constant fraction of its value to be just noticeably different.

(D)   a stimulus must be increased by ten times its amount to be just noticeably different.

(E)   none of the above

36.   All of the following are basic statistical methods for measuring and analyzing thresholds EXCEPT

(A)   the Method of Relative Threshold.

(B)   the Method of Limits.

(C)   the Method of Average Error.

(D)   the frequency method.

(E)   all of the above

37.   The major affective disorders are characterized by

(A)   extreme and inappropriate emotional responses.

(B)   severe depression.

(C)   withdrawal and emotional distortion.

(D)   chronic experience of depression.

(E)   delusional emotional experiences.

38.   Lateral inhibition refers to

(A)   inhibited response following inconsistent negative reinforcement.

(B)   the activity of one nerve cell inhibiting the activity of a neighboring nerve cell.

(C)   inhibited activity in the receptor cells following periods of alternating bright and dim light.

(D)   the inhibition of muscle tissue activity on one side of the brain.

(E)   none of the above

39.   Which of the following problems would require divergent thinking?

(A)   adding a column of numbers

(B)　deciding whether to turn left or right at an intersection while driving a car

(C)　choosing the best move in a card game

(D)　repairing a broken typewriter

(E)　both (A) and (D)

40.　In perceptual research, backward masking refers to

(A)　inhibition of the detection of simple figures in the presence of emotional stimuli.

(B)　an interfering stimulus that closely precedes presentation of the target stimulus.

(C)　an interfering stimulus presented shortly after the target stimulus.

(D)　a longer lasting interfering stimulus that is presented simultaneously with the brief target stimulus.

(E)　none of the above

41.　In sensory systems, a minimum difference between two stimuli is required before we can distinguish between them. This minimum threshold, which can be measured, is called the

(A)　interstimulus difference (ISD).

(B)　differential threshold (DL).

(C)　signal detectability threshold (TSD).

(D)　comparison stimulus threshold (CST).

(E)　subdifferential threshold (SDL).

42.　All of the following are characteristics of light EXCEPT

(A)　photons.　　　　　　　(B)　waves.

(C)　intensity.　　　　　　(D)　photoreception.

(E)　all of the above

43.　A key component of paranoia is usually

(A)　an organized delusional system with jealous content.

(B)　the presence of tactile hallucinations.

(C)　the experiencing of vivid auditory hallucinations.

(D)   the presence of a "dual" personality.

(E)   the experiencing of vivid visual hallucinations.

44.   In perceiving the distance a sound has traveled, a person depends heavily upon

(A)   loudness and intensity.   (B)   resonance.

(C)   brightness and hue.   (D)   saturation.

(E)   frequency.

45.   When light changes from bright to dim the iris of the eye

(A)   dilates.   (B)   constricts.

(C)   remains the same.   (D)   changes in color.

(E)   thickens.

46.   The utterance "ā" is an example of

(A)   a morpheme.   (B)   a phoneme.

(C)   syntax.   (D)   prosody.

(E)   a kernel.

47.   The perception of depth and distance in a 3-dimensional space depends mostly on

(A)   binocular vision.

(B)   texture-density gradient.

(C)   interposition.

(D)   movement detectors.

(E)   the Minimum Principle of Vision.

48.   Organization theory uses theories of reinforcement to increase worker efficiency and satisfaction. According to reinforcement theory, the best time to reward a worker is

(A)   at the end of the year in the form of a bonus.

(B)   never.

(C)   when he first begins work in the company.

(D)   immediately before a task is performed.

(E)   immediately after a task has been performed.

49. A psychologist wants to determine whether one group of 15-year-old girls' I.Q. scores differ significantly from that of a second group of 15-year-old girls. He would use

    (A) a t-test for two independent means.

    (B) a t-test for sample and population means.

    (C) chi-square.

    (D) a factorial design.

    (E) the Pearson product-moment correlation coefficient.

50. The Z-table is derived from

    (A) the standard deviation.   (B) random sampling.

    (C) the normal distribution.   (D) the Z-scores.

    (E) the square root of the t-scores.

51. "Template matching" is a model developed to account for

    (A) neurotransmission.   (B) sensation.

    (C) auditory functions.   (D) language development.

    (E) perception.

52. Individuals rated as "High Anxious" on the Manifest Anxiety Scale

    (A) have a high potential for developing an anxiety disorder at some point in their lifetime.

    (B) display some signs of the learned helplessness phenomenon.

    (C) do better on verbal learning tasks than "Low Anxious" individuals.

    (D) have a shorter attention span than "Low Anxious" individuals.

    (E) none of the above

53. "Hue" can be affected by which of the following?

    (A) wavelength of light   (B) intensity of light

    (C) saturation   (D) brightness of light

    (E) all of the above

54. In drug research, a control group, consisting of subjects administered a "fake" drug with no active ingredients, is usually included. This "fake" drug is known as a

(A)   phoneme.

(B)   null drug.

(C)   blind drug.

(D)   null, dependent variable.

(E)   none of the above

55.   All of the following are important factors in the acquisition of motor skills EXCEPT

(A)   feedback.

(B)   repetition.

(C)   distribution of practice.

(D)   reflex action.

(E)   none of the above

56.   Which of the following describes the correct sequence for learning a perceptual-motor task?

(A)   perception, cognition and automation

(B)   fixation, cognition and automation

(C)   cognition, fixation and automation

(D)   perception, automation and cognition

(E)   fixation, automation and cognition

57.   According to Freud, a developmental halt due to frustration and anxiety is referred to as

(A)   depression.

(B)   fixation.

(C)   regression.

(D)   neurosis.

(E)   learned helplessness.

58.   Defense mechanisms are created by the

(A)   id.

(B)   ego.

(C)   superego.

(D)   anima and animus.

(E)   persona.

59.   *The Interpretation of Dreams* was written by

(A)   Carl Jung.

(B)   Sigmund Freud.

(C)   Ernest Jones.

(D)   Alfred Adler.

(E)   Carl Rogers.

60. According to Jellinek (1952), the prodromal phase of alcoholism is marked by

    (A) heavy social drinking.　　(B) drinking to relieve tension.

    (C) blackouts.　　(D) binge drinking.

    (E) malnutrition.

61. The psychiatrist who has written several influential books questioning the use of the term "mental illness" is

    (A) Bruno Battleheim.　　(B) B.F. Skinner.

    (C) Thomas Szasz.　　(D) Jose Delgado.

    (E) Anna Freud.

62. Modeling is a technique used in

    (A) behavior therapy.　　(B) logotherapy.

    (C) client-centered therapy.　　(D) psychoanalysis.

    (E) rational-emotive therapy.

63. Freud believed that the primary driving force in an individual's life was

    (A) the superego.　　(B) psychosexual development.

    (C) sexual urge.　　(D) bodily functions.

    (E) domination.

64. "The aim of all life is death." This quote from Sigmund Freud's work refers to

    (A) Thanatos.

    (B) Eros.

    (C) the struggle between Eros and Thanatos.

    (D) the death instinct.

    (E) reproduction, a pun on death as sexual orgasm.

65. The psychological point of view which emphasizes "wholeness" and is concerned with questions of how one perceives his environment is

    (A) gestalt psychology.　　(B) psychoanalysis.

    (C) associationism.　　(D) analytic psychology.

    (E) stimulus-response or S-R psychology.

66. A between-subjects design is less efficient than a within-subjects design because

    (A) it has more subjects.   (B) it has less validity.

    (C) it is less reliable.   (D) it is not counterbalanced.

    (E) it must deal with differences among subjects.

67. Sublimation is an example of

    (A) a personality mechanism.

    (B) a defense mechanism.

    (C) the primary personality process.

    (D) the secondary personality process.

    (E) none of the above

68. According to Matina Horner's studies of sex role attitudes and motivation, which of the following is true?

    (A) Women have a motive to succeed which is equivalent to that of men.

    (B) Women have a motive to avoid success.

    (C) Men have a motive to avoid successful women.

    (D) Men have a motive to succeed.

    (E) Women score differently from men in their need to achieve success.

69. As an approach to personality research Gordon Allport favored

    (A) nomothetic studies.   (B) non-parametric studies.

    (C) ideographic studies.   (D) case conference studies.

    (E) cross-cultural studies.

70. A man continues to hunt animals even though he does not need them for food. According to Gordon Allport, this is an example of

    (A) functional autonomy.   (B) ego autonomy.

    (C) motivational autonomy.   (D) self-reinforcement.

    (E) innate, aggressive instinct.

71. The Yerkes-Dodson Law is most closely related to

    (A) Eysenck's biological model of personality.

(B) Skinner's learning model of personality.

(C) Roger's humanistic model of personality.

(D) Sheldon's somatotype model of personality.

(E) Newman's genetic model of hereditary personality.

72. A phenotypic and genotypic basis for personality was theorized by

(A) A. Bandura.   (B) V. Frankl.

(C) A. Adler.   (D) H. Eysenck.

(E) C. Darwin.

73. Which of the following statements is correct?

(A) A factorial design is not based on analysis of variance.

(B) Analysis of covariance is not related to correlation.

(C) Correlation is related to predictability in methodology.

(D) The range of correlation coefficients is −.04 to +.04.

(E) both (B) and (C)

74. The simplest measure of variability is the

(A) standard deviation.   (B) Z-score.

(C) variance.   (D) range.

(E) chi-square.

75. Transference neurosis is an aspect of the therapeutic process most common in

(A) logotherapy.   (B) implosive therapy.

(C) psychoanalysis.   (D) client-centered therapy.

(E) none of the above

76. When the superego becomes a major force in a developing child's personality, the child soon develops

(A) anxieties.   (B) a moral sense.

(C) neurotic conflicts.   (D) an interest in sexual activity.

(E) hedonism.

77. The belief that perception consists of individual sensations meshing with memories of past sensational experiences in different combinations was held by the

    (A) nativists.   (B) empiricists.

    (C) gestaltists.   (D) developmentalists.

    (E) structuralists.

78. All of the following are monocular depth cues EXCEPT

    (A) relative size.   (B) interposition.

    (C) texture-density gradient.   (D) linear perspective.

    (E) minimum form gradient.

79. The general-adaptation syndrome can lead to bodily damage when

    (A) psychosomatic diseases fail to protect one from stress.

    (B) adaptive physiological responses fail.

    (C) the adrenal glands return to normal size before adaptive responses occur.

    (D) one is unable to reduce stress which results in chronic bodily arousal.

    (E) the resistance stage sets in.

80. The arousal theory, stating that emotion precedes overt behavior and consists mainly of a general state of arousal or activation, is called the

    (A) Cannon-Bard theory.   (B) James-Lange theory.

    (C) general-adaptation theory.   (D) Premack principle.

    (E) paired-arousal theory.

81. In which form of conditioning is the conditioned stimulus (CS) presented after the unconditioned stimulus (UCS)?

    (A) higher-order conditioning   (B) forward conditioning

    (C) backward conditioning   (D) second-order conditioning

    (E) delayed conditioning

82. In Freudian dream analysis, the term "dream work" refers to

    (A) the process of dream analysis.

    (B) the underlying symbols in a dream.

    (C)   the repression of unconscious symbols in a dream.

    (D)   the processes that convert wishes and impulses into disguised dream images.

    (E)   none of the above

83.   According to Carl Rogers, the structure of the personality is based upon

    (A)   introversion and extroversion.

    (B)   being and non-being.

    (C)   the organism and the self.

    (D)   the will to meaning and the will to power.

    (E)   expectations and reality.

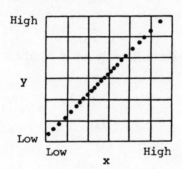

84.   Which of the following choices best describes the correlation pictured above?

    (A)   correlation = +1.00   (B)   correlation = – 1.00

    (C)   correlation = 0.00   (D)   correlation = – 0.45

    (E)   correlation = +0.45

85.   All of the following are factors that influence the intensity of a taste except

    (A)   concentration of the stimulus.

    (B)   amount of tongue area that is stimulated.

    (C)   other tastes that are present at the time.

    (D)   the type of basic taste.

    (E)   amount of saliva.

86. The main function of the vestibular organs is to

    (A) provide a sense of balance.

    (B) provide the ability to taste.

    (C) provide a sense of touch.

    (D) provide an ability to "feel" an emotion.

    (E) none of the above

87. A psychologist wants to study how I.Q., age, and sex affect reading speed. The subjects will be equal numbers of males and females, ages thirty or sixty, and either have an I.Q. of 100 or of 120. The statistical design for this study is

    (A) two factor.   (B) six factor.

    (C) three factor.   (D) nine factor.

    (E) eight factor.

88. Compute the range of the following set of numbers: 5, 692, 415, 17, 63, 200, 145.

    (A) 145   (B) 220

    (C) 687   (D) 5

    (E) 692

89. The greatest concentration of cones occurs in the

    (A) pupil   (B) blind spot.

    (C) optic nerve.   (D) fovea.

    (E) ganglion.

90. Receptor cells that are very sensitive to color are the

    (A) ganglion cells.   (B) rods.

    (C) cones.   (D) bipolar cells.

    (E) chromatic cells.

91. Selfridge's "Pandemonium" model of pattern recognition is an example of a (an) _____ theory.

    (A) template matching   (B) feature analysis

    (C) heuristic   (D) synthetic

    (E) psycholinguistic

92. According to Alfred Adler, man is striving for

    (A) self-actualization.   (B) power.

    (C) superiority and goals.   (D) leadership.

    (E) distinction.

93. Weber's Law ($\Delta I / I = K$) refers to

    (A) stimulus thresholds.   (B) sensory transduction.

    (C) the "tricolor" theory.   (D) reinforcement rate matching.

    (E) none of the above

94. The colored portion of the eye is called the

    (A) lens.   (B) cornea.

    (C) pupil.   (D) iris.

    (E) retina.

95. The role of imitation in social learning was first systematically observed by

    (A) Miller and Dollard.   (B) Bandura and Walters.

    (C) Stanley Milgram.   (D) B.F. Skinner.

    (E) J.B. Watson.

96. Gordon Allport preferred which of the following methods in his personality research?

    (A) factorial design   (B) nomothetic method

    (C) chi-square method   (D) ideographic method

    (E) both (B) and (C)

97. In a positively skewed distribution, which of the following gives the correct relative sequence from left to right of central tendency measures?

    (A) mode, median, mean

    (B) mean, median, mode

    (C) Mean, median, and mode are all at the same point.

    (D) median, mode, mean

    (E) Not enough information is given to determine the sequence.

98. In order to produce effects in experiments, researchers manipulate

    (A) subjects.   (B) dependent variables.

    (C) independent variables.   (D) test variables.

    (E) statistics.

99. In our society, money is an example of a

    (A) primary reinforcer.

    (B) secondary (conditioned) reinforcer.

    (C) socio/reinforcer.

    (D) negative reinforcer.

    (E) simple operant.

100. The field theory of behavior was proposed by

    (A) John Watson.   (B) Ivan Pavlov.

    (C) Wilhelm Wundt.   (D) Kurt Lewin.

    (E) William James.

101. An important function of rehearsal in verbal learning is

    (A) mediation.

    (B) transference of material from short term to long term memory.

    (C) acclimation to the meaning of the material.

    (D) both (A) and (B)

    (E) all of the above

102. Similarity is to difference as generalization is to

    (A) choices.   (B) discrimination.

    (C) detectability.   (D) distinction.

    (E) none of the above

103. The serial-position curve shows that the most material is learned

    (A) at the beginning of a list.

    (B) during all phases of learning.

    (C) at the end of a list.

    (D)   in the middle of a list.

    (E)   during recognition of learned material.

104. A discrete motor task differs from a continuous motor task in

    (A)   difficulty.

    (B)   length.

    (C)   enjoyment of task.

    (D)   the dexterity needed to perform the task.

    (E)   the type of movements performed.

105. Which of the following correlation values is the best predictor for a relationship between x and y?

    (A)   -.70   (B)   +.60

    (C)   +.50   (D)   .10

    (E)   +7.0

106. A measure of variability based upon the differences between each score and the mean is the

    (A)   standard deviation.   (B)   sampling error.

    (C)   Z–score.   (D)   range.

    (E)   t–score.

107. Borrowed from computer programming, the "executive routine" model proposes an explanation for

    (A)   human development.   (B)   language acquisition.

    (C)   human perception.   (D)   human memory.

    (E)   serial learning.

108. The time required to produce associations to pictures is

    (A)   greater than the time required to produce associations to words.

    (B)   less than the time required to produce associations to words.

    (C)   equal to the time required to produce associations to words.

    (D)   dependent on the amount of detail in the pictures.

    (E)   less for women than for men.

109. A founding father of psychology who organized the first psychology lab in 1879 was

    (A)   Sir Charles Sherrington.   (B)   Hermann von Helmholtz.

    (C)   William James.   (D)   Wilhelm Wundt.

    (E)   Eugene Galanter.

110. Historically, gestalt psychologists focused mainly on problems dealing with

    (A)   perception.   (B)   learning.

    (C)   motivation.   (D)   development.

    (E)   cognition.

QUESTIONS 111–113: choose the word or phrase that does not belong in the set.

111. (A)   amnesia   (B)   fugue

    (C)   schizo-affective disorders (D)   somnambulism

    (E)   multiple personality

112. (A)   bipolar cell   (B)   dendrites

    (C)   myelin sheath   (D)   schwann cell

    (E)   axon

113. (A)   decrease in heartbeat

    (B)   ingestion of food

    (C)   constriction of bronchi

    (D)   increased secretion of saliva

    (E)   pupil dilation

QUESTIONS 114–116: select the incorrect pair.

114. (A)   Dollard — social learning   (B)   Wundt — structuralism

    (C)   Guthrie — neobehaviorism (D)   Hull — neobehaviorism

    (E)   Perls — functionalism

115. (A)   Chomsky — semantic differential

(B)   Miller — frustration-aggression hypothesis

(C)   Maslow — hierarchy of needs

(D)   McClelland — achievement motive

(E)   Kraeplin — dementia-praecox

116. (A)   Jung — extroversion-introversion

(B)   Kohlberg — formal operations

(C)   Adler — ruling-dominant type

(D)   Erikson — industry vs. inferiority

(E)   Ellis — rational-emotive therapy

117. A platykurtic curve is

(A)   flat.   (B)   peaked.

(C)   positively skewed.   (D)   negatively skewed.

(E)   hyperbolic.

118. Correlational studies

(A)   indicate causality.

(B)   are more valid than laboratory studies.

(C)   involve manipulations of independent variables.

(D)   indicate some relationship between two variables.

(E)   all of the above

119. The general Graduate Record Examination is an example of a (an)

(A)   projective test.   (B)   cross-cultural test.

(C)   achievement test.   (D)   aptitude test.

(E)   intelligence test

120. The Thematic Apperception Test is an example of a (an)

(A)   intelligence test.   (B)   projective test.

(C)   cross-cultural test.   (D)   aptitude test.

(E)   achievement test.

121. Which of the following is the correct formula for a measure of intelligence quotient in children? [Note: C.A. = Chronological Age, M.A. = Mental Age]

(A) $I.Q. = \dfrac{C.A.}{M.A.} \times 10$

(B) $I.Q. = \dfrac{M.A.}{C.A.} \times 50$

(C) $I.Q. = \dfrac{C.A.}{M.A.} \times 100$

(D) $I.Q. = \dfrac{C.A.}{M.A.} \times 50$

(E) $I.Q. = \dfrac{M.A.}{C.A.} \times 100$

122. Which of the following is not characteristic of the MMPI?

(A) It was developed within a specific theoretical framework.

(B) It consists of ten clinical scales.

(C) It contains validity scales.

(D) It employs a self-report method of answering questions.

(E) It is a type of personality test.

123. Which of the following variables affects conformity?

(A) size of the majority opinion

(B) prior commitment

(C) status of individuals in the group

(D) self-esteem of subject

(E) all of the above

124. The studies of diffusion of responsibility sparked by the Kitty Genovese murder case were pioneered by

(A) Schachter and Festinger.

(B) Darley and Latane.

(C) Rodin and Ross.

(D) Krauss and Deutsch.

(E) Zimbardo and Zajonc.

125. Stanley Milgram, in his landmark study on obedience to authority, found that when subjects were asked to shock a confederate in increasing amounts in order to teach him a word matching task,

(A) 65% of the subjects administered shocks throughout the experiment and gave the maximum 450-volt shock.

(B) 75% of the subjects refused to participate in the experiment.

(C)   30% of the subjects administered shocks throughout the experiment and gave the maximum 450-volt shock.

(D)   people of low intelligence were more likely to apply the maximum 450-volt shock.

(E)   both (A) and (D)

126. Irving Janis is best known for his work on

(A)   social crowding.   (B)   social facilitation.

(C)   emotion and motivation.   (D)   conformity.

(E)   groupthink.

127. Someone who repeatedly washes his hands even when they are not dirty may be said to be suffering from

(A)   learned helplessness.   (B)   a conversion reaction.

(C)   an obsession.   (D)   a phobia.

(E)   a compulsion.

128. Electroconvulsive shock therapy (ECT) has been demonstrated to be effective in the treatment of

(A)   severe depression.   (B)   schizophrenia.

(C)   paranoia.   (D)   fugue.

(E)   all of the above

129. An antisocial reaction is an example of

(A)   a depressive neurosis.   (B)   a neurosis.

(C)   a conduct disorder.   (D)   delusional behavior.

(E)   a psychosis.

130. In reactive schizophrenia, the onset of symptoms is

(A)   inconsistent among this psychiatric population.

(B)   rapid and sudden.

(C)   slow and gradual.

(D)   indirectly related to the prognosis.

(E)   none of the above

131. In DSM-IV, attention deficit/hyperactivity disorder is classified among

    (A) dissociative disorders.   (B) personality disorders.

    (C) mood disorders.   (D) substance-related disorders.

    (E) disorders usually diagnosed in infancy, childhood, or adolescence.

132. An inability to recall one's prior identity and a sudden desire to travel away from one's customary surroundings are the essential features of

    (A) amnesia.   (B) affective disorder.

    (C) depersonalization.   (D) multiple personality.

    (E) a psychogenic fugue.

133. According to the anxiety theory of neurosis, depression is the result of

    (A) not assigning the anxiety to specific problems.

    (B) directing anxiety against the self.

    (C) multiple unresolved anxieties.

    (D) unsuccessful repression of anxieties.

    (E) none of the above

134. Korsakoff's psychosis is a disorder associated with

    (A) alcoholism.   (B) heroin addiction.

    (C) thyroid imbalance.   (D) cocaine addiction.

    (E) old age.

135. A psychologist is studying the relationship between verbal learning and mode of presentation. Upon analyzing the data, the psychologist finds a correlation of +1.50. On the basis of this correlation, he would conclude that there is a

    (A) strong positive correlation.

    (B) strong negative correlation.

    (C) computational error.

    (D) low negative correlation.

    (E) low positive correlation.

136. To convert a standard deviation into a variance, one must

    (A) take the square root of the standard deviation.

(B)   multiply the standard deviation by $1/X$.

(C)   divide the standard deviation by X.

(D)   square the standard deviation.

(E)   multiply the standard deviation by $1/X$.

137. Performance = Expectancy × Value is the symbolic representation of which theorist?

(A)   C. Hull

(B)   E. Tolman

(C)   D. McClelland

(D)   N. Miller

(E)   L. Festinger

138. According to consistency theories of motivation, imbalanced cognitive structures

(A)   are the result of negative learning.

(B)   tend to remain imbalanced.

(C)   will seek expression through contradictory behavior.

(D)   are a major cause of psychosis.

(E)   tend to change and become balanced.

139. The reinforcement schedule that produces the highest rates of performance is a

(A)   fixed-interval schedule.

(B)   variable-interval schedule.

(C)   fixed- ratio schedule.

(D)   variable-ratio schedule.

(E)   none of the above

140. Second-order conditioning is an important phenomenon because it demonstrates how an originally neutral CS used in the first-order conditioning can assume the properties of a (an)

(A)   first-order conditioning stimulus.

(B)   instrumental stimulus.

(C)   reinforcer.

(D)   positive reward.

(E)   negative reward.

141. Each score in a distribution has been multiplied by 5. The standard deviation is

(A) increased by 5.

(B) increased by 10.

(C) unchanged from the original value.

(D) divided by 5.

(E) increased to 5 times its original value.

142. One type of test validity is

(A) the extent to which a test measures a theoretical construct.

(B) the degree of thoroughness in a test.

(C) the extent to which repetitions of a test result in the same score.

(D) the degree to which subjects find a test valid.

(E) the effectiveness of a test.

143. In DSM-IV, bipolar disorder is classified among

(A) somatoform disorders.   (B) mood disorders.

(C) anxiety disorders.   (D) schizophrenias.

(E) sexual and gender identity disorders.

144. Fetishism would be considered a

(A) learning disorder.   (B) dementia.

(C) psychotic disorder.   (D) factitious disorder.

(E) paraphilia.

QUESTIONS 145–147 refer to the following passage.

In a study conducted in 1957 on smoking habits and attitudes, it was discovered that 29% of non-smokers, 20% of light smokers, and only 7% of heavy smokers believed that there was a relationship between smoking and lung cancer.

145. This study was conducted to test

(A) congruity theory.   (B) relational concepts.

(C) ignorance.   (D) balance theory.

(E) cognitive dissonance theory.

146. The theory tested in the study was proposed by

    (A) Heider.   (B) Tannenbaum.

    (C) Osgood.   (D) Milgram.

    (E) Festinger.

147. Only 7% of the heavy smokers believed that smoking was very dangerous because

    (A) they were not aware of the statistics.

    (B) psychological distress would result if they continued to smoke with the strong belief that it is harmful.

    (C) most of the heavy smokers were motivated to change their attitudes to produce consistency.

    (D) both (B) and (C)

    (E) all of the above

QUESTIONS 148–150 refer to the following passage.

Many psychologists believe that aggression is a behavior which is learned through operant conditioning, in which rewards and punishments shape a person's behavior. Modeling, or vicarious conditioning, is also thought to contribute to the development of aggressive behavior. In contrast with this predominant school of thought is the school that believes that aggression is an inborn tendency, and that because humans use their intelligence to aggress, they have never developed natural controls on aggression against their own species, as have other animals.

148. The belief that aggression is learned is held by

    (A) social learning theorists.   (B) phenomenological theorists.

    (C) psychodynamic theorists.   (D) experimental theorists.

    (E) all of the above

149. Which of the following statements is false?

    (A) If a child is rewarded for random, aggressive behavior, chances are good that the behavior will be repeated.

    (B) If a child is punished for acting aggressively, the likelihood of that behavior reoccurring is lessened.

    (C) If aggression is reinforced irregularly, the aggressive behavior is gradually discouraged.

(D) both (B) and (C)

(E) none of the above

150. The approach in which it is believed that aggression is an inborn tendency has been most supported by the work of

(A) Sigmund Freud.   (B) Konrad Lorenz.

(C) Carl Rogers.   (D) Albert Bandura.

(E) B.F. Skinner.

151. The short-term memory can hold how many items at one time?

(A) 7 items, plus or minus two

(B) 10 items, plus or minus two

(C) 10 items, plus or minus five

(D) 5 items

(E) none of the above

152. The earliest studies on record of verbal learning and memory were conducted by

(A) Thorndike.   (B) Pavlov.

(C) Skinner.   (D) Ebbinghaus.

(E) Mowrer.

153. The idea that each instinct is receptive to certain stimuli and contains a disposition to behave in a certain way was proposed by

(A) William McDougall.   (B) Clark Hull.

(C) John Stuart Mill.   (D) Charles Darwin.

(E) David McClelland.

154. The highest level in Maslow's hierarchical model of motivation is

(A) esteem and self-esteem.   (B) love and belonging.

(C) self-satisfaction.   (D) self-actualization.

(E) interpersonal union.

155. Approach-avoidance conflicts are difficult to resolve because

(A) the positive and negative aspects of a situation are equally strong.

(B)   a single goal possesses both positive and negative aspects.

(C)   one must choose the lesser of two evils.

(D)   they produce cognitive dissonance.

(E)   all of the above

156. Studies of male and female responses to erotic material indicate that

(A)   men and women respond the same to erotic material.

(B)   men become sexually aroused but women do not.

(C)   both men and women enjoy scenes of homosexuality involving their own sex.

(D)   men are aroused more by explicit sex while women are aroused by romantic scenes.

(E)   none of the above

157. The first systematic study of operant conditioning was performed in 1938 by

(A)   E.L. Thorndike.   (B)   B.F. Skinner.

(C)   Miller and Dollard.   (D)   A. Bandura.

(E)   I. Pavlov.

158. The reinforcement schedule that yields the lowest performance is the

(A)   fixed-ratio schedule.

(B)   variable-ratio schedule.

(C)   fixed-interval schedule.

(D)   variable-interval schedule.

(E)   intermittent reinforcement schedule.

QUESTIONS 159–160 refer to the following diagrams.

(A)   (B)

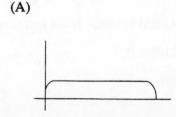 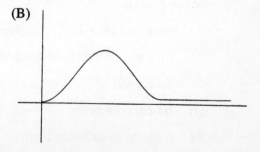

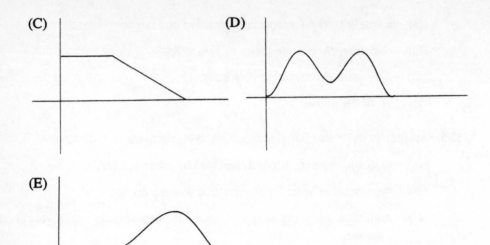

159. Which graph represents a platykurtic distribution?

160. In which graph is the mean greater than the mode and the median?

161. All of the following are human factors and components of the work cycle except

    (A) perceptual processes.   (B) problem solving.

    (C) communication processes.   (D) recall processes.

    (E) muscular (motor) processes.

162. Extreme scores in a distribution most dramatically affect the

    (A) t-score.   (B) mode.

    (C) mean.   (D) median.

    (E) Z-score.

163. During the premoral stage described by Kohlberg's moral development theory, children

    (A) think bad behavior is punished and good behavior is not punished.

    (B) have no conception of good or bad behavior.

    (C) are amoral.

    (D) are uncooperative.

    (E) conform to authority figures.

164. All of the following mark early stages in embryonic development EXCEPT

    (A) zygote.   (B) blastula.

    (C) blastomeres.   (D) morula.

    (E) follicle.

QUESTIONS 165–167 refer to the following passage.

The cerebellum is greatly involved in planning movements as well as in coordinating them. It develops new motor programs which enable slow and deliberate movements to become rapid and automatic after practice. Damage to the cerebellum can lead to inability to perform rapid alternating movements and difficulty in making eye movements.

165. Movements that are rapid and automatic after practice are known as

    (A) feedback-guided movements.

    (B) gross movements.

    (C) ballistic movements.

    (D) fine movements.

    (E) involuntary movements.

166. When someone with cerebellar damage is performing the "finger-to-nose" test, his finger reaches a point just in front of his nose and then begins shaking out of control. This points to the fact that

    (A) putting one's finger on one's nose is a purely ballistic movement.

    (B) the cerebellum is responsible for maintaining the steady, non-relaxed positioning of a limb or other body part.

    (C) the person may be developing Parkinson's disease.

    (D) both (B) and (C)

    (E) both (A) and (B)

167. Which of the following is NOT controlled by the cerebellum?

    (A) speaking   (B) writing

    (C) playing the piano   (D) walking

    (E) playing basketball

168. A rat is trained to run through a maze for food. After several days, extinction is begun by removing the food. Eventually, the rat quits running. After

a delay of several days, the rat is again placed in the maze (without food) and it runs through the maze again for a while. What is this process called?

(A) resensitization

(B) spontaneous recovery

(C) partial extinction

(D) renewed response recovery

(E) generalization

169. First-born children have been shown to

(A) be more dependent than later borns.

(B) be more affiliative when fearful, than later borns.

(C) be more intelligent than later-born children.

(D) both (A) and (B)

(E) all of the above

170. A "normal" average I.Q. score is

(A) 85.

(B) 100.

(C) 115.

(D) 110.

(E) none of the above

171. The reticular activating system (RAS) is thought to be

(A) responsible for hunger and satiation.

(B) unrelated to drive forces in humans.

(C) the central coordinating point for information in the nervous system.

(D) the physiological center for schizophrenic symptoms.

(E) both (A) and (C)

172. In 1959, Festinger and Carlsmith studied the effects of cognitive dissonance on attitude change. Subjects were paid $1 or $20 to lie by telling another subject that a boring task was interesting. In a post-experimental questionnaire, which group showed the most attitude change about the enjoyment of the task?

(A) $20 group

(B) $1 group

(C) Both changed the same amount.

(D) There was no change in either group.

(E) Only "prior commitment" subjects in the $20 group showed no change.

QUESTIONS 173–175 refer to the following diagram.

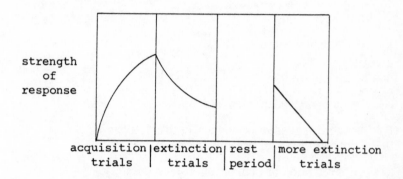

173. According to this diagram,

 (A) a new competing response replaces the original learned response.

 (B) extinction is an inhibition of a learned response.

 (C) conditioned behavior can reappear after extinction without additional conditioning.

 (D) both (B) and (C)

 (E) both (A) and (C)

174. The phenomenon that takes place in the last section is known as

 (A) disinhibition.   (B) counterconditioning.

 (C) spontaneous recovery.   (D) reconditioning.

 (E) second-order conditioning.

175. Extinction of a conditioned response occurs when

 (A) the CS is presented without the UCS several times.

 (B) the UCS is presented without the CS several times.

 (C) the CS is presented for more than five seconds before the start of the UCS.

 (D) the CS terminates before the onset of the UCS.

 (E) the CS begins after the UCS is terminated.

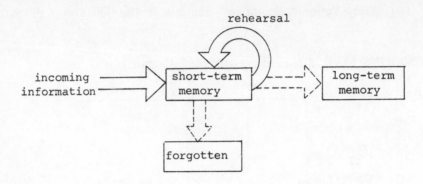

176. In the process of verbal learning, rehearsal

    (A)   aids retention of items in short-term memory.

    (B)   aids retention of sensory representations in short-term memory.

    (C)   facilitates the transfer of material from short-term to long-term memory.

    (D)   both (A) and (C)

    (E)   all of the above

177. Which of the following is not a factor that influences the learning of a list?

    (A)   position of the items   (B)   frequency of the items

    (C)   similarity of the items   (D)   concreteness

    (E)   all are factors that influence learning

178. Which is/are the most important factor(s) in rehearsal?

    (A)   individual presentation rate

    (B)   number of trials

    (C)   time spent learning

    (D)   both (A) and (C)

    (E)   both (B) and (C)

QUESTIONS 179–181 refer to the following passage.

   A person desperately needs to be cured of a phobia. The therapy chosen for him involves the use of learning principles. The goal of this therapy is the elimination of the patient's specific fear, rather than alteration of the patient's entire personality pattern. In the case of a phobia, the approach most often chosen is systematic desensitization.

179. The therapeutic approach described above is that of a

    (A) humanistic therapist.   (B) logotherapist.

    (C) behavior therapist.   (D) psychoanalyst.

    (E) gestalt therapist.

180. Systematic desensitization was developed by

    (A) John Watson.   (B) Frederick Perls.

    (C) Victor Frankl.   (D) Joseph Wolpe.

    (E) Carl Rogers.

181. Systematic desensitization is a (an) _____ technique.

    (A) cognitive restructuring   (B) operant

    (C) counterconditioning   (D) aversive

    (E) counterbalancing

QUESTIONS 182–184 refer to the following passage.

An experiment was performed in which a pigeon was placed in a Skinner box. The pigeon had been trained to peck a key in order to receive grain. Another pigeon was placed in the box during an extinction period (when grain was not being given for pecking) and the trained pigeon attacked the newcomer by pecking at his head, throat, and eyes.

182. Which of the following theorists have performed this experiment?

    (A) Skinner   (B) Burner

    (C) Hull   (D) Dollard

    (E) Guthrie

183. The most common source of aggression is

    (A) deprivation.   (B) frustration.

    (C) conflict.   (D) punishment.

    (E) violence on television.

184. The trained pigeon attacked the newcomer because

    (A) he thought he would be competing for grain.

    (B) his aggression was displaced.

(C)   he was there.   (D)   both (A) and (C)

(E)   both (B) and (C)

185. The human struggle between being and nonbeing is an important theme in which theory of psychology?

(A)   Freudian theory   (B)   existential theory

(C)   humanistic theory   (D)   social psychology theory

(E)   behavioral theory

186. According to Allport, the ego is better termed the

(A)   proprium.   (B)   functional autonomy.

(C)   collective conscious.   (D)   mediator.

(E)   ego functions.

187. According to Erikson, a child four to six years of age is in which stage of development?

(A)   latency stage   (B)   muscular-anal stage

(C)   locomotor- genital stage   (D)   oral-sensory stage

(E)   locomotor-sensory stage

188. In Jungian theory, the "shadow" represents

(A)   unconscious drives.   (B)   the animus.

(C)   the anima.   (D)   the persona.

(E)   motivational drives.

189. In linguistic terminology, the term "boy" is a (an)

(A)   morpheme.   (B)   phoneme.

(C)   stereotype.   (D)   prosody.

(E)   example of syntax.

190. According to Noam Chomsky's theory of transformational grammar, a "kernel" is

(A)   the surface structure of a sentence.

(B)   the smallest unit of meaning in a language.

(C)   the deep structure of a sentence.

(D)   the connotation of a sentence.

(E)   the basic declarative thought of the sentence.

191. According to Sheldon's somatotyping theory, an ectomorph is

    (A) soft and round.   (B) strong and muscular.

    (C) slender and fragile.   (D) tall and thin.

    (E) none of the above

192. The founder of client-centered therapy is

    (A) Victor Frankl.   (B) Carl Rogers.

    (C) Sigmund Freud.   (D) Carl Jung.

    (E) Alfred Adler.

193. Which of the following does NOT describe a true relationship between environmental factors and the stability of the I.Q.?

    (A) There is an increasing stability of I.Q. with age.

    (B) Prerequisite learning skills contribute to the stability of I.Q.

    (C) Changes in family structure have no effect on I.Q.

    (D) Emotional stability has a beneficial effect on I.Q.

    (E) Parental concern over the child's welfare has a stabilizing effect on I.Q.

194. The capacity of a test to measure what it sets out to measure is called its

    (A) standardization.   (B) reliability.

    (C) objectivity level.   (D) validity.

    (E) concurrence.

QUESTIONS 195–197 refer to the following passage.

A classical experiment in conformity research done by Muzafer Sherif involved the effects of group judgments on "the autokinetic phenomenon." A light projected on the wall appears to move although this movement is actually due to the movement of the subject's eyes. It was found that individual's judgments of the rate of movement of the light were influenced very much by the opinions of others. Even when the group was no longer present, the individual estimates were still in agreement with previous group opinions.

195. The fact that the subjects still agreed with the confederate group although they were no longer present shows that

    (A) compliance took place.

(B)   private acceptance took place.

(C)   internalization has occurred.

(D)   both (A) and (B)

(E)   all of the above

196. Which of the following statements is false?

(A)   The more authoritarian a person, the less he or she will conform.

(B)   "External" personalities are more likely to conform than "internals."

(C)   People with low self-esteem are likely to conform.

(D)   If a group is not unanimous there is a large decrease in conformity.

(E)   People with greater intelligence conform less than those with low intelligence.

197. A person who publicly supports an opinion that he does not privately accept will often change his opinion so that it will agree with the publicly expressed one. This occurs as a result of

(A)   compliance.   (B)   internalization.

(C)   dissonance.   (D)   deindividuation.

(E)   hypocrisy.

QUESTIONS 198–200 refer to this distribution of SAT scores.

198. What percent of the SAT scores fall between 500 and 600?

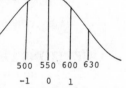

(A)   50%   (B)   68%

(C)   14%   (D)   34%

(E)   98%

199. Which equation could determine the standard deviation of the score 630 from the given mean?

(A) $t = \dfrac{x - \mu}{\sigma}$ (B) $s = \dfrac{\mu - \bar{x}}{\sigma}$

(C) $z = \dfrac{\mu - x}{\sigma}$ (D) $z = \dfrac{x - \mu}{\sigma}$

(E) $s = \dfrac{\bar{x} - \mu}{\sigma}$

200. In this distribution,

  (A) the mean is greater than the mode.

  (B) the mean is greater than the median.

  (C) the mode, median and mean are equal.

  (D) the mode and median are equal and higher than the mean.

  (E) the mean and mode are equal and higher than the median.

201. Konrad Lorenz demonstrated that a newly hatched duckling would follow the first moving object that it sees. He called this instinctive behavior

  (A) autoshaping.   (B) the rooting reflex.

  (C) the autokinetic effect.   (D) imprinting.

  (E) fowl play.

202. The ethologist who spent several years studying the problem-solving abilities of chimpanzees was

  (A) Margaret Mead.   (B) Wolfgang Kohler.

  (C) Joy Adamson.   (D) Aldous Huxley.

  (E) Erik Erikson.

203. The sexual behavior of which of the following species is most affected by hormones?

  (A) humans   (B) apes

  (C) wolves   (D) horses

  (E) rats

204. The fundamental attribution error is a tendency in humans to

  (A) blame people for situationally induced behavior.

  (B) engage in sexist stereotypes.

  (C) emphasize dispositional factors in determining people's behavior.

  (D) accept placebo effects.

  (E) emphasize I.Q. and race when forming opinions.

205. Which of the following variables has the most influence on our being attracted to someone?

(A)   physical attractiveness   (B)   proximity

(C)   similarity   (D)   confidence

(E)   familiarity

206. You are watching television and see a commercial where one of your favorite movie stars is discussing a nutritional cereal that you should buy. Because we like the star's movies, there is a tendency to believe that the star is also an expert on cereals. This tendency is referred to as the _____ effect.

(A)   barnum   (B)   piezoelectric

(C)   star   (D)   halo

(E)   none of the above

207. Humans normally have 46 chromosomes. A person born with an extra 21st chromosome (47 in all) would have

(A)   Klinefelter's syndrome.   (B)   Turner's syndrome.

(C)   Down's syndrome.   (D)   Korsakoff's syndrome.

(E)   a very high I.Q.

208. The fact that a blind infant would smile for the first time at about the same age as a sighted infant is evidence that smiling is

(A)   learned.   (B)   imitative behavior.

(C)   congenital.   (D)   nurtured behavior.

(E)   innate.

209. The primary sex hormones in human females are

(A)   testosterone and androgen.

(B)   progesterone and estrogen.

(C)   progesterone and testosterone.

(D)   testosterone and estrogen.

(E)   estradiol and testosterone.

210. According to Piaget, a person who cannot consistently use abstract logic has NOT reached the stage of

(A)   concrete operations.

(B)   preoperational development.

(C)   formal operations.

(D)   initiative vs. guilt.

(E)   extrovert vs. introvert.

211. The drug that has been a successful treatment for some cases of bipolar disorder is

(A)   thorazine.   (B)   valium.

(C)   seconal.   (D)   lithium carbonate.

(E)   chlorpromazine.

212. *Symptom substitution* and *displacement* refer to the Freudian explanations for

(A)   manic behavior.   (B)   phobias.

(C)   depression.   (D)   schizophrenia.

(E)   obsessive-compulsive disorders.

213. In Freudian psychoanalysis, there is a tendency for patients to show *transference*. This term refers to

(A)   the patients' exhibiting strong emotional responses directed at the analyst.

(B)   transferring blame for their problems from themselves to relatives.

(C)   lying about the nature of their problems.

(D)   their fear of the technique of systematic desensitization as part of their cure.

(E)   substituting one phobia for another.

214. The *critical period* for language acquisition refers to the fact that

(A)   humans are not emotionally stable until they can communicate effectively.

(B)   after a certain age, language skills deteriorate.

(C)   if a person has not acquired a language by puberty, he or she may never learn to speak appropriately.

(D)   humans must acquire one language at a time.

(E)   the brain needs a time frame to develop language centers.

215. Retarded humans frequently show language deficits. Below a measured I.Q. of _____, language acquisition of simple statements and sentences is highly unlikely.

    (A) 100   (B) 80

    (C) 70   (D) 50

    (E) 20

216. Morphemes differ from phonemes in that

    (A) morphemes are utterances that have no meaning.

    (B) phonemes carry meaning while morphemes do not.

    (C) morphemes carry meaning while phonemes do not.

    (D) morphemes refer to animal sounds while phonemes are sounds made only by humans.

    (E) phonemes refer to speech sounds while morphemes refer to sign language gestures.

217. The best demonstrations of language acquisition by apes and chimps show that they function on a level equivalent to a human

    (A) three-year-old.

    (B) child between 7 and 11 years of age.

    (C) adolescent between 12 and 15 years of age.

    (D) adolescent between 16 and 20 years of age.

    (E) adult 21 years of age or older.

TEST 1

ANSWER KEY

1.	(C)	26.	(B)	51.	(E)	76.	(B)
2.	(B)	27.	(E)	52.	(C)	77.	(B)
3.	(C)	28.	(B)	53.	(E)	78.	(E)
4.	(B)	29.	(A)	54.	(E)	79.	(D)
5.	(C)	30.	(B)	55.	(D)	80.	(A)
6.	(D)	31.	(B)	56.	(C)	81.	(C)
7.	(A)	32.	(A)	57.	(B)	82.	(D)
8.	(E)	33.	(C)	58.	(B)	83.	(C)
9.	(A)	34.	(E)	59.	(B)	84.	(A)
10.	(C)	35.	(C)	60.	(C)	85.	(D)
11.	(D)	36.	(A)	61.	(C)	86.	(A)
12.	(B)	37.	(A)	62.	(A)	87.	(C)
13.	(B)	38.	(B)	63.	(C)	88.	(C)
14.	(D)	39.	(C)	64.	(C)	89.	(D)
15.	(D)	40.	(C)	65.	(A)	90.	(C)
16.	(D)	41.	(B)	66.	(E)	91.	(B)
17.	(B)	42.	(D)	67.	(B)	92.	(C)
18.	(A)	43.	(A)	68.	(B)	93.	(A)
19.	(C)	44.	(A)	69.	(C)	94.	(D)
20.	(B)	45.	(A)	70.	(A)	95.	(A)
21.	(B)	46.	(B)	71.	(A)	96.	(D)
22.	(D)	47.	(A)	72.	(D)	97.	(A)
23.	(C)	48.	(E)	73.	(C)	98.	(C)
24.	(C)	49.	(A)	74.	(D)	99.	(B)
25.	(C)	50.	(C)	75.	(C)	100.	(D)

101.	(B)	131.	(E)	161.	(C)	191.	(C)
102.	(B)	132.	(E)	162.	(C)	192.	(B)
103.	(A)	133.	(B)	163.	(A)	193.	(C)
104.	(E)	134.	(A)	164.	(E)	194.	(D)
105.	(A)	135.	(C)	165.	(C)	195.	(D)
106.	(A)	136.	(D)	166.	(B)	196.	(A)
107.	(D)	137.	(B)	167.	(D)	197.	(C)
108.	(A)	138.	(E)	168.	(B)	198.	(B)
109.	(D)	139.	(D)	169.	(E)	199.	(D)
110.	(A)	140.	(C)	170.	(B)	200.	(C)
111.	(C)	141.	(E)	171.	(C)	201.	(D)
112.	(A)	142.	(A)	172.	(B)	202.	(B)
113.	(E)	143.	(B)	173.	(D)	203.	(E)
114.	(E)	144.	(E)	174.	(C)	204.	(A)
115.	(A)	145.	(E)	175.	(A)	205.	(B)
116.	(B)	146.	(E)	176.	(E)	206.	(D)
117.	(A)	147.	(D)	177.	(E)	207.	(C)
118.	(D)	148.	(A)	178.	(C)	208.	(E)
119.	(D)	149.	(C)	179.	(C)	209.	(B)
120.	(B)	150.	(B)	180.	(D)	210.	(C)
121.	(E)	151.	(A)	181.	(C)	211.	(D)
122.	(A)	152.	(D)	182.	(D)	212.	(B)
123.	(E)	153.	(A)	183.	(B)	213.	(A)
124.	(B)	154.	(D)	184.	(E)	214.	(C)
125.	(A)	155.	(B)	185.	(B)	215.	(E)
126.	(E)	156.	(D)	186.	(A)	216.	(C)
127.	(E)	157.	(B)	187.	(C)	217.	(A)
128.	(A)	158.	(C)	188.	(A)		
129.	(C)	159.	(A)	189.	(A)		
130.	(B)	160.	(B)	190.	(E)		

DETAILED EXPLANATIONS
OF ANSWERS

GRE PSYCHOLOGY TEST 1

1.   **(C)**   In the process of sensory transduction, physical information from the environment, in the form of light strikes the specialized receptor cells on the retina. This causes light-sensitive substances to undergo chemical changes. These changes cause an electrical event called a "generator potential" to occur. This "generator potential" then activates nerve cells, which transmit the visual information to the brain.

2.   **(B)**   The retina is composed of photoreceptor nerve cells (rods and cones) which form a photosensitive curtain at the back of the eye. Over 120 million photoreceptor cells are found in the retina of each eye.

3.   **(C)**   Standardization of a test implies that there is a uniformity of procedure in administering and scoring the test. If this uniformity (standardization) exists then one can be assured of only measuring the one independent variable of interest — the person being tested. Without standardization, the examiner cannot be certain that the difference in test scores among individuals is attributable to true individual differences rather than chance factors in the testing environment.

4.   **(B)**   The appropriate significance level is .05. This is the usual cut-off point for determining the significant difference between two means. At the .05 level the difference between the means is considered so great that it is unlikely that it could have occurred by chance. A p value of .05 means that the results obtained could have occurred by chance in only 5 out of 100 replications of the experiment.

5.   **(C)**   Pitch is closely related to the frequency of the stimulus. Sound is basically vibrations of particles in the air. These vibrations are wavelike and are called soundwaves. The frequency of a vibration is a measure of how many times it goes up and down in a single period of time. We generally experience high frequency waves as high pitched tones. Waves with low frequencies correspond to low pitched tones; therefore, pitch is closely related to the frequency of sound.

6.   **(D)**   The cochlea is part of the inner ear concerned with hearing. It consists of three canals, the vestibular, the tympanic and the tectorial, that spiral around inside the cochlea. It also contains the organ of corti which has small,

hair-tipped, receptor cells necessary for hearing. In addition, the cochlea contains the round window, another membrane separating the inner and middle ears.

7.   **(A)**   Whenever items of a list are learned in sequence, serial learning takes place. Associations may be formed between the items, or the proper order of the items may be learned by linking them to a particular position in the list.

8.   **(E)**   Serial learning occurs when a list of items is memorized and re-called in a particular order. In serial-anticipation learning, a list of items, usually nonsense syllables, are presented one at a time for a standard time interval. The first time the list is presented, the subject will not know which successive syl-lables are correct. Beginning with the second trial, he is asked to anticipate the syllable that follows the one he is looking at. This method provides immediate feedback to the subject about accuracy of response. In paired-associate learning, the subject must learn a list of paired items. The left-hand item of the pair is the stimulus item and the right-hand item is the response item. After learning the pairs, the subject should be able to produce the response item when given the stimulus item. Free recall learning is the learning and recall of a list of items. The retrieved items do not need to be in any specific order.

9.   **(A)**   E.L. Thorndike first proposed the law of effect, although B.F. Skin-ner and H. Rachlin did contribute to the study of it. The law of effect is con-cerned with the effects of reward and punishment on behavior. Responses are learned or extinguished as a consequence of their effect on the organism. A response that produces satisfaction becomes associated with the situation in which it occurs, so that whenever this situation occurs, the response is more likely than before to recur. A response that causes discomfort is less likely to recur.

10.   **(C)**   The kinds of numbers that can take on any fractional or integer value between specified limits are categorized as continuous, whereas values that are usually restricted to whole number values are called discrete. Thus, if we identify the number of people who use toothpaste, the data generated is discrete. Heights and weights are continuous.

11.   **(D)**   Ivan P. Pavlov (1849-1936) virtually discovered the phenomenon of classical conditioning and was the first to investigate it systematically. In Pavlov's experiments with the salivating response of his dogs, he established the basic methodology and terminology still used today in classical conditioning experiments. Pavlov referred to food as the unconditional stimulus (UCS) be-cause it naturally and consistently elicited salivation, which he called the uncon-ditioned response (UCR). Pavlov later taught dogs to salivate to light. This was accomplished by presenting the light just prior to presenting the food. After a series of such pairings, the dogs would salivate in response to the light. In this case, the light was a conditioned stimulus (CS) and the salivation in response to

the light was a conditioned response (CR). Hence, Pavlov's research elucidated the process of classical conditioning.

12. **(B)** In classical conditioning the stimulus that elicits a response before any conditioning begins is called the unconditioned stimulus. It reliably elicits the unconditioned response (UCR) before the experiment. During the experimental manipulation the unconditioned stimulus (UCS) is paired with a conditioned stimulus (CS) that originally does not elicit a response. After several such pairings the subject will elicit a conditioned response (CR) to the conditioned stimulus (CS) that is very similar to the unconditioned response (UCR). After this conditioned response (CR) is learned, the unconditioned stimulus (UCS) may be removed, but the subject will keep responding to the conditioned stimulus (CS).

13. **(B)** A type I error equals the significance level. Alpha (α) is the probability of committing a type I error. The type I error is an error of statistical inference that occurs when the null hypothesis is true, but is rejected. The smaller Alpha is, the more confident we are that the results obtained are significant, that is, they did not just happen by chance.

14. **(D)** The theory of association states that learning consists of the formation of associations between responses and the stimuli which are present when those responses are made. The associationists and their descendants, the behaviorists, see learning as automatic, gradual, and as being "favored upon" the organism by the external stimuli demands.

15. **(D)** Adler developed a scheme of personality types based on the degree of social interest and activity level in different personalities. His types were:
1) The ruling dominant (choleric) — this person is assertive, aggressive and active. While he has a high activity level, his social interest is low.
2) The getting-leaning type (phlegmatic) — this type expects others to satisfy his needs and to provide for his interests. He has a low activity level and low social interest.
3) The avoiding type (melancholic) — this person is inclined to achieve success by circumventing a problem or withdrawing from it. He has a very low activity level and low social interest.
4) The socially useful type (sanguine) — this is the most healthy personality type. He is socially oriented and prepared to cooperate with others to master the tasks of life.

16. **(D)** The oral-sensory stage is the first stage in Erikson's developmental theory. During the oral-sensory stage, the basic crisis centers on the development of either trust or mistrust. If these needs are consistently satisfied and if the infant receives love, he will develop a sense of trust, not only in others, but in himself and his ability to handle his needs. If these needs are not met and the infant lacks love, attention, and stimulation, he will develop a sense of mistrust.

Erikson believes that the development of a healthy personality is contingent upon the formation of trust at this early stage.

17. **(B)** The id contains all of man's instinctual urges. The id is dominant during infancy. The infant is pure id — he only feels urges and knows they must be satisfied. He only cares that he is hungry and wants to be fed, or tired, and wants sleep. The id pushes the individual to seek pleasure and avoid pain; it is the seat of human instincts.

18. **(A)** It is correct by definition. While all the answer possibilities are defense mechanisms, only reaction-formation is described.

19. **(C)** Harlow conducted one of the best known studies of mother-child interaction and the effects of maternal deprivation on infant development. In place of their natural mothers, he constructed 2 kinds of surrogates: a bare, wire model with a milk bottle and nipple, and a terrycloth model. Results showed that the monkeys always preferred the terrycloth model except during feeding times when they always preferred the model with the bottle. In fact, the monkeys were so much more attached to the terrycloth model, that they would cling to it while attempting to feed from the wire model. Harlow concluded that food-giving does not render an attachment between mother and child. In other experiments, Harlow demonstrated that monkeys who were deprived of any surrogate during the first 8 months of life were unable to make contact and socialize with other monkeys. He also demonstrated that "contact comfort" was an important variable in mother-child attachment formation.

20. **(B)** In human engineering, the special abilities and limitations of man must be taken into account in such a way that design engineers can effectively incorporate the human operator as a component in the man-machine system. The human factors engineer is concerned with the contriving, designing and producing of structures and machines useful to man. He applies knowledge of the properties of matter to the task of creating equipment for human use.

21. **(B)** Anxiety is an emotional state characterized by non-specific fears and various autonomic symptoms. The effect of anxiety is different for different learning tasks. One major finding is that anxiety does not hinder the learning of simple tasks, such as discrimination learning, but does hinder the learning of more complicated, less familiar tasks.

22. **(D)** When engaging in a serial-learning task, such as learning the alphabet, some parts of the list are usually easier to learn than others. A serial-position effect usually occurs which makes the items at the beginning of the list easiest to learn (primacy effect), the items at the end of the list the next easiest to learn (recency effect), and the items at the middle of the list most difficult to learn.

23. **(C)**   Word length is not an important characteristic influencing the learning of verbal material.

24. **(C)**   While all of the choices are types of human learning, the most distinctly human and significant type of learning is verbal learning. Verbal learning provides an important link between elementary non-verbal learning processes, language, and thought. All formal and informal education in older children and adults involves verbal learning.

25. **(C)**   The "anima" is Jung's theoretical construct of the female image. He believed that the "anima" is the projected image of the female throughout history in man's unconscious. This internalized female image is based on men's real experiences with women, particularly his mother, sister or other family members and on the collective experience of men throughout history. In contrast to the "anima," both the "anima" and the "animus" are archetypes in Jung's theory of the collective unconscious.

26. **(B)**   In general, humans do not have the life experience, cognitive, verbal and motor skills required to complete an I.Q. test before the age of seven. Few people question the reliability of I.Q. tests. The validity of these tests has been questioned.

27. **(E)**   Arousal is a total physiological response to a situation. During arousal, the EEG pattern in the brain changes. The autonomic nervous system (ANS) becomes more active during arousal states. The sympathetic part of the ANS increases heart rate, blood pressure, and distributes more blood to the exterior muscles. It also causes changes in the muscles and internal organs by causing blood to be pumped away from internal organs and muscles. It then rushes toward exterior muscles in the trunk and limbs. The entire body prepares for action when in an aroused state. The results of lie detector tests are not admissible in a court of law because they are only 65% reliable.

28. **(B)**   There are several variations of the lie detector, but practically all lie detectors measure heart rate, respiration, and perspiration rate (galvanic skin response). The assumption behind the use of the lie detector is that a person can hide external emotional expression but not the involuntary, physiological changes that accompany a stressful situation such as lying to police detectives.

29. **(A)**   To state that a distribution is positively skewed is an attempt to describe the curve form of that frequency distribution. A few extreme higher values form a positively skewed graph.

30. **(B)**   Since the median is the single middle score in a distribution, it is not affected by a few extreme scores, unless it is one of those extreme scores. Then it would not be a representative median. In contrast, the mean is an average

of all the scores in a distribution; therefore, it would always be affected by extreme scores.

31. **(B)** Introspection is no longer considered an appropriate method of research in psychology. Introspection involves an examining of one's own thoughts and feelings and making inferences based on this examination. It was thought that if a psychologist could arrive at a clearer understanding of his own psychological functioning, he would also understand human functioning in general, more clearly.

32. **(A)** A longitudinal study is an extended examination of the same subject or subjects over a (usually long) period of time. This approach is particularly useful in examining the stability of a behavior characteristic over time, or the development of a behavior over time.

33. **(C)** In split-half reliability the correlation between the two scores is the reliability coefficient. Usually, the examiner uses scores on odd and even items as two scores. This procedure is preferred to comparing scores from the first and second half of the test due to practice effects and fatigue. The split-half reliability coefficient is often called the coefficient of internal consistency because the comparison of two scores on a test indicates whether the test has an underlying consistency.

34. **(E)** Group testing has definite advantages over individual testing. The reduction of cost, increase in reliability and objectivity of scoring are all considerable advantages that make group testing more practical than individual testing in many situations.

35. **(C)** A constant fraction of the stimulus must be increased for noticeable differences. Their proportion is symbolized as:

$$\Delta I / I = K$$

in which I symbolizes intensity and Delta I the increase necessary to yield the just noticeable difference (j.n.d.).

36. **(A)** The Method of Limits, the Method of Average Error and the frequency method are the three basic statistical methods employed in threshold analysis. They all present a constant Standard stimulus (St) and a variable Comparison stimulus (Co). The three differ in their focus on discriminations. The Method of Limits notes at what level the subject's responses shift from one type to another. The Method of Average Error notes the accuracy of the subject's discriminations. The frequency method notes the relative frequency of the subject's responses.

37. **(A)** Affective disorders are characterized by a disturbance of mood ac-

companied by related symptoms. Mood is defined as a prolonged emotional state which colors the whole psychic life and generally involves either depression or elation. In affective disorders, mood tends to be at one extreme or the other. The patient may be depressed, or he may be manic, or he may exhibit bipolar symptoms, an alternation between depression and mania.

38. **(B)**   The process of lateral inhibition has two major functions in the visual system. It reduces the amount of repetitious information being sent to our brains. In addition, it serves to sharpen the contrast at the edges of objects.

39. **(C)**   In choosing the best move in a card game, one must be able to generate a number of possible solutions; therefore, divergent thinking is the process being utilized. Divergent thinking requires flexibility, fluency of ideas, and originality.

40. **(C)**   The backward masking effect can be achieved in experiments by flashing a letter on a screen and following the letter image (target stimulus) with a flash of bright light (interfering stimulus). The effect the light flash has on the letter image is to "erase" it from one's perception. The backward masking effect demonstrates that the brief life of memory codes can be easily erased by input that is specific to the given sense modality.

41. **(B)**   The concept of a differential threshold (DL) is basic to understanding sensory systems. The differential threshold is not considered constant, even for a specific sensory system. For example, if you are in a room with one person talking, you will definitely notice when a second person begins talking. That additional sound energy will be above the DL. If you are in a room where 20 people are talking, you may not notice if one other person begins to speak. In this case the DL is higher; a greater amount of sound energy is needed in order for the addition to be noticed. In general, the greater the intensity of the original stimulus, the greater is the differential threshold.

42. **(D)**   Photoreception is not a characteristic of light itself, but photons, waves, and intensity are. Another characteristic of light not mentioned above is composition. Light is thought of by physicists as having a dual nature. On the one hand, they see it as composed of *photons* — packets of energies. On the other hand, it is thought to consist of *waves* which are described by their wave lengths. *Intensity* refers to the number of photons of light while *composition* is the number of wave lengths.

43. **(A)**   In the DSM-IV, the essential features of paranoia are persistent, persecutory delusions or delusions of jealousy. The persecutory delusions usually involve a single theme or an organized series of themes, such as being drugged, poisoned, conspired against or harassed.

44.   **(A)**   The loudness of a sound is closely related to the intensity of the physical stimulus. Intensity is a measure of the amount of physical energy a stimulus sends to our senses, in this case our auditory system. We experience a high intensity sound as being loud. Hence, in perceiving the distance of a sound, loudness and intensity are important factors. In addition to these factors, previous psychological and physical experience with the sound is of great importance.

45.   **(A)**   The iris responds to dimmer light by dilating. This adjusts the amount of light entering the eye through the pupil. When the light dims, the iris opens more to allow more light in. Conversely, when the light becomes brighter, the iris constricts to reduce the amount of light entering the pupil.

46.   **(B)**   Phonemes are the smallest units of sound in a language. They are single vowel and consonant sounds found in every language. English has 45 phonemes. Phonemes are the first sounds that an infant makes.

47.   **(A)**   When we view any close, three-dimensional object, each eye receives a slightly different view because each sees the world from a slightly different position. This produces binocular disparity and double imagery. Without binocular vision, it is very difficult to distinguish between a three-dimensional space and a flat surface representing a three-dimensional space.

48.   **(E)**   Reinforcement theory has proven that reinforcement is most effective if it occurs immediately after a task has been performed. End-of-the-year bonuses or quarterly reviews may not be as effective as immediate bonuses. Investigation of optimal schedules of reinforcement is ongoing and diverse; both negative and positive reinforcement schedules have been shown to be quite effective on worker productivity and satisfaction.

49.   **(A)**   The two groups of girls to be compared constitute two independent means. A t-test on these populations would determine the difference, if any, between their mean I.Q. scores. This t-test would not assume that the groups overlap, or that one group of girls is a sample of a larger population of the other girl group. Since the psychologist is only interested in the difference of the two I.Q. means, a factorial design would not be necessary.

50.   **(C)**   The Z-table is derived from the normal distribution. Z-scores are used to compare the test scores of different individuals. They tell us by how many standard deviations a score varies from the mean.

51.   **(E)**   "Template matching" explains how our perceptual system might work. Representations, or templates, of patterns perceived in the environment are stored in memory. Recognition occurs when the internal pattern of a template is compared to the pattern of the external stimulus. This process has been studied mainly for letters and words.

52. **(C)** The Manifest Anxiety Scale (MA) is a self-report inventory that determines an individual's arousal level in comparison to group scores on a test. Because anxiety and arousal level is thought to correlate with drive level, learning theorists have been interested in the performance levels of High versus Low Anxious scorers. Many studies using this scale have shown that High Anxious individuals do better on verbal learning tasks than do Low Anxious individuals.

53. **(E)** Wavelength, intensity/brightness and saturation are all interrelated, and it is the combination of these factors that produce "hue." Wavelength of light is the most important factor determining which hue we perceive. Intensity, or brightness, also differs for different hues. As for saturation, the hue is called "saturated" if only a single wavelength is perceived. As different wavelengths are added, the hue becomes grayer and less "saturated."

54. **(E)** A "fake" drug is known as a placebo. A placebo is used to control for effects caused by the simple ingestion of a pill or injection of a drug. It is also used as a baseline measure against which the effects of the other drugs are compared. In order to demonstrate that a drug is effective, one must show that it had a greater effect on the subject than the placebo.

55. **(D)** Reflex action is not a factor in the acquisition of motor skills. The other choices are all important factors of motor skill acquisition. Feedback is considered one of the strongest variables controlling performance. The more frequently feedback is given, the better is the performance of the task. Repetition refers to practice of the task. Repetition facilitates learning and development of the skill. The distribution of practice, as well as the amount of time spent practicing, will also affect the rate at which a person learns a motor task. Studies have shown that spaced practice results in the most efficient learning.

56. **(C)** Establishing familiarity and integrating basic responses is the first phase of learning a perceptual-motor task. This phase is called cognition and involves becoming familiar with what type of task is at hand, what must be done, what materials are required, what movements must be made. During the next phase — fixation — one receives kinesthetic feedback (information from the muscles) by performing the task. During this phase, one learns to make the task response under appropriate stimulus conditions. During the third phase — automation — one continues to practice the skill while focusing on the fine details and organizing responses into larger units.

57. **(B)** According to Freud, fixation results from abnormal personality development. Freud stated that a person feels a certain amount of frustration and anxiety as he passes from one stage of development to the next. If that frustration and anxiety become too great, development may halt the person becoming fixated at the stage he is trying to grow out of. For example, an overly dependent child is thought to be fixated. Development has ceased at an early stage preventing the child from growing up and becoming independent.

58.　**(B)**　The ego creates defense mechanisms to deal with the excessive anxiety which can result from the clash between the id (and its desires) and the superego (and its moral imperatives). Examples of defense mechanisms include repression, displacement, reaction-formation, intellectualization, projection and denial.

59.　**(B)**　*The Interpretation of Dreams* was one of Sigmund Freud's most famous books, dealing with psychoanalytic and personality theory.

60.　**(C)**　The prodromal phase of alcoholism is the second phase of this disorder. It is characterized by blackouts, in which the drinker remains conscious and does not appear to be greatly intoxicated. However, he later has no recall of the events that transpired. In the prodromal phase, the drinker treats alcohol more as a drug than a beverage. At this point, the individual becomes preoccupied with his drinking.

61.　**(C)**　Thomas Szasz, in books such as *Ideology and Insanity*, believes that mental illness as the term is used is a myth. "Illness" implies a disease model and no one has demonstrated that maladaptive behavior patterns are reliably the result of underlying neurological damage or malfunction.

62.　**(A)**　In modeling, an individual learns by observing and then imitating the behavior of others. For example, to rid a client of a dog phobia, the therapist exposes the client to both live and filmed displays of people interacting fearlessly with dogs. The client then imitates this behavior, eventually overcoming his fear of dogs. As a number of research programs have shown, this kind of learning helps people acquire new resources in a relatively short time.

63.　**(C)**　Freud believed that the primary driving force in an individual's life is the sexual urge (the libido). His theory of motivational development was particularly concerned with sexual gratification, as it changed in relation to the child's body. His theory of personality constructs (the id, ego and superego) also deals with the sexual urge, as it confronts the constraints of the outer world.

64.　**(C)**　Late in his life, Freud proposed that the aim of all life was death, and that human behavior was the outcome of a struggle between Thanatos (the death instinct) and Eros (the life instinct). Freud contended that the goal of all instincts was a return to inorganic matter, to death and the end of all stimulation.

65.　**(A)**　Conceived by Fritz Perls, gestalt psychology tries to help a patient become a whole, integrated person, by expanding the patient's self-awareness to include presently unacceptable and undesirable aspects of his personality. The underlying premise of this approach is that neurotic behavior results from a lack of integration of various aspects of the self. The focus, therefore, is always on the self, although the therapy takes place within a group.

66.   **(E)**   A between-subjects design deals with differences among people, and this decreases efficiency. It is a conservative form of design, but this conservatism does afford at least one advantage. There is no chance of one treatment level affecting another treatment level because the same person never receives both treatments. A tradeoff is thus made between confused subject differences and confused treatment levels.

67.   **(B)**   Sublimation is an example of a defense mechanism. A defense mechanism is a pattern created by the ego to deal with id impulses that contradict social taboos as embodied by the superego. In sublimation, the direct expression of an unacceptable motive is denied, and a related, acceptable behavior is substituted. For example, dancing can be a sublimation for the fulfillment of sexual desires.

68.   **(B)**   Matina Horner studied the attitudes of both men and women towards members of their own sex who have succeeded in traditionally male-dominated occupations. Sixty-five percent of the women believed that success would lead to negative results for the women described, while less than 10% of the men anticipated negative consequences for the successful men. From these results, Horner postulated that women are motivated to avoid success in occupational and intellectual pursuits in order to ensure success in emotional and relational pursuits.

69.   **(C)**   Ideographic study involves selecting methods of study that will not blur or conceal the uniqueness of the individual subject. The ideographic approach emphasizes the importance of individual traits in determining behavior, and thus recommends study of the individual as the most effective approach to understanding behavior. Since Allport did not believe in the validity of general principles of behavior, he preferred to use the ideographic method. Allport was the first psychologist to stress the ideographic approach.

70.   **(A)**   Most theories of motivation point to organic drives or reward-seeking impulses as the fundamental basis of action. However, the principle of *functional autonomy* states that a given activity or behavior may become an end in itself, even though it was originated as the means to some other end. Certain activities, therefore, may be capable of sustaining themselves without biological reinforcement simply because they are enjoyable. For example, according to Allport, although people need no longer hunt for food, they may continue to do so because they like to hunt.

71.   **(A)**   The Yerkes-Dodson Law (1908) argues that a continuum of arousal levels, from very low to very high, can be found to correspond to performance levels in various tasks. Given the level of arousal in a situation, one can predict quality of performance. Eysenck took this a step further, by saying that the introvert/extrovert dimension of personality could be found to correspond to the general level of cortical arousal. Introverts would show the greatest levels of

cortical stimulation, while extroverts would show the lowest. Thus, Eysenck gave this dimension of personality an inherited basis, which has been tested and substantiated by experimentation.

72. **(D)** Eysenck's personality theory is considered hierarchical, consisting of three levels. At the first level, the observable or *phenotypical* level, introversion and extroversion are determined, typically with pen and pencil tests. Qualities such as shyness, sociability, activity and impulsiveness are scored. The second level in Eysenck's theory involves performance tests which assess motor movements and vigilance, as well as conditioning tests, to assess introversion and extroversion. The third level is called the genotypical level and is the causal level for the preceding two levels. At this third level, the basis for personality is conceptualized as a balance of physical excitation and inhibition, and is therefore, considered the biological basis of personality in Eysenck's theory.

73. **(C)** Correlation is related to predictability, through the concept of predictive validity. Predictive validity is the degree to which a test measures what it is supposed to measure. This validity is based on correlational data and cannot be determined without such.

74. **(D)** The range is the simplest measure of variation since it gives the limits within which all the elements of a distribution are confined. The range of a set of scores is the difference between the highest and lowest score in a set of scores. For example if you have the scores 18, 12, 23, 30, 34, then 12 is the lowest score and 34 is the highest score. The difference between the highest and lowest score is 22. Hence, the range is 22.

75. **(C)** The resolution of the transference neurosis is one of the most important parts of the cure in classical psychoanalysis. For it to occur successfully, the analyst must be able to maintain the stance of compassionate neutrality. Transference neurosis refers specifically to displaced and usually intense and inappropriate reactions of the patient to the analyst.

76. **(B)** A moral sense of the world is embodied in the personality component called the superego. The superego represents the taboos and mores or rules of the society in which the child lives. The process by which the child comes to learn cultural norms is called socialization. Hence, the development of the superego represents the child's moral socialization.

77. **(B)** For many years perception was explained by the empiricist theory. This theory assumes that we don't see shapes, distances, or forms at all. We see only points of light arranged in various manners. Some of these arrangements have strong nonvisual memories associated with them which gives us the ability to measure distance. Thus, the empiricist theory relies a great deal on learning as an explanation for our experience of the world. This view of perception has been refuted by the nativists, who believe that human perception is innate.

78. **(E)**   Minimum form gradient is not a monocular depth cue. Monocular depth cues convey to us information about space through one eye only. Relative size refers to figures becoming smaller as they are seen at further distances. Interposition is when one figure interrupts the outline of another. The texture-density gradient is the rate at which some property changes uniformly from one part of the area portrayed to another. Linear perspective is the effect in which lines that would be parallel on the ground appear to converge on the picture plane.

79. **(D)**   General-adaptation syndrome describes the three stages the body passes through in its reaction to stress: the alarm reaction, the stage of resistance, and the stage of exhaustion. The syndrome can ultimately lead to bodily damage during the final stage of exhaustion. At this point, prolonged stress and the resulting physical arousal exhausts the body's resources. This is caused in part by a depletion of the adrenal hormones. When this occurs, disorders such as rheumatism and arthritis can develop. Ultimately, death may result from prolonged exhaustion.

80. **(A)**   The Cannon-Bard theory argues, "if we see a bear, we experience fear, and then we run." Cannon and Bard considered the thalamus the "seat of the emotions." An emotion-producing stimulus first stimulates the thalamus, which then discharges impulses to the lower brain area, which in turn activates the cerebral cortex and the autonomic nervous system. This produces a general state of arousal which is experienced as an emotion. The observable behavior — in this case, running — shortly follows the emotion.

81. **(C)**   In backward conditioning, the CS is presented after the UCS. Backward conditioning is not very effective, if at all. In a classical conditioning experiment, backward conditioning would take place if a light (CS) would be turned on shortly after the food (UCS) was delivered to the dog. This particular procedure has shown that no response is conditioned even though there exists a temporal contiguity between the CS and UCS.

82. **(D)**   Because of the disguised nature of wish-fulfillment in dreams, Freud distinguished between the manifest, literal, content of the dream and the latent, symbolic, and true meaning of the dream. The mental process that converts what is wished into disguised, manifest images is called the "dreamwork." It is the function of the psychoanalyst to undo this dreamwork and reveal the true wishes of the dreamer.

83. **(C)**   Rogers' personality constructs are the organism and the self. The organism is conceived to be the locus of experience; experience includes everything available to the awareness and all that occurs within the organism. The self or self-concept refers to the organized and consistent set of perceptions that is self-referential, i.e., that refer to "I" or "me." It also includes the perceptions of the relationships between the self and the rest of the world. In addition to the self, there is an ideal self which represents what the individual aspires to be.

84. **(A)** The figure depicts a perfect, positive correlation. Note that all the observations fall on the same straight line. This is a perfect "linear relation." Since this is a positive correlation, X increases as Y increases by a proportionate amount.

85. **(D)** There are four basic tastes, but none of these differentially influence the intensity of a taste. The other three choices do influence taste intensity. Generally, the higher the concentration of the stimulus, the more intense is the taste experienced. Also, the larger the area of tongue stimulated, the more intense is the taste. Two different parts of the tongue may be stimulated by two different tastes at the same time. This process is called "contrast" and it can affect taste intensity. Additionally, saliva must mix with the stimuli in order to taste them. Therefore, the amount of saliva is also an important factor in intensity of taste.

86. **(A)** The vestibular organs provide a sense of balance by monitoring the movements and position of the head. There are two groups of vestibular organs. These are the semicircular canals and the otolith organs. They are both located in the inner ear. The semicircular canals do not respond to continuous movement. Rather, they respond only to changes in the rate of motion of the head. The otolith organs do not respond to movements. Instead, they respond to the actual position of one's head. Together, the semicircular canals and otolith organs provide us with a continuous sense of balance.

87. **(C)** I.Q., age, and sex are the three factors in this study. Conceptually, this is a $2 \times 2 \times 2$ factorial design. The different groups (i.e., male/female, thirty/sixty, and 100 I.Q./200 I.Q.) constitute the two levels in each of these factors.

88. **(C)** The range of a set of numbers is defined as the highest score minus the lowest score, in this case, $692 - 5 = 687$. The range is the quickest and least informative measure of variability. The best measure to use is the standard deviation.

89. **(D)** Cones are located primarily in the fovea. There are about 6 to 7 million cones in each eye. Cones require a large amount of light energy to respond to a stimulus.

90. **(C)** Cones respond differentially to different color wavelengths, providing us not only with color perception but also an ability to sense fine gradations of color.

91. **(B)** Feature analysis theories, of which the best known is the "Pandemonium" theory, describe mechanisms whereby the nervous system analyzes small details in sensory input. Feature analysis also describes the cognitive system as being hierarchically organized in its analysis of information.

92. **(C)** To Adler, the goal of behavior is to compensate for a subjectively perceived sense of inferiority by achieving superiority. Therefore, an individual cannot fully comprehend his life without understanding the goal he or she is striving for.

93. **(A)** According to Weber's Law, "a stimulus must be increased by a constant fraction of its value to be just noticeably different." In Weber's equation $\Delta I/I = K$, K is that constant fraction, while I symbolizes intensity and Delta I the increase in intensity necessary to yield the just noticeable difference (j.n.d.), the threshold level. The j.n.d. is also referred to as the difference threshold (DL).

94. **(D)** The colored portion of the eye is called the iris. It is the tissue that surrounds the pupil and regulates its size. By contracting or dilating, the iris adjusts the amount of light entering the eye.

95. **(A)** Experiments with children, in which they were rewarded for imitating a model, formed the basis of Miller and Dollard's conclusions concerning learning from model imitation. They concluded that imitation of social behavior probably derives strength from the fact that conformist behavior is rewarded in many situations, whereas nonconformist behavior often results in punishment.

96. **(D)** Allport stressed the use of the ideographic method in his research on personality. In ideographic study, an effort is made not to conceal or blur the uniqueness of a particular individual. If the emphasis of a study is upon personal dispositions (individual traits) as the primary determinants of behavior, then the only effective theoretical approach is the ideographic method.

97. **(A)** In a positively skewed distribution, the mode is smaller than the median, which is smaller than the mean.

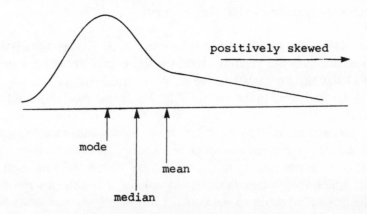

In a positively skewed distribution, the mode and median are more accurate measures of central tendency than the mean.

98. **(C)** In an experiment, the independent variable is the one which the investigator manipulates, hoping to affect the outcome of the dependent variable (usually the subject's response). To determine the effect of the experimental manipulation, one measures the dependent variable.

99. **(B)** Conditioned, or secondary reinforcement, occurs when the reinforcing stimulus is not inherently pleasing or reinforcing, but becomes so through association with other pleasant or reinforcing stimuli. Money is an example of a secondary (conditioned) reinforcer. Coins and paper currency are not in themselves pleasing, but the things they buy are pleasing. Therefore, an association is made between money and inherently pleasing primary reinforcers, such as food and drink. Hence, the term "conditioned reinforcer" is used.

100. **(D)** Kurt Lewin first developed the field theory of behavior, which emphasizes that behavior does not depend on the organism alone or the environment alone, but on what occurs between the two. In field theory, psychological events, like physical events, are thought to represent a balance and interaction of many forces. A change anywhere in the system is seen as affecting the whole system. For psychologists applying this theory, behavior is shaped not by individual chains of cause and effect, but by the interactions of forces which make up the entire field.

101. **(B)** Rehearsal serves two functions. It allows items in short-term memory to be retained. Also, it appears to facilitate material from the short-term to long-term memory. In transference of most contents, rehearsal is necessary for learning.

102. **(B)** Generalization is the application of a response to a whole class or group of stimuli, although the response has been conditioned for only a limited portion of that group. In contrast, discrimination is the ability to recognize differences between similar stimuli. This ability results from learning the different consequences of responding to the similar stimuli.

103. **(A)** In a serial-learning task, some parts of the list are usually easier to learn than others. A serial-position effect usually occurs, in which items at the beginning of the list are easiest to recall, items at the end of the list are next easiest to recall, and items in the middle of the list are the most difficult to recall.

104. **(E)** A discrete motor task differs from a continuous motor task because it involves a series of movements which are separate from each other. Typing is an example of a discrete task. Continuous tasks are made up of a series of smooth movements which merge together. An example of a continuous movement is steering the driving wheel in an automobile. In general, discrete skills are more easily forgotten than continuous skills.

105. **(A)** The correlation of – .70 is the best predictor. Correlations can have

any value between -1.0 and $+1.0$. As the absolute value of the correlation approaches 1.0, the prediction based on the correlation becomes more accurate. A negative correlation shows an inverse relationship between x and y: as x goes up, y goes down, and vice versa. A positive correlation shows a direct relationship between x and y: as x goes up, y goes up, and vice versa.

106. **(A)** By definition, the standard deviation is

$$\sqrt{\sum_i \frac{(x_i - \overline{x})^2}{n}} \ , \text{ where } \overline{x} = \frac{\Sigma x_i}{n}.$$

The standard deviation gives a feeling for how far away from the mean we can expect an observation to be.

107. **(D)** The executive routine model proposes that memory works in a manner similar to that of a computer program. The mind, like a computer, has a set of strategies, component activities or subroutines, and rules for their use. The executive routine is the mechanism which uses the routines to decide on an appropriate action. It has final control over the mind's processes as a whole. It is the mechanism that intervenes between memory and action.

108. **(A)** It has been hypothesized that it takes more time to produce associations to pictures than to words, because pictures first produce visual associations which must then be transformed into words. It has been demonstrated that visual memories may be clustered in memory by their distinctive physical —spatial properties rather than by their names. Thus, the processing time involved for transforming the visual impression into a verbal impression should include a memory "search" for the correct category, and then a specific name.

109. **(D)** Wilhelm Wundt (1832-1920) established the first laboratory of psychology at the University of Leipzig, Germany, in 1879. The establishment of Wundt's laboratory prompted the further establishment of experimental psychology laboratories in several locales.

110. **(A)** A reaction to structuralism, gestalt psychology was founded in 1912 in Germany by Max Wertheimer, and his colleagues K. Koffka and W. Kohler. Gestaltists believed that behavior and experiences are not compounds of simple elements, but rather of patterns or organizations. They believed this theory holds true with most perceived objects; the parts or features of the object are somehow organized through perception so that they are seen as a unified whole. The whole of the phenomenon is seen as more than the sum of its parts. Although perception was its main focus, gestalt psychology can be applied to nearly all forms of behavior.

111. **(C)** Amnesia, fugue, somnambulism, and multiple personality are four types of dissociative reactions. In dissociative reactions, certain mental processes

become detached from the mainstream of consciousness. Schizo-affective disorders are thought of as combinations of schizophrenic and affective disorders.

112. **(A)** Bipolar cells are involved in vision. The other four choices are components of neurons. Dendrites receive information from the axons of other neurons, while axons send information to neurons, glands, or muscles. The myelin sheath surrounds the axon.

113. **(E)** Pupil dilation is controlled by the sympathetic nervous system, whereas the parasympathetic nervous system controls heartbeat, constriction of bronchi, digestion and secretion of saliva.

114. **(E)** Frederick Perls was the founder of gestalt psychology. Its main tenet is that neurotic behavior is a result of a lack of integration of various aspects of an individual. The therapy focuses on the person as a whole and emphasizes the individual's experiences at the moment. The functionalist school emphasized mind-body interactions. Its most influential proponents were William James and John Dewey.

115. **(A)** Noam Chomsky was a linguist who first distinguished between surface and deep structures. He constructed a theory of transformational grammar. Osgood developed a technique for measuring the connotative meanings of words called the semantic differential. Subjects were asked to rate individual words on several scales. Each scale has seven intervals between antonyms.

116. **(B)** Kohlberg is well known for his theory of moral development, which involves three levels: premorality, the morality of conventional role conformity, and the morality of self-accepted principles. The period of formal operations is the final stage in Piaget's system of cognitive development. In this stage, the child's thinking becomes more propositional, logical, and idealistic.

117. **(A)** A platykurtic curve is marked by flatness, indicating a wide dispersion of measurements. It is possible for this kind of curve to be positively or negatively skewed, but skewness in itself does not determine a platykurtic curve. A curve that is peaked is called leptokurtic.

118. **(D)** Correlations are indicative of a relationship between two variables. The higher the absolute value of the correlation, the stronger the relationship between the variables. Correlation measures how well the existence of a variable or some aspect of a variable is predictive of another variable. Unfortunately, correlation tells us nothing about which of the two variables has an effect on the other. Many times, it is a third variable that is affecting both variables together.

119. **(D)** Aptitude tests serve to predict subsequent performance, e.g., to determine if an individual will profit from an education at a particular college. Examiners usually apply the term "aptitude" to tests which measure the effects

of learning under uncontrolled or unknown conditions. In addition, people who take aptitude tests do not usually have a uniform prior experience. All the people taking the Graduate Record Examination have attended college, but not the same college, and they have not all studied the same subjects.

120. **(B)** The Thematic Apperception Test (TAT) was designed by Murray and Morgan in 1935 to determine an individual's major themes of concern by having him respond freely to vague and ambiguous pictures presented on TAT cards. Theoretically, the themes expressed in the responses reflect the subjects' concerns, i.e., the subject projects his concerns on to the TAT pictures.

121. **(E)** For each year of age up to 15 years, there is a set of abilities characteristic to the normal child. If these abilities develop earlier than average, the child is considered more intelligent than the average child; if the abilities develop later, then the child is considered below average in intelligence. The I.Q. for children is computed by dividing the mental age (M.A.) by the chronological age (C.A.) and then multiplying the quotient by 100 to eliminate decimals:

$$I.Q. = \frac{M.A.}{C.A.} \times 100.$$

122. **(A)** The MMPI was not developed within a particular theoretical framework. It is a self-report personality test, consisting of 550 statements to which the subject is asked to answer "true," "false," or "cannot say" in respect to himself. It was originally designed to discriminate between "normals" and people in psychiatric categories. It is now used to assess an individual's personality.

123. **(E)** All of these variables affect an individual's conformity to a group. The greater the number of people in a group that agree to an opinion, the greater the pressure on an individual to conform. Also, groups made up of experts, friends, or people familiar to the subject will increase conformity. To reduce conformity, have the subject make a prior commitment to his opinion, or include people in the group — sometimes even one will do — who agree with his opinion. Finally, a person with low self-esteem is more likely to conform than one with high esteem.

124. **(B)** In 1968, Kitty Genovese was murdered. While 38 people heard her cries for help over a period of half an hour, no one called the police. Shocked by the incident, Darley and Latane studied similar situations in the laboratory and found that people are least likely to help when there are many possible helpers. They called this effect a diffusion of responsibility because all possible helpers shunned personal responsibility, figuring someone else would help.

125. **(A)** In spite of the confederate's "desperate" screams and complaints of a heart condition, most of the subjects reluctantly complied with the orders of the

experimenter — a "legitimate authority" — and eventually applied the maximum shock. Although intelligence of the subject had no effect on compliance, the status of the experimenter showed a strong effect. From this experiment, Milgram concluded that the events in Nazi Germany could have occurred anywhere, even in small-town America, because of people's tendency to obey authority.

126. **(E)**   Janis' focus on group decision-making led him to study powerful decision-makers coming together to decide upon courses of action of potentially historical significance. His description of what happens is called groupthink. Most often, groupthink generates bad decisions because of the group's own characteristics, such as a sense of invulnerability, moral self-righteousness, a tendency towards self-censorship of divergent views and strong conformity pressures.

127. **(E)**   Repeated hand-washing is known as an obsessive-compulsive neurosis, although, as in other obsessive-compulsive disorders, the two components need not exist simultaneously. Repeated hand-washing is termed compulsive if the person feels compelled to perform the behavior, interfering with more appropriate behavior. As opposed to a compulsion, an obsession is a recurring thought, rather than an action, which a person cannot control or stop. This disorder is thought to arise as a defense against anxiety. In the case of repeated hand-washing, the act may be associated with a conflict between masturbation and guilt.

128. **(A)**   Although ECT was once used as a treatment for schizophrenia, it has been shown to be ineffective in the treatment of the disorder. In fact, ECT has been shown to be effective only in the treatment of severe depression. How it works is not known.

129. **(C)**   A conduct disorder is characterized by observed behavior which varies from the norm of acceptable behaviors. An antisocial reaction is a type of conduct disorder. Antisocial reactions are typically characterized by: poor judgment, insensitivity, disregard for authority and law, and emotional immaturity. Psychologists generally agree that such a problem is a function of poor development of the conscience aggravated by environmental factors.

130. **(B)**   A rapid and sudden onset of symptoms is characteristic of reactive schizophrenia. The patient may suffer a pronounced shock, or trauma, just before the outbreak of the schizophrenia. If the patient was moderately well adjusted before the disturbance, the chances for recovery are fairly good.

131. **(E)**   Attention deficit/hyperactivity disorder is characterized by difficulty paying attention, high levels of activity at inappropriate times, difficulty controlling impulses, and impairment in social, academic, or occupational functioning. Although it may last into adulthood, it is typically first diagnosed in childhood,

often due to a child's behavioral problems and poor academic performance in school.

132. **(E)**   Frequently, a person experiencing a psychogenic fugue will move to a new geographic location and try to start an entirely new life. The emerging identity will usually be more gregarious and uninhibited than the prior personality, which was typically quiet and ordinary. Like amnesia, a fugue is usually precipitated by psychosocial stress. The duration of most fugues is brief — hours or days — although in rare cases a fugue will last many months.

133. **(B)**   It is generally accepted that neurotic symptoms are a result of inner, unresolved anxiety, which stirs up conflict within the individual. The symptoms manifested by the neurotic are similar to defense mechanisms in that they usually involve denial and distortion of reality. Depression is usually the result of the neurotic directing his displaced anxiety back at himself instead of at an external object.

134. **(A)**   Korsakoff's psychosis is associated with alcoholism. Major symptoms are loss of memory of recent events, time and space disorientation, and a tendency to make up stories to fill in the forgotten past. Current research indicates that the psychosis probably results from vitamin B deficiencies due to the poor eating habits associated with alcoholism.

135. **(C)**   The strongest possible correlations are +1.0 and –1.0. These are perfect correlations. Any correlation higher than +1.0 or lower than –1.0 is erroneous, and the data should be analyzed again.

136. **(D)**   The standard deviation is the square root of the variance. Hence, if we square the standard deviation we will obtain the variance. The formula for standard deviation is

$$\text{sd} = \sqrt{\frac{\sum_i (x_i - \bar{x})^2}{n}}$$

Therefore, variance $= (\text{sd})^2 = \dfrac{\sum_i (x_i - \bar{x})^2}{n}$

137. **(B)**   In Tolman's view, behavior is elicited by environmental cues, both internal and external, and by a variety of "unbalanced" situations. The motivation theory developed by Tolman is known as an expectancy-value theory. His theory states that behavior results from the interaction of the needs and demands of a person at any given time, with the person's perception of the quality of the environment at that time. Performance is the result of how much the person expected to attain what he wishes for, combined with the value attributed to that wish.

138. **(E)** Consistency or homeostatic theories maintain that the principal motivating force of the organism is to maintain a consistent physical or psychological state. The theory states that imbalanced relationships tend to change and become balanced.

139. **(D)** With the highest rates of performance, the variable-ratio schedule elicits consistently high rates even after prolonged discontinuance of the reinforcement. In fact, once an operant learning response has been established with a variable-ratio reinforcement schedule, it is difficult to extinguish the response.

140. **(C)** In secondary reinforcement, a neutral stimulus is paired with the conditioned stimulus, after that conditioned stimulus can reliably elicit the conditioned response. When this is accomplished, the new or second conditioned stimulus will elicit the conditioned response even though it was never directly paired with the unconditioned stimulus. In this manner, the original, neutral CS comes to work as a reinforcer for the second-order conditioning response.

141. **(E)** The standard deviation (sd) increases by the same multiple as each of its scores. In this case it is the multiple 5.

142. **(A)** The extent to which a test measures a theoretical construct is called construct validity. A psychological construct is a term that represents a set of consistent data about persons. The degree to which a test extracts information about the psychological construct is the degree to which it possesses construct validity, and therefore, the degree to which it is a valid measure of that construct.

143. **(B)** Bipolar disorder (often called manic depression) is characterized by alternating periods of depression and mania. Suicide attempts are most likely during the depression phase. The manic phase may involve an inflated sense of self-esteem, high levels of physical activity, flights of ideas, being unusually talkative, and distractibility.

144. **(E)** Fetishists are people whose preferred method of sexual arousal involves the use of non-living objects (other than those designed specifically for genital stimulation). Paraphilias include this and several other sexually oriented disorders. Frequently, fetishists masturbate while touching or smelling the fetish object, which is commonly a woman's underpants, bra, or other garment (paraphiliacs are almost exclusively male).

145. **(E)** The theory of cognitive dissonance states that individuals are motivated to keep their cognitions — beliefs, attitudes, values — internally and actively consistent. If an inconsistency reaches awareness, "dissonance" is produced. For example, if a person believes there is a positive relationship between smoking and cancer yet continues to smoke heavily, this person will experience psychological discomfort upon realizing this is an inconsistency. He will then be motivated to change his attitude or his behavior.

146. **(E)**   Leon Festinger proposed the theory of cognitive dissonance. Heider's balance theory and Osgood and Tannenbaum's congruity theory are also consistency theories, which maintain that the motivating force of an organism is to achieve consistent physical and psychological states.

147. **(D)**   According to the cognitive dissonance theory, only a small number of the heavy smokers believed that smoking was dangerous because the dissonance created by the inconsistency between attitude and action motivated the majority of the heavy smokers to change their attitudes, which were easier to change than their actions.

148. **(A)**   The social learning theory of aggression holds that most aggression is learned through operant conditioning. Therefore, aggression results only after certain actions are reinforced by rewards and discouraged by punishments. Modeling is another form of social learning that contributes to the development of aggressive behavior.

149. **(C)**   According to the social learning theory of aggression, if a child is rewarded for random aggressive behavior, it is highly probable that the behavior will occur again. On the other hand, if a child is punished for acting aggressively, the likelihood of that behavior occurring again is reduced. It has been found that the schedule of reinforcement is particularly important in the learning of aggressive responses. For example, if aggression is reinforced irregularly, the aggressive behavior will tend to last longer than if the reinforcement is continuous.

150. **(B)**   The belief that aggression is an inborn tendency in all animals, including man, has been most supported by the work of Konrad Lorenz.

151. **(A)**   Short-term memory (STM) is very limited in its capacity. It can only hold about seven items (plus or minus two items) of information at a time. This brief memory span requires deliberate rehearsal to prevent a specific memory from decaying over time.

152. **(D)**   The German philosopher Hermann Ebbinghaus was the first to examine learning and memory scientifically. His experiments in the late 1800s attempted to provide an empirical basis for the study of human learning, memory and association theory.

153. **(A)**   The work of William McDougall was especially important in classifying and understanding instincts. In addition to proposing that each instinct is receptive to certain stimuli, he further argued that the receptivity and behavioral components of each instinct might change as a function of learning. Therefore, as one becomes older, an instinct might be activated by different stimuli and produce many different behaviors.

154. **(D)**   Maslow's Hierarchy of Needs has five levels. These are: physiological needs, safety and security, love and belonging, esteem and self-esteem, and self-actualization. As one type of need is satisfied, the next higher in the hierarchy becomes the dominant motivating factor. According to Maslow, few people achieve the highest stage in the motivation hierarchy.

155. **(B)**   In an approach-avoidance conflict situation, one is both attracted to and repelled by the same goal. For example, one may want to go to college, but may also be fearful of the typical college work load.

156. **(D)**   Schmidt and Sigusch (1972), and others, have measured sexual arousal (penile erections and vaginal lubrication) while subjects view erotic material. Men are more aroused by explicit sexual scenes than romantic scenes, e.g., handholding on a beach. Women showed the opposite responses. Romantic scenes stimulated them while explicit sex scenes did not. Neither men nor women were aroused by homosexual scenes involving their own sex.

157. **(B)**   Skinner developed an apparatus consisting of a small enclosure with a lever device and a food receptacle. A hungry rat was placed in the box, and in time usually pressed the lever by chance, and automatically received food (a reward). After some time, most of the rats learned to make this response (lever-pressing) as soon as they entered the box. This learning was termed operant conditioning because the animal had to perform an operation to get a reward.

158. **(C)**   In the fixed-interval schedule, reinforcement is given after a fixed period of time, no matter how much work is done. This schedule has the lowest yield in terms of performance. However, just before the reinforcement is given, activity increases.

159. **(A)**   A platykurtic distribution is very flat, indicating a wide dispersion of measurements.

160. **(B)**   In a positively skewed distribution the mean is greater than both the median and the mode. In any skewed distribution the mean is affected most and pulled in the direction of the skew.

161. **(C)**   In analyzing the human input into any task, four psychological functions are usually distinguished. These are: perceptual processes, recall processes, problem-solving processes, and muscular processes. These components are considered when forming a step-by-step description of a task in a work cycle.

162. **(C)**   Extreme scores most dramatically affect the mean because the mean is essentially an average of a set of scores. The inclusion of extreme scores changes their average and might therefore, be a less desirable measure of central tendency.

163. **(A)**   According to Kohlberg, the premoral stage is the first level of moral behavior. During the early stage of this level, children have a good-bad conception of behavior. For the early premoral child, moral behavior is based on the subjective consequences.

164. **(E)**   A follicle is the part of the ovary where an egg matures. The other choices represent four early stages of embryonic development. Their correct maturational order is zygote, blastomeres, morula and blastula. There are also later stages which are not listed in this question.

165. **(C)**   Rapid movements that are automatic after practice are known as ballistic movements. In a ballistic movement, a sequence of movements is carried out as an organized whole, in proper order and with proper timing. Sensory feedback kicks in only after a group of movements, and not between each separate movement.

166. **(B)**   The cerebellar nuclei are important for maintaining a limb, or other body parts, in a steady, nonrelaxed position. In the diagnosis of cerebellar damage, the "finger-to-nose" movement is often tested. A normal person creates this movement in three steps. The finger moves ballistically to a point just in front of the nose, where it is then held for a moment. Then, the finger again begins to move toward the nose, slowly and under the control of the basal ganglia.

167. **(D)**   The cerebellum controls the ballistic movements of speaking, writing, playing an instrument, and performing most athletic skills. The basal ganglia control the slower, more gradual movements that are modified by sensory feedback while the movement is still occurring. The basal ganglia are involved with postures and movements of the body as a whole.

168. **(B)**   The recurrence of a response after extinction is called spontaneous recovery. This process makes complete extinction virtually impossible. Several, successive extinction trials minimize the effect of this process, but rarely is it ever permanently extinguished. Spontaneous recovery may demonstrate why it is so difficult to get rid of bad habits.

169. **(E)**   All of these are characteristic of first-born children. Although none of these relationships is especially strong, they do exist and have raised many questions about the factors contributing to them. Schachter and Zajone have suggested that these effects may be due to parents giving more specialized attention to their first-born children than to later-born children.

170. **(B)**   A "normal" I.Q. score is considered to be about 100, while 98% of the people who take I.Q. tests fall in the range between 60 and 140. Someone who scores above 140 is considered a genius.

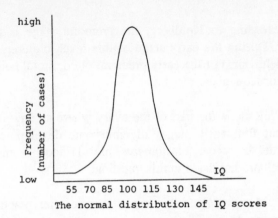

The normal distribution of IQ scores

171. **(C)**   Located in the midbrain, the RAS has abundant complex connections with other parts of the nervous system and sends out large numbers of fibers into the rest of the brain. The RAS also receives information directly from fibers coming from all parts of the nervous system. Due to its functions, the most important of which is modulation of the overall activity of the brain, the reticular activating system is believed to be the central coordinating point for information in the nervous system.

172. **(B)**   All the subjects considered $20 sufficient justification for telling the lie, and $1 inadequate. Those in the $1 group, therefore experienced cognitive dissonance (psychological distress) caused by the inconsistency between their attitude toward the job and their telling the lie.

Subsequently, they rated the job more enjoyable than previously. Those in the $20 group experienced no dissonance — they felt justified in lying — and therefore, reported no attitude change.

Kestinger's (1957) theory of cognitive dissonance can be applied to a wide variety of social situations which challenge a person's desire to maintain cognitive equilibrium.

173. **(D)**   According to Pavlov, a conditioned response is only inhibited during extinction; it is not permanently extinguished. As seen in the last frame of the diagram, conditioned behavior can reappear without additional conditioning, even though extinction appeared successful (frame 2).

174. **(C)**   Spontaneous recovery is the reappearance of a conditioned response after extinction, without extra conditioning. If a rest interval follows extinction, the CR will reappear in a somewhat weaker form. If the original conditioning beings again at this point, the CR will be strengthened very rapidly.

175. **(A)**   Extinction occurs when the conditioned stimulus is repeatedly presented without the unconditioned stimulus. The strength of the response elicited by the CS and its ability to elicit the CR at all, gradually decreases as the CS continues to be presented alone. The CR strength eventually declines to at least the level present before conditioning began.

176. **(E)**   In verbal learning, rehearsal allows items in short-term memory to

be retained and it also facilitates transference of material from short-term to long-term memory. Short-term memory holds the trace of an experience for only a limited amount of time. If there is no rehearsal, the items will be forgotten rapidly.

177. **(E)** Characteristics of verbal materials that influence how effectively they are learned include position in the list, similarity in appearance, meaning or category, frequency, and concreteness. The type and amount of past learning a person has done also affects his rate of acquisition of new material.

178. **(C)** The time spent learning is the important factor in rehearsal. The individual presentation rate and the number of trials are not as important.

179. **(C)** Behavior therapy attacks symptoms of behavioral disorders through the use of learning principles. There is no probing of the unconscious or any attempt to change the entire personality. There are four methods of behavior therapy: counterconditioning, operant conditioning, modeling, and cognitive restructuring.

180. **(D)** Joseph Wolpe developed systematic desensitization. In this procedure, a deeply relaxed person is told to imagine a series of situations producing progressively greater amounts of anxiety. The imagined scene is the stimulus, the anxiety is the undesired response and relaxation is the new response.

181. **(C)** Three of the most frequently used counterconditioning techniques are systematic desensitization, assertive training, and aversive conditioning. Assertive training is used for people who cannot express positive or negative feelings to others. Aversive conditioning tries to attach negative feelings to stimuli that are considered inappropriately attractive.

182. **(D)** Dollard, along with Doob and Miller, is a social learning theorist who proposed the frustration-aggression hypothesis. In this experiment, the absence of grain elicits frustration and aggression, which is taken out on the innocent pigeon.

183. **(B)** According to the frustration-aggression hypothesis, the most common source of aggression is frustration. Frustration concerning a goal not yet achieved can lead to aggression, and if the source of the frustration is nearby, the aggression may be taken out on that person or thing. If the source is unavailable, the aggression will be displaced onto someone or something else.

184. **(E)** The trained pigeon's aggression was displaced because it could not attack the source of its frustration. The newcomer's presence provided an object for the trained pigeon's aggression. Because it was there, the newcomer became the "scapegoat."

185. **(B)** One of the most important themes of existential psychology is the struggle between being and nonbeing. This struggle involves not only life and death, but also full acceptance of oneself versus partial acceptance or even

rejection of aspects of oneself. Psychologists such as Frankl, Laing, May, Tillich, and Maslow were interested in this theme.

186. **(A)**   Allport believed that terms like "ego" or "self" should be used as adjectives. He decided to rename the ego functions of the personality the "proprium" or "propriate functions." These functions include bodily sense, self-identity, self-esteem, rational thinking and cognitive style. The proprium is considered to develop with time; it is not innate.

187. **(C)**   The third stage of Erikson's theory of psychosocial development is called the locomotor-genital stage, lasting from age four to six. This period is characterized by the formation of initiative or guilt, the development of fine motor skills, and an increase in language development and curiosity.

188. **(A)**   The "shadow" represents the repressed unconscious drives and desires of the personal unconscious. Because it is believed to be found in all people, often referred to as a person's "dark side," it is considered part of the collective unconscious.

189. **(A)**   A morpheme is the smallest unit of meaning in a given language. In English, morphemes can be whole words, such as "boy"; prefixes such as "anti-"; or suffixes such as "-ing." There are more than 100,000 morphemes in English.

190. **(E)**   Noam Chomsky (1957) was the first to distinguish between surface and deep structure in language; he constructed a theory of transformational grammar based on these structures. In this system, a "kernel" of a sentence is the basic, declarative thought of the sentence. For example, "The boy hit the girl" could be a kernel sentence. This kernel sentence can be transformed to: "The girl was hit by the boy," "Did the boy hit the girl?," or "Wasn't the girl hit by the boy?" The kernel sentence, along with its transformations, comprise the basic patterns of surface structure.

191. **(C)**   Somatotyping is a system that describes personality in terms of an individual's physique. Sheldon defined three broad categories of body types: endomorph, mesomorph, and ectomorph. An ectomorph is characterized by a slender, fragile physique, and a sensitive, intellectual personality.

192. **(B)**   Carl Rogers developed client-centered therapy based on his theories of the self-actualizing potential in man. He felt that the patient in therapy should bear responsibility for his own self-actualization and wellness. In client-centered therapy, the therapist is non-directive, while the patient is responsible for working out his own problems.

193. **(C)**   Changes in family structure such as divorce, loss of parents, adoption, and severe or prolonged illness of a family member, all have a negative effect on the child's intellectual development. In general, these changes disrupt the stability of the child's intelligence quotient by acting as stressors in the child's life.

194. **(D)** Test validity is generally defined as the capacity of a test to measure what it sets out to measure. In terms of test construction, content validity is built into the test; an analysis of the subject matter or content of the test must be undertaken before the construction of test items. Criterion-related validity must also be established. To do this, one must correlate the test with some objective criterion that is an appropriate measure of the trait or ability that the test is supposed to be measuring.

195. **(D)** Compliance refers to a change in external behavior, while private acceptance refers to a change in attitude. In the presence of a group, the subjects conform with their beliefs outwardly; that is, they show compliance. The fact that they continued to do so in the group's absence shows that private acceptance also took place. Internalization is a very strong social response based on a desire to be "right." Once a belief is internalized it is highly resistant to change.

196. **(A)** Authoritarian persons prove to be greatly influenced by authority figures, and, the more authoritarian a person is, the more he or she will conform. "External" personalities feel their lives are controlled by factors outside their control, while "internals" feel life is in their control. "Externals" tend to conform more than "internals." It has been found that a large decrease in conformity results if even one person in a group disagrees. Tests have shown that conformity varies inversely with intelligence.

197. **(C)** When there is an inconsistency between actions and attitudes, psychological distress occurs. This is known as cognitive dissonance. In order to rid oneself of this dissonance, a person often changes his opinion or attitude so that it is in agreement with his actions.

198. **(B)** In a normal distribution 68% of the population falls within ± 1 standard deviation of the mean. 95% falls within ± 2 standard deviations of the mean, and 99.5% falls within ± 3 standard deviations of the mean.

199. **(D)** The correct formula to find out by how many standard deviations a score deviates from the mean is the formula for the Z-score. Z-scores are used to compare the scores of different individuals. Any normal distribution with a mean, μ, and variance σ^2 can be converted to a standard distribution with a mean $= 0$ and a variance $= 1$. The formula

$$Z = \frac{x - \mu}{\sigma}$$

could be used here as follows.

$$Z = \frac{630 - 550}{50} \qquad Z = 1.6$$

200. **(C)** This is a normal distribution, in which the mode, median, and mean are always equal.

201. **(D)** Lorenz was one of the leading ethologists of his day. Ducks and other species of birds exhibit this tendency to attach themselves to the first

moving object that they see.

202. **(B)**   Kohler spent years studying the problem-solving behavior of chimps. He observed that the animals often exhibited "insight," i.e., the sudden solution to a problem without the use of trial and error learning.

203. **(E)**   The lower a species is on the phylogenetic scale, the more its behavior is controlled by instincts and hormones. Rats are lower on the scale than any of the other species listed.

204. **(A)**   We tend to take credit for our successes. We blame others or situational variables for our errors and mistakes. However, we don't extend that consideration to others. When people make mistakes, we hold them totally responsible and discount any situational variables that may have influenced them.

205. **(B)**   We tend to like people who are similar to us in views and habits. We also like people who we are familiar with and who seem confident. And while physical attractiveness has the most influence on whether or not we will approach a person for the purpose of establishing a relationship, physical proximity dictates who we can see to be attracted to in the first place.

206. **(D)**   Humans tend to believe that if people are proficient in one area, then they are competent in other areas. This is the halo effect. Teachers tend to think that a student that is earning an "A" in their class is an overall "A" student.

207. **(C)**   Down's syndrome is the presence of an extra chromosome on the 21st pair. The incidence of the problem increases with the age of the woman, i.e., women in their 40s or older have a much higher risk of having a Down's syndrome baby than women in their early 20s.

208. **(E)**   Since the blind baby has never seen a smile, he or she can't be imitating it. Likewise, it cannot be a learned or nurtured behavior. Smiling when we are pleased or content must therefore be an innate (inborn) characteristic in humans. Congenital refers to factors being present at birth. Smiling usually doesn't occur for the first few months.

209. **(B)**   Progesterone and estrogen regulate the female reproductive cycle, development of secondary sex characteristics, and mood. Testosterone is the primary male sex hormone.

210. **(C)**   The stage of formal operations is noted for the ability of the individual to deal with abstract problems and concepts. It usually begins around puberty but research shows that some people never develop these skills, and continue to function at the level of concrete operations for life.

211. **(D)** A small quantity of lithium (a white powdered metal) is essential for human functioning. Some people who suffer from manic depression have a lithium deficiency; their bodies don't retain the metal. Lack of lithium produces the mood swings observed. Treatment consists of taking lithium carbonate capsules to maintain their body's lithium levels.

212. **(B)** In Freudian psychoanalysis, the patient has a deep-seated fear that he or she doesn't want to face. He or she displaces this fear by developing a phobia — another irrational fear that is easier to deal with. For example, the patient may have a fear of heights which masks a fear of sex. If we cure the phobia, another will take its place, i.e., symptom substitution. Clinical studies have not supported this theory.

213. **(A)** Patients frequently begin to treat their analyst like a long-time relative or acquaintance. They often transfer to the analyst feelings of hostility and love meant for others.

214. **(C)** Humans are born prewired to acquire language. However, the environment must provide the stimulation for the brain areas associated with language to develop. Cases of children raised by animals or under conditions of extreme language deprivation (kept locked in a room and seldom spoke to) show that if humans don't acquire a language by puberty, they never will acquire any reasonable mastery of language regardless of years spent trying to provide them with remedial language training.

215. **(E)** Humans with an I.Q. of 20 or less barely make reliable contact with their environments and seldom develop abilities beyond those of an infant. Retarded individuals with an I.Q. of 50 or higher can learn to comprehend and make simple statements.

216. **(C)** Phonemes are the forty or so basic sounds that all humans are capable of making. The coos and babbling of a baby are phonemes. Morphemes are the smallest units of speech sounds that carry meaning. Prefixes such as "un," "pro," and "pre" are examples of morphemes.

217. **(A)** Even with years of daily training, the number of vocabulary words and the complexity of the statements that apes and chimps make and comprehend are equivalent to only a human three-year-old. Most statements involve rewards such as "Give me apple." Furthermore, they often act as if word order doesn't matter. "Give me apple," "Apple me give," and "Me apple give" are used interchangeably. Syntax in ape communications is limited.

The Graduate Record Examination in

PSYCHOLOGY

Test 2

THE GRADUATE RECORD EXAMINATION
PSYCHOLOGY TEST 2
ANSWER SHEET

1. (A) (B) (C) (D) (E)
2. (A) (B) (C) (D) (E)
3. (A) (B) (C) (D) (E)
4. (A) (B) (C) (D) (E)
5. (A) (B) (C) (D) (E)
6. (A) (B) (C) (D) (E)
7. (A) (B) (C) (D) (E)
8. (A) (B) (C) (D) (E)
9. (A) (B) (C) (D) (E)
10. (A) (B) (C) (D) (E)
11. (A) (B) (C) (D) (E)
12. (A) (B) (C) (D) (E)
13. (A) (B) (C) (D) (E)
14. (A) (B) (C) (D) (E)
15. (A) (B) (C) (D) (E)
16. (A) (B) (C) (D) (E)
17. (A) (B) (C) (D) (E)
18. (A) (B) (C) (D) (E)
19. (A) (B) (C) (D) (E)
20. (A) (B) (C) (D) (E)
21. (A) (B) (C) (D) (E)
22. (A) (B) (C) (D) (E)
23. (A) (B) (C) (D) (E)
24. (A) (B) (C) (D) (E)
25. (A) (B) (C) (D) (E)
26. (A) (B) (C) (D) (E)
27. (A) (B) (C) (D) (E)
28. (A) (B) (C) (D) (E)
29. (A) (B) (C) (D) (E)
30. (A) (B) (C) (D) (E)
31. (A) (B) (C) (D) (E)
32. (A) (B) (C) (D) (E)
33. (A) (B) (C) (D) (E)

34. (A) (B) (C) (D) (E)
35. (A) (B) (C) (D) (E)
36. (A) (B) (C) (D) (E)
37. (A) (B) (C) (D) (E)
38. (A) (B) (C) (D) (E)
39. (A) (B) (C) (D) (E)
40. (A) (B) (C) (D) (E)
41. (A) (B) (C) (D) (E)
42. (A) (B) (C) (D) (E)
43. (A) (B) (C) (D) (E)
44. (A) (B) (C) (D) (E)
45. (A) (B) (C) (D) (E)
46. (A) (B) (C) (D) (E)
47. (A) (B) (C) (D) (E)
48. (A) (B) (C) (D) (E)
49. (A) (B) (C) (D) (E)
50. (A) (B) (C) (D) (E)
51. (A) (B) (C) (D) (E)
52. (A) (B) (C) (D) (E)
53. (A) (B) (C) (D) (E)
54. (A) (B) (C) (D) (E)
55. (A) (B) (C) (D) (E)
56. (A) (B) (C) (D) (E)
57. (A) (B) (C) (D) (E)
58. (A) (B) (C) (D) (E)
59. (A) (B) (C) (D) (E)
60. (A) (B) (C) (D) (E)
61. (A) (B) (C) (D) (E)
62. (A) (B) (C) (D) (E)
63. (A) (B) (C) (D) (E)
64. (A) (B) (C) (D) (E)
65. (A) (B) (C) (D) (E)
66. (A) (B) (C) (D) (E)

67. (A) (B) (C) (D) (E)
68. (A) (B) (C) (D) (E)
69. (A) (B) (C) (D) (E)
70. (A) (B) (C) (D) (E)
71. (A) (B) (C) (D) (E)
72. (A) (B) (C) (D) (E)
73. (A) (B) (C) (D) (E)
74. (A) (B) (C) (D) (E)
75. (A) (B) (C) (D) (E)
76. (A) (B) (C) (D) (E)
77. (A) (B) (C) (D) (E)
78. (A) (B) (C) (D) (E)
79. (A) (B) (C) (D) (E)
80. (A) (B) (C) (D) (E)
81. (A) (B) (C) (D) (E)
82. (A) (B) (C) (D) (E)
83. (A) (B) (C) (D) (E)
84. (A) (B) (C) (D) (E)
85. (A) (B) (C) (D) (E)
86. (A) (B) (C) (D) (E)
87. (A) (B) (C) (D) (E)
88. (A) (B) (C) (D) (E)
89. (A) (B) (C) (D) (E)
90. (A) (B) (C) (D) (E)
91. (A) (B) (C) (D) (E)
92. (A) (B) (C) (D) (E)
93. (A) (B) (C) (D) (E)
94. (A) (B) (C) (D) (E)
95. (A) (B) (C) (D) (E)
96. (A) (B) (C) (D) (E)
97. (A) (B) (C) (D) (E)
98. (A) (B) (C) (D) (E)
99. (A) (B) (C) (D) (E)

100. (A) (B) (C) (D) (E)	140. (A) (B) (C) (D) (E)	180. (A) (B) (C) (D) (E)
101. (A) (B) (C) (D) (E)	141. (A) (B) (C) (D) (E)	181. (A) (B) (C) (D) (E)
102. (A) (B) (C) (D) (E)	142. (A) (B) (C) (D) (E)	182. (A) (B) (C) (D) (E)
103. (A) (B) (C) (D) (E)	143. (A) (B) (C) (D) (E)	183. (A) (B) (C) (D) (E)
104. (A) (B) (C) (D) (E)	144. (A) (B) (C) (D) (E)	184. (A) (B) (C) (D) (E)
105. (A) (B) (C) (D) (E)	145. (A) (B) (C) (D) (E)	185. (A) (B) (C) (D) (E)
106. (A) (B) (C) (D) (E)	146. (A) (B) (C) (D) (E)	186. (A) (B) (C) (D) (E)
107. (A) (B) (C) (D) (E)	147. (A) (B) (C) (D) (E)	187. (A) (B) (C) (D) (E)
108. (A) (B) (C) (D) (E)	148. (A) (B) (C) (D) (E)	188. (A) (B) (C) (D) (E)
109. (A) (B) (C) (D) (E)	149. (A) (B) (C) (D) (E)	189. (A) (B) (C) (D) (E)
110. (A) (B) (C) (D) (E)	150. (A) (B) (C) (D) (E)	190. (A) (B) (C) (D) (E)
111. (A) (B) (C) (D) (E)	151. (A) (B) (C) (D) (E)	191. (A) (B) (C) (D) (E)
112. (A) (B) (C) (D) (E)	152. (A) (B) (C) (D) (E)	192. (A) (B) (C) (D) (E)
113. (A) (B) (C) (D) (E)	153. (A) (B) (C) (D) (E)	193. (A) (B) (C) (D) (E)
114. (A) (B) (C) (D) (E)	154. (A) (B) (C) (D) (E)	194. (A) (B) (C) (D) (E)
115. (A) (B) (C) (D) (E)	155. (A) (B) (C) (D) (E)	195. (A) (B) (C) (D) (E)
116. (A) (B) (C) (D) (E)	156. (A) (B) (C) (D) (E)	196. (A) (B) (C) (D) (E)
117. (A) (B) (C) (D) (E)	157. (A) (B) (C) (D) (E)	197. (A) (B) (C) (D) (E)
118. (A) (B) (C) (D) (E)	158. (A) (B) (C) (D) (E)	198. (A) (B) (C) (D) (E)
119. (A) (B) (C) (D) (E)	159. (A) (B) (C) (D) (E)	199. (A) (B) (C) (D) (E)
120. (A) (B) (C) (D) (E)	160. (A) (B) (C) (D) (E)	200. (A) (B) (C) (D) (E)
121. (A) (B) (C) (D) (E)	161. (A) (B) (C) (D) (E)	201. (A) (B) (C) (D) (E)
122. (A) (B) (C) (D) (E)	162. (A) (B) (C) (D) (E)	202. (A) (B) (C) (D) (E)
123. (A) (B) (C) (D) (E)	163. (A) (B) (C) (D) (E)	203. (A) (B) (C) (D) (E)
124. (A) (B) (C) (D) (E)	164. (A) (B) (C) (D) (E)	204. (A) (B) (C) (D) (E)
125. (A) (B) (C) (D) (E)	165. (A) (B) (C) (D) (E)	205. (A) (B) (C) (D) (E)
126. (A) (B) (C) (D) (E)	166. (A) (B) (C) (D) (E)	206. (A) (B) (C) (D) (E)
127. (A) (B) (C) (D) (E)	167. (A) (B) (C) (D) (E)	207. (A) (B) (C) (D) (E)
128. (A) (B) (C) (D) (E)	168. (A) (B) (C) (D) (E)	208. (A) (B) (C) (D) (E)
129. (A) (B) (C) (D) (E)	169. (A) (B) (C) (D) (E)	209. (A) (B) (C) (D) (E)
130. (A) (B) (C) (D) (E)	170. (A) (B) (C) (D) (E)	210. (A) (B) (C) (D) (E)
131. (A) (B) (C) (D) (E)	171. (A) (B) (C) (D) (E)	211. (A) (B) (C) (D) (E)
132. (A) (B) (C) (D) (E)	172. (A) (B) (C) (D) (E)	212. (A) (B) (C) (D) (E)
133. (A) (B) (C) (D) (E)	173. (A) (B) (C) (D) (E)	213. (A) (B) (C) (D) (E)
134. (A) (B) (C) (D) (E)	174. (A) (B) (C) (D) (E)	214. (A) (B) (C) (D) (E)
135. (A) (B) (C) (D) (E)	175. (A) (B) (C) (D) (E)	215. (A) (B) (C) (D) (E)
136. (A) (B) (C) (D) (E)	176. (A) (B) (C) (D) (E)	216. (A) (B) (C) (D) (E)
137. (A) (B) (C) (D) (E)	177. (A) (B) (C) (D) (E)	217. (A) (B) (C) (D) (E)
138. (A) (B) (C) (D) (E)	178. (A) (B) (C) (D) (E)	
139. (A) (B) (C) (D) (E)	179. (A) (B) (C) (D) (E)	

GRE

PSYCHOLOGY TEST 2

TIME: 170 Minutes
  217 Questions

DIRECTIONS: Choose the best answer for each question and mark the letter of your selection on the corresponding answer sheet.

---

1. According to Bandura and Walters, all of the following processes are involved in observational learning EXCEPT

    (A) attention process.   (B) retention process.

    (C) reproduction process.   (D) motivation process.

    (E) chaining process.

2. According to Carl Rogers, the structure of personality is based on

    (A) ego and superego.

    (B) organism and self.

    (C) conscious and collective unconscious.

    (D) inferiority and superiority.

    (E) introversion and extroversion.

3. The theory that we all experience a series of psychosocial crises throughout our lives was proposed by

    (A) Freud.   (B) Adler.

    (C) Sheldon.   (D) Erikson.

    (E) Jung.

4. All of the following choices are advantageous of field research EXCEPT

    (A) "real people" are studied.

    (B) reactions of subjects are more natural.

    (C) it has more impact than lab studies.

    (D)   behavior is not influenced by the psychologist.

    (E)   there is an appropriate control involved.

5.   The purpose of the "Q-technique" is

    (A)   to measure accurate norms of population.

    (B)   item analysis in factorial designs.

    (C)   to measure the correlation between language and behavior.

    (D)   to measure a person's opinion of himself.

    (E)   to measure correlation between X and Y variables.

6.   In a cross-sectional study, the researcher examines

    (A)   subjects over extended periods of time.

    (B)   different subjects at different developmental levels.

    (C)   different cultural groups for comparison.

    (D)   the dynamics of relationships with family members.

    (E)   both (A) and (B)

7.   Item analysis is essential to test construction because it provides

    (A)   feedback on the effectiveness of the test.

    (B)   for reliability in the test.

    (C)   for validity in the test.

    (D)   for construct validity in the test.

    (E)   an accurate picture of the subject's knowledge.

8.   Analytical psychology was developed by

    (A)   Frankl.   (B)   Horner.

    (C)   Adler.   (D)   Freud.

    (E)   Jung.

9.   The psychological point of view which emphasizes unconscious motivation as a factor in human behavior is

    (A)   client-centered therapy.

    (B)   gestalt psychology or field theory.

(C)   psychoanalysis.

(D)   stimulus-response or S–R psychology.

(E)   rational-emotive therapy.

10.   In an experiment studying the effects of different drugs on reaction time, each subject is presented with all of the conditions in the experiment. This is an example of a

(A)   factorial design.

(B)   within subjects design.

(C)   between subjects design.

(D)   quasi-experimental design.

(E)   multi-control design.

11.   The MMPI is to psychopathology as the CPI is to

(A)   normalcy.   (B)   childhood.

(C)   I.Q.   (D)   projectivity.

(E)   childhood psychopathology.

12.   What is the value of the median for the numbers: 34, 29, 26, 37, 31 and 34?

(A)   31   (B)   34

(C)   30.1   (D)   32.5

(E)   5.5

13.   Find the range of the sample composed of the observations: 33, 53, 35, 37, 49.

(A)   37   (B)   5

(C)   10   (D)   4

(E)   20

14.   The matching law in animal learning states that

(A)   only highly preferred reinforcers can be used to reward less preferred responses.

(B)   only less preferred reinforcers can be used to reward highly preferred responses.

(C)   only behavior that "matches," that is, is somehow related to the reinforcer will be learned.

(D)   rates of response are relative to rates of reinforcement.

(E)   none of the above

15.   According to Heider's balance theory, which perceptual factors are the most important in liking another person?

(A)   attractiveness and similarity

(B)   associating a person with a feeling

(C)   attitudes and values

(D)   consistency and proximity

(E)   consistency and balance

16.   Rotter's Locus of Control scale attempts to measure

(A)   independence-dependence.

(B)   internality-externality.

(C)   rationality-irrationality.

(D)   masculine-feminine characteristics.

(E)   both (B) and (C)

17.   Based on his study of work performance, Vroom states that an individual's motivation to work is a function of

(A)   job incentives.   (B)   expectation and valence of goal.

(C)   employee status.   (D)   meaningfulness of job.

(E)   managerial style.

18.   The morality of self-accepted principles was proposed by

(A)   Piaget.   (B)   Freud.

(C)   Erikson.   (D)   Kohlberg.

(E)   Bandura.

19.   An "index of centrality" refers to

(A)   a measure of work equality.

(B)   a measure of the extent to which a given individual interacts with others.

(C) a measure of the extent to which individuals are excluded from interaction with others.

(D) a measure of management potential.

(E) the coherence of employee organization in a business.

QUESTIONS 20-21 refer to the following graphs.

(A)

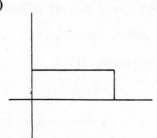

(B)

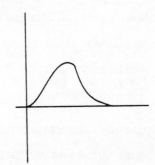

(C)

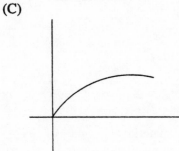

(D)

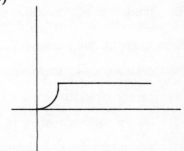

(E)

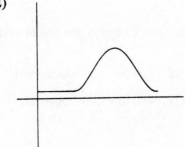

20. Which curve represents an ogive?

21. In which graph does each score occur with the same frequency?

22. Which of these tests did McClelland first use to measure the need for achievement?

(A)   Bayley Scales

(B)   Wechsler Adult Intelligence Scale (WAIS)

(C)   Minnesota Multiphasic Personality Inventory

(D)   Thematic Apperception Test (TAT)

(E)   Rosenzweig Picture-Frustration Study

23.   A stationary point of light that appears to move in the dark refers to the

(A)   autokinetic phenomenon.   (B)   attitude change effect.

(C)   conformity effect.   (D)   automated effect.

(E)   phi phenomenon.

24.   An approving comment made by a boss to his employee is an example of

(A)   generalized reinforcement.   (B)   conditioned reinforcement.

(C)   primary reinforcement.   (D)   social reinforcement.

(E)   positive reinforcement.

25.   Neurons are unique among cells in that they

(A)   cannot conduct impulses.

(B)   cannot reproduce.

(C)   have a nucleus containing genetic material.

(D)   are surrounded by a membrane.

(E)   all of the above

26.   The range of electromagnetic wavelengths to which our visual system can respond ranges from

(A)   500 to 1,500 nanometers.   (B)   100 to 1,000 nanometers.

(C)   300 to 900 nanometers.   (D)   400 to 750 nanometers.

(E)   100 to 5,000 nanometers.

27.   According to Carl Rogers, human motivation is based on the need to

(A)   express one's sexuality and aggressive nature.

(B)   actualize and enhance the self through experiences.

(C)   find meaning in life.

(D)   struggle between being and non-being in the world.

(E)   strive for affection and approval from others.

28. Which of the following best describes the major function(s) of the spinal cord?

    (A) acts as a messenger to the brain

    (B) filters sensory impulses

    (C) directs simple actions independent of the brain

    (D) both (A) and (B)   (E) both (A) and (C)

29. Which of the following tests makes the most prominent use of statistics in its scoring procedures?

    (A) TAT   (B) Rorschach Test

    (C) Locus of Control Test   (D) MMPI

    (E) Sentence Completion Test

30. According to Guilford's model of intelligence, how many dimensions of intelligence are there?

    (A) three dimensions

    (B) a variable number depending on I.Q.

    (C) 120 dimensions

    (D) 10 dimensions   (E) none of the above

31. The type of validity which measures the extent to which a test measures a theoretical construct is

    (A) content validity.   (B) face validity.

    (C) synthetic validity.   (D) criterion validity.

    (E) construct validity.

32. The type of epileptic seizure in which there is only momentary alteration of consciousness and a slight twitching of the muscles is the

    (A) grand-mal seizure.   (B) petit-mal seizure.

    (C) psychomotor seizure.   (D) borderline seizure.

    (E) focal seizure.

33. According to Bruner's theory of cognitive development, the iconic stage is

    (A) concerned with language development.

    (B) concerned with the use of visual images to understand the world.

(C)   concerned with the use of action to understand the world.

(D)   concerned with symbolism in the understanding of the world.

(E)   representative of egocentric activity.

34.   According to Guilford, divergent thinking requires

(A)   one solution.   (B)   arithmetic reasoning.

(C)   fluency of ideas.   (D)   categorization.

(E)   (A) and (B)

35.   The opponent-process theory of color perception was proposed by

(A)   E. Hering.   (B)   H. Helmholtz.

(C)   C. L. Franklin   (D)   E. Land.

(E)   D. Premack.

36.   The region at the base of the brain which is highly involved in most emotional and physiological motivation is the

(A)   medulla.   (B)   rhinencephalon.

(C)   pituitary gland.   (D)   hypothalmus.

(E)   actomyosin.

37.   The sensitivity of the eye to light varies with

(A)   wavelength.   (B)   the eye's state of adaptation.

(C)   the region of the retina.

(D)   the contraction or dilation of the iris.

(E)   all of the above.

QUESTIONS 38-39 refer to this diagram.

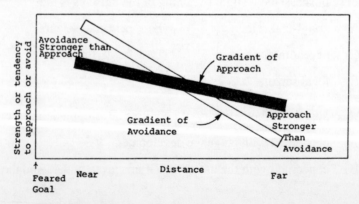

38. Which of the following statements best describes this gradient?

    (A) initial approach is stronger, than avoidance gradient is stronger

    (B) approach gradient is stronger

    (C) avoidance gradient is stronger

    (D) there is an equal attraction and repulsion of the goal

    (E) (A) and (D)

39. Which of the following conflicts best describes the pictured gradient?

    (A) approach avoidance conflict

    (B) multiple approach-avoidance conflict

    (C) approach-approach conflict

    (D) avoidance-avoidance conflict

    (E) vacillation conflict

40. Which types of behavior result from the type of conflict shown below?

    (A) escape   (B) vacillation

    (C) boredom   (D) (A) and (C)

    (E) (A) and (B)

41. Latent-inhibition refers to

    (A) increase in effectiveness of classical conditioning resulting from previous unreinforced exposure to the conditioned stimulus.

    (B) decrease in effectiveness of classical conditioning resulting from previous unreinforced exposure to the conditional stimulus.

    (C) a decrease in response to a repeatedly presented or constant stimulus.

    (D)   an increase in response to a repeatedly presented or constant stimulus.

    (E)   none of the above

42.   All of the following are characteristics of the preoperational stage of development EXCEPT

    (A)   egocentric thought.   (B)   understanding of conservation.

    (C)   static thinking.   (D)   problem solving behavior.

    (E)   intuitive thought.

QUESTIONS 43–44 refer to the following paragraph.

Suppose you are playing monopoly with a group of children. These children understand the basic instructions and will play by the rules. They are not capable of hypothetical transactions dealing with mortgages, loans, and special pacts with other players.

43.   According to Piaget, these children are in which stage of cognitive development?

    (A)   sensorimotor stage

    (B)   formal operations stage

    (C)   preconceptual preoperational stage

    (D)   concrete operational stage

    (E)   intuitive preoperational stage

44. What are the probable ages of these children?

    (A)   8–13   (B)   4–7

    (C)   2–4   (D)   7–11

    (E)   5–10

45.   The Language Acquisition Device was proposed by

    (A)   Piaget.   (B)   Bruner.

    (C)   Kohler.   (D)   Chomsky.

    (E)   Mednick.

46.   When we say that our visual system is 50% crossed, we mean that

    (A)   half of the information from the right visual field is perceived by the left retina.

(B)   half of the fibers from the optic nerve cross over to the opposite side of the brain.

(C)   half of the visual image strikes the left side of the retina, and the other half strikes the right side of the retina.

(D)   half of the visual image is inverted in the retina.

(E)   none of the above

47.   Chris Argyris, an organization theorist, drew on personality theory to formulate his theory regarding the interaction of the work environment and the individual. What was its major focus?

(A)   the active versus passive individual

(B)   the mature versus immature individual

(C)   the ineffective versus effective individual

(D)   inexperienced versus experienced individuals

(E)   formal versus informal work conditions

48.   Robert Rosenthal in his studies on experimenter bias, or "self-fulfilling prophecy," found that

(A)   bias effects are limited to laboratory situations.

(B)   triple-blind experiments are needed to ensure true validity of results.

(C)   bias effects are widespread and have been shown to affect even I.Q. scores.

(D)   bias effects do occur often but are rarely large enough to affect the significance of results.

(E)   both (A) and (B)

49.   In a statistical test, Power $(1-\beta)$ is

(A)   the probability of accepting a false null hypothesis.

(B)   a measure of external and construct validity.

(C)   the probability of rejecting a false null hypothesis.

(D)   a type I error.   (E)   a type II error.

50.   In which form of schizophrenia would you most likely see delusions of grandeur or persecution?

(A)   depressive   (B)   simple

(C)   complex   (D)   catatonic

(E)   paranoid

51.   Korsakoff's psychosis is most often associated with

(A)   excessive alcohol intake.

(B)   changes in the brainstem.

(C)   nutritional deficiencies.

(D)   both (A) and (B)   (E)   both (A) and (C)

52.   All of the following are characteristics of sociopathy EXCEPT

(A)   absence of irrationality or symptoms of psychosis.

(B)   disregard for the truth.

(C)   no sense of shame.

(D)   a history of suicide attempts.

(E)   onset no later than early twenties.

53.   Echoic code is to auditory system as iconic code is to

(A)   tactile experience.   (B)   visual system.

(C)   sensory system.   (D)   olfactory system.

(E)   none of the above

54.   The Theory of Selective Attention was proposed by

(A)   Selfridge.   (B)   Bruner.

(C)   Broadbent.   (D)   Lockhart and Craik.

(E)   Tolman.

55.   Those items that are most likely to be forgotten are those

(A)   that are "concrete."

(B)   with the least digits/letters.

(C)   at the beginning of a long list.

(D)   in the middle of a long list.

(E)   at the end of a long list.

56.   A model in which the internal representation of a pattern is structurally
      similar to the stimulus pattern is called a

(A)   visual feature model.   (B)   constructive model.

(C)   template matching model.   (D)   specific feature model.

(E)   pandemonium model.

57.   Which of the following best describes correlational analysis?

(A)   a measure of association between two variables

(B)   a measure of linear association between two characteristics

(C)   a measure of causation between X and Y

(D)   a measure of causation of X on Y

(E)   a measure of causation of Y on X

58.   Spinal nerves belong to the

(A)   peripheral nervous system.

(B)   central nervous system.

(C)   antagonistic nervous system.

(D)   residual nervous system.

(E)   none of the above

59.   A person who has more difficulty hearing high pitched tones than low pitched tones probably has

(A)   nerve deafness.   (B)   conduction deafness.

(C)   functional deafness.   (D)   tone specific deafness.

(E)   tonotopic deafness.

60.   Abraham Maslow is a chief proponent of the _____ school of human behavior.

(A)   behaviorist   (B)   structuralist

(C)   humanist   (D)   functionalist

(E)   existentialist

61.   When the difference between two means is shown to be significant

(A)   the null hypothesis is rejected.

(B)   the null hypothesis is disproved.

(C)   the alternative hypothesis is disproved.

(D) the independent variable is proved.

(E) both (A) and (B)

62. The All-or-None Law refers to

(A) stimulation of the Schwann cell.

(B) the size of the signal produced in the nerve cell.

(C) K^+ being all inside or all outside the nerve cell.

(D) Na^+ being all inside or all outside the nerve cell.

(E) stimulation of the unmyelinated axons.

63. During the relative refractory period,

(A) the nerve cell will not respond to any new stimulation.

(B) the nerve cell will respond to chemical changes in Na^+.

(C) the nerve cell requires a stronger stimulus to fire.

(D) the nerve cell requires an influx of Na^+ and an efflux of K^+.

(E) both (B) and (C)

64. Conjunctive, disjunctive, and relational concepts refer to

(A) simple concepts.   (B) complex concepts.

(C) percepts.   (D) imagery concepts.

(E) symbols.

QUESTIONS 65-67 refer to the following passage.

Most American psychologists favor the component process theory of cognitive development. The theory is based on the assumption that a child's cognition develops as he reaches certain levels of competence in various cognitive skills. As the child gains cognitive abilities, they are integrated into a general cognitive ability. The component process is concerned with problem solving. The degree of success achieved is used as an index for measuring cognitive ability. Before a child is fully competent to solve problems, he must be able to use the following five mental processes: encoding, memory, evaluation, deduction, and mediation.

65. The component process theory probably developed out of a tradition of _____ research.

(A) cognition   (B) emotion

(C) motivation   (D) behavioral

(E) information processing

66. This theory of cognitive development assumes that cognitive ability will be reflected in _____ .

    (A) cognition   (B) encoding

    (C) deduction   (D) performance

    (E) memory

67. This theory deemphasizes the importance of _____ in the cognitive development of the child.

    (A) language   (B) thinking

    (C) emotion   (D) performance

    (E) using indexes

68. The autokinetic effect is most commonly demonstrated with which of the following stimuli?

    (A) a spot of light in a darkened room

    (B) lights flashing on and off in a patterned sequence

    (C) lights rotating around a single, central spot of light

    (D) a steady blue light consistently viewed

    (E) a light flashing on and off at a speed of .03 seconds

69. The Minimum Principle was proposed by which school of thought?

    (A) functionalist   (B) psychoanalytic

    (C) behaviorist   (D) gestalt

    (E) structuralist

70. A man walking to work counts the number of stop signs he sees on the street. As he arrives at the entrance to his office, he fears that he has miscounted and that his children will die unless he counts the signs correctly. He runs back home and starts recounting the stop signs as he walks. This man would be diagnosed as having a(an)

    (A) hypochondriacal reaction.

    (B) systematic reaction.

    (C) obsessive-compulsive reaction.

    (D) conversion reaction.   (E) dissociative reaction.

71. The ego, in contrast to the id,

(A)   mediates between wish-fulfilling desires and the outer reality.

(B)   is composed of only wish-fulfilling desires.

(C)   mediates between reality and internal rules.

(D)   cannot mediate with the superego.

(E)   is innate, not learned.

72.   Alcohol dependence would be considered a type of

(A)   anxiety disorder.   (B)   mood disorder.

(C)   somatoform disorder.   (D)   personality disorder.

(E)   substance-related disorder.

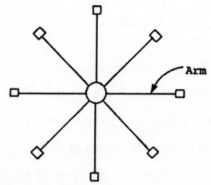

Radial Arm Maze

73.   In a radial arm maze, food was placed at the end of each arm and a rat was placed in the center. The rat's food-searching behavior indicated that

(A)   the rat could smell the food and therefore, knew where to find it.

(B)   the rat visited each arm in a fixed, systematic pattern.

(C)   the rat visited each arm in an almost random fashion.

(D)   the rat rarely revisited an arm because it learned spatially which arms it had visited.

(E)   both (C) and (D)

74.   Stanley Schachter (1959), in his studies on the human affiliative need, found that

(A)   highly fearful people are much more likely to affiliate than less fearful people.

(B)   first-born children are more likely to affiliate than later-born children.

(C)   when given a choice, highly fearful people preferred to affiliate only with those who were in the same experimental condition.

(D)   people affiliate to reduce fear.

(E)   all of the above

75.   According to Guilford's model of intelligence, which of the following is true?

(A)   The Stanford-Binet test is wrong to use as a performance measure.

(B)   Intelligence is a function of experience, not of genetic endowment.

(C)   Intelligence consists of a specific set of traits that can be classified.

(D)   Intelligence is a unitary characteristic.

(E)   Intelligence is a function of contents × contexts.

76.   The Thematic Apperception Test supposedly reflects

(A)   how one organizes ambiguous stimuli.

(B)   one's overall level of introversion-extroversion.

(C)   interpersonal conflicts and needs.

(D)   one's relative ranking on several trait scales.

(E)   one's possible latent psychosis.

77.   Cross-sectional studies differ from longitudinal studies in that the former

(A)   are more time consuming and expensive.

(B)   are not susceptible to changing generational experiences.

(C)   are more susceptible to changing generational experiences.

(D)   use data from samples of varying age levels.

(E)   are less efficient than the latter.

78.   The test used to assess an infant's current developmental status and to discriminate between mentally retarded children and normal children is the

(A)   Wechsler Intelligence Scale for Children.

(B)   Stanford-Binet Intelligence Test.

(C)   Motor Activity Test.

(D)   Guilford Factor Test.

(E)   Bayley Scales.

79. Which of the following psychoanalytic theorists proposed the need to move toward people, move against people, and move away from people?

   (A) Sullivan   (B) Horney

   (C) Fromm   (D) Anderson

   (E) Adler

80. The repeated presentation of the CS without the UCS results in

   (A) spontaneous recovery.   (B) inhibition.

   (C) extinction.   (D) higher-order conditioning.

   (E) negative reinforcement.

81. William James, James Cattell, John Dewey and E.L. Thorndike all belonged to which school of thought?

   (A) structuralist   (B) behaviorist

   (C) gestaltist   (D) mentalist

   (E) none of the above

82. Doob, Dollard, Miller, Mowrer and Sears (1939) suggested that all aggressive acts are caused by

   (A) anger.   (B) tension.

   (C) stress.   (D) frustration.

   (E) both (A) and (D)

83. The classic social psychology experiments that demonstrated that most people would perform acts in direct contradiction to their morals and beliefs, if a legitimate authority figure accepted responsibility for those acts, was performed by

   (A) B.F. Skinner.   (B) Sigmund Freud.

   (C) Stanley Milgram.   (D) Leon Festinger.

   (E) Rollo May.

84. In psychology, the concept of motivation was first described in terms of instinctive behavior. On whose theory was this concept largely based?

   (A) Hume   (B) Descartes

   (C) James   (D) Darwin

   (E) Freud

85. Auditory processes in humans are sensitive to auditory frequencies ranging from

    (A) 10 Hz – 50,000 Hz   (B) 20 Hz – 20,000 Hz

    (C) 5,000 Hz – 100,000 Hz   (D) 5,000 Hz – 50,000 Hz

    (E) 1 Hz – 20 Hz

86. The taste buds on the tip of the tongue are most sensitive to

    (A) salty tastes.   (B) sweet tastes.

    (C) bitter tastes.   (D) sour tastes.

    (E) both (C) and (D)

87. The blocking experiment performed by Leon Kamin suggests that

    (A) organisms condition to all stimuli involved in a contingency.

    (B) organisms only condition to one stimulus involved in a contingency.

    (C) organisms condition to some, but not all, stimuli in a contingency.

    (D) organisms condition by trial and error.

    (E) both (A) and (D)

88. An EPSP causes the nerve cell to

    (A) polarize.   (B) contract.

    (C) become more negative.   (D) become less negative.

    (E) none of the above

89. The pituitary gland secretes which of the following hormones?

    (A) TSH (thyroid stimulating hormone)

    (B) ACTH (adrenocorticotrophic hormone)

    (C) FSH (follicle stimulating hormone)

    (D) LH (luteinizing hormone)

    (E) all of the above

90. Problems that have more than one correct solution require

    (A) divergent thinking.   (B) symbolic thought.

    (C) disjunctive thinking.   (D) convergent thinking.

    (E) complex concepts.

91. A frequency-distribution will often approach the normal distribution as

    (A) the number of scores included gets very large.

    (B) the number of scores included gets very small.

    (C) more variables are included in the frequency distribution.

    (D) certain scores are eliminated from the distribution.

    (E) the distribution normalizes in shape.

92. Given a sample mean, the range of values within which the parametric mean must lie, can be computed. This is known as the

    (A) parametric deviation.　　(B) variability range.

    (C) mode.　　(D) confidence interval.

    (E) parametric range.

93. According to Freud, memories and drives that can be easily recalled but are not within consciousness at the moment are in the

    (A) personal unconscious.　　(B) collective unconscious.

    (C) unconscious.　　(D) preconscious.

    (E) ego.

94. A hostile person comes to believe that other people are "out to get" him. According to Freudian theory this man is

    (A) sublimating.　　(B) identifying.

    (C) projecting.　　(D) rationalizing.

    (E) displacing.

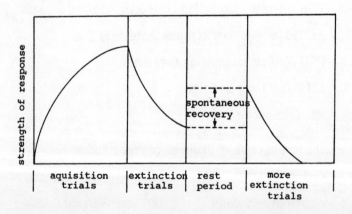

95. According to the above diagram, which of the following best describes the occurrence of spontaneous recovery?

    (A) New learning takes place during the rest period.

    (B) CR reappears in weaker form than before extinction was begun.

    (C) CR reappears in full strength.

    (D) There is memory of learning.

    (E) (A) and (C)

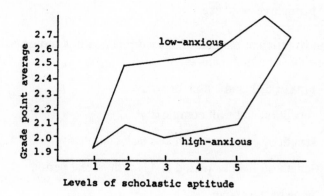

96. According to the above diagram, which of the following statements is true?

    (A) Levels of scholastic aptitude are not related to grade point average.

    (B) Low-anxiety students have higher grade point averages and higher scholastic aptitudes.

    (C) High anxiety students have higher grade point averages and higher scholastic aptitudes.

    (D) (A) and (B)   (E) (A) and (C)

97. Because the id seeks to gratify its desires without delay, it operates on the

    (A) satisfaction principle.   (B) pleasure principle.

    (C) ego.   (D) superego.

    (E) unconscious desires.

98. An obese person refuses to diet and insists that dieting is unhealthy and that he needs to eat as much as he does to sustain his energy level. According to Freud, this person is

    (A) sublimating.   (B) identifying.

(C) projecting.   (D) rationalizing.

(E) displacing.

99. In classical conditioning, the response that automatically occurs whenever the unconditioned stimulus is presented without any training is called a (an)

(A) behavioral response.   (B) unconditioned response.

(C) preconditioned response.   (D) unlearned response.

(E) instinctive response.

100. The most efficient method of spaced practice in a motor task varies which of the following two features?

(A) type of task and length of study

(B) repetition and skill complexity

(C) length of practice period and task complexity

(D) length of practice period and length of rest period

(E) none of the above

101. Social learning theory was first proposed by

(A) Bandura and Walters.

(B) B.F. Skinner.

(C) Miller and Dollard.

(D) J.B. Watson.

(E) Carl Rogers.

102. Which of the following psychologists places special emphasis on the need for positive regard and the need for self-regard?

(A) Maslow   (B) Rogers

(C) Adler   (D) Sheldon

(E) Frankl

103. According to Allport, which of the following are the two important components of behavior?

(A) ego body and superego components

(B) adaptive and expressive components

(C)   organism and self

(D)   personal conscious and collective conscious

(E)   introversion and extroversion components

104. In contrast to the cones,

(A)   rods function mainly in night vision.

(B)   rods are concentrated in the fovea.

(C)   rods produce color images, as well as black and white images.

(D)   rods are connected to bipolar cells in a one-to-one ratio.

(E)   rods are unimportant to night vision.

105. The behavioral modification technique that uses repeated exposure to aversive stimuli or disturbing scenes to extinguish the emotional responses associated with those stimuli is

(A)   systematic desensitization.   (B)   implosive therapy.

(C)   reciprocal inhibition.   (D)   token economy system.

(E)   negative reinforcement.

106. If 70% of the variance found in the scores in a population are attributable to genetic factors, then the heritability index would be

(A)   .30.   (B)   .03.

(C)   .07.   (D)   .70.

(E)   2.3.

107. The opponent-process theory of color vision

(A)   proposed that there are three types of receptors in the eye.

(B)   stated that there are two kinds of receptors in the eye.

(C)   was proposed by B. Young.

(D)   explains color vision as the process of mixing the light of different colors.

(E)   contradicted psychophysics theory about the perception of color thresholds.

108. Psychodrama, a form of group therapy in which participants act out their feelings as if they were actors, was introduced by

(A) Perls.

(B) Moreno.

(C) Frankl.

(D) Jung.

(E) Erikson.

109. According to Freud, the main function of dreams is

(A) to bridge the unconscious with the conscious mind.

(B) the assimilation of conscious memories into the unconscious.

(C) the release of unconscious materials into preconscious.

(D) wish fulfillment of the individual.

(E) release of sexual and social tensions.

110. Which of the following is true of a normal distribution?

(A) It has two modes.

(B) It has one mode.

(C) It has a skewed curve.

(D) The mode and the mean are equal.

(E) both (B) and (D)

111. Alfred Binet is famous for developing the first

(A) item analysis.

(B) adult intelligence test.

(C) projective test.

(D) fixed alternative test.

(E) child intelligence test.

112. For this series of observations find the mean, median, and mode (in that order)

500, 600, 800, 800, 900, 900, 900, 900, 900, 1000, 1100.

(A) 845.45, 600, 900

(B) 845.45, 900, 900

(C) 845.45, 900, 850

(D) 854.54, 600, 900

(E) 854.54, 900, 850

113. The Law of Effect is concerned with the effects of

(A) hormones in behavior.

(B) internal drive states on behavior.

(C) rewards and punishments on behavior.

(D)   activity states on behavior.

(E)   perceptual learning techniques.

114. In "Psychology as the Behaviorist Views It," Watson (1913) made his final break with the structuralists and functionalists. What insight that has affected behaviorism today can be credited to him?

(A)   Behavior constitutes the most important source of information that psychologists possess regarding human nature.

(B)   The contents and operations of the mind are of primary importance.

(C)   Psychology cannot be viewed as a "natural" science.

(D)   Laboratory experiments severely limit the validity of psychology; field studies should be conducted.

(E)   both (A) and (B)

115. Sandra Bem devised a scale to measure feminine and masculine characteristics. Her research shows that people who score high on an androgyny scale tend to have

(A)   low self-esteem.   (B)   confusion concerning sexuality.

(C)   high self-esteem.   (D)   high anxiety.

(E)   maladaptive problems.

116. The Milgram experiments indicate that

(A)   reward and punishment increases compliance.

(B)   pressure from legitimate authorities in a situation increases compliance.

(C)   social pressure increases compliance.

(D)   justification increases compliance.

(E)   group pressure on individuals increases compliance toward group decisions.

117. According to Herzberg's two factor theory of job satisfaction, which of the following choices are important factors?

(A)   maintenance and motivator factors

(B)   job specialization and responsibility

(C)   management and organizational development

(D)   authority and decision making

(E)   communication and motivator factors

118. According to Baumrind's 1967 study of the family as a socializing agent,

    (A) children's personality was related to the type of discipline received from parents.

    (B) parental discipline was not related to child's personality.

    (C) there was a correlation between parental personalities and children's personalities.

    (D) there was an inverse relationship between the amount of discipline the child received and the amount of behavioral control he exhibited.

    (E) none of the above

119. Rensis Likert developed the "linking-pin" concept to provide a method for

    (A) increasing productivity.

    (B) increasing job satisfaction.

    (C) instituting pay incentives.

    (D) improving communication and group effort.

    (E) both (A) and (C)

120. Harlow and Zimmerman (1959) demonstrated that female monkeys raised in isolation

    (A) made good mothers once their offspring were born.

    (B) could not display maternal attachment.

    (C) killed their offspring.

    (D) displayed infant-like behavior themselves.

    (E) became overattached to their offspring.

121. Which of the following developmental periods is characterized by indifference to sexually related matters?

    (A) latency stage   (B) oral stage

    (C) anal stage   (D) tactile stage

    (E) phallic stage

122. The "Oedipus Complex" is to the "Electra Complex" as

    (A) girl is to boy.   (B) girl is to mother.

    (C) id is to ego.   (D) boy is to father.

    (E) boy is to girl.

123. The state of internal discomfort that is created by an inconsistency between actions and attitudes is referred to as

(A) conformity.   (B) social pressure effect.

(C) cognitive dissonance.   (D) punishment conformity.

(E) conformity dissonance.

124. The manifest content of a dream refers to

(A) the hidden, symbolic, actual meaning of a dream.

(B) the manifestation of psychic tensions in a dream.

(C) the literal content of the dream as experienced by the dreamer.

(D) the realization of symbolic meanings in a dream.

(E) both (A) and (C)

125. In any sensory system, the strength of a stimulus may be coded in the _____ of firing of the individual neuron.

(A) frequency   (B) pattern

(C) strength   (D) all of the above

(E) none of the above

QUESTIONS 126-128 are based on the following paragraph.

A woman visits a psychologist for the following problem. She is extremely afraid of pigeons and is overcome with fear and anxiety every time she sees a pigeon. She tells the psychologist that her fear is irrational and she cannot control it. She first remembers being afraid of pigeons at age eight when she fell off her bicycle in the street and landed on a dead pigeon. Her fear is growing more intense, and earlier that week a pigeon flew past her and sent her huddling in a doorway crying with fear.

126. The most probable diagnosis of this woman's case is

(A) anxiety neurosis.   (B) hysterical neurosis.

(C) dissociative reaction.   (D) phobic reaction.

(E) obsessive-compulsive neurosis.

127. The most likely treatment prescribed for this disorder is

(A) aversion therapy.

(B) token economy techniques.

(C) systematic desensitization. (D) modeling techniques.

(E) client-centered therapy.

128. Within a learning theory paradigm, the origin of this disorder could be explained by stating that fear associated with falling from the bike was the UCS and that the bird lying in the street was the

(A) US.

(B) CR.

(C) UCR.

(D) CS.

(E) SS.

129. The "persona" is the mask of conscious intentions behind which an individual hides. This personality construct was proposed by

(A) A. Bandura.

(B) G. Allport.

(C) C. Rogers.

(D) C. Jung.

(E) S. Schachter.

130. Of the following tests, the most suitable for determining the I.Q. of most 12-year-olds is the

(A) Bayley Scales.

(B) WAIS.

(C) WISC.

(D) WPPSI.

(E) Raven Progressive Matrices.

131. The double-blind technique refers to a method of experimentation

(A) where neither the experimental nor control group know the purpose of the study.

(B) often used in perceptual research.

(C) where there are two control groups.

(D) where neither the subject nor the experimenter knows whether the subject is in the experimental or control group.

(E) involving the absence of sight in both eyes.

132. Which of the following is not characteristic of the neurotic depressive?

(A) rigid conscience

(B) considerable stress tolerance

(C) tendency to feel guilty

(D) use of symptoms to gain sympathy from others

(E) feelings of hopelessness

QUESTIONS 133-135 refer to parts of the brain pictured in this diagram.

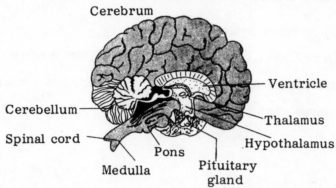

133. The part of the brain which regulates and coordinates muscle movement is the

    (A) cerebellum.   (B) pons.

    (C) ventricle.   (D) medulla.

    (E) thalamus.

134. The fourth ventricle is located in the

    (A) hypothalamus.   (B) medulla.

    (C) spinal cord.   (D) pons.

    (E) ventricle.

135. The part of the brain which coordinates muscle movements on the two sides of the body is the

    (A) thalamus.   (B) hypothalamus.

    (C) medulla.   (D) cerebellum.

    (E) pons.

136. Which of the following acts as a relay station for information coming from the mid and hindbrains and going to the cortex?

    (A) parietal lobe   (B) spinal cord

    (C) pons   (D) cerebellum

    (E) thalamus

137. All of the following are cells of the retina except

    (A) ganglion cells.   (B) bipolar cells.

(C) rod and cone cells.   (D) granule cells.

(E) amacrine cells.

138. The diagram below depicts the

(A) Law of Effect.   (B) Yerkes-Dodson effect.

(C) motivation conflict.   (D) general-adaptation syndrome

(E) optimal effect.

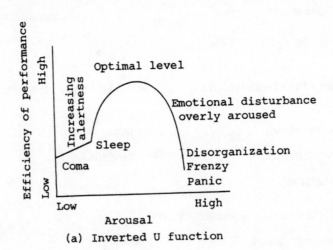

(a) Inverted U function

139. After the apex of the inverted U is reached, performance

(A) becomes variable.   (B) increases.

(C) declines.   (D) is not relevant.

(E) none of the above

140. How many stages are there in the general-adaptation syndrome?

(A) 1   (B) 2

(C) 3   (D) 4

(E) 5

141. The Skinner box is used for studies of

(A) chaining behavior.   (B) forward conditioning.

(C) classical conditioning.   (D) operant conditioning.

(E) second-order conditioning.

142. Perhaps the oldest systematic theory of human development was developed by Sigmund Freud. It assumes that development is made up of which of the following components?

    (A) instinctive, psychosexual, maturative

    (B) sensorimotor, preoperational, concrete operational

    (C) compensation, reversibility, identity

    (D) dynamic, sequential, structural

    (E) enactive, iconic, symbolic

QUESTIONS 143-145 refer to the following passage.

In a study, subjects watched a person in an unpleasant situation. The person was hooked up to an array of electrical apparati. Upon hearing a buzzer, the person feigned pain which the subjects watched. The physiological responses of the subjects witnessing this behavior were recorded. After the subjects watched the person "suffer" a few times, the subjects demonstrated an increased emotional response when the buzzer sounded.

143. The study shows the effects of

    (A) vicarious conditioning. (B) operant conditioning.

    (C) conditioned empathy. (D) perceptual conditioning.

    (E) none of the above

144. The emotional responses of subjects were probably recorded by a

    (A) SR. (B) SRG.

    (C) GR. (D) GSR.

    (E) both (A) and (B)

145. This study presents the modeling theory of _____ disorders.

    (A) anxiety (B) phobic

    (C) depressive (D) affective

    (E) compulsive

146. All of the following are morphemes EXCEPT

    (A) "pre-" (B) "girl"

    (C) "-ing" (D) "n"

    (E) "re-"

QUESTIONS 147-149 refer to the following paragraph.

There are important factors to be considered in the study of abnormal behavior. First, hypotheses or claims must be testable. For example, if it is asserted that traumatic experiences in childhood lead to problems in adulthood, this idea must be testable to be confirmed or disconfirmed by scientific methods. Second, observations and experiments must be reproducible under the same experimental conditions by other scientists.

147. The point of view expressed above could best be called

    (A) structuralism.   (B) introspection.

    (C) holism.   (D) scientific empiricism.

    (E) objective functionalism.

148. Lines 6–7 in the above paragraph refer to the concept of

    (A) experimental construction.

    (B) validity.   (C) reliability

    (D) construct validity.   (E) testing measures.

149. This point of view holds that

    (A) conscious experience does not exist.

    (B) clinical theory and method constitute the basic techniques in the study of abnormal behavior.

    (C) the study of abnormal behavior is hindered by clinical methodology.

    (D) theoretical accounts of abnormal behavior must be subject to scientific methodology.

    (E) conscious experience cannot be studied scientifically.

QUESTIONS 150-152 refer to the following figure.

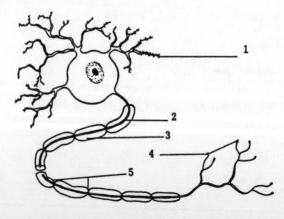

150. The above diagram pictures a "typical neuron." Which of the following choices identifies the Nodes of Ranvier?

(A) 1   (B) 2

(C) 3   (D) 4

(E) 5

151. Which of the following choices identifies the synaptic boutons which contain neurotransmitters?

(A) 1   (B) 2

(C) 3   (D) 4

(E) 5

152. Which of the following choices identifies the dendrites, neural fibers that receive electrical impulses?

(A) 1   (B) 2

(C) 3   (D) 4

(E) 5

153. The phenomenon of backward masking provides evidence for

(A) long-term memory.   (B) short-term memory.

(C) latent inhibition.   (D) information processing.

(E) iconic coding.

154. Motor activity is stored in

(A) enactive codes.   (B) visual codes.

(C) verbal codes.   (D) tactile codes.

(E) active codes.

155. Material in long-term memory

(A) may be lost if the person is interrupted while retrieving it.

(B) is hypothesized to involve ongoing electrical processes in the brain rather than changes in the brain cells.

(C) includes all memory that is not currently active.

(D) may include information that never passed through short-term memory.

(E) both (A) and (C)

QUESTIONS 156-158 refer to the following passage.

A 35-year-old male office worker enters a psychiatric hospital in an agitated and hyperactive state. While the psychiatrist is interviewing the patient, he paces about the room unable to sit down. His speech is accelerated, and he has difficulty staying on one topic of conversation. He tells the psychiatrist why his fellow workers nominated him to be president of his company and about his numerous degrees in physics, chemistry, and medicine. Following the interview the psychiatrist makes a diagnosis and treatment plan.

156. The probable diagnosis for this patient's case is

    (A) paranoid schizophrenia.

    (B) bipolar disorder.

    (C) catatonic schizophrenia.

    (D) obsessive-compulsive disorder.

    (E) atypical psychosis.

157. The salient symptoms that led the psychiatrist to make this specific diagnosis were

    (A) delusions of grandeur.   (B) accelerated speech and thought.

    (C) both (A) and (B)   (D) agitated, hyperactive behavior.

    (E) both (B) and (D)

158. The most probable psychotropic medication prescribed in the treatment plan was (were)

    (A) antidepressants.   (B) lithium.

    (C) sedatives.   (D) phenothiazines.

    (E) butyrophenes.

IN QUESTIONS 159-164, identify the pair which represents an INCORRECT association.

159. (A) Latané — diffusion of responsibility

    (B) Krauss — trucking game conflict

    (C) Anderson — conformity

    (D) Festinger — social comparison theory

    (E) Bem — group decision making

160. (A) Kohlberg — morality development

(B) Erikson — psychosocial development

(C) Sheldon — child cognition

(D) Bandura — social learning

(E) Gall — trait approach to personality

161. (A) Rescorla — two-process learning theory

(B) Premack — response probability

(C) Köhler — matching law

(D) Guthrie — one-trial learning

(E) Watson — motor theory

162. (A) Szazs — ethical model

(B) Graham — attitudes and illnesses

(C) Kallman — heredity of manic depression

(D) Asch — central traits of personality

(E) Alexander — impression formation

163. (A) Luchins — mental set

(B) Wertheimer — trait approach to personality

(C) Johnson — problem solving

(D) Osgood — semantic differentials

(E) Cattell — factor analysis of personality

164. (A) Schachter — emotion and motivation

(B) Piaget — cognition development

(C) Stevens — power law

(D) Murray — Thematic Apperception Test (TAT)

(E) Seligman — social exchange theory

165. Two kinds of change that occur to the cell body of a neuron during an action potential are

    (A) electrical and chemical.

    (B) spontaneous and stimulated.

    (C) hormonal and mechanical.

    (D) summation and subtraction.

    (E) chemical and hormonal.

166. Which of the following chemicals is responsible for the transmission of an impulse between neurons?

    (A) actomyosin

    (B) acetylcholine

    (C) acetylcholinesterase

    (D) luteinizing hormone

    (E) (A) and (C)

167. Which of the following are not innervated by the autonomic nervous system?

    (A) leg muscles

    (B) pupillary muscles

    (C) adrenal glands

    (D) pituitary glands

    (E) heart muscles

168. "Visual Cliff" experiments suggest that

    (A) tactile perceptions are an important aspect of depth perception.

    (B) depth perception improves with experience in the environment.

    (C) depth perception is innate in certain species.

    (D) (A) and (B)

    (E) (A) and (C)

169. The figures represented by A and B are classically known as

    (A) constancy patterns.

    (B) parallel patterns.

    (C) Kohler line equivalents.

    (D) McCollough effect.

    (E) Müller-Lyer patterns.

QUESTIONS 170-172 refer to the following passage.

In an experiment, 30 students were asked to perform several repetitive, tedious, and boring tasks. Ten of the students were offered a reward of $1 to go out of the lab into a waiting room to tell the next person about the exciting tasks they had performed. Ten other students were paid $20 for doing exactly the same thing. Another 10 students were not asked to "sell" anything. Afterwards, each of the 30 students filled out a questionnaire rating their attitudes about the boring tasks they had performed. The students who were paid $1 reported that they thought the tasks were exciting and interesting. The students who were paid $20 rated the tasks as dull. The group of students who were asked not to "sell" anything to the other students also rated their tasks as dull.

170. This experiment is a study of which phenomenon?

    (A) social comparison   (B) social facilitation

    (C) social learning   (D) rationalization

    (E) cognitive dissonance

171. Which group showed the most attitude change?

    (A) the group that was paid $1   (B) the group that was paid $20

    (C) the group that was unpaid   (D) the enthusiastic group

    (E) There was no change in any condition.

172. The highly paid group might be said to represent a case of

    (A) over-justification.   (B) insufficient justification.

    (C) sufficient justification.   (D) pro-attitudinal justification

    (E) none of the above

QUESTIONS 173–174 refer to the following passage.

In an experiment investigating hemispheric specializations (1968), split-brain subjects were told to feel a three-dimensional object without looking at it. They were then shown two-dimensional representations of objects and asked to point to the pattern corresponding to the object they felt. They were much more accurate when using the left hand than when using the right.

173. A split-brain person is one who had his corpus callosum cut as treatment for a severe case of

    (A) Parkinson's disease.   (B) Huntington's chorea.

    (C) schizophrenia.   (D) epilepsy.

    (E) insomnia.

174. From this experiment it can be seen that

    (A) the right hemisphere is specialized for complex visual and spatial tasks.

    (B) the left hemisphere is specialized for complex visual and spatial tasks.

    (C) sensory information from the left hand travels to the left hemisphere of the brain.

    (D) the split brain person cannot relate a three-dimensional object to its two-dimensional representation.

    (E) both (B) and (C)

175. In a particular study, young children were asked to feel two fabrics, either with the same or the opposite hands, and say whether they were the same or different materials. Three-year-olds made 90% more errors with different hands than with the same hand, and five-year-olds made only 10% more errors with different hands. A probable reason for this would be that

    (A) the sense of touch is more developed in five-year-olds.

    (B) the corpus callosum matures between ages three and five.

    (C) the right hemisphere is not sufficiently developed in three-year-olds.

    (D) both (A) and (B)   (E) all of the above

176. Intelligence tests measure

    (A) innate ability.   (B) performance.

    (C) educational level.   (D) both (A) and (B)

    (E) both (A) and (C)

177. In factor analysis, separateness of factors is assessed by

    (A) degree of correlation.

    (B) task analysis.

    (C) similarity of distribution.

    (D) both (A) and (B)   (E) both (B) and (C)

178. Which of the following is NOT a projective test?

    (A) TAT   (B) DAP

    (C) Rorschach   (D) Rosenweig P-F

    (E) WAIS

179. Which of the following theorists stressed the "proprium" or conscious ego functions as being most influencial in behavior?

    (A)   Allport   (B)   Horney

    (C)   Adler   (D)   Rogers

    (E)   Jung

180. Second-order conditioning is an important phenomenon because it demonstrates how an originally neutral CS can assume properties of

    (A)   first-order conditioning.   (B)   instrumental stimuli.

    (C)   a reinforcer.   (D)   a positive reward.

    (E)   a negative reward.

181. In 1915, Cannon and Bard sharply criticized the James-Lange theory on emotion by showing that

    (A)   there were not different physiological patterns for different emotions.

    (B)   there were different physiological patterns for different emotions.

    (C)   the hypothalamus was not the "seat of emotions."

    (D)   we experience the emotion after perceiving the physiological change.

    (E)   both (A) and (C)

182. Imprinting is the phenomenon describing

    (A)   visual memory coding in the brain.

    (B)   the neural effect of light on the retina.

    (C)   how the young of many species follow whatever conspicuous object that is first presented to them.

    (D)   Jung's theory of collective unconscious symbols in the mind.

    (E)   the almost immediate effect of a strong punishment on the curtailment of an operant response.

183. Stanley Milgram (1970), interpreted the unique behavior and habits of city dwellers in terms of which hypothesis?

    (A)   situation-appropriate   (B)   privacy deprivation

    (C)   diffusion of responsibility (D)   information-overload

    (E)   social conflict

184. Another phrase which might be used to describe the concept of instinctive behavior is

    (A) innate fixed-action pattern.

    (B) stimulus releaser.   (C) vacuum activity.

    (D) internal precipitater.   (E) both (A) and (C)

185. The vibrations of the eardrum are transmitted to the inner ear by the

    (A) cochlea.   (B) malleus, incus, and stapes.

    (C) basilar membrane.   (D) hair cells.

    (E) all of the above

186. The two major functions of smell are

    (A) evaluation of food and protection.

    (B) evaluation of food and communication.

    (C) evaluation of food and prey detection.

    (D) prey detection and protection.

    (E) none of the above

187. Allen Wagner argued that CS-UCS relationships are learned only if

    (A) they are expected.

    (B) there is a contingency between the two.

    (C) they are rehearsed.

    (D) there is a contiguity between the two.

    (E) both (A) and (C)

QUESTIONS 188-190 are based on the following diagrams.

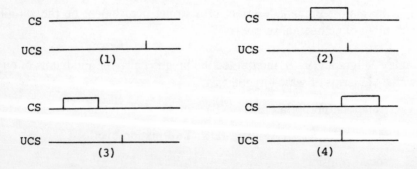

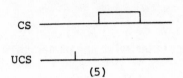

CS

UCS

(5)

Note: Upward deflections of the lines represent the on-set of a stimulus, a flat line means no stimulus is being presented.

188. The forward classical conditioning method is

(A) 1   (B) 2

(C) 3   (D) 4

(E) 5

189. Trace classical conditioning is represented by figure

(A) 1   (B) 2

(C) 3   (D) 4

(E) 5

190. The temporal classical conditioning method is represented by figure

(A) 1   (B) 2

(C) 3   (D) 4

(E) 5

191. A significant correlation means that

(A) a high correlation is more likely to exist between significant variables.

(B) the likelihood of getting a correlation that large is very probable.

(C) a relationship is likely to exist between two variables in the general population.

(D) none of the above   (E) (A) and (C)

192. Graphically presented material in which a bar represents the number of cases in an interval of measurement is a (an)

(A) polygon.   (B) histogram.

    (C)   cumulative frequency.   (D)   interval.

    (E)   standard norm.

QUESTIONS 193-196 refer to the following paragraph.

    The American Psychiatric Association (APA) has developed a classification system for mental illnesses known as the *Diagnostic and Statistical Manual of Mental Disorders* (DSM). The most recent edition is DSM-IV. Earlier versions of the diagnostic classification system had been criticized on the grounds that (1) the diagnostic classes were not homogeneous, (2) the system was not reliable, and (3) the system lacked validity.

193. In terms of diagnosis, reliability should be determined by

    (A)   the number of people with the disorder.

    (B)   the amount of agreement between diagnosticians concerning the diagnosis of a patient.

    (C)   the number of symptoms corresponding to the behaviors of patients.

    (D)   the total number of patients diagnosed with the classification.

    (E)   a combination of the total number of patients diagnosed and the correspondence of symptoms.

194. A lack of homogeneity of diagnoses is a problem because

    (A)   it is difficult to separate different diagnostic categories from each other.

    (B)   people diagnosed under one category of disorder might display significantly different behaviors.

    (C)   an inexperienced clinician may make an incorrect diagnosis.

    (D)   both (A) and (B)   (E)   both (A) and (C)

195. Whether or not predictions can be made about a diagnostic class once it has been formed is the test of

    (A)   reliability.   (B)   diagnostic strength.

    (C)   face validity.   (D)   validity.

    (E)   operational definitions.

196. Which of the following describe reasons why diagnosticians might disagree?

    (A)   collection of different information due to patient inconsistencies

(B)   unclear criteria in the diagnostic system

(C)   different interview styles

(D)   all of the above   (E)   none of the above

QUESTIONS 197-200 refer to the following paragraph.

To some extent, individuals lose their personal sense of identity when they are in a group. Instead of feeling that they personally are morally responsible for their actions, groups tend to share the responsibility. No single member feels this sense of responsibility as strongly as he would if he were acting alone. The members respond, and are responded to, as a group. This effect differs considerably among different types of groups. There is evidence that the greater the loss of personal identity in a group, the more free and uninhibited is the behavior of its members.

197. To what social phenomenon does this paragraph refer?

(A)   deindividuation   (B)   social exchange

(C)   Groupthink   (D)   cohesiveness

(E)   fusional responsibility

198. In an experiment studying this phenomenon, what would be the likely independent variable?

(A)   amount of attitude change

(B)   amount of responsibility placed on the group

(C)   the size of the group

(D)   amount of uninhibited behavior displayed

(E)   identifiability of subjects

199. One implication of this phenomenon is that

(A)   the more responsibility given to the group, the less responsibility each individual feels.

(B)   the more responsibility given to the group, the more responsibility each individual feels.

(C)   anything that makes the members of a group less identifiable increases the effect.

(D)   the larger the group, the smaller the effect.

(E)   none of the above

200. This paragraph implies that the effect

    (A)   usually has positive consequences.

    (B)   usually has negative consequences.

    (C)   has either positive or negative consequences depending on the situation.

    (D)   is equal for all groups.

    (E)   disappears with time.

201. Species-specific behavior patterns is an ethological term that refers to

    (A)   the preferred diet of different species of birds.

    (B)   instinctive social behavior patterns of animals and insects.

    (C)   the study of animal behavior in the natural environment.

    (D)   the relative intelligence of different species.

    (E)   all of the above

202. Bees can signal the location and distance of pollen to other bees. They communicate this information in the form of a dance. The Nobel Prize winner who spent years studying and deciphering the "bee dance" is

    (A)   Konrad Lorenz.   (B)   Charles Darwin.

    (C)   Edward Wilson.   (D)   Karl von Frisch.

    (E)   Niko Tinbergen

203. The Nobel Prize-winning ethologist who studied the mating rituals of the three-spined stickleback fish was

    (A)   Konrad Lorenz.   (B)   Charles Darwin.

    (C)   Edward Wilson.   (D)   Karl von Frisch.

    (E)   Niko Tinbergen.

204. A genetic defect known as Klinefelter's syndrome typically produces a tall, thin, sterile male with underdeveloped testes and breast development. This sex chromosome make up is

    (A)   XXY.   (B)   XY.

    (C)   XX.   (D)   XO.

    (E)   XYY.

205. A genetic defect known as Turner's syndrome typically produces a short female with a webbed neck, broad body, and no ovaries who won't develop secondary sex characteristics. This sex chromosome make-up is

(A) XXY.   (B) XY.

(C) XO.   (D) YY.

(E) YO.

206. Recent studies have indicated that women who smoke cigarettes during pregnancy

(A) transmit nicotine to their babies through the placenta.

(B) are twice as likely to give birth prematurely.

(C) have a higher incidence of babies with congenital defects.

(D) have a higher risk of miscarriage.

(E) all of the above

207. The normalcy of a baby at birth is assessed by the _____, which measures heart rate, respiration, muscle tone, reflexes, and body color.

(A) Apgar Scoring System.

(B) Thematic Apperception Test.

(C) Minnesota Multiphasic Inventory.

(D) Life Stress Scale.   (E) Polygraph.

208. From the Freudian perspective, making fun of someone at a social function just to be humorous and make others laugh is

(A) an attempt to just be humorous.

(B) indicative of a sexual desire for the person.

(C) camouflaged aggression.

(D) a mask for an inferiority complex.

(E) a desire to be teased ourselves.

209. According to social learning theory, one of the primary means of socializing our children is

(A) taming their instincts.   (B) developing their superegos.

(C) helping them self-actualize. (D) observational learning.

(E) providing minimum discipline.

210. According to the DSM-IV (*Diagnostic and Statistical Manual of Mental Disorders*) of the American Psychiatric Association, homosexuality is

    (A) a neurosis.

    (B) not sufficient grounds to warrant therapy.

    (C) a psychosis.

    (D) a dissociative disorder.

    (E) an antisocial personality.

211. The data on the average rapist indicates that he is

    (A) a single, teenage black man.

    (B) a single, teenage white man.

    (C) a married, white male in his 20s.

    (D) a gang member of any race.

    (E) in his 30s with several arrests on record.

212. The linguistic differences in the world's languages are produced by

    (A) different combinations of morphemes.

    (B) the fact that different races can produce different phonemes.

    (C) the different syntax rules that were developed by different nations.

    (D) different combinations of phonemes.

    (E) all of the above

213. Criticisms of the claims that apes and chimps can learn to communicate using American Sign Language include

    (A) the animals seldom make up novel statements they weren't specifically taught.

    (B) word order doesn't seem important to the animal.

    (C) they appear to fail to grasp syntax.

    (D) trainers have inadvertently cued the animals so they would emit certain signs.

    (E) all of the above

214. The vocal apparatus for producing speech sounds (vocal cords, muscle control of lips, throat, tongue, and jaw) are useless unless the organism has which area in its brain developed in order to coordinate these movements?

(A)   hypothalamus   (B)   thalamus

(C)   Broca's area   (D)   lateral ventricles

(E)   fissure of Rolando

215. Remembering precisely where you were, and what you were doing, when you first heard shocking news about a national event or the death of a close friend is characteristic of _____ memory.

(A)   eidetic   (B)   flashbulb

(C)   iconic   (D)   echoic

(E)   anterograde

216. Mnemonics are

(A)   a characteristic of sound.

(B)   the sound produced when two notes an octave apart are played simultaneously.

(C)   techniques used to improve memory.

(D)   the seven individual elements in short-term memory.

(E)   the scientific term for a memory location in the brain.

217. Testimony obtained while a subject is hypnotized

(A)   is accepted in a court of law.

(B)   is very detailed and accurate.

(C)   is evidence for reincarnation.

(D)   is often a combination of the truth and fantasy.

(E)   all of the above

TEST 2

ANSWER KEY

1.	(E)	26.	(D)	51.	(E)	76.	(C)
2.	(B)	27.	(B)	52.	(D)	77.	(D)
3.	(D)	28.	(E)	53.	(B)	78.	(E)
4.	(E)	29.	(D)	54.	(C)	79.	(B)
5.	(D)	30.	(A)	55.	(D)	80.	(C)
6.	(B)	31.	(E)	56.	(C)	81.	(E)
7.	(A)	32.	(B)	57.	(B)	82.	(D)
8.	(E)	33.	(B)	58.	(A)	83.	(C)
9.	(C)	34.	(C)	59.	(A)	84.	(D)
10.	(B)	35.	(A)	60.	(C)	85.	(B)
11.	(A)	36.	(D)	61.	(A)	86.	(B)
12.	(D)	37.	(E)	62.	(B)	87.	(C)
13.	(E)	38.	(E)	63.	(C)	88.	(D)
14.	(D)	39.	(A)	64.	(B)	89.	(E)
15.	(E)	40.	(E)	65.	(E)	90.	(A)
16.	(B)	41.	(B)	66.	(D)	91.	(A)
17.	(B)	42.	(B)	67.	(C)	92.	(D)
18.	(D)	43.	(D)	68.	(A)	93.	(D)
19.	(B)	44.	(D)	69.	(D)	94.	(C)
20.	(D)	45.	(D)	70.	(C)	95.	(B)
21.	(A)	46.	(B)	71.	(A)	96.	(B)
22.	(D)	47.	(B)	72.	(E)	97.	(B)
23.	(A)	48.	(C)	73.	(E)	98.	(D)
24.	(D)	49.	(C)	74.	(E)	99.	(B)
25.	(B)	50.	(E)	75.	(C)	100.	(D)

101.	(C)	131.	(D)	161.	(C)	191.	(C)
102.	(B)	132.	(B)	162.	(E)	192.	(B)
103.	(B)	133.	(A)	163.	(B)	193.	(B)
104.	(A)	134.	(B)	164.	(E)	194.	(B)
105.	(B)	135.	(E)	165.	(A)	195.	(D)
106.	(D)	136.	(E)	166.	(B)	196.	(D)
107.	(A)	137.	(D)	167.	(A)	197.	(A)
108.	(B)	138.	(B)	168.	(C)	198.	(E)
109.	(D)	139.	(C)	169.	(E)	199.	(C)
110.	(E)	140.	(C)	170.	(E)	200.	(C)
111.	(E)	141.	(D)	171.	(B)	201.	(B)
112.	(B)	142.	(D)	172.	(A)	202.	(D)
113.	(C)	143.	(A)	173.	(D)	203.	(E)
114.	(A)	144.	(D)	174.	(A)	204.	(A)
115.	(C)	145.	(B)	175.	(B)	205.	(C)
116.	(B)	146.	(D)	176.	(B)	206.	(E)
117.	(A)	147.	(D)	177.	(A)	207.	(A)
118.	(A)	148.	(C)	178.	(E)	208.	(C)
119.	(D)	149.	(D)	179.	(A)	209.	(D)
120.	(B)	150.	(E)	180.	(C)	210.	(B)
121.	(A)	151.	(D)	181.	(A)	211.	(C)
122.	(E)	152.	(A)	182.	(C)	212.	(D)
123.	(C)	153.	(E)	183.	(D)	213.	(E)
124.	(C)	154.	(A)	184.	(E)	214.	(C)
125.	(A)	155.	(C)	185.	(B)	215.	(B)
126.	(D)	156.	(B)	186.	(B)	216.	(C)
127.	(C)	157.	(E)	187.	(C)	217.	(D)
128.	(D)	158.	(B)	188.	(B)		
129.	(D)	159.	(C)	189.	(C)		
130.	(C)	160.	(C)	190.	(A)		

DETAILED EXPLANATIONS
OF ANSWERS

GRE PSYCHOLOGY TEST 2

1.   **(E)**   Chaining is not a process involved in observational learning. According to Bandura, attention, retention, reproduction, and motivation are all critical processes in observational learning or modeling. A person must attend to the behavior being shown and retain the information observed. The person must use memory to guide the reproduction of the behavior previously shown, and be motivated to reproduce the behavior.

2.   **(B)**   According to Carl Rogers, the organism and the self are the two constructs of personality. The organism is conceived to be the locus of experience; experience includes everything available to awareness and all that occurs within the organism. The self or self-concept refers to the organized and consistent set of perceptions that are self-referential, i.e., that refer to "I" or "me." These two constructs interact to form the personality.

3.   **(D)**   Erikson determined that there were eight developmental crises in our lives that corresponded to the eight developmental periods. These crises in their developmental order are: (1) trust vs. mistrust, (2) autonomy vs. doubt and shame, (3) initiative vs. guilt, (4) industry vs. inferiority, (5) identity crisis, (6) intimacy vs. isolation, (7) crisis of child rearing, and (8) integrity vs. despair in old age.

4.   **(E)**   The issue of control in field research is problematic. Control is not an advantage of field studies because there isn't appropriate control involved in these types of studies. Control is a tradeoff for the other advantages in field research.

5.   **(D)**   Carl Rogers used the "Q-technique" for research purposes. The Q-technique is essentially a method of systematically analyzing a person's attitudes or opinions about a matter. Usually, the Q-technique is used to measure a person's opinions about him-/herself.

6.   **(B)**   A cross-sectional study is one in which different subjects at different developmental levels are compared. For example, a researcher could examine language development by comparing the linguistic ability of different groups of children at different stages of development.

7.   **(A)**   Item analysis is a method of analyzing individual items on a par-

ticular test. This method is used for the purpose of discovering problems and failures in the instructor's teaching and the student's studying and for the purpose of improving test construction. Item analysis is important because it provides the examiner with feedback on the effectiveness of his test and teaching method.

8.   **(E)**   Analytic psychology is the term applied to the form of psychoanalysis developed by Carl Jung. In Jung's analytic psychology, he postulated the conscious, the personal unconscious and the collective unconscious as the basic elements of mental existence rather than the id, ego and superego of Freud's psychoanalysis.

9.   **(C)**   In psychoanalysis, the material of the unconscious mind needs to be brought into the conscious mind so that it no longer serves as a source of anxiety and confusion for the patient. By bringing the unconscious motivations into consciousness, the analyst seeks to reconstruct the patient's personality, to enable him to deal more effectively in relationships.

10.   **(B)**   In a within-subjects design, each subject is tested in all the conditions of the experiment at one time or another. In this example, each subject would ingest each of the drugs separately and perform the same task each time.

11.   **(A)**   The CPI (California Psychological Inventory), as developed by Gough, is an objective personality inventory developed for use with less clinical and deviant groups of subjects than the MMPI. Some of the representative scales included are: Self-control, Responsibility, Flexibility, Achievement via Independence, Tolerance, and Intellectual efficiency. The items are not designed to measure gross psychopathology, but to measure more minor forms of maladjustment.

12.   **(D)**   The sample arranged in order is 26, 29, 31, 34, 34, 37. The number of observations is even and thus the median, or middle number, is chosen halfway between the third and fourth number. In this case the median is

$$\frac{31 + 34}{2} = 32.5$$

13.   **(E)**   The range is a measure of dispersion of the sample and is defined to be the difference between the largest and smallest observations. In this example, the largest observation is 53 and the smallest is 33. The difference is $53 - 33 = 20$ and the range is 20.

14.   **(D)**   The matching law states that an animal will respond (perform an operant response) proportionately to the amount it is reinforced. Suppose a rat had the option of pulling a chain for food pellets on a V1–5 ratio or pressing a lever for food on a U1–10 ratio. According to this law, the rat should both pull the chain and press the lever, but it would pull the chain more than press the

lever because it matches the number of responses to how much reinforcement it receives per response.

15. **(E)** Fritz Heider proposed that the key to understanding interpersonal attraction is "balance," a harmonious and non-stress-producing state. He also contended that our perception of the attributes of a person controls the way we behave toward that person, as well as what we expect from him or her. The perceptual factors that are most important in Heider's theory are balance and consistency. According to Heider, we seek to achieve a harmonious balance in our relations with our friends. Any imbalance, such as disagreement with a friend, creates psychological discomfort which motivates people to restore balance by either rejecting the friend or changing one's own attitude.

16. **(B)** "Locus of Control" as a determinant of behavior is predicated on the notion that an important determinant of an individual's action is the degree to which the individual perceives that a reward follows from his or her own behavior (internality) or is controlled by forces outside him- or herself (externality). According to Rotter's Locus of Control Scale, people with an internal orientation tend to take responsibility for what happens to them, while people with an external orientation see the events of life as due to chance and beyond their control.

17. **(B)** Vroom states that an individual's motivation is a function of two factors: (1) the "expectation" that a particular behavior will lead to a desired goal and (2) the "valence" or desirability of the goal. This is called the Expectancy Theory. This proposal is not directly related to motivation in the work place, but has received attention by Human Resource Development departments in companies.

18. **(D)** Kohlberg devised an extensive theory of moral development. The morality of self-accepted principles is the third and highest level of morality according to Kohlberg. This level initiates the beginning of the individual's moral standards and takes place during adolescence. The adolescent arrives at an understanding of individual rights, ideals and principles. He or she can see beyond the literal interpretation of rules and laws. Kohlberg believes that morality is a decision making process rather than a fixed behavioral trait.

19. **(B)** The "index of centrality" is a mathematical measure developed by H. Leavitt. It provides a measure of the extent to which a given individual interacts with others. The higher a person scores on this index, the more that person participates in the communications that occur. High scores on this index of centrality arc always associated with those in leadership positions. Leavitt also created the "index of peripherality" which measures the extent to which individuals are excluded from interaction with others.

20. **(D)** An ogive is an S-shaped curve.

21. **(A)**   A rectangular distribution is one in which each score occurs with the same frequency.

22. **(D)**   McClelland first used the Thematic Apperception Test to measure the need for achievement (n Ach). This is a projective test in which people are asked to tell a story about a variety of pictures they see. McClelland was interested in the degree to which people projected achievement needs into the picture stories. The stories are scored and the degree of achievement imagery is assessed by content analysis.

23. **(A)**   The autokinetic phenomenon is of importance because of its use in conformity studies. People viewing the stationary point of light with a group of people were dramatically influenced in their perceptions by the opinions of others in the group. These studies of the autokinetic phenomenon were conducted by Muzafer Sherif and have become classic studies of conformity behavior.

24. **(D)**   Social reinforcement occurs when the reinforcer consists of feedback from individuals in one's environment. Approval from a boss is clearly an example of positive social reinforcement. Other examples of positive social reinforcement would be attention and affection, while examples of negative social reinforcement would be indifference or enmity.

25. **(B)**   Neurons are the basic structural and functional units of the nervous system. There are many types, each having a specific function. Despite their diversity, there are certain characteristics common to all neurons. They all conduct impulses and consist of a cell body, an axon and dendrites. They are different from all other types of cells in the body in that they cannot reproduce.

26. **(D)**   The range of wavelengths to which we can respond is called the visible spectrum. It extends from approximately 400 nanometers (violet) to about 750 nanometers (red). This energy is called light because the eye can convert it into nerve impulses.

27. **(B)**   Carl Roger's theory of human motivation is based on the assumption that the organism is a purely monistic dynamic system. This means that there is one universal, all encompassing drive. According to Rogers, the one drive is the desire to "actualize, maintain, and enhance the experiencing organism." The basic tendency is to grow and expand oneself. To actualize means to have a person's real self, or essence, emerge and replace any false aspects of his personality.

28. **(E)**   The spinal cord has two major functions. It acts as a messenger, relaying information from the body to the brain and back to the body. It also directs simple reflex actions without input from the brain.

29. **(D)** The Minnesota Multiphasic Personality Inventory (MMPI) consists of 550 statements to which the subject is asked to answer true, false, or cannot say in respect to himself. The test has 10 subscales of behaviors and is standardized. Groupings of answers in the 10 subscales are statistically analyzed. The MMPI, due to its standardization and method of statistical analysis, has a high degree of empirical validity and criterion related validity.

30. **(A)** The three dimensions of intelligence are operations, contents, and products. Operations help describe what mental activity a person is using to approach a problem, for example, memory or cognition. Operations like memory or cognition are performed on some specific kind of content, like reading material. Products are the end results of the operations. More specifically, a product is the form in which information is processed.

31. **(E)** Construct validity is concerned with the degree to which a test measures a theoretical construct or an underlying trait. It also raises the question of what a test score reveals about an individual; will the test score help the examiner to understand the examinee by providing meaningful information about the individual's personality or intellectual characteristics? Meaningful information is essential to construct validity.

32. **(B)** In petit-mal epileptic attacks, there is neither an aura nor are there convulsions. Such an attack is only a momentary alteration of consciousness. The person stops what he is doing and his eyes roll up. There may be a few twitches of the eye and face muscles, but in most cases such seizures are difficult to recognize. As with other seizures, the petit-mal seizure is caused by excessive brain activity due to discharges of neurons.

33. **(B)** The iconic mode is the second stage in Bruner's theory of cognitive development. In this stage, knowledge of the world is based heavily on images which stand for perceptual events. A picture, for example, may stand for an actual event. While the emphasis is usually on visual images, other sensory images are possible.

34. **(C)** Divergent thinking involves generating a number of possible solutions. It requires a fluency of ideas, flexibility, and originality. The solution of complex chess problems, for example, requires divergent thinking. This is true because there are always many possibilities to consider before making a move.

35. **(A)** Ewald Hering (1878), a German physiologist, proposed that there were three different receptor types, each composed of a pair of opponent processes. He thought there was a white-black receptor, a red-green receptor, and a blue-yellow receptor. If one member of the opponent pairs was stimulated more than the other, that color was seen. If red was stimulated more than green, red was the color observed.

36. **(D)**   The hypothalamus, located under the thalamus, is a collection of nuclei concerned with homeostatic regulations. Electrical stimulation of certain cells in the hypothalamus produces sensations of hunger, thirst, pain, pleasure, or sexual drives. These are all important emotional and physiological motivators of behavior.

37. **(E)**   Several factors influence the sensitivity of the eye to light. The eyes are affected by the nature of light, which itself is a function of wavelength, intensity, and composition. The eye's state of adaptation varies with the surrounding stimuli and is subject to great variability. The region of the retina is directly associated with light sensitivity because it contains the rod and cone photoreceptor cells. The iris regulates the amount of light entering through the pupil.

38. **(E)**   Both choices (A) and (D) are true. Here the individual is equally attracted and repelled by the goal. The person is trapped in an approach-avoidance conflict. The gradient shows that the person's initial tendency is to approach the goal, but as he gets closer to it, the tendency to avoid it becomes stronger.

39. **(A)**   The gradient shown depicts an approach-avoidance conflict. In this type of conflict, the goal object has both positive and negative qualities for the individual; hence, he is both attracted to it and repelled by it at the same time. Thus, this type of conflict involves making a sometimes difficult decision. Approach-avoidance conflicts usually produce the greatest amount of frustration.

40. **(E)**   Two kinds of behavior are likely to result from an avoidance-avoidance conflict. One is vascillation and the other is escape or attempting to leave the conflict situation. In vascillation, the individual wavers between the two negative goals for an indefinite period of time. In escape behavior, the person tries to run away from the conflict or problem. Attempting to leave the conflict often has greater negative consequences than staying in the avoidance-avoidance conflict situation.

41. **(B)**   Latent-inhibition is an important learning principle in animals as well as in people. For example, if a rat is periodically exposed to a tone but receives no reinforcement for any response, it will habituate to the tone and ignore it. If this tone was then used to classically condition the rat, the conditioning would not be very successful.

42. **(B)**   An understanding of conservation is not characteristic of the preoperational stage of development. This occurs later during the concrete operational stage. During the preoperational stage, the child first views the world through an egocentric thinking style. As he develops, the child develops problem solving abilities which are based on intuitive thinking. The thinking process is static with respect to reversibility and permanence of thought in this stage. This

is one of the four developmental periods that Piaget defined in his cognitive development theory.

43.   **(D)**   Based on the description of the way these children understood the game rules, one could determine that they are in the concrete operational stage of development. This stage emphasizes concrete understanding of rules, and logical thinking as it relates to real concrete objects. Abstract and hypothetical thinking are largely undeveloped.

44.   **(D)**   The concrete operational stage lasts from ages seven to eleven years. This is the usual age span, but it may be shorter or longer in an individual child.

45.   **(D)**   Noam Chomsky believes that children are born with a certain "something," a certain genetic predisposition that enables them to learn grammar. Chomsky called this predisposition the Language Acquisition Device (LAD). It is believed to exist at birth. Chomsky used this concept to explain the relative ease with which normal children learn grammar.

46.   **(B)**   The retina sends visual information it receives from the environment to the brain through various nerve fibers. These fibers are known collectively as the optic nerve. There is a right and left optic nerve, one from each eye. These join in a region called the optic chiasm. At this point, half of the fibers of each optic nerve cross over to the opposite side of the brain. This is what we mean when we say our visual system is 50% crossed.

47.   **(B)**   While activity levels and effectiveness of the worker are discussed in Argyris's theory, his major categorization is mature versus immature individuals in the work environment. The immature person is described as passive, distractible, dependent, and shallow. The mature person is described as active, having focused attention, independent, and deeply interested. He used this categorization to study how a worker stays satisfied on the job; an immature worker is much more easily satisfied because of his shallowness.

48.   **(C)**   Rosenthal conducted a study showing that teachers can affect their pupil's I.Q. test scores. He told a group of teachers that certain students had high intellectual potential. In reality, these students were randomly selected. At the end of the year, these pupils showed a much larger I.Q. gain than students not identified as high in potential. Because the teachers expected the pupils to do better, they unconsciously took steps along the way to make sure that they did. Needless to say, this study shook the foundations of psychological research and caused many to doubt the validity of much of the research up to that point not using double-blind techniques.

49.   **(C)**   (C) is the answer by definition. β is the probability of committing a Type II error, whereas $1 - \beta$ is the power of the test. One test of significance is

said to be more powerful than another if it is more likely to result in the rejection of a false null hypothesis. The more powerful test is more likely to detect a difference between two means.

50. **(E)** The paranoid schizophrenic is characterized by the presence of numerous and systematized delusions, usually of persecution or grandeur. They may sometimes have the delusion of being controlled by an alien force. Auditory and visual hallucinations may accompany the delusions. Generally, paranoid schizophrenics are more alert and verbal than other schizophrenics. They tend to intellectualize, building up an organized set of beliefs based on the wrong (paranoid) assumptions.

51. **(E)** Korsakoff's psychosis is a disorder associated with alcoholism. Current research has indicated that nutritional and vitamin deficiencies associated with excessive alcohol intake are the basis for the disorder. The major symptoms of this psychosis are loss of memory for recent events, time and space disorientation, and a tendency to fabricate stories to fill in forgotten past events.

52. **(D)** A history of suicide attempts is not characteristic of sociopathy. In fact, a history of no sincere suicide attempts is part of the diagnostic criteria for sociopathy. Sociopathy is the term used to refer to the antisocial personality syndrome, which describes a person who is basically unsocialized and often in conflict with society.

53. **(B)** Iconic coding represents a fleeting, visual experience that is of great importance in the study of information processing. In the visual realm, the iconic image is that which occurs during a single glance. Usually lasting about 1/15 of a second, iconic storage consists of a series of successive glances each representing a small section of a larger object.

54. **(C)** The theory of Selective Attention was proposed by Broadbent. Broadbent's approach also became known as the filter theory, because it generally hypothesized that certain sensory inputs are rejected, while others are "allowed in" for further processing. According to the theory, information passes through a selective filter which only attends to the important aspects of stimuli. This filtered information then passes through channels into a limited-capacity short-term memory bank where it is retained by the processing system.

55. **(D)** Generally, the items that are forgotten are those in the middle of the list. This is because what is learned first usually interferes with what comes later (productive interference) and what is learned later usually interferes with what came earlier (retroactive interference). Thus, the items in the middle are most susceptible to being forgotten because they are subject to both kinds of interference.

56. **(C)** Template matching theories purport that each pattern is recognized

by noting its similarity with a basic, internal model. It is considered a problematic theory due to its rigidity. For example, people recognize an "R" even if it is upside down, very small, or huge. The template theory would have to be expanded to include a new template for every possible size and orientation of the letter to provide a viable explanation of the capabilities of the human pattern-recognition system.

57. **(B)** Correlational analysis measures the degree of linear association between two characteristics, X and Y. Correlation should not be confused with causation. Correlation is a mathematical technique for showing whether elements in two sets of data are linearly related to each other, while causality implies that one of the variables has a causal effect on the other.

58. **(A)** Spinal nerves belong to the peripheral nervous system (PNS). They arise as pairs at regular intervals from the spinal cord, branch, and run to various parts of the body to innervate them. In humans, there are 31 symmetrical pairs of spinal nerves.

59. **(A)** A person suffering from nerve deafness will have more difficulty hearing high pitched tones. This type of deafness results from damage to the auditory nervous system. Hair cells in the cochlea translate sound vibrations into electrical messages our brain can "understand." Specific hair cells respond to specific tones. If some are damaged, the vibrations of certain tones will not be properly translated into electrical messages.

60. **(C)** Maslow is a chief proponent of the humanist school of human behavior. His most popular theory concerns the hierarchical nature of the human motivational structure. He set forth a five-stage model in which the lower, most dominant needs control human motivation until they are satisfied. The next needs then come into play. Maslow's theory, though popular and innovative, lacks empirical support. In this respect it is similar to other humanistic theories of behavior.

61. **(A)** A null hypothesis is analyzed in terms of its acceptance or rejection rather than in terms of its proof or disproof. The null hypothesis cannot be proved anymore than disproved because there always exists the possibility of Type I or Type II errors. A null hypothesis can only be accepted or rejected according to the level of significance of the results. A significant result means only that the difference obtained probably did not occur by chance.

62. **(B)** A minimum amount of stimulation is needed for a nerve cell to begin sending signals. But once this threshold value is reached, the All-or-None Law states that the size of the signal produced is always the same, regardless of the size of the stimulus. Signal frequency determines our perception of stimulus intensity.

63.   **(C)**   When the nerve cell has finished responding to past stimulation, it may again be responsive to new stimulation. However, it takes a much stronger stimulus to get the neuron to fire. This is called the relative refractory period. During this period, the nerve cell can respond if a strong enough stimulus is provided. The length of the relative refractory period varies from nerve to nerve.

64.   **(B)**   Concepts are symbols of connections between two or more objects, events, or ideas. They allow the mind to distinguish relations among objects and events. When multiple stimuli are considered simultaneously, a concept is complex. Conjunctive, disjunctive, and relational concepts all constitute complex concepts. Conjunctive concepts exist when the objects possess two or more common properties. Disjunctive concepts are based on entities in which only one property, or a combination of properties is necessary to fulfill the concept. Comparisons between two properties express a relational concept.

65.   **(E)**   The inclusion of encoding, memory, evaluation, deduction, and mediation indicate that the component process theory is based on work in information processing. Each of these areas is of interest to the psychologist studying information processing. The component process theory is an interesting assimilation of these concepts.

66.   **(D)**   This theory assumes that the knowledge and ability of the child to perform problem solving tasks will appear in the child's performance on objective indexes that test problem solving. This question taps into the debate of competence versus performance that is of concern to many areas of psychology.

67.   **(C)**   You will notice in the reading of the passage, that there is no mention of the emotional effects and experience of the child on its cognitive development. This theory is limited to looking at the progressive problem solving ability in the child. It does not examine the emotional or psychosocial development of the child.

68.   **(A)**   The autokinetic effect is a perceptual experiment most famously used for studying conforming behavior. A light is projected on the wall of a dark room and it appears to move. The movement is, however, due to the movement of the viewer's eyes. This apparent movement is called the "autokinetic effect" or phenomenon. This phenomenon was used in a landmark study by Sherif and Hood (1962), testing social informational influence on conformity.

69.   **(D)**   The gestalists developed from their observations and experiments numerous "laws" of perceptual organization. These laws are actually an outline of the factors which seem to influence our perception of space. They can mainly be summarized by the "law" of simplicity, commonly called the Minimum Principle. The Minimum Principle states that our nervous systems are constructed in any given scene, to see what is simplest to see.

70. **(C)**   Although they are separate symptoms, obsession and compulsion often occur together as a neurotic reaction pattern. Obsessions are persistent, often unreasonable thoughts which cannot be banished. A person may become so obsessed with an idea that he or she will count stoplights, and cracks in the pavement, or will swear inappropriately or even commit murder as a defense mechanism against it. A compulsion is a persistent act which is committed over and over again. Virtually any behavior may be viewed as a compulsion if the individual reports an irresistible urge to perform the behavior. Obsessive-compulsive behavior prevents a person from thinking anxiety-provoking thoughts.

71. **(A)**   The ego is the intermediary between the id and reality. It develops between the ages of eight months and eighteen months, as the child acquires an understanding of what is possible in the outer world. The ego also distinguishes between long-range and short-range goals and decides which activities will be most profitable to the individual. The id and ego work together to determine the individual's goals.

72. **(E)**   Although the misuse of alcohol is likely to occur with some other disorders, perhaps as a way of "self-medicating," dependence on alcohol is a distinct problem in itself. As with other substances on which people may become dependent (e.g., marijuana, cocaine, sedatives, nicotine), alcohol dependence involves use of the drug despite significant behavioral, social, physical, or cognitive problems caused by that use. Further, the alcoholic uses it frequently enough and in high enough volumes to produce tolerance, withdrawal, and consequent compulsive drinking.

73. **(E)**   These characteristics of animal learning have been repeatedly demonstrated with rats in a radial arm maze. Many animals have a sophisticated spatial memory on which they rely to search for prey and to find caches of food they have hidden for the winter. In nature, spatial cues such as trees, hills and rocks are used by many animals, such as birds and bees, to remember where they have seen or hidden food.

74. **(E)**   All of these are characteristics of affiliation. Schachter had 2 conditions in his experiment: High versus Low fear, in which he warned subjects that they were going to receive a shock that was either extremely painful or just a tickle. After announcing a ten minute delay before the shocks, he gave them a questionnaire that indicated their desire to affiliate. High fear subjects wanted to affiliate much more than the Low fear subjects. He also found that first-born children affiliate more when fearful and that "misery only loves misery's company," that is, fearful subjects prefer to affiliate with others in the same situation.

75. **(C)**   Guilford's concept of intelligence is based on a multiple factor theory, which means that he describes intelligence as consisting of a specific set of traits or factors. He classified intelligence along three dimensions, which are operations, contents, and products.

76. **(C)** The Thematic Apperception Test was designed by Murray and Morgan in 1935, to determine the major themes of concern for a particular individual by allowing him to respond freely to the vague and ambiguous pictures presented on TAT cards. Theoretically, the themes expressed in the responses reflect the subject's present motivational, emotional, and conflicted condition.

77. **(D)** A cross-sectional study is one in which different subjects at different developmental levels are compared. Instead of using a longitudinal approach, for example, a researcher could investigate language development with children of different developmental levels. The obvious advantage of a cross-sectional study over a longitudinal study is that it is much less time consuming. It is also less expensive.

78. **(E)** Bayley Scales of Infant Development assess the developmental status at the time they are administered. The assessment is carried out by determining if the infant engages in normative behavior for his age. There are three scales of assessment: the Mental Scale, the Motor Scale, and the Infant Behavior Record.

79. **(B)** Karen Horney, an analyst who broke from classical psychoanalysis, developed a theory concerning the neurotic needs of the individual. She identified ten neurotic needs which fall under three general categories: 1) moving toward people, 2) moving away from people, 3) moving against people. She thought most people achieve an integration and balance of these forces, but the neurotic individual lacks this balance and integration.

80. **(C)** Extinction of conditioned respondent behavior occurs when the CS is presented without the UCS a number of times. The magnitude of the response elicited by the CS and the percentage of presentations of the CS which elicits responses, gradually decreases as the CS continues to be presented without the UCS. If CS presentation continues without the UCS, the CR will decline to at least the level present before the classical conditioning was begun.

81. **(E)** All of these important figures in psychology were adherents to the functionalist school of thought. They studied how and why the mind works. Strongly influenced by Darwin, they emphasized the use of the mind as a tool for adaptation to the environment. They were among the first to emphasize learning and the scientific method.

82. **(D)** Although almost always accompanied by anger, it is solely frustration which is the root of all aggressive acts. This theory is known as the frustration-aggression hypothesis. Further investigation studying aggressive instincts and predispositions to fight, as well as behavior modeling, suggest that much more is at work. In all likelihood, frustration is sufficient, but not necessary, to produce aggression.

83. **(C)** Milgram designed an experiment where a subject (the teacher) would give electric shocks to another human (the learner) whenever the learner gave the wrong answer on a word association task. Each shock was stronger than the one before. Although the shock apparatus was labelled "WARNING–INTENSE SHOCK," and the learner begged the teacher to stop, 63% of the subjects continued the experiment because the researcher told them that he would take full responsibility for the results.

84. **(D)** The concept of instinctive human motivation was based on Darwin's evolutionary theory, which stressed the survival value of instinctive animal behaviors. Since Darwin claimed that humans were descendants of lower animals, psychologists such as McDougall and James, used Darwin's theory in their studies on human motivation. Eventually the concept of instinct was abandoned and in its place came the concept of drive as the motivational force.

85. **(B)** Human auditory processes are sensitive to a fairly broad range of frequencies, from 20 Hz – 20,000 Hz. Frequency is the number of cycles completed by a sound wave in one second. A cycle is made up of two components: compression and refraction. The time that it takes to complete one cycle is called the period of sound. Frequencies below 20 Hz are felt as vibrations, rather than heard.

86. **(B)** There are different sensitivities to different kinds of taste in different areas of the tongue. Unlike the tip, the back surface is most sensitive to bitter tastes, and the sides of the tongue are most sensitive to salty and sour tastes. Each taste bud contains 10-15 individual receptor cells that are sensitive to and absorb specific molecules of substances tasted. There are 10,000 taste buds on the tongue.

87. **(C)** Kamin's research suggests that organisms do not condition to all stimuli in a contingency because of a process called blocking. In his experiment, one group of subjects received a CS composed of a tone and light paired with shock. Tests showed that both the tone and light shown separately, produced a strong fear response. The second group had an initial pairing of only tone with shock and then a subsequent pairing of tone and light with shock. Tests showed that the light produced no fear response, because it was not paired with the shock due to blocking. The pairing of the tone with the shock, blocked out subsequent learning on the tone and light pairing with shock.

88. **(D)** An EPSP is an excitatory postsynaptic potential, and refers to changes in a nerve cell's charge relative to the environment. An EPSP occurs when stimulation makes the nerve cell less negative, as would occur if the cell membrane now begins to allow positive charges to pass through. It is considered excitatory because if it is large enough, it may cause the nerve cell to become sufficiently positive in order to fire.

89.   **(E)**   The pituitary gland produces TSH, ACTH, FSH, and LH. TSH induces secretion of another hormone in the thyroid gland. ACTH stimulates the adrenal cortex to secrete cortisol. Both LH and FSH control the secretion of the sex hormones by the gonads. They also regulate the growth and development of sperm and ovum. Hence, the pituitary is in a sense a master gland that directs the hormone secretions to other glands and organs.

90.   **(A)**   Problems with more than one correct solution require divergent thinking. Divergent thinking produces several different solutions for a problem. This type of thinking requires flexibility, fluency of ideas, and originality. Divergent thinking is believed to be the basis for creativity.

91.   **(A)**   The normal distribution is the most important distribution in statistics. As the number of scores in a frequency distribution grows, the curve will approach the shape of the normal distribution curve. It is also important to note that every population which is normally distributed may be characterized by two population parameters: the mean and the variance.

92.   **(D)**   The confidence interval is a statistic which specifies at some known probability level the range within which the population mean must lie, given a known sample measure. The limits of the range of acceptance are called confidence limits and specifically, the distance between these limits is termed the confidence interval.

93.   **(D)**   In Freud's system, three levels of consciousness were distinguished: the conscious, the preconscious, and the unconscious. In terms of this question, the preconscious is midway between the conscious and the unconscious. The preconscious contains memories and drives that can easily be recalled but are not within consciousness at the moment.

94.   **(C)**   The person described in this question is exhibiting a defense mechanism which Freud termed projection. Projection may be defined as attributing one's unacceptable motives to another person or group of people. The person in the example attributes his hostility, which he perceives as unacceptable, to others who are "out to get" him.

95.   **(B)**   Conditioned behavior can later reappear without additional conditioning, even though extinction had appeared to be successful. This is known as spontaneous recovery. If a rest interval follows the extinction of a CR, it will reappear spontaneously but in a weaker form. Then if conditioning is done again, using the same stimuli, the original response will be strengthened quickly.

96.   **(B)**   Based on the reading of the graph in the diagram, low-anxiety students have higher grade point averages and higher levels of scholastic aptitude than high-anxiety students. Notice the performance jump from level 1 to

level 2 of scholastic aptitude. Usually, the more anxious a person is, the lower his performance level on a verbal learning task.

97. **(B)** The pleasure principle might be translated as "if it feels good, do it." This principle is what guides the id to seek gratification of its desires and to avoid unpleasurable stimuli leading to pain. The id is basically an instinctive pleasure seeker.

98. **(D)** Rationalization is a Freudian defense mechanism that involves attempts by a person who is not conscious of the real reasons for his inappropriate or unacceptable behavior, to justify or explain the behavior, by reference to socially acceptable motives. It occurs whenever an individual fears that a behavior he has engaged in might be abnormal.

99. **(B)** Examples of unconditioned responses are salivation to food and adrenal gland responses to fear stimuli.

100. **(D)** The most efficient method of spaced practice varies two features: 1) the length of the practice period, and 2) the length of the rest period. In general, short practice periods result in more efficient learning of a motor task. Periods should not be so short, however, that the task is separated into meaningless units. Very long rest periods, however, do not increase the learning rate. Most tasks do not require rest periods of more than a few minutes. Beyond this optimal time, learning rate will not increase.

101. **(C)** Social learning theory, first described by Miller and Dollard, is an attempt to combine the principles of social analysis of behavior with principles of learning taken from the behavior scientist's animal laboratory. In this respect, Miller and Dollard took important steps in integrating these two previously separate areas of inquiry in psychology. Based on this theory, Bandura and Walters created another social learning theory that emphasized the role of "modeling" in the acquisition of behavior.

102. **(B)** Carl Rogers places special emphasis on the need for positive regard and the need for self regard. He considers both to be learned needs. Positive regard refers to the positive assessment an individual receives from other people. The need for self regard is established as a result of receiving positive regard from others.

103. **(B)** Allport stated that there are two components of behavior, adaptive and expressive. The adaptive component refers to the function of the act and the expressive component accounts for the individuality of an act. Allport was especially interested in the individual and the study of expressive behavior. Allport believed in a general unity underlying personality, and, therefore, he maintained that studying an individual's expressive behavior would lead to an understanding of the central aspects of his personality.

104. **(A)**   Rods are more sensitive to light than cones, and thus will respond to very dim lights to which cones cannot respond. Due to this sensitivity, rods function mainly in night vision. They also produce only black and white images. This explains why, though we usually can see everything in a dark room, little appears in color.

105. **(B)**   Implosive therapy is an effective technique in reducing the adversiveness of stimuli. Once the client understands the procedure, the therapist begins to describe scenes known to produce strong negative emotions. The idea is to emotionally "flood" the client by describing the stimuli vividly. The client is not permitted to avoid the imagined disturbing scene; he or she must withstand the repeated exposure if the therapist is to extinguish the associated emotional response. Therapy is concluded when the adversive images no longer produce negative emotional responses in the client.

106. **(D)**   A high heritability index, .70, would mean that 70% of the variance in scores is due to genetic factors. Heritability is a statistical concept that reflects the percentage of variability in a trait associated with differences in the genetic composition of the individuals in a given group.

107. **(A)**   The opponent-process theory stated that there are only three kinds of color receptors in the eye. Each color receptor was thought to represent a pair of colors — red-green, yellow-blue, and black-white. These receptors were thought to respond to these colors in an "opponent" fashion. This means that they would be excited in response to one of the colors, and inhibited in response to the other color.

108. **(B)**   Psychodrama was introduced by a Viennese psychiatrist named J. L. Moreno. The assumption of psychodrama is that different kinds of role playing promote the expression of true feelings and thoughts that are troubling to the person. To facilitate the therapeutic role playing, attempts are made to produce a theatrical atmosphere. A real stage is used and an audience is frequently present.

109. **(D)**   Freud reasoned that the dream is a hallucinatory state that structures events, not as they would be in reality, but as the dreamer wishes them to be. When unconscious desires conflict with conscious restraints, however, it is necessary for the "dream work" to pursue devious paths to express the wish.

110. **(E)**   A normal distribution has a number of defining characteristics. It is represented by a bell shaped curve, it has one mode, and the mean, mode, and median are equal. This curve is the graphic representation of the normal probability distribution.

111. **(E)**   In 1904 Alfred Binet was asked by the French government to construct a test that would distinguish between normal children and children with severe learning disabilities. Binet conceived of intelligence as the relationship of mental ability and chronological age. For each age up to 15 years, there is a set

of characteristic abilities that develop in the normal child. If they developed earlier than average, the child is more intelligent than average; if the abilities develop later, then the child is considered to be of below average intelligence.

112. **(B)**   The mean is the value obtained by adding all the measurements and dividing by the numbers of measurements

$$\text{mean} \ (\overline{x}) = \frac{500+600+800+800+900+900+900+900+900+1000+1100}{11}$$

$$\overline{x} = \frac{9300}{11} = 845.45$$

The median is the observation in the middle. We have 11, so here it is the sixth, 900. The mode is the observation that appears most frequently. That is also 900, which has 5 appearances. All three of these numbers are measures of central tendency.

113. **(C)**   The Law of Effect states that responses which are followed by pleasurable events or satisfaction, are more likely to occur again as behavioral responses. Responses that are followed by displeasure, will be less likely to occur again. In general, the principle proposes that positive reinforcement–reward–facilitates learning, and negative reinforcement–punishment–inhibits learning.

114. **(A)**   Watson made his break with the structuralists and functionalists because he was against their preoccupation with the contents and operations of the mind. He felt that while consciousness probably does exist, we can only study *observable* behavior. His preference was to focus on environmental manipulations as they related to the adaptation of organisms. In most of his research on learning, he employed the experimental-manipulative strategy.

115. **(C)**   In Bem's research, people were determined androgynous if they described themselves primarily with adjectives that were neither masculine nor feminine, but were neutral. Based on her research, androgynous people tend to have high self-esteem and were more adaptable. They were found to function well in situations which call for typically masculine, independent behavior, as well as those that require more tender, helpful feminine behavior.

116. **(B)**   In his studies on the nature of obedience, Stanley Milgram discovered that the average middle-class American male would, under direction of a legitimate authority figure, administer severe shocks to other individuals in an experimental setting. This alarming finding, demonstrated the extent to which ordinary people would comply with the orders of a legitimate authority figure, even to the point of harming his fellow man.

117. **(A)**   Herzberg postulated that there are two groups of factors that have a significant impact on worker satisfaction. These are what he calls "maintenance

or hygiene" factors and "motivator" factors. The hygiene/maintenance factors are concerned mainly with the work environment, including company policy, administration, supervision, employee relations, salary, status, and security. The motivational factors are concerned mainly with the job itself. They include achievement, recognition, the quality of work, responsibility, and growth or advancement. Together, these two general factors determine job satisfaction.

118. **(A)**   In his study, Baumrind (1967) found a relationship between type of discipline and child's personality. Children in a preschool were categorized into three personality groups. The children who were friendly, self-controlled, and self-reliant were found to have parents who were demanding, controlling and loving. Children who were withdrawn and unhappy, were found to have de-manding but unaffectionate parents. The children who lacked self-control and self-reliance, had parents who were both permissive and affectionate.

119. **(D)**   The linking-pin concept is based on the idea that management will make full use of its potential only when each individual is a functioning member of one or more work groups. The linking-pin concept requires that a person of top management also be accepted as a member of the middle management group. The key point is that these individuals be accepted as legitimate members of both groups. In this manner, communication and group effort are greatly improved.

120. **(B)**   The females raised in isolation made poor mothers. They did not display nurturant behavior toward their offspring. While some were abusive toward their offspring, none of the mothers actually killed them.

121. **(A)**   The latency stage lasts about five years, from ages six to eleven. During this period the child's identification with the parent of his own sex becomes stronger. The child also incorporates more of the beliefs and values of his culture, hence, the superego is developing to a greater degree. The child comes to distinguish between acceptable and unacceptable behavior in his society. During this period children generally seek out more playmates of their own sex.

122. **(E)**   The Oedipus Complex is to the Electra Complex as boy is to girl. In the Oedipal Complex, the boy wants his mother for himself and wants to be rid of the competing father, but he fears castration from the father. In order to deal with that fear, he represses it and identifies with his father. In the Electra Complex, the girl desires the father and wants to be rid of the mother, but with time, her devaluation of her mother and her jealousy fade, as she develops the female behaviors of appealing to the father and desiring a baby as a substitute for the penis she is lacking.

123. **(C)**   Cognitive dissonance was first proposed by Leon Festinger, and is an important concept within the field of social psychology. Cognitive dissonance

is an uncomfortable psychological state due to an inconsistency between beliefs and behavior. For example, a person publicly states that he will vote for candidate X due to pressures to agree with friends, but secretly he believes that candidate Y is the better politician. This situation would cause dissonance and the person would seek some outlet such as attitude change to restore cognitive balance.

124. **(C)**   When a person dreams, his memory of what actually happened is the manifest content of the dream. According to Freud, it is the function of the psychoanalyst to interpret and unravel the manifest content and reveal the more fundamental latent content from which the dream was derived.

125. **(A)**   Differences in stimuli intensity are encoded by the number of action potentials occurring in a given amount of time. For example, if a dull red box and a bright red box were sitting on a table, viewing the brighter box would cause more signals per unit time to be sent to the brain, than would viewing the dull box.

126. **(D)**   Phobic reactions are strong, irrational fears of specific objects or situations. For example, when a person is extremely fearful of birds, snakes, heights or closed places, provided that there is no objective danger, the label phobia is applied to the person's fear and avoidance. A person suffering from phobic neurosis knows what he is afraid of and usually recognizes that his fear is irrational but cannot control it.

127. **(C)**   Systematic desensitization is a behavioral procedure whereby the therapist reinforces a behavior which is in opposition to the behavior the patient wants to eliminate. The behavior reinforced is usually a relaxation response. In this problem, the patient would be asked to relax and continue relaxing as she imagined fearful situations with pigeons. Eventually, the previously anxiety-arousing stimulus is associated with relaxation and the behavior (fear of pigeons) ceases to be maladaptive.

128. **(D)**   In terms of this example, falling off one's bicycle (UCS), reliably elicits fear and anxiety (UCR). The single pairing of the sight of a dead pigeon (CS), with the act of falling (UCS), created a conditioned response (CR) of fear and anxiety elicited upon seeing pigeons in future situations. The UCS of falling off the bicycle, was no longer needed to be present to create the CR of fear and anxiety. Although this theory sounds like a good explanation for the occurrence of phobias, in many cases phobics have never had any early traumatic experiences with the phobic object.

129. **(D)**   While all the choices list personality theorists, C. Jung proposed the "persona" as a basic personality element. He believed that an individual's persona is one aspect of the collective psyche — it comes into existence to mitigate an individual's realization of being part of the collective mass of humanity.

130. **(C)**   The Wechsler Intelligence Scale for Children (WISC) would be the most appropriate choice for the majority of 12-year-olds. The WISC is normally administered to children from the ages of $6^1/_2 - 16^1/_2$. There are subscales which measure mathematical ability, vocabulary, problem solving and digit span problems.

131. **(D)**   The double-blind technique is most often used in drug research. This method assures that neither the experimenter nor the subject can affect the results, thus biases are reduced.

132. **(B)**   Considerable stress tolerance is not characteristic of neurotic depression. Neurotically depressed people generally have a considerable intolerance to stressful situations. A rigid conscience, feelings of guilt, hopelessness, and manipulative use of symptoms for sympathy, are all characteristics of neurotic depression.

133. **(A)**   The cerebellum is made up of a central part and two hemispheres extending sideways. The size of the cerebellum in different animals is roughly correlated with the amount of muscular activity. The cerebellum coordinates muscle contraction. Injury to the cerebellum results in the inability to coordinate muscle movements, although the muscles can still move.

134. **(B)**   The medulla is connected to the spinal cord and is the most posterior part of the brain. Here the central canal of the spinal cord (spinal lumen) enlarges to form a fluid-filled cavity called the fourth ventricle. The medulla also has numerous nerve tracts which bring impulses to and from the brain.

135. **(E)**   The pons is an area of the hindbrain containing a large number of nerve fibers which pass through it and make connections between the two hemispheres of the cerebellum, thus coordinating muscle movements on the two sides of the body. The pons also contains the nerve centers that aid in the regulation of breathing.

136. **(E)**   The thalamus, a part of the forebrain located just above the midbrain, functions mainly as a major relay station of the brain. Information from sensory receptors which travels through the spinal cord, or information coming from the forebrain and midbrain usually arrives at the thalamus and is then relayed to the appropriate areas in the cortex.

137. **(D)**   Granule cells are in the cerebellum, not in the retina. The retina is composed of three cell layers — a transparent layer of ganglion cells, transparent bipolar cells, and rod and cone receptor cells. The ends of the bipolar cells are interconnected through amacrine cells. The receptor cell layer is located on the side of the retina away from the light. Light must travel through the rest of the retina before reaching the light-sensitive rods and cones.

138. **(B)**   Yerkes and Dodson, studied the relationship between arousal levels and performance on various tasks. The diagram depicts the Yerkes-Dodson Law, which states that performance is a curvilinear function of arousal or motivation, showing first an increase and then a decrease in performance as arousal is increased.

139. **(C)**   After the optimum level (the apex of the inverted U-) is reached, as arousal becomes greater, anxiety and emotional disturbance increases, and performance declines. This is the negative arousal side of the Yerkes-Dodson effect.

140. **(C)**   There are three stages in the general adaptation syndrome. The first stage is the alarm reaction, which is the initial reaction to stress. This reaction consists of bodily reactions including increased heart rate and blood pressure. The second stage is the stage of resistance. Here the body recovers from the initial stress and attempts to endure. The third stage is exhaustion and the body is no longer able to tolerate any further stress.

141. **(D)**   Operant conditioning is a learning process in which the frequency of a specific response is shaped and maintained by the consequences of the response. For the specific demonstration of such a process, Skinner developed an apparatus designed to give a signal (to respond) and a method for delivering the reinforcement. This device is nicknamed the "Skinner box."

142. **(D)**   Freud viewed humans as passive organisms whose psychological development is initiated and maintained through "intrapsychic" events, that is, internal events. The dynamic component includes the expression of the basic instincts. The sequential component includes the five psychosexual stages: oral, anal, phallic, latency and genital. The structural component includes the concept of the id, ego and superego. Although abstract and absent of the study of observational behavior, Freud's theory is a major force in developmental psychology.

143. **(A)**   This study, done by Bandura and Rosenthal demonstrated the effects of vicarious conditioning, which is observing a model. In this study, the subjects learned that the buzzer was aversive by watching someone else (model) being "shocked," as the buzzer rang. The subjects learned the aversion to the buzzer so well that they responded physiologically to the buzzer sound.

144. **(D)**   The GSR (galvanic skin response) is a well documented method of measuring physiological responses to arousal. In this study the GSR would measure the subjects' physiological arousal to the aversive sound of the buzzer, achieved through vicarious conditioning. The inferred state of physiological arousal is fear in response to buzzer sound.

145. **(B)**   The modeling theory of phobic disorders assumes that phobic responses may be learned through the imitation of others. The learning of phobic reactions through modeling is generally referred to as vicarious conditioning.

Vicarious conditioning can take place through both observation and verbal instruction. In this study, the phobic reaction conditioned was fear in response to a
buzzer, and the conditioning took place through observation.

146. **(D)**   Morphemes are the smallest units of meaning in a language. All of
the question choices were morphemes except "n," which is a phoneme. Phonemes combine to form morphemes. In English, morphemes can be whole words
such as "girl" or prefixes and suffixes like "re-" and "-ing." There are more than
100,000 morphemes in the English language.

147. **(D)**   The point of view expressed in the paragraph is best termed scientific empiricism. The focus is on making theory, subject to the laws of scientific
method. The theories of abnormal functioning must be subject to verifiable scientific methods of experimentation, such as disconfirmability.

148. **(C)**   Reliability is an important aspect of the scientific-empirical method.
If only one experiment is performed, conclusions cannot securely be drawn from
the data. Experimental results must be repeated numerous times to verify the
reliability of results and the ensuing conclusions.

149. **(D)**   The point of view expressed in the paragraph stresses that theoretical accounts of abnormal behavior must be subject to scientific methodology.
This was the main idea presented in choice (D)

150. **(E)**   The Nodes of Ranvier are identified as the points at which the
myelin sheath covers the axon ends. Note the indentations in the myelin sheath.
The Nodes of Ranvier are important in the propagation of action potentials along
the axon. Impulses are propagated (or transmitted) from one Node of Ranvier to
another, thus proceeding much more rapidly than if the entire length of the axon
had to depolarize progressively.

151. **(D)**   Synaptic boutons, also called axonic terminals, are the end tips of
the axon. They almost make contact with the dendrites of another neuron. The
neurotransmitters produced in the boutons travel across the synaptic cleft to
interact with the membrane of the receiving cell, changing the membrane permeability.

152. **(A)**   Dendrites are numerous in the neuron. They receive information,
either from other neurons or directly from the environment, and then divert the
electrical impulses (information) toward the cell body of the neuron. Action
potentials are not generated along the dendrites.

153. **(E)**   In the backward masking procedure, a letter (an icon) is flashed on a
screen. After the letter is flashed, there is a brief period of about five seconds
during which the impression can be completely erased by the flash of a bright

light coding interference. This backward masking effect demonstrates the brief life of memory codes, that they can be easily erased by subsequent input that is specific to the given sense modality.

154. **(A)**   Codes in the memory system that store motor activity are called "enactive codes." Because most studies on problem solving have focused on visual and verbal codes, very little is known about how enactive codes affect thinking.

155. **(C)**   Long-term memory is complex and possesses a virtually limitless capacity. It is therefore difficult for theorists to study. Long-term memory can be slow and difficult. Past events that relate to a current situation have to be searched for out of billions of stored items. It usually requires effort to put new information into long-term memory. Material that is in long-term memory can be brought into active memory and will not be lost if it is interrupted.

156. **(B)**   The paragraph describes the manic phase of this two-sided disorder. The manic attack is an extreme and exuberant upswing in mood and activity. The manic person is hyperactive and agitated. His speech and flow of ideas are accelerated. The depressive attack is characterized by the opposite tendencies.

157. **(E)**   Accelerated speech and thought, and an agitated, hyperactive behavioral state are the most salient combination of symptoms for a diagnosis of bipolar disorder. Delusions of grandeur are symptomatic of manic-depressive psychosis, as well as other psychotic states. This choice would therefore not be helpful in differentiating the disorder for diagnostic purposes.

158. **(B)**   Lithium is the drug most often used to control manic symptoms. Present studies are trying to determine whether continued use of the drug could prevent the onset of further attacks. Results indicate that lithium medication is effective in prevention of both manic and depressive episodes.

159. **(C)**   Anderson was known for his work on impression formation. He resolved the controversy between averaging versus adding models of impression formation by creating a weighted averaging model. In his model, traits are averaged but more value is given to polarized traits.

160. **(C)**   Sheldon related behavioral dispositions to physical characteristics to form a body-type theory of personality. His system involved three body types: endomorphic, mesomorphic, and ectomorphic. Sheldon's theory does not currently receive much support and is no longer very influential.

161. **(C)**   Kohler was a gestalt psychologist who primarily studied the behavior of problem solving in chimpanzees. Kohler argued that learning and problem solving are largely a function of organizational processes. He stated that problem

solving involves a sudden "moment of insight" when the solution is figured out.

162. **(E)**   Franz Alexander is best known for his work on psychosomatic illness. He is called the father of psychosomatic medicine. He proposed that specific psychosomatic illnesses are associated with specific conflicts, e.g., asthma is caused by excessive, unresolved dependence on the mother.

163. **(B)**   Wertheimer is known as the father of gestalt psychology. Gestalt psychology was a reaction against structuralism that began in Germany at the turn of the century. This school emphasized organizational processes in behavior. Kohler, Koffka, and Wertheimer were its main proponents.

164. **(E)**   Seligman is best known for his research on depression using the learned helplessness model. If a person comes to believe that he has no personal control over events in life — especially aversive events — he may give up and become depressed due to learned helplessness.

165. **(A)**   Both electrical and chemical changes occur — the change from a resting state to an action potential. In the neuron, the action potential is caused first by a change from a negative to a positive charge inside the cell. A chemical change occurs when the change in the electrical charge causes the permeability of the cell membrane to change, allowing sodium ions to rush in.

166. **(B)**   Nerves of the parasympathetic system secrete a neurotransmitter called acetylcholine. Acetycholine is the transmitter chemical for synapses between neurons of the peripheral nervous system outside the autonomic system.

167. **(A)**   The leg muscles are innervated by the somatic nervous system. The other choices are innervated by the autonomic nervous system. The somatic nervous system includes the sensory nerves that bring all sensory information into the central nervous system, plus the motor nerves that control the activity of the skeletal muscles. The autonomic system directs the activity of smooth and cardiac muscles and of glands.

Figure 1

168. **(C)** "Visual Cliff" experiments, first conducted by Gibson and Walk, indicate that depth perception is probably innate. The experiment involves placing the infant on a large sheet of glass, under half of which checked linoleum has been placed. (See Figure 1 in previous page) At the edge where the linoleum stops, it appears that a cliff occurs. The infants systematically avoid the apparent cliff. While this does not prove that the ability is innate, it does indicate that depth perception is not a purely learned experience.

169. **(E)** The Müller-Lyer patterns are a classic example of an illusion. The two lines are of the same length, though B appears to be shorter than A. One attempt to explain this illusion is that the converging lines in line B, suggest the depth cue of linear perspective, which makes that line appear to be nearer to the viewer than line A. This explains the illusion as being due to the unconscious action of a depth cue.

170. **(E)** Cognitive dissonance was first proposed by Festinger. This theory states that there is a tendency towards cognitive consistency. When two or more cognitions exist that are inconsistent with one another, a state of dissonance exists. Since this tendency for consonance (consistency) exists, the individual will strive to remove the dissonance through an attitudinal or behavioral change.

171. **(B)** This group is in a state of cognitive dissonance. Therefore, its members' attitudes should change to maintain cognitive consistency. One cognition, "I think the task is boring," is in direct conflict with the other cognition, "I think the task is exciting." Even though the task in fact was boring and tedious, the dissonance created was dissolved by a subsequent attitude change that may be expressed thusly: the task is not as boring as people think.

172. **(A)** This condition is a case of overjustification. In the highly paid group, the subject believes s/he has a good reason for performing a discrepant act. Therefore, very little dissonance is aroused.

173. **(D)** In severe cases of epilepsy, the corpus callosum is cut, thus isolating the two cerebral hemispheres from each other. The corpus callosum consists of two bundles of axons through which neurons in each hemisphere communicate.

174. **(A)** The left hemisphere of the cerebral cortex is connected to sensory receptors in the right half of the body, and the right hemisphere is connected to receptors in the left half of the body. Thus, in this experiment, when the subject feels the object with his left hand, the information travels to the right hemisphere, but cannot get to the left hemisphere, since the corpus callosum is severed. The fact that he performs better with the left hand, shows that it must be the right hemisphere that is specialized for complex visual and spatial tasks.

175. **(B)**   In humans the corpus callosum is immature at birth. Due to the low maturation of the corpus callosum, the behavior of young children can be similar to that of split-brain adults in some instances. From this study, it is seen that the corpus callosum matures between the ages of three and five.

176. **(B)**   All intelligence tests, and psychological tests in general, measure the performance or behavior of the subject. From the measure of performance, we infer the knowledge and ability, as well as predict future performance, of the subject. It is important to consider that factors such as motivation, can affect the performance on tests by either enhancing it or deterring it.

177. **(A)**   Factor analysis is a complex statistical procedure which is used to identify a small number of underlying mental factors or psychological traits. Its purpose is to simplify the description of behavior by reducing the number of categories used in the description. Usually, the investigator administers a large number of tests to many individuals and then sets up a table of correlations in which he could show the extent to which each test correlates with every other test. The correlation coefficient is a measure of how well one test score (factor) predicts another score.

178. **(E)**   The WAIS is an intellectual test for adults. The other choices are all projective tests that attempt to identify unconscious desires, conflicts, and impulses. The subject "projects" into the stimulus material his needs and attitudes. In all these tests (TAT, DAP, Rorschach, and Rosenweig P-F), it is assumed that when a person's mind is free to wander, it will "fix" on those issues that are important.

179. **(A)**   Allport claimed that in order to understand an individual, it is necessary to know what his conscious intentions are; he stressed ego functioning, also called the proprium, as being the most influential in behavior. Allport focuses on the current thoughts and goals of the individual. He regarded the past as insignificant in the assessment of an individual's behavior.

180. **(C)**   Second-order conditioning is based on secondary reinforcement. In second-order conditioning, a neutral stimulus is paired with the conditioned stimulus, after that conditioned stimulus can reliably elicit the conditioned response. When this is accomplished, the new or second-conditioned stimulus will elicit the conditioned response even though it was never paired directly with the unconditioned stimulus.

181. **(A)**   The James-Lange theory, proposed that we first experience a specific, psychological state in reaction to some stimulus and then perceive an emotion on this state. For example, we see a huge bear running towards us, we run

and then we feel afraid, because we see that we are running. Cannon and Bard compiled evidence that showed that there are not specific, physiological patterns for different emotions. They proposed that we see the bear, we experience fear, and then we run. They thought it was stimulus stimulation of the hypothalamus that created the emotion.

182. **(C)**   Imprinting is one of the most striking of all behavior phenomena. A typical experiment exposes young chicks to a moving object as soon as they are born. No other object, including the mother, is presented. Later, most animals will follow this object and emit "distress" calls in its absence and "contentment" calls in its presence.

183. **(D)**   Milgram argues that those living in big cities are often subjected to an overwhelming influx of stimulation and information. People in turn, develop strategies to protect themselves against this. Some of his findings are (1) the more dense the environment, the less children interact; (2) violations of privacy lead to withdrawal; (3) adults in crowded situations look at each other's faces less and like others less.

184. **(E)**   Both of these terms are used in ethology, the study of instinctive behavior, to describe species-specific fixed-action pattern behavior. The crucial aspects of an innate fixed-action pattern are (1) it is innate, (2) it is always the same response, (3) all of the members of a species (categorized by sex, situation, etc.) have it, and (4) it is a species-specific pattern. Vacuum activity, a concept developed by Lorenz, describes the eliciting of a fixed pattern response in the absence of a releasing stimulus due to the buildup of action-specific energies.

185. **(B)**   Otherwise known as the hammer, anvil, and stirrup, these three bones (ossicles) of the middle ear are responsible for transmitting the vibrations of the eardrum to the inner ear, where they are transformed into nerve signals. These nerve signals are sent to the brain and are interpreted as sound.

186. **(B)**   The first function, evaluation of food, is obvious. The second function, communication, is an especially important use for smell in animals. Smell is used for territorial marking and sexual attraction. Chemicals produced for the purpose of communication are called pheromones. Many times an animal can smell these pheromones several miles away. The study of the perception of smell is still crude and a satisfactory model of this process is nonexistent.

187. **(C)**   Rehearsal means going over something again and again in one's memory. Wagner argued that perhaps only surprising or unexpected UCS's promote rehearsal. There is a limit, on how many things an organism can rehearse at one time and therefore, a limit, on how much an animal can learn in a given

situation. This theory was used to explain the results of Leon Kamin's blocking experiment.

188. **(B)**   In the procedure called forward classical conditioning, the CS is presented and within five seconds of its onset, the UCS is presented. Of all the various experimental time relations possible between the CS and UCS, the simultaneous conditioning procedure, within which the CS is presented for less than 0.5 seconds before the USC is presented, leads to the quickest production of the CR.

189. **(C)**   The classical Pavlovian experiments employ a simultaneous or nearly simultaneous presentation of the CS with the UCS. In Trace classical conditioning, the CS is presented and then withdrawn. After a brief delay, the UCS is presented. The CR typically occurs during the delay between CS offset and UCS onset.

190. **(A)**   The temporal classical conditioning procedure provides no explicit CS. The UCS is presented at regular intervals, for example, every five minutes, exactly. After a few trials, the CR occurs just before the five minutes are up. Theoretically, time serves as the CS, hence the name, temporal classical conditioning. Figures 4 and 5 represent versions of backward classical conditioning where the UCS is presented before the CS. No CR develops because the CS signals the end of, or non-occurrence of the UCS.

191. **(C)**   A significant correlation whether positive or negative, describes the relationship between two variables in such a way that change in one is associated with change in the other. A positive correlation indicates that the two variables change in the same direction. A negative correlation indicates that the two variables change in opposite directions.

192. **(B)**   A histogram is a graphic representation of a frequency distribution in which the cases falling in each score category are represented by a bar whose size is proportional to the number of cases. Since each bar is the full width of the score category, the bars make a continuous "pile" showing the form of the frequency distribution.

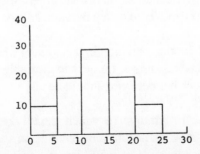

193. **(B)** Whether or not different diagnosticians will agree that a given diagnostic label should be applied to a particular patient, is the test of reliability. For a classification system to work, those applying it must be able to agree on what is and what is not an instance of a particular class of behaviors.

194. **(B)** Whenever a class is formed, the behavior of all its members should be similar along the dimensions distinguishing the classification. There should be behavioral homogeneity. A lack of homogeneity is a problem because people diagnosed under one category may display significantly different types of behaviors. Many studies have found that knowing what diagnostic category a patient falls into tells relatively little about the behavior of the patient. The problem is that the previous diagnostic system did not adequately specify how many of the various symptoms must be present or the degree to which they must manifest to make a diagnosis.

195. **(D)** A major criticism of the DSM-III-R was its lack of validity. Whether or not predictions can be made about a class of behaviors once formed, is the test of validity. Validity has a specific relationship to reliability: the less reliable a category is, the more difficult it is to make valid statements about the category. Since the DSM-III-R lacked reliability, it also had inadequate validity.

196. **(D)** Diagnosticians may disagree for a variety of reasons. As indicated in the paragraph, unclear criteria in the diagnostic system is a problem. Another issue to consider is what the patient tells one doctor, but not another. The interviewer's style can also result in differing information, which gets translated into differential diagnoses.

197. **(A)** Many times people do things in a group that they would not normally do alone. This is because they become deindividuated to some extent, because they lose a sense of personal responsibility and identity. Deindividuation is sometimes referred to as responsibility diffusion.

198. **(E)** Identity is the key concept. An experiment would vary the extent to which a person is identifiable. Many experiments have been conducted in which the subjects put on identical clothing and were not called by name. These groups produced far more deindividuation than control groups in which the subjects wore their normal clothes and were called by name.

199. **(C)** As stated in the paragraph, the greater the deindividuation of a group, the greater the effect. Hence, the less identifiable a member is, the more free and uninhibited his or her behavior should be.

200. **(C)** The action of groups, in which deindividuation exists, has been shown to be either positive or negative depending on the circumstances. Many groups perform great deeds, such as rebuilding a house destroyed by fire, that a

single individual would not necessarily do alone. Unfortunately, much of the time the consequences are negative, as in the case of lynchings and racial strife.

201. **(B)** Nest building, mating rituals, and similar behavior that is instinctive and performed by all members of a particular species is referred to as species-specific behavior. Answer (C) is the definition of ethology.

202. **(D)** Karl von Frisch demonstrated that bees dance around in particular muscular movements in order to communicate the location and distance of food to other members of the hive.

203. **(E)** Niko Tinbergen studied the mating rituals of the three-spined stickleback fish. Lorenz studied animal aggression, while von Frisch worked with bees.

204. **(A)** Males with Klinefelter's syndrome have an extra X chromosome so their genetic makeup is XXY instead of XY as in a normal male. Females possess an XX genetic pair. XO refers to Turner's syndrome.

205. **(C)** The twenty third chromosome pair of the normal female has two X chromosomes (XX). Victims of Turner's syndrome have only one X so their genetic code is XO. XXY refers to Kleinfelter's syndrome. YO doesn't exist.

206. **(E)** Smoking cigarettes has been linked with all four problems listed. Cigarette companies place a warning label on their products cautioning pregnant women about these risks.

207. **(A)** The Apgar Scoring System, developed by Virginia Apgar in 1953, is administered to newborns twice: one minute after birth and, again, four minutes later. Low scores on this test signal potential congenital problems.

208. **(C)** In classic Freudian theory, all behavior is motivated by subconscious sexual and aggressive drives. Therefore all behavior is obviously sexual, aggressive, or a substitute for them. Humor is considered camouflaged aggression because we can lash out at people under the guise of just telling a joke. We are serious about the criticisms that we are supposedly just kidding about.

209. **(D)** In behaviorism, the environment shapes our behavior through the use of rewards and punishments. We also learn by observing other people who serve as models for us. Choices (A) and (B) represent the Freudian approach, while choice (C) comes from the Humanistic approach.

210. **(B)** Since 1973, the American Psychiatric Association has considered homosexuality to be an alternate lifestyle (ego-syntonic homosexuality) and not symptomatic of mental illness unless the person is unhappy with his or her sexual orientation. In the latter case, where stress, anxiety, or depression is

caused by sexual orientation, the diagnosis is ego-dystonic homosexuality, and worthy of treatment.

211. **(C)** Contrary to the depictions on television and in the movies, the average rapist is a married, white male. Rape is not motivated by sexual needs. Sexual partners are available at home, in bars, or can be paid. The rapist is motivated by an aggressive desire to dominate and intimidate his victim, not out of a sense of sexual need.

212. **(D)** Phonemes are the 40 or so speech sounds all humans are capable of making. Regardless of nationality or race, all humans are members of the same species. The differences in languages is the result of using phonemes in different combinations.

213. **(E)** Several reports have questioned the original claims made concerning the ability of apes and chimps to acquire and use symbolic language. All four of the criticisms listed have been made.

214. **(C)** Broca's area, located in the left frontal lobe of the brain, coordinates speech. Damage to this area produces expressive aphasia, i.e., difficulty in making statements. Paul Broca discovered the function of this part of the brain in 1861.

215. **(B)** Flashbulb memories refer to vivid recollections in memory because of their association with significant events in our lives. For most of us, our early childhood memories are scanty except for exceptional events such as birthday parties. Eidetic memory is photographic memory.

216. **(C)** Mnemonics are techniques used to improve memory. They typically teach us to associate new material with familiar memories so our retrieval of the new material will be better.

217. **(D)** Studies have shown that recollections of events described while under hypnosis aren't reliable. Although the subject is convinced that he or she is telling the truth, their description of an event is often a mixture of fantasy and the truth. Consequently, hypnotic testimony is not admissible in a court of law, and is not considered proof of reincarnation because the subject talks about "former lives."

The Graduate Record Examination in

PSYCHOLOGY

Test 3

THE GRADUATE RECORD EXAMINATION
PSYCHOLOGY TEST 3
ANSWER SHEET

1. Ⓐ Ⓑ Ⓒ Ⓓ Ⓔ
2. Ⓐ Ⓑ Ⓒ Ⓓ Ⓔ
3. Ⓐ Ⓑ Ⓒ Ⓓ Ⓔ
4. Ⓐ Ⓑ Ⓒ Ⓓ Ⓔ
5. Ⓐ Ⓑ Ⓒ Ⓓ Ⓔ
6. Ⓐ Ⓑ Ⓒ Ⓓ Ⓔ
7. Ⓐ Ⓑ Ⓒ Ⓓ Ⓔ
8. Ⓐ Ⓑ Ⓒ Ⓓ Ⓔ
9. Ⓐ Ⓑ Ⓒ Ⓓ Ⓔ
10. Ⓐ Ⓑ Ⓒ Ⓓ Ⓔ
11. Ⓐ Ⓑ Ⓒ Ⓓ Ⓔ
12. Ⓐ Ⓑ Ⓒ Ⓓ Ⓔ
13. Ⓐ Ⓑ Ⓒ Ⓓ Ⓔ
14. Ⓐ Ⓑ Ⓒ Ⓓ Ⓔ
15. Ⓐ Ⓑ Ⓒ Ⓓ Ⓔ
16. Ⓐ Ⓑ Ⓒ Ⓓ Ⓔ
17. Ⓐ Ⓑ Ⓒ Ⓓ Ⓔ
18. Ⓐ Ⓑ Ⓒ Ⓓ Ⓔ
19. Ⓐ Ⓑ Ⓒ Ⓓ Ⓔ
20. Ⓐ Ⓑ Ⓒ Ⓓ Ⓔ
21. Ⓐ Ⓑ Ⓒ Ⓓ Ⓔ
22. Ⓐ Ⓑ Ⓒ Ⓓ Ⓔ
23. Ⓐ Ⓑ Ⓒ Ⓓ Ⓔ
24. Ⓐ Ⓑ Ⓒ Ⓓ Ⓔ
25. Ⓐ Ⓑ Ⓒ Ⓓ Ⓔ
26. Ⓐ Ⓑ Ⓒ Ⓓ Ⓔ
27. Ⓐ Ⓑ Ⓒ Ⓓ Ⓔ
28. Ⓐ Ⓑ Ⓒ Ⓓ Ⓔ
29. Ⓐ Ⓑ Ⓒ Ⓓ Ⓔ
30. Ⓐ Ⓑ Ⓒ Ⓓ Ⓔ
31. Ⓐ Ⓑ Ⓒ Ⓓ Ⓔ
32. Ⓐ Ⓑ Ⓒ Ⓓ Ⓔ
33. Ⓐ Ⓑ Ⓒ Ⓓ Ⓔ

34. Ⓐ Ⓑ Ⓒ Ⓓ Ⓔ
35. Ⓐ Ⓑ Ⓒ Ⓓ Ⓔ
36. Ⓐ Ⓑ Ⓒ Ⓓ Ⓔ
37. Ⓐ Ⓑ Ⓒ Ⓓ Ⓔ
38. Ⓐ Ⓑ Ⓒ Ⓓ Ⓔ
39. Ⓐ Ⓑ Ⓒ Ⓓ Ⓔ
40. Ⓐ Ⓑ Ⓒ Ⓓ Ⓔ
41. Ⓐ Ⓑ Ⓒ Ⓓ Ⓔ
42. Ⓐ Ⓑ Ⓒ Ⓓ Ⓔ
43. Ⓐ Ⓑ Ⓒ Ⓓ Ⓔ
44. Ⓐ Ⓑ Ⓒ Ⓓ Ⓔ
45. Ⓐ Ⓑ Ⓒ Ⓓ Ⓔ
46. Ⓐ Ⓑ Ⓒ Ⓓ Ⓔ
47. Ⓐ Ⓑ Ⓒ Ⓓ Ⓔ
48. Ⓐ Ⓑ Ⓒ Ⓓ Ⓔ
49. Ⓐ Ⓑ Ⓒ Ⓓ Ⓔ
50. Ⓐ Ⓑ Ⓒ Ⓓ Ⓔ
51. Ⓐ Ⓑ Ⓒ Ⓓ Ⓔ
52. Ⓐ Ⓑ Ⓒ Ⓓ Ⓔ
53. Ⓐ Ⓑ Ⓒ Ⓓ Ⓔ
54. Ⓐ Ⓑ Ⓒ Ⓓ Ⓔ
55. Ⓐ Ⓑ Ⓒ Ⓓ Ⓔ
56. Ⓐ Ⓑ Ⓒ Ⓓ Ⓔ
57. Ⓐ Ⓑ Ⓒ Ⓓ Ⓔ
58. Ⓐ Ⓑ Ⓒ Ⓓ Ⓔ
59. Ⓐ Ⓑ Ⓒ Ⓓ Ⓔ
60. Ⓐ Ⓑ Ⓒ Ⓓ Ⓔ
61. Ⓐ Ⓑ Ⓒ Ⓓ Ⓔ
62. Ⓐ Ⓑ Ⓒ Ⓓ Ⓔ
63. Ⓐ Ⓑ Ⓒ Ⓓ Ⓔ
64. Ⓐ Ⓑ Ⓒ Ⓓ Ⓔ
65. Ⓐ Ⓑ Ⓒ Ⓓ Ⓔ
66. Ⓐ Ⓑ Ⓒ Ⓓ Ⓔ

67. Ⓐ Ⓑ Ⓒ Ⓓ Ⓔ
68. Ⓐ Ⓑ Ⓒ Ⓓ Ⓔ
69. Ⓐ Ⓑ Ⓒ Ⓓ Ⓔ
70. Ⓐ Ⓑ Ⓒ Ⓓ Ⓔ
71. Ⓐ Ⓑ Ⓒ Ⓓ Ⓔ
72. Ⓐ Ⓑ Ⓒ Ⓓ Ⓔ
73. Ⓐ Ⓑ Ⓒ Ⓓ Ⓔ
74. Ⓐ Ⓑ Ⓒ Ⓓ Ⓔ
75. Ⓐ Ⓑ Ⓒ Ⓓ Ⓔ
76. Ⓐ Ⓑ Ⓒ Ⓓ Ⓔ
77. Ⓐ Ⓑ Ⓒ Ⓓ Ⓔ
78. Ⓐ Ⓑ Ⓒ Ⓓ Ⓔ
79. Ⓐ Ⓑ Ⓒ Ⓓ Ⓔ
80. Ⓐ Ⓑ Ⓒ Ⓓ Ⓔ
81. Ⓐ Ⓑ Ⓒ Ⓓ Ⓔ
82. Ⓐ Ⓑ Ⓒ Ⓓ Ⓔ
83. Ⓐ Ⓑ Ⓒ Ⓓ Ⓔ
84. Ⓐ Ⓑ Ⓒ Ⓓ Ⓔ
85. Ⓐ Ⓑ Ⓒ Ⓓ Ⓔ
86. Ⓐ Ⓑ Ⓒ Ⓓ Ⓔ
87. Ⓐ Ⓑ Ⓒ Ⓓ Ⓔ
88. Ⓐ Ⓑ Ⓒ Ⓓ Ⓔ
89. Ⓐ Ⓑ Ⓒ Ⓓ Ⓔ
90. Ⓐ Ⓑ Ⓒ Ⓓ Ⓔ
91. Ⓐ Ⓑ Ⓒ Ⓓ Ⓔ
92. Ⓐ Ⓑ Ⓒ Ⓓ Ⓔ
93. Ⓐ Ⓑ Ⓒ Ⓓ Ⓔ
94. Ⓐ Ⓑ Ⓒ Ⓓ Ⓔ
95. Ⓐ Ⓑ Ⓒ Ⓓ Ⓔ
96. Ⓐ Ⓑ Ⓒ Ⓓ Ⓔ
97. Ⓐ Ⓑ Ⓒ Ⓓ Ⓔ
98. Ⓐ Ⓑ Ⓒ Ⓓ Ⓔ
99. Ⓐ Ⓑ Ⓒ Ⓓ Ⓔ

100. Ⓐ Ⓑ Ⓒ Ⓓ Ⓔ
101. Ⓐ Ⓑ Ⓒ Ⓓ Ⓔ
102. Ⓐ Ⓑ Ⓒ Ⓓ Ⓔ
103. Ⓐ Ⓑ Ⓒ Ⓓ Ⓔ
104. Ⓐ Ⓑ Ⓒ Ⓓ Ⓔ
105. Ⓐ Ⓑ Ⓒ Ⓓ Ⓔ
106. Ⓐ Ⓑ Ⓒ Ⓓ Ⓔ
107. Ⓐ Ⓑ Ⓒ Ⓓ Ⓔ
108. Ⓐ Ⓑ Ⓒ Ⓓ Ⓔ
109. Ⓐ Ⓑ Ⓒ Ⓓ Ⓔ
110. Ⓐ Ⓑ Ⓒ Ⓓ Ⓔ
111. Ⓐ Ⓑ Ⓒ Ⓓ Ⓔ
112. Ⓐ Ⓑ Ⓒ Ⓓ Ⓔ
113. Ⓐ Ⓑ Ⓒ Ⓓ Ⓔ
114. Ⓐ Ⓑ Ⓒ Ⓓ Ⓔ
115. Ⓐ Ⓑ Ⓒ Ⓓ Ⓔ
116. Ⓐ Ⓑ Ⓒ Ⓓ Ⓔ
117. Ⓐ Ⓑ Ⓒ Ⓓ Ⓔ
118. Ⓐ Ⓑ Ⓒ Ⓓ Ⓔ
119. Ⓐ Ⓑ Ⓒ Ⓓ Ⓔ
120. Ⓐ Ⓑ Ⓒ Ⓓ Ⓔ
121. Ⓐ Ⓑ Ⓒ Ⓓ Ⓔ
122. Ⓐ Ⓑ Ⓒ Ⓓ Ⓔ
123. Ⓐ Ⓑ Ⓒ Ⓓ Ⓔ
124. Ⓐ Ⓑ Ⓒ Ⓓ Ⓔ
125. Ⓐ Ⓑ Ⓒ Ⓓ Ⓔ
126. Ⓐ Ⓑ Ⓒ Ⓓ Ⓔ
127. Ⓐ Ⓑ Ⓒ Ⓓ Ⓔ
128. Ⓐ Ⓑ Ⓒ Ⓓ Ⓔ
129. Ⓐ Ⓑ Ⓒ Ⓓ Ⓔ
130. Ⓐ Ⓑ Ⓒ Ⓓ Ⓔ
131. Ⓐ Ⓑ Ⓒ Ⓓ Ⓔ
132. Ⓐ Ⓑ Ⓒ Ⓓ Ⓔ
133. Ⓐ Ⓑ Ⓒ Ⓓ Ⓔ
134. Ⓐ Ⓑ Ⓒ Ⓓ Ⓔ
135. Ⓐ Ⓑ Ⓒ Ⓓ Ⓔ
136. Ⓐ Ⓑ Ⓒ Ⓓ Ⓔ
137. Ⓐ Ⓑ Ⓒ Ⓓ Ⓔ
138. Ⓐ Ⓑ Ⓒ Ⓓ Ⓔ
139. Ⓐ Ⓑ Ⓒ Ⓓ Ⓔ

140. Ⓐ Ⓑ Ⓒ Ⓓ Ⓔ
141. Ⓐ Ⓑ Ⓒ Ⓓ Ⓔ
142. Ⓐ Ⓑ Ⓒ Ⓓ Ⓔ
143. Ⓐ Ⓑ Ⓒ Ⓓ Ⓔ
144. Ⓐ Ⓑ Ⓒ Ⓓ Ⓔ
145. Ⓐ Ⓑ Ⓒ Ⓓ Ⓔ
146. Ⓐ Ⓑ Ⓒ Ⓓ Ⓔ
147. Ⓐ Ⓑ Ⓒ Ⓓ Ⓔ
148. Ⓐ Ⓑ Ⓒ Ⓓ Ⓔ
149. Ⓐ Ⓑ Ⓒ Ⓓ Ⓔ
150. Ⓐ Ⓑ Ⓒ Ⓓ Ⓔ
151. Ⓐ Ⓑ Ⓒ Ⓓ Ⓔ
152. Ⓐ Ⓑ Ⓒ Ⓓ Ⓔ
153. Ⓐ Ⓑ Ⓒ Ⓓ Ⓔ
154. Ⓐ Ⓑ Ⓒ Ⓓ Ⓔ
155. Ⓐ Ⓑ Ⓒ Ⓓ Ⓔ
156. Ⓐ Ⓑ Ⓒ Ⓓ Ⓔ
157. Ⓐ Ⓑ Ⓒ Ⓓ Ⓔ
158. Ⓐ Ⓑ Ⓒ Ⓓ Ⓔ
159. Ⓐ Ⓑ Ⓒ Ⓓ Ⓔ
160. Ⓐ Ⓑ Ⓒ Ⓓ Ⓔ
161. Ⓐ Ⓑ Ⓒ Ⓓ Ⓔ
162. Ⓐ Ⓑ Ⓒ Ⓓ Ⓔ
163. Ⓐ Ⓑ Ⓒ Ⓓ Ⓔ
164. Ⓐ Ⓑ Ⓒ Ⓓ Ⓔ
165. Ⓐ Ⓑ Ⓒ Ⓓ Ⓔ
166. Ⓐ Ⓑ Ⓒ Ⓓ Ⓔ
167. Ⓐ Ⓑ Ⓒ Ⓓ Ⓔ
168. Ⓐ Ⓑ Ⓒ Ⓓ Ⓔ
169. Ⓐ Ⓑ Ⓒ Ⓓ Ⓔ
170. Ⓐ Ⓑ Ⓒ Ⓓ Ⓔ
171. Ⓐ Ⓑ Ⓒ Ⓓ Ⓔ
172. Ⓐ Ⓑ Ⓒ Ⓓ Ⓔ
173. Ⓐ Ⓑ Ⓒ Ⓓ Ⓔ
174. Ⓐ Ⓑ Ⓒ Ⓓ Ⓔ
175. Ⓐ Ⓑ Ⓒ Ⓓ Ⓔ
176. Ⓐ Ⓑ Ⓒ Ⓓ Ⓔ
177. Ⓐ Ⓑ Ⓒ Ⓓ Ⓔ
178. Ⓐ Ⓑ Ⓒ Ⓓ Ⓔ
179. Ⓐ Ⓑ Ⓒ Ⓓ Ⓔ

180. Ⓐ Ⓑ Ⓒ Ⓓ Ⓔ
181. Ⓐ Ⓑ Ⓒ Ⓓ Ⓔ
182. Ⓐ Ⓑ Ⓒ Ⓓ Ⓔ
183. Ⓐ Ⓑ Ⓒ Ⓓ Ⓔ
184. Ⓐ Ⓑ Ⓒ Ⓓ Ⓔ
185. Ⓐ Ⓑ Ⓒ Ⓓ Ⓔ
186. Ⓐ Ⓑ Ⓒ Ⓓ Ⓔ
187. Ⓐ Ⓑ Ⓒ Ⓓ Ⓔ
188. Ⓐ Ⓑ Ⓒ Ⓓ Ⓔ
189. Ⓐ Ⓑ Ⓒ Ⓓ Ⓔ
190. Ⓐ Ⓑ Ⓒ Ⓓ Ⓔ
191. Ⓐ Ⓑ Ⓒ Ⓓ Ⓔ
192. Ⓐ Ⓑ Ⓒ Ⓓ Ⓔ
193. Ⓐ Ⓑ Ⓒ Ⓓ Ⓔ
194. Ⓐ Ⓑ Ⓒ Ⓓ Ⓔ
195. Ⓐ Ⓑ Ⓒ Ⓓ Ⓔ
196. Ⓐ Ⓑ Ⓒ Ⓓ Ⓔ
197. Ⓐ Ⓑ Ⓒ Ⓓ Ⓔ
198. Ⓐ Ⓑ Ⓒ Ⓓ Ⓔ
199. Ⓐ Ⓑ Ⓒ Ⓓ Ⓔ
200. Ⓐ Ⓑ Ⓒ Ⓓ Ⓔ
201. Ⓐ Ⓑ Ⓒ Ⓓ Ⓔ
202. Ⓐ Ⓑ Ⓒ Ⓓ Ⓔ
203. Ⓐ Ⓑ Ⓒ Ⓓ Ⓔ
204. Ⓐ Ⓑ Ⓒ Ⓓ Ⓔ
205. Ⓐ Ⓑ Ⓒ Ⓓ Ⓔ
206. Ⓐ Ⓑ Ⓒ Ⓓ Ⓔ
207. Ⓐ Ⓑ Ⓒ Ⓓ Ⓔ
208. Ⓐ Ⓑ Ⓒ Ⓓ Ⓔ
209. Ⓐ Ⓑ Ⓒ Ⓓ Ⓔ
210. Ⓐ Ⓑ Ⓒ Ⓓ Ⓔ
211. Ⓐ Ⓑ Ⓒ Ⓓ Ⓔ
212. Ⓐ Ⓑ Ⓒ Ⓓ Ⓔ
213. Ⓐ Ⓑ Ⓒ Ⓓ Ⓔ
214. Ⓐ Ⓑ Ⓒ Ⓓ Ⓔ
215. Ⓐ Ⓑ Ⓒ Ⓓ Ⓔ
216. Ⓐ Ⓑ Ⓒ Ⓓ Ⓔ
217. Ⓐ Ⓑ Ⓒ Ⓓ Ⓔ

GRE

PSYCHOLOGY TEST 3

TIME: 170 Minutes
217 Questions

DIRECTIONS: Choose the best answer for each question and mark the letter of your selection on the corresponding answer sheet.

---

1. The manifest content of dreams refers to the

    (A) symbolic content.

    (B) actual meaning of the dream.

    (C) literal content as experienced by the dreamer.

    (D) psychoanalytic interpretations of content.

    (E) sexual content.

2. A knee jerk is an example of a

    (A) disynaptic reflex.　　(B) spastic movement.

    (C) monosynaptic reflex.　　(D) parasympathetic reflex.

    (E) double innervation.

3. The thalamus serves which of the following functions?

    (A) relay center for sensory impulses

    (B) relay center from spinal cord to cerebrum

    (C) regulates external expression of emotion

    (D) all of the above

    (E) none of the above

4. Which of the following effects does adrenalin have on the human body?

    (A) constriction of the pupils　　(B) increased rate of digestion

    (C) accelerated heart beat　　(D) increased hormone production

    (E) decreased hormone production

5. Which of the following plays an important role in the regulation of respiration?

    (A) pons   (B) hypothalamus

    (C) thalamus   (D) forebrain

    (E) midbrain

6. Which of the following constitutes monocular depth cues?

    (A) relative size   (B) linear perspective

    (C) interposition   (D) all of the above

    (E) none of the above

7. Laws of perceptual organization were formulated by the _____ school of psychology.

    (A) behaviorist   (B) structuralist

    (C) nativist   (D) psychoanalytic

    (E) gestalt

8. Once two wavelengths of light combine, which of the following occurs?

    (A) You see two colors.   (B) You see a deeper hue.

    (C) You see a new color.   (D) You see a purer saturation.

    (E) both (B) and (D)

9. Intellectualization is a defense mechanism that is also known as

    (A) reaction formation.   (B) rationalization.

    (C) compensation.   (D) projection.

    (E) rejection.

10. Responses on the Rorschach Inkblot Test are evaluated in terms of

    (A) locations.   (B) determinants.

    (C) content.   (D) all of the above

    (E) none of the above

11. The first stage of ego development is considered to be

    (A) id, ego, superego conflicts.

    (B) primary identification with the mother.

(C)   autonomous ego functions.

(D)   ego introjects.

(E)   ego boundary settings.

12.   Distributions with extreme values at one end are said to be

(A)   positively skewed.   (B)   negatively skewed.

(C)   skewed.   (D)   histograms.

(E)   measures of noncentral tendency.

13.   All secondary sources of drive are

(A)   homeostatic.   (B)   physiogenic.

(C)   goal-seeking.   (D)   self-propelling.

(E)   learned.

14.   Which of the following developmental psychologists most strongly favors
       a stage theory of development?

(A)   Maccoby   (B)   Gelman

(C)   Piaget   (D)   Spock

(E)   Spitz

15.   According to Edward Tolman, Expectation × Value =

(A)   Performance.   (B)   Achievement.

(C)   Need for Achievement.   (D)   Goal.

(E)   Activation — Arousal.

16.   The frustration-aggression hypothesis was proposed by

(A)   Festinger.   (B)   Hull.

(C)   Doob, Dollard, and Miller. (D)   Tolman.

(E)   McClelland.

17.   Eidetic memory is most often found in

(A)   adults.   (B)   children.

(C)   psychotic adults.   (D)   mentally-retarded children.

(E)   depressed adults.

18. A grown man's fear of dogs developed after having been bitten by the neighbor's dog when he was a child. This is an example of

    (A) forward conditioning.   (B) stimulus generalization.

    (C) backward conditioning.   (D) UCS.

    (E) negative reinforcement.

19. Any behavior that can be engaged in without much concentration and effort is called

    (A) autonomic behavior.   (B) learned behavior.

    (C) overlearned behavior.   (D) automatic behavior.

    (E) conscious process.

20. Which of these is NOT characteristic of narcissistic personality disorder?

    (A) a grandiose sense of self-importance

    (B) a lack of empathy

    (C) fantasies of unlimited power

    (D) a strong need for admiration from others

    (E) shallow and rapidly changing expressions of emotions

21. According to Adler's theory of personality, the Oedipus Complex involves

    (A) strivings to escape the father.

    (B) strivings to become superior to the father.

    (C) strivings to become superior to the mother.

    (D) mainly a sexual phenomenon.

    (E) an expression of latent sexuality.

22. The "conscience" is the part of the superego that

    (A) mediates with the id.   (B) punishes.

    (C) gratifies.   (D) controls the ego.

    (E) contains the sexual urges.

23. Which of the following represents a measure and method of analyzing perceptual thresholds?

    (A) Method of Limits   (B) Method of Average Error

(C)   frequency method   (D)   all of the above

(E)   none of the above

24.   According to the anxiety theory of neurosis, depression is

(A)   not an anxiety neurosis.

(B)   directing displaced anxiety back at oneself.

(C)   a result of denying anxiety.

(D)   due to an extended anxiety state.

(E)   none of the above

25.   Anima, according to Jung, is

(A)   a male's unconscious feminine characteristics.

(B)   the developmental phase of mid-life.

(C)   the dark side of the personal unconscious.

(D)   a female's unconscious male characteristics.

(E)   the developmental phase of late life.

26.   In the technique of shaping behavior, which of the following is used?

(A)   differential reinforcement   (B)   positive reinforcement

(C)   neutral acknowledgment   (D)   negative reinforcement

(E)   punishment procedures

27.   Which researcher developed the Culture Fair Intelligence Test?

(A)   Spearman   (B)   Raven

(C)   Cattell   (D)   Wechsler

(E)   Rorschach

28.   In learning motor skills, the most efficient method of spaced practice varies which of the following features?

(A)   length of practice period

(B)   length of rest period

(C)   type of practice technique

(D)   both (A) and (B)

(E)   both (B) and (C)

29. Freud developed the concept of Eros, which is the

(A) death instinct.

(B) life instinct.

(C) third developmental stage.

(D) sex instinct.   (E) regressive potential.

30. Structuralism, the first theoretical school in psychology, evolved primarily from the work of

(A) Wundt.   (B) Kohler.

(C) Watson.   (D) Tolman.

(E) Wertheimer.

31. Our perceptual processes have an ability to maintain a stable internal representation of objects even when the environment is constantly changing. For which of the following stimulus dimensions does this statement hold true?

(A) shape   (B) size

(C) brightness   (D) both (A) and (B)

(E) all of the above

32. The Milgram experiments on social power figures indicate that

(A) the use of reward and punishment increases compliance.

(B) pressure from an authority figure in the situation increases compliance.

(C) social pressure increases compliance.

(D) justification increases compliance.

(E) lack of justification increases compliance.

33. Propinquity or the degree of physical closeness is the strongest determining factor in

(A) interpersonal attractiveness. (B) friendship.

(C) social interdependence.   (D) all of the above

(E) none of the above

34. A research design which contains features of both between-subjects and within-subjects designs is

(A) factorial design.   (B) omnibus design.

(C) mixed factorial design.   (D) bidirectional statistical design.

(E) multiple design.

35. Any procedural variable which can cause a subset of the population to be nonrepresentative of the population is a

(A) sample error.   (B) sample bias.

(C) population error.   (D) sample shift.

(E) population bias.

36. The number of independent pieces of information remaining following an estimation of population parameters is the

(A) degrees of freedom (df).   (B) error term.

(C) critical value (Fα).   (D) data reduction.

(E) Scheffe critical value (Fs).

37. Psychologists and educators have come to realize that creativity and intelligence

(A) are synonymous.   (B) are not synonymous.

(C) are negatively correlated.   (D) appear as bimodal functions.

(E) are both measured by I.Q. tests.

38. All of the following are examples of popularly administered crosscultural tests EXCEPT the

(A) Leiter International Performance Scale.

(B) Culture Fair Test.

(C) Progressive Matrices.

(D) Goodenough Draw-A-Man Test.

(E) all of the above

39. In Karen Horney's psychoanalytic theory, the fundamental concept is

(A) basic anxiety.   (B) need to love.

(C) self actualization.   (D) need to be loved.

(E) libidinal instincts.

40. According to Piaget, a child capable of hypothetical thinking is in which developmental stage?

    (A) sensorimotor stage   (B) preoperational stage

    (C) intuitive preoperational stage

    (D) concrete operations stage

    (E) formal operations stage

41. Anna Freud continued her father's work by making contributions to our understanding of

    (A) ego-defense mechanisms.   (B) eros and thanatos.

    (C) the id.   (D) the phallic stage.

    (E) anal-retentive personality.

42. During an interview a person may focus on the interviewer's remarks and reactions. However, at some future occasion he may be able to remember the visual details of the room in which the interview took place. This ability refers to

    (A) multiple encoding.   (B) parallel storage.

    (C) visual memory.   (D) none of the above

    (E) all of the above

43. According to the Central Limit Theorem, which of the following is true?

    (A) A frequency distribution may have two modes.

    (B) A different chi-square distribution exists for each number of df.

    (C) A statistical analysis involving comparison of variance is incomplete.

    (D) Sampling distribution of the mean approaches the normal distribution in shape as sample size increases.

    (E) There must be a standard deviation of -1.0 or $+1.0$.

44. According to Piaget's theory of cognitive development, middle childhood is characterized by

    (A) hypothetical reasoning.   (B) deductive thinking.

    (C) concrete operations.   (D) egocentric thinking.

    (E) INRC binary grouping.

45. The California Psychological Inventory differs from the Minnesota Multiphasic Personality Inventory in that it is used

   (A) on more clinically deviant groups.

   (B) with children.

   (C) with adolescents.

   (D) on less clinically deviant groups.

   (E) none of the above

46. Of the following, which is NOT true of self-report personality measures?

   (A) Subjects rate simple behavioral statements as true or false.

   (B) The test measures usually have extensive norms.

   (C) Subjects are given little freedom in responding.

   (D) Most of the measures provide accurate behavioral prediction.

   (E) The Q-sort is a common technique.

47. Given a sample of data that is homogeneous, you can expect the standard deviation to be

   (A) large.

   (B) small.

   (C) above 0.05.

   (D) small if the sample size is small.

   (E) large if the sample size is large.

48. The Rorschach and TAT tests are types of _____ tests.

   (A) aptitude   (B) projective

   (C) sociogram   (D) developmental

   (E) objective

49. Word association tests and sentence completion tests are examples of

   (A) verbal techniques.   (B) objective tests.

   (C) subjective tests.   (D) projective techniques.

   (E) verbal projective tests.

50. Ninety-eight percent of the people who take a standardized intelligence test have scores which fall between

    (A) 85 – 115.   (B) 55 – 145.

    (C) 70 – 130.   (D) 100 – 150.

    (E) none of the above

51. A child who wins a game and gains peer approval is receiving

    (A) primary reinforcement.   (B) secondary reinforcement.

    (C) social reinforcement.   (D) both (A) and (B)

    (E) both (B) and (C)

52. Another name for the successive method of approximation is

    (A) reinforcement.   (B) shaping.

    (C) fixed reinforcement.   (D) chaining.

    (E) operant conditioning.

53. Hermann Ebbinghaus is best known for his historical work in

    (A) neuroanatomy.

    (B) sensory processes.

    (C) visual perception of patterns.

    (D) learning and memory performance.

    (E) visical attention processes.

54. Perceptual constancies are primarily thought to be a function of

    (A) reflex.   (B) convergence.

    (C) instinct.   (D) divergence.

    (E) learning.

55. Which of the following is NOT a Gestalt Law of Organization?

    (A) area   (B) closedness

    (C) proximity   (D) continuation

    (E) all of the above are Laws of Organization

56. Dollard, Doob, Miller, Mowrer and Sears have suggested that all aggressive acts are caused by

(A) confusion.

(B) poor social learning.

(C) frustration.

(D) stress.

(E) pain.

57. An I.Q. range of 20-35 would indicate what degree of retardation?

(A) mild

(B) moderate

(C) severe

(D) profound

(E) none of the above

58. In the equation $\dfrac{MA}{CA} \times 100 = I.Q.$, MA assesses

(A) an absolute level of cognitive capacity.

(B) the amount of information known.

(C) the level of maturity attainment.

(D) all of the above

(E) none of the above

59. Identify the diagnostic category which is NOT appropriately grouped with the others.

(A) obsessive-compulsive disorder

(B) phobic reaction

(C) affective bipolar disorder

(D) conversion disorder

(E) anxiety reaction

60. The disorder in which the musculature or sensory functions are impaired, although the bodily organs are themselves normal, is called

(A) a hysteric reaction.

(B) a conversion reaction.

(C) psychosomatic disorder.

(D) stress-induced fatigue.

(E) dissociative disorder.

61. Guilford's model of intelligence is

(A) specifically geared toward the learning disabled.

(B) a two-factor theory.

(C) a multiple-factor theory.

(D) not based on unique, individual differences.

(E) based on group testing measures.

62. The Rotter Incomplete Sentence Blank is a (an)

    (A) objective testing technique.

    (B) intelligence test.

    (C) internality /externality assessment scale.

    (D) projective test.   (E) literary competence exam.

63. According to psychoanalytic thinking, the personality structure consists of

    (A) habits.   (B) drives.

    (C) self.   (D) id, ego, and superego.

    (E) consciousness.

64. The sympathetic and parasympathetic nervous systems constitute the

    (A) autonomic nervous system.

    (B) central nervous system.

    (C) peripheral nervous system.

    (D) somatic nervous system.

    (E) antagonistic nervous system.

65. The "white matter" of the central nervous system is actually

    (A) nerve fiber pathways.   (B) cell bodies.

    (C) cell centers.   (D) cortical tissue.

    (E) cerebral tissue.

66. Which of the following is present in the synaptic vesicles?

    (A) action potential   (B) neurotransmitters

    (C) Na^+ (D) synaptic inhibitors

    (E) K^+

67. Which of the following has direct control over the function of the pituitary gland?

    (A) pons   (B) cerebral cortex

    (C) hypothalamus   (D) midbrain

    (E) cerebellum

68. Which stimulus cue(s) is(are) NOT involved in depth perception?

     (A) light and shadow   (B) color intensity

     (C) relative position   (D) linear perspective

     (E) texture-density gradient

69. Emmert's Law refers to the

     (A) constancy of an elliptical figure.

     (B) interpretation of sensory data.

     (C) Muller-Lyer pattern illusions.

     (D) effect of context on size perception.

     (E) apparent size of a projected afterimage.

70. The wavelength of green is

     (A) greater than yellow but less than blue.

     (B) greater than either yellow or blue.

     (C) the same wavelength as yellow.

     (D) greater than blue but less than yellow.

     (E) greater than red.

71. Physical sounds from our environment are translated into electrical messages in the

     (A) spiral geniculate.   (B) trapezoid body.

     (C) cochlea.   (D) spiral ganglion.

     (E) eustachian tube.

72. In a factor analysis, separateness of factors is assessed by

     (A) degree of correlation.   (B) task analysis.

     (C) similarity of distribution. (D) both (A) and (B)

     (E) both (B) and (C)

73. The proportion of total variation in a population that is due to genetic variation is

     (A) phenotype.   (B) genotype.

     (C) heritability.   (D) absolute heritability.

     (E) relative heritability.

74. Which of the following best describes the alternative hypothesis?

    (A) The hypothesis that there is no effect.

    (B) The hypothesis that there is only one effect.

    (C) The hypothesis that there are two effects.

    (D) The null hypothesis is false.

    (E) none of the above

75. According to Fromm, a truly healthy person manifests a (an)

    (A) receptive orientation.   (B) exploitative orientation.

    (C) productive orientation.   (D) marketing orientation.

    (E) hoarding orientation.

76. A teratogen refers to a (an)

    (A) stage of embryonic development.

    (B) birth defect involving CNS activity.

    (C) environmental agent which produces birth defects.

    (D) part of the deep brain.

    (E) part of the RAS in the brain stem.

77. According to Clark Hull, Drive × Habit =

    (A) Performance.   (B) Achievement.

    (C) Need for Achievement.   (D) Goal.

    (E) Activation-Arousal.

78. Freud pointed out that an important influence upon behavior is

    (A) unconscious dissonance.   (B) level of aspiration.

    (C) cognitive dissonance.   (D) unconscious motivation.

    (E) none of the above

79. Echoic memory refers to

    (A) visual perception.   (B) eidetic perception.

    (C) verbal codes.   (D) auditory perception.

    (E) enactive codes.

80. Which of the following reinforcement schedules has the lowest yield of performance?

    (A) fixed-ratio schedule   (B) variable-ratio schedule

    (C) fixed-interval schedule   (D) variable-interval schedule

    (E) systematic-interval schedule

81. During stage 4 sleep, which brain wave pattern predominates?

    (A) beta waves   (B) sleep spindles

    (C) alpha waves   (D) irregular wave patterns

    (E) delta waves

82. The chromosomal abnormality in which there is a trisomy of chromosome 21 is the cause of

    (A) borderline brain dysfunction.

    (B) epilepsy.

    (C) Down's Syndrome.

    (D) Korsakoff's syndrome.

    (E) both (A) and (B)

83. Which of the following "needs" did Carl Rogers place special emphasis on?

    (A) need for social support   (B) need for positive regard

    (C) need for self-regard   (D) both (A) and (B)

    (E) both (B) and (C)

84. An unathletic man becomes a career sportswriter. This situation is an example of what defense mechanism?

    (A) compensation   (B) sublimation

    (C) displacement   (D) identification

    (E) projection

85. Which part of the eye inverts the image of objects?

    (A) fovea   (B) cornea

    (C) lens   (D) retina

    (E) blind spot

86. According to the DSM-IV, multiple personality is a _____ disorder.

    (A) neurotic   (B) psychotic

    (C) personality   (D) dissociative

    (E) conduct

87. According to Erikson's developmental theory, the maturity stage deals with which of the following crises?

    (A) initiative vs. guilt   (B) identity crisis

    (C) autonomy vs. doubt   (D) intimacy vs. isolation

    (E) integrity vs. despair

88. Autonomic conditioning refers to

    (A) operant conditioning of voluntary muscles.

    (B) operant conditioning of responses like heart rate or intestinal contractions.

    (C) classical conditioning of voluntary muscles.

    (D) classical conditioning of responses like heart rate or intestinal contractions.

    (E) a nonexistent procedure.

89. What is the main disadvantage of cross-cultural tests?

    (A) reliability problems

    (B) They compare people of different cultures.

    (C) Predictive and diagnostic value is lost.

    (D) none of the above

    (E) all of the above

90. Which of the following is true of Short-Term Memory (STM)?

    (A) It has a storage capacity of ten items.

    (B) It does not require rehearsals.

    (C) STM is highly susceptible to interference.

    (D) Information always travels from STM to Long-Term Memory.

    (E) It is a permanent record of experience.

91. According to Freud, the main function of dreams is

    (A)   release of the ego.   (B)   sexual instinct release.

    (C)   unconscious urges.   (D)   to balance psychic forces.

    (E)   wish fulfillment.

92. In psychology, measurement devices must be

    (A)   reliable.   (B)   valid.

    (C)   conclusive.   (D)   both (A) and (B)

    (E)   both (B) and (C)

93. Prominent among monocular depth cues is

    (A)   accommodation.   (B)   texture-density gradient.

    (C)   retinal disparity.   (D)   retinal polarity.

    (E)   mono-polarity.

94. Deindividuation refers to

    (A)   antisocial acts.

    (B)   disinhibition.

    (C)   anonymity in a group situation.

    (D)   aggression.   (E)   group aggression.

95. Cognitive dissonance theory was proposed by

    (A)   Solomon Asch.   (B)   Kurt Lewin.

    (C)   Jerome Bruner.   (D)   Leon Festinger.

    (E)   Stanley Milgram.

96. The probability of committing a type I error is defined as

    (A)   beta (β).   (B)   mu (μ).

    (C) χ^2 (chi).   (D) $\hat{\omega}^2 A$ (omega).

    (E)   alpha (α).

97. Which of the following describes attributes of color?

    (A)   hue   (B)   brightness

    (C)   saturation   (D)   both (A) and (B)

    (E)   all of the above

98. A Z distribution refers to

    (A) a measure of variability; an average of the sum of the squares deviations from the mean.

    (B) coefficients used in calculating the sum of squares for single-df comparisons.

    (C) the normal distribution expressed in terms of deviations from the mean divided by the standard deviation.

    (D) a theoretical distribution used in conjunction with the t-test and in the establishment of a confidence interval.

    (E) a distribution always used in conjunction with the chi-square test of correlation.

99. Which of the following variables should be taken into account when a psychological test is to be administered?

    (A) tester's rapport with subjects

    (B) the subject's amount of anxiety

    (C) the subject's understanding of test directions

    (D) (A) and (C) only

    (E) all of the above

100. The "Kent-Rosanoff" Test is a (an)

    (A) projective test.

    (B) factor analysis test.

    (C) word association test.

    (D) intelligence test.

    (E) language aptitude test for babies.

101. According to Erich Fromm, man has needs that arise from conditions of his lonely existence. Which of the following did Fromm identify as a human need?

    (A) the need for a sense of individual identity

    (B) the need for belonging to a society

    (C) the need to relate satisfactorily to his fellow beings

    (D) all of the above

    (E) none of the above

102. According to Kohlberg's theory of moral development, the morality of self-accepted principles is characterized by

    (A) a focus on good and bad behavior.

    (B) premoral behavior.

    (C) an understanding of individual rights, ideals, and principles.

    (D) important peer and social relations.

    (E) none of the above

103. The Palmar reflex, present in neonates, refers to which behavior?

    (A) sucking   (B) startle response

    (C) head turning   (D) hand grasping

    (E) swallowing

104. With reference to short-term memory, rehearsal

    (A) assists in the transfer of information from short-term to long-term memory.

    (B) allows material to remain in short-term memory indefinitely.

    (C) is not primarily an acoustic phenomenon.

    (D) both (A) and (B)

    (E) both (B) and (C)

105. The mean of the squared differences from the mean of the distribution is a definition of the

    (A) Z-score.   (B) mode.

    (C) median.   (D) standard deviation.

    (E) variance.

106. Which of the following choices correctly traces the initial stages of prenatal development?

    (A) blastomeres, blastula, morula

    (B) zygote, gastrula, morula

    (C) blastomeres, zygote, morula

    (D) blastomeres, gastrula, blastula

    (E) zygote, blastomeres, morula

107. The Rosenzweig Picture Study is a psychological test based on the theory of

    (A) closure.   (B) aggression and frustration.

    (C) developmental temperance. (D) factor analysis.

    (E) personality change.

108. "The Measurement of Adult Intelligence" was written by

    (A) Binet.   (B) Wechsler.

    (C) Skinner.   (D) Guilford.

    (E) Terman.

109. A psychological theoretician in the process of developing a theory would be most interested in test measures in terms of their

    (A) construct validity.   (B) face validity.

    (C) predictive validity.   (D) concurrent validity.

    (E) theoretical validity.

110. To obtain norms for a testing measure, the test is first administered to a large group of the population on which this test will be used. This group is known as the

    (A) test group.   (B) control group.

    (C) standardization sample.   (D) construct sample.

    (E) criterion sample.

111. In the hierarchical theory of intelligence which of the following is placed at the top of the hierarchy?

    (A) "s" factors   (B) verbal-education

    (C) practical-mechanical   (D) Spearman's g-factor

    (E) general reasoning

112. Cattell considered crystallized intelligence to be a (an)

    (A) developmental process.

    (B) ability to deal with new problems.

    (C) function of brain damage.

    (D) inability to deal with new problems.

    (E) repertoire of information, cognitive skills, and strategies.

113. Which of the following behavior theorists proposed that behavior may be controlled by internal, symbolic processes?

    (A) Bandura   (B) Watson

    (C) Skinner   (D) Thorndike

    (E) Pavlov

114. Which of the following statements does not describe a feature of classical conditioning?

    (A) Behavior affected is usually experienced as involuntary.

    (B) Unconditioned and conditioned stimuli are presented to the organism.

    (C) In the absence of key stimuli the behavior does not occur.

    (D) Reinforcement and punishment are produced by the organism's behavior.

    (E) The unconditioned stimulus occurs without regard to the organism's behavior.

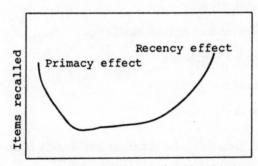

115. The above diagram depicts which of the following choices?

    (A) learning curve   (B) threshold effect

    (C) serial position curve   (D) memory curve

    (E) none of the above

116. Figure-ground organization is not a function of

    (A) the background against which a stimulus is perceived.

    (B) preference for white as figure.

    (C) size of different regions.

(D)   symmetry of stimulus.

(E)   interposition cues.

117. In perceptual research, the McCollough Effect refers to

(A)   the figure-ground relationship.

(B)   an illusion of size constancy.

(C)   an illusion of movement.

(D)   template matching.

(E)   the aftereffects of strong visual stimulation.

118. The most difficult conflicts to resolve are

(A)   approach-approach.   (B)   double approach-avoidance.

(C)   avoidance-avoidance.   (D)   double avoidance-approach.

(E)   approach-avoidance.

119. Phenylketonuria or PKU refers to a (an)

(A)   neurotransmitter.

(B)   severe form of mental retardation.

(C)   inner ear membrane.

(D)   rare form of psychosis.

(E)   none of the above

120. A test that measures what a person has already learned in prior training is an

(A)   aptitude test.   (B)   objective test.

(C)   experimental test.   (D)   intelligence test.

(E)   achievement test.

121. A person is completely unresponsive, stares blankly into space, and never moves. He or she is showing symptoms related to

(A)   paranoia.   (B)   hebephrenic schizophrenia.

(C)   catatonic schizophrenia.   (D)   dyssocial reaction.

(E)   mania.

122. Which of the following choices is NOT characteristic of infantile autism?

    (A) early onset   (B) extreme aloneness

    (C) language problems   (D) bizarre behavior

    (E) brain lesions

QUESTIONS 123–124 refer to the following paragraph.

   The Aplysia, an invertebrate related to a slug, has been the subject of many experiments on the psychology of learning. These animals have fewer neurons than vertebrates, making it easier for scientists to observe their biochemical mechanisms. These observations can then be applied to the study of vertebrate learning. In one experiment, a weak, repetitive stimulus presented at any point on the animal led to a decline of the withdrawal response at that point. It was also found that with the repetition of a sensitizing stimulus, there is a high level of AMP present in the sensory neuron, which leads to the production of a protein responsible for long-term sensitization.

123. The decrease in the withdrawal response after a stimulus is presented repeatedly is known as

    (A) sensitization.   (B) habituation.

    (C) classical conditioning.   (D) operant conditioning.

    (E) preparedness.

124. This paragraph implies that

    (A) the stronger the original stimulus, the greater the eventual habituation.

    (B) short-term sensitization can be prevented by blocking protein synthesis.

    (C) there is a connection between protein synthesis and long-term learning.

    (D) none of the above

    (E) all of the above

QUESTIONS 125–126 refer to the following paragraph.

   In a particular personality test a subject is given a group of self-referential statements and is asked to sort them into piles based on whether the statement is highly characteristic or very uncharacteristic of his personality. It is expected that the sorting will approximate a normal distribution — most of the statements will be considered fairly neutral in terms of the subject's personality.

125. This method of testing is known as a (an)

    (A) t-test.   (B) Q-technique.

    (C) MMPI.   (D) aptitude test.

    (E) projective test.

126. Self-reports have been criticized because

    (A) they have low reliability.

    (B) the subject can deceive the researcher.

    (C) they have low validity.

    (D) both (A) and (B)   (E) all of the above

QUESTIONS 127–128 refer to the following paragraph.

A researcher has tested a new drug for reducing anxiety on a sample of 100 people. After a treatment period of two weeks, 70 people reported feeling much less anxious and certain physiological tests showed them to be less anxious. The researcher now wants to claim that the drug is effective.

127. In order for this researcher's results to be valid he must have

    (A) chosen a random sample.

    (B) had a placebo group.

    (C) used the double-blind group.

    (D) both (A) and (B)   (E) all of the above

128. If the researcher rejects the null hypothesis that the drug is not effective, but in reality the null hypothesis is true, he has

    (A) increased the power of the test.

    (B) made a Type I error.   (C) made a Type II error.

    (D) increased α.   (E) none of the above

129. According to psychoanalytic theory, when an unpleasant or threatening thought or idea is not permitted into awareness, it is due to

    (A) repression.   (B) projection.

    (C) displacement.   (D) reaction formation.

    (E) compensation.

130. The "Oedipus Complex" occurs during which stage of psychosexual development?

   (A) oral   (B) genital

   (C) anal   (D) phallic

   (E) latency

131. Scales in which equal differences between scores can be treated as equal units are called

   (A) categorical scales.   (B) nominal scales.

   (C) ordinal scales.   (D) interval scales.

   (E) unitary scales.

132. In an experiment, the subject's response is best known as the

   (A) dependent variable.   (B) independent variable.

   (C) experimental variable.   (D) dependent response.

   (E) independent response.

133. The theoretical constructs of a phenotypic and genotypic basis of personality were developed by

   (A) Rogers.   (B) Jung.

   (C) Eysenck.   (D) Pearls.

   (E) Adler.

134. The Yerkes-Dodson Law is most closely related to which of the following personality theories?

   (A) Freud's psychosexual stages

   (B) Eysenck's phenotypic/genotypic personality

   (C) Jung's introversion and extroversion types

   (D) Roger's self-actualization stages

   (E) Erikson's stages of psychosocial development

135. During a child's development, if the amount of frustration and anxiety becomes too great concerning movement to the next stage, development may come to a halt. The individual is said to become

   (A) dependent.   (B) passive.

(C) fixated.

(D) regressive.

(E) repressed.

136. Allport proposed a number of essential requirements for a theory of human motivation. Which of the following choices is NOT a requirement ?

(A) The theory must acknowledge the contemporaneity of motives.

(B) The theory must account for the ego in motivational acts.

(C) The theory must be pluralistic, allowing for many types of motivation.

(D) The theory must invest cognitive processes with dynamic force.

(E) The theory must recognize that each individual can have a unique set of motives.

137. According to Sheldon's somatotype theory, a person who is strong, muscular, active, and aggressive is probably

(A) andomorphic.

(B) ectomorphic.

(C) daomorphic.

(D) endomorphic.

(E) mesomorphic.

138. Learning not to respond to stimuli in some form or another occurs in

(A) habituation.

(B) extinction.

(C) systematic desensitization.

(D) all of the above

(E) none of the above

QUESTIONS 139–141 refer to the following paragraph.

In a learning experiment subjects were presented with a list of words paired with cues. Some words were paired with strong cues and others with weak cues. After the presentation they were given a cued recall test in which some of the cues were the same as before, but others did not match the original cues. The results, of course, were best for those words presented with a strong cue and retrieved with the same strong cue. Recall was found to be superior for words rehearsed and retrieved with the same weak cue rather than those rehearsed with a weak cue and retrieved with a strong cue.

139. The results of this experiment demonstrate the principle of

(A)   paired-associate learning.   (B)   parallel processing.

(C)   encoding specificity.   (D)   reconstructive memory.

(E)   nonspecific transfer.

140. This principle implies that

(A)   items are stored in memory the way they are first perceived.

(B)   memory is context dependent.

(C)   the uniqueness of the link between retrieval cues and the information to be recalled is a major factor in recall ability.

(D)   both (A) and (B)

(E)   all of the above

141. A major proponent of the concept of a unique memory trace was

(A)   Ebbinghaus.   (B)   Treisman.

(C)   Watson.   (D)   Craik.

(E)   Bem.

QUESTIONS 142–144 refer to the following paragraph.

An early experiment by Kohler (1926), investigating the mentality of chimpanzees, involved placing a banana outside the cage beyond the ape's reach and giving him several short, hollow sticks which would have to be pushed together in order to reach the banana. The brightest ape in the experiment tried at first to get the banana with one stick, then he pushed the stick out as far as possible with a second stick without success. Eventually, he saw that the sticks could be connected to form a longer stick, thus perceiving a completely new relationship between the sticks.

142. The results of this experiment were interpreted in terms of

(A)   trial-and-error learning.   (B)   gestalt principles.

(C)   behaviorist principles.   (D)   organizational behavior.

(E)   high-order conditioning.

143. Kohler's viewpoint was most incompatible with the theories held by

(A)   Thorndike.   (B)   Watson.

(C)   Wertheimer.   (D)   Wendt.

(E)   Lewin.

144. According to Kohler, problem solving involves

    (A) restructuring the perceptual field.

    (B) insight.

    (C) a long process of trial-and-error.

    (D) both (A) and (B)   (E) all of the above.

145. In his personality theory, Gordon Allport stressed the importance of

    (A) conscious motivation.   (B) unconscious motivation.

    (C) ego control.   (D) self-esteem.

    (E) psychodynamics.

146. In Piaget's theory of child development, object permanence occurs at the end of the _____ stage.

    (A) sensorimotor   (B) preoperational

    (C) formal operational   (D) concrete operational

    (E) intuitive preoperational

147. According to Adler, the central core of personality functioning is a (an)

    (A) denial of neurotic needs.

    (B) compensatory behavior due to neurotic needs.

    (C) perceived sense of inferiority for which the person attempts to compensate.

    (D) actualizing self.

    (E) autonomous functioning ego.

148. Because the _____ seeks to gratify its desires without delay, it operates on the _____.

    (A) ego, pleasure principle   (B) id, pleasure principle

    (C) id, reality principle   (D) ego, reality principle

    (E) superego, punishment principle

149. According to Piaget, the child's basic developmental process includes

    (A) assimilation.   (B) schemas.

    (C) accommodation.   (D) both (A) and (B)

    (E) all of the above

150. In Allport's theory of motivation, functional autonomy is a principle that refers to

    (A) activities being able to sustain themselves without biological rein-forcement.

    (B) the uniqueness of human motivations.

    (C) a self-sustaining ego.

    (D) both (A) and (C)

    (E) none of the above

151. People with a strong androgyny score on Bem's Sex Role Inventory tend to

    (A) demonstrate low anxiety.

    (B) have low self-esteem and acceptance.

    (C) demonstrate high anxiety.

    (D) have high self-esteem and acceptance.

    (E) both (A) and (D)

152. The personality test that is used mainly as a diagnostic instrument to differ-entiate between normal people and those with psychiatric problems is the

    (A) CPI.   (B) TAT.

    (C) MMPI.   (D) Q-technique.

    (E) 16 Personality Factors Test.

QUESTIONS 153–155 refer to the following passage.

    Sensory feedback has been found to be vital in the control of movement. Walking produces many kinds of sensory feedback. It is possible to eliminate this feedback from arm and leg movements by means of surgery. One can cut all the sensory nerves for part of the body without harming the motor nerves because of their segregation. Sensory nerves enter the spinal cord in the dorsal root, and the motor nerves leave the spinal cord in the ventral root.

153. Cutting the sensory nerves in a limb of an animal to eliminate feedback is called

    (A) denervation.   (B) deactivation.

    (C) deafferentation.   (D) deefferentation.

    (E) decerebration.

154. If the sensory nerves of both forelegs of a monkey are cut, the animal will most probably

   (A) be paralyzed for life.

   (B) recover the use of the stronger limb.

   (C) have to be trained to walk again.

   (D) gradually recover the use of both limbs.

   (E) both (C) and (D)

155. In humans, the _____ control(s) slow gradual movements that are modified by sensory feedback.

   (A) cerebellum   (B) spinal cord

   (C) basal ganglia   (D) hippocampus

   (E) hypothalamus

QUESTIONS 156–157 refer to the following paragraph.

The epigenetic approach to the study of behavior development concentrates on the interaction of nature and nurture. The basis of this approach is that there is an ongoing interplay between behaviors that are genetically controlled and the environment. The result of this interplay is the observed behavior.

156. Another term for the observed behavior is

   (A) nature.   (B) phenotype.

   (C) genotype.   (D) nurture.

   (E) biological determinism.

157. Which of the following statements is FALSE?

   (A) Nurture determines the extent to which potentialities for behavior will be realized.

   (B) The genotype sets fixed genetic limits for behavior.

   (C) A deprived environment has a detrimental effect on intellectual development.

   (D) A child's I.Q. can be raised with an improvement in environment.

   (E) none of the above

158. A newly developed children's intelligence test is reported in the literature to be correlated +.25 with the Wechsler Intelligence Scale for Children —

Revised form (WISC-R). Which of the following statements provides the best assessment of the above information?

(A)   The new intelligence test has high criterion validity.

(B)   The new intelligence test is relatively content-independent of the WISC-R.

(C)   The new intelligence test has low concurrent validity.

(D)   The new intelligence test has high reliability.

(E)   The new intelligence test has low reliability.

159. All of the following are requirements of the response measure EXCEPT

(A)   observability.   (B)   numerical transformability.

(C)   economic feasibility.   (D)   stability, reliability.

(E)   adaptability for a wide variety of experiments.

160. Which is the most consistent measure of central tendency?

(A)   mean   (B)   mode

(C)   median   (D)   variance

(E)   standard distribution

161. Which of the following factors would NOT affect the reliability of a test?

(A)   test length   (B)   test-retest interval

(C)   guessing   (D)   content of questions

(E)   variation within a test situation

162. A Z-score is one type of standard score with a mean of _____ and a variance of _____ .

(A)   50, 10   (B)   0, 2

(C)   100, 50   (D)   0, 1

(E)   100, 10

163. Bandura's research on aggressive behavior mostly focused on aggression as

(A)   an innate, inherited trait.

(B)   a result of modeling.

(C)   an instinctual drive common to most everyone.

    (D)   unrelated to rewards and punishments

    (E)   both (B) and (D)

164. Which one of these psychologists thinks that aggression is an inborn tendency in all animals, including man?

    (A)   Freud   (B)   Lorenz

    (C)   Bandura   (D)   Ross

    (E)   both (A) and (B)

165. Social Comparison Theory was first introduced by

    (A)   Bandura.   (B)   Krauss.

    (C)   Schachter.   (D)   Festinger.

    (E)   Aronson.

166. The factor that has been found to be the most predictive of interpersonal attraction is

    (A)   similarity.   (B)   proximity.

    (C)   status.   (D)   honesty.

    (E)   physical attractiveness.

167. A test is termed homogeneous if

    (A)   it is utilized on a homogeneous population.

    (B)   scores among heterogeneous populations tested look the same.

    (C)   the standard error of measurement indicates 0.0 error.

    (D)   one common factor underlies performance on all items in the test.

    (E)   norm-referenced measures have been used in test construction.

168. In a ratio scale, there are

    (A)   rankings of data.   (B)   equal intervals.

    (C)   absolute zero points. (D)   both (A) and (B)

    (E)   both (B) and (C)

QUESTIONS 169–172 refer to the following paragraph.

    In a neuron, the action potential is caused by changes in the relative concentration of positive charges inside and outside the cell body. During its resting state, the nerve cell has an electrical potential slightly negative with respect to the outside. When the cell is stimulated, the permeability of the membrane changes to allow almost all of the positive charges to rush in. This state is very brief and the original resting potential is soon restored by the action of the sodium pump.

169. During the resting potential, the charge on the inside of the cell relative to the outside is about

   (A)   +10 millivolts.   (B)   −20 millivolts.

   (C)   −70 millivolts.   (D)   +70 millivolts.

   (E)   −100 millivolts.

170. When the positive charges rush into the cell, the cell becomes

   (A)   polarized.   (B)   hyperpolarized.

   (C)   hypopolarized.   (D)   depolarized.

   (E)   unpolarized.

171. The sodium-potassium pump

   (A)   allows for passive diffusion of sodium and potassium across the cell membrane.

   (B)   actively transports sodium ions out of the cell while simultaneously drawing potassium ions into the cell.

   (C)   actively transports potassium ions out of the cell while simultaneously drawing sodium ions into the cell.

   (D)   promotes a net movement of positive ions into the cell.

   (E)   both (C) and (D)

172. Within a given cell, all action potentials

   (A)   are equal in size, but different in shape (amplitude).

   (B)   are equal in shape, but different in size.

   (C)   are approximately equal in size and shape.

   (D)   differ from each other in size and shape.

   (E)   are also called hyperpolarizations.

QUESTIONS 173–175: Choose the item that does NOT belong with the others.

173. (A)   schizophrenic personality

    (B)   manic-depressive personality

    (C)   hysterical personality

    (D)   anxiety neurosis

    (E)   depressive neurosis

174. (A)   cognitive restructuring   (B)   positive regard

    (C)   non-directive therapy   (D)   self-theory

    (E)   Q-technique

175. (A)   TAT   (B)   Rorschach Test

    (C)   word association test   (D)   MMPI

    (E)   Draw-a-Person Test

QUESTIONS 176–178 refer to the following paragraph.

It has been found that a cut through the hindbrain near the locus impairs REM sleep. Descending fibers from the caudal locus coeruleus extend into the spinal cord where they inhibit motor neurons. After damage to this area in the brain of a cat, the cat can still have REM sleep, but the muscles do not relax. The locus coeruleus also releases what are called FTG neurons which are in the reticular formation of the pons. These neurons produce rapid eye movements and desynchronization of the EEG. Just prior to REM sleep, certain inhibiting cells of the locus coeruleus decrease their activity and remove inhibition from the FTG cells.

176. Based on the above paragraph, one can safely say that

    (A)   FTG neurons show a significant amount of activity during REM sleep.

    (B)   damage to the locus coeruleus may cause an increase in REM sleep time.

    (C)   damage to the locus coeruleus causes an increase in muscle relaxation during REM sleep.

    (D)   both (A) and (B)   (E)   both (A) and (C)

177. REM sleep is also known as

    (A)   paradoxical sleep.   (B)   inactive sleep.

    (C)   desynchronized sleep.   (D)   both (A) and (C)

    (E)   all of the above

178. The reticular formation of the brain

    (A) has definite boundaries.

    (B) is critical for wakefulness and alertness.

    (C) can only be activated by certain stimuli.

    (D) is important for conveying precise information.

    (E)   all of the above

179. The function of the vestibular organs is to provide

    (A) auditory conduction to the brain.

    (B) visual conduction to the brain.

    (C) a kinesthetic response.

    (D) electrical transmission to receptor cells.

    (E) a sense of balance.

180. Conscience and morality are conceptually defined within the Freudian theory as the

    (A) conscious.   (B) id.

    (C) preconscious.   (D) ego.

    (E) superego.

181. The type of scale that is used for a variable such as political party affiliation or religion is a (an) _____ scale.

    (A) ratio   (B) interval

    (C) ordinal   (D) nominal

    (E) reversible

182. Freud referred to libido energy invested in the ego as

    (A) instinct.   (B) object libido.

    (C) regressive libido.   (D) catharsis.

    (E) narcissistic libido.

183. Fromm's concept of the "hoarding orientation" refers most closely to

    (A) a person's need for profit.

    (B) a person's style of taking from others.

(C)   the need to maintain a strong identification with others.

(D)   the need to save and possess.

(E)   the need for submission and dependence.

184. The learning theory explanation of acquired motives is based upon

(A)   sublimation.   (B)   secondary reinforcement.

(C)   primary reinforcement.   (D)   cognitive dissonance.

(E)   response to salient stimuli.

185. Which theorist believes that all neurotic needs can be reduced to one or another of three categories: toward people, away from people, and against people?

(A)   Rogers   (B)   Erikson

(C)   Sullivan   (D)   Horney

(E)   Fromm

186. Which of the following was particularly interested in the effect of birth order on personality?

(A)   Rogers   (B)   Adler

(C)   Fromm   (D)   Sullivan

(E)   Sheldon

187. Which of the following is true?

(A)   33% of the scores fall between the median and 3rd quartile.

(B)   50% of the scores fall between the median and 3rd quartile.

(C)   25% of the scores fall between the median and 3rd quartile.

(D)   66% of the scores fall between the median and 3rd quartile.

(E)   75% of the scores fall between the median and 3rd quartile.

188. The type of study construction in which different subjects at different developmental levels are compared is a

(A)   longitudinal study.   (B)   cross-sectional study.

(C)   field study.   (D)   group construction.

(E)   naturalistic study.

QUESTIONS 189–190 refer to the following information.

Nine rats run through a maze. The time each rat took to traverse the maze is recorded and these times are listed below.

1 min.	1.5 min.	1 min.
2.5 min.	2 min.	0.9 min.
3 min.	1.25 min.	30 min.

189. Which of the three measures of central tendency would be most appropriate for this data?

(A) mean

(B) median

(C) mode

(D) both (B) and (C)

(E) all of the above

190. What is the median of these observations?

(A) 1.25

(B) 2.0

(C) 1.5

(D) 1.0

(E) 4.79

QUESTIONS 191-193 refer to the following paragraph.

In order to understand an individual, it is necessary to know what his conscious intentions are. The ego functions are the most influential in behavior; and unconscious motivation plays no part in a normal person's behavior patterns. The personality structure is largely represented by traits which motivate behavior. These traits develop as a result of an individual's interaction with the environment, and are responsible for adaptive, expressive, and stylistic behavior.

191. The viewpoint expressed above is held by

(A) Allport.

(B) Rogers.

(C) Freud.

(D) Jung.

(E) Ellis.

192. This theorist's approach to psychology is _____ rather than _____ .

(A) behavioral, organismic

(B) scientific, humanistic

(C) psychoanalytic, behavioral

(D) humanistic, scientific

(E) humanistic, behavioral

193. Which of the following statements would NOT be true, according to this theorist?

    (A) A theory of human motivation must acknowledge the contemporaneity of motives.

    (B) An individual's wishes and aspirations are important keys to his or her present behavior.

    (C) An individual's past is important in understanding his or her present behavior.

    (D) A given activity may become an end or goal in itself even though it was originally begun for some other reason.

    (E) Many types of motive may occur simultaneously.

QUESTIONS 194–197 are based on the following information.

    CS (tone)

                        CR (eye-blink)

    UCS (air puff)

194. The conditioned response is elicited by the

    (A) unconditioned stimulus before and after conditioning.

    (B) previously neutral stimulus after conditioning.

    (C) unconditioned stimulus only after conditioning.

    (D) both (A) and (B)   (E) both (B) and (C)

195. Classical conditioning

    (A) results in behaviors which operate on the environment to produce an effect.

    (B) is the most significant kind of learning.

    (C) involves reward and punishment.

    (D) always involves two stimuli presented simultaneously.

    (E) none of the above

196. Forward conditioning refers to

    (A) presentation of the UCS prior to the CS.

    (B) the onset of the CS before the onset of the UCS.

    (C) termination of the UCS prior to the onset of the CS.

(D)   presentation of the UCS for more than five seconds before the start of the CS.

(E)   none of the above

197. Which of the following theorists built upon Pavlov's work in conditioning?

(A) E. Fromm   (B) M. Wertheimer

(C) C. Hull   (D) J.B. Watson

(E) K. Lashley

The following represents the results of a conformity experiment developed by Solomon Asch, in which subjects were to choose from three lines of different sizes, the one with the same length as line X. Each subject was on a panel with confederates who all gave the same wrong answer.

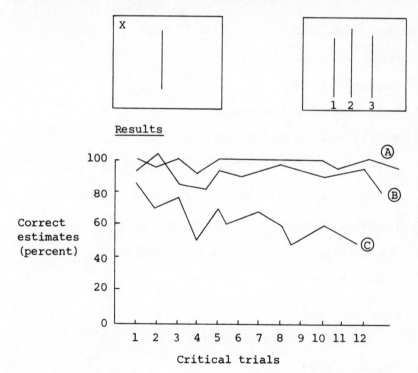

198. When alone against the majority, as seen in the line marked _____ people tend to conform _____ of the time.

(A) C, 1/3   (B) B, 1/10

(C) C, all   (D) A, none

(E) B, 1/3

199. Which of the following characteristics have been found to be strong predictors of conformity to social pressure?

    (A) authoritarian personality (B) "external" personality

    (C) high need for approval (D) both (B) and (C)

    (E) all of the above

200. Which of the following is NOT a controlling factor of conformity?

    (A) whether or not the opinion of the majority is unanimous

    (B) self-esteem of the subjects

    (C) the desire to give the correct answer

    (D) whether or not the group consists of people similar to the subject

    (E) all of the above are controlling factors

201. In language, grammar refers to

    (A) the morphemes used.

    (B) the phonemes used.

    (C) both morphemes and phonemes.

    (D) the rules used to connect phrases.

    (E) the morphology of the statement.

202. Psychologists who specialize in the study of language are called

    (A) psychogrammartists. (B) psycholinguists.

    (C) psychometricians. (D) morphemologists.

    (E) phonemologists.

203. Morphology refers to the

    (A) relationship between sounds and their meanings.

    (B) origins of words.

    (C) relationship between different languages.

    (D) study of infant babbling.

    (E) non-verbal forms of communication.

204. Ethologists insist that

    (A) animals be studied under laboratory conditions.

    (B)   the natural environment must be included in an analysis of animal behavior.

    (C)   teaching language to chimps is immoral.

    (D)   evolution is irrelevant to the study of instincts.

    (E)   all of the above

205. In ethology, an ethogram refers to

    (A)   a catalog of a particular species' behavior.

    (B)   the place a species occupies on the phylogenetic scale.

    (C)   the mating call of a species.

    (D)   the intelligence of a species.

    (E)   the longevity of a species.

206. In ethology, fixed action patterns (FAPs) refer to

    (A)   the way a group of neurons fire.

    (B)   limits on an animal's ability to learn.

    (C)   instinctive behavior.

    (D)   group behavior among humans.

    (E)   the study of sports psychology.

207. Sociometry refers to the study of

    (A)   how sociable a person is.

    (B)   measuring how extroverted a person is.

    (C)   a nation's national character.

    (D)   leadership qualities.

    (E)   the structure of small groups.

208. Social psychologists study _____, while sociologists study _____.

    (A)   groups, individuals

    (B)   group norms, national norms

    (C)   individuals, groups

    (D)   abnormal people, normal people

    (E)   introverts, extroverts

209. The Zimbardo prison studies showed that

    (A) prisons do not rehabilitate people.

    (B) prisons are too lenient.

    (C) prisoners live better than the general population.

    (D) absolute power corrupts absolutely.

    (E) the guards are minimally trained.

210. Behavior deliberately intended to injure or destroy is the psychological definition of

    (A) sociopathy.   (B) hostility.

    (C) frustration.   (D) instinct.

    (E) aggression.

211. Which of the following is a technique used in psychoanalysis?

    (A) client-centered therapy   (B) systematic desensitization

    (C) dream analysis   (D) implosion therapy

    (E) modelling

212. Aversion therapy would be used for which of the following problems?

    (A) alcoholism   (B) paranoia

    (C) anxiety   (D) phobias

    (E) all of the above

213. Which class of drugs would be prescribed for children who have been diagnosed as hyperactive?

    (A) narcotics   (B) depressants

    (C) hallucinogens   (D) stimulants

    (E) anti-anxiety

214. Free association is the cornerstone of the _____ approach to therapy.

    (A) humanistic   (B) psychoanalytic

    (C) neurobiological   (D) behavioristic

    (E) cognitive

215. A psychologist who assesses the effects of noise levels in a factory and the incidence of accidents is probably a(n) _____ psychologist.

    (A) psychoanalytic

    (B) social

    (C) behavioral

    (D) commercial

    (E) industrial

216. Sports psychology is concerned with

    (A) instituting fair rules.

    (B) improving the players' performance.

    (C) making sure that the game isn't beyond the capability of the players.

    (D) the dangers of injury.

    (E) all of the above.

217. A parapsychologist would study which of the following phenomena?

    (A) clairvoyance

    (B) precognition

    (C) telepathy

    (D) psychokinesis

    (E) all of the above

TEST 3

ANSWER KEY

1.	(C)	26.	(A)	51.	(E)	76.	(C)
2.	(C)	27.	(C)	52.	(B)	77.	(A)
3.	(D)	28.	(D)	53.	(D)	78.	(D)
4.	(C)	29.	(B)	54.	(E)	79.	(D)
5.	(A)	30.	(A)	55.	(E)	80.	(C)
6.	(D)	31.	(E)	56.	(C)	81.	(E)
7.	(E)	32.	(B)	57.	(C)	82.	(C)
8.	(C)	33.	(A)	58.	(A)	83.	(E)
9.	(B)	34.	(C)	59.	(C)	84.	(A)
10.	(D)	35.	(B)	60.	(B)	85.	(C)
11.	(B)	36.	(A)	61.	(C)	86.	(D)
12.	(C)	37.	(B)	62.	(D)	87.	(E)
13.	(E)	38.	(E)	63.	(D)	88.	(B)
14.	(C)	39.	(A)	64.	(A)	89.	(C)
15.	(A)	40.	(E)	65.	(A)	90.	(C)
16.	(C)	41.	(A)	66.	(B)	91.	(E)
17.	(B)	42.	(B)	67.	(C)	92.	(D)
18.	(B)	43.	(D)	68.	(B)	93.	(B)
19.	(D)	44.	(C)	69.	(E)	94.	(C)
20.	(E)	45.	(D)	70.	(D)	95.	(D)
21.	(B)	46.	(D)	71.	(C)	96.	(E)
22.	(B)	47.	(B)	72.	(A)	97.	(E)
23.	(D)	48.	(B)	73.	(C)	98.	(C)
24.	(B)	49.	(E)	74.	(D)	99.	(E)
25.	(A)	50.	(C)	75.	(C)	100.	(C)

101.	(D)	131.	(D)	161.	(D)	191.	(A)
102.	(C)	132.	(A)	162.	(D)	192.	(D)
103.	(D)	133.	(C)	163.	(B)	193.	(C)
104.	(D)	134.	(B)	164.	(E)	194.	(D)
105.	(E)	135.	(C)	165.	(D)	195.	(E)
106.	(E)	136.	(B)	166.	(B)	196.	(B)
107.	(B)	137.	(E)	167.	(D)	197.	(D)
108.	(B)	138.	(D)	168.	(E)	198.	(A)
109.	(A)	139.	(C)	169.	(C)	199.	(E)
110.	(C)	140.	(E)	170.	(D)	200.	(C)
111.	(D)	141.	(D)	171.	(B)	201.	(D)
112.	(E)	142.	(B)	172.	(C)	202.	(B)
113.	(A)	143.	(A)	173.	(C)	203.	(A)
114.	(D)	144.	(D)	174.	(A)	204.	(B)
115.	(C)	145.	(A)	175.	(D)	205.	(A)
116.	(B)	146.	(A)	176.	(D)	206.	(C)
117.	(E)	147.	(C)	177.	(D)	207.	(E)
118.	(B)	148.	(B)	178.	(B)	208.	(C)
119.	(B)	149.	(E)	179.	(E)	209.	(D)
120.	(E)	150.	(A)	180.	(E)	210.	(E)
121.	(C)	151.	(E)	181.	(D)	211.	(C)
122.	(E)	152.	(C)	182.	(E)	212.	(A)
123.	(B)	153.	(C)	183.	(D)	213.	(D)
124.	(C)	154.	(D)	184.	(B)	214.	(B)
125.	(B)	155.	(C)	185.	(D)	215.	(E)
126.	(D)	156.	(B)	186.	(B)	216.	(B)
127.	(E)	157.	(B)	187.	(C)	217.	(E)
128.	(B)	158.	(C)	188.	(B)		
129.	(A)	159.	(E)	189.	(D)		
130.	(D)	160.	(A)	190.	(C)		

DETAILED EXPLANATIONS OF ANSWERS

GRE PSYCHOLOGY TEST 3

1.   **(C)**   Because of the disguised nature of wish fulfillment in dreams, Freud distinguished between the manifest content and latent content of dreams. The manifest content refers to the literal content of the dream as experienced by the dreamer. It is the conscious manifestation of the hidden, symbolic desires and fears in the unconscious.

2.   **(C)**   A knee jerk is an example of a monosynaptic reflex. This is the simplest type of reflex arc because there is only one synapse between the sensory and motor neurons. In the knee jerk reflex, the tendon of the knee cap is tapped and thereby stretched, and receptors in the tendon are stimulated. An impulse travels along the sensory neuron to the spinal cord, where it synapses directly with a motor neuron and is then transmitted to the effector muscle in the leg, causing it to contract.

3.   **(D)**   The thalamus serves a number of functions. It serves as a relay center for sensory impulses. Fibers from the spinal cord and parts of the brain synapse here with other neurons going to the various sensory areas of the cerebrum. The thalamus seems to regulate and coordinate the external signs of emotion. The thalamus is in the forebrain, located on top of the hypothalamus.

4.   **(C)**   Adrenalin is a hormone which stimulates the sympathetic nervous system. One of the many resulting effects of adrenalin on the body is the stimulation of the heart. When stimulated, the sympathetic branch to the muscles of the heart causes the heart to beat more rapidly and vigorously. Thus, adrenalin has the effect of accelerating and strengthening the heart beat.

5.   **(A)**   The pons is an area of the hindbrain containing a large number of nerve fibers which pass through it and make connections between the two hemispheres of the cerebellum, thus coordinating muscle movements on the two sides of the body. It is also especially important in aiding the regulation of breathing.

6.   **(D)**   All of the choices are monocular depth cues, meaning that they all convey information about space through one eye only. Relative size involves figures becoming smaller as they are seen at a greater and greater distance. Due to linear perspective, lines that would be parallel on the ground converge on the picture plane. Interposition is when one figure interrupts the outline of another and a strong depth cue is produced, indicating the relative positions.

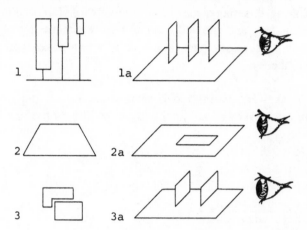

7.   **(E)**   The gestalt school of psychology proposed laws of perceptual organization. They concerned themselves with large units of perception such as form, and the figures and contexts in which forms are set. From this study emerged a group of "laws" of organization. The laws deal with area, closedness of figure, proximity of figures, continuation of line, and symmetry.

8.   **(C)**   The full color spectrum is red-orange-yellow-green-blue-indigo-violet. Note that there are a number of colors, like pink or brown, that do not appear in the spectrum. These colors are formed by the combining of two wavelengths of light which are colors from the spectrum. Once the wavelengths combine, it is impossible for our eye to separate out the colors that went into the production of the new color.

9.   **(B)**   Intellectualization, or rationalization, may be defined as an attempt by a person who is unaware of the real reasons underlying his inappropriate behavior to explain his behavior by using socially acceptable motives. One of the classic rationalizations is the "sour grapes" phenomenon. As the story goes, the fox could not reach the grapes he wanted and rationalized that it was just as well because they were sour anyway.

10.   **(D)**   In the Rorschach Inkblot Test, there are three different aspects to each response: location, determinant, and content. Location refers to the area of the blot that the subject responds to. The determinant refers to the characteristic of the blot that determined the subject's response (form, color, and movement). The content category refers to what was seen in the blot: human or animal, male or female, etc. The examiner tabulates the total number of responses and the total in each of the three categories.

11.   **(B)**   Primary identification with the mother occurs during the first few weeks of life. At first it is thought that the infant cannot distinguish itself from its mother. During this stage, the infant's level of differentiation between himself, and the mother, and himself, and the environment, increases. This early identification is a necessary part of the child's ego development according to psychoanalytic theory.

12.   **(C)**   A skewed distribution is a nonsymmetrical frequency distribution. A distribution can be skewed at either end, in the direction of the longer tail.

Positively Skewed   Negatively Skewed

The positively and negatively skewed distributions are specific forms of the skewed distribution.

13.   **(E)**   All secondary sources of drive are learned. These are acquired drives responses that have been acquired in a particular environmental situation. These sources of drive include such learned drives as success, money, power, appearance and security. These responses have motivational consequences similar to the primary sources of motivation in that they influence and direct behavior.

14.   **(C)**   Piaget proposed a stage theory of cognitive development. He proposed that the child goes through a sensorimotor period (0–2 yrs.), a preoperational period (2–7 yrs.), a concrete operational period (7–11 yrs.), and finally a formal operational period (12–16 yrs.). At each stage there is an emergence of new and important cognitive skills, until the child reaches the end of formal operations and is capable of adult cognition.

15.   **(A)**   In Tolman's view, behavior is precipitated by environmental cues, both internal and external, and by a variety of unbalanced situations. Specifically, Tolman believed that performance is a function of the individual's *expectancies* of achieving his goal in the environment, the level of demand or *value* for that particular goal, and the availability of the goal in the environment. He translates his theory into the equation Expectancy $\times$ Value = Performance.

16.   **(C)**   Doob, Dollard and Miller proposed the frustration-aggression hypothesis which argues that all aggressive acts are caused by frustration, which is almost always accompanied by anger. There is strong evidence to indicate that frustration alone can produce aggression, although it is impossible to determine

whether frustration is a necessary component, that is, if all aggressive acts require frustration.

17. **(B)** Eidetic memory refers to the capacity to retain the details of visual scenes to a greater degree than the average person. This capacity is also called "photographic memory." This ability occurs most frequently in children. It is rare in adults of this culture, believed to be the case because it is not useful in our society.

18. **(B)** This problem describes a stimulus generalization response. Stimulus generalization may be defined as the elicitation of a learned response by a stimulus similar to, but not identical with, the conditioned stimulus. In the example, a man generalizes his fear of one specific dog to all other dogs, but not to cats, birds, etc., which are too different to elicit the fear response.

19. **(D)** This choice is correct by definition. The term automatic behavior refers to any behavior that can be engaged in without much concentration and effort. For example, activities like bicycle riding are performed automatically. Motor responses in such activities are automatic because the person does not need to think about them to perform them. When riding a bicycle, the person is conscious of such responses as steering, pedaling, and braking, but he or she does not think about them — they are automatic.

20. **(E)** As exemplified by response options (A) through (D), narcissists see themselves as superior to others but need a lot of support to maintain that belief. Histrionics may or may not think they are wonderful, but they do want a lot of attention. They try to achieve this through theatrical, over-emotional, and inappropriately sexual or provocative behavior. Because they use excessive emotionality to get noticed, the emotional behavior changes as the requirements for attention change, and audiences eventually come to recognize the histrionic's emotional displays as shallow and inauthentic.

21. **(B)** Adler differed from Freud concerning the purpose of the Oedipus Complex. Instead of being a purely sexual phenomenon, the Oedipal conflicts were seen by Adler to involve strivings to become superior to the father, to compete with the father. This relates to Adler's larger theory of personality which was concerned with overcoming a perceived sense of inferiority for which the individual strives to compensate by gaining superiority in many areas of functioning.

22. **(B)** The superego develops from the ages of eighteen months to six years. It is often described as having two divisions. One is the "conscience" which consists of the child's internalized rules. This is the part of the superego which mentally punishes, based on the known internalized rules of what is right

and wrong. The other division of the superego is the "ego ideal." This division represents strivings and goals highly regarded by the parents.

23. **(D)** In order to reliably measure and analyze perceptual thresholds, statistical methods were developed. There are three basic methods used for this purpose, which are the Method of Limits, the Method of Average Error, and the frequency method. They are alike in that they all present (for comparison) a constant Standard stimulus (St), and a variable Comparison stimulus (Co).

24. **(B)** According to the anxiety theory of neurosis, the symptoms exhibited by a neurotic are usually one of three stages of unresolved anxiety. The symptom can be a normal response to anxiety, a way to avoid anxiety, or a reaction to the original conflict which caused the anxiety. In the case of depression, the person is thought to direct his displaced anxiety back at himself instead of at an external object.

25. **(A)** The projected image of the female throughout history in man's unconscious is the "anima." This internalized image is based on his real experiences with women, particularly his mother or sisters, and the collective experience of men throughout history. The anima determines a man's relationship to women throughout his life. The anima helps a man compensate for his otherwise one-sided view of his interactions with and perceptions of others.

26. **(A)** The shaping of a new behavior involves the reinforcement of acts similar to the desired one (an approximation). The method involves differential reinforcement, which means that the same act is not continually reinforced. During each successive trial, reinforcement is given only if the subject engages in an act of behavior that more closely resembles the desired behavior. As the training or shaping proceeds, closer and closer approximations are required for reinforcement.

27. **(C)** R.B. Cattell developed the Culture Fair Intelligence Test, a paper-and-pencil test available on three levels, each having a varying number of subtests. Unfortunately, Cattell's test does not completely compensate for cultural disadvantages. In cultures different from the one in which the test was designed, performance was considerably lower than the original norms.

28. **(D)** Spaced practice results in more efficient learning than massed practice. The most efficient method of spaced practice varies two features: (1) the length of the practice period, and (2) the length of the rest period. In general, short practice periods result in more efficient learning of a motor task. Periods should not be so short, however, that the task is separated into meaningless units. The optimal rest period length is about two or three minutes.

29. **(B)** Freud defined two instincts in man, one of which is Eros. Eros is the life instinct or the will to live, which includes the libidinal urges. Eros

competes with Thanatos, the death instinct, once an individual is fully developed. It is the life-giving urges of Eros that are most intimately connected with the child's development.

30. **(A)**   Wilhelm Wundt started the structuralist school of psychology. He established the first psychology lab in 1879. Wundt believed that the proper object of study for psychology was the content of the conscious mind. He wanted to divide the mind into compartments or mental elements in order to identify and analyze them. He concluded that the three basic structures were sensations, images and feelings.

31. **(E)**   An object's shape, size and brightness, as well as color, remain constant in our perceptual processes in spite of changes in both the environment and in the retinal image. Most of this constancy relies on memory and interpretation of context.

32. **(B)**   In his studies on the nature of obedience, Stanley Milgram discovered that the average middle-class American male would, under the direction of a legitimate power and authority figure, administer severe shocks to other individuals in an experimental setting. This somewhat alarming finding demonstrated the extent to which ordinary people will comply with orders from a legitimate source of social power and authority, even to the point of committing cruel and harmful actions toward their fellow man.

33. **(A)**   The factor that is found to be most predictive of interpersonal attractiveness is propinquity or degree of physical closeness. The closer two individuals are geographically, the more likely it is that they will like each other. A repeated finding concerning mate selection is that individuals find mates who live close by them.

34. **(C)**   A mixed factorial design incorporates features of within-subjects and between-subjects design styles. In a within-subjects design, the same subjects receive all the levels of treatment conditions. In a between-subjects design, different subjects are in each of the treatment conditions. A mixed factorial design will use a certain amount of repetition in the treatment conditions to which subjects are exposed, but not all subjects will receive all treatments.

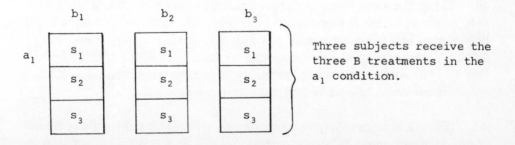

Three subjects receive the three B treatments in the a_1 condition.

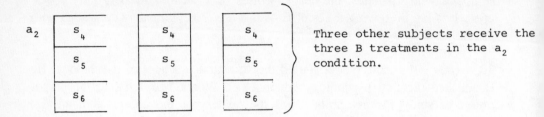

Three other subjects receive the three B treatments in the a_2 condition.

35. **(B)**   A sample bias is any procedural variable which causes the sample to be unrepresentative of the population. A sample bias often yields inaccurate predictions about the population under study. Hence, it reduces the statistical power of the analysis on this population.

36. **(A)**   This choice is correct by definition. In general, degrees of freedom can be defined in terms of the number of scores in a set that are free to vary, meaning that they do not have restrictions placed on them. Once the process of statistical inference is begun and a sum of squares calculated, all the scores in a set are not completely free. The general rule for calculating the degrees of freedom is

$$df = \begin{pmatrix} \# \text{ of indep.} \\ \text{observations} \end{pmatrix} - \begin{pmatrix} \# \text{ of population} \\ \text{estimates} \end{pmatrix}$$

37. **(B)**   Specialists in the fields of psychology and education have come to recognize that creativity and intelligence are not synonymous. Creativity is certainly not measurable by standard I.Q. tests. Creativity is influenced by many non-intellectual, temperamental characteristics, such as a receptive attitude toward novel ideas, specific perceptual tendencies, and ideational fluency.

38. **(E)**   Traditionally, cross-cultural tests have tried to eliminate those factors which differentiate between two cultures. The Leiter International Performance Scale, Cattell's Culture Fair Intelligence Test, Raven's Progressive Matrices factor test, and the Goodenough Draw-A-Man Test, all attempt to overcome cultural biases.

39. **(A)**   The fundamental concept in Karen Horney's psychoanalytic theory is basic anxiety. This is experienced in childhood as a feeling of isolation and helplessness in a potentially hostile world. The anxiety results from parental attitudes toward the child which may take the form of dominance, lack of affection, lack of protective behavior, and many other negative affect states. Horney considers anxiety to be a learned response, not an innate response.

40. **(E)**   The stage of formal operations is the final step in Piaget's system of cognitive development. It begins at about age eleven when the child begins to

free himself from the period of concrete operations. He can now imagine hypothetical states and he realizes that there are many possible solutions to a problem. Thinking becomes increasingly propositional, logical, and idealistic.

41. **(A)**   Anna Freud, daughter of Sigmund, was a disciple of the psychoanalytic approach developed by her father. One of her contributions was several works detailing the mechanics of ego-defense mechanisms.

42. **(B)**   Whenever new information is encoded, the internal and external environment in which it occurred is also assimilated. Even when one is specifically concerned with a particular aspect of an event, surrounding input also enters the memory system. This simultaneous storage of information in memory is called parallel storage and it is of prime importance in the study of both memory and thinking.

43. **(D)**   The Central Limit Theorem is a theorem of statistical theory stating that the sampling distribution of the mean approaches the normal distribution in shape as the size of the random sample on which the means are based is increased. This theorem is the statistical justification for any statements made about the sampling distribution of the mean.

44. **(C)**   In Piaget's theory, an operation is a thought. Thought refers to the mental representation of something that is not immediately perceived. During this period of concrete operations, the child is capable of invoking a mental representation or image of an object or event. This representation is linked to a mental image of the "concrete" perceptual experience. It must exist in the physical sense and not be hypothetical.

45. **(D)**   The California Psychological Inventory (CPI), as developed by Gough (1957), is an objective personality inventory developed for use with less clinically deviant groups of subjects. Most of the CPI was developed using the method of contrasted groups and internal consistency analysis. Some of the representative scales are: Self-control, Responsibility, Flexibility, Achievement via Independence, Tolerance, and Intellectual efficiency. The items measure minor forms of maladjustment.

46. **(D)**   Personality tests usually have a limited range of responses or are designed with true/false choices. They may assess a wide range of personality characteristics. Objective personality tests are generally structured with well-documented norms of responding. The Q-sort is one of the techniques used with self–report referential tests. While these tests are well structured and documented, they may not be accurate predictors of future behavior.

47. **(B)**   The standard deviation is a measure of the variability or spread of scores in a group. If the grouping sample is homogeneous, there would be little variation among the subjects; therefore, the standard deviation should be small.

The standard deviation is expressed as the square root of the average of the squared deviations from the mean of the group.

48. **(B)** Projective tests allow the subject to freely associate the stimuli presented. It is assumed that the responses are expressions (projections) of unconscious desires, conflicts, and impulses. Another basic assumption of projective methods is that the production of responses depends largely upon personality factors. The Rorschach test uses inkblots as the stimuli to project experiences, while the TAT uses pictures of ambiguous situations between people as the test stimuli. Despite the difference in test stimuli, both the Rorschach and TAT use projective methods to assess personality.

49. **(E)** Both the word association test and the sentence completion test are referred to as verbal projective tests because both stimulus materials and responses are verbal in nature. The administration of these two tests presupposes a minimum reading level and thorough familiarity with the language in which the test was developed. Both measures permit an almost unlimited variety of responding. Due to the limitations of these tests, they should not be administered to children, illiterates, and people from foreign cultures.

50. **(C)** A "normal" I.Q. is considered to be about 100, and 99 percent of the people who take intelligence tests fall in the range between 55 and 145. A person who scores below 70 is considered to be mentally retarded.

51. **(E)** Social reinforcement is a type of secondary reinforcement that occurs when the reinforcer consists of feedback from individuals in one's surrounding environment. Examples of this include attention, approval, affection, indifference and enmity. Hence, social reinforcement can be positive or negative, Each social reinforcement either strengthens or weakens particular behaviors. In the example of a child winning a game and gaining peer approval, the child is receiving positive social reinforcement which should strengthen game-winning behaviors.

52. **(B)** The successive method of approximation involves the reinforcement of acts similar to the desired one (an approximation). The method uses differential reinforcement for behaviors that are successively closer to the desired behavior. The shaping of responses is the teaching of behavior by reinforcing successively closer approximations of the desired behavior until the desired behavior is attained. Hence, both are, by definition, the same behavioral technique.

53. **(D)** Hermann Ebbinghaus, a young German philosopher, was the first to examine learning and memory scientifically. His experiments in the late 1800's attempted to give an empirical basis for the study of human learning. Ebbinghaus measured learning difficulty by presenting a subject with a series of items to learn and counting the number of presentations necessary to learn the

material and recall it. He measured memory by requiring subjects to relearn material they knew but had forgotten. He recorded the number of times something had to be rehearsed before perfect recitation of the material occurred.

54.   **(E)**   Perceptual constancy is commonly believed to be a function of learning and experience. A problem with this is that if constancy were based upon past experience, we would assume that our experience would teach us to always perceive correctly. However, our perceptions are sometimes tricked by illusions of size constancy, due to inaccurate estimations of object distance. This phenomenon is called "misapplied constancy" and has been studied in an effort to challenge this accepted theory of perceptual constancy.

55.   **(E)**   All of these are examples of Gestalt Laws of Organization. The smaller the enclosed *area* of representation, the more it is likely to look like a figure. Areas that are *closed* are more likely to be seen as figures. Items that are placed in close *proximity* are likely to be visually grouped together in a logical manner. An arrangement that has *continuation* with the fewest interruptions of line or curve will be organized as a figure. Lastly, the more *symmetrical* a closed area is, the more likely it is to be viewed as a figure.

56.   **(C)**   This research group proposed the frustration-aggression hypothesis, which argues that all aggressive acts are caused by frustration. Frustration is almost always thought to be accompanied by anger. There is strong evidence, much of which is provided by these researchers, that frustration alone can produce aggression.

57.   **(C)**   An I.Q. range of 20–35 indicates a severe degree of mental retardation. School-age children would be expected to learn to talk or use sign language. They can be trained in elementary health and self-care habits. Adults with this functioning level may contribute to their daily maintenance, but need complete supervision. They require a controlled environment.

58.   **(A)**   MA is the abbreviation for mental age. MA assesses an absolute level of cognitive capacity. This level of cognitive capacity is determined by the test level that a child can pass. For example, if the highest test level that a child could pass is the test level that all average nine-year-olds passed and no average eight-year-old passed, then the child is presumed to have a mental age of nine. If the child's chronological age is seven, then he would be considered "bright," but if his age is twelve, he would be considered "slow."

59.   **(C)**   Affective bipolar disorder is a psychotic state characterized by extreme moods of both elation and extreme depression. The other choices all describe neurotic disorders. Psychosis is a more extreme state and break from reality, while neurotic disorders generally arise out of a stress and anxiety experience. Behavior is preoccupied with the avoiding of stress and anxiety. It is characterized by rigid and unsuccessful attempts to reduce the anxiety state.

60.   **(B)**   In conversion reactions, the operations of the musculature or sensory functions are impaired, although the bodily organs are healthy. Patients with conversion disorders have reported symptoms such as paralysis, blindness, seizures, coordination disturbances, and anesthesia, all without any sign of physiological cause. Although the symptoms are usually psychosomatic, conversion reaction is the best answer. Hysteria can be a subtype of a conversion reaction if it is marked with these symptoms. The symptoms are not under the patient's voluntary control.

61.   **(C)**   Guilford's model of intelligence is based on a multiple-factor theory. His theory contains 120 different factors of intelligence. He described these traits or factors of intelligence by classifying them along three dimensions that interact. These dimensions are: operations, contents, and products. Operations describe what a person does when he uses a specific trait. Contents are the base of information on which operations are performed. Products describe the end results of the operations. Hence, operations × contents × products = intelligence in Guilford's model.

62.   **(D)**   The Rotter Incomplete Sentence Blank is a verbal projective technique. The sentence completion test permits an almost unlimited variety of responses. This test consists of 40 sentence stems which require completion to such items as: What worries one...; My mother...; My ambition.... The responses are rated on a 7-point scale of adjustment/maladjustment. Some argue that this test is more objectively scored than other such verbal projective tests.

63.   **(D)**   The personality structure consists of id, ego, and superego. According to Freud, the id is the most fundamental component of personality and is comprised of drives, needs, and instinctual impulses. It is unable to tolerate tension, is obedient only to the pleasure principle and is in constant conflict with the superego. The superego develops out of the ego during childhood. It contains values, morals and basic attitudes as learned from parents and society. The ego mediates between the id and superego. The ego is sometimes called the executive agency of the personality because it controls actions and decides how needs should be satisfied.

64.   **(A)**   The autonomic nervous system is divided into two parts, both structurally and functionally. One part is called the sympathetic nervous system and the other is known as the parasympathetic nervous system. These two branches act antagonistically to each other. If one system stimulates an effector, the other would inhibit its action. The basis for homeostatic regulation by the autonomic system lies in the fact that the sympathetic and parasympathetic system each send a branch to the same organ, causing double innervation.

65.   **(A)**   The "white matter" of the central nervous system is actually the nerve fiber pathways. The white matter consists mainly of axons. The axons are

surrounded by a fatty, white covering called the myelin sheath, hence their nick-name, white matter.

66.   **(B)**   Synaptic vesicles are small, sac-like structures located at the axon of the neuron. They contain neurotransmitters, which are chemicals that permit unidirectional transmission of an action potential from one neuron to another. Acetylcholine and noradrenaline are two types of neurotransmitters.

67.   **(C)**   The hypothalamus, located under the thalamus, is a collection of nuclei concerned with many important homeostatic regulations. Electrical stimulation of certain cells in the hypothalamus produces sensations of hunger, thirst, pain, pleasure, or sexual drive. The hypothalamus is also important for its influence on the pituitary gland, which is functionally under its control. Cells of the hypothalamus synthesize chemical factors that modulate the release of hormones produced and stored in the pituitary.

68.   **(B)**   Color intensity is not a stimulus cue involved in the perception of depth. The other choices are all factors involved in depth perception.

69.   **(E)**   According to Emmert's Law, the apparent size of a projected after-image is directly proportional to the distance between the eye and the surface onto which the image is projected. To test this perceptual law, stand in front of a bright window and gaze at it from a distance of two feet. This should produce an afterimage when you look away. If you project the afterimage from a distance of four feet to a plain white surface you will see an image that is the same size as the window. If, however, you project the afterimage from a distance of two feet, the image will appear to be half the size of the original window image.

70.   **(D)**   Within the color spectrum, blue is perceived at 470–475 nanometers wavelength, green at 495–535 nanometers, yellow at 575–580 nanometers, and red at 595–770 nanometers wavelength. Hence, with reference to the question, the wavelength of green is greater than blue but less than yellow or red.

71.   **(C)**   Physical sounds from the environment in the form of waves are translated into electrical messages in the cochlea. The cochlea contains special hair cells which are bent as part of a chain reaction due to the vibrations of the ossicles, namely the stapes, which pushes against the oval window on the cochlea. As these hairs are bent, an electrical event called a generator potential occurs. This potential stimulates nearby nerve cells. The activated nerve cells then carry an electrical message about the original sound wave vibrations along to the brain.

72.   **(A)**   Factor analysis is a mathematical procedure designed to analyze the degree of correlation between different factors underlying a psychological phenomenon. The purpose is to simplify the description of behavior by reducing the

number of descriptive categories used. Separateness of factors is assessed by the degree of correlation present between variables. Specifically, the correlation co-efficient is a measure of how well one score predicts another. The more positive a correlation is, the more the variables are related to one another; the more negative a correlation is, the greater the separation of factors.

73. **(C)** This choice is correct by definition. Heritability is defined as the proportion of the total variation in a population that is due to genetic variation. Since heritability is dependent on a ratio of genetic to nongenetic variation, its value is affected by both factors. Heritability can be increased by either an increase in genetic variation or by a decrease in nongenetic or environmental variation.

74. **(D)** The two hypotheses tested in statistics are called the alternative hypothesis and the null hypothesis. The null hypothesis states that there is no experimental effect. The alternative hypothesis asserts that there is an experimental effect and, therefore, the null hypothesis is false.

75. **(C)** Fromm believed that a healthy individual manifests the productive orientation in which he achieves goals and, thereby, realizes and actualizes his full potential in life. The essential component of a productive orientation is making a creative contribution to one's family life, career, and to the betterment of society. The other choices are pathological orientations developed by Fromm to characterize neurotic styles of coping with insecurity and isolation.

76. **(C)** Teratogens are environmental agents that produce abnormalities in the developing fetus. A teratogen can be a disease contracted during pregnancy, a chemical (drug or hormone) an expectant mother takes, or the radiation to which a pregnant woman may be exposed.

77. **(A)** Hull's theory accounted for the appetitive drives of hunger, thirst and sex, and for the aversive drive of pain avoidance. A physiological need was believed to produce a drive that sought to initiate a behavior that would reduce the drive and satisfy the need. The behavior employed depended on the degree of success with which the behavior had reduced drive in the past. This learned association between the drive and the behavior that reduces it is called a "habit." This theoretical relationship was expressed as Performance = Drive × Habit.

78. **(D)** Freud's theory of motivational processes represents only a limited segment of his life work, but it is a segment on which much of his other work is built. Freud believed that behavior was motivated largely by unconscious instincts. These instincts were collectively referred to as the "id." The id unconsciously motivates behavior by giving rise to tensions, which the person is motivated to satisfy and reduce.

79. **(D)** Echoic memory deals with information taken in through auditory

perception. Because auditory perception takes place over a period of time, some kind of memory must preserve it long enough for speech processing to occur. The medium for the temporary storage of auditory information is the echoic memory. The maximum duration of echoic memory has been difficult to determine. This transitory memory decays gradually, and its duration has varied inversely with the difficulty of the task that was used to measure it. Estimates of its duration range from one to ten seconds.

80. **(C)** In a fixed-interval schedule, reinforcement occurs after a fixed period of time. No matter how much work is done, reinforcement is given after a set period of time. This schedule has the lowest yield in terms of performance. However, just before reinforcement time, activity increases.

81. **(E)** During stage 4 sleep, delta waves predominate. Delta waves are very slow, occurring about once every second. During this stage of sleep, the sleeper is virtually immobile and not easily woken. Stage 4 sleep is the deepest stage of sleep with no REM activity; therefore, no dreaming occurs during this sleep stage.

82. **(C)** Down's syndrome is the most prevalent single-factor cause of mental retardation. It is caused by a chromosomal abnormality. The vast majority of Down's children have forty-seven chromosomes instead of forty-six. During the earliest stage of an egg's development the two chromosomes of pair 21 fail to separate. When the sperm and egg unite, chromosome pair 21 has three chromosomes instead of the usual two. This is referred to as a trisomy of chromosome 21.

83. **(E)** In his theory of motivation, Carl Rogers places special emphasis on two needs: the need for positive regard and the need for self-regard. Both are learned needs. Positive regard refers to the positive assessment an individual receives from other people; the need for positive regard develops in infancy as a result of the love and care a baby receives. The need for self-regard is established as a result of receiving positive regard from others. These two needs are not always in congruence and can, therefore, interfere with the actualizing tendency.

84. **(A)** When a personal shortcoming is overcome by an intense effort to become successful in another field, the person is displaying compensation. In this example, the man chose a field related to his personal shortcoming, but that is not always the case.

85. **(C)** The lens is a transparent tissue that focuses the image by changing shape — thickening for near objects and thinning for distant ones. This process is called accommodation. Like the cornea, the lens is curved in shape. It bends, inverts, and focuses light rays onto the retina.

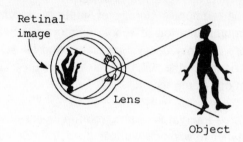

Retinal image

Lens

Object

86. **(D)** Multiple personality, the presence of separate and different personalities within the same individual, is perhaps the most dramatic type of dissociative reaction. The individual personalities in this disorder are generally quite discrepant and usually the primary personality remains unaware of the secondary personalities. Generally in dissociative disorders, a group of mental processes splits off from the mainstream of consciousness, or a behavior is incompatible with the rest of the personality.

87. **(E)** The eighth and final stage of Erikson's scheme is maturity. The basic crisis during this stage is ego integrity vs. disgust and despair. A sense of integrity develops if the individual, having looked back on his life, believes that it has been meaningful and relatively successful. He feels good about his past and is prepared to live the rest of his life in peace. A feeling of disgust, however, may arise if the individual sees his life as meaningless, wasted, and generally unsuccessful.

88. **(B)** Autonomic conditioning refers to the operant conditioning of autonomic responses such as heart rate and intestinal contractions. Through conditioning, a subject could alter the rate of an autonomic response. It was known for a long time that autonomic responses could be classically conditioned. It was believed that this could not be done with an operant conditioning procedure until Miller's (1969) experiment. The experiment showed autonomic conditioning was possible and led to research that examined cures for problems like high blood pressure, using operant conditioning methods.

89. **(C)** The disadvantage of cross-cultural tests is that the predictive and diagnostic value of the intelligence test is lost. There is little gained by administering culture fair tests if they do not provide useful information concerning the culturally relevant knowledge and abilities of a student. Cross-cultural tests often miss this relevant information and, therefore have little meaningful predictive value.

90. **(C)** STM is highly susceptible to interference. For instance, when a

person begins dialing a telephone number but is interrupted, the number may be forgotten or dialed incorrectly. Interference can disrupt STM because there is no rehearsal time after a response. Information may also be interrupted because the interfering activity could also enter STM and cause it to reach its capacity for stored items. In either case, displacement of old, unrehearsed items will occur.

91. **(E)** To Freud, dreams represented attempts at wish fulfillment. He reasoned that the dream is a hallucinatory state that structures events not as they would be in reality, but as the dreamer wishes them to be. When unconscious desires conflict with conscious restraints, it is necessary for the dreamwork to disguise the meaning of the dream in order to express the wish.

92. **(D)** Measuring devices must have two characteristics. First, they must be reliable. This means that an individual's score or rating should not vary with repeated testings. For example, an intelligence test which yields highly different scores each time the subject takes the test is useless. Second, a measuring device must be valid. This means that it should measure what it was designed to measure. An I.Q. test, for example, would not yield an accurate measure of anxiety, but it should be an accurate measure of intelligence.

93. **(B)** The texture-density gradient is a monocular depth cue. A gradient is the rate at which some property changes uniformly from one part of the area portrayed to another. The texture gradient of this impression becomes denser as it becomes more distant. This effect is achieved on a pictorial plane by drawing the horizontal parallel lines closer and closer together as greater distance is portrayed.

94. **(C)** Deindividuation is a state in which a person feels a lessened sense of personal identity and responsibility. It is a state likely to be experienced by a person in a large group or crowd situation.

95. **(D)** Proposed by Leon Festinger, the theory of cognitive dissonance states that people are motivated to keep their cognitions — beliefs, attitudes, opinions, and values — consistent. If the relationship between their cognitions becomes inconsistent, it causes psychological distress which is called "dissonance." Cognitive dissonance is an uncomfortable psychological state which motivates a person to regain psychological consistency.

96. **(E)** Alpha (α) is the probability of committing a Type I error. This is the probability with which an experimenter is willing to reject the null when it is, in fact, correct. α is also known as the significance level. Generally, $\alpha \leq .05$ is an acceptable significance level.

97. **(E)** Hue, brightness, and saturation are all attributes of color. The wavelength of the light determines which "hue" we will perceive. When a single wavelength of light is perceived, the hue appears pure or "saturated." As the

intensity of the light increases, the light will appear brighter. These three factors interact to determine the actual color we see.

98. **(C)** This choice is correct by definition. If all raw scores are transformed into Z-scores

$$Z = \frac{\text{deviation}}{\text{standard deviation}},$$

the resulting distribution will also be normal with a mean of 0 and a standard deviation of 1.0. This distribution is called the standard normal distribution or the Z distribution. A picture of the Z distribution is presented below.

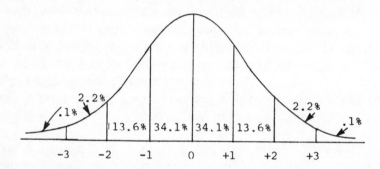

99. **(E)** Many variables must be taken into account when a test is administered. The subject's understanding of the test, test directions, examiner's rapport, subject's level of anxiety concerning the test, personality type of examiner, and the subject's experience with practice tests are all important variables to consider before the actual test administration. If such variables are not taken into account, there is likely to be systematic bias in the test samples, which will interfere with the factors that the test is specifically trying to examine.

100. **(C)** The Kent-Rosanoff Test is a word association test which consists of 100 neutral words. These words were chosen because they elicit the same reaction from most people. For instance, the word "dark" usually elicits the response "light." The purpose of this test is to see to what degree a given subject's responses agree with the norms of common responses. A low number of common responses has been found among schizophrenics as compared with normals. Hence, this word association test is often used as a phychiatric screening instrument.

101. **(D)** Erich Fromm believes that man has five basic needs which result from conditions of a lonely existence. Three of these needs were listed in the question. The five needs are: the need for a sense of identity; the need to feel that one belongs to society; the need to transcend animal nature as a creative human being; the need to relate to fellow beings; and the need for a stable and consistent frame of reference.

102. **(C)**   The third and highest level of morality according to Kohlberg's scheme is called the morality of self-accepted principles. This level initiates the beginning of the individual's moral standards. The child arrives at an understanding of individual rights, ideals, and principles. He can see beyond the literal interpretation of rules and laws. This level of morality is characteristic of the adolescent.

103. **(D)**   A neonate is a newborn infant. Most of the behavior of the neonate is reflexive. One significant reflexive behavior is the Palmar reflex which refers to hand grasping and occurs when an object is placed in the infant's hand. Other important reflexes are sucking, startle response, head turning and swallowing.

104. **(D)**   Rehearsal appears to serve two main functions. The first is to allow material to remain in short-term memory indefinitely. The second appears to be assisting in the transfer of information from short-term to long-term memory. The limited capacities of short-term memory affect the amount of information that can be successfully rehearsed. It is a relatively small amount of material that can be remembered and kept alive through rehearsal.

105. **(E)**   The variance of the sample of data is the mean of the squared differences from the mean of the distribution. It is expressed in equation form as:

$$s^2 = \frac{\Sigma(x_i - \bar{x})^2}{n}$$

In general terms, the variance is the measure of dispersion of scores around some measure of central tendency.

106. **(E)**   Prenatal development occurs in the following order: zygote, blastomeres, morula, blastula, early and late gastrula, endoderm, ectoderm, and finally mesoderm development. These changes in form and cell division characterize the development from zygote to embryo.

107. **(B)**   The Rosenzweig Picture Study was derived from Rosenzweig's theory of frustration and aggression, which emphasized different types of aggression and different ways of expressing aggression. The test consists of a set of cartoons in which one person frustrates another. The first person says something which provokes aggression or frustration in the second person. There is a blank space in which the second person responds to the aggression of the first person. The examinee fills in what the second person, the frustrated person, responds. This method seems to be a fairly robust measurement of attitudes and feelings concerning aggression.

108. **(B)**   David Wechsler, founder of the first adult intelligence scale wrote, "The Measurement of Adult Intelligence," in which he put forth his arguments on the nature of intelligence and its appropriate measurement in adults. He argued that intelligence is not predominantly verbal. Wechsler designed a meas-

ure of intelligence that included subsets of verbal and nonverbal performance areas.

109. **(A)**   When a test is designed to measure a theoretical idea or construct, its validity is judged by the extent to which it conforms to the requirements of the theory. Unlike predictive validity and concurrent validity, construct validity is a matter of logical analysis, not correlation.

110. **(C)**   A test is standardized by administering it to a large sample of the population on which the test is to be used. This initial group is called the standardization sample. The scores of this group provide the norms against which other individuals' scores will be compared. A key factor in the standardization sample is that the group accurately reflects the population on which further testing will be performed. If this is not strictly followed, then the norms obtained from the standardization sample will be useless.

111. **(D)**   The hierarchical theory of intelligence is basically an alternative method of organizing the factors that determine intelligence. Spearman's g-factor, which is the general intelligence factor, is placed at the top of the hierarchy. Two broad group factors, verbal-educational and practical-mechanical are at the next level. Below that are more specific group factors. Finally, on the last level, there is a multiplicity of specific factors. In many ways, the hierarchical theory of intelligence is basically an extension of Spearman's two-factor theory of intelligence.

112. **(E)**   Cattell distinguished between fluid intelligence, which refers to the ability to deal with new problems, and crystallized intelligence. Crystallized intelligence is the repertoire of information, cognitive skills and problem—solving strategies developed by the application of fluid intelligence to various areas of experience. Hence, the two are distinguished from each other, but they interact in the environment and thereby constitute intelligence. Cattell indicates that as we age, fluid intelligence drops off, but crystallized intelligence remains.

113. **(A)**   Bandura maintained that there were three types of behavior control systems, one of which is controlled by internal symbolic processes. Man has the ability to visualize or predict the outcomes and long-range consequences of various behaviors. This level of behavior is most frequently found in adults and adolescents, since it requires a certain level of maturation. Infants and pre-schoolers are not capable of setting long-range goals for themselves. Rule internalization, which is another aspect of this control system, also requires a degree of maturation.

114. **(D)**   Choice (D) is a characteristic of operant conditioning. It is not characteristic of classical conditioning. Classical conditioning is the process of substituting a conditioned stimulus for an unconditioned stimulus to evoke an innate, involuntary or previously-learned response. This procedure involves pair-

ing the conditioned stimulus with the unconditioned stimulus repeatedly. Eventually, the conditioned stimulus alone will elicit or evoke the behavior. The presence of either the CS or the UCS is needed for the behavior to occur.

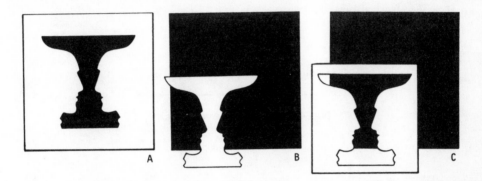

115. **(C)** The diagram depicts a serial position curve which always has this characteristic shape. Psychologists suggest that the curve is due to a primacy-recency effect. A primacy effect occurs when the items at the beginning of the list are the most easily remembered. A recency effect occurs when items near the end of the list are remembered well. When both effects occur, it is called a primacy-recency effect. It is believed that the accuracy of recalling. the last few items in a list is a result of the short-term memory store, and that recall of early items which subjects had been able to rehearse, reflects the contribution of long-term memory.

116. **(B)** Figure-ground organization was a perceptual phenomenon of great interest to the Gestalt psychologists. The background against which a stimulus is perceived is as important to figure-ground organization as is the symmetry of the stimulus. The size of different regions determines which image we will see first. Interposition cues determine whether we perceive the stimuli as having a figure-ground relationship at all. Color does not seem to be significant in the perception of figure-ground patterns as long as the figure and the ground are two different colors. Hence, the preference for white as a figure is not a significant characteristic of figure-ground organization.

117. **(E)** The McCollough Effect refers to the after-effects of strong stimulation. After looking intensely at a brightly colored light, if the gaze is directed at a smooth white surface, the same light will be seen, only in the complementary color. If the original light was red, a green light will be seen. The explanation of the effect comes from a consideration of colored-line feature detectors. Thus, if there is a complementary set of red and green line detectors, prolonged exposure to red lines would make white lines appear greenish. The McCollough Effect demonstrates the existence of two complementary systems sensitive to certain colors.

118. **(B)**   A double approach-avoidance conflict is one in which the individual is caught between two goals, both of which have positive and negative qualities. In this type of conflict, the two alternatives are usually similar. These conflicts are usually complicated and involve complex social factors which produce a great deal of frustration.

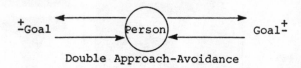

Double Approach-Avoidance

119. **(B)**   Phenylketonuria or PKU refers to a severe form of mental retardation, which is determined by a single recessive gene. PKU occurs when there is a deficiency in the enzyme that normally allows the body to metabolize the amino acid phenylalinine. When the enzyme deficiency is present, phenylalinine is converted into a toxin which damages the infant's developing nervous system. This problem can be treated by introducing a diet restricted in phenylalinine to the infant early on in its life. In this manner, the damage can be reduced or eliminated.

120. **(E)**   A test that measures primarily what a person has already learned in prior training (a uniform prior experience), is an achievement test. Achievement tests are usually administered after training in order to evaluate what the individual has gained through training. An example of a uniform prior experience is a geometry class; the New York State Regents Examination in Geometry is an achievement test given to all who have undergone the uniform prior experience of taking a geometry class in a New York State public high school.

121. **(C)**   Disturbances in motor functions are the most obvious symptoms of catatonic schizophrenia. A catatonic schizophrenic sometimes alternates between immobility and wild excitement, but the two types can also predominate. The immobile state is more common and is characterized by physical rigidity, muteness, and unresponsiveness. Despite the severity of its symptoms, catatonia is more likely than other forms of schizophrenia to "cure itself" without treatment.

122. **(E)**   Brain lesions are not characteristic of early infantile autism. Autism refers to an absorption in the self as a means of avoiding communication or escaping reality. Infantile autism, classified as one of the pervasive developmental disorders in DSM-IV, is a childhood psychosis characterized by a very early onset, extreme aloneness, language problems such as mutism, echolalia, or pronoun reversal, and bizarre behavioral responses to various aspects of the environment, such as a refusal to accept any changes in daily routine or physical setting.

123. **(B)** Eric Kandel performed many experiments with Aplysia. He traced the neural path from the touch receptors to the motor neurons that control the withdrawal response. Three types of learning were found, *habituation* — repetitive weak touch at a point leading to a decline in the response, *sensitization* — a strong stimulus leading to a prolonged facilitation of the withdrawal response, and *classical conditioning* — pairing a weaker stimulus with a stronger one, thus increasing the later effectiveness of the weak stimulus.

124. **(C)** Among several other chemical changes that take place in the neuron, there is a new protein produced which is responsible for long-term sensitization. Long-term sensitization can be prevented by drugs that block protein synthesis, whereas short-term sensitization would not be affected. Thus protein synthesis was found to be important for long-term changes in Aplysia, and there now exists evidence for the importance of protein synthesis in vertebrate learning.

125. **(B)** The Q-technique is an objective personality test which elicits a person's own analysis of his personality. In the Q-sort, used by Carl Rogers, the subject is asked to sort statements into a specified number of piles based on whether they are characteristic of his personality or not.

126. **(D)** Self-reports, such as the Q-sort, have low reliability because it is expected that the subject will try to deceive the researcher either consciously or unconsciously. The subject may give a distorted picture of himself in order to "defend" himself. He may also base his decisions on social desirability.

127. **(E)** In a true experiment, the sample should be chosen randomly and divided into groups by random assignment. It is necessary in drug research to have an experimental group and a control group in order to be able to measure the effects of the drug. The double-blind technique, assures that neither the experimenter nor the subject can affect the results, because neither knows which person is in which group.

128. **(B)** A Type I error is when one rejects the null hypothesis when it is true. A Type II error is accepting it when it is false. In this experiment the null hypothesis was that the drug was not effective. Rejecting the null hypothesis means that one's results were significant and not merely due to chance.

129. **(A)** Repression is a major defense mechanism in psychoanalytic theory. Repression describes the mechanism whereby an unpleasant or threatening thought or idea is not permitted into awareness. Repression occurs when an individual experiences a painful event and tries to forget it. He represses the experience by burying it in his unconscious mind. The unconscious mind is replete with repressed feelings toward painful experiences.

130. **(D)** The "Oedipus Complex" occurs during the phallic stage of psycho-

sexual development. It is considered a substage. The Oedipus Complex occurs due to the boy's growing sexual interest in his mother and his growing jealousy and fear of castration associated with his father.

131. **(D)** In an interval scale, numbers are arranged to order a variable in such a way that equal changes in the variable are represented by equal differences in the numbers. Reaction time is a common psychological variable which is usually treated as an interval scale. This scale has the properties of order and additivity of numbers.

132. **(A)** The dependent variable is the subject's response. It is the factor which the experimenter wants to measure, which may be affected by the independent variable. The independent variable is the variable which is manipulated by the experimenter. Hence, if the independent variable is task difficulty in a motor construction task such as a three-dimensional puzzle, the dependent variable may be construction time, i.e., how fast the subject can construct the puzzle, or it may be the number of correct pieces placed in the puzzle.

133. **(C)** Hans Eysenck developed the phenotypic and genotypic basis of personality. His theory had three levels. At the first, phenotypic level, personality types of introversion and extroversion are measured with personality inventories. At the second level, introversion and extroversion are measured with motor and conditioning task performance. At the third, genotypic level, personality is conceptualized as a physiological excitation/inhibition balance. This is considered the biological basis for personality.

134. **(B)** The Yerkes-Dodson Law is most closely related to Eysenck's phenotypic/genotypic theory of personality because both are concerned with arousal levels. Eysenck believes that the introvert/extrovert dimension of personality has an inherited basis; that it can be measured by the level of cortical arousal within a person; and that by measuring this characteristic, certain modes of behavior are predictable. The Yerkes-Dodson predictions about the relationship between arousal level and performance provide a framework in which to test the hypothesis set forth by Eysenck.

135. **(C)** According to Freud, fixation is the result of abnormal personality development. In his scheme of personality development, consisting of progressive stages, Freud stated that there is a certain amount of frustration and anxiety as the person passes from one stage to the next. If the amount of frustration and anxiety over the next stage is too great, development will halt, and the person becomes fixated at one stage. A very dependent child is an example of an early fixation preventing him from becoming independent.

136. **(B)** This choice is not a requirement for Allport's motivational theory. Allport did not like to use the term ego because he did not want to be involved in the confusion of hypothesizing the existence of an agent inside man's head that

organizes and controls the personality. He preferred to think in terms of a number of ego functions that he called propriate functions.

137. **(E)** Somatotyping is a system, developed by Sheldon, that attempts to describe personality in terms of an individual's physique. A mesomorph has a strong, muscular, and athletic physique. Their temperament or personality is generally active, energetic, and aggressive. They usually are more achievement oriented and less religious than other somatotypes. Psychopathology in this type manifests itself in delinquency, criminal behavior, and mood alterations.

138. **(D)** Habituation, extinction, and systematic desensitization are all variations on the applications of learning theory. All three contain the essential component of learning not to respond to stimuli. Habituation involves a decreased response to a stimulus because it has become familiar. Extinction involves learning not to respond to a specific stimulus that was previously learned and responded to. Systematic desensitization envolves reconditioning so that a previously learned aversive stimulus is no longer responded to with fear.

139. **(C)** The encoding specificity principle states that recall is highly dependent on the congruity between encoding and retrieval cues. Thus, even though a strong cue is better than a weak cue by itself, it is not effective at retrieval if the word was encoded with a weak cue. The uniqueness of the encoding leads to better recall.

140. **(E)** According to the encoding specificity principle, items are stored in memory the way they are first perceived. Uniqueness of the connection made between the word and the cue is very important, as is the context in which the item was presented.

141. **(D)** F.I.M. Craik is known for his research on the precision of encoding and the importance of a unique link between retrieval cues and the encoded information. Craik and Lockhart stressed the importance of depth of processing, which leads to better recall.

142. **(B)** Kohler, a well known spokesman for the Gestalt movement, interpreted the results of his experiments in terms of the whole situation. He considered problem solving a matter of reconstructing the perceptual field. He attributed the eventual success of the chimp to insight — the spontaneous seeing of relations.

143. **(A)** In problem solving, Kohler believed that the solutions came suddenly, and the insight remained a permanent possession. Thorndike held that trial-and-error behavior led to learning. Kohler outwardly criticized Thorndike's work, claiming that his experiments allowed only blind and random behavior on the part of the animal. An animal in a maze cannot see the entire pattern and so he has no choice but to engage in trial-and-error learning.

144. **(D)**   As a Gestalt theorist, Kohler held that problem solving involves restructuring the perceptual field. This can only be accomplished when the subject can view the task as a whole. He believed that true problem solving requires insight and realistic thinking.

145. **(A)**   The most important tenet of Allport's personality theory is his stress on conscious motivation. He claimed that in order to understand an individual, it is necessary to know what his conscious intentions are. Allport stressed the proprium or ego functions as being most influential in behavior. Allport regards the past as insignificant in the assessment of an individual's behavior.

146. **(A)**   In the Piagetian theory of child development, object permanence occurs at the end of the sensorimotor stage. This is a critical achievement of this early period of life. Object permanence is the awareness that objects exist outside of the child's own sensory experiences and motor manipulations and that they endure even when he neither sees them nor moves them around.

147. **(C)**   According to Adler, the central core of personality functioning is a subjectively perceived sense of inferiority for which an individual strives to compensate by gaining superiority. Because of this, an individual's life-meaning could not be fully comprehended without knowledge of the goal toward which he or she was striving. Furthermore, Adler felt that the normal, healthy individual was motivated by a goal that was related to his fellow man.

148. **(B)**   The pleasure principle is a concept originated by Freud. It is the idea that man strives to avoid pain and seek pleasure. It is on this principle that the id operates, seeking immediate gratification. The id is the most fundamental component of personality, comprising drives, needs and instinctual impulses. The id is unable to tolerate tension or to compromise and,therefore, is obedient only to the pleasure principle.

149. **(E)**   According to Piaget's theory of child development, the infant at birth has very basic schemas, such as sucking reflexes, as well as the ability to assimilate and accommodate to his environment. These later produce more complex schemas. Assimilation is the taking in of information. It eventually results in the accommodation of information. Accommodation is the adaptive modification of the child's cognitive structures in order to deal with new experiences. A schema is an organized pattern of behavior.

150. **(A)**   Allport's requirements for a theory of motivation are met by his concept of functional autonomy. The principle of functional autonomy states that a given activity or form of behavior may become an end or goal in itself, in spite of the fact that it was originally engaged for some other reason. Activities are capable of sustaining themselves without biological reinforcement. An example of this principle is Allport's explanation for the reason a man would continue to hunt animals even though he does not need them for food. Allport maintains that

the man hunts simply because he likes to hunt.

151. **(E)**   The Bem Sex Role Inventory contains 60 adjectives which are associated with strongly masculine or strongly feminine characteristics or which are applicable to either sex. Someone who finds that the more neutral adjectives apply to himself is called androgynous. This sex typing is the most positive because it contains the good qualities of both sexes. On top of having higher self-esteem, androgynous people also are more adaptable and can function well in situations which call for masculine or feminine behavior.

152. **(C)**   The MMPI (Minnesota Multiphasic Personality Inventory) is the most widely used personality test. It consists of 550 self-report "true/false" questions. Normal people answer these questions differently than psychiatric patients. Although sometimes used to assess individual differences among those with normal personalities, it is mostly used to distinguish between normal people and those with psychiatric problems.

153. **(C)**   Cutting the sensory (afferent) nerves in a limb to eliminate feedback is referred to as deafferentation. The animal loses all sensation in the affected part of the body, but the motor nerves remain totally intact.

154. **(D)**   In 1968, Taub and Berman cut all the afferent nerves from one arm of a monkey, after which the animal did not spontaneously use the limb for anything. However, when the afferent nerves of both forelimbs were cut, the monkey recovered use of both. It was concluded that if one forelimb is deafferented, the monkey does not use it only because it is easier to use the normal limb alone. When both are deafferented, the monkey is forced to use both, thus showing that voluntary movements are still possible after sensory feedback has been greatly reduced.

155. **(C)**   The basal ganglia, which consists of the caudate nucleus, the putamen, and the globus pallidus, are important for slow, gradual movements that can be modified by sensory feedback while the movement is occurring. Damage to the basal ganglia can lead to Parkinson's disease, a progressive deterioration of walking, standing, and other movements of the body as a whole.

156. **(B)**   Genotype refers to the genetic constitution of an organism. The phenotype refers to the observable characteristics of an organism, or the extent to which its potential is realized.

157. **(B)**   The genotype, nature, does not set fixed genetic limits for behavior. Limits do not exist because the genotype must act through the environment to produce a particular behavior. Nature or inheritance sets the potentialities for behavior, and nurture or the environment determines the extent to which potentialities will be realized. A deprived environment can greatly retard intellectual development, and an enriched environment can enhance intellectual abilities.

158. **(C)**   The WISC-R is known to have good validity as a measure of intelligence. If the new intelligence test has only a +. 25 correlation with the WISC-R, it has low concurrent validity. Concurrent validity refers to whether or not test scores are related to some already available criterion measure, in this case the WISC-R. There is a relatively low correlation and, therefore, a poor relationship between these two measures.

159. **(E)**   A response measure (also called the dependent variable) need not be adaptable to a wide variety of experiments. Each research chooses the response measure most appropriate for a specific study of the behavior. Observability, numerical transformability, and economic feasibility are all important considerations for a specific response measure.

160. **(A)**   In comparison with other measures of central tendency, the mean is the most consistent measure. If you take large independent sets of data and analyze the measures of central tendency, the mean varies less from data set to set than do other measures of central tendency. Therefore, the mean is more consistent as a measure over many data sets and is the most commonly used of all the measures of central tendency.

161. **(D)**   The actual content of the questions in a test should not affect the reliability of the test as long as the questions remain the same over testing periods. If questions change, the content changes and essentially, you have a different test with different reliability measures. The five factors that do affect reliability are: test length, test-retest interval, variability of scores, guessing, and variation within a test situation.

162. **(D)**   A Z score is a type of standard score with a mean of 0 and a variance of 1. In general, standard scores are raw scores that have been transformed into a normal distribution with a specific mean and standard deviation. The Z scores express how far scores lie from the mean in terms of the standard deviation.

163. **(B)**   Most psychologists today believe that aggression is a learned behavior. Bandura, a social learning theorist, studied the effects of modeling on aggression. Modeling is simply a process whereby a person learns a new behavior by watching another person engage in it. He found that children exposed to aggressive models (either live, filmed or cartoon) were significantly more likely to demonstrate aggressive behavior than those not exposed to aggressive models. He also found that reward contingencies played a very important role in the effectiveness of model learning.

164. **(E)**   Freud originally introduced this idea in his psychoanalytic theory in the 1930s. Today this approach to aggressive behavior has been most supported by the work of Lorenz. Lorenz is an ethologist — that is, one who studies the behavior of animals in their natural habitat. He believes that because humans use

their intelligence to aggress, they have never developed natural controls on aggression against their own species.

165. **(D)** Festinger (1954) proposed that all people have a drive to evaluate themselves. In situations lacking in objective, nonsocial means of evaluation, people evaluate themselves by comparison with other people. This is Social Comparison Theory. Much research has been performed using this phenomenon, most notably, Stanley Schachter's studies on emotion and affiliation.

166. **(B)** The closer two individuals are geographically, the more likely it is that they will like each other. A repeated finding concerning mate selection is that individuals find mates who live close to them. Another function of proximity is that it makes possible the operation of other factors that can increase attraction, such as attitude similarity.

167. **(D)** Through the process of factor analysis, the number of underlying factors in a test can be determined. If only one factor underlies the performance on all the test items, the test is considered homogeneous. All scores can be attributed to the single factor being assessed.

168. **(E)** Equal intervals and an absolute zero point characterize ratio scales. Weight is an example of a measurement mode on a ratio scale. There is an absolute 0 (no weight) and equal intervals can be spoken of 50 pounds compared to 100 pounds. This might be useful in the measurement and observation of feeding behaviors in animals and humans.

169. **(C)** The membrane of a neuron is selectively permeable. Potassium ions and chloride ions cross the membrane less easily than water, and sodium ions cross with still more difficulty. The inside of the neuron has an electrical potential slightly negative with respect to the outside. This resting potential is about –70 millivolts.

170. **(D)** When the nerve cell is stimulated, the cell becomes less negative. If a charge of about +10 millivolts is reached, we say that the "threshold" has been reached. Positive charges (sodium ions) can now rush into the cell, and the cell becomes positive relative to its surroundings — it has been depolarized.

171. **(B)** The sodium-potassium pump is important for maintaining the negative charge inside the neuron. Sodium is heavily concentrated outside the cell and should, like potassium, be strongly attracted by the negative charge inside the neuron. However, the pump actively transports sodium ions out of the cell, while simultaneously drawing potassium ions into the cell. The potassium can then diffuse out again more freely than the sodium can diffuse back in, thus promoting a net movement of positive ions out of the cell.

172. **(C)** An action potential is also referred to as a depolarization. Accord-

ing to the all-or-none law, all action potentials within a given cell are approximately equal in size and shape. The size and shape are independent of the intensity of the stimulus that initiated the action potential.

173. **(C)** The hysterical personality type is a type of personality disorder. A personality or character disorder is on the borderline between normal and neurotic behavior. Schizophrenia and manic-depression are forms of psychosis and are severe mental disorders. Neuroses can be treated using psychotherapy. Individuals with personality disorders are able to meet the demands of life and usually do not seek therapeutic treatment. The hysterical personality type is often found in young women and is characterized by high excitability, self-centeredness, lack of stability and coquettish behavior with a nonresponsive frigidity underlying the flirting.

174. **(A)** Cognitive restructuring is a technique of behavior modification which attempts to manipulate the thinking and reasoning processes of the patient. The other four choices are part of Carl Rogers' client-centered therapy. This therapy is as non-directive as possible so that the client can develop his own solutions to problems. It is important to form a realistic self-image. The Q-technique, developed by Rogers, is a method of systematically analyzing a person's attitudes about anything. It measures a person's opinion about himself.

175. **(D)** The MMPI is an objective personality test which consists of 550 statements to which the subject is to answer "true," "false," or "cannot say" with respect to himself. The TAT, Rorschach, word-association, and Draw-a-person tests are projective personality tests which are unstructured and thus demand originality.

176. **(D)** The current theory on REM (rapid eye movement) sleep is that there are certain locus coeruleus neurons that steadily inhibit FTG neurons. Right before REM sleep, they decrease their activity, thus removing inhibition from the FTG cells. The FTG cells produce the rapid eye movements and desynchronization of the EEG characteristic of this stage of sleep. At the end of REM sleep, the locus coeruleus cells continue their usual activity inhibiting the FTG cells. This implies that damage to the locus coeruleus causes an increase in REM sleep time because of decreased inhibition of the FTG cells; however, this sleep lacks the normal muscle relaxation.

177. **(D)** REM sleep is known as paradoxical sleep because although the EEG pattern resembles wakefulness, the person is more difficult to awaken than in any other stage. The EEG is desynchronized, thus the term desynchronized sleep. It is also known as active sleep.

178. **(B)** The reticular formation is critical for wakefulness and alertness. The input and output of the reticular formation are diffuse. The area appears more irregular and disorderly than most of the rest of the brain. Any strong

stimulation activates the system and thus diffusely activates the entire cerebral cortex.

179. **(E)**　Our vestibular organs provide us with a sense of balance. They do this through information about the movements and position of the head. There are two groups of vestibular organs. These are the semicircular canals and the otolith organs, both located in the inner ear. The three semicircular canals are fluid filled and respond to the changes in rate of motion of the head. The otolith organs are small stone-like crystals which respond to the actual position of one's head.

180. **(E)**　Morality and conscience are conceptually defined as the superego functions. The superego represents the taboos and mores or rules of the society in which the child lives. It may encompass religious rules as well. The process by which the child learns cultural norms and identifies with them is called socialization. Hence, the development of the superego represents the socialization functions in the child.

181. **(D)**　Nominal scaling is the assignment of numbers to groups as names, used to distinguish between logically separated groups. For example, one can assign the numbers 1, 2, and 3 to Democrats, Republicans, and Independents, respectively, but there is no continuous relationship between them as in interval data, nor is there a particular rank order as in ordinal data.

182. **(E)**　According to Freudian theory, the libido invested in the ego is called narcissistic libido. The formation of narcissistic libido is a normal part of the ego's development. In developing out of the id, the ego takes a share of the libidinal energy for itself. To the extent that the ego has the libido invested in itself, it is called narcissistic and is a form of self love.

183. **(D)**　The "hoarding orientation," one of four pathological dynamic styles identified by Fromm, is characterized by the need to save and possess. This orientation involves the perception of the outside world as threatening, which leads to distrust of and rigidity toward people. The hoarding person tends to be frugal, miserly, letting out as little as possible of both material things and emotions.

184. **(B)**　Acquired or secondary motives do not have inherently reinforcing or motivating properties; they must be learned through a process of secondary reinforcement. For example, money is a secondary source of drive learned in this way. Money is associated with primary reinforcers like food and shelter. It therefore becomes a secondary or acquired motive, independent of what it can buy.

185. **(D)**　Karen Horney postulated ten different neurotic needs which could all be reduced to three categories of neurotic styles. They are: 1) a movement toward people, indicating a need for love; 2) a movement away from people,

indicating a need for independence; and 3) a movement against people, indicating a need for power.

186. **(B)** Of the theorists in the neo-Freudian movement, it was Adler who placed the emphasis on the relationship between personality and birth order. He believed that the oldest, middle, and youngest children have very different social experiences resulting in different personality formations. The eldest child is believed to feel "dethroned" upon the birth of a sibling. This leads to lifelong feelings of insecurity and hostility. The middle child is believed to be very ambitious and have a tendency for jealousy. The youngest child is most likely to be spoiled and to have a lifelong behavior problem.

187. **(C)** The median represents the 50th percentile and the third quartile represents the 75th percentile. Therefore, 25% of the scores fall between the median and third quartile. Check a normal distribution curve for these figures and their relative positions.

188. **(B)** A cross-sectional study is one in which different subjects at different developmental levels are compared. For example, instead of using a longitudinal approach to a study, a researcher could investigate language development by comparing the linguistic ability of different groups of children at different stages of development. This approach would certainly hasten the study and reduce the cost of studying language development as compared to using the longitudinal approach, which takes years.

189. **(D)** The mean is not appropriate here since only one rat took longer than 4.79 minutes. This rat actually took 30 minutes, thus the mean was distorted. The median or mode describes this set of data much more appropriately.

190. **(C)** When the times are arranged in order from lowest to highest, the median, which is the middle number in an array, turns out to be 1.5. 0.9, 1.0, 1.0, 1.25, 1.5, 2.0, 2.5, 3.0, 30.0.

191. **(A)** Gordon Allport's personality theory stresses conscious motivation. In order to understand an individual, it is necessary to know what his conscious intentions are. Unlike the Freudians and the behaviorists, Allport does not see the past as significant to the assessment of a person's behavior. The personality structure is represented by common traits and individual traits, which are responsible for a person's uniqueness.

192. **(D)** Allport's approach to psychology is humanistic, as opposed to scientific. He does not believe in the application of scientific principles to psychology. His approach puts emphasis on the importance of personal dispositions as the foremost determinants of behavior.

193. **(C)** According to Allport, a theory of human motivation must acknowl-

edge the contemporaneity of motives. People are not motivated by their past experiences. The theory must also be pluralistic, allowing for several motives to occur simultaneously. An individual's conscious motives (wishes, aspirations) are keys to his present behavior. Allport's concept of functional autonomy states that activities may be capable of sustaining themselves without biological reinforcement. For example, a man can continue to hunt even though he does not need to in order to get food. Thus an activity becomes a goal in itself.

194. **(D)** Classical conditioning involves the repeated pairing of some conditioned stimulus with the unconditioned stimulus. After a while, the conditioned stimulus, when presented alone, will elicit the unconditioned response. Thus, the conditioned response is basically the same as the unconditioned response. It is elicited by the unconditioned stimulus before and after conditioning, and by the previously neutral stimulus after conditioning.

195. **(E)** Classical conditioning is the learning of a response to a particular stimulus which previously could not elicit that response. It does not involve reward and punishment as does discrimination learning, and it does not result in behaviors which produce an effect on the environment as does operant conditioning. The two stimuli are not always presented simultaneously. The most significant kind of learning for human beings is verbal learning.

196. **(B)** In forward conditioning, the onset of the CS (conditioned stimulus), precedes the onset of the UCS (unconditioned stimulus). This results in strong CS-produced responses. There are two types of forward conditioning. Delayed conditioning involves presentation of the CS for more than five seconds before the start of the UCS. Trace conditioning involves the termination of the CS prior to the onset of the UCS.

197. **(D)** J.B. Watson expanded Pavlov's work. He applied conditioning principles to emotions, mental disease, language, and learning. In his theory, complex learning was considered to be the chaining of conditioned reflexes.

198. **(A)** When alone against the majority, approximately 35%, (about $1/_3$) of the real subjects chose to give an obviously incorrect, but conforming, response. A shows the response when there was no opposition, and B shows the response when there was one other person against the majority. It has been a consistent finding in social psychology that people conform one-third of the time to the opinion of a unanimous majority. However, if the subject even has just one ally, his probability of conforming to the majority is sharply reduced.

199. **(E)** Three personality characteristics that have proven to be predictive of conformity behavior are:
1) An authoritarian person is greatly influenced by authority figures; thus, the more authoritarian a person is the more he or she will conform.
2) People who believe that the circumstances of life are under their control

are called "internals," while those that feel that what happens to them is beyond their control are "externals." "Externals" are more likely to conform than "internals."

3) People who are high in need for approval conform more than people who are low in this need.

200. **(C)** Controlling factors of conformity include whether or not the opinion of the majority is unanimous, whether or not the group consists of the subjects' friends or of experts or peers, and the self-esteem of the subjects. The desire to give the correct answer is not a factor since subjects will choose an obviously incorrect answer so as to avoid group rejection.

201. **(D)** Grammar, which includes syntax, refers to the rules used to connect meaningful phases.

202. **(B)** The branch of psychology concerned with language development and use is psycholinguistics. How we speak is indicative of how we think. To study language is to explore brain logic and function.

203. **(A)** Morphology is the study of how particular sounds are related to the meanings that they convey.

204. **(B)** Ethology is the study of the instincts, habits, mating rituals, and other behaviors of animals. The ethologists insist that the natural environment provides complex cues for a species that are sacrificed under laboratory conditions.

205. **(A)** An ethologist would catalog the feeding, mating, nesting, and other vital behaviors of a species in their natural habitat. From this information he/she would a catalog of the species behavior, an ethogram.

206. **(C)** Fixed action patterns refer to instinctive behaviors that are triggered by environmental cues. The "bee dance" which signals to other bees the position and distance of pollen; particular mating rituals of elk and various species of fish are examples of FAPs.

207. **(E)** Sociometry refers to the study of the organization and hierarchial structure of small groups. It is concerned with the position various people play in the group.

208. **(C)** Social psychologists study how the individual is affected by the group. They would be interested in how peer pressure influences the individual. Sociologists, on the other hand, are interested in group behavior.

209. **(D)** Zimbardo set up a mock prison, complete with bars, in the basement of the college. Student volunteers were assigned roles as "prisoners" or

"guards," and wore the appropriate uniforms. Zimbardo wanted to assess the effects of the prison environment on personality. The experiment had to be cancelled after a few days because the prisoners had become morose or rebellious, and the guards were beginning to act sadistically.

210. **(E)** Aggression is defined as behavior intended to hurt living things for purposes other than survival, or the destruction of property. Instrumental aggression refers to cases where aggression is socially sanctioned, such as a fireman breaking down a door.

211. **(C)** In psychoanalysis, all problems stem from unresolved childhood conflicts and subconscious influences. Dreams are an avenue for the subconscious to manifest itself on the conscious mind. Choice (A) is the humanistic approach. The other choices are from the behavioral approach to therapy.

212. **(A)** Aversion therapy pairs unpleasant outcomes with undesirable behavior. Rapid smoking is one form. A smoker has one cigarette after another until he or she feels sick. They learn to associate cigarettes with illness. Alcoholics are given a drug (antabuse) that makes them ill if they have an alcoholic beverage. They learn to avoid alcohol.

213. **(D)** Children are not miniature adults. They often respond to drugs differently than adults. Stimulants, which make adults hyper, act like tranquilizers on children. Hence, they are prescribed for hyperactivity.

214. **(B)** The patient lying on the couch, speaking freely about any subject, is the technique called free association. It is believed that he or she will reveal important facts in their dialogue.

215. **(E)** An industrial psychologist works to improve performance in the work place.

216. **(B)** Sports' psychologists have no power over the rules of any sport. They analyze a player's performance and devise methods, some physical, some psychological, to aid the player in improving his or her game.

217. **(E)** A parapsychologist studies all paranormal phenomana. That includes clairvoyance (perceiving objects from a distance), precognition (seeing the future), telepathy (mind reading), and psychokinesis (moving objects with the mind).

The Graduate Record Examination in

PSYCHOLOGY

Test 4

Test 4 is also on CD-ROM as part of REA's exclusive interactive GRE Psychology TEST*ware*®. We recommend that you take the computerized exam first. This will give you the additional study features and benefits of enforced timed conditions, individual diagnostic analysis, and instantaneous scoring. See page vi for guidance on how to get the most out of our GRE Psychology book and software.

THE GRADUATE RECORD EXAMINATION
PSYCHOLOGY TEST 4
ANSWER SHEET

1. Ⓐ Ⓑ Ⓒ Ⓓ Ⓔ
2. Ⓐ Ⓑ Ⓒ Ⓓ Ⓔ
3. Ⓐ Ⓑ Ⓒ Ⓓ Ⓔ
4. Ⓐ Ⓑ Ⓒ Ⓓ Ⓔ
5. Ⓐ Ⓑ Ⓒ Ⓓ Ⓔ
6. Ⓐ Ⓑ Ⓒ Ⓓ Ⓔ
7. Ⓐ Ⓑ Ⓒ Ⓓ Ⓔ
8. Ⓐ Ⓑ Ⓒ Ⓓ Ⓔ
9. Ⓐ Ⓑ Ⓒ Ⓓ Ⓔ
10. Ⓐ Ⓑ Ⓒ Ⓓ Ⓔ
11. Ⓐ Ⓑ Ⓒ Ⓓ Ⓔ
12. Ⓐ Ⓑ Ⓒ Ⓓ Ⓔ
13. Ⓐ Ⓑ Ⓒ Ⓓ Ⓔ
14. Ⓐ Ⓑ Ⓒ Ⓓ Ⓔ
15. Ⓐ Ⓑ Ⓒ Ⓓ Ⓔ
16. Ⓐ Ⓑ Ⓒ Ⓓ Ⓔ
17. Ⓐ Ⓑ Ⓒ Ⓓ Ⓔ
18. Ⓐ Ⓑ Ⓒ Ⓓ Ⓔ
19. Ⓐ Ⓑ Ⓒ Ⓓ Ⓔ
20. Ⓐ Ⓑ Ⓒ Ⓓ Ⓔ
21. Ⓐ Ⓑ Ⓒ Ⓓ Ⓔ
22. Ⓐ Ⓑ Ⓒ Ⓓ Ⓔ
23. Ⓐ Ⓑ Ⓒ Ⓓ Ⓔ
24. Ⓐ Ⓑ Ⓒ Ⓓ Ⓔ
25. Ⓟ Ⓑ Ⓨ Ⓓ Ⓔ
26. Ⓐ Ⓑ Ⓒ Ⓓ Ⓔ
27. Ⓐ Ⓑ Ⓒ Ⓓ Ⓔ
28. Ⓐ Ⓑ Ⓒ Ⓓ Ⓔ
29. Ⓐ Ⓑ Ⓒ Ⓓ Ⓔ
30. Ⓐ Ⓑ Ⓒ Ⓓ Ⓔ
31. Ⓐ Ⓑ Ⓒ Ⓓ Ⓔ
32. Ⓐ Ⓑ Ⓒ Ⓓ Ⓔ
33. Ⓐ Ⓑ Ⓒ Ⓓ Ⓔ

34. Ⓐ Ⓑ Ⓒ Ⓓ Ⓔ
35. Ⓐ Ⓑ Ⓒ Ⓓ Ⓔ
36. Ⓐ Ⓑ Ⓒ Ⓓ Ⓔ
37. Ⓐ Ⓑ Ⓒ Ⓓ Ⓔ
38. Ⓐ Ⓑ Ⓒ Ⓓ Ⓔ
39. Ⓐ Ⓑ Ⓒ Ⓓ Ⓔ
40. Ⓐ Ⓑ Ⓒ Ⓓ Ⓔ
41. Ⓐ Ⓑ Ⓒ Ⓓ Ⓔ
42. Ⓐ Ⓑ Ⓒ Ⓓ Ⓔ
43. Ⓐ Ⓑ Ⓒ Ⓓ Ⓔ
44. Ⓐ Ⓑ Ⓒ Ⓓ Ⓔ
45. Ⓐ Ⓑ Ⓒ Ⓓ Ⓔ
46. Ⓐ Ⓑ Ⓒ Ⓓ Ⓔ
47. Ⓐ Ⓑ Ⓒ Ⓓ Ⓔ
48. Ⓐ Ⓑ Ⓒ Ⓓ Ⓔ
49. Ⓐ Ⓑ Ⓒ Ⓓ Ⓔ
50. Ⓐ Ⓑ Ⓒ Ⓓ Ⓔ
51. Ⓐ Ⓑ Ⓒ Ⓓ Ⓔ
52. Ⓐ Ⓑ Ⓒ Ⓓ Ⓔ
53. Ⓐ Ⓑ Ⓒ Ⓓ Ⓔ
54. Ⓐ Ⓑ Ⓒ Ⓓ Ⓔ
55. Ⓐ Ⓑ Ⓒ Ⓓ Ⓔ
56. Ⓐ Ⓑ Ⓒ Ⓓ Ⓔ
57. Ⓐ Ⓑ Ⓒ Ⓓ Ⓔ
58. Ⓐ Ⓑ Ⓒ Ⓓ Ⓔ
59. Ⓐ Ⓑ Ⓒ Ⓓ Ⓔ
60. Ⓐ Ⓑ Ⓒ Ⓓ Ⓔ
61. Ⓐ Ⓑ Ⓒ Ⓓ Ⓔ
62. Ⓐ Ⓑ Ⓒ Ⓓ Ⓔ
63. Ⓐ Ⓑ Ⓒ Ⓓ Ⓔ
64. Ⓐ Ⓑ Ⓒ Ⓓ Ⓔ
65. Ⓐ Ⓑ Ⓒ Ⓓ Ⓔ
66. Ⓐ Ⓑ Ⓒ Ⓓ Ⓔ

67. Ⓐ Ⓑ Ⓒ Ⓓ Ⓔ
68. Ⓐ Ⓑ Ⓒ Ⓓ Ⓔ
69. Ⓐ Ⓑ Ⓒ Ⓓ Ⓔ
70. Ⓐ Ⓑ Ⓒ Ⓓ Ⓔ
71. Ⓐ Ⓑ Ⓒ Ⓓ Ⓔ
72. Ⓐ Ⓑ Ⓒ Ⓓ Ⓔ
73. Ⓐ Ⓑ Ⓒ Ⓓ Ⓔ
74. Ⓐ Ⓑ Ⓒ Ⓓ Ⓔ
75. Ⓐ Ⓑ Ⓒ Ⓓ Ⓔ
76. Ⓐ Ⓑ Ⓒ Ⓓ Ⓔ
77. Ⓐ Ⓑ Ⓒ Ⓓ Ⓔ
78. Ⓐ Ⓑ Ⓒ Ⓓ Ⓔ
79. Ⓐ Ⓑ Ⓒ Ⓓ Ⓔ
80. Ⓐ Ⓑ Ⓒ Ⓓ Ⓔ
81. Ⓐ Ⓑ Ⓒ Ⓓ Ⓔ
82. Ⓐ Ⓑ Ⓒ Ⓓ Ⓔ
83. Ⓐ Ⓑ Ⓒ Ⓓ Ⓔ
84. Ⓐ Ⓑ Ⓒ Ⓓ Ⓔ
85. Ⓐ Ⓑ Ⓒ Ⓓ Ⓔ
86. Ⓐ Ⓑ Ⓒ Ⓓ Ⓔ
87. Ⓐ Ⓑ Ⓒ Ⓓ Ⓔ
88. Ⓐ Ⓑ Ⓒ Ⓓ Ⓔ
89. Ⓐ Ⓑ Ⓒ Ⓓ Ⓔ
90. Ⓐ Ⓑ Ⓒ Ⓓ Ⓔ
91. Ⓐ Ⓑ Ⓒ Ⓓ Ⓔ
92. Ⓐ Ⓑ Ⓒ Ⓓ Ⓔ
93. Ⓐ Ⓑ Ⓒ Ⓓ Ⓔ
94. Ⓐ Ⓑ Ⓒ Ⓓ Ⓔ
95. Ⓐ Ⓑ Ⓒ Ⓓ Ⓔ
96. Ⓐ Ⓑ Ⓒ Ⓓ Ⓔ
97. Ⓐ Ⓑ Ⓒ Ⓓ Ⓔ
98. Ⓐ Ⓑ Ⓒ Ⓓ Ⓔ
99. Ⓐ Ⓑ Ⓒ Ⓓ Ⓔ

100. Ⓐ Ⓑ Ⓒ Ⓓ Ⓔ	140. Ⓐ Ⓑ Ⓒ Ⓓ Ⓔ	180. Ⓐ Ⓑ Ⓒ Ⓓ Ⓔ
101. Ⓐ Ⓑ Ⓒ Ⓓ Ⓔ	141. Ⓐ Ⓑ Ⓒ Ⓓ Ⓔ	181. Ⓐ Ⓑ Ⓒ Ⓓ Ⓔ
102. Ⓐ Ⓑ Ⓒ Ⓓ Ⓔ	142. Ⓐ Ⓑ Ⓒ Ⓓ Ⓔ	182. Ⓐ Ⓑ Ⓒ Ⓓ Ⓔ
103. Ⓐ Ⓑ Ⓒ Ⓓ Ⓔ	143. Ⓐ Ⓑ Ⓒ Ⓓ Ⓔ	183. Ⓐ Ⓑ Ⓒ Ⓓ Ⓔ
104. Ⓐ Ⓑ Ⓒ Ⓓ Ⓔ	144. Ⓐ Ⓑ Ⓒ Ⓓ Ⓔ	184. Ⓐ Ⓑ Ⓒ Ⓓ Ⓔ
105. Ⓐ Ⓑ Ⓒ Ⓓ Ⓔ	145. Ⓐ Ⓑ Ⓒ Ⓓ Ⓔ	185. Ⓐ Ⓑ Ⓒ Ⓓ Ⓔ
106. Ⓐ Ⓑ Ⓒ Ⓓ Ⓔ	146. Ⓐ Ⓑ Ⓒ Ⓓ Ⓔ	186. Ⓐ Ⓑ Ⓒ Ⓓ Ⓔ
107. Ⓐ Ⓑ Ⓒ Ⓓ Ⓔ	147. Ⓐ Ⓑ Ⓒ Ⓓ Ⓔ	187. Ⓐ Ⓑ Ⓒ Ⓓ Ⓔ
108. Ⓐ Ⓑ Ⓒ Ⓓ Ⓔ	148. Ⓐ Ⓑ Ⓒ Ⓓ Ⓔ	188. Ⓐ Ⓑ Ⓒ Ⓓ Ⓔ
109. Ⓐ Ⓑ Ⓒ Ⓓ Ⓔ	149. Ⓐ Ⓑ Ⓒ Ⓓ Ⓔ	189. Ⓐ Ⓑ Ⓒ Ⓓ Ⓔ
110. Ⓐ Ⓑ Ⓒ Ⓓ Ⓔ	150. Ⓐ Ⓑ Ⓒ Ⓓ Ⓔ	190. Ⓐ Ⓑ Ⓒ Ⓓ Ⓔ
111. Ⓐ Ⓑ Ⓒ Ⓓ Ⓔ	151. Ⓐ Ⓑ Ⓒ Ⓓ Ⓔ	191. Ⓐ Ⓑ Ⓒ Ⓓ Ⓔ
112. Ⓐ Ⓑ Ⓒ Ⓓ Ⓔ	152. Ⓐ Ⓑ Ⓒ Ⓓ Ⓔ	192. Ⓐ Ⓑ Ⓒ Ⓓ Ⓔ
113. Ⓐ Ⓑ Ⓒ Ⓓ Ⓔ	153. Ⓐ Ⓑ Ⓒ Ⓓ Ⓔ	193. Ⓐ Ⓑ Ⓒ Ⓓ Ⓔ
114. Ⓐ Ⓑ Ⓒ Ⓓ Ⓔ	154. Ⓐ Ⓑ Ⓒ Ⓓ Ⓔ	194. Ⓐ Ⓑ Ⓒ Ⓓ Ⓔ
115. Ⓐ Ⓑ Ⓒ Ⓓ Ⓔ	155. Ⓐ Ⓑ Ⓒ Ⓓ Ⓔ	195. Ⓐ Ⓑ Ⓒ Ⓓ Ⓔ
116. Ⓐ Ⓑ Ⓒ Ⓓ Ⓔ	156. Ⓐ Ⓑ Ⓒ Ⓓ Ⓔ	196. Ⓐ Ⓑ Ⓒ Ⓓ Ⓔ
117. Ⓐ Ⓑ Ⓒ Ⓓ Ⓔ	157. Ⓐ Ⓑ Ⓒ Ⓓ Ⓔ	197. Ⓐ Ⓑ Ⓒ Ⓓ Ⓔ
118. Ⓐ Ⓑ Ⓒ Ⓓ Ⓔ	158. Ⓐ Ⓑ Ⓒ Ⓓ Ⓔ	198. Ⓐ Ⓑ Ⓒ Ⓓ Ⓔ
119. Ⓐ Ⓑ Ⓒ Ⓓ Ⓔ	159. Ⓐ Ⓑ Ⓒ Ⓓ Ⓔ	199. Ⓐ Ⓑ Ⓒ Ⓓ Ⓔ
120. Ⓐ Ⓑ Ⓒ Ⓓ Ⓔ	160. Ⓐ Ⓑ Ⓒ Ⓓ Ⓔ	200. Ⓐ Ⓑ Ⓒ Ⓓ Ⓔ
121. Ⓐ Ⓑ Ⓒ Ⓓ Ⓔ	161. Ⓐ Ⓑ Ⓒ Ⓓ Ⓔ	201. Ⓐ Ⓑ Ⓒ Ⓓ Ⓔ
122. Ⓐ Ⓑ Ⓒ Ⓓ Ⓔ	162. Ⓐ Ⓑ Ⓒ Ⓓ Ⓔ	202. Ⓐ Ⓑ Ⓒ Ⓓ Ⓔ
123. Ⓐ Ⓑ Ⓒ Ⓓ Ⓔ	163. Ⓐ Ⓑ Ⓒ Ⓓ Ⓔ	203. Ⓐ Ⓑ Ⓒ Ⓓ Ⓔ
124. Ⓐ Ⓑ Ⓒ Ⓓ Ⓔ	164. Ⓐ Ⓑ Ⓒ Ⓓ Ⓔ	204. Ⓐ Ⓑ Ⓒ Ⓓ Ⓔ
125. Ⓐ Ⓑ Ⓒ Ⓓ Ⓔ	165. Ⓐ Ⓑ Ⓒ Ⓓ Ⓔ	205. Ⓐ Ⓑ Ⓒ Ⓓ Ⓔ
126. Ⓐ Ⓑ Ⓒ Ⓓ Ⓔ	166. Ⓐ Ⓑ Ⓒ Ⓓ Ⓔ	206. Ⓐ Ⓑ Ⓒ Ⓓ Ⓔ
127. Ⓐ Ⓑ Ⓒ Ⓓ Ⓔ	167. Ⓐ Ⓑ Ⓒ Ⓓ Ⓔ	207. Ⓐ Ⓑ Ⓒ Ⓓ Ⓔ
128. Ⓐ Ⓑ Ⓒ Ⓓ Ⓔ	168. Ⓐ Ⓑ Ⓒ Ⓓ Ⓔ	208. Ⓐ Ⓑ Ⓒ Ⓓ Ⓔ
129. Ⓐ Ⓑ Ⓒ Ⓓ Ⓔ	169. Ⓐ Ⓑ Ⓒ Ⓓ Ⓔ	209. Ⓐ Ⓑ Ⓒ Ⓓ Ⓔ
130. Ⓐ Ⓑ Ⓒ Ⓓ Ⓔ	170. Ⓐ Ⓑ Ⓒ Ⓓ Ⓔ	210. Ⓐ Ⓑ Ⓒ Ⓓ Ⓔ
131. Ⓐ Ⓑ Ⓒ Ⓓ Ⓔ	171. Ⓐ Ⓑ Ⓒ Ⓓ Ⓔ	211. Ⓐ Ⓑ Ⓒ Ⓓ Ⓔ
132. Ⓐ Ⓑ Ⓒ Ⓓ Ⓔ	172. Ⓐ Ⓑ Ⓒ Ⓓ Ⓔ	212. Ⓐ Ⓑ Ⓒ Ⓓ Ⓔ
133. Ⓐ Ⓑ Ⓒ Ⓓ Ⓔ	173. Ⓐ Ⓑ Ⓒ Ⓓ Ⓔ	213. Ⓐ Ⓑ Ⓒ Ⓓ Ⓔ
134. Ⓐ Ⓑ Ⓒ Ⓓ Ⓔ	174. Ⓐ Ⓑ Ⓒ Ⓓ Ⓔ	214. Ⓐ Ⓑ Ⓒ Ⓓ Ⓔ
135. Ⓐ Ⓑ Ⓒ Ⓓ Ⓔ	175. Ⓐ Ⓑ Ⓒ Ⓓ Ⓔ	215. Ⓐ Ⓑ Ⓒ Ⓓ Ⓔ
136. Ⓐ Ⓑ Ⓒ Ⓓ Ⓔ	176. Ⓐ Ⓑ Ⓒ Ⓓ Ⓔ	216. Ⓐ Ⓑ Ⓒ Ⓓ Ⓔ
137. Ⓐ Ⓑ Ⓒ Ⓓ Ⓔ	177. Ⓐ Ⓑ Ⓒ Ⓓ Ⓔ	217. Ⓐ Ⓑ Ⓒ Ⓓ Ⓔ
138. Ⓐ Ⓑ Ⓒ Ⓓ Ⓔ	178. Ⓐ Ⓑ Ⓒ Ⓓ Ⓔ	
139. Ⓐ Ⓑ Ⓒ Ⓓ Ⓔ	179. Ⓐ Ⓑ Ⓒ Ⓓ Ⓔ	

GRE

PSYCHOLOGY TEST 4

TIME: 170 Minutes
217 Questions

DIRECTIONS: Choose the best answer for each question and mark the letter of your selection on the corresponding answer sheet.

---

1. A person threatened by his own fascination with pornography becomes an advocate of censorship. This is an example of the defense mechanism known as

    (A) projection.   (B) displacement.

    (C) reaction formation.   (D) compensation.

    (E) sublimation.

2. Suspicious and rigid thinking are most characteristic of

    (A) depression.   (B) autism.

    (C) paranoia.   (D) histrionic personality.

    (E) character disorder.

3. In a positively skewed distribution, the median is

    (A) larger than the mode.   (B) larger than the mean.

    (C) equal to the mean.   (D) negatively skewed.

    (E) equal to the mode.

4. The ability to withstand conflict is considered a guard against

    (A) conflict resolution.   (B) conversion reaction.

    (C) developing neurosis.   (D) all of the above

    (E) none of the above

5. A prominent characteristic of paranoid schizophrenia is

    (A) delusions of grandeur.   (B) flat affect.

(C)   disorganized speech.   (D)   disorganized behavior.

(E)   echolalia.

6.   Defense mechanisms are created by the

(A)   id.   (B)   ego.

(C)   superego.   (D)   repression.

(E)   eros instinct.

7.   Which of the following is NOT characteristic of sociopathy?

(A)   low intelligence   (B)   no sense of responsibility

(C)   lack of genuine insight   (D)   unconventional sex life

(E)   antisocial behavior without regret

8.   To Freud, dreams represented attempts at

(A)   conflict release.   (B)   control of the id.

(C)   preconscious expression.   (D)   wish fulfillment.

(E)   control of the ego.

9.   Which of the following choices best describes a sociogram?

(A)   an open-ended test in which subjects describe social goals

(B)   a test that asks the subject to specify reasons for social choices and rejections

(C)   a diagram that exposes the social structure of a group

(D)   both (A) and (B)

(E)   none of the above

10.   Interpretation of the Thematic Apperception Test (TAT) is usually

(A)   factor analysis.   (B)   content analysis.

(C)   quantitative analysis.   (D)   qualitative analysis.

(E)   structured analysis.

11.   Sir Francis Galton greatly contributed to the field of psychology by developing the

(A)   first laboratory.

    (B)   first sensory-motor psychological tests.

    (C)   early neuroanatomy procedures.

    (D)   phrenology movement.

    (E)   concept of mental illness.

12.   According to Freud, paranoia is caused by

    (A)   a fixation at the anal stage.

    (B)   an unresolved Oedipal Complex.

    (C)   destruction of the superego.

    (D)   unacceptable homosexual impulses.

    (E)   sublimation of feelings of guilt.

13.   Who began the study of the measurement of infant intelligence in the United States?

    (A)   Wechsler   (B)   Cattell

    (C)   Gesell   (D)   Bayley

    (E)   Binet

14.   Which of the following is no longer classified as a mental disorder?

    (A)   mental retardation   (B)   Alzheimer's disease

    (C)   homosexuality   (D)   aphasia

    (E)   all of the above

15.   Responses in the Rorschach Inkblot Test are scored with reference to

    (A)   location.   (B)   determinant.

    (C)   content.   (D)   all of the above

    (E)   none of the above

16.   The medulla oblongata, pons, midbrain, and diencephalon are all parts of the

    (A)   cerebellum.   (B)   cortex.

    (C)   left hemisphere.   (D)   right hemisphere.

    (E)   brainstem.

17.   The greater the deindividuation of any group the

(A) less anonymous the group members are.

(B) more irresponsibly its members behave.

(C) more responsibly its members behave.

(D) greater the chance for antisocial behavior.

(E) both (B) and (D)

18. A theory formulated by Freud which supports aggression as a means of releasing inner tension is known as

(A) congruity theory.   (B) catharsis theory.

(C) rationalization.   (D) frustration-aggression theory.

(E) instrumental aggression.

19. Slot machines are an example of which type of reinforcement schedule?

(A) fixed-interval   (B) variable-ratio

(C) fixed-ratio   (D) variable-interval

(E) none of the above

20. In which of Piaget's stages of cognitive development will a child realize that when a volume of water is poured from a tall, narrow beaker, to a wide beaker, the volume remains the same even though it reaches a lower level?

(A) preoperational   (B) sensorimotor

(C) concrete operational   (D) latency

(E) formal operations

21. According to Craik and Lockhart's approach to memory

(A) retention is determined by depth of analysis.

(B) there is an unlimited capacity of memory.

(C) rote learning is superior to elaborate learning.

(D) there is a perceptual filter which handles one channel at a time.

(E) the search for a probe item in a list is serial self-terminating.

22. The cerebral cortex receives information from the

(A) auditory system.   (B) visual system.

(C) motor system.   (D) all of the above

(E) both (A) and (B)

23. Which of the following is NOT one of the categories of dissociative disorders according to the DSM-IV?

    (A) psychogenic amnesia

    (B) multiple personality

    (C) catatonic schizophrenia

    (D) psychogenic fugue

    (E) depersonalization disorder

24. Random assignment of numbers to members of a group is an example of a (an)

    (A) ratio scale.   (B) nominal scale.

    (C) ordinal scale.   (D) interval scale.

    (E) none of the above

25. REM sleep is also known as

    (A) paradoxical sleep.   (B) desynchronized sleep.

    (C) passive sleep.   (D) both (A) and (B)

    (E) none of the above

26. Which group represents the three ways to measure the amount of long-term memory retention?

    (A) recognition, recall, and rehearsal

    (B) recall, recognition, and savings

    (C) recognition, savings, and rate of forgetting

    (D) savings, recall, and retrieval

    (E) recognition, recall, and retrieval

27. In studies of attention, shadowing is used to

    (A) mask all information from attention.

    (B) differentially mask irrelevant information.

    (C) be sure the subject's attention is concentrated on a single task.

    (D) mediate the subject's attention between 2 or more tasks.

    (E) stimulate retroactive inhibition.

28. According to Allport's theory of motivation, people are motivated

(A) by past and current experiences.

(B) toward future goals.

(C) by social reinforcement.

(D) by current experiences.

(E) by the ego ruling over the superego.

QUESTIONS 29–30 refer to the following passage.

To use the F-table, you would need information about the body of data which you are analyzing. It is important to know the degrees of freedom for the numerator mean square of the F ratio. You also need to know the denominator degrees of freedom for the F ratio. Finally it is important to know the significance level (α). All of this knowledge is necessary to successfully determine F.

29. The degrees of freedom (df) represent

(A) the difference between a score and a mean of the set of data scores.

(B) an error term.

(C) the number of independent pieces of information.

(D) a value obtained for a sampling distribution that specifies a critical region.

(E) the denominator term of an F ratio.

30. In an Analysis of Variance, the significance level indicates

(A) the probability of making a Type I error.

(B) that F is correct.

(C) the probability of making a Type II error.

(D) (A) and (B) (E) (B) and (C)

QUESTIONS 31–35 refer to the following curves. Match each curve with its corresponding description.

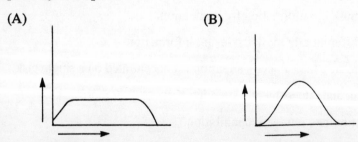

(A) (B)

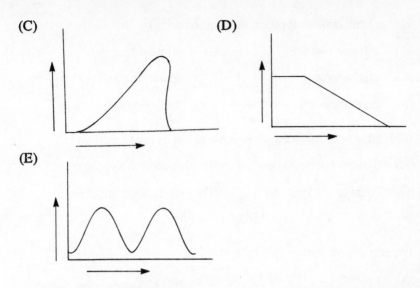

(C)

(D)

(E)

31.   The successful extinction curve.

32.   The curve which has the mean, median, and mode in the same place.

33.   The distribution of weights in a representative random sample of female adults.

34.   The negatively skewed distribution.

35.   The platykurtic distribution.

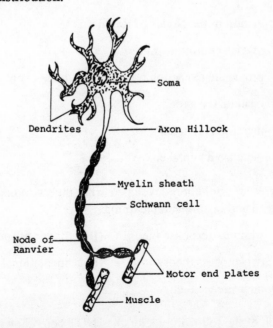

QUESTIONS 36–40 refer to the above diagram.

36. This neuron is most appropriately called a (an)

    (A) afferent neuron.　　　　　(B) efferent neuron.

    (C) glial neuron.　　　　　　(D) spinal neuron.

    (E) connector cell.

37. Within the neuron, electrochemical messages travel from the

    (A) axon to the dendrite.　　(B) axon to the synapse.

    (C) soma to the synapse.　　(D) dendrite to the axon.

    (E) dendrite to the axon hillock.

38. The action potential begins in the

    (A) neuron.　　　　　　　(B) soma.

    (C) dendrite.　　　　　　(D) axon hillock.

    (E) myelin sheath.

39. If the pictured neuron is stimulated with an electrode, it will

    (A) hyperpolarize.　　　　(B) depolarize.

    (C) initiate an action potential.　(D) both (A) and (B)

    (E) both (B) and (C)

40. The function of the Nodes of Ranvier is to

    (A) release neurotransmitters.

    (B) propagate the action potential down the axon.

    (C) insulate the axon.

    (D) increase Na^+ uptake.

    (E) increase K^+ uptake.

41. Mowrer and Solomon developed what theory to explain the interaction of classical and instrumental learning?

    (A) stimulus-response theory　(B) opponent-process theory

    (C) two-process theory　　　(E) mediational theory

    (D) interference theory

42. Which of the following factors has NOT been shown to affect the desire to affiliate?

(A) intelligence   (B) birth-order

(C) uncertainty   (D) fear

(E) hunger

43. If a person stops practicing a skill, takes a rest, and begins again, he will usually perform better than he did during the first practice period. This is due to a phenomenon called

(A) primary feedback.   (B) secondary feedback.

(C) transfer of training.   (D) distribution of practice.

(E) reminiscence.

44. A social learning theorist would say that television

(A) has a cathartic effect on viewers.

(B) has no influence on aggressive behavior.

(C) increases aggression that is not related to reward and punishment.

(D) provides models for aggressive behavior.

(E) both (C) and (D)

45. The child as a "tabula rasa" was first introduced by

(A) Freud.   (B) Hall.

(C) Rousseau.   (D) Locke.

(E) Watson.

46. According to the tropistic theory, the animal's response is

(A) always contingent on some reinforcer.

(B) a direct function of the stimulus.

(C) perfected through practice and repetition.

(D) shaped in part by consciousness.

(E) both (A) and (C)

47. Which of these was NOT offered by Freud as part of his explanation of depression?

(A) "symbolic loss"

(B) fixation at the oral stage of development

(C)   introjection

(D)   mourning

(E)   all of these concepts are a part of Freud's theory of depression

48.   One way to increase the likelihood of compliance with a request is to induce a person to agree first to a much smaller request. This is known as the

(A)   Hawthorne effect.   (B)   innoculation technique.

(C)   foot-in-the-door technique. (D)   sleeper effect.

(E)   cognitive consistency technique.

49.   Someone who is faced with a discrepant communication can reduce the stress by

(A)   derogating the source.   (B)   rationalization.

(C)   assimilation and contrast.   (D)   (A) and (B) only

(E)   all of the above

50.   Which therapy offers little advice, if any, and prescribes no "right" way of behaving?

(A)   Gestalt   (B)   rational-emotive

(C)   client-centered   (D)   behavior

(E)   implosive

51.   The hypnagogic state refers to the

(A)   state one experiences when going from a sleep state to wakefulness.

(B)   state one experiences when going from a wakeful state to sleep.

(C)   state experienced during hypnosis.

(D)   normal wakeful state.

(E)   normal sleep state.

52.   The tendency of a patient to react to a therapist with the same childhood emotions he used to experience toward his parents is called

(A)   transference.   (B)   free association.

(C)   implosion.   (D)   counter-repression.

(E)   modeling.

53. Which of the following behaviors is characteristic of infantile autism?

    (A) social isolation

    (B) extreme sensitivity to pain

    (C) stereotyped behavior

    (D) both (A) and (C)

    (E) all of the above

54. The rationalist approach of Chomsky in explaining language development is also referred to as

    (A) nativist.

    (B) empiricist.

    (C) cognitive.

    (D) culture-bound.

    (E) none of the above

55. Visual information travels from the optic nerve to the

    (A) lateral geniculate nucleus.

    (B) occipital lobe.

    (C) superior colliculus.

    (D) both (A) and (B)

    (E) all of the above

56. Which type of reliability involves the examiner obtaining two scores for a subject with one administration of a test?

    (A) test-retest reliability

    (B) alternate form reliability

    (C) split-half reliability

    (D) scorer reliability

    (E) content reliability

57. Of the following psychologists, who described the identity crisis as a major problem faced by the adolescent?

    (A) Erikson

    (B) Freud

    (C) Piaget

    (D) Horney

    (E) none of the above

58. According to Adler, the basis of personality functioning is a

    (A) tendency toward self-centeredness.

    (B) subjectively perceived sense of inferiority.

    (C) subjectively perceived sense of superiority.

    (D) "will to pleasure."

    (E) none of the above

59. In order to measure how much information remained in visual memory immediately after a brief visual display went off and before any information decayed, Sperling used a sampling technique known as

(A) selective report.　　(B) whole report.

(C) partial report.　　(D) shadowing.

(E) backward masking.

60. Which of the following plays an important role in programming rapid ballistic movements?

(A) the cerebellar cortex　　(B) the basal ganglia

(C) the thalamus　　(D) the medulla

(E) the reticular formation

61. In Vroom's "Expectancy Theory," the term "valence" refers to

(A) expected rewards.

(B) the desirability of a goal.

(C) the behavior that will lead to a desired goal.

(D) motivation.

(E) the charge on an ion.

62. Parkinson's disease is a gradual degeneration of a particular path of

(A) serotonin-containing axons.

(B) motor neurons.

(C) dopamine-containing axons.

(D) acetylcholine-containing axons.

(E) mescaline receptors.

QUESTIONS 63–65 refer to the following passage.

Signal detection theory was originally developed to account for the unreliability of sensory detection at or near threshold intensities. Signal strength, d', would determine the detection rates along with the subject's criterion level, B. Detection theory has been extended analogously to recognition memory experiments. Within this analogy, d' is a measure of trace strength, where "strength" is understood as an expression of encoding distinctiveness, a critical factor in recognition accuracy.

63. The field of psychology in which this theory is prominent is known as

    (A) behaviorism.   (B) psychophysics.

    (C) cognitive psychology.   (D) biopsychology.

    (E) perception.

64. When a subject reports a signal when none actually occurred, it is called a

    (A) miss.   (B) hit.

    (C) false alarm.   (D) tradeoff.

    (E) mistake.

65. Which of the following statements regarding signal detection is FALSE?

    (A) With the strict criterion of paying subjects 10¢ for each hit, but fining them $2.00 for each false alarm, the amount of misses will be greater.

    (B) The larger the familiarity of an item (d') is, the greater the likelihood of correctly accepting or rejecting that item as belonging to a recently learned list.

    (C) In recognition memory the size of d' will be smaller if the test items were given a deep, elaborate processing.

    (D) both (A) and (C)

    (E) All of the above are true statements.

66. The Draw-a-Person Test (DAP) is a (an)

    (A) diagnostic test for nonverbal children.

    (B) intelligence test for nonverbal children.

    (C) expressive, projective test.

    (D) intelligence test for prelinguistic children.

    (E) creativity test for school age children.

67. A test of the capacity to learn a particular skill and to learn within a specific area of knowledge is called a (an)

    (A) aptitude test.   (B) achievement test.

    (C) projective test.   (D) acquisition test.

    (E) intelligence test.

QUESTIONS 68–69 Refer to the following graph.

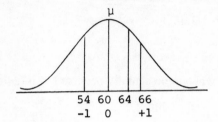

standard deviation = 6

68. What is the Z-score for the obtained raw score, 64?

(A) + 1   (B) – .66

(C) + .66   (D) + .99

(E) –1

69. What percent of the values in this distribution fall between 54 and 66?

(A) 34.14%   (B) 95.44%

(C) 99.74%   (D) 68.26%

(E) none of the above

QUESTIONS 70–72: identify the pair which shows an incorrect association.

70. (A) Cattell — factor analysis

(B) Bandura — social learning theory

(C) Rogers — rational emotive therapy

(D) Lewin — field theory

(E) Premack — reinforcement

71. (A) Allport — Q-technique

(B) Maslow — self-actualization

(C) Kohlberg — moral development

(D) Kohler — problem solving

(E) Allport — factor analysis

72. (A) Perls — non-directive therapy

(B) Toffler — information overload

(C)   Mischel — social learning theory

(D)   Szasz — ethical model

(E)   Erikson — psychosocial development

73.   The experimental chamber called the Skinner box is used for many studies of

(A)   habituation.   (B)   latent habituation.

(C)   operant conditioning.   (D)   backward conditioning.

(E)   sensitization control.

74.   According to John B. Watson, complex learning was considered to be

(A)   the chaining of conditioned reflexes.

(B)   associative learning of behaviors.

(C)   simultaneous conditioning of responses.

(D)   second-order conditioning of behavior.

(E)   higher-order conditioning of responses.

75.   Performance = Drive × Habit is a symbolic representation proposed by

(A)   David McClelland.   (B)   Henry Murray.

(C)   Abraham Maslow.   (D)   Sigmund Freud.

(E)   Clark Hull.

76.   Which of the following psychologists studied the tool use of apes?

(A)   Tolman   (B)   Kohler

(C)   Lewine   (D)   Wundt

(E)   Watson

77.   Which of the following behavioral theorists believed in a one-trial learning theory?

(A)   Tolman   (B)   Lashley

(C)   Watson   (D)   Skinner

(E)   Guthrie

78. Which of the following equations expresses Fechner's Law of psychophysics?

(A) $\frac{\Delta I}{I} = C$

(B) $\frac{\Delta I}{K} = S$

(C) $S = K \log I$

(D) $S = I \log K$

(E) $\frac{\Delta I}{\log K} = S$

79. What is the best treatment for bipolar disorder?

(A) electroconvulsive therapy

(B) psychosurgery

(C) lithium chloride

(D) chlorpromazine

(E) iproniazid

80. Avoidance conditioning can produce

(A) active avoidance.

(B) extinction.

(C) passive avoidance.

(D) suppression.

(E) both (A) and (C)

81. Which of the following types of learning CANNOT be directly observed?

(A) operant conditioning

(B) response learning

(C) verbal learning

(D) perceptual learning

(E) classical conditioning

82. The drive-reduction theory was proposed by

(A) Clark Hull.

(B) B.F. Skinner.

(C) Harry Harlow.

(D) Erik Erikson.

(E) Kurt Lewin.

83. The following graph depicts the response pattern for a pigeon's pecking to a yellow light. Note what happens on day 6 with the introduction of the green light. The pigeon's response to the lights after the ninth day shows that it learned

(A) stimulus generalization.

(B) stimulus discrimination.

(C) perceptual differences.

(D) operant conditioning.

(E) negative reinforcement.

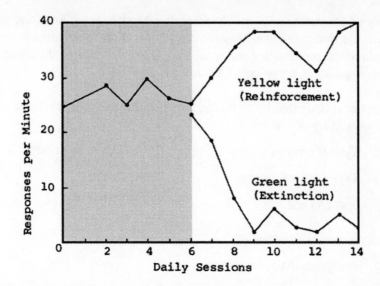

84. Saturation refers to

    (A) hue.   (B) taste.

    (C) brightness.   (D) sound.

    (E) smell.

85. A little girl with an I.Q. of 100 would have a mental age that is

    (A) much lower than her chronological age.

    (B) slightly lower than her chronological age.

    (C) much higher than her chronological age.

    (D) slightly higher than her chronological age.

    (E) equal to her chronological age.

86. *Prior* to training in the classical conditioning paradigm, which of the following is true?

    (A) CS → UCR   (B) CS → UCS

    (C) CS → CR   (D) UCS → UCR

    (E) UCS → CR

QUESTIONS 87–89 refer to the following passage.

The power of a statistical test is the probability of correctly rejecting the null hypothesis when it is false. It is defined by the value $1-\beta$ where β (beta) is the probability of not rejecting the null hypothesis when it is false. In testing the null hypothesis, it is compared to alternative conditions. If this alternative hypothesis specifies direction, a one-tailed test is utilized. If the direction of the alternative values is not specified, a two-tailed test is used.

87. If power is increased by changing the critical level, α, from .01 to .05 then the probability of making a

(A) Type II error increases.   (B) Type II error decreases.

(C) Type I error increases.   (D) both (B) and (C)

(E) both (A) and (C)

88. Using a one-tailed test will

(A) always increase the power.

(B) increase the power when the true mean is in the direction of the tail.

(C) always increase the probability of rejecting the null hypothesis.

(D) both (A) and (C)

(E) never increase the power.

89. In order to increase the power of a test, a researcher can

(A) decrease the sample size.   (B) increase β.

(C) increase the sample size.   (D) both (B) and (C)

(E) both (A) and (B)

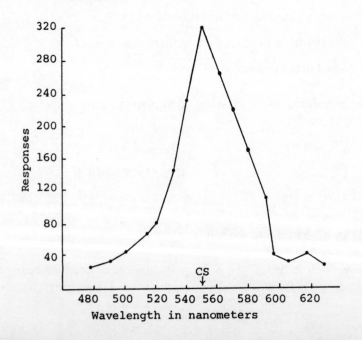

90. The gradient in the preceding figure is shown for a group of pigeons trained to peck a button illuminated with a 550 nanometer light, and then presented with test buttons of several colors ranging from 480 to 620 nanometers. This gradient depicts the principle of

    (A) Skinnerian learning techniques.

    (B) backward conditioning.

    (C) forward conditioning.

    (D) higher-order learning.

    (E) stimulus generalization.

91. Albert Ellis created which method of therapy?

    (A) Erhard seminar training   (B) Gestalt therapy

    (C) primal therapy   (D) misconception therapy

    (E) rational-emotive therapy

92. In negative reinforcement,

    (A) an aversive stimulus is administered.

    (B) a pleasing stimulus is removed.

    (C) response learning is faster than escape training.

    (D) an aversive stimulus is removed.

    (E) response learning is slower than escape training.

93. The Law of Effect suggests that

    (A) practice produces learning.

    (B) performance does not indicate learning.

    (C) there must be practice and purpose for learning.

    (D) neither practice nor reward are important to learning.

    (E) reinforcement affects behavior.

94. Which of the following leads to the quickest and easiest learning of the conditioned response (CR)?

    (A) forward conditioning   (B) simultaneous conditioning

    (C) trace conditioning   (D) delay conditioning

    (E) backward conditioning

QUESTIONS 95–97 refer to the following passage.

A person sees the world as a jungle in which everyone is against one another. In this dangerous world he believes human beings are primarily selfish or evil. He is very prejudice and tends to be unperceptive about the feelings and ideas of others. At times he can be very aggressive and at other times, submissive.

95. The person described above has many characteristics of a (an)

   (A) paranoid personality.   (B) manic-depressive.

   (C) authoritarian personality. (D) egocentric personality.

   (E) androgynous personality.

96. This type of personality would be measured by the

   (A) F scale.   (B) CPI.

   (C) Bayley scales.   (D) Q-technique.

   (E) MMPI.

97. Which of the following true/false questions is/are typical of this test?

   (A) I have trouble making new friends.

   (B) If people would talk less and work more, everybody would be better off.

   (C) Most people don't realize how much our lives are controlled by plots hidden in secret places.

   (D) both (B) and (C)

   (E) all of the above

QUESTIONS 98–100 refer to the following passage.

The study of the human being as he adapts to his environment is highly important. Consciousness guides the organism to the ends required for survival and is thus thought of as an organ which is specifically appropriate to the needs of a complex organism in a complex environment.

98. This concept is central to which school of thought?

   (A) functionalist   (B) behavioristic

   (C) Gestalt psychology   (D) structuralist

   (E) phenomenological

99. Which of the following psychologists had a great influence in this approach?

    (A) Wilhelm Wundt   (B) Henry James

    (C) John B. Watson   (D) William James

    (E) Max Wertheimer

100. Which of the following statements regarding this school of thought is FALSE?

    (A) It was influenced by Darwin's theory of evolution.

    (B) It is concerned with the components of the mind.

    (C) Learning is an important adaptive process.

    (D) both (A) and (B)

    (E) All of the above are true statements.

101. According to Freud, there is one defense mechanism that leads to socially adaptive behavior. Which of the following is it?

    (A) displacement   (B) reaction formation

    (C) projection   (D) rationalization

    (E) sublimation

102. Maintaining a rigid posture, even against attempts by others to be moved, is characteristic of

    (A) somatoform disorders.   (B) catatonic schizophrenia.

    (C) dissociative disorders.   (D) antisocial personality disorder.

    (E) obsessive-compulsive disorder.

103. A test score that has NOT been converted into a form permitting comparison with scores of other tests is known as a

    (A) rank score.   (B) percentile score.

    (C) raw score.   (D) T-score.

    (E) Z-score.

104. All of the following are often psychosomatic disorders EXCEPT

    (A) hypertension.   (B) gastrointestinal disorder.

    (C) migraines.   (D) paranoia.

    (E) asthma.

105. The most obvious symptom of the catatonic schizophrenic is

    (A) disturbances in language. (B) delusional systems.

    (C) auditory hallucinations. (D) disorganization of behavior.

    (E) disturbances in motor functions.

106. When Freud stated that "The aim of all life is death" he was referring to

    (A) developmental conflicts. (B) libido.

    (C) id conflicts. (D) Thanatos.

    (E) instincts.

107. The type of disorder associated with alcoholism that involves *pathological changes* in the brain stem is

    (A) Korsakoff's psychosis. (B) prodromal psychosis.

    (C) Wernicke's syndrome. (D) cyclothymic disorder.

    (E) Broca's syndrome.

108. Defense mechanisms are defensive in that they

    (A) defend against external stressors.

    (B) guard against conflicts between the id and superego.

    (C) protect the ego from the instincts.

    (D) protect the developing child from stressful experiences.

    (E) protect individuals from anxiety that they might not be able to tolerate.

109. All of the following are projective tests EXCEPT the

    (A) Rorschach Inkblot Test. (B) Thematic Apperception Test.

    (C) Word association test. (D) Draw-a-Person Test.

    (E) They are all examples of projective tests.

110. Which of the following is NOT indicative of Alzheimer's disease?

    (A) rapid deterioration of mental ability

    (B) development of aphasias and aproxias

    (C) very old age at onset; usually 60-70 years old

    (D) extreme emotional distress and agitation

    (E) both (B) and (D)

111. The semantic differential, developed by Charles Osgood,

    (A)   made the first distinction between phonemes and morphemes.

    (B)   is a technique for assessing denotative meaning.

    (C)   is a technique for assessing connotative meaning.

    (D)   is also known as the atmosphere effect.

    (E)   is also known as the halo effect.

112. Pierre Janet is most well known for

    (A)   extensive research on hysteria.

    (B)   use of hypnosis.

    (C)   developing the first psychological theory of neurosis.

    (D)   being one of the first to attract attention to mental illness.

    (E)   all of the above

113. When taking an intelligence test, a child with the disorder agraphia would have difficulty with

    (A)   perception of the test stimuli.

    (B)   verbal portions of the exam.

    (C)   understanding verbal directions.

    (D)   comprehending the meaning of directions.

    (E)   writing answers to the problems.

114. Which therapy uses role-playing in a group setting as one of its main techniques?

    (A)   Gestalt   (B)   Rational-emotive

    (C)   Implosive   (D)   Client-centered

    (E)   all of the above

115. The "hero" in the Thematic Apperception Test is

    (A)   the subject taking the test.

    (B)   the subject's idealized self.

    (C)   the subject's identified self.

    (D)   arbitrary.

    (E)   the figure in the picture around whom the subject thinks the action revolves.

116. Homeostatic regulation is achieved by the

   (A)   central nervous system.

   (B)   peripheral nervous system.

   (C)   autonomic nervous system

   (D)   sympathetic nervous system

   (E)   parasympathetic nervous system

117. Autistic children usually

   (A)   resist any change in routine.

   (B)   have inappropriate emotional expressions.

   (C)   respond well to chlorpromazine.

   (D)   both (A) and (C)

   (E)   both (A) and (B)

118. Among the findings on Rotter's Locus of Control scale is the fact that

   (A)   individuals with high achievement motivation are more internal in their dispositions.

   (B)   individuals with low achievement motivation are more internal in their dispositions.

   (C)   whites are less internal than blacks.

   (D)   females are less external than males.

   (E)   locus of control is an innate characteristic.

119. The reinforcement schedule which would most probably lead to the strongest and most lasting response is

   (A)   variable-interval.   (B)   fixed-interval.

   (C)   fixed-ratio.   (D)   variable-ratio.

   (E)   both (A) and (D)

120. According to Kohlberg's theory of moral development, which of the following concepts is characteristic of a child at the second level of morality?

   (A)   Good behavior is characteristic of someone who obeys authority and society's laws.

   (B)   The child understands individual rights and democratic principles.

(C)   Evil behavior is that which is punished, and good is that which is not punished.

(D)   Good behavior is that which is praised by society.

(E)   both (A) and (D)

121. A task in which performance fails to improve even with the application of increasing resources is said to be

(A)   attenuated.

(B)   data-limited.

(C)   resource-limited.

(D)   context dependent.

(E)   none of the above

122. Coding for pitch in the auditory system is accomplished by

(A)   hair cells on the basilar membrane that produce action potentials at the same frequency as sound waves.

(B)   sounds at different pitches which activate hair cells at different locations on the basilar membrane.

(C)   vibrations which are formed in the cochlea.

(D)   both (A) and (B)

(E)   both (B) and (C)

123. Which of the following psychologists is a proponent of the phenomenological model of psychopathology?

(A)   Maslow

(B)   Szasz

(C)   Bandura

(D)   Dollard

(E)   none of the above

124. The neurotransmitter _____, present almost exclusively in the _____, has a great influence on sleep.

(A)   serotonin, reticular activating system

(B)   dopamine, basal ganglia

(C)   serotonin, raphe system

(D)   acetylcholine, hypothalamus

(E)   norepinephrine, hypothalamus

125. In a negatively skewed distribution the

    (A) mean is lower than the median.

    (B) mode is lower than the median.

    (C) median and the mean are equal.

    (D) median and the mode are equal.

    (E) mean is between the mode and the median.

126. Which of the following are postulates of the encoding specificity principle?

    (A) Items are stored in memory the way they are first perceived.

    (B) The particular manner of encoding determines the type of retrieval
         cues that will allow access to the stored information.

    (C) The closer coding and retrieval cues match each other, the better the
         recall will be.

    (D) both (B) and (C)   (E) all of the above

127. The Gestalt experience of perceiving an array of equally spaced dots as
     rows and columns is attributed to

    (A) proximity.   (B) wholistic functions.

    (C) continuity.   (D) additive vision.

    (E) none of the above

128. The personality structure, according to Allport, is represented largely by

    (A) unconscious motivation.

    (B) the ego.

    (C) issues of internality and externality.

    (D) self-identity congruence.

    (E) traits.

QUESTIONS 129–130 refer to the following passage.

Every effect has a cause and all causal sequences are located within the realm
of nature. These causal sequences can be comprehended and analyzed by a
particular human faculty — reason. The power to understand and control the
world is the faculty that separates human beings from animals. This faculty is
what gives humans the superior advantage in the realm of created being.

129. This paragraph best describes the basic tenets of which?

    (A)   rationalism   (B)   structuralism

    (C)   functionalism   (D)   dualism

    (E)   phenomenalism

130. Which one of the following was a major proponent of this philosophy?

    (A)   Locke   (B)   Aquinas

    (C)   Aristotle   (D)   Comte

    (E)   both (B) and (C)

QUESTIONS 131–135 refer to the following equations. Match each equation with its corresponding description.

(A) $\dfrac{\Sigma x_i}{n}$ (B) $\dfrac{\Sigma(x_i - \bar{x})^2}{n-1}$

(C) $\dfrac{\Sigma(x_i - \bar{x})^3}{n}$ (D) $\dfrac{x - \mu}{\sigma}$

(E) $\dfrac{\mu - M}{n - x_i}$

131. The equation essential to analyzing the relative measure of symmetry.

132. The probability of standardized Z-scores can be found with this equation.

133. The equation which is INCORRECT.

134. The equation which represents the mean of a data sample.

135. The equation which represents the standard deviation squared.

QUESTIONS 136–140 refer to the following passage.

The thalamus, a part of the forebrain located just above the midbrain, functions mainly as a relay station of the brain. Sensory information from the environment travels through the spinal cord, or information coming from areas of the midbrain and hindbrain usually arrives at the thalamus and is then relayed to appropriate areas of the cortex. The thalamus is organized into various centers called nuclei. Specific nuclei send information to specific areas of the cortex.

136. Sensory information from the environment travels to the spinal cord and thalamus by way of the

(A)   afferent nerves.   (B)   spinal nerves.

(C)   thalmidic neurons.   (D)   efferent neurons.

(E)   central nervous system.

137. The part of the thalamus that sends information to the visual cortex is the

(A)   lateral posterior nucleus.   (B)   anterior body.

(C)   dorsomedial.   (D)   lateral geniculate nucleus.

(E)   intralaminar nuclei.

138. The thalamus differs from the reticular activating system in that

(A)   it contains more white matter.

(B)   it is a relay station for information on the way to the cerebral cortex.

(C)   the different sensory systems are kept rigidly separate.

(D)   it contains more gray matter.

(E)   it produces ADH.

139. The hypothalamus is to homeostatic regulation, as the thalamus is to the regulation of

(A)   external signs of emotion.   (B)   muscle tone.

(C)   breathing.   (D)   hormone production.

(E)   none of the above

140. The thalamus is considered to be part of the

(A)   peripheral nervous system.

(B)   autonomic nervous system.

(C)   haptic system.

(D)   central nervous system.

(E)   somatic nervous system.

141. The routine of replacing one habit with another, rather than simply extinguishing a habit, is called

(A)   counterconditioning.   (B)   discrimination.

(C)   higher-order conditioning.   (D)   stimulus control.

(E)   shaping.

142. Which of the following statements is FALSE?

    (A) Subjects in high fear situations have a greater tendency to affiliate than subjects in low fear situations.

    (B) The greater the degree of uncertainty, the greater the tendency to affiliate.

    (C) The greater the anxiety, the weaker the tendency to affiliate.

    (D) As hunger increases, the desire to affiliate increases.

    (E) In terms of birth order, later-born children have a greater tendency to affiliate when fearful than first-born children.

143. Many times, previous learning can influence learning in new situations. This phenomenon is known as

    (A) reminiscence.   (B) coherence.

    (C) cognitive learning.   (D) secondary feedback.

    (E) transfer of training.

144. Research has shown that children who are reared by strict punishment usually

    (A) become criminals.   (B) grow up to be passive.

    (C) grow up to be aggressive. (D) enlist in the armed forces.

    (E) both (A) and (D)

145. Which name does NOT belong in this group?

    (A) Kohler   (B) Tolman

    (C) Hull   (D) Watson

    (E) Thorndike

146. Omission training uses

    (A) reward to elicit a desired response.

    (B) negative reinforcement to increase the frequency of a desired response.

    (C) unpleasant stimuli to stop an undesired response.

    (D) reward to get the learner to withhold a response that is not desired.

    (E) none of the above

147. In children, the presence of bizarre and repetitive activities, a fascination with unusual objects, and an obsession with maintaining the sameness of their environment are signs of

    (A) autism.

    (B) obsessive-compulsive disorder.

    (C) mania.

    (D) hyperactivity.

    (E) enuresis.

148. If someone is told ahead of time that he is going to be exposed to a persuasive communication

    (A) cognitive dissonance is greatly increased.

    (B) cognitive dissonance is only slightly increased.

    (C) he will be less able to resist persuasion.

    (D) he will be more able to resist persuasion.

    (E) both (A) and (C)

149. In both the Trucking Game (Deutsch and Krauss, 1960) and the Prisoner's Dilemma game,

    (A) there was a strong tendency for the players to compete.

    (B) there was a strong tendency for the players to cooperate.

    (C) there was an equal tendency for the players to compete and to cooperate.

    (D) early in the game there was a strong tendency to compete and later in the game there was a strong tendency to cooperate.

    (E) early in the game there was a strong tendency to cooperate and later in the game there was a strong tendency to compete.

150. Systematic desensitization operates on the basic assumption that

    (A) all phobias are undesirable behaviors that are unconsciously positively reinforced.

    (B) most neurotic patterns are conditioned anxiety responses.

    (C) the ego sometimes develops bizarre neurotic patterns to deal with anxiety caused by the id-superego conflict.

    (D) the best way to eliminate an unwanted behavior is to merely remove the reinforcement for it.

    (E) both (A) and (D)

151. Which of the following statements about REM-deprived subjects is NOT true?

    (A) These subjects experience greater difficulties in concentration and memory during the day than non-REM-deprived controls.

    (B) These subjects experience greater tension and irritability during the day than non-REM-deprived controls.

    (C) These subjects entered into fewer REM periods on successive nights of the experiment than did non-REM-deprived controls.

    (D) When allowed to sleep without interruption these subjects dreamed 60 percent more than usual.

    (E) All of the above statements are true.

152. Which of the following statements are true?

    I. Delirium tremens is an alcoholic psychotic reaction.

    II. Trisomy 21 causes cretinism in children.

    III. Compulsive reactions are obsessive thought patterns.

    IV. In conversion reactions, anxiety is expressed in the form of physical symptoms.

    (A) I only   (B) II only

    (C) I and IV only   (D) I, II and III only

    (E) All are true.

153. The phenomenon in which individuals lose their personal sense of responsibility when they are in a group is known as

    (A) adaptive conformity.   (B) disinhibition.

    (C) deindividuation.   (D) impulsiveness.

    (E) none of the above

154. The generative grammar of a language is

    (A) the same as the restrictive rules of a language.

    (B) the set of rules that determine the structure of the language.

    (C) believed to be acquired spontaneously according to the structuralists.

    (D) both (A) and (C)

    (E) both (B) and (C)

155. Upon reaching our sense organs, physical energy is converted to a form that can be processed in our brains. When light energy is converted to a change in the receptor membranes' polarization, which step in the transformation is taking place?

    (A) coding   (B) transduction

    (C) reception   (D) excitation

    (E) none of the above

156. The concept of _____ validity is concerned with tests used for diagnosis of an existing situation.

    (A) predictive   (B) face

    (C) concurrent   (D) construct

    (E) content

157. Which of the following maintains that unconscious motivation does NOT belong in a "normal" person's behavior?

    (A) Jung   (B) Allport

    (C) Freud   (D) Skinner

    (E) Rogers

158. Rogers believes that a major factor in emotional maladjustment is a (an)

    (A) lack of self-approval.   (B) need for approval from others.

    (C) unrealistic self-concept. (D) both (A) and (C)

    (E) all of the above

159. In a memory experiment, subjects were presented with short stories, each containing a critical sentence. Later they were shown sentences and asked whether or not they were identical to those they had just seen. The subjects were more likely to detect change from the original when

    (A) tested immediately after learning the sentence in the story.

    (B) the wording was changed but the meaning was the same.

    (C) they were tested after a long interval and there were semantic changes.

    (D) both (A) and (B)

    (E) both (A) and (C)

160. Apraxia is characterized by an inability to

(A)   organize movements in terms of purpose.

(B)   make movements.

(C)   do something when instructed verbally.

(D)   both (A) and (C)   (E)   all of the above

161. Overspecialization in businesses

(A)   requires greater supervision within departments.

(B)   leads to greater output.

(C)   leads to poor management-employee relations.

(D)   both (A) and (B)   (E)   both (A) and (C)

162. "Each neuron synthesizes, stores, and uses only one transmitter (or the
same combination of transmitters) at all synapses formed by all branches
of its axon." This is known as

(A)   Dale's Law.

(B)   Boyle's Law.

(C)   the law of specific nerve energies.

(D)   Thorndike's Law of Effect. (E)   none of the above

QUESTIONS 163–165 refer to the following passage.

In a particular experiment, a person was shown a picture on the left side of a
screen and then told to put one hand behind a curtain to feel several objects and
find the one that had just been flashed on the screen. If allowed to use the left
hand, the person performed correctly, but if told to use the right hand accuracy
fell to the level of chance. Also, when the display was flashed in the right visual
field, the person could name the object easily, but when it was flashed in the left
visual field the person could not name it or describe it.

163. The person in this experiment has had an operation on which part of the
brain?

(A)   occipital lobe   (B)   corpus callosum

(C)   hypothalamus   (D)   pons

(E)   superior colliculus

164. For most people the ability to speak depends on

(A)   the left hemisphere of the cerebral cortex.

(B)   the right hemisphere of the cerebral cortex.

(C)   both hemispheres of the cerebral cortex.

(D)   the lateral hypothalamus.

(E)   the hippocampus.

165. Information seen in the left visual field travels to

(A)   the left hemisphere.   (B)   the corpus callosum.

(C)   the right hemisphere.   (D)   both hemispheres.

(E)   the cerebellum.

QUESTIONS 166–167 refer to the following passage.

A person who has extreme test anxiety is instructed to imagine being told
when an upcoming exam is to take place, and then to think of himself studying
for it and eventually imagine himself actually taking the exam.

166. This person is undergoing

(A)   cognitive restructuring.   (B)   assertive training.

(C)   transference.   (D)   systematic desensitization.

(E)   aversive conditioning.

167. This type of counterconditioning technique was developed by

(A)   J. Wolpe.   (B)   V. Frankl.

(C)   A. Ellis.   (D)   F. Perls.

(E)   V. Raimy.

QUESTIONS 168–169 refer to the following graph.

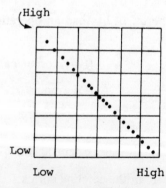

Correlation = – 1.00

168. According to this graph,

    (A) t = +1.   (B) r = -1.

    (C) r = +1.   (D) t = -1.

    (E) r = 0.

169. This type of analysis is used to

    (A) analyze reliability from experiments with several levels on one or more independent variables.

    (B) measure the degree of linear association between two characteristics.

    (C) determine whether a distribution is significantly different from the expected distribution.

    (D) measure the difference between variances.

    (E) none of the above

QUESTIONS 170–172: Identify which term does NOT belong with the others.

170. (A) conduct disorder   (B) enuresis

    (C) conversion disorder   (D) opppositional defiant disorder

    (E) attention deficit/hyperactivity disorder

171. (A) secondary circular reactions

    (B) coordination of secondary schemes

    (C) internalization of thought

    (D) reflex

    (E) decentration

172. (A) anterior pituitary   (B) adrenal cortex

    (C) hypothalamus   (D) ovary

    (E) parathyroid

173. *Beyond Freedom and Dignity*, a book which deals with the philosophical issues of operant conditioning, was written by

    (A) John B. Watson.   (B) E.L. Thorndike.

    (C) Miller and Dollard.   (D) A. Bandura.

    (E) B.F. Skinner.

174. In forward conditioning onset of the

    (A) CS precedes onset of the UCS.

    (B) CS occurs simultaneously with the CR.

    (C) UCS precedes onset of the CS.

    (D) CR precedes onset of the CS.

    (E) CR precedes onset of UCS.

175. Achievement motivation (nAch) was proposed by

    (A) Clark Hull.   (B) David McClelland.

    (C) Abraham Maslow.   (D) Sigmund Freud.

    (E) Henry Murray.

176. In studies on learned helplessness, previous exposure to uncontrollable, aversive events results in

    (A) little or no learning on a subsequent task in which control is possible.

    (B) a moderate level of learning on a subsequent task in which control is possible.

    (C) a high level of learning on a subsequent task in which control is possible.

    (D) sophisticated avoidance skills.

    (E) low level contingency responses.

177. Which of the following theorists proposed that classical conditioning was unable to account for many learning experiences?

    (A) Pavlov   (B) Thorndike

    (C) Watson   (D) Skinner

    (E) Wickens

178. The human eye is insensitive to light waves shorter than about _____ and longer than _____ nanometers.

    (A) 450, 850   (B) 350, 750

    (C) 100, 2,000   (D) 150, 1,050

    (E) none of the above

QUESTIONS 179–182 refer to the following passage.

Information in short-term memory has a very short life span if it is not rehearsed constantly. Two theories that offer explanations for this are the interference model and the time-decay model. According to the interference model. there is only a certain amount of space available in STM, so when information entering exceeds the amount of space, some items are forgotten or replaced by the new information. The items that are forgotten are usually in the middle of the list.

179. According to the interference model, what factors contribute to poorer memory for the middle of a list?

    (A)   serial position effect   (B)   proactive interference

    (C)   retroactive interference   (D)   all of the above

    (E)   both (B) and (C)

180. Proactive interference is defined as the

    (A)   detrimental effect of prior learning on retention of recently learned material.

    (B)   rapid decay of more recently learned material.

    (C)   detrimental effect of recent learning on the recall of previously learned material.

    (D)   rapid decay of previously learned material.

    (E)   detrimental effect of the similarity between old items and new items.

181. When the category of the items to be remembered is changed after several trials, there is

    (A)   a release from retroactive interference.

    (B)   a release from proactive interference.

    (C)   no change in recall.

    (D)   a decrease in retroactive interference.

    (E)   both (A) and (B)

182. In one study, subjects were shown pictures of simple objects. One group of subjects was told to classify them by color, another by shape, and the third was to make no classification. When asked to recall the items, it was found that the

    (A)   speed of recall was better for those who were allowed to recall using the same categories.

(B)   accuracy of recall was superior for those who had classified by color and were allowed to recall by color.

(C)   accuracy of recall was the same for those who classified by shape and recalled by shape than those who did not make a classification but were told to recall by shape.

(D)   both (A) and (B)

(E)   none of the above

183. You have statistically tested the difference between two means in your experiment. You would have the most confidence in them if you found the differences to be significant on what significance level?

(A)   .05   (B)   .1

(C)   .2   (D)   .01

(E)   .95

184. Laws of perceptual organization were formulated by workers in which school of psychology?

(A)   Behaviorist   (B)   Gestalt

(C)   Nativists   (D)   Empiricist

(E)   Structuralist

185. Factor analysis is central to which of the following theorists' positions on intelligence?

(A)   Spearman   (B)   Guilford

(C)   Burt   (D)   all of the above

(E)   none of the above

186. Approach-avoidance conflicts often result in

(A)   frustration.   (B)   oscillation.

(C)   forgetting.   (D)   avoidance learning.

(E)   erratic behavior.

QUESTIONS 187–189 are based on the following passage.

In a particular learning experiment the effect of elaborate (involving meaning) rehearsal versus rote (just repeating the words) rehearsal on later recall is being tested. There are two groups of subjects. All subjects will be given 25 words to study in the rote condition and 25 words to study in the elaborate condition. One group will be tested immediately after the last word is presented. The second group will be tested after a short delay in which they will be given a distractor task involving simple arithmetic.

187. What are the independent variables?

    (A) method of study

    (B) time of testing (immediate or delayed)

    (C) amount of words recalled

    (D) both (A) and (B)   (E) all of the above

188. In this experiment the variable of delayed testing vs. immediate testing is a

    (A) between-subjects variable.

    (B) within-subjects variable.

    (C) counterbalancing variable.

    (D) matching technique.   (E) control.

189. The order in which the 50 words will be presented to the subjects in the rote or elaborate condition should be determined by

    (A) randomization.   (B) matching.

    (C) counterbalancing.   (D) the difficulty of the words.

    (E) none of the above

190. Avoidance conditioning is characterized by

    (A) slow extinction.   (B) rapid extinction.

    (C) response suppression.   (D) response recovery.

    (E) both (A) and (C)

QUESTIONS 191–194 refer to the following passage.

In the earlier shadowing experiments, results led to the conclusion that people can only attend to one thing at a time. According to the perceptual filter model, a person could only pay attention to one channel at a time and only information that has passed through the filter can enter memory. Further experimentation led to the finding that the unattended message would be attended to if it contained the subject's own name or had information that would be expected contextually in the message receiving attention.

191. The concept of a perceptual filter model was proposed by

(A) Kahneman.   (B) Craik.

(C) Broadbent.   (D) Funkhouser.

(E) Loftus.

192. If the name of the subject is presented on the passive (unattended) channel, attention switches to that channel. This is known as

(A) transference.

(B) the smorgasbord phenomenon.

(C) the cocktail party phenomenon.

(D) a reversal shift.   (E) the threshold effect.

193. Which of the following statements about attention is (are) true?

(A) Attention is selective.

(B) Some analysis of meaning can occur without conscious attention.

(C) An individual can only allocate his attentional resources to one stimulus at a time.

(D) both (A) and (B)   (E) all of the above

194. In a typical shadowing experiment the

(A) subject must repeat everything she hears out loud.

(B) material to be shadowed is presented in one ear of an earphone.

(C) subject is tested on material that was not attended to.

(D) both (A) and (B)   (E) all of the above

QUESTIONS 195–197 refer to the following passage.

A consistent cycle lasting approximately 24 hours is called a circadian rhythm. The body's circadian rhythm appears to be generated internally. If an animal is kept in an environment with constant temperature, constant humidity, constant level of light, and an unchanging noise level, it continues to go to sleep approximately every 24 hours. In a study involving a blind person with a sleep-wakefulness disorder, it was found that he had a spontaneous rhythm of 24.9 hours for body temperature, alertness, and other functions. When his rhythm was in phase with the outside world, he functioned effectively, but when it was out of phase, he had sleeping and waking problems.

195. From this passage it can be concluded that

    (A) light is the generating mechanism of the biological clock.

    (B) light plays an important role in controlling the biological clock.

    (C) an individual can be trained to maintain a cycle which is other than 24 hours.

    (D) both (A) and (B)

    (E) none of the above

196. Which gland is responsible for releasing large amounts of melatonin at night and small amounts in the daytime?

    (A) Hypothalamus   (B) Thyroid

    (C) Pineal   (D) Adrenal cortex

    (E) Adrenal medulla

197. In order for the biological clock to be reset by light, a small part of the hypothalamus, called the suprachiasmatic nucleus, receives direct input from the

    (A) occipital lobe.   (B) pituitary gland.

    (C) retina.   (D) optic nerve.

    (E) environment.

QUESTIONS 198–200 refer to the following passage.

The concept of a psychological field or "life space" is analogous to the field theory of physics. The "life space" includes all the events at any time, past, present, or future, that can influence a person. Thus analysis of behavior requires analysis of the total situation. There exists a state of equilibrium between the person and his environment and when this equilibrium is disturbed a tension arises. The organism then acts to release the tension by restoring the equilibrium. Tension is the motivation or need that is created and when a goal is reached the tension is released.

198. The application of field theory to psychology was proposed by

    (A) Wertheimer.   (B) Lewin.

    (C) Kohler.   (D) Tolman.

    (E) Hull.

199. In order to mathematically represent the direction of relationships within the life space, the concept of _____ was used.

    (A) Fourier analysis   (B) topology

    (C) hodological space   (D) Euclidian space

    (E) vector analysis

200. This approach holds that

    (A) the various factors that determine subsequent behavior are independent of one another.

    (B) the way in which an object (event) influences behavior is determined by the context in which it exists.

    (C) when a state of tension arises, equilibrium is restored automatically.

    (D) both (A) and (B)

    (E) both (B) and (C)

201. The ability of young children to use two-word sentences is referred to as

    (A) telegraphic speech.   (B) aphasia.

    (C) babbling.   (D) morpheme induction.

    (E) Broca's language.

202. In order to acquire a language, a species must have the following ability:

    (A) latent learning   (B) concept formation

    (C) hearing   (D) trial and error learning

    (E) all of the above

203. The belief that humans have innate abilities to use syntax and grammar correctly is _____ position.

    (A) the learning theory   (B) the humanistic

    (C) Chomsky's   (D) B.F. Skinner's

    (E) Broca's

204. Donna makes statements such as "my milk," and "Daddy working." Donna is probably _____ year(s) old.

    (A) one   (B) two

    (C) three   (D) four

    (E) five

205. The brain uses which of the following to determine depth?

(A) parallax   (B) convergence

(C) phi phenomenon   (D) retinal disparity

(E) size constancy

206. Humans are most sensitive to the taste of _____ and least sensitive to _____.

(A) saltiness, sweetness   (B) sourness, saltiness

(C) bitterness, sourness   (D) sourness, sweetness

(E) bitterness, sweetness

207. Which one of the following phenomena has NOT been scientifically proven to exist?

(A) clairvoyance   (B) precognition

(C) psychokinesis   (D) telepathy

(E) all of the above

208. Covertly observing gorillas in their natural environment would be a goal of

(A) behavioral psychology.   (B) ecological psychology.

(C) ethology.   (D) simian psychologists.

(E) anthropologists.

209. Belief in the id would be the _____ view, whereas recording the frequency of acts of aggression would represent the _____ approach.

(A) functionalist, structuralist   (B) structuralist, a priori

(C) structuralist, functionalist   (D) gestalt, introspection

(E) dynamist, gestalt

210. A psychologist who studies the variables that contribute to effective reading skills is a (an) _____ psychologist.

(A) applied   (B) clinical

(C) industrial   (D) counseling

(E) social

211. The fundamental attribution error states that we credit success to _____ causes, and failures to _____ causes.

    (A) social, emotional   (B) external, internal

    (C) internal, external   (D) emotional, social

    (E) personal, political

212. We usually recommend a film to friends if it started well and had a terrific ending, even though the middle was slow and boring. The film's producer is taking advantage of the _____ and _____ effect.

    (A) primacy, recency   (B) cognitive, primacy

    (C) cognitive, inertial   (D) recency, overgeneralization

    (E) personal bias, halo

213. The fact that peer pressure can make a new worker put out less effort than if he or she was working alone is an example of

    (A) social facilitation.   (B) social loafing.

    (C) goldbricking.   (D) cognitive reappraisal.

    (E) inductive laziness.

214. In biological terms, when a woman first sees her newborn baby she is looking at a

    (A) fetus.   (B) zygote.

    (C) progeny.   (D) neonate.

    (E) child.

215. Stimulation of the cheek will cause a newborn to begin making sucking responses. This illustrates the _____ reflex.

    (A) perkinjie   (B) korsakoff

    (C) startle   (D) feeding

    (E) rooting

216. In general, biological adolescence begins at

    (A) 13 years of age.   (B) puberty.

    (C) 10 years of age.   (D) 15 years of age.

    (E) 12 years of age.

217. Which one of the following is a "Western" concept?

    (A)   infancy   (B)   puberty

    (C)   adolescence   (D)   teenagers

    (E)   juvenile delinquency

TEST 4

ANSWER KEY

1.	(C)	26.	(B)	51.	(B)	76.	(B)
2.	(C)	27.	(C)	52.	(A)	77.	(E)
3.	(A)	28.	(D)	53.	(D)	78.	(C)
4.	(C)	29.	(C)	54.	(A)	79.	(C)
5.	(A)	30.	(A)	55.	(D)	80.	(E)
6.	(B)	31.	(D)	56.	(C)	81.	(D)
7.	(A)	32.	(B)	57.	(A)	82.	(A)
8.	(D)	33.	(B)	58.	(B)	83.	(B)
9.	(C)	34.	(C)	59.	(C)	84.	(A)
10.	(B)	35.	(A)	60.	(A)	85.	(E)
11.	(B)	36.	(B)	61.	(B)	86.	(D)
12.	(D)	37.	(D)	62.	(C)	87.	(D)
13.	(C)	38.	(D)	63.	(B)	88.	(B)
14.	(C)	39.	(E)	64.	(C)	89.	(C)
15.	(D)	40.	(B)	65.	(C)	90.	(E)
16.	(E)	41.	(C)	66.	(C)	91.	(E)
17.	(E)	42.	(A)	67.	(A)	92.	(D)
18.	(B)	43.	(E)	68.	(C)	93.	(E)
19.	(B)	44.	(D)	69.	(D)	94.	(B)
20.	(C)	45.	(D)	70.	(C)	95.	(C)
21.	(A)	46.	(B)	71.	(A)	96.	(A)
22.	(D)	47.	(E)	72.	(A)	97.	(D)
23.	(C)	48.	(C)	73.	(C)	98.	(A)
24.	(B)	49.	(E)	74.	(A)	99.	(D)
25.	(D)	50.	(C)	75.	(E)	100.	(B)

101.	(E)	131.	(C)	161.	(E)	191.	(C)
102.	(B)	132.	(D)	162.	(A)	192.	(C)
103.	(C)	133.	(E)	163.	(B)	193.	(D)
104.	(D)	134.	(A)	164.	(A)	194.	(E)
105.	(E)	135.	(B)	165.	(C)	195.	(B)
106.	(D)	136.	(A)	166.	(D)	196.	(C)
107.	(C)	137.	(D)	167.	(A)	197.	(C)
108.	(E)	138.	(C)	168.	(B)	198.	(B)
109.	(E)	139.	(A)	169.	(B)	199.	(C)
110.	(C)	140.	(D)	170.	(C)	200.	(B)
111.	(C)	141.	(A)	171.	(E)	201.	(A)
112.	(E)	142.	(E)	172.	(E)	202.	(B)
113.	(E)	143.	(E)	173.	(E)	203.	(C)
114.	(A)	144.	(C)	174.	(A)	204.	(B)
115.	(E)	145.	(A)	175.	(B)	205.	(D)
116.	(C)	146.	(D)	176.	(A)	206.	(E)
117.	(E)	147.	(A)	177.	(D)	207.	(E)
118.	(A)	148.	(D)	178.	(B)	208.	(C)
119.	(D)	149.	(A)	179.	(E)	209.	(C)
120.	(E)	150.	(B)	180.	(A)	210.	(A)
121.	(B)	151.	(C)	181.	(B)	211.	(C)
122.	(D)	152.	(C)	182.	(D)	212.	(A)
123.	(A)	153.	(C)	183.	(D)	213.	(B)
124.	(C)	154.	(E)	184.	(B)	214.	(D)
125.	(A)	155.	(B)	185.	(D)	215.	(E)
126.	(E)	156.	(C)	186.	(B)	216.	(B)
127.	(A)	157.	(B)	187.	(D)	217.	(C)
128.	(E)	158.	(D)	188.	(A)		
129.	(A)	159.	(E)	189.	(C)		
130.	(E)	160.	(D)	190.	(A)		

DETAILED EXPLANATIONS
OF ANSWERS
GRE PSYCHOLOGY TEST 4

1. **(C)** Reaction formation is a defense mechanism, first described by Freud, in which an individual asserts a motive that is opposite in character to the one that threatens him or her. As in the question, where a person threatened by his or her own attraction to pornography defends against this threat by advocating censorship.

2. **(C)** The paranoid individual is characterized by a cognitive mode which is both suspicious and rigid in its interpretations of events. Information is consistently and rigidly interpreted in a suspicious manner by the paranoid individual. Other possible interpretations are ignored by the paranoid as being false or as a "cover-up" because only negative assaults against the individual by others validate his or her suspicious thinking.

3. **(A)** In a skewed distribution, the median moves in the direction of the skew, and the mode occurs at the distribution's highest point. The mean moves more in the tail direction than the median does.

4. **(C)** The ability to withstand conflict is considered a guard against neurosis. The two significant factors in tolerance are 1) the actual amount of conflict which a person can handle adequately and 2) the ability to withstand stress as a function of life experiences. This factor of tolerance combines with the current amount of stress to determine the likelihood of neurosis from resultant anxieties.

5. **(A)** Paranoid schizophrenics can appear fairly normal at first, but typically have delusions of persecution ("My phone is tapped by the CIA") or grandeur ("I'm the king of the universe") that give them away. Response options (B) through (E) are typical of catatonic schizophrenics. Echolalia is the parrot-like and pointless repetition of words or phrases spoken by other people.

6. **(B)** A defense mechanism is a process an individual employs to compensate for a desire which cannot be fulfilled because of social taboos. Defense mechanisms are created by the ego in an attempt to deal with the unfulfilled wish by mediating between the id and the superego. When conflict between these forces becomes excessive, the individual must find means of dealing with it. Defense mechanisms are these means. Examples of defense mechanisms are repression, displacement, reaction formation, rationalization, and projection.

7.   **(A)**   Low intelligence is not characteristic of sociopathy. Rather average or superior intelligence is considered characteristic of this behavioral disorder. Along with the characteristics listed in this question, one of the most important aspects of sociopathy is the lack of emotional response from the individual after committing an antisocial act. Sociopaths have little or no regard for social values and norms. They are incapable of significant loyalty to others and tend to be selfish individuals.

8.   **(D)**   Freud thought that dreams represented attempts at wish fulfillment. He reasoned that the dream is an hallucinatory state, which structures events not as they would be in reality but as the dreamer wishes them to be. When unconscious desires conflict with conscious restraints, however, it is necessary for the "dream work" to pursue indirect symbolic paths to express the wish. Because of the disguised nature of wish fulfillment, the analyst must interpret the manifest dream to discover the latent content of wishes.

9.   **(C)**   A sociogram is a diagram that plots the social structure of a group. It is an aid in understanding group structure through visual means. The sociogram is useful in assigning people to subgroups within the group, which could result in a more effective group structure. This type of diagram can help to identify leaders within a group or isolated members who obtain little support through the group structure.

10.   **(B)**   Interpretation of the Thematic Apperception Test is generally performed with a content analysis. The examiner listens to the stories which the subject makes up for each of the visual test cards. The contents of the subject's story are then interpreted and analyzed, primarily with reference to Murray's lists of "needs" for achievement, affiliation, and aggression and "press." Press refers to forces which affect the satisfaction of needs.

11.   **(B)**   Galton was one of the earliest figures in the development of the testing of movement. He thought that people with the highest intelligence should have the best sensory discrimination abilities because knowledge of the environment reaches us through our senses. To test this proposition, Galton developed sensory discrimination and motor coordination tests. Although the proposition is considered questionable, the development of such measurement tests and equipment is of historical significance. Galton is also credited with the discovery of correlation.

12.   **(D)**   Freud stated that paranoia was a mixture of two defense mechanisms created by the ego to deal with unacceptable homosexual impulses. "I love him" is rejected and transformed into "I hate him" by the process of reaction formation. The cognition "I hate him" is then rejected because of its aggressive, anti-social content. By the process of projection, this is changed into "He hates me and is persecuting me" and, thus, paranoia is created.

13.   **(C)**   Arnold Gesell launched a monumental study of infant behavior in the early 1920s. His main focus was mental development from birth to the age of ten. His creation of a series of behavior and ability norms by age spawned many studies such as the Berkeley Growth Study and tests such as the Cattell Baby Test.

14.   **(C)**   All of the other disorders are still listed in the APA manual. Homosexuality is no longer considered a sexual deviation or a mental disorder. In fact, most findings indicate that homosexuals have no more personality maladjustment problems than their heterosexual peers.

15.   **(D)**   In the Rorschach, the scorer must pay attention to three different aspects of each response. These are location, determinant, and content. Location refers to the area of the blot on which the subject is focused. The determinant refers to the characteristic of the blot that determined the subject's response. The content categories refer to what was seen in the blot.

16.   **(E)**   The brain stem has four divisions. They are the medulla oblongata, which contains ascending and descending traits of interneurons and motor neurons, and serves integrative functions for the respiratory and cardiovascular system; the pons, which connects the two hemispheres of the cerebellum and contains nerve centers that aid in the regulation of breathing; the midbrain which contains centers for certain visual and auditory reflexes; and the diencephalon, a paired organ connected to the cerebrum.

17.   **(E)**   Deindividuation occurs when individuals lose their personal sense of responsibility when they are in a group. In a group, people feel more anonymous and thus less morally accountable for their actions. This loss of individuality has been found to be the cause of violent, antisocial behavior that is sometimes seen in large groups.

18.   **(B)**   Catharsis theorists believe that aggression can be minimized and channeled into more productive or neutral outlets than retaliating against the cause of the frustration. Aggressive energy can be displaced onto another object. Expressing aggressive impulses tends to reduce subsequent aggression. Acceptable ways to reduce an aggressive feeling are through sports, watching violent movies, or more constructive behaviors like throwing oneself into one's work or writing an essay.

19.   **(B)**   In a variable-ratio schedule, the number of responses required before reinforcement is given, is intermittent and irregular. This type of schedule produces the highest rates of performance. At the slot machine, a gambler never knows when he will receive the reward so he continues to play indefinitely.

20.   **(C)**   In Piaget's concrete operational period which lasts from age 7 to 11 years, the child consistently conserves such qualities as length, quantity, weight,

and volume. The child also classifies concrete objects by category and begins to understand the relationships among categories.

21. **(A)** In Craik and Lockhart's levels of processing model of memory, the greater the depth of analysis, the higher the probability of later recall. Information processing takes place in stages. First it is analyzed in terms of physical characteristics and then in terms of context, meaning and recognition. They developed the idea of a "limited capacity central processor" to account for the limited capacity of memory.

22. **(D)** The cerebral cortex consists of two hemispheres, each organized to receive information from the opposite side of the body. There are four lobes: the occipital, which contains visual areas; the parietal, which receives touch information; the frontal lobe which contains the precentral gyrus which is specialized for the control of movement; and the temporal lobe which receives auditory information.

23. **(C)** In dissociative reactions a group of mental processes splits off from the mainstream of consciousness. The specific categories of dissociative disorders are dissociative amnesia, dissociative fugue, dissociative identity (also known as multiple personality), and depersonalization disorder. A fifth category is reserved for individuals who do not satisfy the specific criteria for any of the other four. Dissociative amnesia involves loss of memory for a period of time during which the person cannot remember his previous life but knows how to function in the world. In dissociative fugue, the individual suddenly travels away from his usual surroundings and cannot recall his prior identity. In multiple personality, the various personalities can be quite discrepant. Depersonalization is characterized by the feeling of one's own reality being temporarily lost.

24. **(B)** In a nominal scale, numbers can be assigned to members of a group randomly. The members are not ranked in any particular order as in an ordinal scale, and they are not related to each other on a continuous scale as with interval data. There is also no absolute zero point as on a ratio scale.

25. **(D)** There are four stages of sleep. The later periods of stage 1 are called paradoxical sleep because the EEG shows a desynchronized pattern resembling wakefulness, yet at this stage a person is more difficult to awaken than in any other stage. During this stage the eyes move rapidly back and forth, thus the term rapid eye movement, also known as desynchronized sleep, D sleep, or active sleep.

26. **(B)** There are three ways by which to measure the amount of retention in long-term memory. The recall method requires that the subject reproduce something previously learned with a minimum of cues. The smallest amount of retention is measured with this method. In recognition the subject must recognize whether or not he has seen the information before. This method is used in

multiple-choice exams. In the savings method, the subject learns something that he has already learned before to see if the amount of trials it takes has decreased.

27. **(C)** "Shadowing" is the name given to the popular technique for being sure that a subject's attention is concentrated on a single task. This is done to study the limits of attention capacity. In a shadowing task, a series of words is read to the subject and the subject is asked to repeat everything he hears out loud.

28. **(D)** One of the essential components of Allport's theory of motivation is the contemporaneity of motives. Allport believed that whatever moves a person to think or act moves him now, in the current situation. He did not believe that people are motivated by their past experiences. On this point, Allport differs greatly from psychodynamic theorists.

29. **(C)** The degrees of freedom (dF), in general terms, represent the number of independent pieces of information remaining, following the estimation of population parameters. There are specific degrees of freedom associated with particular sources of variance and variance estimates, such as dfA, the degrees of freedom associated with factor A, or df num, the degrees of freedom associated with the numerator of the F ratio.

30. **(A)** The significance level (α) indicates the probability of making a Type I error. It is the probability with which an experimenter is willing to reject the null hypothesis when it is in fact correct. Usually α is set at .05, so there is a 5% probability of rejecting H_0 (and accepting H_1) when H_0 is true and there is no experimental effect.

ANSWERS 31–35 all refer to the grouped curves.

31. **(D)** A successful extinction curve should begin at a learning acquisition curve level and then drop off to zero as reinforcement is stopped and the behavior extinguishes.

32. **(B)** Only the normal distribution curve can have an equivalent mode, mean, and median. Curve B is the only curve representing the normal distribution.

33. **(B)** The normal distribution is a bell-shaped curve. It is thought to approximate the distribution of many biological and psychological characteristics, including weight distributions for random samples of the population.

34. **(C)** The negatively skewed distribution has extreme values distributed in the lower half of the curve. Thus, the distribution is negatively skewed or skewed to the left.

35. **(A)** A distribution that is flat is called platykurtic. The distribution's flatness indicates a wide dispersion of measurements.

36. **(B)** The neuron pictured is a motor-effector or efferent neuron. As can be seen in the diagram, the axon sends electrochemical messages down to the muscle and motor end plates. The efferent neuron sends the message from brain to the muscles.

37. **(D)** Electrochemical messages travel from the dendrites through the axon within a neuron. The dendrites transmit information to the soma. When the net excitation in the soma reaches a certain threshold, the electrochemical impulse is initiated and it passes down the axon by means of the action potential. The action potential is generated by changes in the permeability of the membrane towards Na+ ions. The ions enter the axon and depolarize the membrane in the neighboring areas. The action potential travels through the axon as a wave.

38. **(D)** The point at which an axon and soma are joined is called the axon hillock. It is here that the action potential is first generated. At this point in the neuron (the beginning of the axon), the polarization of the cell changes, resulting in the action potential. The cable properties of the axon allow the electrical message to travel down the length of the axon.

39. **(E)** When sufficiently stimulated, the neuron will depolarize, thereby becoming positive in charge relative to the outside. Due to stimulation, the permeability to Na+ increases which causes a rushing in of positive ions. The depolarization across the neuron membrane causes the action potential that initiates the nerve impulse's progress along the axon. The depolarization initiates an action potential.

40. **(B)** The function of the Nodes of Ranvier is to rapidly propagate the action potential down the axon. The Nodes of Ranvier are actually gaps in the myelin sheath along the length of the axon. The action potential jumps over the parts of the axon that are covered with myelin sheath. So, instead of being regenerated at every point of the axon's membrane, the action potential is recreated only at the Nodes of Ranvier. This increases the speed with which action potentials are generated down the length of the axon.

41. **(C)** Mowrer and Solomon argued that emotional states become classically conditioned. They said that the occurrence of these classically conditioned states motivates instrumental responses and that the termination of these states reinforces instrumental responses. They called this interaction a two-process theory.

42. **(A)** Intelligence has not been shown to affect affiliation. All the other factors have been experimentally manipulated in the lab and have been shown to

affect the desire to affiliate. Similarity of co-affiliators and the degree of possible verbal communication have also been shown to affect affiliation.

43. **(E)** While this phenomenon is affected by the distribution of practice, it is specifically called reminiscence. Reminiscence can occur after spaced or massed practice. Rest periods dissolve fatigue, but not the learning of correct responses. This accounts for the fact that reminiscence enhances motor learning.

44. **(D)** Social learning theorists claim that television provides models for aggressive behavior and thereby reinforces already acquired aggressive acts and helps to instill new ones in the viewers. Lab studies showed that modeling does indeed play a large part in aggression and that an important variable is whether or not the behavior is rewarded. The majority of laboratory experiments conducted in this area have shown an increase in aggression as the result of watching television.

45. **(D)** Although J.B. Watson was a strong proponent of environmental determinism, John Locke was the first major figure to stress the importance of environment in influencing human development. "Tabula Rasa" means "blank slate." In other words, a child is born as a blank slate upon which environmental experiences would determine the course of his development. Locke urged parents to use intelligent, rational thinking when rearing their children.

46. **(B)** Physiologist Jacques Loeb (1859–1924) developed a theory of animal behavior based on tropisms. A tropism is a response that is a forced, involuntary movement, a direct function of the stimulus. The concepts of reinforcers and consciousness are not used in this theory; there is always a set response for a set stimulus. Loeb's theory was a completely mechanistic one and was highly influential to Watson.

47. **(E)** Freud saw the potential for depression as being created during the oral period. If the child receives too much or too little oral gratification, he may become fixated at this stage. This fixation may result in his being overly dependent on other people for the maintenance of his self-esteem. For these individuals, the process of mourning the loss of a loved one may go astray because the individual introjects the deceased and identifies with him. This may result in self-blame and depression. The anger toward the death of the lost one is directed upon himself. "Symbolic loss" occurs in a depression in which no one has died. An example of this is rejection symbolized as a total withdrawal of love.

48. **(C)** Once a person has agreed to a small request, he is more likely to agree to a large one. Freedman and Fraser (1966) went door-to-door asking housewives to sign a petition for a "safe-driving campaign." Many weeks later, the experimenters returned and asked these women who signed, as well as a control group that was never asked to sign, to display a large unattractive sign,

"Drive Carefully" in their front yard. Fifty-five percent of the women who had signed (small request) agreed to display the sign (large request), while only 17 percent of those who had not been asked to sign the petition agreed to display the sign. The initial smaller compliance tripled the amount of compliance to a larger request.

49.   **(E)**   All of these are correct. Derogating the source means dismissing the communicator as unreliable, biased or incompetent. Therefore, no stress is felt by disagreeing with the message. Rationalization is a method of avoiding the issue by distorting the meaning of the message. Assimilation is distorting the message by perceiving it as closer to one's own position than it actually is. Contrast is distorting the message by perceiving it as farther away from one's own position than it actually is. Both of these extremes reduce stress by allowing one to either accept or dismiss the discrepant message.

50.   **(C)**   Client-centered therapy, developed by Carl Rogers (1951, 1961, 1966), is a humanistic nondirective approach to therapy. The prime goal is to help the client to accept and to become comfortable with himself. The therapist usually offers no advice or interpretation, rather she reflects and clarifies what the client says to add insight and to promote self-understanding.

51.   **(B)**   A hypnagogic state is the state one experiences going from wakefulness to sleep. The hypnagogic state is usually described in terms of three ego states: intact ego state, destructuralized ego state, and restructuralized ego state. These states establish a pattern in which contact with the external environment is gradually lost as sleep begins and progresses. Mental content is at first logical, then becomes bizarre, and is then followed by a final stage that exhibits some logic, but no perceived contact with the outside world.

52.   **(A)**   Transference is an integral part of the psychoanalytic process. One of the main roles of the therapist is to serve as a transference object. This emotional attachment usually develops during free-association when the patient reports whatever feelings, thoughts, etc. come to mind. Transference brings hostilities and problems out into the open where they can be analyzed in a rational manner. Resolution of this "transference neurosis" is one of the most important parts of the cure in psychoanalysis.

53.   **(D)**   Autism is characterized by social isolation, stereotyped behaviors, and insensitivity to pain along with several other behaviors. Some autistic children never develop any spoken language and have abnormal responses to sensory stimuli. It is usually noticed at a very early age and shows little improvement over time with or without any of the current treatments available.

54.   **(A)**   The rationalist approach of Chomsky is referred to as a nativist because it states that the ability to learn and use language is innate, or native to

the human brain. This idea of "innate schema" holds that certain universal principles of language are built right into the brain.

55.   **(E)**   Axons from the ganglion cells form the optic nerve, which extends to the lateral geniculate nucleus of the thalamus. From there they extend to the visual cortex in the occipital lobe. Fibers of the optic nerve also go to the superior colliculus which functions in location information.

56.   **(C)**   Split-half reliability involves obtaining two scores with one administration of a test. The correlation between these scores is the reliability coefficient. Usually the test is split according to odd-even items. The split-half reliability coefficient is also known as the coefficient of internal consistency since the comparison of the two halves shows whether there is an underlying consistency among the items on the test.

57.   **(A)**   According to Erikson, the fifth stage of psychosocial development is adolescence. The major problem faced in this stage is the identity crisis. Confusion about what role the adolescent is to play can cause much anxiety and stress.

58.   **(B)**   According to Adler, the central core of personality functioning is a subjectively perceived sense of inferiority which leads the individual to strive to compensate by gaining superiority. To him, the "will to power" is central to the personality whereas Freud believed that the "will to pleasure" was important. He also felt that the normal individual was motivated by a goal rooted in social interest, whereas the neurotic personality had self-centered goals.

59.   **(C)**   Sperling used the technique of partial report in order to sample the information present in visual memory. The logic of doing this rather than a whole report in which subjects are required to report all the items they could, is that if a subject is required to recall a part of the total information presented, this could be used to estimate how much of the total display was still in storage at the moment of testing.

60.   **(A)**   It is known that the neurons of the cerebellum are active prior to movement, not just during and after movement. In 1974 Hans Kornhuber proposed that the cerebellum plays an important part in all voluntary ballistic movements. This includes the development of motor programs that allow slow movements to become fast and automatic after practice. Damage to the cerebellum results in difficulty in writing, speaking, and doing most athletics.

61.   **(B)**   Vroom explained that there are motivational and nonmotivational determinants of work performance. The nonmotivational determinant is a person's ability to do a task. His performance is an interaction of his motivation and his abilities. An individual's motivation is a function of the "expectation"

that a certain behavior will lead to a desired goal, and of the "valence" which is the desirability of the goal. This is known as the "Expectancy Theory."

62. **(C)** Parkinson's disease usually occurs in the elderly. Its symptoms are slow movements, rigidity, and tremors. There is a slow and gradual degeneration of dopamine-containing axons which lead to the basal ganglia. The therapy for this consists of trying to restore the missing dopamine by taking L-DOPA pills, the precursor to dopamine. There are, however, harmful side effects of L-DOPA.

63. **(B)** The use of psychophysics is an important approach to understanding the process of recognition. In a typical experiment a subject hears or sees a weak stimulus while the experimenter varies the intensity. The purpose is to find the lowest intensity at which the signal becomes barely detectable. This is known as the sensory threshold. In recognition memory. the signal of variable strength is the memory trace and detection represents the process whereby the decision is made as to whether or not a particular stimulus exceeds a certain threshold of familiarity.

64. **(C)** In a detection experiment, if a signal is presented and the subject says "yes" to whether he thought he detected a signal, it is called a hit. If he says "no" it is called a miss. If there is no signal present and the subject says "yes" it is a false alarm, and if he says "no" it is a correct rejection. The subject's criterion, β (beta) can be calculated by analysis of the hit rate and false alarm rate for a given intensity.

65. **(C)** According to the signal detection theory, the criterion is set along the intensity dimension. If an observation results in more activity than the criterion the subject reports that a signal has occurred since it is above the threshold. If there is a lower level of activity than the criterion, no signal is reported. With a strict criterion the subject will be less willing to report a signal, so there will be more misses. The detectability of the signal, which is the strength of the memory trace in recognition is represented by the distance between the two distributions, d'. The distributions are the noise distribution and the signal plus noise distribution. In recognition the distributions are that of "old" items and that of "new" or recently learned items. The size of d' will be greater if the test items were given elaborate processing since that will make them more distinguishable from old items.

66. **(C)** The draw-a-person test (DAP) is referred to as an expressive projective testing technique because it has both diagnostic and therapeutic purposes. The subject not only reveals his emotional difficulties, but also relieves them through free self-expression. The procedure involves asking the subject to draw a person. The examiner then notes the subject's comments, the sequence of parts drawn, and the subject's attitude. The subject then draws a person of the opposite sex. The two drawings are compared for relative size, use of lines, details,

and symmetry. The test is qualitatively evaluated in developing the subject's personality profile.

67.   **(A)**   Aptitude tests generally assess the capacity to learn a skill or a specific area of knowledge. They generally measure the effects of learning under uncontrolled or unknown conditions. The focus of aptitude tests is to predict subsequent performance in an area, e.g., to determine if an individual will profit from the education at a particular college, if someone will perform well in a specific training program, etc. A well-known example is the SAT, which is administered to college-bound students across the United States with a variety of educational backgrounds.

68.   **(C)**   The z-score is obtained from the formula

$$z = \frac{x - \mu}{\sigma}.$$

Here, x is the obtain score, 64, and σ is the distance between the mean and 66 or between the mean and 54. The standard deviation is thus 6. The answer +.66 is obtained from

$$\frac{64 - 60}{6}.$$

69.   **(D)**   In a normal curve approximately 68% of the values fall between +1 and –1 standard deviation away from the mean, 95% of the values fall between +2 and –2 and about 99% fall between +3 and –3 standard deviations.

70.   **(C)**   Carl Rogers is a client-centered therapist who believes that the goal of psychotherapy is to allow the client to establish a realistic self-image. Rational-emotive therapy was developed by Albert Ellis. It is a method of behavior modification known as cognitive restructuring.

71.   **(A)**   Allport proposed the concept of functional autonomy which holds that activities are capable of maintaining themselves without biological reinforcement. He stresses conscious motivation, and believes that the personality structure is represented largely by traits. The Q-techniques is used by Rogers. It is a method of systematically analyzing a person's attitudes, usually about himself.

72.   **(A)**   Frederick Perls was the beginner of Gestalt psychology which aims at helping an individual become a whole, integrated person. Non-directive therapy is another term for Rogers' client-centered therapy because the therapist does not direct the client at all. The client does the thinking and talking and solves his own problem.

73.   **(C)**   In a typical operant conditioning process, the organism is signalled to perform a specific response. When the response is performed the organism is reinforced through a process known as shaping, the organism learns the exact

response required for the reinforcer. B.F. Skinner developed an apparatus designed to give a signal to the animal, a means of responding to the signal, and a method of delivering the reinforcement. This device is nicknamed "the Skinner box."

74. **(A)** John B. Watson expanded and built upon Pavlov's work studying conditioned reflexes. Watson applied conditioning principles to emotions, mental disease, language, and learning. He employed the concept of conditioning as a central theoretical construct in which complex learning was considered to be simply the chaining of conditioned reflexes.

75. **(E)** Clark Hull's theory accounted for the appetitive drives of hunger, thirst, sex, and for the drive to avoid pain. A physiological survival-oriented need was believed to produce a drive that led to behavior that would reduce the drive and therefore satisfy the need. The behavior performed would depend on the degree of success with which the behavior had reduced the drive in the past. This learned association between the drive and the behavior that reduces it is called a "habit." To explain this process, Hull constructed the formula Performance = Drive × Habit or $P = D \times H$. It was the basis for an objective and mathematical model of motivation.

76. **(B)** Wolfgang Kohler believed that animals behaved intelligently when conditions were optimal. He used a procedure to test this idea in which chimpanzees were placed in an enclosed area with a desirable object (banana) out of reach. To reach the banana, the chimpanzees had to utilize objects such as sticks and boxes that were spread out in the area as tools. Kohler found that the chimpanzees were very successful at making use of tools in the retrieval of food (bananas).

77. **(E)** Guthrie believed that one-trial learning takes place. For this reason, as compared with other behavior theorists, Guthrie placed little emphasis on practice as related to learning. He believed that learning was an all or nothing endeavor. To Guthrie, all learning was solely based on the contiguity of stimulus and response.

78. **(C)** Fechner's Law states that the strength of a sensation grows as the logarithm of the stimulus intensity. This is expressed in equation form as

$$S = K \log I$$

S represents psychological magnitude, I represents stimulus intensity, K represents a constant.

79. **(C)** Lithium is the drug used most often to control this disorder. It is by far the most effective treatment available. Unfortunately, lithium does not cure manic-depression, it only controls the symptoms which usually reappear.

Electroconvulsive Therapy (ECT) is sometimes used to bring a patient out of the severe depressive side of the disorder, but this treatment is not nearly as effective in controlling the entire disorder.

80.   **(E)**   Avoidance conditioning can produce active avoidance in which the organism must demonstrate a certain response — jumping over a bar or pressing a lever — to avoid shock. It can also produce passive avoidance in which the organism must not respond — not press a lever or not step on a section of the box, in order to avoid the aversive stimulus.

81.   **(D)**   Perceptual learning involves the formation of relationships between stimuli. The formation of relationships is an internal process. As such, it cannot be directly observed. In order to determine if perceptual learning has occurred, *indirect* methods of study are required.

82.   **(A)**   Clark Hull and his students were interested in the idea that many motives seem directed at the reduction of some internal state of bodily tension which, if continued, would lead to injury or death. His drive-reduction theory was a homeostatic concept which proposed that anything an organism does is ultimately directed at getting rid of or avoiding some unpleasant physiological state.

83.   **(B)**   The pigeon has learned to discriminate between the yellow light (for which it receives reinforcement) and the green light (for which it does not receive reinforcement). After three days (days 6–9), the pigeon appears to have learned the discrimination.

84.   **(A)**   Saturation is one of the three attributes of color experience. It is the psychological correlate of purity, or the number of different wavelengths in a color mixture. When a single wavelength of light is perceived, the hue is said to be pure, or saturated, but as other wavelengths are added, the hue becomes distilled and appears less saturated.

85.   **(E)**   A child with an I.Q. of 100 would have a mental age equal to his or her chronological age. Here's why it is so;

$$100 = \frac{M.\,A.}{C.\,A.} \times 100$$

divide each side by 100

$$1 = \frac{M.\,A.}{C.\,A.}$$

multiply each side by C.A.

$$C.A. = M.A.$$

86.   **(D)**   Prior to training the animal in the classical conditioning paradigm, only the unconditioned stimulus (UCS) can elicit the unconditioned response (UCR). Conditioned stimuli (CS) are not yet effective because training in the CS

+ UCS pairing has not yet taken place. For the same reason, a conditioned response (CR) cannot be elicited, as this is defined as the response elicited by the presentation of the CS.

87.   **(D)**   If the critical level, α, which indicates the probability of making a Type I error, is increased, then the probability of making that error is increased. Since the larger the value of α, the smaller the value of β, the probability of making a Type II error decreases. A Type I error is rejecting the null hypothesis when it is actually true, and a Type II error is not rejecting the null hypothesis when it is false.

88.   **(B)**   Using a one-tailed test will only increase the power when the true mean is in the direction of the tail. This is quite logical since if the mean were in the opposite direction of the tail, the one-tailed test would be totally useless.

89.   **(C)**   In order to increase the power of a test one can either increase α, or increase the sample size. The larger the sample, the smaller the probability of a Type I and Type II error.

90.   **(E)**   After an organism has learned a specific response to a stimulus, it will make this response to stimuli which are similar to the original stimulus. The graph shows that the closer the test stimulus was to the training stimulus of 550 nanometers, the more the birds pecked. The more similar the new stimulus is to the original stimulus, the more likely it is that the learned response will be generalized.

91.   **(E)**   Ellis' therapy is based on the idea that a person's cognitive understanding of events, when mistaken, can lead him to maladaptive behavior. People make such irrational self-statements as "I would be really stupid if I made a mistake" and therefore view the world in these self-destructing, anxiety-provoking ways. He treats this through the use of extensive talking that leads the patient to realize the irrationality of his self-statements. In addition, the patient is asked to fantasize about coping with an anxiety-provoking situation.

92.   **(D)**   Negative reinforcement is used to increase the likelihood of a certain behavior. In learning theory terms, negative reinforcement involves the termination of an aversive stimulus contingent upon the occurrence of a desired behavior. Giving a prisoner time off for good behavior is an example of negative reinforcement. The aversive stimulus (jail) is terminated if the desired behavior (good social, obedient behavior) occurs, thereby increasing the likelihood of the behavior (obedience).

93.   **(E)**   Thorndike's Law of Effect emphasizes the importance of reinforcement in the learning process. According to Thorndike, behavior which is satisfying or pleasing is "stamped in," while behavior that leads to annoyance or

unpleasantness is "stamped out." In general, the principle that reinforcement is necessary for and facilitates learning.

94. **(B)** Nearly all possible time relations have been used in conditioning research. Of all theses various experimental time relationships, simultaneous conditioning is the quickest and most efficient. In simultaneous conditioning, the conditioned stimulus is presented continuously. Then, after a small delay, the unconditioned stimulus is presented. Finally both terminate together. This procedure rapidly produces the conditioned response.

95. **(C)** An authoritarian individual views the world as a jungle and sees it as dangerous and threatening. The person is highly ethnocentric and prejudiced. Authoritarians tend to be opposed to self-examination and unperceptive of the feelings of others. They are dominant to those they perceive as weaker, and submissive to those they perceive as more powerful than themselves.

96. **(A)** The F (fascist) Scale is used to measure the authoritarian personality. It was developed in the late 1940s by Adorno in order to identify the type of personality that would be responsive to fascist ideology. Scores on the F scale correlate highly with anti-semitism and ethnocentrism. It measures the following characteristics: Conventionalism, authoritarian submission, authoritarian aggression, anti-introspection, superstition and stereotyping, power and toughness destruction and cynicism, projectivity, and sexual concerns.

97. **(D)** The F scale is an attitude-trait scale. It has to do with others in the person's social world. Typical questions also include: Human nature being what it is, there will always be war and conflict, and obedience and respect for authority are the most important virtues children should learn.

98. **(A)** A main concept of functionalism is the study of a person as he adapts to his environment. The functionalists believed that behavior and mental processes are adaptive, and they studied mind-body interactions. Consciousness was thought of as an organ.

99. **(D)** The concept of functionalism was influenced very much by William James, although he did not find it. He was concerned with conscious processes as activities of an organism that produced a difference in that organism's life. Wundt was a leader in the structuralist school of psychology, and Watson's ideas led to behaviorism. Wertheimer founded Gestalt psychology. Henry James, William's brother, is, of course, the famous writer.

100. **(B)** Structuralists were concerned with the components of the mind. Functionalism was influenced by Darwin's theory of evolution and one of its basic tenets is that learning is an important adaptive process.

101. **(E)**   Sublimation is the expression of undesirable id impulses through creative and productive means. Examples of these socially adaptive behaviors are painting and sculpture which are theorized to be an expression of sexual impulses. This defense mechanism sometimes provides a fairly permanent solution to the need for protection from anxiety caused by undesirable impulses.

102. **(B)**   Maintenance of a rigid posture is typical of the odd muscular activity (or lack of it) of the catatonic schizophrenic. Catatonics may also strike an unusual pose and hold it for long periods of time (called "waxy flexibility"), engage in purposeless and excessive motor activity, develop odd, stereotyped mannerisms, or remain immobile for much of the time.

103. **(C)**   A test score that has not been converted into a form permitting comparison with other scores is a raw score. Raw scores constitute the raw data base which is to be statistically analyzed. Before data analysis can begin, raw scores must be converted into Z-scores or something similar.

104. **(D)**   Psychosomatic disorders are those in which an individual's psychological problems play a major factor in an organic disease, or pathology. Common disorders which are often psychosomatic in nature are hypertension, migraine headaches, asthma, gastrointestinal problems, and ulcers. These disorders are no less real or dangerous than disorders with a firm organic basis. The treatment is therefore both psychological and medical.

105. **(E)**   Disturbances in motor functions are the most obvious symptoms of the catatonic type of schizophrenia. A catatonic schizophrenic typically alternates between immobility and wild excitement, but often either one or the other type of motor symptoms may predominate. In the excited state the catatonic may shout and talk continuously and incoherently, all the while pacing back and forth. The immobile state is characterized by physical rigidity, muteness, and unresponsiveness.

106. **(D)**   In this quote, Freud was referring to Thanatos, the death instinct. He believed that all human behavior was the result of a struggle between Eros, the life instinct, and Thanatos. In the end, Thanatos wins the struggle. Freud observed that the ultimate aim of an instinct was to return to the unstimulable state of inorganic matter, more specifically, to death. Thanatos is rarely observed in pure form. It can only be inferred from the observation of its derivatives — aggressive and violent tendencies.

107. **(C)**   Wernicke's syndrome is an alcohol-related disorder. Very often this disorder is classified with organic pathologies since it involves pathological changes in the brain stem. The characteristic symptoms are memory loss, confusion, eye dysfunctions, and apathy. It is easily confused with Korsakoff's psychosis, but is differentiated from it due to the pathological organic changes in the

brain. Wernicke's syndrome is related to alcoholism through a thiamine vitamin deficiency. Treatment involves vitamin therapy and attempted reduction of alcohol consumption.

108. **(E)** Defense mechanisms are defensive in that they protect the individual from anxiety they may not be able to tolerate. The anxiety results not from external events, but rather from conflicts between the id and superego which have become excessive in dealing with a situation. Defense mechanisms are created by the ego to deal with these anxieties. These mechanisms may be strong or mild depending on the individual and the anxiety-producing situation.

109. **(E)** All of these various tests are projective in nature. Projective tests evaluate the total personality for its uniqueness. They are fairly unstructured, and the stimulus situations are meant to evoke a broad range of answers. In addition, nonverbal behavior is analyzed under fairly standardized conditions.

110. **(C)** Alzheimer's disease starts at an early age, usually in the 40's or 50's. All the other choices are common symptoms. This form of presenile dementia is unfortunately incurable, and can take anywhere from a few months to five years to progress to full loss of intellectual function.

111. **(C)** The connotation of a word includes the qualities and characteristics associated with the word that are not part of the literal definition (denotation). For example, "Teacher" may have a connotation of "strict, smart, and impatient." Osgood developed a method of assessing connotation using as many as 50 scalar ratings. All of these scales are grouped under three basic dimensions: evaluation (good-bad), potency (weak-strong) and activity (fast-slow). The word is then rated as to where it stands along these dimensions.

112. **(E)** Janet (1859–1947) was one of the original psychologically oriented scientists to study and treat mental illness. A forerunner of the psychoanalysts, he researched hysteria and used hypnosis as his major investigative technique. He was also the first to develop a psychological theory of neurosis.

113. **(E)** Agraphia is a form of organic brain damage in which there is an impairment in the ability to write. It is a communicative disorder under the general heading of aphasia and may often occur in conjunction with alexia.

114. **(A)** Gestalt therapy, introduced by Frederick Perls (1967, 1969), uses a group setting, but emphasizes each individual's perception of self and world. To increase self-awareness, the person acts out fantasies and situations, sometimes even acting out the roles of inanimate objects. Perls also places great emphasis on the interpretation of dreams.

115. **(E)** The "hero" in the Thematic Apperception Test is the figure in the picture around whom the subject assumes the action revolves. Traditionally, the

TATs are interpreted according to the needs of the "hero" and predominant, recurrent themes. Type and extent of fantasy imagery as well as the outcome of the story described are also analyzed.

116. **(C)** The autonomic system regulates homeostatic functions in the body. The autonomic system is divided into two parts, which are called the sympathetic nervous system and the parasympathetic nervous system. These two branches act antagonistically to each other. If one system stimulates an effector, the other inhibits its action. They act to keep each other in check and maintain homeostasis by balancing activation and inhibition of the two systems.

117. **(E)** Autistic children are resistant to changes in routine and often have sudden incidents of fear and crying for no apparent reason. Their emotions seem to arise from spontaneous, internal sources rather than from any occurrence in the environment. Chlorpromazine, which usually reduces symptoms in schizophrenics, has little effect in autistic children besides sedation.

118. **(A)** Rotter's Locus of Control scale attempts to measure the extent to which a person has an internal or external orientation. A person with an internal orientation tends to take responsibility for what happens to him whereas the "external" sees his life events as due to chance or some other factor beyond his control. Consistent findings have been found, some of which are: people with high achievement motivation are more internal, generally, males are more internal than females, whites are more internal than blacks. Locus of control is a learned or acquired characteristic and can be changed by new experiences.

119. **(D)** The variable-ratio schedule produces the highest rates of performance. Because reinforcement is intermittent and irregular, response continues at a high, almost constant rate, sometimes approaching the maximum physical capacity of the organism. The fixed-interval schedule produces the lowest yield in terms of performance. The fixed-ratio schedule produces a strong response pattern, but response drops off immediately after reinforcement. The variable-interval schedule tends to have consistent performance but a slightly lower frequency than a variable-ratio schedule.

120. **(E)** According to Kohlberg, there are three levels in the emergence of morality. The first is premoral, in which the child believes that bad behavior is that which is punished, and good, that which is not punished. The second level is called morality of conventional role conformity in which good behavior is obeying to authority and society's laws and thus is praised by society. The third level is the morality of self-accepted principles in which the child, now an adolescent, recognizes democratic principles and develops his own notions of right and wrong which reflect individual principles of conscience.

121. **(B)** Norman and Bobrow said that in any task the level of performance may be either resource-limited or data-limited. When a continuous increase in

effort, or processing resources, yields a continual improvement the task is re-source-limited. On the other hand, when the upper limit on performance is determined solely by the quality of the data, the task is data-limited. In this case, no matter how much capacity you may allocate to the task, the task still remains virtually impossible.

122. **(D)**   The currently prevalent theory of pitch perception incorporates aspects of both the frequency and place theories. The frequency theory holds that the basilar membrane vibrates in synchrony with a sound and causes the hair cells to produce action potentials at the same frequency. The place theory holds that each portion along the membrane is tuned to specific pitch and vibrates when that pitch is present. For low pitched sounds the frequency theory applies, but for high pitched sounds the neurons cannot fire at the same rate as the frequency of sound waves, but can produce action potentials occurring at the same phase in the sound wave.

123. **(A)**   Abraham Maslow, Carl Rogers, and Fritz Perls proposed the phenomenological model which emphasizes the importance of a person's existence in the here and now, placing heavy stress on the individual's own efforts to actualize his or her potential. Feelings and intuition become important in the understanding of causes of behavior.

124. **(C)**   The sleep-promoting area of the brain has been identified as the raphe system. It is located medially in the hindbrain. Axons from the raphe system use serotonin almost exclusively as their synaptic transmitter. If the synthesis of serotonin is blocked, insomnia ensues. This insomnia can be reversed by giving 5-HTP, the precursor to serotonin.

125. **(A)**   In a skewed distribution, the median and the mean move in the direction of the skew. The mean is pulled towards the tail the most. The mode occurs at the highest point of the distribution.

126. **(E)**   The encoding specificity principle implies the importance of the uniqueness of the link between retrieval cues and the encoded information in recall ability. In order to be an effective retrieval cue, the information used in retrieval must be stored with the to-be-remembered information at the time of learning.

127. **(A)**   Gestaltists believe that we organize an impression to simpler forms. One of the major components of simplicity is proximity. Dots or objects placed closely together tend to be grouped together in some kind of meaningful configuration. Columns and rows are organized figures that the eye sees easily, and it tends to organize unconnected, yet closely placed objects into a familiar pattern. Whether this tendency is inborn or learned is not currently known.

128. **(E)**   The personality structure, according to Allport, is represented

largely by traits; these traits motivate behavior. A trait is regarded as a neuropsychic structure which causes an individual to behave in a meaningfully consistent manner. These traits develop as a result of a person's interaction with the environment. There are common traits which are often referred to simply as traits and there is the individual trait which has been referred to as a personal disposition. All traits are responsible for adaptive and expressive behaviors.

129. **(A)**   Rationalism focuses on exclusive causal relationships between events and states that the faculty of reason is the prime tool for understanding potentially every event that occurs in the universe. One problem with this philosophy is that it always relies on primary assumptions that are usually subjective and somewhat circular. Many times these assumptions are not explained, but dismissed as "self-evident." In spite of these problems, rationalism's original premise that the universe is orderly, provided the basis for all subsequent philosophical and scientific thought.

130. **(E)**   Both Aristotle and Thomas Aquinas, as well as Thomas Jefferson were among the first and best known proponents of the rationalist philosophy.

ANSWERS TO QUESTIONS 131–135 refer to the group of five equations.

131. **(C)**   The equation:

$$\frac{\Sigma(x_i - \overline{x})^3}{n} = m^3.$$

m^3 is also called the third moment. The third moment (m^3) is an essential part of computing the relative measure of symmetry:

$$a^3 = \frac{m^3}{s^3}.$$

132. **(D)**   The transformation of X (raw score) to Z (standard score) is given by the equation

$$Z = \frac{x - \mu}{\sigma}.$$

Any normal distribution with a mean μ (mu) and a variance σ^2 (sigma squared) can be converted into the standard normal distribution. The probability of X in the distribution with μ and σ^2 is equivalent to the probability of Z in the normal distribution with mean 0 and variance 1. Hence, given X, its Z probability can be found.

133. **(E)**   The equation

$$\frac{\mu - M}{n - X_i}$$

is false. It is not used in statistical analysis.

134. **(A)** The mean is the arithmetic average. It is obtained by adding up all the scores and dividing by the number of scores in the data sample. It is expressed statistically as

$$\frac{\Sigma(x_i)}{n}$$

where ΣX_i represents the summation of scores and n represents the number of scores in the sample.

135. **(B)** The equation which represents the standard deviation squared is the variance. It is expressed as:

$$\frac{\Sigma(x_i - \overline{x})^2}{n - 1}$$

Variance is a measure of the dispersion of scores around some measure of central tendency.

136. **(A)** Sensory information from the environment travels to the spinal cord and the thalamus by way of afferent nerves. Afferent nerves are nerves carried by the dorsal root which relay information about the environment (sensory impulses) to the central nervous system. Afferent nerves are composed of afferent neurons.

137. **(D)** The lateral geniculate nucleus (or body) relays all messages from visual reception to the visual area of the cortex.

138. **(C)** In the thalamic system, the different sensory systems are kept rigidly separate, whereas the reticular activating system treats all the senses as one group providing arousal information. Thus the thalamus has specific nuclei to receive only certain kinds of information. The reticular activating system is not organized in this way. In the RAS, the same information will activate wide regions of the cortex, and not just specific sensory areas.

139. **(A)** The hypothalamus has the important function of homeostatic regulation and the thalamus has the function of regulating and coordinating the external signs of emotion. By stimulating the thalamus with an electrode, a sham rage can be elicited in a cat — the hair stands on end, the claws protrude, and the back becomes humped. However, as soon as the stimulation ceases, the rage responses disappear.

140. **(D)** The thalamus is part of the brain; therefore, it is part of the central nervous system (CNS). The central nervous system includes the brain and spinal cord.

141. **(A)** Counterconditioning is the weakening or elimination of a conditioned response by the learning of a new response that is incompatible with, and

stronger than the one being extinguished. This procedure is better than extinction alone for getting rid of unwanted responses.

142. **(E)** The reverse of this statement is true: *first-born children* have a greater tendency to affiliate when fearful than later-born children. Stanley Schachter (1959), a major affiliation theorist, found that first-borns, when afraid, affiliate more than second-borns, who, in turn, affiliate more than third-borns, and so on. The most popular explanation for this effect is that first-born children are more dependent on their parents for security and comfort in fearful situations due to being the only child and therefore the main target of the parents' concern and attention.

143. **(E)** Positive transfer occurs when previous learning makes new learning easier. Negative transfer occurs when previous learning interferes with new learning. In both verbal and motor learning, the more similar the two tasks are, the greater the positive transfer will be between them.

144. **(C)** This adverse effect has generally been attributed to the frustrating effect of severe punishment. Mild punishment is a far more effective tool for reducing aggression in children.

145. **(A)** Wolfgang Kohler (1887–1967) was one of the early founders of Gestalt psychology along with Max Wertheimer (1880–1943) and Kurt Koffka (1886–1941). All of the others listed are behaviorists or well known antecedent influences (Thorndike). Tolman (1886–1959) had his own style of behaviorism that focused on goal–directed, purposive behavior. Hull (1884–1952) defined behavior in terms of a biological adaptation to a unique environment. Watson (1878–1958) is the founder of behaviorism and its methods and Thorndike's (1874–1949) connectionism was a powerful antecedent influence on behaviorism.

146. **(D)** An example of omission training: a parent allows a child to stay out late (reward) only if he stops drinking beer (undesired response). The reward is contingent on not making a response. Other types of training are reward, escape, and punishment.

147. **(A)** In autism, a child seems aloof during the earliest stages of life. Usually the child prefers isolation and does not communicate with or show affection towards his parents. The child has no real concept of self and shows serious difficulties in four major areas: social attachment, perceptual-cognitive functioning, language development, formation of self-identity.

148. **(D)** This effect is operating on the principle that "Forewarned is forearmed." Forewarning helps build up a person's defenses against a discrepant message. Most likely, this can be explained by the person mentally preparing to

refute the argument ahead of time. If there is no forewarning, the person has no time to organize a mental defense against the persuasive message.

149. **(A)** Even though the optimal strategy in both of these games is obviously to cooperate, there was a strong tendency to compete. In fact, in the Prisoner's Dilemma game, cooperation decreased even further as the game progressed. In both games, the player's competed and lost, instead of cooperating and winning.

150. **(B)** Systematic desensitization, developed by Wolpe (1961), treats behavior that is being negatively reinforced — that is, reinforced by the successful avoidance of a painful situation. It involves a counterconditioning approach in which the therapist trains the client to relax in situations that previously produced anxiety. The therapy involves three easy steps: training in the relaxation procedure, the construction of an anxiety hierarchy, and the desensitization procedure in which relaxation is paired with imagined, anxiety-provoking situations.

151. **(C)** REM-deprived subjects entered into more REM periods during each successive night of the experiment. Since most dreaming occurs during REM periods, these subjects dream 60% more than usual. Experiments performed on REM deprivation indicate that man has a need to dream.

152. **(C)** Trisomy 21 causes mongolism (also called Down's syndrome). Instead of a pair of #21 chromosomes, there exists a triplet due to a defect in the egg's development. Compulsive reactions are persistent acts which are uncontrollably repeated over and over. The individual feels an irresistible urge to perform the act and experiences extreme distress if prevented from doing so.

153. **(C)** Deindividuation is a state in which a person feels a lessened sense of personal identity and a decreased concern about what others think of him/her. This occurs when a person is part of a group and thus feels less responsible for his actions. This is also known as responsibility diffusion.

154. **(E)** The generative grammar of a language is the set of rules that determine how the language is structured. It is not the same as the restrictive rules of a language. Generative rules are believed to be automatically incorporated into the child's cognitive structure early in development.

155. **(B)** The conversion of physical energy into a form that can be processed by our brains has three steps. *Reception* is the absorption of physical energy. *Transduction* is the conversion of energy from the absorbed stimulus to an electrochemical pattern in the neurons. *Coding* is the one-to-one correspondence between an aspect of the physical stimulus and an aspect of the nervous system's activity.

156. **(C)**   Concurrent validity is one type of criterion-related validity. The other type is predictive validity. The purpose of a test with only concurrent validity is to make available a simpler and faster substitute for the criterion data. In criterion-related validity, a comparison is made between performance on the test and some independent measure of validity. If the test is the SAT, an appropriate criterion would be future college grades.

157. **(B)**   Gordon Allport's theory of personality stresses conscious motivation. Allport regards the past as unimportant in assessing a person's behavior. He maintains that unconscious motivation is only a major determinant of behavior in the case of neurotic and psychotic individuals. Whereas most theorists, including Freud and Skinner, regard people showing abnormal behavior as only quantitatively different from those who don't; Allport believes that the difference is qualitative.

158. **(D)**   According to Rogers, an unrealistic self-concept contributes greatly to emotional maladjustment. In his client-centered therapy, Rogers aims at changing the person's self-references from mostly negative to mostly positive. It was found that the conditions of clients who gained more self-approval had been clinically judged to have improved.

159. **(E)**   It is known that memory for the idea of a passage is better than memory for its verbatim contents. This experiment shows that semantic coding is the more common form of memory storage. When tested right after hearing the sentence in the story, any change from the original wording or semantic, was detected. After longer intervals, subjects were able to recognize changes in meaning, but not changes in wording when the same meaning was preserved.

160. **(D)**   Damage to the cerebral cortex outside the motor cortex leads to a complex movement deficit called apraxia. This involves an ability to make movements, but an inability to organize them. A person with apraxia can do something spontaneously but is not able to do it when instructed verbally.

161. **(E)**   J.C. Worthy conducted studies within Sears, Roebuck and Company, and found that overspecialization is a great cause of poor management-employee relations. When jobs are broken down too finely there exists low morale and low output. Conflicts result because greater supervision and more formal controls are needed. Worthy suggested that a simpler structure with less administrative centralization would create an environment conducive to better attitudes and greater individual responsibility.

162. **(A)**   Dale's Law states that each neuron synthesizes, stores, and uses only one transmitter at all synapses formed by all branches of its axon. A modified version of that would add that each neuron releases the same combination of transmitters at every synapse it forms. The synapses using any particular trans-

mitter are found to be located in discrete paths and groups rather than being scattered throughout the brain.

163. **(B)** Some people have their corpus callosum cut as a treatment for severe epilepsy. This results in isolation of the two cerebral hemispheres from each other. Information that enters one hemisphere cannot pass to the other. Thus, information seen on the left side of a screen going to the right hemisphere cannot be described by the person even though he or she is able to point out the object with his or her left hand.

164. **(A)** For the majority of people, the ability to speak depends on the left hemisphere of the cerebral cortex. Principal language areas are Broca's Area, located in the left frontal lobe; Wernicke's Area, in the left temporal lobe; and an area known as the arcuate fasciculus which connects the two.

165. **(C)** Each hemisphere is connected to the eyes in a way that it gets input from the opposite half of the visual world. Light from the right visual field shines onto the left half of each retina. The left half of each retina connects to the left hemisphere. The right half of each retina, which sees the left half of the visual field, connects to the right hemisphere. Normally, the left and right hemispheres exchange information through the corpus callosum and other smaller bundles of fibers.

166. **(D)** Systematic desensitization involves asking a deeply relaxed person to imagine a series of anxiety-provoking situations, along a continuum. The situations range from only mild-fear provoking to intense-fear provoking. When a scene is imagined without anxiety, the person can then move to the next level in the hierarchy.

167. **(A)** Joseph Wolpe developed the procedure of systematic desensitization. It is one of the three most frequently used counterconditioning techniques. The other two are assertive training and aversive conditioning.

168. **(B)** In correlational analysis, the correlation coefficient is r. The graph shows that as y decreases, x increases by a proportionate amount; thus, the line has a negative slope and $r = -1$.

169. **(B)** Correlation analysis measures the degree of linear association between two characteristics, x and y. When the correlation coefficient, r, is $+1$, as x increases, y increases by a proportionate amount; and when $r = -1$, as y decreases, x increases by a proportionate amount. When there is no correlation, $r = 0$ and x and y are independent.

170. **(C)** Conversion disorder is a type of somatoform disorder that involves real motor or sensory deficits that nevertheless have no neurological or medical

basis. The other disorders all fall under the category of attention deficit and disruptive behavior disorders, which is itself a subcategory of disorders usually first diagnosed in infancy, childhood, or adolescence. Enuresis is more commonly known as "bedwetting."

171. **(E)** According to Piaget's theory of cognitive development, decentration occurs in the concrete operational period. The child is able to focus his attention from one part of a situation to another. The earliest period of cognitive development, the sensorimotor period, includes the reflex stage, primary circular reactions, secondary circular reactions, coordination of secondary schemes, tertiary circular reactions, and internalization of thought.

172. **(E)** The parathyroid secretes parathyroid hormone which increases blood calcium and decreases potassium. The other four organs are involved in some way with reproduction. The anterior pituitary releases luteinizing hormone, follicle-stimulating hormone, adrenocorticotropic hormone (ACTH), growth hormone, thyroid-stimulating hormone, and prolactin. The adrenal cortex secretes androgens and estrogens and also aldosterone and cortisol. The hypothalamus secretes the releasing hormones for TSH, LH, FSH, GH, and the inhibiting hormones for GH and prolactin. The ovary releases estrogens.

173. **(E)** In his later years, B. F. Skinner's attention had extended to philosophical issues based on his operant conditioning theory. The result was his book *Beyond Freedom and Dignity* in which he subscribed to the doctrine of determinism. From his laboratory experiments with rats, he came to the belief that societies, as well as individuals, can be controlled.

174. **(A)** The onset of the CS precedes the onset of the UCS in forward conditioning. Forward conditioning results in strong CS-produced responses. Also in forward conditioning, CR strength increases as the onset of CS occurs closer in time to the onset of the UCS. An optimal time interval exists between the CS onset and the UCS onset. Both relatively long and quite short time intervals between CS onset and UCS onset result in weaker CRs than otherwise.

175. **(B)** Achievement motivation may be defined as the need, or drive, to perform a task successfully as judged against standards of excellence. Since individuals differ in the amount of satisfaction they receive from achievement, much attention is focused on the differences in environments as providing more or less achievement opportunities. This theory was proposed by David McClelland as part of his Achievement Motivation model of behavior.

176. **(A)** A series of studies by Seligman and Maier demonstrated the consequences of exposure to aversive events that cannot be controlled. One group of dogs was administered shocks that they could control by pressing a panel. A second group had no control over the shocks. The dogs were then placed in a different situation in which shock could be escaped by jumping over a hurdle.

The first group learned to jump quickly. The second group failed to learn because of their previous exposure to shock they could not control. Instead, these dogs acted passively and whined. This phenomenon is called learned helplessness.

177. **(D)** B. F. Skinner was the chief figure of a group of behaviorists who thought that classical conditioning theory was unable to explain the whole range of learning phenomena. Skinner thought that it was especially inadequate at explaining operant learning. He thought it was necessary to consider the organism's past reinforcement history to better understand instrumental conditioning. Skinner believed that operant conditioning was the basis of most real-life behavior.

178. **(B)** The eye is insensitive to light waves below and beyond the range of 350 to 750 nanometers. In between this range, the rods and cones are differentially sensitive to wavelengths of light. Generally, the cones are less sensitive than the rods to middle wavelength light. The maximal sensitivity for cones is 560 nanometers and the maximal sensitivity for rods is 510 nanometers.

179. **(E)** Proactive interference is the detrimental effect of prior learning on the retention of recently learned material. Retroactive interference is when the last few items learned interfere with the earlier items. The items in the middle of a list are thus subject to both types of interference so they are least likely to be recalled.

180. **(A)** By definition, proactive interference is the detrimental effect of prior learning on the retention of recently learned material.

181. **(B)** It has been found that when the category of the items to be remembered is changed, there is a release from proactive interference. Thus there is a large increase in recall because the previous items are no longer interfering with memory of recent items, since they are no longer similar to each other.

182. **(D)** This study, done by Funkhouser showed how classification at time of input affects retention. It was found that the speed and accuracy of recall for subjects who were permitted to recall using the same categories by which they had studied the information were superior to that of the subjects who had to use different categories. This study indicates that the categorization made at the time of study restricts the way in which the material can be readily used (recalled).

183. **(D)** The smaller the significance level, the more confident one is that the differences obtained are significant. A significance level (p-value) of .01 means that there is only a 1% probability that the differences you obtained could have occurred by chance. Similarly a level of .05 would mean that there is a 5% probability that the differences obtained are not real but occurred by chance. Most psychological experiments, except for some clinical research, require a

level of .05 or less to demonstrate significant results. Here, significance refers to non-chance occurrences.

184. **(B)**   Gestalt theory followed structuralism as a leading explanation for the human perceptual system. Gestalt theorists rejected the structuralist idea that our perceptions were based on an assemblage of separate points of sensation, and concerned themselves with larger units of perception. From their study emerged a group of "Laws of Organization." Some of the central laws are the perception of area, closedness, proximity, continuation, and symmetry.

185. **(D)**   Spearman, Guilford, and Burt have all used factor analysis in the development of theories and tests, though they have used it in different ways. In general, psychologists use factor analysis in an attempt to identify underlying intellectual traits, or descriptive categories. The names of the traits "uncovered" by factor analysis have been used to establish categories which are useful in describing intelligence. Spearman focused on 2 main factors, a general factor and specific factors. Guilford's model addressed 120 separate factors. Burt's development of the hierarchical theory represents a midpoint between the extremes of 2 and 120 factors.

186. **(B)**   In approach-avoidance conflicts, the goal that attracts is the same as the one that repels. This type of conflict often results in behavioral oscillation. The organism oscillates between approaching the goal and avoiding the goal. This phenomenon was first systematically studied by Neal Miller. He analyzed differences in the animal's response to approach-avoidance situations as a function of the distance from the goal. He called these gradients of approach and gradients of avoidance.

187. **(D)**   Independent variables are manipulated by the experimenter. In this experiment the researcher wants to observe the effects that various methods of study and time of testing will have on the dependent variable of amount of words recalled.

188. **(A)**   In a between-subjects design half of the subjects are exposed to one level of the variable and half are exposed to the other. In this experiment one group receives delayed testing and one group receives an immediate test. This type of design must deal with individual differences. One way to do this is by administering a pre-test for memory and then form pairs of subjects with similar scores and then randomly assign one member of the pair to one group and the other member to the second group. In a within-subjects design in which all subjects are treated with both levels of the independent variable, this problem of individual differences is eliminated, but there are other disadvantages.

189. **(C)**   When dealing with a within-subjects variable such as method of study in this experiment, one has to make sure that all possible treatment orders are used. This is known as counterbalancing.

190. **(A)** In avoidance conditioning the subject's response to a neutral stimulus delays the occurrence of an aversive stimulus. Eventually, to maintain the avoidance behavior, only the neutral stimulus needs to be presented for it to occur, hence, the extinction of the behavior is very slow.

191. **(C)** The filter theory of selective attention was suggested by Broadbent. This filter was capable of handling only one channel at a time, but one could switch back and forth in order to follow each one. According to this theory only the information which gets past the filter can be analyzed for meaning, so the only way one would hear one's name on the unattended channel would be if the filter happened to be switched on to that channel at that particular moment.

192. **(C)** The cocktail party phenomenon is the name given to the phenomenon in which a person's attention switches from the active channel to the passive channel when his name is presented on the passive (unattended) channel. This is a familiar occurrence at cocktail parties and the like. Although one may not be paying attention to other conversations, he is still able to notice when his name is mentioned.

193. **(D)** Attention is a selective process, and it has been shown that some analysis of meaning can occur without conscious attention. This has been demonstrated in several shadowing experiments in which the subject's interpretation of what they heard in the attended message was influenced by certain contextually related words presented to the unattended ear. An individual can allocate his attentional resources proportionally to several stimuli at a time.

194. **(E)** In a typical shadowing, experiment the subject repeats everything that is heard, out loud. The material to be shadowed is presented in one ear of an earphone and test material is presented in the other ear or visually. The subject is then tested on the material presented to the nonshadowing ear.

195. **(B)** Changes in light and dark do not run the biological clock. Light is involved in "resetting" the clock, but the free-running rhythm of the clock continues to work even in an unchanging environment. As seen in the paragraph, the blind man's spontaneous rhythm continues even when it is out of phase with the outside world, but it does require light in order to be reset.

196. **(C)** The pineal gland releases large amounts of melatonin at night and small amounts in the daytime. Light inhibits the production of melatonin during the day and it has been found that the high levels present at night promote sleep.

197. **(C)** It is now being accepted that the suprachiasmatic nucleus generates the biological clock. This portion of the hypothalamus receives direct input from the retina. If all input to the SCN is eliminated it continues to generate a free-running rhythm but it cannot be reset by light.

198. **(B)** The field theory of behavior was developed by Kurt Lewin and named as an analogy to a theory of electricity and magnetism. It emphasizes that behavior depends on interactions between the organism and the environment. Behavior is shaped by a combination of forces which make up the entire field, or "life space."

199. **(C)** Lewin used a form of geometry known as topology in order to map the life space. This deals with the order of relationships, but not with their direction or distance. To represent direction he developed a new form of qualitative geometry called hodological space, in which he utilized vectors to represent directions of movement toward goals.

200. **(B)** The field theory approach holds that the way in which an object influences behavior is determined by the context of which it is a part. This is in agreement with the basic idea that behavior requires an analysis of the situation as a whole.

201. **(A)** The ability of young children to use two-word sentences is referred to as telegraphic speech. Inclusion of articles, i.e., "the," "a," comes later. Aphasia refers to a speech disorder. Choices (D) and (E) do not exist.

202. **(B)** Concept formation refers to the ability to learn to classify objects by common properties, and to generalize novel instances of the concept. Concepts are symbolic precursors to the acquisition of language.

203. **(C)** Noam Chomsky is one of the leaders in the field of psycholinguistics. His research suggests that humans acquire language too rapidly to be explained by imitation and trial-and-error learning models.

204. **(B)** The use of telegraphic speech (two-word statements) is typical of two-year-olds.

205. **(D)** Retinal disparity refers to the fact that each eye sends a slightly different image to the brain. The brain uses the differences between the two images as a cue to perceive depth.

206. **(E)** The sense of taste in humans is most sensitive to bitterness and least sensitive to sweetness. Bitter tastes trigger the gag reflex, a tendency to vomit. It is not a coincidence that most poisons taste bitter. The gag reflex would have saved the life of a primitive human sampling a novel food. Only the tip of the tongue is sensitive to "sweet" which is the reason children lick lollipops with the tip of their tongues. Adults, on the other hand, place aspirin and other bitter pills on the back of their tongues in the area of the tongue most sensitive to bitterness.

207. **(E)** Clairvoyance is the ability to perceive objects from a distance, for example, a subject perceiving the contents of a sealed envelope. Precognition refers to predicting the future. Psychokinesis is the ability to move objects with the mind, while telepathy refers to mind reading. Most of the people who claim to have these abilities have been shown to be frauds or clever magicians. Hence, the scientific community is skeptical of these claims.

208. **(C)** Ethology is the study of various species in their natural environment. Ethologists believe that knowledge of a species obtained in laboratories or zoos is limited, artificial, and incomplete. A simian psychologist would be an ape with a Ph.D.

209. **(C)** Structuralism believes that mental structures exist (such as the id, ego, and superego) and introspection (self-examination) is the means to explore these structures. Psychoanalysis uses the structural approach. Functionalism limits scientific inquiry to observable phenomena. The behaviorists use this approach.

210. **(A)** Applied psychologists attempt to apply psychological principles discovered through research to "real world" problems. Clinical psychologists typically provide therapy.

211. **(C)** We take credit for our successes (internal causes), and assign blame for our failures to environmental variables (external causes). The Freudian ego-defense mechanisms of reaction formation and projection make similar points.

212. **(A)** The primacy and recency effects, respectively, refer to our remembering best the first and the last bits of information that we were given. The middle information is distorted by proactive and retroactive interference effects.

213. **(B)** People have an inherent need to be accepted by others. If co-workers frown on our performance, the average person will slow down in order to avoid censure from peers. The opposite is true also. A mediocre worker will improve his or her performance if put in with good workers. This is social facilitation.

214. **(D)** A newborn is referred to as a neonate. A zygote refers to the fertilized egg before it takes on human form. The fetus is the term that applies to an unborn creature that has developed the majority of its organs and limbs.

215. **(E)** Stimulation of the cheek of a newborn elicits the rooting reflex. The baby turns to the source of stimulation and begins to suck.

216. **(B)** Menstruation in the female and the production of live sperm in the male mark the beginning of biological puberty. Puberty can begin as early as nine years of age (precocious puberty) or as late as 16 years of age.

217. **(C)** Adolescence, a period between infancy and adulthood, is a Western concept that was developed during this century. In many cultures, children are given adult responsibilities at puberty. They marry, are apprenticed, or join the military as early as 10 years of age. Allowing young people the luxury of a few years to develop before assuming the responsibilities of adults is a Western concept. Some psychologists believe that these freedoms can be detrimental, rather than fostering the development of maturity.

The Graduate Record Examination in

PSYCHOLOGY

Test 5

Test 5 is also on CD-ROM as part of REA's exclusive interactive GRE Psychology TEST*ware*®. We recommend that you take the computerized exam first. This will give you the additional study features and benefits of enforced timed conditions, individual diagnostic analysis, and instantaneous scoring. See page vi for guidance on how to get the most out of our GRE Psychology book and software.

THE GRADUATE RECORD EXAMINATION
PSYCHOLOGY TEST 5
ANSWER SHEET

1. Ⓐ Ⓑ Ⓒ Ⓓ Ⓔ
2. Ⓐ Ⓑ Ⓒ Ⓓ Ⓔ
3. Ⓐ Ⓑ Ⓒ Ⓓ Ⓔ
4. Ⓐ Ⓑ Ⓒ Ⓓ Ⓔ
5. Ⓐ Ⓑ Ⓒ Ⓓ Ⓔ
6. Ⓐ Ⓑ Ⓒ Ⓓ Ⓔ
7. Ⓐ Ⓑ Ⓒ Ⓓ Ⓔ
8. Ⓐ Ⓑ Ⓒ Ⓓ Ⓔ
9. Ⓐ Ⓑ Ⓒ Ⓓ Ⓔ
10. Ⓐ Ⓑ Ⓒ Ⓓ Ⓔ
11. Ⓐ Ⓑ Ⓒ Ⓓ Ⓔ
12. Ⓐ Ⓑ Ⓒ Ⓓ Ⓔ
13. Ⓐ Ⓑ Ⓒ Ⓓ Ⓔ
14. Ⓐ Ⓑ Ⓒ Ⓓ Ⓔ
15. Ⓐ Ⓑ Ⓒ Ⓓ Ⓔ
16. Ⓐ Ⓑ Ⓒ Ⓓ Ⓔ
17. Ⓐ Ⓑ Ⓒ Ⓓ Ⓔ
18. Ⓐ Ⓑ Ⓒ Ⓓ Ⓔ
19. Ⓐ Ⓑ Ⓒ Ⓓ Ⓔ
20. Ⓐ Ⓑ Ⓒ Ⓓ Ⓔ
21. Ⓐ Ⓑ Ⓒ Ⓓ Ⓔ
22. Ⓐ Ⓑ Ⓒ Ⓓ Ⓔ
23. Ⓐ Ⓑ Ⓒ Ⓓ Ⓔ
24. Ⓐ Ⓑ Ⓒ Ⓓ Ⓔ
25. Ⓐ Ⓑ Ⓒ Ⓓ Ⓔ
26. Ⓐ Ⓑ Ⓒ Ⓓ Ⓔ
27. Ⓐ Ⓑ Ⓒ Ⓓ Ⓔ
28. Ⓐ Ⓑ Ⓒ Ⓓ Ⓔ
29. Ⓐ Ⓑ Ⓒ Ⓓ Ⓔ
30. Ⓐ Ⓑ Ⓒ Ⓓ Ⓔ
31. Ⓐ Ⓑ Ⓒ Ⓓ Ⓔ
32. Ⓐ Ⓑ Ⓒ Ⓓ Ⓔ
33. Ⓐ Ⓑ Ⓒ Ⓓ Ⓔ

34. Ⓐ Ⓑ Ⓒ Ⓓ Ⓔ
35. Ⓐ Ⓑ Ⓒ Ⓓ Ⓔ
36. Ⓐ Ⓑ Ⓒ Ⓓ Ⓔ
37. Ⓐ Ⓑ Ⓒ Ⓓ Ⓔ
38. Ⓐ Ⓑ Ⓒ Ⓓ Ⓔ
39. Ⓐ Ⓑ Ⓒ Ⓓ Ⓔ
40. Ⓐ Ⓑ Ⓒ Ⓓ Ⓔ
41. Ⓐ Ⓑ Ⓒ Ⓓ Ⓔ
42. Ⓐ Ⓑ Ⓒ Ⓓ Ⓔ
43. Ⓐ Ⓑ Ⓒ Ⓓ Ⓔ
44. Ⓐ Ⓑ Ⓒ Ⓓ Ⓔ
45. Ⓐ Ⓑ Ⓒ Ⓓ Ⓔ
46. Ⓐ Ⓑ Ⓒ Ⓓ Ⓔ
47. Ⓐ Ⓑ Ⓒ Ⓓ Ⓔ
48. Ⓐ Ⓑ Ⓒ Ⓓ Ⓔ
49. Ⓐ Ⓑ Ⓒ Ⓓ Ⓔ
50. Ⓐ Ⓑ Ⓒ Ⓓ Ⓔ
51. Ⓐ Ⓑ Ⓒ Ⓓ Ⓔ
52. Ⓐ Ⓑ Ⓒ Ⓓ Ⓔ
53. Ⓐ Ⓑ Ⓒ Ⓓ Ⓔ
54. Ⓐ Ⓑ Ⓒ Ⓓ Ⓔ
55. Ⓐ Ⓑ Ⓒ Ⓓ Ⓔ
56. Ⓐ Ⓑ Ⓒ Ⓓ Ⓔ
57. Ⓐ Ⓑ Ⓒ Ⓓ Ⓔ
58. Ⓐ Ⓑ Ⓒ Ⓓ Ⓔ
59. Ⓐ Ⓑ Ⓒ Ⓓ Ⓔ
60. Ⓐ Ⓑ Ⓒ Ⓓ Ⓔ
61. Ⓐ Ⓑ Ⓒ Ⓓ Ⓔ
62. Ⓐ Ⓑ Ⓒ Ⓓ Ⓔ
63. Ⓐ Ⓑ Ⓒ Ⓓ Ⓔ
64. Ⓐ Ⓑ Ⓒ Ⓓ Ⓔ
65. Ⓐ Ⓑ Ⓒ Ⓓ Ⓔ
66. Ⓐ Ⓑ Ⓒ Ⓓ Ⓔ

67. Ⓐ Ⓑ Ⓒ Ⓓ Ⓔ
68. Ⓐ Ⓑ Ⓒ Ⓓ Ⓔ
69. Ⓐ Ⓑ Ⓒ Ⓓ Ⓔ
70. Ⓐ Ⓑ Ⓒ Ⓓ Ⓔ
71. Ⓐ Ⓑ Ⓒ Ⓓ Ⓔ
72. Ⓐ Ⓑ Ⓒ Ⓓ Ⓔ
73. Ⓐ Ⓑ Ⓒ Ⓓ Ⓔ
74. Ⓐ Ⓑ Ⓒ Ⓓ Ⓔ
75. Ⓐ Ⓑ Ⓒ Ⓓ Ⓔ
76. Ⓐ Ⓑ Ⓒ Ⓓ Ⓔ
77. Ⓐ Ⓑ Ⓒ Ⓓ Ⓔ
78. Ⓐ Ⓑ Ⓒ Ⓓ Ⓔ
79. Ⓐ Ⓑ Ⓒ Ⓓ Ⓔ
80. Ⓐ Ⓑ Ⓒ Ⓓ Ⓔ
81. Ⓐ Ⓑ Ⓒ Ⓓ Ⓔ
82. Ⓐ Ⓑ Ⓒ Ⓓ Ⓔ
83. Ⓐ Ⓑ Ⓒ Ⓓ Ⓔ
84. Ⓐ Ⓑ Ⓒ Ⓓ Ⓔ
85. Ⓐ Ⓑ Ⓒ Ⓓ Ⓔ
86. Ⓐ Ⓑ Ⓒ Ⓓ Ⓔ
87. Ⓐ Ⓑ Ⓒ Ⓓ Ⓔ
88. Ⓐ Ⓑ Ⓒ Ⓓ Ⓔ
89. Ⓐ Ⓑ Ⓒ Ⓓ Ⓔ
90. Ⓐ Ⓑ Ⓒ Ⓓ Ⓔ
91. Ⓐ Ⓑ Ⓒ Ⓓ Ⓔ
92. Ⓐ Ⓑ Ⓒ Ⓓ Ⓔ
93. Ⓐ Ⓑ Ⓒ Ⓓ Ⓔ
94. Ⓐ Ⓑ Ⓒ Ⓓ Ⓔ
95. Ⓐ Ⓑ Ⓒ Ⓓ Ⓔ
96. Ⓐ Ⓑ Ⓒ Ⓓ Ⓔ
97. Ⓐ Ⓑ Ⓒ Ⓓ Ⓔ
98. Ⓐ Ⓑ Ⓒ Ⓓ Ⓔ
99. Ⓐ Ⓑ Ⓒ Ⓓ Ⓔ

100. Ⓐ Ⓑ Ⓒ Ⓓ Ⓔ	140. Ⓐ Ⓑ Ⓒ Ⓓ Ⓔ	180. Ⓐ Ⓑ Ⓒ Ⓓ Ⓔ
101. Ⓐ Ⓑ Ⓒ Ⓓ Ⓔ	141. Ⓐ Ⓑ Ⓒ Ⓓ Ⓔ	181. Ⓐ Ⓑ Ⓒ Ⓓ Ⓔ
102. Ⓐ Ⓑ Ⓒ Ⓓ Ⓔ	142. Ⓐ Ⓑ Ⓒ Ⓓ Ⓔ	182. Ⓐ Ⓑ Ⓒ Ⓓ Ⓔ
103. Ⓐ Ⓑ Ⓒ Ⓓ Ⓔ	143. Ⓐ Ⓑ Ⓒ Ⓓ Ⓔ	183. Ⓐ Ⓑ Ⓒ Ⓓ Ⓔ
104. Ⓐ Ⓑ Ⓒ Ⓓ Ⓔ	144. Ⓐ Ⓑ Ⓒ Ⓓ Ⓔ	184. Ⓐ Ⓑ Ⓒ Ⓓ Ⓔ
105. Ⓐ Ⓑ Ⓒ Ⓓ Ⓔ	145. Ⓐ Ⓑ Ⓒ Ⓓ Ⓔ	185. Ⓐ Ⓑ Ⓒ Ⓓ Ⓔ
106. Ⓐ Ⓑ Ⓒ Ⓓ Ⓔ	146. Ⓐ Ⓑ Ⓒ Ⓓ Ⓔ	186. Ⓐ Ⓑ Ⓒ Ⓓ Ⓔ
107. Ⓐ Ⓑ Ⓒ Ⓓ Ⓔ	147. Ⓐ Ⓑ Ⓒ Ⓓ Ⓔ	187. Ⓐ Ⓑ Ⓒ Ⓓ Ⓔ
108. Ⓐ Ⓑ Ⓒ Ⓓ Ⓔ	148. Ⓐ Ⓑ Ⓒ Ⓓ Ⓔ	188. Ⓐ Ⓑ Ⓒ Ⓓ Ⓔ
109. Ⓐ Ⓑ Ⓒ Ⓓ Ⓔ	149. Ⓐ Ⓑ Ⓒ Ⓓ Ⓔ	189. Ⓐ Ⓑ Ⓒ Ⓓ Ⓔ
110. Ⓐ Ⓑ Ⓒ Ⓓ Ⓔ	150. Ⓐ Ⓑ Ⓒ Ⓓ Ⓔ	190. Ⓐ Ⓑ Ⓒ Ⓓ Ⓔ
111. Ⓐ Ⓑ Ⓒ Ⓓ Ⓔ	151. Ⓐ Ⓑ Ⓒ Ⓓ Ⓔ	191. Ⓐ Ⓑ Ⓒ Ⓓ Ⓔ
112. Ⓐ Ⓑ Ⓒ Ⓓ Ⓔ	152. Ⓐ Ⓑ Ⓒ Ⓓ Ⓔ	192. Ⓐ Ⓑ Ⓒ Ⓓ Ⓔ
113. Ⓐ Ⓑ Ⓒ Ⓓ Ⓔ	153. Ⓐ Ⓑ Ⓒ Ⓓ Ⓔ	193. Ⓐ Ⓑ Ⓒ Ⓓ Ⓔ
114. Ⓐ Ⓑ Ⓒ Ⓓ Ⓔ	154. Ⓐ Ⓑ Ⓒ Ⓓ Ⓔ	194. Ⓐ Ⓑ Ⓒ Ⓓ Ⓔ
115. Ⓐ Ⓑ Ⓒ Ⓓ Ⓔ	155. Ⓐ Ⓑ Ⓒ Ⓓ Ⓔ	195. Ⓐ Ⓑ Ⓒ Ⓓ Ⓔ
116. Ⓐ Ⓑ Ⓒ Ⓓ Ⓔ	156. Ⓐ Ⓑ Ⓒ Ⓓ Ⓔ	196. Ⓐ Ⓑ Ⓒ Ⓓ Ⓔ
117. Ⓐ Ⓑ Ⓒ Ⓓ Ⓔ	157. Ⓐ Ⓑ Ⓒ Ⓓ Ⓔ	197. Ⓐ Ⓑ Ⓒ Ⓓ Ⓔ
118. Ⓐ Ⓑ Ⓒ Ⓓ Ⓔ	158. Ⓐ Ⓑ Ⓒ Ⓓ Ⓔ	198. Ⓐ Ⓑ Ⓒ Ⓓ Ⓔ
119. Ⓐ Ⓑ Ⓒ Ⓓ Ⓔ	159. Ⓐ Ⓑ Ⓒ Ⓓ Ⓔ	199. Ⓐ Ⓑ Ⓒ Ⓓ Ⓔ
120. Ⓐ Ⓑ Ⓒ Ⓓ Ⓔ	160. Ⓐ Ⓑ Ⓒ Ⓓ Ⓔ	200. Ⓐ Ⓑ Ⓒ Ⓓ Ⓔ
121. Ⓐ Ⓑ Ⓒ Ⓓ Ⓔ	161. Ⓐ Ⓑ Ⓒ Ⓓ Ⓔ	201. Ⓐ Ⓑ Ⓒ Ⓓ Ⓔ
122. Ⓐ Ⓑ Ⓒ Ⓓ Ⓔ	162. Ⓐ Ⓑ Ⓒ Ⓓ Ⓔ	202. Ⓐ Ⓑ Ⓒ Ⓓ Ⓔ
123. Ⓐ Ⓑ Ⓒ Ⓓ Ⓔ	163. Ⓐ Ⓑ Ⓒ Ⓓ Ⓔ	203. Ⓐ Ⓑ Ⓒ Ⓓ Ⓔ
124. Ⓐ Ⓑ Ⓒ Ⓓ Ⓔ	164. Ⓐ Ⓑ Ⓒ Ⓓ Ⓔ	204. Ⓐ Ⓑ Ⓒ Ⓓ Ⓔ
125. Ⓐ Ⓑ Ⓒ Ⓓ Ⓔ	165. Ⓐ Ⓑ Ⓒ Ⓓ Ⓔ	205. Ⓐ Ⓑ Ⓒ Ⓓ Ⓔ
126. Ⓐ Ⓑ Ⓒ Ⓓ Ⓔ	166. Ⓐ Ⓑ Ⓒ Ⓓ Ⓔ	206. Ⓐ Ⓑ Ⓒ Ⓓ Ⓔ
127. Ⓐ Ⓑ Ⓒ Ⓓ Ⓔ	167. Ⓐ Ⓑ Ⓒ Ⓓ Ⓔ	207. Ⓐ Ⓑ Ⓒ Ⓓ Ⓔ
128. Ⓐ Ⓑ Ⓒ Ⓓ Ⓔ	168. Ⓐ Ⓑ Ⓒ Ⓓ Ⓔ	208. Ⓐ Ⓑ Ⓒ Ⓓ Ⓔ
129. Ⓐ Ⓑ Ⓒ Ⓓ Ⓔ	169. Ⓐ Ⓑ Ⓒ Ⓓ Ⓔ	209. Ⓐ Ⓑ Ⓒ Ⓓ Ⓔ
130. Ⓐ Ⓑ Ⓒ Ⓓ Ⓔ	170. Ⓐ Ⓑ Ⓒ Ⓓ Ⓔ	210. Ⓐ Ⓑ Ⓒ Ⓓ Ⓔ
131. Ⓐ Ⓑ Ⓒ Ⓓ Ⓔ	171. Ⓐ Ⓑ Ⓒ Ⓓ Ⓔ	211. Ⓐ Ⓑ Ⓒ Ⓓ Ⓔ
132. Ⓐ Ⓑ Ⓒ Ⓓ Ⓔ	172. Ⓐ Ⓑ Ⓒ Ⓓ Ⓔ	212. Ⓐ Ⓑ Ⓒ Ⓓ Ⓔ
133. Ⓐ Ⓑ Ⓒ Ⓓ Ⓔ	173. Ⓐ Ⓑ Ⓒ Ⓓ Ⓔ	213. Ⓐ Ⓑ Ⓒ Ⓓ Ⓔ
134. Ⓐ Ⓑ Ⓒ Ⓓ Ⓔ	174. Ⓐ Ⓑ Ⓒ Ⓓ Ⓔ	214. Ⓐ Ⓑ Ⓒ Ⓓ Ⓔ
135. Ⓐ Ⓑ Ⓒ Ⓓ Ⓔ	175. Ⓐ Ⓑ Ⓒ Ⓓ Ⓔ	215. Ⓐ Ⓑ Ⓒ Ⓓ Ⓔ
136. Ⓐ Ⓑ Ⓒ Ⓓ Ⓔ	176. Ⓐ Ⓑ Ⓒ Ⓓ Ⓔ	216. Ⓐ Ⓑ Ⓒ Ⓓ Ⓔ
137. Ⓐ Ⓑ Ⓒ Ⓓ Ⓔ	177. Ⓐ Ⓑ Ⓒ Ⓓ Ⓔ	217. Ⓐ Ⓑ Ⓒ Ⓓ Ⓔ
138. Ⓐ Ⓑ Ⓒ Ⓓ Ⓔ	178. Ⓐ Ⓑ Ⓒ Ⓓ Ⓔ	
139. Ⓐ Ⓑ Ⓒ Ⓓ Ⓔ	179. Ⓐ Ⓑ Ⓒ Ⓓ Ⓔ	

GRE

PSYCHOLOGY TEST 5

TIME: 170 Minutes
217 Questions

DIRECTIONS: Choose the best answer for each question and mark the letter of your selection on the corresponding answer sheet.

---

1. Suppose that you wished to have a right handed "split-brain" patient read and comprehend a written passage. To which visual field should you most likely present the material?

   (A) right

   (B) left

   (C) it makes no difference which field

   (D) it depends on the size of letters

   (E) it depends on the content of the material

2. A personnel department developed a typing test for prospective secretaries. They gave the test to a group of job applicants on two occasions and found that the correlation between typing scores was +.89. From this outcome it should be concluded that the test is

   (A) valid.   (B) invalid.

   (C) reliable.   (D) unreliable.

   (E) in need of additional development and evaluation.

3. An individual who goes "blind" suddenly yet seems unconcerned about this dramatic loss and shows no underlying organic reason for the loss is probably suffering from

   (A) agoraphobia.   (B) conversion disorder.

   (C) dissociative disorder.   (D) occipital phobia.

   (E) post-traumatic stress syndrome.

4. Which personality theorist placed emphasis on the importance of a person's cognitive interpretations of the world, called personal constructs?

    (A) George Kelly   (B) Albert Bandura

    (C) Carl Rogers   (D) Carl Jung

    (E) Abraham Maslow

5. Which of the following concepts helps to explain the bystander effect, as exemplified in the Kitty Genovese murder case?

    (A) cognitive dissonance   (B) tragedy of the commons

    (C) risky shift   (D) actor - observer bias

    (E) diffusion of responsibility

6. If a psychologist went into a restaurant lounge and observed people's drinking habits, the psychologist would be using which of the methods of research?

    (A) survey   (B) experiment

    (C) natural observation   (D) case study

    (E) interview

7. In Stanley Milgram's classic study of the effect of authority on social compliance, what do the variations in (a) the physical remoteness of the victim and (b) the level of shocks the subject was willing to administer represent, respectively?

    (A) independent variable and dependent variable

    (B) independent variable and independent variable

    (C) independent variable and confounding variable

    (D) dependent variable and confounding variable

    (E) confounding variable and dependent variable

8. Suppose you are told that two conditions in an experiment differ at the .05 level of significance. What does this imply?

    (A) the difference occurs only 5% of the time

    (B) the difference can be generalized to 5% of the population

    (C) the difference is not very reliable

    (D) the difference is probably correlational, not causal

    (E) the difference occurs by chance only 5% of the time

9. If the correlation coefficient between two variables equals .98, what can you conclude?

   (A) the variables are causally related

   (B) there is relatively little unexplained error variance

   (C) as one variable increases in value the other decreases

   (D) the means of the variables are equal

   (E) the standard deviations of the variables are large, close to 1.0

10. Suppose that a young woman is anxious about the fact that she no longer loves her boyfriend. She copes by telling him: "You don't love me anymore." Which defense mechanism is she using?

    (A) denial   (B) repression

    (C) reaction formation   (D) transference

    (E) projection

11. In Freud's theory, which stage occurs after the phallic stage of development?

    (A) anal   (B) latent

    (C) self-actualization   (D) oral

    (E) concrete operations

12. Suppose that a young woman is anxious about the fact that she no longer loves her boyfriend. She copes by telling him: "I love you." Which defense mechanism is she using?

    (A) denial   (B) rationalization

    (C) intellectualization   (D) reaction formation

    (E) cognitive dissonance

13. Which of the following problems would Freud regard as fixation and regression to the oral stage?

    (A) antisocial aggression (B) alcoholism

    (C) compulsive gambling   (D) obsessive neatness

    (E) reoccurring nightmares

14. Human factors psychology is most closely related to which of the following areas of psychology?

(A) clinical   (B) industrial

(C) social   (D) personality

(E) physiological

15. Which approach to psychology stresses the person's inner drive to develop to his or her full potential?

(A) psychodynamic   (B) humanistic

(C) behavioristic   (D) cognitive

(E) psychobiological

16. Cattell distinguished between two types of intelligence. The type that deals with a person's skill at processing novel problems and relationships is called

(A) contextual.   (B) fluid.

(C) crystallized.   (D) componential.

(E) experiential.

17. Gardner has proposed a theory of multiple intelligences. Which of the following is NOT one of the dimensions in his theory?

(A) musical   (B) verbal

(C) bodily skill   (D) mathematical

(E) performance

18. The Stanford-Binet test of intelligence would assign which of the following values to a child who is chronologically 5 years old and mentally 10 years old.

(A) 50   (B) 100

(C) 150   (D) 200

(E) 250

19. Spearman explained the positive correlation among abilities measured on most intelligence tests in terms of

(A) poor validity of test procedures.

(B) poor reliability of test procedures.

(C) a common ability, called the Q-factor.

(D) a common ability, called the c-factor.

(E) multiple dimensions of intelligence.

20. If the questions on a paper-and-pencil test about honesty directly address how a person would react in situations requiring honesty, the test possesses

    (A) normative validity.   (B) face validity.

    (C) construct validity.   (D) predictive validity.

    (E) split-half reliability.

21. The consensus of opinion is that about _____ of an individual's intelligence is determined by his or her heredity.

    (A) 10%   (B) 25%

    (C) 50%   (D) 75%

    (E) 90%

22. Which of the following is NOT a projective test?

    (A) Inkblot   (B) TAT

    (C) Draw-a-Person   (D) MMPI

    (E) Rorschach

23. Which of the following items has content validity for a test of mental disturbance?

    (A) I like to sleep.   (B) I hate to take tests.

    (C) I often feel afraid.   (D) I enjoy playing Monopoly.

    (E) I like to watch T.V.

24. Test-retest and _____ are techniques for assessing the _____ of a psychological test.

    (A) split-half, reliability   (B) split-half, validity

    (C) item analysis, reliability   (D) item analysis, validity

    (E) correlation, significance

25. Suppose a psychologist correlates scores on an honesty test administered by a personnel department at the time of hiring with an observational measure of theft on the job during the second year of employment. What is he or she attempting to establish?

    (A) test-retest reliability   (B) criterion validity

    (C) construct validity   (D) face validity

    (E) content validity

26. Which of the following is an argument against the use of multiple choice tests?

    (A) They rarely have predictive validity.

    (B) Only creative people do well on multiple choice tests.

    (C) When asked to explain their choices, people give odd and incorrect reasons for why they selected the correct choice.

    (D) Recognition of the correct answer is often harder than recalling it.

    (E) They are more expensive to administer than alternative formats.

27. Which of the following is NOT a way to detect or prevent lying or cheating on the MMPI?

    (A) empirically keyed scoring

    (B) forced choice techniques

    (C) use bizarre questions as lures

    (D) use of psychopathic deviance scale

    (E) all of the above detect lying

28. Which of the following best describes a clinical psychologist?

    (A) prescribes psychoactive medication

    (B) conducts mostly basic research, not applied

    (C) holds an M.D. degree

    (D) holds a PsyD degree

    (E) holds a Ph.D. degree

29. About 2/3 of all mental hospital admissions are for

    (A) mania.   (B) depression.

    (C) schizophrenia.   (D) obsessive-compulsive disorder.

    (E) hypochondria.

30. Tardive dyskinesia is a side effect of

    (A) psychosurgery on the frontal lobes.

    (B) psychosurgery on the limbic system.

    (C) phenothiazines.

    (D) alcoholism.

    (E) tricyclic anti-pressants.

31. Which of the following concepts concerns descriptive statistics?

    (A) Chi square   (B) Analysis of variance

    (C) T–test   (D) F test

    (E) Mode

32. Which of the following is needed in computing a t-test?

    (A) Median   (B) Standard deviation

    (C) Correlation coefficient (D) Chi square

    (E) Interquartile range

33. Suppose that two treatment groups produce frequency distributions that do not overlap. What can you conclude?

    (A) The difference in means of the two groups occurs by chance less than one time in a hundred.

    (B) The difference in means of the two groups is less than their standard deviations.

    (C) The difference in the standard deviations of the two groups is negligible.

    (D) The difference in the standard deviations of the two groups is likely to occur less than one time in a hundred.

    (E) The difference in means of the two groups is most likely due to chance.

34. If two variables are correlated and yield an r value equal to $-.75$, then which of the following statements is true?

    (A) The negative value implies a chance relationship between the variables.

    (B) About 50% of the variance in the scores of one variable can be explained in terms of the other variable.

    (C) The standardized mean of one variable differs from the standardized mean of the other variable by .75.

    (D) The probability that the correlation occurred by chance is less than .001.

    (E) An analysis of variance on the data would reveal a significant causal relationship.

35. Which of the following pairs of concepts are most closely related in social psychology?

    (A) cognitive dissonance — bystander effect

    (B) attribution bias — tragedy of the commons

    (C) internal locus of control — fundamental attribution error

    (D) risky shift — belief bias

    (E) anonymity — deindividuation

36. Which of the following concepts is LEAST related to prejudice?

    (A) cognitive dissonance

    (B) stereotypes

    (C) familiarity effect

    (D) racial differences in face recognition

    (E) socialization

37. When two people are introduced for the first time, an initial impression is formed. Which factor most powerfully affects this first impression?

    (A) method of handshake   (B) physical appearance

    (C) nonverbal communication   (D) external locus of control

    (E) speech mannerisms

38. Which of the following concepts is more physical than psychological?

    (A) crowding   (B) noisiness

    (C) density   (D) loudness

    (E) personal space

39. Which of the following is a measure of variability in test scores?

    (A) standard error of the mean   (B) central tendency

    (C) percentile score   (D) mode

    (E) beta weight

40. Which of the following correlation coefficients represents the strongest relation between two variables?

    (A) .01   (B) −.28

(C) .38   (D) .58

(E) −.68

41. Which of the following concepts are most closely related?

(A) repression — motivated forgetting

(B) denial — self fulfilling prophecy

(C) primacy — recognition failure

(D) delay of reinforcement — transfer of training

(E) Premack principle — interference theory

42. Suppose a pigeon is trained to peck a key when a red light is presented on the key. Then the key color is changed to pink. If the pigeon pecks the pink key, what principle is illustrated?

(A) stimulus generalization   (B) response generalization

(C) primary reinforcement   (D) secondary reinforcement

(E) partial reinforcement

43. Which method of assessing memory is most sensitive?

(A) recognition   (B) forced choice recognition

(C) cued recall   (D) free recall

(E) savings or relearning

44. Besides the lens, what other structure is responsible for bringing an image into focus on the retina?

(A) cornea   (B) iris

(C) fovea   (D) sclera

(E) vitreous humour

45. Which theory best explains pitch perception for high frequency sounds?

(A) frequency theory   (B) place theory

(C) inhibition theory   (D) opponent process theory

(E) modulation theory

46. Which theory best accounts for color vision at the level of the visual cortex, as opposed to the retinal level?

(A) frequency theory   (B) trichromatic theory

(C) opponent process theory   (D) chromatic disparity theory

(E) hemispheric fusion theory

47. Which structure is located in the middle ear?

(A) incus   (B) basilar membrane

(C) tympanic membrane   (D) pinna

(E) semi-circular canals

48. Which of the following is NOT a Gestalt grouping principle of perception?

(A) closure   (B) proximity

(C) disparity   (D) unity

(E) similarity

49. _____ refers to changes in the focal length of the eye to bring a retinal image into focus.

(A) Binocular disparity   (B) Linear perspective

(C) Adaptation   (D) Assimilation

(E) Accommodation

50. In signal detection theory, beta refers to _____ and d' refers to _____ .

(A) response criterion, perceptual sensitivity

(B) perceptual sensitivity, response criterion

(C) hit rate, false alarm rate

(D) false alarm rate, hit rate

(E) subjective sensitivity, objective sensitivity

51. Suppose you are viewing two cars of identical brightness, one red and one blue, under daylight conditions. As night falls what would happen?

(A) The blue car would look brighter.

(B) The red car would look brighter.

(C) Both would look brighter.

(D) The red car would look green.

(E) The blue car would look green.

52. Which of the following is true about photoreceptors called rods?

    (A) They are most sensitive under daylight.

    (B) They are most sensitive under night time conditions.

    (C) They are responsible for color vision.

    (D) They are responsible for the Muella-Lyer illusion.

    (E) They are clustered in the fovea.

53. Which concept refers to the meaning of language?

    (A) pragmatics   (B) syntax

    (C) grammar   (D) semantics

    (E) diction

54. Chomsky distinguished between linguistic _____ and _____.

    (A) generativity, grammar   (B) speech, text

    (C) competence, performance   (D) grammar, syntax

    (E) knowledge, skill

55. Which of the following is a theory of forgetting that stresses the similarity of items in memory?

    (A) interference   (B) decay

    (C) consolidation   (D) psychodynamic

    (E) Gestalt

56. The limitation of short-term memory of 7± 2 chunks can be observed in an

    (A) face recognition task.   (B) absolute judgment task.

    (C) signal detection task.   (D) just-noticeable-difference task.

    (E) none of the above.

57. Which of the following memory stores has a decay time of about 250 milliseconds?

    (A) short-term memory   (B) echoic memory

    (C) tactile memory   (D) iconic memory

    (E) working memory

58. Which of the following is true about judgments of the frequency of occurrence of events?

    (A) High frequency events tend to be overestimated.

    (B) High frequency events tend to be underestimated.

    (C) Low frequency events tend to be underestimated.

    (D) Low frequency events tend to be judged least accurately.

    (E) High frequency events tend to be judged least accurately.

59. In a concept identification task, all examples of a concept are either red, or square, or both red and square. This illustrates a _____ conceptual rule.

    (A) conjunctive   (B) exclusive disjunctive

    (C) inclusive disjunctive (D) conditional

    (E) biconditional

60. A rule of thumb that sometimes helps one to solve a problem is called a _____ .

    (A) algorithm   (B) mnemonic

    (C) acronym   (D) heuristic

    (E) acrostic

61. Which operant conditioning procedure increases the rate of a response by terminating an aversive stimulus?

    (A) positive reinforcement (B) negative reinforcement

    (C) punishment   (D) omission training

    (E) shaping

62. In classical conditioning, the conditioned response occurs after the presentation of the

    (A) unconditioned response.   (B) primary reinforcer.

    (C) unconditioned stimulus.   (D) conditioned response.

    (E) conditioned stimulus.

63. Which of the following concepts are most closely related?

    (A) operant conditioning — blocking

    (B) classical conditioning — partial reinforcement

(C)   Shaping — backward conditioning

(D)   Theory X — operant conditioning

(E)   Theory Y — classical conditioning

64.   How are operant and classical conditioning different?

(A)   Only operant conditioning requires voluntary behavior.

(B)   Only classical conditioning undergoes extinction.

(C)   Only operant conditioning involves a conditional stimulus.

(D)   Only classical conditioning involves a conditioned stimulus.

(E)   Only classical conditioning involves aversive stimuli.

65.   Which structure connects the left and right hemispheres of the brain?

(A)   Thalamus   (B)   Reticular formation

(C)   Limbic system   (D)   Corpus callosum

(E)   Temporal cortex

66.   The frontal lobes are most likely to be highly active during

(A)   auditory perception.   (B)   walking.

(C)   visual perception.   (D)   abstract problem solving.

(E)   olfactory perception.

67.   In a right-handed individual, where is Broca's area most likely to be located?

(A)   Left hemisphere   (B)   Right hemisphere

(C)   Visual cortex   (D)   Limbic system

(E)   Parietal cortex

68.   Which of the following is NOT a part of the peripheral nervous system?

(A)   Parasympathetic system (B)   Limbic system

(C)   Sympathetic system   (D)   Sensory neurons

(E)   Motor neurons

69.   Self-deprecation, sadness, and _____ are symptoms of depression.

(A)   private language   (B)   repetitive behavior

(C)   confused decision making   (D)   catatonic postures

(E)   visual hallucination

70.   A behaviorist would contend that depression is caused by

(A)   unconscious conflicts.

(B)   failure to learn the proper way to behave.

(C)   failure to become self-actualized.

(D)   society labeling people as abnormal.

(E)   life problems.

71.   Which of the following is NOT an anxiety disorder?

(A)   post traumatic stress syndrome

(B)   social phobia

(C)   panic disorder

(D)   agoraphobia

(E)   manic depression

72.   Which of the following is a common symptom of anxiety disorders?

(A)   hallucinations   (B)   illusions

(C)   bodily complaints   (D)   delusions

(E)   paranoia

73.   Which of the following concepts are most closely related?

(A)   thought disorder — schizophrenia

(B)   multiple personality — schizophrenia

(C)   hallucinations — depression

(D)   amnesia — catatonia

(E)   drug abuse — autism

74.   Disorganized, catatonic, and paranoid are types of

(A)   schizophrenia.   (B)   multiple personality.

(C)   dissociative disorders. (D)   phobias.

(E)   depression.

75. Which of the following is NOT a characteristic of schizophrenia?

    (A) hallucinations   (B) delusions

    (C) extreme mood swings   (D) autism

    (E) aberrant speech

76. Suppose that an individual is brought to a mental hospital by police. They picked him up for singing extremely loudly and rapidly on a city bus, harassing riders with obscenities, and promising to give large sums of money to the driver. Based on this information alone, what would be your preliminary diagnosis.

    (A) paranoia   (B) fugue

    (C) bipolar affective disorder (D) schizophrenia

    (E) multiple personalities

77. Schizophrenia is most closely related to

    (A) phobia.   (B) multiple personalities.

    (C) alcoholism.   (D) post traumatic stress disorder.

    (E) affective psychosis.

78. Suppose that a housewife comes to a therapist complaining of extreme fear about leaving her home. Based only on this information, what would the therapist's preliminary diagnosis be?

    (A) free floating anxiety   (B) agoraphobia

    (C) social phobia   (D) zoophobia

    (E) depression

79. Suppose a therapist treats a fear of heights by asking the client to imagine being at the top of a roller coaster after inducing a state of deep relaxation. What type of therapy is probably being used?

    (A) client centered   (B) systematic densensitization

    (C) psychodynamic   (D) cognitive relaxation

    (E) social learning

80. Cognitive therapy developed by Aaron Beck has been successfully used in treating

    (A) phobias.   (B) schizophrenia.

(C)   manic reactions.   (D)   alcoholism.

(E)   depression.

81.   Shortly after birth a duck will follow the first object that walks by it. This illustrates

(A)   conditioned responses.   (B)   super stimuli.

(C)   sign stimuli.   (D)   imprinting.

(E)   shaping.

82.   Which of the following shows the largest ratio of brain size to body mass?

(A)   chimpanzees   (B)   humans

(C)   dolphins   (D)   elephants

(E)   whales

83.   Which of the following areas of applied psychology is largest in terms of the number of psychologists employed?

(A)   school   (B)   community

(C)   clinical   (D)   industrial/organizational

(E)   human factors

84.   One of the pioneers of the psychology of perception was

(A)   McDougall.   (B)   Helmholtz.

(C)   Skinner.   (D)   Jung.

(E)   Watson.

85.   Suppose that a psychologist is employed by a computer firm to design the keyboard of a personal computer. The employee would best be classified as a

(A)   behavioral psychologist.

(B)   an industrial psychologist.

(C)   a human factors psychologist.

(D)   a clinical psychologist.

(E)   a social psychologist.

86.   Which individual is correctly matched with their theory?

(A)   Lewin — Field Theory

(B)   James — Law of Effect

(C)   Freud — Personal Construct Theory

(D)   Wundt — Pragmatism

(E)   Watson — Adaptation Theory

87.   In Steven's Law, subjective experience is equated with a power function of stimulus intensity. Which type of stimulus shows the greatest exponent in this power function?

(A)   light intensity   (B)   sound waves

(C)   line length   (D)   electric shock intensity

(E)   color hue

88.   Which of the following is true of cone vision?

(A)   called scotopic

(B)   more sensitive to dim light than rod vision

(C)   poorer visual acuity than rod vision

(D)   suffers from damage in the periphery of the retina

(E)   responsible for color vision

89.   Which of the following is NOT a cue for depth perception?

(A)   relative motion   (B)   texture gradient

(C)   similarity gradient   (D)   familiar size

(E)   binocular disparity

90.   Suppose a piano and a trumpet sound middle C at an equal loudness. Though they are equal in frequency they differ in _____ .

(A)   timbre   (B)   pitch

(C)   loudness   (D)   noisiness

(E)   vibrations

91.   Suppose that a mother brings her five year old son to the doctor and complains about his sleepwalking. What should the doctor say to her about this problem?

(A)   It is a sign of an organic disorder.

(B) It is a normal consequence of REM sleep.

(C) It will probably be outgrown.

(D) It is an early sign of psychosis.

(E) It is caused by REM sleep deprivation.

92. Repetition of a mantra or phrase is a procedure of

(A) Zen meditation.   (B) transcendental meditation.

(C) deep reflection.   (D) lucid dreaming.

(E) hypnosis.

93. Suppose you have a dream about the GRE examination you took that morning. Freud would have labeled this as

(A) latent content.   (B) manifest content.

(C) spurious content.   (D) archetypical content.

(E) anxious content.

94. When a right handed individual is engaged in a writing task, which type of brain waves would likely be recorded from the right hemisphere?

(A) alpha   (B) beta

(C) gamma   (D) delta

(E) epsilon

95. Which of the following is true about REM sleep?

(A) it occurs about every 30 minutes

(B) it is rare among newborn infants

(C) it is rare among the congenitally blind

(D) it is characterized by delta waves

(E) it is characterized by beta waves

96. Suppose you observe a subject sleeping while wired to an EEG machine. If you arouse the person during stage II sleep, what conscious experience is the subject likely to report?

(A) a bizarre event   (B) a mundane event

(C) an auditory hallucination (D) a visual hallucination

(E) a nightmare

97. The gate control theory of pain perception presumes that pain signals are blocked by

    (A) nonmyelinated neurons.   (B) myelinated neurons.

    (C) efferent neurons.   (D) afferent neurons.

    (E) motor neurons.

98. In listening to two conversations simultaneously, it is possible to attend to one and ignore the other if they differ in

    (A) pitch.   (B) semantics.

    (C) pragmatics.   (D) syntax.

    (E) diction.

99. George Sperling's well known experiment on iconic memory showed that subjects had trouble remembering more than five or so items because of

    (A) retroactive interference.   (B) proactive interference.

    (C) masking.   (D) repression.

    (E) rapid decay.

100. Endel Tulving has proposed three memory systems. They are

    (A) mnemonic, dichotic, and melodic.

    (B) sensory, short-term, and long-term.

    (C) semantic, syntactic, and pragmatic.

    (D) procedural, semantic, and episodic.

    (E) declarative, procedural, and episodic.

101. The technology of biofeedback is based on the principle of

    (A) backward conditioning.   (B) punishment.

    (C) negative reinforcement.   (D) positive reinforcement.

    (E) chaining.

102. Which of the following leads to a decrease in the likelihood of a behavior occurring in the future?

    (A) shaping   (B) negative reinforcement

    (C) continuous reinforcement   (D) omission training

    (E) all operant conditioning methods

103. The slowest rate of extinction is achieved with

    (A) partial reinforcement.   (B) continuous reinforcement.

    (C) symbolic reinforcement.   (D) primary reinforcement.

    (E) secondary reinforcement.

104. Suppose you observe at an Atlantic City casino that a slot machine pays off the first pull that comes after, on average, an interval of 15 minutes. What type of reinforcement schedule is this?

    (A) fixed interval   (B) variable interval

    (C) fixed ratio   (D) variable ratio

    (E) none of the above

105. Another name for operant conditioning is

    (A) social learning.   (B) classical conditioning.

    (C) instrumental conditioning.   (D) latent conditioning.

    (E) instinctive conditioning.

106. Making logical guesses about what happened at a party you attended on New Year's Eve fifteen years ago is called

    (A) consolidation.   (B) trace retrieval.

    (C) memory replay.   (D) reconstructive retrieval.

    (E) logical retrieval.

107. Based on principles of learning and memory which of the following should be a good study habit?

    (A) spend considerable amounts of time in self-test

    (B) massive study or cramming the night before a test

    (C) read each assignment slowly several times from first word to last

    (D) spend the most study time on the first parts of a reading assignment

    (E) spend the most study time on the final parts of a reading assignment

108. Which memory holds a large amount of information for about 2 seconds?

    (A) tactile memory   (B) echoic memory

    (C) iconic memory   (D) short-term memory

    (E) working memory

109. The levels of processing theory predicts that you will remember the word "train" best if you first

    (A) repeat it over and over.

    (B) categorize it as a type of transportation.

    (C) consider its size and color in your mind's eye.

    (D) count the number of vowels the word contains.

    (E) think of a word that it rhymes with.

110. If you say that an apple illustrates the category of fruit better than a grape, what type of conceptual knowledge are you using most directly?

    (A) defining features   (B) typicality gradient

    (C) conjunctive relations   (D) fuzzy boundaries

    (E) theoretical constraints

111. Which of the following illustrates a basic level of categorization to use Eleanor Rosch's term.

    (A) living thing   (B) animal

    (C) collie   (D) dog

    (E) tricolor collie

112. Which of the following is true of speed reading rates compared with normal reading rates?

    (A) results in fewer regressive eye movements

    (B) results in entire sentences of all types being encoded in single fixations

    (C) results in a higher comprehension rate

    (D) produces more subvocalization

    (E) is better for studying highly technical material

113. Noticing relations between a list material to be remembered and information already stored in long-term memory is called

    (A) maintenance rehearsal.   (B) mnemonic rehearsal.

    (C) elaborative rehearsal.   (D) categorical rehearsal.

    (E) pragmatic rehearsal.

114. Suppose you compare free recall performance under four memory conditions, in which the person is either sober or intoxicated with alcohol during study or test. Which condition is most likely to show the poorest level of performance?

    (A) sober at study; sober at test

    (B) sober at study; intoxicated at test

    (C) intoxicated at study; intoxicated at test

    (D) intoxicated at study; sober at test

    (E) all conditions except sober at study and sober at test will perform equally poorly

115. According to decay theory, forgetting is due to a(n)

    (A) availability problem.   (B) consolidation problem.

    (C) encoding problem.   (D) retrieval problem.

    (E) accessibility problem.

116. Suppose that you incorrectly believe that death from a tornado is more likely than death from asthma. Which of the following can explain your error.

    (A) conservative bias   (B) minimax strategy

    (C) means-end analysis   (D) availability heuristic

    (E) representativeness heuristic

117. According to the atmosphere hypothesis in syllogistic reasoning

    (A) people usually reason carefully but sometimes make mistakes.

    (B) people fail to reason at all, but jump to conclusions based on the form of syllogism.

    (C) people reason well on invalid syllogisms, but not valid.

    (D) people reason well on valid syllogisms, but not invalid.

    (E) people reason well with false premises.

118. Suppose that your car fan belt breaks and you fail to realize that your wife's pantyhose might serve as a temporary replacement belt. Which concept explains your failure?

    (A) domain specific knowledge

    (B) Einstellung

(C) limited capacity of short-term memory

(D) perceptual set

(E) functional fixedness

119. Which of the following functions is the neurotransmitter epinephrine NOT responsible for?

(A) increased heart rate

(B) consolidation of memory

(C) dilation of pupils

(D) relaxed breathing

(E) relaxation of stomach muscles

120. Consider these two sentences. "The suit was made by the tailor." "The tailor made the suit." How do these sentences differ most clearly?

(A) semantics   (B) pragmatics

(C) deep structure   (D) surface structure

(E) verb tense

121. Suppose you absent-mindedly step off a curb in a city and a passing truck narrowly misses you. Which branch of the nervous system mediates the increase in heart rate you experience?

(A) left hemisphere   (B) right hemisphere

(C) parasympathetic   (D) sympathetic

(E) central

122. The signal-receiving end of a neuron is called a (an)

(A) cell body.   (B) dendrite.

(C) axon.   (D) myelinated sheath.

(E) medulla.

123. The adrenal gland releases _____ .

(A) serotonin   (B) acetylcholine

(C) growth hormone   (D) dopamine

(E) epinephrine

124. Which brain structure is important in causing a person to awaken from sleep?

    (A) limbic activating system

    (B) cerebral activating system

    (C) reticular activating system

    (D) thalamic activating system

    (E) parietal activating system

125. Suppose that psychosurgery is tried to remedy the uncontrollable violent behavior of a convicted serial murderer. Which brain structure should probably be operated on?

    (A) thalamus   (B) cerebellum

    (C) pituitary   (D) medulla

    (E) amygdala

126. Damage to Wernicke's area in the brain is likely to cause difficulties with?

    (A) visual acuity.   (B) color vision.

    (C) speech production.   (D) speech recognition.

    (E) motor movements.

127. The trichromatic theory of color vision presumes people possess which three types of photoreceptors?

    (A) red, green and blue rods

    (B) red, yellow and blue rods

    (C) red, green and blue cones

    (D) red, yellow and blue cones

    (E) green, yellow and blue cones

128. Suppose you stare at a yellow square for two minutes, then shift your gaze to a white piece of paper. You will see a _____ afterimage as predicted by _____ theory.

    (A) blue, opponent process   (B) red, opponent process

    (C) blue, trichromatic   (D) green, trichromatic

    (E) yellow, saturation

129. Suppose you are an audiophile and a stereo salesman advises you to spend an extra $1,000 on a system that faithfully reproduces the frequencies on a compact disk from 5 to 25,000 Hz. As a sensory psychologist, what is your wisest response?

    (A)   state that the ear drum would be punctured by 25,000 Hz

    (B)   state that an ideal human ear can only detect from 20 to 20,000 Hz

    (C)   state that an ideal human ear can only detect from 500 to 15,000 Hz

    (D)   state that frequencies above 10,000 Hz are rarely found in music

    (E)   state that most music falls in a range of 1,000 to 5,000 Hz

130. Suppose you just stepped off a ride at an amusement park in which you were spinning rapidly. Which part of the sensory system is related to the disorientation you now experience?

    (A)   cochlea   (B)   semicircular canals

    (C)   visual cortex   (D)   eustachian tubes

    (E)   stapes

131. Our ability to distinguish pitches at very high frequencies is best explained by

    (A)   Steven's theory.   (B)   frequency theory.

    (C)   Young-Helmhotz theory.   (D)   vibration theory.

    (E)   place theory.

132. If you took sound level measurements about 200 feet from the commercial jet taking off, what would your recording register?

    (A)   25,000 Hz   (B)   20,000 Hz

    (C)   80 dB   (D)   120 dB

    (E)   160 dB

133. Suppose that you were fired from your job. While driving home on the freeway, you tailgate a slow moving car and yell obscenities at the driver. Which concept best accounts for your behavior?

    (A)   reaction formation

    (B)   tragedy of the commons

    (C)   frustration-aggression hypothesis

    (D)   just-world phenomenon   (E)   projection

134. Suppose you meet a person at a party. Which theory assumes you calculate the costs and benefits of developing a relationship with the person?

    (A) social exchange

    (B) attribution

    (C) two factor

    (D) altruism

    (E) social judgment

135. Suppose that a father believes his first born daughter will be more intelligent than his second born. This belief then influences how he behaves toward his daughters, giving more time and attention to his first born. What does this illustrate?

    (A) prejudice

    (B) social schema

    (C) social reality

    (D) self-fulfilling prophecy

    (E) primacy effect

136. When we think of an extrovert, we automatically think of a person who is outgoing, assertive and talks a great deal. We do so because of

    (A) conformity.

    (B) attribution bias.

    (C) prototypes.

    (D) actor-observer bias.

    (E) prejudice.

137. According to the fundamental attribution error, how would you explain the behavior of a stranger who gives a $100 bill to a Salvation Army collector outside a department store?

    (A) presume the person is kind and generous

    (B) presume the person is trying to impress others

    (C) presume the person's employer requires such contributions

    (D) presume the person used to receive support from the Salvation Army

    (E) presume the person was ordered to do so by a court as part of a criminal sentence

138. According to the actor-observer bias, which of the following would likely occur after a student fails a professor's exam?

    (A) The student would blame himself for not being intelligent.

    (B) The student would blame the professor for creating too difficult of an exam.

    (C) The student would blame himself for not trying hard enough.

(D) The professor would blame himself for creating too difficult of an exam.

(E) The professor would blame the university for a classroom that is too noisy for taking exams.

139. A predisposition to behave in a particular way is called a(n)

(A) orienting reflex.   (B) prototype.

(C) stereotype.   (D) attributional bias.

(E) attitude.

140. Denial, anger, bargaining, and acceptance are stages associated with

(A) menopause.   (B) puberty.

(C) retirement.   (D) mid life crisis.

(E) dying.

141. Suppose that you were opposed to drinking alcohol because of your religious background. In which situation is your attitude most likely to change toward more tolerance of drinking following an incident in which you publicly have a drink?

(A) when your friends paid you $50 to take one drink

(B) when you were forced at gun point to take a drink

(C) when you decided freely to take a drink just for the novelty of it

(D) when you took a drink in order to irritate your elderly parents

(E) when you took a drink because you were with friends in a bar and had to be sociable

142. As _____ increases a person's need for social affiliation increases.

(A) cognitive dissonance   (B) fear

(C) anxiety   (D) depression

(E) none of the above

143. The concept of social facilitation implies that

(A) friendships are easier to make in large groups than in small ones.

(B) prejudices are more easily overcome in sociable settings.

(C) the presence of other people improves individual performance.

(D) first impressions are formed more rapidly when many other people are present.

(E) conformity is greatest when other people are present.

144. Which of the following is NOT a factor that influences the degree to which two people like each other?

(A) familiarity   (B) physical attractiveness

(C) similarity   (D) conformity

(E) proximity

145. Solomon Asch conducted a classic experiment in which he asked a group of college students to decide which of three lines was equal in length to a standard line. What was Asch studying?

(A) the mere exposure effect   (B) conformity

(C) social facilitation   (D) reference groups

(E) difference thresholds

146. Suppose you join a pickup basketball game at the gym in which the teams are randomly chosen. As the game progresses you notice that you and the other members of your team begin to believe your team is superior and express signs of hostility toward your opponents. What accounts for this?

(A) conformity   (B) prejudice

(C) stereotypes   (D) actor-observer bias

(E) in-group bias

147. The process of one person becoming differentiated from others in a particular social situation is called

(A) individuation.   (B) differentiation.

(C) prototyping.   (D) modeling.

(E) social learning.

148. Anonymity has been shown to increase

(A) test performance.   (B) aggression.

(C) conformity.   (D) loving.

(E) prejudice.

149. Military strategists can plan a nuclear war, in which millions would be killed, without thinking about the human loss in a meaningful way. Which concept best explains how they can do this?

    (A) suppression   (B) dehumanization

    (C) prejudice   (D) social reality

    (E) equity theory

150. In Stanley Milgram's famous experiment on obedience about what percent of the subjects administered the maximum dangerous shock level of 450 volts to the victim?

    (A) 15   (B) 45

    (C) 65   (D) 85

    (E) 100

151. According to the _____ hypothesis, watching pornographic movies should decrease the tendency of rapists to commit their crimes.

    (A) aggression   (B) modeling

    (C) frustration   (D) freedom of speech

    (E) catharsis

152. Konrad Lorenz contended that aggression is

    (A) socially learned.

    (B) the result of prejudice.

    (C) a direct result of territoriality.

    (D) a direct result of personal space.

    (E) an innate readiness to fight for survival.

153. When two dogs are fighting, the loser will roll over and expose its neck to a bite from the winner. This is called a(n)

    (A) appeasement signal.   (B) death instinct.

    (C) cathartic gesture.   (D) frustration signal.

    (E) pro-social gesture.

154. Which of the following statements is true?

    (A) Tool usage is found only in humans.

    (B) All species exhibit territorial behavior.

(C) Males dominate females in all species.

(D) Various instances of within-species killing among animals have been observed.

(E) Aggression is primarily an inherited trait in all species.

155. A central controversy in the debate about whether chimpanzees can learn language is

(A) whether they can generate numerous novel expressions.

(B) whether they can speak clearly enough to be understood.

(C) whether they can learn more than one type of syntax.

(D) whether their mental lexicons are large enough.

(E) whether their sentences are sufficiently pragmatic.

156. Which species shows a brain structure as complex as that of humans?

(A) elephants   (B) baboons

(C) chimpanzees   (D) dolphins

(E) none of the above

157. Stanley Schachter proposed that emotion is a product of _____ and _____ .

(A) instincts, physical states

(B) heredity, environment

(C) motivation, learning

(D) physiological arousal, cognitive appraisal

(E) testosterone levels, epinephrine levels

158. Who wrote the classic book entitled *The Expression of Emotions in Man and Animals?*

(A) James   (B) Darwin

(C) Lorenz   (D) McDougall

(E) Freud

159. The social norms concerning the public expression of various emotions are called

(A) display rules.   (B) species-specific rules.

(C)   conformity rules.   (D)   stereotypical rules.

(E)   affective rules.

160. A person's full set of genes is called the

(A)   phenotype.   (B)   genotype.

(C)   germ cells.   (D)   poly genes.

(E)   none of the above.

161. The process through which heredity causes development of bodily functions is called

(A)   accommodation.   (B)   tracking.

(C)   maturation.   (D)   adaptation.

(E)   channeling.

162. A famous study by Eleanor Gibson employed a visual cliff with a checkered pattern. The results suggested that

(A)   depth perception is learned.

(B)   pattern perception is learned.

(C)   depth perception is innate.

(D)   pattern perception is innate.

(E)   visual perception shows critical periods of development.

163. Which of the following would be a highly unusual event in human development?

(A)   walking at 12 months

(B)   rolling over at 2 months

(C)   distinguishing different consonants at 1 month

(D)   babbling at 1 month

(E)   speaking first words at 1 month

164. Which of the following is NOT a well defined stage of language acquisition?

(A)   babbling   (B)   one word

(C)   two words   (D)   three words

(E)   telegraphic speech

165. Suppose a nursing infant is given a pacifier for the first time. She must modify her sucking response slightly through a process called

    (A) modeling.

    (B) assimilation.

    (C) maturation.

    (D) restructuring.

    (E) accommodation.

166. Which of the following is attained during the sensorimotor stage of development?

    (A) object permanence

    (B) reversibility

    (C) concrete operations

    (D) decentration

    (E) socialization

167. Egocentrism is observed in children during the _____ stage.

    (A) formal operational

    (B) one word

    (C) telegraphic speech

    (D) preoperational

    (E) sensorimotor

168. Which stage comes last in Piaget's theory of cognitive development?

    (A) conventional

    (B) preoperational

    (C) preconventional

    (D) sensorimotor

    (E) formal operational

169. In Harry Harlow's experiments with surrogate mothers found that baby monkeys

    (A) preferred proximity to cloth mothers over eating.

    (B) preferred eating over interacting with peers.

    (C) preferred interaction with peers over surrogate mothers.

    (D) preferred proximity to wire mothers over interacting with peers.

    (E) preferred playing alone over interacting with surrogate mothers.

170. Which of the following refers to biological differences between males and females present at birth?

    (A) gender

    (B) gender identity

    (C) sex

    (D) gender role

    (E) genotype

171. During which stage of moral development, according to Kohlberg, are moral judgments based on a need for acceptance from others?

    (A) 1   (B) 2

    (C) 3   (D) 4

    (E) 5

172. Suppose a business executive decides it is morally wrong to dump his company's toxic waste in a rural wooded area because the law prohibits it. Kolhberg would say that he is at the _____ stage of moral development.

    (A) 3   (B) 4

    (C) 5   (D) 6

    (E) 7

173. Freud postulated that a child enters the _____ stage of psychosexual development at about age two.

    (A) latent   (B) phallic

    (C) anal   (D) oral

    (E) pleasure/pain

174. Either too much or too little gratification at a particular stage of development, thought Freud, leads to _____ .

    (A) anger   (B) identity complex

    (C) regression   (D) denial

    (E) fixation

175. Which of the following is a key difference between Freud and Erikson's theories of development?

    (A) Only Freud saw that development might be arrested.

    (B) Only Erikson saw that development might be arrested.

    (C) Only Erikson saw development as a lifelong process.

    (D) Only Freud saw development as a lifelong process.

    (E) Only Freud was concerned with development of autonomy at age 2.

176. An elderly person looking back on life is unlikely to feel futility or despair if he or she has achieved a sense of

    (A) ego-integrity.   (B) genital gratification.

(C) generativity.   (D) identity.

(E) competence.

177. Which of the following is a normal consequence of growing old?

    (A) severe memory loss

    (B) eccentricity

    (C) loss of I.Q.

    (D) loss of speed of information processing

    (E) loss of vocabulary

178. Which is the final stage of development in Freud's theory?

    (A) phallic   (B) genital

    (C) intimacy   (D) formal

    (E) latent

179. Scents or chemical signals that are released in the air to control various forms of behavior among animals are called

    (A) hormones.   (B) catecholamines.

    (C) neuropeptides.   (D) enkephalines.

    (E) pheromones.

180. Suppose you hear a child saying incorrect words like "breaked," "foots," and "mouses." What does this show?

    (A) The child has learned a rule, but overgeneralizes.

    (B) The child' s diction is poorly developed.

    (C) The child's understanding of pragmatics is substandard.

    (D) The child' s understanding of syntax is substandard.

    (E) The child's understanding of semantics is substandard.

181. Which of the following concepts are most closely related?

    (A) anima — ego

    (B) id — gamma types

    (C) prototypes — collective unconscious

    (D) archetypes — superego

    (E) collective unconscious — archetypes

182. Which of the following is NOT a stage of the General Adaptation Syndrome?

    (A) resistance   (B) arousal

    (C) alarm   (D) exhaustion

    (E) all are stages

183. Suppose you believe that people are capable of developing personally throughout life and that, given the opportunity, they will achieve their full potential. Which approach to personality does this describe?

    (A) humanistic   (B) cognitive

    (C) psychodynamic   (D) behavioristic

    (E) social learning

184. Which of the following concepts is NOT relevant to explaining the moon illusion?

    (A) depth perception   (B) familiar size

    (C) relative motion parallax (D) texture gradient

    (E) apparent shape of the sky

185. Learning theorists have explained the formation and maintenance of a phobia in terms of

    (A) backward conditioning and positive reinforcement.

    (B) classical conditioning and negative reinforcement.

    (C) blocking and classical conditioning.

    (D) negative reinforcement and punishment.

    (E) classical conditioning and positive reinforcement.

186. Suppose you met three strangers from Europe, Africa, and Asia. Which of the following would you notice about them?

    (A) Their hand gestures for expressing anger would be the same.

    (B) Their body language would in general be the same.

    (C) Their facial expressions for expressing happiness would be the same.

    (D) Their vocal expressions for expressing surprise would be the same.

    (E) The ratio of their heights and weights would be the same.

187. Pupil diameter varies as a function of

    (A) mental effort.   (B) serotonin levels.

    (C) hunger.   (D) tactile perception.

    (E) none of the above.

188. Which of the following theories denies that a single absolute threshold for visual perception can be established?

    (A) adaptation   (B) Weber's

    (C) Fechner's   (D) signal detection

    (E) Steven's

189. According to one theory of hunger, whenever fats stored in special fat cells fall below a certain level, called the _____, eating ensues.

    (A) lipostatic threshold   (B) absolute threshold

    (C) critical set point   (D) eating threshold

    (E) metabolic level

190. Maslow would contend that a person must first satisfy _____ needs before satisfying _____ needs.

    (A) congnitive, attachment   (B) attachment, esteem

    (C) esthetic, esteem   (D) safety, biological

    (E) transcendence, self-actualization

191. Self-efficacy is a key concept in which theory of personality?

    (A) psychodynamic   (B) personal construct

    (C) humanistic   (D) behavioristic

    (E) social learning

192. Which theorist distinguished between deficiency motivation and growth motivation?

    (A) Maslow   (B) Jung

    (C) Kelly   (D) Bandura

    (E) Rogers

193. Freud understood aggression in terms of

    (A) repression.   (B) Thanatos.

(C)   ego threats.   (D)   projection.

(E)   Eros.

194. Which of the following concepts from Freud's theory of personality did Adler reject as being of major significance?

(A)   conflict   (B)   compensation

(C)   Eros   (D)   unconscious

(E)   inferiority complex

195. Maslow and _____ both emphasized the concept of self-actualization.

(A)   Kelly   (B)   James

(C)   Rogers   (D)   Fromm

(E)   Sullivan

196. Suppose you find yourself very anxious while visiting your parents at Christmas. Freud would attribute this to

(A)   unconscious intentions intruding on the superego.

(B)   an overactivation of Thanatos.

(C)   an overactivation of Eros.

(D)   a failure of repression.

(E)   a failure to sublimate libido.

197. Suppose that your neighbor checks whether he locked his front door, begins to walk away, and returns to check again. He repeats this 20-30 times. He may suffer from

(A)   anxiety attacks.   (B)   post traumatic stress disorder.

(C)   free floating anxiety.   (D)   phobia.

(E)   obsessive-compulsive disorder.

198. Suppose a friend is constantly going to the doctor because she misinterprets normal bodily reactions as symptoms of serious illness. She may suffer from

(A)   hypochondriasis.

(B)   conversion disorder.

(C)   generalized anxiety disorder.

(D)   xenophobia.   (E)   monophobia.

199. Which of the following has shown a dramatic increase in reported frequency in recent years?

    (A) hypochondriasis   (B) schizophrenia

    (C) conversion disorder   (D) multiple personality

    (E) phobia

200. Some schizophrenia patients show abnormally high levels of _____.

    (A) dopamine   (B) epinephrine

    (C) norepinephrine   (D) acetylcholine

    (E) serotonin

201. Suppose you are extremely afraid of going to a dentist. How would a behavioral therapist treat this fear?

    (A) punishment   (B) systematic desensitization

    (C) rational-emotive therapy   (D) omission training

    (E) stress-inoculation training

202. Freud would probably criticize behavioral therapies on which of the following grounds?

    (A) They are not client-centered.

    (B) They overemphasize ego control.

    (C) They overemphasize parental influence on development.

    (D) They treat symptoms but not underlying causes.

    (E) They take too long to help the patient.

203. Suppose that a female friend of yours is receiving therapy from a male psychoanalyst and she is beginning to feel strong feelings of hostility toward him. What is most likely happening?

    (A) countertransference   (B) compensation

    (C) transference   (D) displacement

    (E) insight

204. Suppose you are terrified of public speaking and your therapist has you repeatedly rehearse giving speeches and provides specific feedback. What type of therapist are you most likely seeing?

(A)   psychodynamic   (B)   social learning

(C)   behaviorist   (D)   therapist centered

(E)   Rogerian

205. Which of the following concepts are most closely related?

(A)   aversion therapy — insight therapy

(B)   client centered therapy — psychoanalysis

(C)   implosion — catharsis

(D)   token economy — positive reinforcement

(E)   extinction strategies — self-actualization

206. Tricyclics and MAO inhibitors are

(A)   personality disorder drugs.

(B)   antianxiety drugs.

(C)   aversive conditioning drugs.

(D)   antipsychotic drugs.

(E)   antidepressant drugs.

207. For unknown reasons some mental patients improve without receiving any treatment. This is called a _____ effect.

(A)   halo   (B)   spontaneous recovery

(C)   placebo   (D)   self-fulfilling prophecy

(E)   labeling

208. Eysenck's theory of personality includes a dimension of introverted-extroverted and a dimension of

(A)   stable-unstable.   (B)   anxious-relaxed.

(C)   depressed-manic.   (D)   endomorphic-ectomorphic.

(E)   strong-weak.

209. Cardinal, central, and secondary traits of personality are most closely connected with

(A)   Rogers.   (B)   Fromm.

(C)   Jung.   (D)   Allport.

(E)   Sullivan.

210. One valid criticism of using the MMPI as a screening tool for measuring the personality of job applicants is that it

    (A) was designed to detect psychopathology only.

    (B) consists of only three personality scales.

    (C) cannot detect lying.

    (D) does not assess social introversion.

    (E) has not been researched as well as most tests.

211. Suppose a friend of yours frequently finishes your sentences for you, always hurries, rarely relaxes, and competes intensely at work and at sports. How would your friend best be classified?

    (A) alpha type   (B) beta type

    (C) gamma type   (D) type-A

    (E) type-B

212. According to DSM-IV, all mental disorders are characterized by either distress or _____ .

    (A) depression   (B) anxiety

    (C) hallucination   (D) disability

    (E) fear

213. Suppose a friend's 18-year-old son has been repeatedly suspended from school, frequently fights his peers, cannot keep a job, and several times has stolen money from his parents. How would a psychologist probably label him?

    (A) narcissistic personality disorder

    (B) manic disorder

    (C) juvenile delinquent

    (D) antisocial personality disorder

    (E) schizoid personality type

214. Suppose you teach preschool and you break Joe's candy bar into three pieces and Mike's candy bar into two pieces. Mike complains that he received less than Joe. What does Mike lack?

    (A) conservation   (B) constancy

(C) object permanence (D) egocentrism

(E) accommodation

215. A classic experiment with kittens wearing collars around their necks and being exposed to only horizontal lines provided evidence on

(A) perceptual constancy. (B) critical periods.

(C) imprinting. (D) accommodation.

(E) depth perception.

216. Complete social isolation of monkeys during their first six months of life can cause

(A) learned helplessness.

(B) delayed attachment with peers.

(C) delayed imprinting with mother.

(D) fear or aggression around mother.

(E) fear or aggression around peers.

217. The growth of facial hair in an adolescent male is an example of a

(A) primary sex characteristic.

(B) secondary sex characteristic.

(C) characteristic of menarche.

(D) latent stage trait.

(E) sex-linked trait.

TEST 5

ANSWER KEY

1.	(A)	26.	(C)	51.	(B)	76.	(C)
2.	(C)	27.	(D)	52.	(B)	77.	(E)
3.	(B)	28.	(E)	53.	(D)	78.	(B)
4.	(A)	29.	(B)	54.	(C)	79.	(B)
5.	(E)	30.	(C)	55.	(A)	80.	(E)
6.	(C)	31.	(E)	56.	(B)	81.	(D)
7.	(A)	32.	(B)	57.	(D)	82.	(B)
8.	(E)	33.	(A)	58.	(B)	83.	(C)
9.	(B)	34.	(B)	59.	(C)	84.	(B)
10.	(E)	35.	(E)	60.	(D)	85.	(C)
11.	(B)	36.	(A)	61.	(B)	86.	(A)
12.	(D)	37.	(B)	62.	(E)	87.	(D)
13.	(B)	38.	(C)	63.	(D)	88.	(E)
14.	(B)	39.	(A)	64.	(A)	89.	(C)
15.	(B)	40.	(E)	65.	(D)	90.	(A)
16.	(B)	41.	(A)	66.	(D)	91.	(C)
17.	(E)	42.	(A)	67.	(A)	92.	(B)
18.	(D)	43.	(E)	68.	(B)	93.	(B)
19.	(C)	44.	(A)	69.	(C)	94.	(A)
20.	(B)	45.	(B)	70.	(B)	95.	(E)
21.	(C)	46.	(C)	71.	(E)	96.	(B)
22.	(D)	47.	(A)	72.	(C)	97.	(C)
23.	(C)	48.	(C)	73.	(A)	98.	(A)
24.	(A)	49.	(E)	74.	(A)	99.	(E)
25.	(B)	50.	(A)	75.	(C)	100.	(D)

101.	(D)	131.	(E)	161.	(C)	191.	(E)
102.	(D)	132.	(D)	162.	(C)	192.	(A)
103.	(A)	133.	(C)	163.	(E)	193.	(B)
104.	(B)	134.	(A)	164.	(D)	194.	(C)
105.	(C)	135.	(D)	165.	(E)	195.	(C)
106.	(D)	136.	(C)	166.	(A)	196.	(D)
107.	(A)	137.	(A)	167.	(D)	197.	(E)
108.	(B)	138.	(B)	168.	(E)	198.	(A)
109.	(B)	139.	(E)	169.	(A)	199.	(D)
110.	(B)	140.	(E)	170.	(C)	200.	(A)
111.	(D)	141.	(C)	171.	(C)	201.	(B)
112.	(A)	142.	(B)	172.	(B)	202.	(D)
113.	(C)	143.	(C)	173.	(C)	203.	(C)
114.	(D)	144.	(D)	174.	(E)	204.	(B)
115.	(A)	145.	(B)	175.	(C)	205.	(D)
116.	(D)	146.	(E)	176.	(A)	206.	(E)
117.	(B)	147.	(A)	177.	(D)	207.	(B)
118.	(E)	148.	(B)	178.	(B)	208.	(A)
119.	(D)	149.	(B)	179.	(E)	209.	(D)
120.	(D)	150.	(C)	180.	(A)	210.	(A)
121.	(D)	151.	(E)	181.	(E)	211.	(D)
122.	(B)	152.	(E)	182.	(B)	212.	(D)
123.	(E)	153.	(A)	183.	(A)	213.	(D)
124.	(C)	154.	(D)	184.	(C)	214.	(A)
125.	(E)	155.	(A)	185.	(B)	215.	(B)
126.	(D)	156.	(D)	186.	(C)	216.	(E)
127.	(C)	157.	(D)	187.	(A)	217.	(B)
128.	(A)	158.	(B)	188.	(D)		
129.	(B)	159.	(A)	189.	(C)		
130.	(B)	160.	(B)	190.	(B)		

DETAILED EXPLANATIONS
OF ANSWERS

GRE PSYCHOLOGY TEST 5

1.   **(A)**   Given that the split brain patient was right-handed it is very likely that he or she has a language center in the left hemisphere. It would, therefore, be necessary to present the material to the right visual field. This would enter the side of the left eye nearest the temple, which in turn maps onto the left hemisphere, resulting in comprehension by the language center.

2.   **(C)**   A correlation greater than .80 is considered a strong relationship for behavioral data. Because of this and because the direction of the relationship is positive, the test-retest correlation indicates the test is reliable. Reliability refers to the consistency of measurement. Validity, in contrast, refers to whether a test measures what it is supposed to measure. To establish validity, one would have to correlate test performance with some other relevant variable, such as on-the-job typing performance.

3.   **(B)**   Physical problems that have no apparent organic basis are called somatoform disorders. In extreme cases, called conversion disorders, there is a sudden loss of a sensory or motor function. Going "blind" despite a functional visual system is an example of a conversion disorder. Dissociative disorders, on the other hand, refer to a sudden loss of mental functions or loss of personal identity. Amnesia and multiple personality are examples.

4.   **(A)**   George Kelly was a pioneer of cognitive theoretical approaches to the study of personality. He argued that people actively interpret reality by developing personal constructs — beliefs about how two things are alike and different from a third. These constructs are idiosyncratic, unlike the unconscious archetypes studied by Carl Jung. Albert Bandura was a social learning theorist. Abraham Maslow and Carl Rogers were humanistic theorists.

5.   **(E)**   The bystander effect refers to individuals watching a brutal attack without helping the victim, calling the police, or in any way intervening. One factor that helps account for this social phenomenon is diffusion of responsibility. No one feels personally responsible for taking action because they believe someone else should handle the situation. Ironically, helping is more likely when there is only one witness than when there is a group of witnesses. Two other relevant factors are that people (1) judge the costs of intervening as too high and, (2) ignorantly assume that because no one else is intervening there really is not a problem, despite appearances.

6.   **(C)**   Observing behavior in a field setting without intervening in any fashion is called naturalistic observation. Because the psychologist did not engage customers in dialogue, did not focus on a single subject, did not ask a fixed set of questions, and did not manipulate any independent variables, interview, case study, survey, and experiment are incorrect alternatives.

7.   **(A)**   Independent variables are variables that the experimenter manipulates to see what effect they have on dependent variables. Dependent variables are measures of how an organism acts, thinks, or feels. In Milgram's experiment, the variations in the experimenter's behavior, such as the authoritative nature of the statements made to participants comprised the independent variable. The level of shock administered by subjects was a measure of compliance.

8.   **(E)**   In inferential statistics the alpha level refers to the probability that the observed value of a particular statistic, such as a t-test, would occur by chance. By convention, research outcomes, such as the difference between two conditions, are considered statistically significant if the observed value would occur by chance less than 5% of the time. Stated differently, the outcome is considered real or reliable rather than as a random event. Whether causal explanations for the outcome can be inferred depends on whether the experimental design ruled out confounding variables.

9.   **(B)**   Correlation coefficients vary between −1.0 and +1.0. Positive coefficients indicate that as the value of one variable increases, so do the values of the other variable. Negative coefficients indicate that as the values of one variable increases, the value of the other decreases. A correlation of zero represents no relation between the values. If the absolute value reaches 1.0, it means one can account for all the variance of variable in terms of variations in the other. Even a perfect correlation, and 0.98 is considered essentially perfect, does not permit one to conclude a causal relationship.

10.   **(E)**   Denial, repression, reaction formation, and projection are all defense mechanisms identified by psychoanalytic theory. Projection refers to transferring one's own feelings and reactions onto others as a way of protecting the ego from anxiety. Here the young woman is made anxious by the realization that she no longer loves her boyfriend and copes by projecting this feeling onto her boyfriend. Transference is a process that occurs during psychotherapy, according to Freud.

11.   **(B)**   The Freudian stages of development are oral, anal, phallic, latent, and genital. The latent stage is characterized by a lack of concern with the psychosexual development and takes place between age 5 and the onset of puberty. Self-actualization is a level of motivation identified by Maslow and concrete operations is a stage of cognitive development identified by Piaget.

12. **(D)** Denial, rationalization, intellectualization, and reaction formation are all defense mechanisms identified by psychoanalytical theory. Reaction format refers to transforming one's true feelings and reactions into their opposites as a way of protecting the ego from anxiety. Here the young woman is made anxious by the realization that she no longer loves her boyfriend and copes by expressing the exact opposite. Cognitive dissonance is a social psychological concept.

13. **(B)** Freud postulated that either failure to satisfy the needs of a particular stage of development or overindulgence in those needs can produce a fixation on that stage. Later in life stressful events can cause the person to regress to the fixated stage of development as a coping device. Alcoholism, characterized by a high degree of oral stimulation, therefore could represent a fixation at the oral stage.

14. **(B)** Human factors, clinical, and industrial are areas of applied psychology. Human factors concerns the design of human-machine systems. Industrial is closely related but focuses more on the selection and training of personnel who use a system than on the design of system itself. Clinical, of course, concerns the treatment of abnormal behavior and problems in living. Social, personality, and physiological are all basic areas of research.

15. **(B)** The humanistic approach, as exemplified by theorists such as Carl Rogers and Abraham Maslow, stresses the self-actualization of an individual's potential. Psychodynamic theory stresses the inner conflicts of personality, whereas behaviorism focuses on the external shaping of personality by the environment. The cognitive approach stresses the active construction of knowledge and beliefs about the world, and the psychobiological approach focuses on neural mechanisms of behavior.

16. **(B)** Crystallized intelligence in Cattel's theory represents accumulated knowledge and facts that are a stable intellectual resource. Fluid intelligence, in contrast, represents skill at processing new problems and relations. Componential, contextual, and experiential are dimensions of Sternberg's triarchic theory of intelligence.

17. **(E)** Gardner's theory of multiple intelligence posits verbal, spatial, mathematical, musical, bodily skill, personal relations, interpersonal relations domains of intelligence. Performance is a subscale of the Wechsler Adult Intelligence Scale.

18. **(D)** The Stanford-Binet intelligence quotient is equal to mental age divided by chronological age, which is then multiplied by 100. Thus, the average or normal I.Q. equals 100 and an individual whose mental age is twice chronological age possesses an I.Q. of 200.

19 **(C)** Spearman theorized a general component of intelligence, named the Q-factor that underlies performance on numerous tests included in intelligence batteries. Correlations among these various tests are typically positive, lending credence to this theory. Critics note, however, that the diversity of the tests usually included is too limited to draw a strong conclusion about the q factor.

20. **(B)** Face validity implies that, based on a surface reading of questions, a test appears to measure what it is supposed to measure. Predictive and construct validity require a deeper analysis in which test performance is correlated with real world indicators of honest behavior.

21. **(C)** There is no question that both genetic and environmental factors determine a person's intelligence. Most psychologists would agree that the two factors are about equally weighted.

22. **(D)** The Rorschach Inkblot, the Thematic Apperception Test (TAT), and the Draw-a-Person tests are classic examples of projective tests in which there is no single correct answer and responses are generated by the test taker. The Minnesota Multiphasic Personality Inventory is a classic objective test in which the person chooses a response from a limited number of alternatives.

23. **(C)** Content validity refers to whether the content of test items is clearly related to the construct being measured. In this case excessive fear is clearly related to mental disturbance whereas the other alternatives are not. Enjoying sleep, games, and T.V. and disliking tests are within the range of normal attitudes.

24. **(A)** Test-retest involves correlating performance across two administrations of a psychological test and split-half involves correlating related items within a single test administration. Both techniques assess the consistency of responding-known as reliability, not validity.

25. **(B)** Criterion or predictive validity refers to correlating performance on a test with a single real word index of the construct being measured. Construct validity also seeks to establish that the test measures what it supposed to measure, but involves multiple real world indices of the contrast.

26. **(C)** Multiple choice tests are relatively inexpensive to administer and they can show predictive validity. But choosing a correct answer does not guarantee that a person understands the concepts being tested; a person could simply guess correctly or select the right answer for reasons that are flawed.

27. **(D)** Empirically keyed scoring involves using items that possess low content validity, in which the desirable or undesirable answer is not apparent. Forced choice items require one to pick one of two responses that are both

undesirable. Bizarre questions can lure respondents who are lying in an effort to look abnormal. The psychopathic deviance scale measures antisocial behavior. It is not a direct check on lying on the test items.

28. **(E)** A clinical psychologist holds a Ph.D. degree and is chiefly involved in applied research and therapy. Unlike M.D.–holding psychiatrists, clinical psychologists cannot presently prescribe medication or other somatic therapies.

29. **(B)** Depression has been called the common cold of mental illness, accounting for 2/3 of all psychiatric hospital admissions. Schizophrenia, in contrast, affects only about 1% of the population. Mania, obsessive-compulsive disorders, and hypochondria are also relatively uncommon.

30. **(C)** Tardive dyskinesia refers to a peculiar gait and other bizarre motor movements; it is a side effect of the class of antipsychotic medications called phenothiazines. Thorazine is an example and is commonly prescribed for schizophrenia.

31. **(E)** The mode, median, and mean describe the central tendency of a frequency distribution. Chi square, analysis of variance (F test), and t-test are examples of inferential statistics, permitting inferences about the statistical significance of observed samples of data.

32. **(B)** A t-test is a parametric type of inferential statistic. It is related to the F test or analysis of variance. Computation requires a measure of variance, the standard deviation, and the mean of a sample. Usually, a t-test involves two means and two standard deviations.

33. **(A)** Inferential statistics allow one to draw conclusions about the probability that data in different groups are reliably different and not the result of chance. Such statistics are necessary when groups differ in their means, but still overlap to some degree in their frequency distributions. Nonoverlap automatically implies a statistically significant difference. One could readily conclude that the difference would occur by chance less than one time in a hundred.

34. **(B)** Pearson's r varies between −1.0 and +1.0. The sign implies the direction of the relation between the two variables, not their statistical significance. The proportion of variance in one variable that can be accounted for by knowing the values of the other variable is equal to r^2 (in this case close to .50). Without knowing how large the sample sizes are, one cannot safely conclude whether the result was significant at the .001 level.

35. **(E)** Anonymity is one condition that leads to deindividuation. This means a person loses a sense of individual identity and responsibility. Being an anonymous member of a large crowd, losing one's self in the group, illustrates deindividuation.

36. **(A)**   Prejudice is a product of social upbringing and draws on stereotypes of the stigmatized groups. The familiarity effect is also relevant; the less familiar another group is, the more we fear that group. The lack of familiarity across different racial groups also makes face recognition more difficult between groups compared to within a single group. This, too, feeds prejudice. Cognitive dissonance, in contrast, has no clear connection.

37. **(B)**   Research in social psychology indicates that physical appearance is the most important determinant of first impressions. It is also relevant in social attraction and effectiveness in persuading others to change their beliefs.

38. **(C)**   Density refers to the number of people occupying a certain size of space, such as a square mile. In contrast to this physical concept, crowding is a psychological concept referring to subjective reactions to high density. Personal space, loudness and noisiness are also psychological concepts.

39. **(A)**   The standard error of the mean is calculated by dividing the standard deviation by the square root of the sample size. Thus, it is closely related to standard deviation and variance, both measures of variability.

40. **(E)**   Correlation coefficients vary between –1.0 and +1.0. The closer the absolute value is to 1.0, the stronger the relation between the variables. The sign of the coefficient indicates the direction of the relation. A –.68 coefficient indicates a reasonably strong relationship in which the values of variable A increase as the values of variable B decrease.

41. **(A)**   Motivated forgetting is one major explanation of memory failures based on psychoanalytic thought. Specifically, the defense mechanism of repression causes a person to forget disturbing events in an effort to avoid conscious anxiety.

42. **(A)**   Stimulus generalization refers to the degree to which an organism responds to stimuli that are similar to the original training stimulus. Primary reinforcers refer to natural reinforcers that require no conditioning, e.g., food or water. Secondary reinforcers refer to stimuli that the organism is taught are rewards. e.g., medals, trophies, or certificates. Partial reinforcement refers to a reinforcement schedule that does not reinforce every response.

43. **(E)**   The least sensitive method for assessing whether a person has stored information in long-term memory is free recall. Cued recall comes next, followed by recognition tests. The most sensitive is the method of savings or relearning. This refers to how rapidly a person can relearn the information or perform a task that uses the information. The method can reveal that information is available in long-term memory even if it cannot be recalled or recognized.

44. **(A)** The cornea is a clear, curved structure at the front of the eye. The curvature refracts the incoming light, which is then further refracted by the lens, in order to bring an image into focus on the retina. The cornea actually bends the light to a greater degree than does the lens.

45. **(B)** Two theories have received empirical support in explaining pitch perception. Frequency theory posits that the entire basilar membrane vibrates in response to the frequency of the incoming sound waves. For low- to mid-range frequencies, this is correct. Place theory contends that a particular position on the basilar membrane responds maximally to a particular frequency. For mid-range to high frequencies, this is also correct. Both frequency and place mechanisms operate in mid-range frequencies, those most common in human speech.

46. **(C)** The trichromatic theory, also known as the Young-Helmholtz theory, explains certain aspects of color perception at the retinal level by postulating three types of cones tuned to red, green, and blue wavelengths. The opponent process theory explains other aspects of color perception at the visual cortex level by postulating three sets of opponent mechanisms. One responds to differences in white-black, another to yellow-blue, and a third to red-green.

47. **(A)** The pinna, ear canal, and tympanic membrane constitute the outer ear. The three small bones, the malleus, incus, and stapes, transmit the sound waves in the middle ear to the cochlea in the inner ear. Other inner ear structures include the basilar membrane and semicircular canals.

48. **(C)** The Gestalt grouping principles explain how visual elements are combined to form meaningful objects and events. Closure, proximity, unity, and similarity are four such principles. Retinal disparity is a cue used in depth perception.

49. **(E)** The focal length of the eye is altered by changing the shape of the lens, a process called accommodation. This term also refers to a Piagetian concept of development, along with assimilation. Binocular disparity and linear perspective are depth perception cues.

50. **(A)** Signal detection theory allows one to separate mathematically a person's sensitivity to the presence of a stimulus (d') and the response criterion or bias toward saying that a stimulus either is or is not present (beta). Hit rates and false alarm rates are used to compute these independent parameters.

51. **(B)** The Purkinje shift refers to the shift in sensitivity of the eye from short wavelengths or blue under daylight conditions to long wavelengths or red under twilight conditions. Red and blue stimuli of equal brightness in daylight would no longer be identical as darkness falls because of this shift.

52. **(B)**   Rods are sensitive under low light conditions (called scotopic vision). The cones are most sensitive under high light conditions (photopic vision). They are responsible for color vision, and are clustered in the fovea.

53. **(D)**   Semantics is concerned with meaning, whereas syntax or grammar is concerned with linguistic structure. Pragmatics, the third broad area of language is concerned with the uses of language in context to achieve specific intentions.

54. **(C)**   Chomsky's linguistic theory of transformational grammar aimed to specify how all acceptable sentences could be generated by an ideal speaker. This theory concerned linguistic competence. It made no claims about psycholinguistic issues of how well or poorly people actually generate particular types of sentences. These were matters of linguistic performance.

55. **(A)**   The key assumption of interference theory is that highly similar events interfere with each other at the time of retrieval from memory. Decay theory concerns memory loss that occurs after storage but prior to retrieval. Consolidation theory concerns failure to store material well in the first place.

56. **(B)**   The short-term memory limitation of 7± 2 chunks of information can be seen in a digit span test and in an absolute judgment task. The latter requires the assignment of perceptual stimuli to response categories. Although the stimuli can be easily distinguished, errors are made if more than seven response categories are needed because of memory failure.

57. **(D)**   Sperling's classic experiments on iconic memory demonstrated that decay time is about 250 milliseconds. Echoic memory has a decay time on the order of 2-3 seconds. The decay time of tactile sensory memory is not well established. Of course, short-term and working memory show much longer decay times.

58. **(B)**   Judgments of frequency of occurrence tend to be most accurate for moderately frequent events. High frequency events are underestimated and low frequency events overestimated.

59. **(C)**   Either one property or another property or both defines the inclusive disjunctive rule. Either one or the other, but not both, is the exclusive disjunctive rule. The conjunctive rule requires both properties, and the conditional and biconditional require contingencies between a primary and secondary property.

60. **(D)**   Heuristics are rules of thumb that may allow one to solve a problem. They often speed solution of a problem by ruling out certain portions of the problem space as not worth exploring. They sometimes fail, however, if a re-

jected portion of the problem space actually contains the solution. Algorithms are rules that always successfully solve problems, though they may be slow and tedious.

61. **(B)** Negative reinforcement involves terminating an aversive stimulus (escape), or postponing the occurrence (avoidance) of a particular response. This increases the likelihood of the response. Negative reinforcement is often confused with punishment in which an aversive stimulus is introduced to decrease the rate of a response.

62. **(E)** During acquisition in classical conditioning, a conditioned stimulus (tone) is presented just before an unconditioned stimulus (food) and an unconditioned response (salivating) occurs automatically. After learning, presentation of the conditioned stimulus (tone) alone elicits the conditioned response (salivating).

63. **(D)** Theory X refers to a motivational perspective in management that employees must be properly rewarded and punished or they will not work hard. It presumes operant conditioning is necessary in the work place. Theory Y contends that people are self-motivated and the use of rewards and punishments is not necessary and may be counterproductive.

64. **(A)** Both classical and operant conditioning involve conditioned stimuli and responses and unconditioned stimuli and responses. The difference is in the order of occurrence. Only operant conditioning requires that an organism must voluntarily act before a reward or punishment can be presented.

65. **(D)** The corpus callosum is a band of fibers that connects the right and left hemispheres. The temporal cortex is a part of the left and right neocortex. The reticular formation is part of the brainstem. The limbic system, including the thalamus, is part of the midbrain.

66. **(D)** The frontal lobes are known as the association areas and are active during associative thinking, such as that required by abstract problem solving. Perception is mediated by other specific areas, such as the visual cortex, and motor skills are supported by the cerebellum.

67. **(A)** The principle of contralateral action dictates the left hemisphere controls the right side of the body. Being right handed implies that the left hemisphere is dominant. Broca's area is generally located in the dominant left hemisphere and is responsible for speech production.

68. **(B)** The limbic system is part of the midbrain. The brain and spinal cord make up the central nervous system, which contrasts with the peripheral nervous system.

69. **(C)**   Confused decision making, sadness, and self-deprecation are classic symptoms of depression, the major affective disorder. Catatonic postures, hallucinations, private language, and repetitive behavior are symptomatic of psychotic disorders, such as schizophrenia.

70. **(B)**   Behaviorism contends that the environment controls a person's behavior through the process of learning. Abnormal behaviors, such as depression, must be attributed to a failure to learn how to behave in ways that are acceptable and fulfilling. Further, these inappropriate responses are reinforced with attention and concern by friends and relatives. Psychoanalysis would point to unconscious conflicts, and humanism would blame a failure to self-actualize or satisfy other fundamental needs.

71. **(E)**   Manic depression or bipolar affective disorder is not in the same class as the others. Phobias, panic disorders, and post traumatic stress disorder are all linked to intense anxiety.

72. **(C)**   Bodily complaints, such as tense and sore muscles, and digestive problems are commonly connected with anxiety disorders. In contrast, hallucinations, delusions, and paranoia are symptoms of psychotic disorders.

73. **(A)**   The defining feature of schizophrenia is thought disorder. Multiple personality, a form of dissociative disorder in the general class of anxiety disorders, is often confused with schizophrenia. Although delusions may occur in severe depression, hallucinations are symptoms of psychosis, not affective disorders.

74. **(A)**   Paranoid schizophrenia is characterized by delusional fears of persecution. Catatonic schizophrenia is characterized by bizarre, fixed postures and lack of response to stimuli. Disorganized schizophrenia is characterized by severe thought disorder, such as hallucinations and meaningless speech

75. **(C)**   Extreme mood swings are the defining characteristic of affective disorders. Hallucinations, delusions, aberrant speech, and autism are characteristic of schizophrenia or psychotic disorders.

76. **(C)**   Bipolar affective disorder is another name for manic depression. The symptoms described are typical of someone in the manic phase of this disease. Such frenetic behavior would not be expected from someone suffering from paranoia, fugue, schizophrenia, or hysteria.

77. **(E)**   Schizophrenia is the major form of psychotic disorder. Affective disorders, both unipolar and bipolar, can be so intense and disturb thought organization so much that they are considered forms of psychosis. In contrast, phobia and post traumatic stress disorders are nonpsychotic anxiety disorders.

Contrary to popular belief, so is multiple personality, which is a form of dissociative disorder.

78. **(B)** Agoraphobia refers to the fear of open spaces. It is often called the housewife's disease because it most frequently occurs among women who are housewives who become, in a sense, prisoners of their own home.

79. **(B)** Systematic desensitization is based on the principle that the parasympathetic (relaxation) response is incompatible with the sympathetic (arousal) response. The client progresses through a hierarchy of gradually arousing imaginary scenes related to the phobia after entering a state of deep relaxation. As predicted by learning theory, this results in extinction of the fear.

80. **(E)** Beck pioneered cognitive therapy for the treatment of depression. He analyzed the cognitive dysfunctions that lead to the low self-esteem characteristic of depression. One example is selectively attending to negative information. By correcting these cognitive dysfunctions through reprogramming, the depression is alleviated.

81. **(D)** Konrad Lorenz observed that newborn ducks would follow him if they saw him before encountering their mother. He termed this phenomenon *imprinting* and argued that it illustrated the importance of instinctual behavior. This concept, along with sign stimuli that release fixed patterns, comprised some of the central ideas of ethology.

82. **(B)** Human beings have the largest brain size relative to body size. Dolphins are very close to our ratio, however, and actually possess larger brains that are equal to ours in complexity (remember that their body size is larger than that of humans). Elephants have much larger brains than humans, but of course their body size is massive as well. It may be that human intelligence is an emergent property of packing such a large complex brain in such a small head cavity.

83. **(C)** The largest group of psychologists, whether engaged in basic research or applied work, work in clinical psychology.

84. **(B)** Helmholtz contributed in several ways to understanding visual and auditory perception in the 19th century. He is best known for the Young-Helmholtz theory of color vision. Also known as the trichromatic theory, it postulated three types of cones — red, green, and blue — which interact to mediate color perception.

85. **(C)** Human factors psychology, also known as ergonomics is concerned with the design of human-machine interfaces. A classic example would be the design of a keyboard. The field aims to design systems that people can use safely and efficiently. An industrial psychologist might well be employed by the computer firm to select and train personnel.

86. **(A)** Kurt Lewin developed a phenomenological approach to psychology known as Field Theory. He was heavily influenced by gestalt psychology in formulating his theory. Thorndyke is connected with the Law of Effect, Kelly with Pragmatism, and Helson with Adaptation Theory.

87. **(D)** Steven's Law holds that subjective experience $= kI^n$, where k and n differ for various senses. This is a more general relationship than the Fechner-Weber law and accounts for their psychophysical observations. The exponent n equals .33 for light intensity, 1.0 for line length, and 3.67 for electric shock intensity (the largest of any sensation studied).

88. **(E)** Red, green, and blue cones mediate color vision; deficiencies of one type are responsible for color blindness or dichromatic vision. Cones located in the central fovea permit a high degree of visual acuity, but they require high levels of illumination to operate effectively (called photopic vision).

89. **(C)** Similarity gradient is not a depth cue. Relative motion permits an inference about distance relations based on parallax. Texture gradient refers to a given unit of texture, such as the size of a tree, which gradually decreases as one looks toward the horizon. Familiar size also helps. As a familiar object moves away from the eye, its familiar size decreases, which the brain interprets as an increase of distance. Binocular disparity, simply phrased, refers to the depth information provided by the disparate views of an object from the left and right eyes, the degree of which varies with distance from the object.

90. **(A)** The harmonics or overtones of an instrument refer to the higher frequencies produced when a fundamental frequency is played. These harmonics represent multiples of the fundamental frequency; for example, a middle C at 256 Hz would generate energy at 512 Hz, 768 Hz, and so on. Two instruments differ in the amplitude or amount of energy at these higher frequencies. The resulting difference in sound is called timbre. Pitch refers to the fundamental frequency, and loudness is the psychological experience from a particular sound intensity and pitch.

91. **(C)** In young children, sleepwalking and sleeptalking are common and are gradually outgrown. Occasionally, these conditions persist in adulthood and are viewed as dissociative states of consciousness. Sleep research indicates that they occur during Stage IV sleep. This is the deepest stage of non-REM sleep and is characterized by theta and delta brain waves.

92. **(B)** Transcendental meditation is a method for altering consciousness by focusing attention on a mantra or phrase and repeating it silently. Research indicates that this procedure induces a relaxation response and generates alpha brain rhythms. Zen meditation generally entails enhancing alertness and atten-

tiveness to the immediate environment. This, too, alters consciousness with practice. Hypnosis involves focusing the attention of and suggesting thoughts to the person undergoing the procedure. Deep reflection was a form of meditation practiced by the writer Aldous Huxley.

93. **(B)** Day residues include important or trivial events plus bodily sensations that find their way into dream content. These were considered manifest content by Freud. Latent content referred to symbolic representations of unconscious conflicts that were central to psychosexual development. Archetypes were universal symbols that Carl Jung believed came from a collective unconscious shared by humanity.

94. **(A)** Voltage changes recorded from the scalp are classified as beta, alpha, theta, and delta, going from high frequency to low frequency. The amplitude of these waves varies inversely with frequency. The high frequency, low amplitude beta waves reflect alert, active processing of information. Alpha waves are seen when a portion of the brain is idling in an awake subject. A right-handed individual would be using the left hemisphere to control motor movements and those structures in the left hemisphere that mediate language production. Hence, the right hemisphere probably would be relatively inactive and showing alpha rhythms.

95. **(E)** Rapid eye movement (REM) sleep takes place about every 90 minutes. It is considered paradoxical sleep because several physiological signs suggest the person is highly aroused and alert yet the person's eyes remain closed and he/she cannot easily be awakened. One of these signs is the presence of beta waves in an EEG recording, which normally reflects alert, active information processing. Subjective reports of people awakened just after REM sleep typically indicate that they were dreaming.

96. **(B)** Stage II sleep is characterized by alpha and theta brain waves. It is one of four stages in non-REM sleep that precede onset of REM sleep. Although REM sleep is associated with the often bizarre world of dreaming, research indicated that mental experiences occur during non-REM sleep as well. A subject aroused from Stage II sleep is likely to report some mundane event from the previous day that is not as unusual or memorable as REM dreams.

97. **(C)** The gate control theory of pain perception contends that incoming pain signals carried by afferent nerves are either transmitted or blocked at the spinal cord. Those transmitted are registered in the brain leading to the subjective experience of pain. The "gate" in the spinal cord can be closed by efferent nerves coming from the brain.

98. **(A)** Research on dichotic listening indicates that attention cannot be given simultaneously to two independent channels of speech. The ability to

attend selectively to one channel and ignore the other is enhanced when the two messages differ in pitch. Differences in semantics, syntax, diction, and pragmatics do not help. These results indicate that preattentive processing that support selective attention operate chiefly on sensory characteristics such as pitch.

99. **(E)** In Sperling's classic studies he presented an array of letters and digits tachistoscopically. When asked to report the entire array subjects could retrieve four or five items and then began to forget everything else they had seen. When cued immediately to report only a particular row of the array, however, they were uniformly accurate. This indicated they could recall any four items in a particular row on command because all the array was briefly available in memory. But after a brief period the nonreported rows began to decay from sensory storage.

100. **(D)** Tulving has proposed a multiple memory system consisting of procedural, semantic and episodic subsystems. These are viewed as embedded with procedural being the most basic. A subset of procedural is semantic, and in turn a subset of semantic is episodic. Procedural memory concerns knowledge of activities and processes. Semantic memory is conceptual knowledge. Episodic memory consists of specific, dated objects and events.

101. **(D)** Biofeedback involves providing an informative signal to the client when they successfully lower blood pressure, relax a particular muscle, or lower body temperature. The signal serves as a positive reinforcer. With practice the client learns through operant conditioning to sustain the desirable physiological response. The technique is used to treat some cases of high blood pressure and anxiety disorders.

102. **(D)** Omission training is a type of operant conditioning in which a pleasant or appetitive stimulus is omitted following the occurrence of a response. This leads to a decrease in this behavioral response. Punishment also decreases response frequency using an aversive stimulus. Negative reinforcement leads to an increase in response frequency, such as escape response, by withdrawing an aversive stimulus.

103. **(A)** Extinction takes place when reinforcers are no longer given following the occurrence of a behavior. If an organism was previously on a continuous reinforcement schedule, it is salient when reinforcers are suddenly not forthcoming. The conditioned response quickly extinguishes. But if an organism was previously on a partial reinforcement schedule, then the transition to extinction is not as easily detected. The conditioned response persists longer in this case.

104. **(B)** With interval schedules of partial reinforcement, a response is reinforced following an interval of time. This can be a fixed interval or it may be variable, with the different intervals averaging to some value. Ratio schedules

involve providing a reinforcer after a certain number of responses have occurred. Again, this can be a fixed value or an average.

105. **(C)**   Operant conditioning is a synonym for instrumental conditioning. An organism's behavior is instrumental in achieving some effect; the organism operates on its environment. Social learning refers to modeling or observational learning. Classical conditioning does not require the organism to act on its environment for learning to occur; it involves passive learning.

106. **(D)**   Retrieval from long-term memory involves a reconstruction of original events. Inferences are logical deductions, and guesses are as much of a part of such remembering as verbatim recall. Retrieval is not a simple replay of a memory recording. Consolidation refers to a process of stabilizing memory trace after initial encoding.

107. **(A)**   Research indicated that self-test is important for checking understanding and for improving memory by practicing retrieval. Massed practice or cramming is known to be ineffective. Skilled reading calls for skimming over material to get a sense of organization and reading difficult passages more often and more carefully than easy passages. Finally, the serial position effect would suggest that the most study time should be devoted to the middle parts of a reading assignment.

108. **(B)**   Sensory memory holds incoming stimuli for a brief period of time. Iconic memory has a duration of only about 250 milliseconds whereas echoic memory has a duration of about 2 seconds. The duration of tactile sensory memory is not well established. Short-term or working memory have much longer durations.

109. **(B)**   The levels of processing theory of memory contends that the depth of encoding operation determines the degree of retention. Encoding at the level of sensory or physical attributes (e.g., size, color, sound) produces poorer retention than encoding at the level of semantic attributes. Categorizing the word train as a form of transportation achieves semantic encoding.

110. **(B)**   Natural categories consist of examples that vary in degrees of membership. A certain instance (apple), called the prototype, best exemplifies the category (fruit). The various degrees of membership is called the typicality gradient. Natural categories also possess fuzzy boundaries (e.g., is a tomato a fruit?). However, both apples and grapes clearly fall within the boundary and so fuzzy boundaries are not at issue here.

111. **(D)**   Rosch's research indicated that superordinate (animal), basic (dog), and subordinate (collie) levels of categorization are processed differently by people. Children appear to learn and use the basic level first. Also, adults are

able to answer questions about basic level categories faster than about superordinate and subordinate categories.

112. **(A)**   Despite commercial claims to the contrary, research shows that speed reading decreases comprehension and would be ill advised for studying technical material. Speed reading amounts to trained skimming. It does reduce the amount of subvocalization and regressive eye movements. It does not permit encoding of entire sentences in a single fixation — unless, of course, the sentence is very short and simple.

113. **(C)**   Noticing relations or making connections between long-term memory and new material is called elaborative rehearsal. Maintenance rehearsal refers to repeating information over and over. Whereas elaborative rehearsal leads to storage in long-term memory, maintenance rehearsal primarily maintains information in short-term memory.

114. **(D)**   State dependent learning refers to the interaction of states of consciousness at the time of the study and test in free recall performance. Alcohol and other drug intoxication shows this phenomenon. Specifically, performance is best when states of consciousness are the same at study and test and worst when they differ. Moreover, the interaction is not symmetrical because original learning is substantially better when the subject studies while sober. Hence, recall performance is worse when the subject is intoxicated at study and sober at test than when he is sober at study and intoxicated at test.

115. **(A)**   Decay theory holds that the information is encoded and consolidated in memory. Then, it begins to decay unless rehearsal or retrieval operations preserve the memory trace. Decay theory contends, therefore, that forgotten material is no longer available. Consolidation theory also attributes forgetting to an availability problem. In contrast, interference theory and motivated forgetting theory claim the information is available in memory, but is inaccessible to retrieval.

116. **(D)**   People make errors in risk judgments because they do not have reliable sources of information about the true probabilities of events. Instead, they draw from memory episodes that are available to them and generalize from this limited information. Because of news coverage and the vividness of destruction, natural disasters are generally more available in memory than events such as death from asthma.

117. **(B)**   The atmosphere hypothesis contends that people do not really evaluate premises and conclusions at all. Instead, they accept a conclusion if its form seems consistent with the form of the premises. For example, universal affirmative conclusion (e.g., All A are B) will be accepted as valid if premises contain universal affirmative quantifiers (All A are B; All B are not C).

118. **(E)**   Functional fixedness refers to thinking only of the standard use of some object and not realizing the object might serve other novel functions. Possessing much domain specific knowledge about auto mechanics would not necessarily help you creatively solve the fan belt problem. In fact it may increase your functional fixedness if you work frequently with fan belts and other parts of an engine. Perceptual set or Einstellung is a related concept to functional fixedness. It refers to the more general constraint on problem solving in which people rely automatically on solutions that have worked in the past, even though they may not be the best solutions.

119. **(D)**   Epinephrine functions to create effects similar to those of the sympathetic nervous system and has been shown to increase memory retention.

120. **(D)**   The two sentences differ in surface structure, but are identical semantically and pragmatically. They show the same deep structure in Chomsky's theory of transformational grammar.

121. **(D)**   The increase in heart rate is part of the fight or flight reaction mediated by the sympathetic branch of the autonomic nervous system. The autonomic nervous system and the somatic system constitute the peripheral nervous system. The sympathetic branch energizes, preparing one to react. The parasympathetic branch, in contrast, relaxes. The two branches are reciprocally innervated, meaning both cannot be stimulated at the same time.

122. **(B)**   A neuron is composed of three main parts: the dendrites, the cell body, and the axon. Nerve impulses are received by the dendrites and transmitted to the cell body. The elongated axon then transmits the impulse to the next neuron. It exits the axon through the terminal buttons and chemically crosses a synapse to the dendrites of the next neuron.

123. **(E)**   Epinephrine is another name for adrenaline. This hormone is secreted by the adrenal gland in response to signals from the sympathetic nervous system. It energizes the muscular system as part of the fight or flight reaction by increasing the heart rate and discharging sugar from the liver into the bloodstream. Norepinephrine is a related hormone secreted by the adrenal gland during this reaction.

124. **(C)**   In the brain stem, the most primitive part of the human brain, lies the reticular activating system. It regulates the general arousal level of the brain and is important in governing alertness, attention, and sleep. At the upper end of the brain stem lies the limbic system, which controls emotion and motivation. Near the limbic is the thalamus, which relays incoming sensory signals to higher brain structure.

125. **(E)**   The amygdala is a portion of the limbic system that plays a central role in aggression. Creating a lesion in the amygdala has actually been tried in violent prisoners for whom psychosurgery appeared to be the last option available. The thalamus is a sensory center while the medulla is responsible for basic repetitive processes such as breathing. The cerebellum controls motor coordination. The pituitary is known as the master gland.

126. **(D)**   Wernicke's area is important in the comprehension of spoken language. It is related to Broca's area, which controls the production of speech.

127. **(C)**   The trichromatic or Young-Helmholtz theory of color vision posits red, green, and blue cones that are maximally responsive to those portions of the visible light spectrum. Depending on the degree to which each type of cone is stimulated, a person perceives a particular hue using the logic of additive color mixing. The rods have no function in color vision. One strong form of evidence supporting the theory is the ability to account for different types of color blindness.

128. **(A)**   The opponent process theory posits three opponent mechanisms in the visual cortex. The first responds to the amount of red versus green light, the second to blue versus yellow, and the third to white versus black. By staring at yellow, one fatigues the yellow half of the yellow-blue mechanism. Then, when an after image forms on white paper, which reflects all wavelengths, the mechanism is more sensitive to blue wavelengths than it is to yellow.

129. **(B)**   An ideal human ear can detect a range of 20 Hz to 20,000 Hz under ideal listening conditions. Given that most listening environments are not noise proof and given that most individuals have suffered at least minor degrees of hearing loss at very high frequencies, it is doubtful that a stereo needs to reproduce 20,000 Hz with high fidelity, let alone 25,000 Hz.

130. **(B)**   The vestibular sense permits the head and body to maintain orientation with respect to gravity. It also monitors acceleration of the body, sensing changes in direction or rate of motion. Tiny hairs bend when fluid moves within the semicircular canals. These are at right angles to one another, allowing motion in any direction to be detected.

131. **(E)**   Place theory holds that a particular place on the basilar membrane vibrates most vigorously in response to a particular frequency. This contrasts with frequency theory. Although evidence supports frequency theory at low frequencies, place theory is firmly supported at mid range to high frequencies.

132. **(D)**   Sound level measurements are taken on a decibel or dB scale. Hertz (Hz) measures sound frequency. The dB scale is logarithmic, to accommodate the tremendous range in sound pressure levels that the human ear can hear without

immediate damage. Over 150 dB, however, would damage the tympanic membrane. A jet would probably be about 120 dB, a very loud sound. We are commonly exposed to 80 dB in a typical office or urban environment.

133. **(C)**   The frustration-aggression hypothesis contends that aggression develops when an organism is prevented from moving toward and achieving a goal. Frustration can accumulate, leading to aggressive acts in the future. This hypothesis regards external factors as critical in understanding aggression. Ethology and psychoanalytic theories, in contrast, blame internal instructs for aggression.

134. **(A)**   Social exchange theory views human interactions in economic terms. When two people meet, they each calculate the costs and benefits of developing a relationship. If the benefits outweigh the costs, then the two people will be attracted to each other. Attribution theory concerns judgments about the factors responsible for our own and others' behavior.

135. **(D)**   Self-fulfilling prophecy refers to behaving in a way that is consistent with a belief or hypotheses, which then results in the hypothesis coming true. Prejudice is strong hatred or dislike for members of a group. Social schemata are mental structures that represent our social beliefs. They construct our sense of social reality.

136. **(C)**   A prototype is an ideal example of a concept or schema. It represents all the characteristics that are most typical of the concept. Prototypes are important in pattern recognition and memory. Beliefs about personality traits such as extroversion are also organized about prototypes.

137. **(A)**   The fundamental attribution error refers to the tendency to assume another person's personality or beliefs cause his or her behavior. We underestimate the power of external factors in controlling behavior and overestimate the power of internal factors. Here attributing the gift of $100 to the trait of kindness is likely. The other attributions listed are related to various external pressures.

138. **(B)**   The actor-observer bias provides a qualification to the fundamental attribution error. As observers of others, we overestimate the power of internal factors in controlling their behavior. As actors, however, we are less susceptible to this error in making attributions about our own behavior. In fact, psychologically healthy (nondepressed) individuals are likely to attribute their failure on an exam to an external factor, such as the professor creating too difficult an exam.

139. **(E)**   An attitude is defined as a predisposition to behave in a certain way. An attitude involves both cognition and emotion. Behavior is not always consistent with attitudes, despite the predisposition. A prototype is the best example of a concept. A stereotype is an overgeneralized belief about a group of

people. An orienting reflex is a reaction to novel, unexpected stimuli.

140. **(E)**   Elizabeth Kubler-Ross theorized that the process of dying in terminally ill patients generally consists of four stages. First, the person denies that he or she is dying. Next, anger is expressed. Third, the person bargains with God or family to live longer. Finally, the person may come to accept death and make peace with it.

141. **(C)**   The theory of cognitive dissonance predicts that attitude change should occur when we freely engage in a behavior inconsistent with our attitudes. If free choice is involved with no external award or coercion then we re-assess our original attitude and change it in the direction of making the new attitude and the past behavior more consistent. Theoretically, we are motivated to change the attitude because of the cognitive dissonance we feel when we freely behave in a manner at odds with our attitudes.

142. **(B)**   The need for social affiliation or desire to be with other people is great when we are afraid. In a classic series of studies, Stanley Schachter manipulated the fear level of college women by leading them to believe they would receive electric shocks in a laboratory experiment. He then measured whether the women preferred to wait for the experiment to begin either alone or with others. Cognitive dissonance has no known effect on affiliation. Anxiety in general may or may not affect social affiliation, while depression decreases the desire to be with others.

143. **(C)**   Social facilitation refers to improvements in an individual's performance when other people are present. This phenomenon occurs both when the person is competing with others and when there is no interaction with others at all; however, it is limited to well learned tasks. The presence of others can increase arousal to non-optimal levels for difficult novel tasks.

144. **(D)**   Research on social attraction indicates that proximity is important for the obvious reason that social interaction is more likely when two people live nearby. Physical attraction and similarity are critical factors. All else being equal, the greater the familiarity, the greater the social attraction.

145. **(B)**   Asch studied conformity by having a group of college students make perceptual judgments. All but one member of the group were confederates of the experimenter. On cue they made erroneous judgments about line lengths — judgments the real subject could readily see were wrong. He found that people conformed out of a need to either internalize the group's beliefs, to identify with the group, or to merely comply with the group.

146. **(E)**   In-group bias refers to the "we versus them" phenomenon. Members of a group, even one formed as quickly and as randomly as in a pickup

game, identify with each other. Outsiders to the group, particularly members of a competing group, are viewed as inferior and objects of aggression.

147. **(A)**   Individuation is defined as a state and a process in which a person's uniqueness from others is established in a particular social context. The person's identity is salient in a group. The individuation involves a blending into a group and can be included by insuring personal anonymity.

148. **(B)**   Social psychology studies suggest that aggression can be increased by making the aggressor anonymous. Anonymity, if anything, could tend to decrease test performance, conformity, loving, and prejudice.

149. **(B)**   Dehumanization is a defense mechanism in which we strip away human qualities of those we aggress against. We refuse to admit that our enemies share the same thoughts, beliefs, fears, and values that we do. We begin to regard the enemy as subhuman animals who are not worthy of living. Obviously dehumanization can be one consequence of extreme prejudice. Suppression is another defense mechanism in which a person tries to forget an anxiety provoking event.

150. **(C)**   Astonishingly, nearly two-thirds of the participants in Milgram's study administered what they thought was a 450 volt shock to another human being at the command of the experimenter. They obeyed the experimenter even though they knew that such a level of shock was extremely dangerous. Milgram used this experimental procedure to examine the factors that influence obedience and to shed light on how atrocities such as the Holocaust are made possible.

151. **(E)**   Freud's theory held that pent-up psychic drives could be relieved through catharsis. Thus, the sexual and aggressive drives of the rapist might be reduced if he vicariously is satisfied through viewing pornography. No evidence supports this. If anything, pornography tends to increase the incidence of rape by dehumanizing women and making such aggression easily modeled and more acceptable.

152. **(E)**   Konrad Lorenz, the well-known ethologist, contended that aggression was an instinctive readiness to fight for one's own survival. He studied how most species engage in aggression, though serious injury or death is usually avoided (unlike the case with human aggression). Other ethologists viewed aggression as a derivative of territoriality. All ethnological views contrast with the frustration-aggression hypothesis of learning theory.

153. **(A)**   Lorenz and other ethologists have cataloged a variety of species-specific behavior patterns. These instinctive responses are triggered by sign stimuli that release the patterns automatically. In the case of aggression most animal species avoid serious injury by displaying an appeasement signal, in

which one animal quits fighting and exposes itself to a fatal attack. This triggers the aggressor to stop fighting as well.

154. **(D)** It is true that species other than humans have been observed killing members of their own species on occasion. Although tool usage is most advanced in humans, chimpanzees have been observed in the wild making and using simple tools for hunting termites. Territoriality, though common, is not universal. Males do not always dominate in the animal kingdom. Aggression involves both inherited and learned tendencies.

155. **(A)** One controversy regarding language usage by chimpanzees, gorillas, and dolphins is grounded in the concept of linguistic generativity. Humans are capable of generating an infinite number of syntactically correct sentences. It is less clear that other species can generate novel expressions that have not been prompted in some fashion. Presuming the evidence eventually suggests they can generate some novel expressions, it remains to be seen whether they show the power and flexibility of human language generation.

156. **(D)** Neuroscientists have concluded that the neocortex of a dolphin is as convoluted and intricate in design as that of humans. The overall size of a dolphin brain is slightly larger than a human brain, but their body size is larger than ours. The ratio of brain size to body size is only slightly less in dolphins compared to humans. The relation of brain complexity to intelligence and consciousness is probably positive, but is not well understood.

157. **(D)** Schachter proposed and reported evidence in favor of a two-factor theory of emotion. General, undifferentiated arousal from sympathetic activation is the first factor. The second is our cognitive appraisal about the causes of our bodily arousal. If the arousal is attributed to emotional sources, then emotion is experienced.

158. **(B)** Charles Darwin wrote *The Expression of Emotions in Man and Animals*. Although not as well-known as his *Origin of Species*, Darwin's book on emotions set the stage for the development of ethology as a field and for modern research on emotional expression.

159. **(A)** Display rules are norms for how to express an emotion in a particular public setting. Research suggests that some aspects of emotional expression are present at birth or are common across cultures. For example, facial expressions of happiness, sadness, anger, fear, surprise, and disgust are universal. However, different cultures hold different norms for the public display of emotion.

160. **(B)** Normal human body cells contain 46 chromosomes. Each chromosome contains numerous genes that provide instructions for the development of physical and psychological characteristics. Half of the chromosomes come from

each parent. The full complement of genes is called the genotype. The actual characteristics of the developed person are called the phenotype.

161. **(C)** Maturation is the process of reorganizing bodily structures and functions under the direction of the genotype. Channeling is a concept in behavioral genetics that concerns the interaction of environmental and genetic factors. Accommodation is a visual process involving the lens and also a concept from Piaget's theory of cognitive development.

162. **(C)** Eleanor Gibson's work with the visual cliff concerned the development of depth perception. She found that infants of various species avoid moving over the cliff, indicating they could visually perceive a drop even though tactilely they were supported by clear glass. Humans are not crawling until between 6 and 10 months, making it unclear whether they might have learned depth perception by that time. Goats, however, show the response within a day of birth. This strongly suggests depth perception is innate.

163. **(E)** The one word stage of speech development does not typically occur until a child is nearly a year old. This is preceded by a babbling stage that begins at about four or five months. Very young infants are capable of cooing and are able to perceive differences among consonants, judging from habituation studies.

164. **(D)** The basic stages of language learning are babbling, one word, two word, and telegraphic-speech stages. There is no three word stage. After the two word stage, children utter short simple sentences that convey the basic content words only. Subject-verb agreement, verb tense, number agreement, and function words are missing from such speech.

165. **(E)** According to Piaget, mental schemata are altered through a process of accommodation. This occurs when some novel situation cannot be assimilated by an existing schema without some modification. The relevant schema is changed to accommodate the new situation. Donald Norman has described three ways such new learning can occur: accretion, tuning, and restructuring. The pacifier example would illustrate tuning.

166. **(A)** One of the primary achievements of the sensorimotor stage, which covers from birth to about 24 months, is the development of an object permanence. The infant learns that objects exist independent of his of her interactions with them. This requires developing a symbolic representation of an object. Prior to achieving object permanence, an object out of sight is out of mind for a young infant.

167. **(D)** Egocentrism does not refer to self-centeredness in its usual sense. Children in the preoperational stage, roughly two to seven years, are characterized by centrism. They cannot take more than one perceptual dimension into their perspective on the world at a single time. Egocentrism means they focus on

how things look from their perspective and cannot imagine how they look from someone else's perspective.

168. **(E)** Formal operations is the final stage in Piaget's theory of cognitive development. The earliest one achieves this stage is typically age eleven and many grown adults do not achieve it. Formal operational thought entails abstract logical reasoning and hypothesis testing. The four stages of Piaget's theory in order are sensorimotor, preoperational, concrete operational, and formal operational.

169. **(A)** Harlow removed infant monkeys from their mothers and provided them with nonliving surrogate mothers. One type was made of wire and the other was wire with a soft terrycloth covering. He found that the monkeys spent the most time with the cloth mother, regardless of which one provided milk. Thus, the need for contact comfort was as important as the need for food.

170. **(C)** In normal infants there is a clear physical differentiation in sexual organs present at birth. This defines the infant's sex. Gender identity is established through a learning process. Depending on the child's environment and hereditary predispositions, the child identifies with either males or females. Depending on gender, different behavioral roles are expected by society. These roles are not stable, however, and change with cultural evolution.

171. **(C)** Stage 3 of Kohlberg's theory of moral development is part of the conventional morality level of ethical reasoning. The individual is motivated to be "good" so as to avoid the disapproval of others and gain their acceptance. Stage 2 is a cost-benefit orientation whereby one behaves morally to obtain rewards.

172. **(B)** Stage 4 is a law and order orientation in which one is motivated to follow the rules laid down by authorities. The business executive behaves morally to avoid a fine and jail sentence imposed by criminal law. He has not yet achieved what Kohlberg calls the stages of principled morality. For example, stage 5 is the beginning of principled morality in which a person behaves morally to promote society's welfare.

173. **(C)** During the first two years of life, according to Freud, the mouth is the main source of gratification. The infant explores the environment and is nourished through the mouth during this oral stage. About the age of two the anal stage begins as the primary source of gratification comes from elimination and later retention of feces. Social demands eventually come to govern the child's pleasure in excretion.

174. **(E)** Both overindulgence and underindulgence at a particular stage of gratification in Freud's theory could cause a person to fixate on that stage. In short it takes a far greater significance than is normal. Such fixation is an im-

pediment to healthy development to the next stage. Regression is a closely related concept. It is a defense mechanism in which excessive stress can cause a person to return to an earlier fixated stage of development.

175. **(C)** Erikson's stages of development cover the entire life span from birth to late adulthood. Freud regarded psychosexual development as complete in adolescence with the finalization of the genital stage of development. Both theorists presumed that development might be arrested and were concerned, in various ways, with the development of autonomy about the age of two.

176. **(A)** Erikson's final stage of development in late adulthood is the crisis of ego integrity versus despair. A successful coping with this crisis involves achieving a sense of satisfaction and wholeness with life. Failure to do so leads to negative views on life and despair.

177. **(D)** The elderly are unable to process information as fast as they once were. This is a normal consequence of an aging nervous system. Contrary to popular belief severe memory loss is not inevitable. It typically occurs only because of an organic disorder, such a Alzheimer's disease. Intelligence and vocabulary size can be just as great or greater in old age. Eccentricity is a matter of personality, not age.

178. **(B)** Freud's stages of psychosexual development begin with the oral stage (birth to age 2), which is followed by the anal stage (age 2 to age 3). Next comes the phallic stage (age 4 to age 5). The latent stage follows (age 6 to puberty). The final development, the genital stage, takes place during puberty.

179. **(E)** Pheromones are chemical signals released by one individual to communicate with other members of the same species. Catecholamines are neurotransmitters and include dopamine, norepinephrine, and epinephrine. Neuropeptides are amino acids found in the brain and include enkephalins.

180. **(A)** This misusage indicated the child has learned rules for forming past tense and plurals and then overregularizes all words in accordance with the rule. The error is especially interesting because it often appears after the child had properly used the irregular forms (broke, feet, mice). After learning these and other specifications, the child derives the rule through a process of hypothesis testing. The rule is then overextended to irregular forms. Eventually these overregularizations are eliminated.

181. **(E)** Carl Jung departed from Freud's psychoanalytic theory in several respects. One of his most influential innovations was the concept of the collective unconscious, which is shared by all humanity. He theorized that certain concepts are symbolically represented in all human memory systems. The symbols he called archetypes.

182. **(B)** Hans Seyle proposed three stages to the General Adaptation Syndrome. The alarm stage occurs first, when a stressor overwhelms an organism's normal level of resistance. This resistance level is then increased to cope with the stressor during the resistance stage. Eventually the stressor must be eliminated in some fashion or resistance breaks down, leading to the exhaustion stage.

183. **(A)** The humanistic approach, as exemplified by the work of Rogers, stresses the process of self-actualization. The cognitive approach, as seen in George Kelly's personal construct theory, stresses the construction of meaning, interpretations, and beliefs. The Freudian psychodynamic approach stresses unconscious conflicts. The behavioristic approach, as seen in Skinner's writings, stresses environmental stimulus control of behavior. Lastly, Bandura's social learning theory stresses the importance of self-regulation of behavior.

184. **(C)** Relative motion parallax refers to differences in how much an object moves across the retinal image depending on its distance. Though it is a source of information about depth perception, relative motion parallax has no bearing on the moon illusion. This famous illusion is caused by misinterpretations in depth perception. Texture gradient, familiar size, and the apparent shape of the sky all play a role.

185. **(B)** A phobia can develop in a two-stage process, according to learning theorists. First, the appearance of an object (a conditioned stimulus) just prior to an unconditioned stimulus elicits an unconditioned fear response. Each time the object appears a conditioned fear reaction occurs. Second, escaping from the object (a conditioned response) would be followed by a reduction in fear. This can produce an operantly conditioned escape response, following the tenets of negative reinforcement.

186. **(C)** Cross-cultural research suggests that the facial expressions for basic emotions, including happiness, are the same. This strongly suggests that some aspects of emotional expression are innately determined. Vocal expressions, hand gestures, and other forms of body language can be shaped by particular cultural norms, however.

187. **(A)** Pupil diameter is mediated by the autonomic nervous system. Several factors affect the diameter, such as general arousal, emotional state, and ambient light levels. Mental effort is one of these factors. Pupil diameter is commonly used as a physiological measure of mental effort.

188. **(D)** Early psychophysical research attempted to establish particular energy levels needed to stimulate different senses. Signal detection theory developed in the 1950s contested whether such absolute thresholds can be specified. The theory holds that psychophysical judgments can be characterized by signal sensitivity (d') and response bias (beta). The absolute threshold can appear to change with either of these factors.

189. **(C)**   The critical set point is the level of fat in specialized fat cells that triggers eating signals when not met. Each person maintains a stable body weight over a lifetime depending on this set point. Successful weight loss requires changing the set point.

190. **(B)**   Maslow's hierarchy of needs include the following, starting with the most basic: biological, safety, attachment, esteem, cognitive, esthetic, self-actualization, transcendence. Theoretically, a person must satisfy basic needs before moving up the hierarchy to satisfy higher order needs.

191. **(E)**   Social learning theory stresses the importance of observational learning and self regulation. It differs from behaviorism in recognizing that an individual is not completely at the mercy of their environment. Self-efficacy refers to the beliefs about one's self worth, competence, and ability to control the environment, rather than be driven by it.

192. **(A)**   Abraham Maslow presumed that people are motivated in two ways. Deficiency motivation refers to restoring physical or psychological equilibrium. Growth motivation refers to moving beyond stability to new challenges and satisfactions.

193. **(B)**   Freud theorized that people are driven by two unconscious forces. Eros motivates sexual urges and obviously relates to preservation of the species. Thanatos, the death instinct, motivates destructive and aggressive urges.

194. **(C)**   Alfred Adler was a neo-Freudian theorists who agreed with the notion of unconscious motivation. However, he rejected the notion that Eros and the pleasure principle were central. Instead he contended that feelings of helplessness, inferiority, and dependency drive people throughout life. Sometimes this drive leads to healthy compensation and other times to neurosis.

195. **(C)**   Carl Rogers developed a new form of psychotherapy based on the premise that people constantly strive to fulfill their inherent potential. Client-centered therapy viewed the therapist as an aide to the client's striving for self-actualization. Similarly, Rogers conceptualized personality theory as being person-centered.

196. **(D)**   Freud speculated that anxiety is a signal that some powerful unconscious conflict is about to burst into consciousness. Anxiety, then, is a preconscious signal that repression is failing and additional defense mechanisms are needed.

197. **(E)**   Obsessive-compulsive disorders are characterized by unusual or bizarre thoughts or fears that are temporarily relieved by performing some action. The relief is brief, however, and the obsessive thoughts quickly return and are again followed by the compulsive act.

198. **(A)**   Hypochondriasis is a type of somatoform disorder in which the victim is preoccupied with potential signs of serious disease. Regardless of negative medical tests and reassurances from physicians, the sufferer remains convinced that something is wrong with them. It is related to conversion disorder in which some actual physical symptom is present despite the lack of any organic basis for it.

199. **(D)**   Multiple personality is a form of dissociative disorder in which several distinctive personalities reside in the same person. It used to be considered extremely rare. However, in the 1970s and 1980s an increasing number of cases have been reported, including well-known cases involving murder suspects. There is some question about whether these are legitimate cases or frauds. For example, the Hill Side Strangler in Los Angeles was initially diagnosed as a multiple personality but was later shown to be faking illness to avoid prosecution for murder.

200. **(A)**   The dopamine hypothesis asserts that schizophrenia is caused by excessive levels of dopamine at specific receptor sites in the brain. Symptoms of thought disorder and hallucinations are linked to increased activity of neurons that use dopamine as a neurotransmitter. Interestingly, heavy dosages of phenothiazines eliminate schizophrenic symptoms and also decrease dopamine levels. The bizarre motor movements of tardive dyskinesia are one side effect of over dosages of these drugs. These motor problems resemble those of Parkinson's disease, which is associated with excessively low levels of dopamine.

201. **(B)**   Behavioral therapists treat phobias effectively using systematic desensitization. This involves an extinction of the learned fear response. Punishment and omission training are behavioral techniques but they would not be useful in treating phobias. Rational-emotive therapy is a form of cognitive not behavioral therapy.

202. **(D)**   Psychoanalysis aims to remove the deeply seated unconscious conflicts that cause neurotic behavior. This process can take years of analysis. Behavioral therapies that fairly rapidly eliminate, say, phobic behavior deal only with symptoms and not unconscious causes, according to proponents of psychoanalysis. Neither psychoanalysis nor behavioral therapy are client centered. Moreover, both approaches to therapy recognize the importance of parental influence on development.

203. **(C)**   This situation illustrates the psychoanalytic concept of transference. The patient begins to perceive the therapist as a significant person in his or her life, such as a father figure, and early conflicts with that person then surface. Counter transference refers to the therapist's perception of and reactions to the patient.

204. **(B)** Social learning therapy is an extension of behavioral techniques. They stress the importance of observational learning and behavioral rehearsal. Any skill such as public speaking can be taught by modeling, instruction, practice, and feedback. A behavioral therapist would probably use systematic desensitization or perhaps a behavioral contract involving positive reinforcement. A psychodynamic therapist would probe early childhood experiences that underly your fear. A Rogerian would help you to understand the significance of your fear and explore how you might overcome the fear as part of your personal growth.

205. **(D)** A token economy is an application of positive reinforcement to an institutional setting. For example in a prison, inmates might earn tokens for good behavior, doing their job well, and so on. The token could then be redeemed for primary or secondary rewards such as special food, cigarettes, or recreational privileges.

206. **(E)** Two ways of chemically treating depression involve tricyclics and MAO inhibitors. Tricyclics increase the availability of serotonin and norepinephrine by preventing the re-uptake of these neurotransmitters by the neurons that released them. MAO inhibitors achieve the same result by inhibiting the action of monoamine oxidase, an enzyme that inactivates serotonin and norepinephrine.

207. **(B)** Spontaneous recovery refers to the remission of a disorder in the absence of any medical or psychological treatment intervention. Spontaneous remission rates form a baseline for judging the effectiveness of a particular chemotherapy or psychotherapy. The placebo effect involves administering an inert treatment, which causes improvement merely because the patient believes the treatment will help.

208. **(A)** Eysenck's theory contends that the stable-unstable dimension, which relates to neuroticism, is independent of the extroversion-introversion dimension. The combination of these dimensions defines four personality types. An individual who is high on introversion and low on stability would be moody, anxious, and rigid — in short, neurotic.

209. **(D)** Gordon Allport distinguished three types of personality traits. A cardinal trait is the focal point of one's life, in cases where there is such an encompassing focus. For instance, a person may focus heavily on personal achievement. Central traits are the basic characteristics of a person, such as punctuality and honesty. Secondary traits are similar but less important than central traits. The combination of all three types of traits are what makes an individual unique.

210. **(A)** The Minnesota Multiphasic Personality Inventory (MMPI) was designed to diagnose mental disorders. It includes 10 clinical scales of psychopa-

thology. They were developed by giving the tests to normative groups of mentally disturbed and normal subjects. Questions that were answered similarly by, say, schizophrenic subjects but differently by normal subjects were then included in the schizophrenia scale. If an individual scores high on this scale, it means he or she shows signs of schizophrenia. The MMPI is very widely used but it was never intended as an all-purpose personality test for making personnel decisions. It is biased somewhat to identifying psychopathology even when none exists.

211. **(D)**   The type-A behavior pattern refers to a coping style in which the individual strives intensely to achieve; rarely relaxes; speaks, walks, and works rapidly; and is highly competitive, compulsive, and hostile. It contrasts with the type-B pattern. Type-A has been linked with higher risk of cardiovascular disease. Recent research suggests that type-As may actually do better than Bs when recovering from heart attacks, however. Alpha, beta, and gamma personality types refer to different temperaments. A person's energy level and behavioral tempo are linked to temperament.

212. **(D)**   Disability refers in this case to an individual being unable to function normally in society. The inability to hold a job or interact with others in a social setting are examples. Distress refers to internal signs of mental disorder, such as fear, sadness, anxiety and other forms of suffering. Some mental disorders cause disability without distress, whereas others cause the reverse.

213. **(D)**   The symptoms are typical of an antisocial personality disorder. Such individuals are self-centered, Machiavellian, and unremorseful of their often disruptive and harmful actions. A high percentage of prison inmates are antisocial. A juvenile delinquent may well fit this personality disorder, but the term is not a diagnostic category in the DSM-IV.

214. **(A)**   Conservation is a Piagetian concept of recognizing the identity of number, mass, and volume despite transformations that alter their perceptual properties. Mike lacks conservation of mass in not realizing that his candy bar is equal to Joe's despite the perceptual difference of two versus three pieces. Learning conservation is a key indicator of progression from the preoperational to the concrete operations stage of development. However, learning conservation in one domain, like mass, does not imply that other domains, like volume, are understood.

215. **(B)**   By putting collars on kittens to restrict their movement and visual perspective and by placing them in a special environment characterized by only horizontal or only vertical lines, researchers studied the tuning of feature detectors in the visual cortex. It was shown that there are critical periods in the kittens' development when they must be exposed to particular environmental stimuli if

the appropriate feature detectors are to develop normally. The research shows the interaction of maturational and environmental influences on development.

216. **(E)**   Complete social isolation prevents the development of attachment and socialization in primates. Monkeys so raised either display fear or aggression when suddenly placed in the companionship of peers.

217. **(B)**   Primary sex characteristics refer to sexual organs. Secondary sex characteristics emerge during puberty as a normal consequence of maturation. Males experience growth of facial and other body hair and a deepening of their voice.

The Graduate Record Examination in

PSYCHOLOGY

Test 6

Test 6 is also on CD-ROM as part of REA's exclusive interactive GRE Psychology TEST*ware*®. We recommend that you take the computerized exam first. This will give you the additional study features and benefits of enforced timed conditions, individual diagnostic analysis, and instantaneous scoring. See page vi for guidance on how to get the most out of our GRE Psychology book and software.

THE GRADUATE RECORD EXAMINATION
PSYCHOLOGY TEST 6
ANSWER SHEET

1. Ⓐ Ⓑ Ⓒ Ⓓ Ⓔ
2. Ⓐ Ⓑ Ⓒ Ⓓ Ⓔ
3. Ⓐ Ⓑ Ⓒ Ⓓ Ⓔ
4. Ⓐ Ⓑ Ⓒ Ⓓ Ⓔ
5. Ⓐ Ⓑ Ⓒ Ⓓ Ⓔ
6. Ⓐ Ⓑ Ⓒ Ⓓ Ⓔ
7. Ⓐ Ⓑ Ⓒ Ⓓ Ⓔ
8. Ⓐ Ⓑ Ⓒ Ⓓ Ⓔ
9. Ⓐ Ⓑ Ⓒ Ⓓ Ⓔ
10. Ⓐ Ⓑ Ⓒ Ⓓ Ⓔ
11. Ⓐ Ⓑ Ⓒ Ⓓ Ⓔ
12. Ⓐ Ⓑ Ⓒ Ⓓ Ⓔ
13. Ⓐ Ⓑ Ⓒ Ⓓ Ⓔ
14. Ⓐ Ⓑ Ⓒ Ⓓ Ⓔ
15. Ⓐ Ⓑ Ⓒ Ⓓ Ⓔ
16. Ⓐ Ⓑ Ⓒ Ⓓ Ⓔ
17. Ⓐ Ⓑ Ⓒ Ⓓ Ⓔ
18. Ⓐ Ⓑ Ⓒ Ⓓ Ⓔ
19. Ⓐ Ⓑ Ⓒ Ⓓ Ⓔ
20. Ⓐ Ⓑ Ⓒ Ⓓ Ⓔ
21. Ⓐ Ⓑ Ⓒ Ⓓ Ⓔ
22. Ⓐ Ⓑ Ⓒ Ⓓ Ⓔ
23. Ⓐ Ⓑ Ⓒ Ⓓ Ⓔ
24. Ⓐ Ⓑ Ⓒ Ⓓ Ⓔ
25. Ⓐ Ⓑ Ⓒ Ⓓ Ⓔ
26. Ⓐ Ⓑ Ⓒ Ⓓ Ⓔ
27. Ⓐ Ⓑ Ⓒ Ⓓ Ⓔ
28. Ⓐ Ⓑ Ⓒ Ⓓ Ⓔ
29. Ⓐ Ⓑ Ⓒ Ⓓ Ⓔ
30. Ⓐ Ⓑ Ⓒ Ⓓ Ⓔ
31. Ⓐ Ⓑ Ⓒ Ⓓ Ⓔ
32. Ⓐ Ⓑ Ⓒ Ⓓ Ⓔ
33. Ⓐ Ⓑ Ⓒ Ⓓ Ⓔ

34. Ⓐ Ⓑ Ⓒ Ⓓ Ⓔ
35. Ⓐ Ⓑ Ⓒ Ⓓ Ⓔ
36. Ⓐ Ⓑ Ⓒ Ⓓ Ⓔ
37. Ⓐ Ⓑ Ⓒ Ⓓ Ⓔ
38. Ⓐ Ⓑ Ⓒ Ⓓ Ⓔ
39. Ⓐ Ⓑ Ⓒ Ⓓ Ⓔ
40. Ⓐ Ⓑ Ⓒ Ⓓ Ⓔ
41. Ⓐ Ⓑ Ⓒ Ⓓ Ⓔ
42. Ⓐ Ⓑ Ⓒ Ⓓ Ⓔ
43. Ⓐ Ⓑ Ⓒ Ⓓ Ⓔ
44. Ⓐ Ⓑ Ⓒ Ⓓ Ⓔ
45. Ⓐ Ⓑ Ⓒ Ⓓ Ⓔ
46. Ⓐ Ⓑ Ⓒ Ⓓ Ⓔ
47. Ⓐ Ⓑ Ⓒ Ⓓ Ⓔ
48. Ⓐ Ⓑ Ⓒ Ⓓ Ⓔ
49. Ⓐ Ⓑ Ⓒ Ⓓ Ⓔ
50. Ⓐ Ⓑ Ⓒ Ⓓ Ⓔ
51. Ⓐ Ⓑ Ⓒ Ⓓ Ⓔ
52. Ⓐ Ⓑ Ⓒ Ⓓ Ⓔ
53. Ⓐ Ⓑ Ⓒ Ⓓ Ⓔ
54. Ⓐ Ⓑ Ⓒ Ⓓ Ⓔ
55. Ⓐ Ⓑ Ⓒ Ⓓ Ⓔ
56. Ⓐ Ⓑ Ⓒ Ⓓ Ⓔ
57. Ⓐ Ⓑ Ⓒ Ⓓ Ⓔ
58. Ⓐ Ⓑ Ⓒ Ⓓ Ⓔ
59. Ⓐ Ⓑ Ⓒ Ⓓ Ⓔ
60. Ⓐ Ⓑ Ⓒ Ⓓ Ⓔ
61. Ⓐ Ⓑ Ⓒ Ⓓ Ⓔ
62. Ⓐ Ⓑ Ⓒ Ⓓ Ⓔ
63. Ⓐ Ⓑ Ⓒ Ⓓ Ⓔ
64. Ⓐ Ⓑ Ⓒ Ⓓ Ⓔ
65. Ⓐ Ⓑ Ⓒ Ⓓ Ⓔ
66. Ⓐ Ⓑ Ⓒ Ⓓ Ⓔ

67. Ⓐ Ⓑ Ⓒ Ⓓ Ⓔ
68. Ⓐ Ⓑ Ⓒ Ⓓ Ⓔ
69. Ⓐ Ⓑ Ⓒ Ⓓ Ⓔ
70. Ⓐ Ⓑ Ⓒ Ⓓ Ⓔ
71. Ⓐ Ⓑ Ⓒ Ⓓ Ⓔ
72. Ⓐ Ⓑ Ⓒ Ⓓ Ⓔ
73. Ⓐ Ⓑ Ⓒ Ⓓ Ⓔ
74. Ⓐ Ⓑ Ⓒ Ⓓ Ⓔ
75. Ⓐ Ⓑ Ⓒ Ⓓ Ⓔ
76. Ⓐ Ⓑ Ⓒ Ⓓ Ⓔ
77. Ⓐ Ⓑ Ⓒ Ⓓ Ⓔ
78. Ⓐ Ⓑ Ⓒ Ⓓ Ⓔ
79. Ⓐ Ⓑ Ⓒ Ⓓ Ⓔ
80. Ⓐ Ⓑ Ⓒ Ⓓ Ⓔ
81. Ⓐ Ⓑ Ⓒ Ⓓ Ⓔ
82. Ⓐ Ⓑ Ⓒ Ⓓ Ⓔ
83. Ⓐ Ⓑ Ⓒ Ⓓ Ⓔ
84. Ⓐ Ⓑ Ⓒ Ⓓ Ⓔ
85. Ⓐ Ⓑ Ⓒ Ⓓ Ⓔ
86. Ⓐ Ⓑ Ⓒ Ⓓ Ⓔ
87. Ⓐ Ⓑ Ⓒ Ⓓ Ⓔ
88. Ⓐ Ⓑ Ⓒ Ⓓ Ⓔ
89. Ⓐ Ⓑ Ⓒ Ⓓ Ⓔ
90. Ⓐ Ⓑ Ⓒ Ⓓ Ⓔ
91. Ⓐ Ⓑ Ⓒ Ⓓ Ⓔ
92. Ⓐ Ⓑ Ⓒ Ⓓ Ⓔ
93. Ⓐ Ⓑ Ⓒ Ⓓ Ⓔ
94. Ⓐ Ⓑ Ⓒ Ⓓ Ⓔ
95. Ⓐ Ⓑ Ⓒ Ⓓ Ⓔ
96. Ⓐ Ⓑ Ⓒ Ⓓ Ⓔ
97. Ⓐ Ⓑ Ⓒ Ⓓ Ⓔ
98. Ⓐ Ⓑ Ⓒ Ⓓ Ⓔ
99. Ⓐ Ⓑ Ⓒ Ⓓ Ⓔ

100. Ⓐ Ⓑ Ⓒ Ⓓ Ⓔ   140. Ⓐ Ⓑ Ⓒ Ⓓ Ⓔ   180. Ⓐ Ⓑ Ⓒ Ⓓ Ⓔ
101. Ⓐ Ⓑ Ⓒ Ⓓ Ⓔ   141. Ⓐ Ⓑ Ⓒ Ⓓ Ⓔ   181. Ⓐ Ⓑ Ⓒ Ⓓ Ⓔ
102. Ⓐ Ⓑ Ⓒ Ⓓ Ⓔ   142. Ⓐ Ⓑ Ⓒ Ⓓ Ⓔ   182. Ⓐ Ⓑ Ⓒ Ⓓ Ⓔ
103. Ⓐ Ⓑ Ⓒ Ⓓ Ⓔ   143. Ⓐ Ⓑ Ⓒ Ⓓ Ⓔ   183. Ⓐ Ⓑ Ⓒ Ⓓ Ⓔ
104. Ⓐ Ⓑ Ⓒ Ⓓ Ⓔ   144. Ⓐ Ⓑ Ⓒ Ⓓ Ⓔ   184. Ⓐ Ⓑ Ⓒ Ⓓ Ⓔ
105. Ⓐ Ⓑ Ⓒ Ⓓ Ⓔ   145. Ⓐ Ⓑ Ⓒ Ⓓ Ⓔ   185. Ⓐ Ⓑ Ⓒ Ⓓ Ⓔ
106. Ⓐ Ⓑ Ⓒ Ⓓ Ⓔ   146. Ⓐ Ⓑ Ⓒ Ⓓ Ⓔ   186. Ⓐ Ⓑ Ⓒ Ⓓ Ⓔ
107. Ⓐ Ⓑ Ⓒ Ⓓ Ⓔ   147. Ⓐ Ⓑ Ⓒ Ⓓ Ⓔ   187. Ⓐ Ⓑ Ⓒ Ⓓ Ⓔ
108. Ⓐ Ⓑ Ⓒ Ⓓ Ⓔ   148. Ⓐ Ⓑ Ⓒ Ⓓ Ⓔ   188. Ⓐ Ⓑ Ⓒ Ⓓ Ⓔ
109. Ⓐ Ⓑ Ⓒ Ⓓ Ⓔ   149. Ⓐ Ⓑ Ⓒ Ⓓ Ⓔ   189. Ⓐ Ⓑ Ⓒ Ⓓ Ⓔ
110. Ⓐ Ⓑ Ⓒ Ⓓ Ⓔ   150. Ⓐ Ⓑ Ⓒ Ⓓ Ⓔ   190. Ⓐ Ⓑ Ⓒ Ⓓ Ⓔ
111. Ⓐ Ⓑ Ⓒ Ⓓ Ⓔ   151. Ⓐ Ⓑ Ⓒ Ⓓ Ⓔ   191. Ⓐ Ⓑ Ⓒ Ⓓ Ⓔ
112. Ⓐ Ⓑ Ⓒ Ⓓ Ⓔ   152. Ⓐ Ⓑ Ⓒ Ⓓ Ⓔ   192. Ⓐ Ⓑ Ⓒ Ⓓ Ⓔ
113. Ⓐ Ⓑ Ⓒ Ⓓ Ⓔ   153. Ⓐ Ⓑ Ⓒ Ⓓ Ⓔ   193. Ⓐ Ⓑ Ⓒ Ⓓ Ⓔ
114. Ⓐ Ⓑ Ⓒ Ⓓ Ⓔ   154. Ⓐ Ⓑ Ⓒ Ⓓ Ⓔ   194. Ⓐ Ⓑ Ⓒ Ⓓ Ⓔ
115. Ⓐ Ⓑ Ⓒ Ⓓ Ⓔ   155. Ⓐ Ⓑ Ⓒ Ⓓ Ⓔ   195. Ⓐ Ⓑ Ⓒ Ⓓ Ⓔ
116. Ⓐ Ⓑ Ⓒ Ⓓ Ⓔ   156. Ⓐ Ⓑ Ⓒ Ⓓ Ⓔ   196. Ⓐ Ⓑ Ⓒ Ⓓ Ⓔ
117. Ⓐ Ⓑ Ⓒ Ⓓ Ⓔ   157. Ⓐ Ⓑ Ⓒ Ⓓ Ⓔ   197. Ⓐ Ⓑ Ⓒ Ⓓ Ⓔ
118. Ⓐ Ⓑ Ⓒ Ⓓ Ⓔ   158. Ⓐ Ⓑ Ⓒ Ⓓ Ⓔ   198. Ⓐ Ⓑ Ⓒ Ⓓ Ⓔ
119. Ⓐ Ⓑ Ⓒ Ⓓ Ⓔ   159. Ⓐ Ⓑ Ⓒ Ⓓ Ⓔ   199. Ⓐ Ⓑ Ⓒ Ⓓ Ⓔ
120. Ⓐ Ⓑ Ⓒ Ⓓ Ⓔ   160. Ⓐ Ⓑ Ⓒ Ⓓ Ⓔ   200. Ⓐ Ⓑ Ⓒ Ⓓ Ⓔ
121. Ⓐ Ⓑ Ⓒ Ⓓ Ⓔ   161. Ⓐ Ⓑ Ⓒ Ⓓ Ⓔ   201. Ⓐ Ⓑ Ⓒ Ⓓ Ⓔ
122. Ⓐ Ⓑ Ⓒ Ⓓ Ⓔ   162. Ⓐ Ⓑ Ⓒ Ⓓ Ⓔ   202. Ⓐ Ⓑ Ⓒ Ⓓ Ⓔ
123. Ⓐ Ⓑ Ⓒ Ⓓ Ⓔ   163. Ⓐ Ⓑ Ⓒ Ⓓ Ⓔ   203. Ⓐ Ⓑ Ⓒ Ⓓ Ⓔ
124. Ⓐ Ⓑ Ⓒ Ⓓ Ⓔ   164. Ⓐ Ⓑ Ⓒ Ⓓ Ⓔ   204. Ⓐ Ⓑ Ⓒ Ⓓ Ⓔ
125. Ⓐ Ⓑ Ⓒ Ⓓ Ⓔ   165. Ⓐ Ⓑ Ⓒ Ⓓ Ⓔ   205. Ⓐ Ⓑ Ⓒ Ⓓ Ⓔ
126. Ⓐ Ⓑ Ⓒ Ⓓ Ⓔ   166. Ⓐ Ⓑ Ⓒ Ⓓ Ⓔ   206. Ⓐ Ⓑ Ⓒ Ⓓ Ⓔ
127. Ⓐ Ⓑ Ⓒ Ⓓ Ⓔ   167. Ⓐ Ⓑ Ⓒ Ⓓ Ⓔ   207. Ⓐ Ⓑ Ⓒ Ⓓ Ⓔ
128. Ⓐ Ⓑ Ⓒ Ⓓ Ⓔ   168. Ⓐ Ⓑ Ⓒ Ⓓ Ⓔ   208. Ⓐ Ⓑ Ⓒ Ⓓ Ⓔ
129. Ⓐ Ⓑ Ⓒ Ⓓ Ⓔ   169. Ⓐ Ⓑ Ⓒ Ⓓ Ⓔ   209. Ⓐ Ⓑ Ⓒ Ⓓ Ⓔ
130. Ⓐ Ⓑ Ⓒ Ⓓ Ⓔ   170. Ⓐ Ⓑ Ⓒ Ⓓ Ⓔ   210. Ⓐ Ⓑ Ⓒ Ⓓ Ⓔ
131. Ⓐ Ⓑ Ⓒ Ⓓ Ⓔ   171. Ⓐ Ⓑ Ⓒ Ⓓ Ⓔ   211. Ⓐ Ⓑ Ⓒ Ⓓ Ⓔ
132. Ⓐ Ⓑ Ⓒ Ⓓ Ⓔ   172. Ⓐ Ⓑ Ⓒ Ⓓ Ⓔ   212. Ⓐ Ⓑ Ⓒ Ⓓ Ⓔ
133. Ⓐ Ⓑ Ⓒ Ⓓ Ⓔ   173. Ⓐ Ⓑ Ⓒ Ⓓ Ⓔ   213. Ⓐ Ⓑ Ⓒ Ⓓ Ⓔ
134. Ⓐ Ⓑ Ⓒ Ⓓ Ⓔ   174. Ⓐ Ⓑ Ⓒ Ⓓ Ⓔ   214. Ⓐ Ⓑ Ⓒ Ⓓ Ⓔ
135. Ⓐ Ⓑ Ⓒ Ⓓ Ⓔ   175. Ⓐ Ⓑ Ⓒ Ⓓ Ⓔ   215. Ⓐ Ⓑ Ⓒ Ⓓ Ⓔ
136. Ⓐ Ⓑ Ⓒ Ⓓ Ⓔ   176. Ⓐ Ⓑ Ⓒ Ⓓ Ⓔ   216. Ⓐ Ⓑ Ⓒ Ⓓ Ⓔ
137. Ⓐ Ⓑ Ⓒ Ⓓ Ⓔ   177. Ⓐ Ⓑ Ⓒ Ⓓ Ⓔ   217. Ⓐ Ⓑ Ⓒ Ⓓ Ⓔ
138. Ⓐ Ⓑ Ⓒ Ⓓ Ⓔ   178. Ⓐ Ⓑ Ⓒ Ⓓ Ⓔ
139. Ⓐ Ⓑ Ⓒ Ⓓ Ⓔ   179. Ⓐ Ⓑ Ⓒ Ⓓ Ⓔ

GRE

PSYCHOLOGY TEST 6

TIME: 170 Minutes
217 Questions

DIRECTIONS: Choose the best answer for each question and mark the letter of your selection on the corresponding answer sheet.

---

1. The light sensitive cells on the retina are the

    (A) rods and cones.

    (B) bipolar cells and neurons.

    (C) olfactory receptors and cones.

    (D) chromocells and phototrons.

    (E) efferent neurons.

2. Ivan Pavlov is famous for

    (A) the discovery of the principles of operant conditioning.

    (B) his theories on child development.

    (C) discovering the mechanisms underlying conditioned reflexes.

    (D) proving that animals can learn language.

    (E) his theories on aggression.

3. Which of the following statements about homosexuality is true?

    (A) It occurs more often in warmer climates.

    (B) It is caused by hormonal imbalances.

    (C) Most homosexuals have had heterosexual experiences.

    (D) Hormone shots can alter sexual preference.

    (E) all of the above

4. According to the psychoanalytic approach to personality

(A) humans strive towards self-actualization.

(B) we are controlled by strong subconscious forces.

(C) our behavior patterns are shaped by rewards and punishments.

(D) we are information processing creatures.

(E) brain chemistry and hormones control behavior.

5. N. Chomsky and B.F. Skinner disagree on

(A) the importance of animal research.

(B) how language is acquired by humans.

(C) the difference between phonemes and morphemes.

(D) dyslexia in infants.

(E) whether chimps can acquire language.

6. After ten years, your parents get a new phone number but you keep dialing the old number. This is an example of

(A) conduct aphasia.   (B) dyslexia.

(C) Broca's syndrome.   (D) retrograde inhibition.

(E) proactive inhibition.

7. Which of the following is considered a dissociative reaction?

(A) psychogenic pain   (B) multiple personality

(C) anxiety neurosis   (D) paranoid schizophrenia

(E) acrophobia

8. Subjects in an experiment are asked to look at a sample line and then pick one of three line lengths that they believe is the same length as the sample line. Many subjects will make an incorrect choice because other people did so before them. These studies by Solomon Ashe demonstrate that

(A) people are not good at judging line lengths.

(B) errors are made when people are nervous.

(C) subjects for social psychology experiments will have to be more carefully selected.

(D) peer pressure will influence our perceptions.

(E) people need to obey authority.

9. The early _____ relied on _____ as their philosophical approach.

    (A) behaviorists, functionalism

    (B) Freudians, functionalism

    (C) behaviorists, structuralism

    (D) humanists, dualism

    (E) Freudians, interactionism

10. The only class of drugs that is NOT physically addicting is

    (A) stimulants.   (B) depressants.

    (C) narcotics.   (D) hallucinogens.

    (E) alcohol.

11. Describing what you see in a series of inkblots represents a (an) _____ personality test.

    (A) structured   (B) trait

    (C) MMPI   (D) endomorphic

    (E) projective

12. Systematic desensitization is a therapy technique that developed from the _____ approach.

    (A) behavioral   (B) Freudian

    (C) cognitive   (D) neurobiological

    (E) humanistic

13. Sailors on lookout duty at night are instructed not to stare directly at the horizon when looking for other ships because

    (A) the cones are more sensitive to light than the rods.

    (B) there are no cones in the fovea.

    (C) night blindness will occur.

    (D) the fovea is seriously impaired in dim light.

    (E) rods only function when they stare directly at an object.

14. The phenomenon of imprinting in geese was discovered by

    (A) Margaret Mead.   (B) Konrad Lorenz.

(C)   Stanley Milgram.   (D)   Erik Erikson.

(E)   Jean Piaget.

15.   Fetal alcohol syndrome refers to

(A)   infants that are born alcoholic.

(B)   a baby that was conceived when its mother was drunk.

(C)   infants that are allergic to alcohol.

(D)   infants born mentally retarded because the mother drank heavily during the pregnancy.

(E)   any of the above conditions.

16.   Which of the following is a psychosomatic disorder?

(A)   blindness where there is nothing organically wrong

(B)   ulcers

(C)   paralyzed legs that have no physical damage

(D)   mutism

(E)   (A), (C), and (D) are all psychosomatic disorders

17.   The correlation between a person's weight and height is NOT +1.00 because

(A)   there is no relationship between weight and height.

(B)   there are tall thin people, and short overweight people.

(C)   not enough people have been tested for this hypothesis.

(D)   this question is beyond statistical measurement.

(E)   weight and height vary with age.

18.   A slot machine operating on a Fixed Ratio 50 reinforcement schedule would pay a jackpot

(A)   the first time someone played it after 50 minutes had elapsed.

(B)   on the average of every 50 minutes.

(C)   after the 50th time it was played.

(D)   only during the first 50 plays.

(E)   continuously after the 50th play.

19. The lobes of the brain located in the back of the head are the

    (A) temporal lobes.   (B) parietal lobes.

    (C) frontal lobes.   (D) hippocampal lobes.

    (E) occipital lobes.

20. Maturation refers to

    (A) the fact that children are genetically pre-programmed to learn to walk and talk at certain ages.

    (B) how well-adjusted a teenager becomes as they grow to adulthood.

    (C) the physical problems associated with aging.

    (D) how well a person's physical age matches their chronological age.

    (E) how early a person tries sex and drugs.

21. The attempts to teach sign language to chimps by Premack, Rumbaugh, and others, suggest that

    (A) chimps can sign as well as humans.

    (B) their performance is equivalent to about a three-year-old human child.

    (C) chimps cannot learn to sign at all.

    (D) the animals prefer to use their own language.

    (E) the mind of chimps is comparable to the mind of humans.

22. Chronic depression has been successfully treated with

    (A) lithium.   (B) thorazine.

    (C) electric shock therapy.   (D) covert sensitization.

    (E) both (A) and (C)

23. The correct order of the stages of Freud's theory of development is

    (A) oral, phallic, latency, anal, and genital.

    (B) oral, latency, genital, phallic, and anal.

    (C) oral, anal, phallic, latency, and genital.

    (D) sensorimotor, concrete operations, trust, oedipal, and genital.

    (E) none of the above

24. The cornerstone of behaviorism is the Law of Effect which states that behavior that is followed by a positive outcome will occur more often in the future. The person who formulated the law after doing research with cats and puzzle boxes was

   (A) Harry Harlow.   (B) Anton Mesmer.

   (C) John Watson.   (D) B. F. Skinner.

   (E) Edward Thorndike.

25. The dull and sharp pain sensations that accompany an injury are produced by _____ and _____ neurons, respectively.

   (A) unmyelinated, myelinated

   (B) axons, dendrites

   (C) soma cells, dopaminergic

   (D) sensory, motor

   (E) negative, positive

26. A one-year-old child is sitting in his high chair playing with his favorite doll. The boy drops the doll to the floor. The fact that the boy looks over the rim of his food tray in an attempt to locate his toy indicates that he has achieved

   (A) conservation of matter.

   (B) conventional morality.

   (C) conservation of number.

   (D) object permanence.

   (E) conservation of objects.

27. In the Milgram obedience studies, the "teachers" would give painful electric shocks to the "learners" even though the learners begged them to stop. The results suggest that

   (A) people are basically sadists.

   (B) the subjects were ignorant about the dangers of electric shock.

   (C) people learn faster if they are punished with electric shock whenever they give a wrong answer.

   (D) people will obey legitimate authority even if the orders are against their moral codes.

   (E) corporal punishment does not work.

28.   Long term studies indicate that personality

(A)   is constantly changing as a result of experience.

(B)   is predominantly innate and little influenced by environment.

(C)   remains fairly consistent after the first seven years.

(D)   is too complex a subject to systematically study.

(E)   develops as Freud said it does.

29.   The part of the auditory system that changes mechanical vibrations into neural signals that the brain can interpret as sound is the

(A)   stapes.   (B)   papilla.

(C)   cochlea.   (D)   tympanic membrane.

(E)   cilia.

30.   Each of the following is a symptom of schizophrenia EXCEPT

(A)   lack of conscience.   (B)   delusions.

(C)   hallucinations.   (D)   emotional blunting.

(E)   word salads.

31.   The man who inadvertently discovered hypnotism and tried to make a living from it was

(A)   Benjamin Spock.   (B)   Bruno Battleheim.

(C)   Sigmund Freud.   (D)   Anton Mesmer.

(E)   Fritz Perls.

32.   The fact that a crowd of people will stand by and watch a person on a building ledge consider suicide, and few of the people in the crowd will intervene or call the police, is an example of

(A)   diffusion of responsibility.

(B)   bystander intervention.

(C)   people's fascination with death.

(D)   Milgram's obedience law.

(E)   cognitive dissonance.

33.   Establishing a fear hierarchy list is the first step in

(A)   psychoanalysis.   (B)   client-centered therapy.

(C)   rational-emotive therapy.   (D)   hypnosis therapy.

(E)   systematic desensitization therapy.

34.   Within the framework of classical conditioning, which one of the follow-
      ing is an example of a conditioned response?

      (A)   paying for a meal with a credit card.

      (B)   a dog responding to verbal commands.

      (C)   experiencing fear when the telephone rings at 3:00 AM.

      (D)   practicing your tennis serve.

      (E)   all of the above

35.   We typically remember the beginning and the end of a film after seeing it
      once. These phenomena are known as the _____ and _____ effects, re-
      spectively.

      (A)   primacy, recency   (B)   decay, consolidation

      (C)   echoic, iconic   (D)   amnesia, suffix

      (E)   displacement, serial position

36.   A person who believes that he or she is Jesus Christ and has come to Earth
      in order to fulfill the scriptures is suffering from

      (A)   the hallucination of being a diety.

      (B)   catatonic schizophrenia.

      (C)   a delusion of grandeur.

      (D)   nihilistic psychosis.

      (E)   obsessive-compulsive behavior.

37.   The sex of a baby, male or female, is determined by

      (A)   the mother.

      (B)   the father.

      (C)   hormone balance at conception.

      (D)   the sixth chromosome.

      (E)   testosterone.

38.   The speed that neural impulses travel is

(A) 3 to 200 miles an hour.   (B) the speed of light.

(C) 600 miles an hour.   (D) 200 miles a second.

(E) too fast to measure.

39. The fact that we can probably get someone to drive us 50 miles if we promise them a dinner and a movie is an example of

(A) the law of latency.   (B) Premack's principle.

(C) Skinner's postulate.   (D) Pavlov's theory of mutual returns.

(E) a classically conditioned response.

40. Before this century, treatment for mental illness included

(A) psychoactive drugs.   (B) exorcism rituals.

(C) group therapy.   (D) orgies.

(E) a safe haven in a well–kept state asylum,

41. Many young children believe that the sun goes down so their father will come home and play with them; "Sesame Street" is only received by their TV set; and the mailman delivers only to their home. These are examples of

(A) conservation of causes.   (B) nativist maturation.

(C) ego defense mechanisms.   (D) egocentricism.

(E) assimilation.

42. It is not uncommon for a rape victim to fear all men for a while, even relatives and familiar men. This is an example of the phenomena of

(A) discrimination.   (B) matching-to-sample.

(C) secondary reinforcement.   (D) generalization.

(E) overshadowing.

43. The order in which visual information is processed is

(A) echoic memory, short-term memory, long-term memory.

(B) short-term memory, episodic memory, long-term memory.

(C) iconic memory, short-term memory, long-term memory.

(D) episodic memory, short-term memory, long-term memory.

(E) semantic memory, short-term memory, long-term memory.

44. During a lecture, smoke begins to enter the room from under a closet door. The students wait until the professor tells them to leave before they respond to the situation. This scene illustrates the principle of

    (A) diffusion of responsibility. (B) social politeness.

    (C) obedience to authority.   (D) pluralistic ignorance.

    (E) anticipatory inertia.

45. The research on the effects of early childhood experiences on adult personality traits suggests that

    (A) childhood experiences have little effect on adult behavior.

    (B) the ability to love and other basic emotional characteristics are learned early in life.

    (C) personality is predominantly genetically determined so the influence of childhood experiences is minimal.

    (D) only extremely good or extremely bad experiences have any lasting effect.

    (E) only physical and sexual abuse influence personality development.

46. You are leaving an evening class at 9:00 PM. The parking lot is dimly lighted. All the vehicles look grey but you can see your yellow car. You are experiencing the perceptual phenomena of

    (A) the stroboscopic effect.

    (B) the phi effect.

    (C) nocturnal chromatic integrity.

    (D) color constancy.

    (E) binocular disparity.

47. Intelligence tests have been accused of being unfair for the following reason(s)

    (A) they do not measure intelligence.

    (B) they are culturally biased.

    (C) too much weight is put on the score.

    (D) they are an invasion of privacy.

    (E) all of the above

48. Zimbardo set up a mock prison and had half of the college students in his

experiment pretend to be guards. The other students served as prisoners. The results of the research indicated that

(A) even an artificial prison environment creates hostility and aggression.

(B) real prison guards should all be college graduates.

(C) college educated prisoners are better behaved.

(D) the situation was too artificial to trust the results.

(E) the prisoners and guards cooperated because they could relate to each other.

49. Which of the senses does the majority of hallucinations occur in?

(A) sight   (B) smell

(C) taste   (D) hearing

(E) touch

50. The two essential conditions for a physical drug addiction to be in evidence are

(A) criminality and ill health.   (B) tolerance and withdrawal.

(C) tolerance and ill health.   (D) mental illness and insomnia.

(E) withdrawal and poor hygiene.

51. There are five recognized senses in human beings. Two other abilities that may be added to the list include

(A) telepathy and precognition.

(B) psychokinesis and clairvoyance.

(C) psychokinesis and kinesthesis.

(D) premonition and deja vu.

(E) balance and kinesthesis.

52. Parents who beat their children severely and frequently

(A) believe the bible mandates it.

(B) are honestly trying to teach their children good discipline.

(C) were seldom disciplined themselves as children.

(D) are following modern theories of child rearing.

(E) were probably victims themselves of the battered child syndrome.

53. All of the following techniques can be successful for memory improvement EXCEPT

    (A) chunking.   (B) the method of loci.

    (C) rehearsal.   (D) state dependent learning.

    (E) the use of mnemonics.

54. Abreaction, insight, and working through, are three steps in _____ therapy.

    (A) cognitive   (B) neurobiological

    (C) psychoanalytic   (D) humanistic

    (E) behavioral

55. In the Freudian scheme of things, the part of the mind that represents our subconscious sexual and aggressive drives is the

    (A) superego.   (B) ego.

    (C) collective unconscious.   (D) shadow.

    (E) id.

56. Myopia, or near-sightedness is caused by

    (A) a malfunction of the lens of the eye.

    (B) a cloudy cornea.

    (C) an elongated eyeball.

    (D) an eyeball that has become shortened.

    (E) faulty cones in the fovea.

57. Nightmares typically occur during _____ sleep.

    (A) stage 4   (B) REM

    (C) stage 3   (D) stage 6

    (E) alpha

58. An experiment is designed to assess the effects of marijuana on memory. The _____ group is given marijuana.

    (A) lucky   (B) experimental

    (C) control   (D) random

    (E) larger

59. According to Freud's Oedipus complex, a _____ lusts for _____

    (A) young girl, her father.   (B) man, his wife.

    (C) brother, his sister.   (D) young boy, his mother.

    (E) both (A) and (D)

60. Harry Harlow raised monkeys with dolls instead of their natural mothers. One of the results of his studies suggested that

    (A) the monkeys preferred the doll to their natural mothers.

    (B) adult sexual receptivity and ability to nurture your own children are learned early in life.

    (C) there were no behavioral differences in animals raised with dolls relative to those monkeys raised with their mothers.

    (D) the presence of the father was more important than that of the mother.

    (E) the monkeys will refuse to eat, and eventually die, if raised only with dolls.

61. In Wolfgang Kohler's experiments, a chimp is put in a cage containing three boxes and a banana suspended high above the animal's head. After first trying to jump up to reach the banana, the chimp looks around then stacks the three boxes so it can climb up to the banana. This is an example of

    (A) trial and error learning.   (B) latent learning.

    (C) classical conditioning.   (D) shaping.

    (E) insight learning.

62. Running indoors when it starts raining is an example of

    (A) positive reinforcement.   (B) punishment.

    (C) escape.   (D) secondary reinforcement.

    (E) a primary reinforcer.

63. Recently, the most frequently rented costume for Halloween was Batman. A few years earlier it was an Indiana Jones costume. This tendency in some humans represents the Freudian defense mechanism of

    (A) rationalization.   (B) identification.

    (C) denial.   (D) projection.

    (E) reaction formation.

64. The sequence in which infants first attempt to communicate is

    (A) crying, cooing, babbling, then patterned speech.

    (B) babbling, cooing, laughing, then consonant speech.

    (C) crying, babbling, hand gestures, then simple speech.

    (D) babbling, laughing, simple speech, words.

    (E) crying, babbling, use of vowels, simple words.

65. You decide to go up on your roof to realign your TV antenna. You get out
    your ladder and climb up on the roof. As you approach the antenna, you
    lose your footing and fall off the roof. Twenty minutes later, you wake up
    on your lawn. You cannot recall anything that occurred during the last 45
    minutes, i.e., thinking about the roof, getting out the ladder, climbing it,
    etc. This is an example of

    (A) anterograde amnesia.   (B) post-trauma depression.

    (C) regression.   (D) a fugue state.

    (E) retrograde amnesia.

66. Applied psychologists would do each of the following EXCEPT

    (A) write psychological profiles of foreign leaders for the CIA.

    (B) help design television commercials.

    (C) counsel the members of a football team.

    (D) study the visual systems of birds in order to design a better optical
        system.

    (E) help accident victims adjust to their injuries.

67. The only illness that electroconvulsive therapy (shock treatments) has been
    successful in treating is

    (A) chronic headaches.   (B) compulsive gambling.

    (C) mania.   (D) schizophrenia.

    (E) depression.

68. Piaget's stages of cognitive development include

    (A) sensorimotor, preoperational, concrete operations, and formal opera-
        tions.

    (B) trust vs. distrust, autonomy vs. doubt, initiative vs. guilt, and inti-
        macy vs. isolation.

    (C)   preconventional, conventional, and postconventional cognitive operations.

    (D)   simple, compound, complex, and abstract thinking.

    (E)   simple logic, deductive reasoning, and inductive reasoning.

69.   In the English language, "pre," "un," and "pro" are examples of

    (A)   phonemes.   (B)   babbling.

    (C)   syntactic forms.   (D)   morphemes.

    (E)   concepts.

70.   In Pavlov's classic experiment, a dog hears the sound of a bell and then is given food powder. After a few trials, the dog salivates to both the bell and the food powder. The conditioned response is _____ while the unconditioned response is _____.

    (A)   the bell, salivation   (B)   salivation, also salivation

    (C)   the bell, the food   (D)   the bell, salivation

    (E)   the dog, the bell

71.   A personality test within which a person is shown pictures of people in ambiguous situations and is asked to interpret what the scene depicts, is taking the _____ test.

    (A)   Wasserman social skills   (B)   Rorschach

    (C)   Thematic Apperception   (D)   California Personality

    (E)   Minnesota Mutiphasic Personality Inventory

72.   Which of the following is NOT an example of parental sex role development strategies?

    (A)   Pink for girls and blue for boys

    (B)   Refusing to buy a six-year-old boy a doll

    (C)   Teaching your daughter to defer to your son

    (D)   Buying your son a set of plastic tools

    (E)   Encouraging little girls to pretend that they are doctors

73.   Which of the following is an example of a conditioned reinforcer?

    (A)   sex   (B)   water

    (C)   a bowling trophy   (D)   praise

    (E)   all of the above

74. The area of the brain where short-term memories are transferred to long-term memory is the

    (A) medulla.   (B) pons.

    (C) hypothalmus.   (D) hippocampus.

    (E) amygdala.

75. All of the following are problems with the survey method of doing research EXCEPT

    (A) its cost relative to other methods.

    (B) experimenter bias.

    (C) the fact that people lie.

    (D) ambiguous questions.

    (E) its validity.

76. Young children are shown a movie of an adult hitting and kicking a rubber doll. Later, they are given access to the doll. Videotapes of the children made with a hidden camera reveal that

    (A) they treat the doll like they do their own toys.

    (B) they hit and kick the doll.

    (C) the boys hit the doll while the girls play gently with it

    (D) the children avoid the doll.

    (E) the girls console the doll.

77. Client-centered therapy is the cornerstone of the _____ approach to therapy.

    (A) neurobiological   (B) behavioral

    (C) humanistic   (D) cognitive

    (E) psychoanalytic

78. When an infant learns to call his father "daddy" and then calls all men "daddy," this is an example of

    (A) overgeneralization.   (B) overdiscrimination.

    (C) undergeneralization.   (D) telegraphic speech.

    (E) a home sign.

79. Within a neuron, the neural impulse travels from

   (A) dendrites to axons.   (B) axons to the nucleus.

   (C) axons to dendrites.   (D) dendrites to the synapse.

   (E) the cell body to the synapse.

80. The fact that people will work harder for a while after a supervisor speaks to them is an example of

   (A) social loafing.   (B) obedience.

   (C) peer compliance.   (D) social facilitation.

   (E) deindividuation.

81. In a classroom demonstration, a teacher moves a piece of chalk from five feet away to within a foot of your eyes. The fact that we perceive the chalk as getting closer, rather than growing, is an example of _____ constancy.

   (A) location   (B) size

   (C) color   (D) shape

   (E) contrast

82. A man gets a job at a factory. He wants to make a good impression so he works quickly and efficiently. He notices that some of the other employees are frowning at him so he slows down his work output. This is an example of _____.

   (A) social facilitation   (B) bystander apathy

   (C) learned helplessness   (D) consolidation

   (E) social loafing

83. The stage of development within which a child can reliably demonstrate conservation of mass and number is the _____ stage.

   (A) preoperational   (B) formal operations

   (C) operational   (D) sensorimotor

   (E) concrete

84. The part of the brain involved in emotional responses such as rage and aggression is the

   (A) parasympathetic system.   (B) reticular activating system.

   (C) limbic system.   (D) sympathetic system.

   (E) Broca reflex loop.

85. One of the main criticisms that psychologists present concerning whether or not chimps can learn language is the fact that the animals seldom use the correct _____.

    (A) aphasias   (B) syllogisms

    (C) propositional thoughts   (D) syntax

    (E) phonemes

86. Everything under the control of the researcher is known as a(n) _____ variable. The behavior of the subject is the _____ variable.

    (A) planned, random   (B) independent, dependent

    (C) dependent, random   (D) dependent, independent

    (E) relevant, dominant

87. Carl Jung believed that

    (A) sex and aggression were the basic components of human personality.

    (B) rewards and punishments shape personality.

    (C) we unconsciously carry the memories of our ancestors.

    (D) fantasies are unhealthy.

    (E) computers would help analyze personality traits.

88. A three-year-old obeys rules in order to gain rewards and avoid punishment. This child is at Kohlberg's _____ stage of moral development.

    (A) preconventional   (B) societal

    (C) conventional   (D) level six

    (E) altruistic

89. You are at a self-serve car wash. A warning bell goes on for five seconds and then stops. It signals that you have a minute to put more coins in or the equipment will turn off. The emotional responses of apprehension and anxiety to finish washing your car that you feel between the time that the bell stops ringing and the machine turns off is an example of _____ classical conditioning.

    (A) simple   (B) delayed

    (C) simultaneous   (D) backward

    (E) trace

90. An increase in the intensity of a stimulus causes

    (A) a decrease in the action potential of a neuron.

    (B) an increase in the neural refractory period.

    (C) a decrease in the resting potential of a neuron.

    (D) a decrease in the neural refractory period.

    (E) a neuron to fire more frequently.

91. Assertive training would be prescribed for which of the following problems?

    (A) a superiority complex   (B) delusions of paranoia

    (C) speaking in word salads   (D) an aggressive personality

    (E) an inferiority complex

92. One of the primary differences between an algorithm and a heuristic is

    (A) algorithms take longer to find a solution.

    (B) heuristics work most, but not all of the time.

    (C) algorithms are used less often than heuristics in artificial intelligence.

    (D) humans depend more on heuristics than algorithms when playing games.

    (E) all of the above

93. The average score on an I.Q. test is 100, and the standard deviation is 15. A person who scores a 120 on the test would be considered

    (A) average.   (B) above average.

    (C) a genius.   (D) mildly retarded.

    (E) this score is not possible

94. The ego defense mechanism that children rely on to reduce fear of their same sex parent during the latency period of development is

    (A) identification.   (B) reaction formation.

    (C) projection.   (D) denial.

    (E) rationalization.

95. You have a dream that your car is stalled in a tunnel, and you cannot find the key to start it. The manifest content of the dream

    (A) is a fear of the inability to perform sexually.

    (B) is your car stalling in a tunnel.

    (C) refers to your concern about making your car payments.

    (D) is a subconscious wish to travel.

    (E) cannot be determined with this information.

96. The natural painkillers manufactured by the brain are called

    (A) morphines.   (B) dopamines.

    (C) endorphins.   (D) adrenaline.

    (E) serotonins.

97. Which of the following species has a brain more anatomically complex than humans?

    (A) dolphins   (B) elephants

    (C) gorillas   (D) chimpanzees

    (E) whales

98. The most radical form of therapy ever provided for people is

    (A) psychosurgery.   (B) systematic desensitization.

    (C) primal scream therapy.   (D) antipsychotic drugs.

    (E) client centered therapy.

99. People who take credit for their successes but blame others for their failures (for example, "I got an A in biology, she failed me in math") are using the ego defense mechanism of

    (A) fantasy.   (B) rationalization.

    (C) denial.   (D) projection.

    (E) displacement.

100. The ability to move objects with mental concentration is an example of

    (A) clairvoyance.   (B) kinethesis.

    (C) ESP.   (D) precognition.

    (E) psychokinesis.

101. Many people have trouble solving riddles or other mental puzzles because they can only perceive of certain objects as being useful in only particular ways. This tendency is known as

    (A) repression.   (B) functional fixedness.

    (C) visual thinking.   (D) incubation.

    (E) spatial thinking.

102. A group of people take an intelligence test at ten in the morning. The same group is retested at three in the afternoon. The scores on both exams are within 5% of each other. These results would support a claim for the test's

    (A) reliability.   (B) ability to assess z scores.

    (C) validity.   (D) ability to measure intelligence.

    (E) fairness.

103. The fact that planet Earth is in serious trouble environmentally, and few of us attempt to pressure the government into reversing the situation is an example of

    (A) climatic indifference.   (B) pluralistic ignorance.

    (C) diffusion of responsibility.   (D) both (A) and (C)

    (E) both (B) and (C)

104. If a child misses the "critical period" for some personal development such as talking or cognitive skills

    (A) they can make it up if they are provided with remedial training.

    (B) they will develop other comparable skills.

    (C) the skill may never develop or, at best, be severely limited.

    (D) the child will become homosexually oriented.

    (E) it will not matter, because humans can learn throughout their lives.

105. Which of the following behaviors would drive reduction theory have trouble explaining?

    (A) a dog drinking from its water bowl

    (B) a human putting on a heavy sweater on a cold day

    (C) a person who missed lunch having a snack

    (D) a person riding on a roller coaster

    (E) going to a restaurant for dinner

106. The absolute threshold for vision refers to

    (A) the colors we see best.

    (B) the minimum decibel level required to see.

    (C) the maximum number of colors that we can simultaneously process.

    (D) the minimum amount of light for us to see the stimulus.

    (E) the best saturation values a stimulus can possess.

107. Each of the following sexual problems is illegal EXCEPT

    (A) pedophilia.   (B) impotence.

    (C) necrophilia.   (D) voyeurism.

    (E) exhibitionism.

108. Most psychotherapists use _____ approach.

    (A) the psychoanalytic   (B) a behavioral

    (C) an eclectic   (D) a humanistic

    (E) the medical

109. The research technique that allows the most control of variables by the experimenter is

    (A) the survey.   (B) naturalistic observation.

    (C) a test.   (D) the formal experiment.

    (E) the case study.

110. The visual-cliff experiment within which an infant will not crawl out and possibly fall down a cliff, although his or her parent is encouraging him or her to do so, demonstrates that

    (A) depth perception is learned.

    (B) infants have no phobias.

    (C) depth perception is innate.

    (D) infants do not trust their parents.

    (E) parental approval is not important to infants.

111. Which of the following is an example of inductive reasoning?

    (A) deciding if you can afford a new car

(B) planning the seating arrangements for a dinner

(C) organizing a mailing list

(D) inventing a better screwdriver

(E) all of the above

112. Festinger demonstrated in a number of experiments that if our actions are at odds with our beliefs, we alter our beliefs in order to justify our behavior. This phenomenon is known as

(A) cognitive appraisal.

(B) reactionary justification.

(C) anxiety consolidation.

(D) cognitive dissonance.

(E) incongruence.

113. Physiognomy, the belief that there is a relationship between personality traits (being criminal, for example) and having certain physical characteristics (shifty-eyes, bushy eyebrows)

(A) has not been supported by research.

(B) is true.

(C) is true for certain racial groups.

(D) has been criticized by Lombroso.

(E) is true for certain ethnic groups.

114. A brain tumor in the hippocampus of the brain would impair a person's ability to learn new things while leaving their old memories intact. This condition is known as

(A) anterograde amnesia.

(B) retroactive inhibition.

(C) retrograde amnesia.

(D) proactive inhibition.

(E) dyslexia.

115. Each of the following is an authentic speciality of the American Psychiatric Association EXCEPT

(A) industrial and organizational psychology.

(B) mental retardation.

(C) astrological psychology.

(D) tests and measurements.

(E) psychology and the law.

116. Washing your hands 50 times a day is an example of _____ behavior.

    (A) obsessive   (B) compulsive

    (C) phobic   (D) dissociative

    (E) schizophrenic

117. An example of a conjunction fallacy is believing that

    (A) stress leads to heart attacks.

    (B) constantly pushing the elevator button makes it come sooner.

    (C) smoking leads to lung cancer.

    (D) alcohol can cause birth defects.

    (E) all of the above

118. Chimps have been taught to use a language in all of the following ways EXCEPT

    (A) American Sign Language.

    (B) speech.

    (C) pushing buttons with symbols for words on them.

    (D) arranging colored plastic forms that represent words.

    (E) both (C) and (D)

119. The fact that blind babies begin to smile at about the same time as sighted babies supports the _____ view of emotional development.

    (A) cognitive   (B) behavioral

    (C) empirical   (D) nativist

    (E) functional

120. A seven-year-old girl looks through an illustrated book about *Alice in Wonderland*. She is then asked, "How many stripes did the cat on page nine have on its tail?" After a moment she correctly says, "twelve." This impressive demonstration is called _____ memory.

    (A) flashbulb   (B) eidetic

    (C) semantic   (D) localized

    (E) spatial

121. A patient that stays perfectly still for hours at a time and is unresponsive to other people is a _____ schizophrenic.

(A)   paranoid   (B)   hebephrenic

(C)   simple   (D)   catatonic

(E)   hypochondriac

122. The only type of psychotherapist that can prescribe drugs is a

(A)   clinical psychologist.   (B)   psychiatric nurse.

(C)   psychiatric social worker. (D)   psychiatrist.

(E)   both (A) and (D)

123. A new drug has been developed that may improve memory in elderly people. The double-blind research design is used in order to prevent bias. This means

(A)   both the experimental and control group subjects are blind.

(B)   only the researchers know which subjects are getting the drug.

(C)   the subjects are not aware of the fact that they are participating in the experiment.

(D)   neither the subjects nor the researchers know who is receiving the drug.

(E)   both the experimenters and the subjects are blindfolded during the memory tests.

124. A rat in a Skinner box has learned that pressing a lever will produce food pellets, but only if the light above the lever is on. The animal consistently presses the lever when the light is on. When it is turned off, the rat immediately walks away from the lever until the light is turned on again. The rat's behavior is an example of

(A)   generalization.   (B)   a fear of the dark phobia.

(C)   the phi phenomenon.   (D)   a discrimination.

(E)   classical conditioning.

125. A person diagnosed as an anxiety neurotic would receive _____ according to the _____ approach to therapy.

(A)   group therapy, humanistic   (B)   aversion therapy, Freudian

(C)   valium, medical   (D)   psychoanalysis, cognitive

(E)   electric shock treatments, behavioral

126. Early personality assessment attempts included phrenology, the belief that

    (A) personality depended on the proportions of four fluids (humors) in the body.

    (B) traits could be ascertained by an examination of the shape and bumps on the skull.

    (C) the stars and your birth sign molded personality.

    (D) certain brain areas produced phrenons, a substance that controlled emotions.

    (E) dreams were wishes and should be carried out in reality or neuroses would result.

127. Most people remember where they were, and what they were doing, when they heard of extraordinary events such as President Kennedy's assassination, or the space shuttle disaster. These vivid memories are examples of _____ memory.

    (A) mnemonic   (B) conjunctive

    (C) repressed   (D) eidetic

    (E) flashbulb

128. When the brain decides on an incorrect perceptual hypothesis, it is referred to as

    (A) the phi phenomenon.   (B) a delusion.

    (C) an illusion.   (D) perceptual incentive.

    (E) the corealis effect.

129. According to the psychoanalytic approach

    (A) the life force is stronger than the death wish.

    (B) the need for sex is acquired during our lifetime.

    (C) physical needs must be met before esteem needs.

    (D) humans are innately afraid of violence.

    (E) the death wish is stronger than the life force.

130. The branch of psychology that designs tests to assess I.Q., aptitude, and other measures of human potential is

    (A) parapsychology.   (B) psychometrics.

(C)   measurecology.   (D)   social psychology.

(E)   statistics.

131.   Artificial intelligence refers to attempts

(A)   at teaching people to think abstractly.

(B)   to measure intelligence in animals.

(C)   to measure intelligence in plants.

(D)   to use genetic engineering to produce more intelligent humans.

(E)   to teach computers to make decisions for which they are not specifically programmed.

132.   Each of the following is a neurotransmitter EXCEPT

(A)   serotonin.   (B)   endorphins.

(C)   norepinephrine.   (D)   dopamine.

(E)   insulin.

133.   The fact that under certain circumstances many people immerse themselves totally into a group, and behave as the group dictates is called

(A)   deindividuation.   (B)   mob control.

(C)   a fugue state.   (D)   groupthink.

(E)   dictatorial herding.

134.   The experiences a person has while being brainwashed by a cult are

(A)   torture, fear, and threat.

(B)   deprivation, terror, reeducations.

(C)   loneliness, religion, fanaticism.

(D)   rejection, dominance, and acceptance.

(E)   compliance, identification, and internalization.

135.   Which of the following famous people insisted that psychology be restricted to observable behavior?

(A)   Sigmund Freud   (B)   Carl Rogers

(C)   Abraham Maslow   (D)   John B. Watson

(E)   Harry Stack Sullivan

136. Jane Goodall spent years living in the wilds of Africa with gorillas. A scientist who does research in the natural environment of the species they are studying is referred to as a(n)

    (A) animal psychologist.   (B) experimental psychologist.

    (C) ethologist.   (D) applied psychologist.

    (E) psychoanalytic psychologist.

137. The phrases "me milk," and "give ball" are examples of _____ speech.

    (A) semantic   (B) syntactic

    (C) incongruent   (D) telegraphic

    (E) congruent

138. Cathy is desperately afraid of gaining weight, thinks that she's fat, and is actually 20% below the average weight for a woman of her height and age. Which disorder does Cathy have?

    (A) encopresis   (B) agoraphobia

    (C) bulimia   (D) hypochondriasis

    (E) anorexia

139. The nativist explanation of the fact that one-week-old babies already exhibit different personality traits would be

    (A) personality is already being shaped by the environment.

    (B) an easy or difficult delivery makes the differences.

    (C) personality is predominantly genetically inherited.

    (D) temperament is a matter of glandular function so it varies from baby to baby.

    (E) all of the above are relevant factors to the nativist position.

140. A subject in an experiment sits in a chair facing a slide screen. Twenty words are projected on the screen, one at a time. Then the subject is asked to report as many of the twenty words, in any order, that they can remember seeing. This is an example of a _____ memory experiment.

    (A) paired associate   (B) recognition task

    (C) serial learning   (D) free recall

    (E) symbolic matching

141. Most people are introduced to drugs by

    (A)   drug dealers.

    (B)   their parents.

    (C)   buying them out of curiosity.

    (D)   their friends.

    (E)   accident.

142. Which one of the following scientists did NOT receive a Nobel Prize?

    (A)   I. P. Pavlov   (B)   D. Huble

    (C)   B. F. Skinner   (D)   R.W. Sperry

    (E)   T. Wiesel

143. You go to a restaurant and are given a table under a noisy fan. After awhile, you no longer notice the noise. This is an example of the phenomenon of

    (A)   habituation.   (B)   spontaneous recovery.

    (C)   extinction.   (D)   punishment.

    (E)   latent learning.

144. The "cocktail party" effect refers to the fact that

    (A)   people tend to drink more at parties than they do at home.

    (B)   we focus on the person talking to us and ignore other voices.

    (C)   we are more apt to give in to peer pressure.

    (D)   we are more conscious of how we look and act.

    (E)   some people are very nervous at parties.

145. What are the effects of excessive levels of noise?

    (A)   None, people adapt to them

    (B)   People prefer noise to silence

    (C)   There is no research on this subject

    (D)   People perform better

    (E)   They disrupt people's ability to concentrate

146. According to Kohlberg's theory of moral development, a person who makes up their own mind about sex, drugs, and other issues is functioning at

   (A)   level 6.   (B)   autonomy.

   (C)   concrete operations.   (D)   level 3.

   (E)   the primary stage.

147. I.Q. tests have been shown to be useful for

   (A)   predicting school performance.

   (B)   measuring innate abilities.

   (C)   predicting financial success.

   (D)   measuring personality traits.

   (E)   all of the above

148. In order to acquire and use verbal language skills, a species must have

   (A)   brain centers designated for fine control of the throat, lips, and tongue.

   (B)   concept learning ability.

   (C)   a brain area capable of comprehending speech.

   (D)   Broca's area or its equivalent.

   (E)   all of the above

149. The ethologist who wrote the book *On Aggression*, and believed that aggression in non-human species frequently serves a positive function was

   (A)   Konrad Lorenz.   (B)   Niko Tinbergen.

   (C)   Robert Bolles.   (D)   William James.

   (E)   Gustav Le Bon.

150. Two groups of infants are provided the same basic care, diaper changes, food etc. The infants in one group are picked up, rocked and spoken to more frequently than the babies in the control group. The result is

   (A)   no differences between the groups.

   (B)   the babies in the experimental group become irritable.

   (C)   the babies in the experimental group gain weight faster than the control group.

   (D)   the control group sleeps more often out of boredom.

(E)   the control group becomes irritable.

151.   A person is at a party surrounded by friends. They are encouraging her to try smoking marijuana. Although she is reluctant to do so, she accepts the joint and begins to smoke it. She is a victim of

(A)   social facilitation.

(B)   peer pressure.

(C)   cognitive dissonance.

(D)   immoral influence.

(E)   regression.

152.   Korsakoff's syndrome, a memory disorder, has been associated with

(A)   a brain tumor.

(B)   venereal disease.

(C)   a bad reaction to LSD.

(D)   mental illness.

(E)   alcoholism.

153.   The largest sense organ of the body is (are) the

(A)   eyes.

(B)   ears.

(C)   tongue.

(D)   skin.

(E)   basal membrane.

154.   The American Psychiatric Association considers homosexuality to be

(A)   perverted.

(B)   immoral.

(C)   abnormal.

(D)   an alternate lifestyle.

(E)   indicative of psychosis.

155.   A statement made by a transsexual would be,

(A)   "I always felt like a woman trapped in a man's body."

(B)   "I am looking for sexual experiences that transcend life."

(C)   "Casual sex with several partners is the only way to be."

(D)   "I don't need or want sex in order to be happy."

(E)   "Prostitution is an honorable profession."

156.   Cases of children raised by animals, or under similar circumstances where they receive no exposure to language, suggests that the critical period for language acquisition appears to be

(A)   seven years of age.

(B)   two years of age.

(C)   puberty.   (D)   eighteen years of age.

(E)   twenty five years of age.

157. The process by which subconscious sexual and aggressive drives are chan-
      neled into acceptable social behaviors is called

(A)   reaction formation.   (B)   intellectualization.

(C)   sublimation.   (D)   denial.

(E)   repression.

158. Which one of the following people had a son or daughter who became a
      famous psychologist?

(A)   John Watson   (B)   Sigmund Freud

(C)   B.F. Skinner   (D)   Rene Descartes

(E)   Ivan Pavlov

159. Aggressive gestures in animals are performed for each of the following
      reasons EXCEPT

(A)   mating rituals.   (B)   hatred and murder.

(C)   to establish territoriality.   (D)   ritual fighting.

(E)   threat displays.

160. Biological constraints on learning refer to situations within which

(A)   you try to teach an animal to do something beyond its capabilities.

(B)   the experiment requires that the animal be restrained.

(C)   the instinctive behavior of the animal interferes with its performance.

(D)   drugs that retard learning are used.

(E)   normal animals are compared to drugged animals.

161. The _____ view believes that rewards, punishments, and vicarious learning
      shape personality.

(A)   cognitive   (B)   humanistic

(C)   psychoanalytic   (D)   neurobiological

(E)   behavioral

162. In order to call yourself a psychotherapist, and hang up a shingle advertis-
      ing counseling services, you are required by law to have a _____ degree.

(A)   B.A.   (B)   M.A.

(C)   M.S.W.   (D)   Ph.D.

(E)   no degree is required in psychology

163. The mean, mode, and range are measures of

(A)   independent variables.   (B)   nominal artifacts.

(C)   distal tendency.   (D)   central tendency.

(E)   deviation.

164. A tennis instructor who first praises any serve that you get over the net but
      eventually reinforces only the best serves is using the behavioral technique
      called

(A)   shaping.   (B)   flooding.

(C)   systematic desensitization. (D)   a fixed ratio schedule.

(E)   assertion training.

165. In which species would sexual behavior be most controlled by hormones?

(A)   apes   (B)   humans

(C)   dogs   (D)   dolphins

(E)   mice

166. You are visiting with neighbors. Their son comes in staggering and you
      smell liquor. You remark to your neighbors that you think their son is
      drunk. They reply that "Bob is just tired," and they actually believe what
      they are saying. This is an example of the ego defense mechanism called

(A)   repression.   (B)   denial.

(C)   reaction formation.   (D)   projection.

(E)   sublimation.

167. The humanistic explanation for deviant behavior is

(A)   an id not adequately controlled by the superego.

(B)   that the behavior was reinforced in the past.

(C)   excessive use of punishment.

(D)   blocked goals.

(E)   a hormone imbalance.

168. Huble and Wiesel's research on receptor fields suggests that

    (A) the closer a person stands to us, the more receptive we are to their ideas.

    (B) certain neurons never fire regardless of stimulation.

    (C) some cells in the visual system respond to particular shapes.

    (D) we are more receptive to certain sounds.

    (E) none of the above

169. Auditory sensory memory is called _____ memory.

    (A) short-term   (B) echoic

    (C) long-term   (D) semantic

    (E) flashbulb

170. The Freudian explanation for certain individuals' desires to become police officers would be

    (A) it's an attempt to satisfy their death wish.

    (B) they realize they are best suited for that type of work.

    (C) they were reinforced for wanting to be police officers.

    (D) they perceive police work as satisfying and admirable.

    (E) they look forward to the adrenaline rushes.

171. A friend arranges a blind date for you. When you are told that the person is a woman truck driver, you become reluctant to meet her. She is the victim of

    (A) sexism.   (B) erroneous appraisal.

    (C) a stereotype.   (D) social inertia.

    (E) projection.

172. A string of lights is flashed in sequence. We perceive the situation as a light that moves along the string. This is a demonstration of

    (A) location constancy.   (B) brightness constancy.

    (C) binocular disparity.   (D) the phi phenomenon.

    (E) the remus effect.

173. The study of twins indicates that

    (A) the environment, has the greatest influence on I.Q.

    (B) intelligence is innate and little influenced by environment.

    (C) genetics and environment have equal influence on I.Q.

    (D) genetics has more influence for some races.

    (E) the results are inconclusive.

174. Crack cocaine is classified as a(n)

    (A) hallucinogen.   (B) depressant.

    (C) narcotic.   (D) analgesic.

    (E) stimulant.

175. The fact that we expect good looking people to also be competent, good humored, and intelligent is an example of

    (A) the Barnum effect.   (B) a social advantage.

    (C) conformity.   (D) the halo effect.

    (E) group support.

176. The behavioral explanation for smoking would be

    (A) a physiological need for nicotine.

    (B) you get attention and status among your smoking friends.

    (C) it is a manifestation of the death wish.

    (D) it is a perception that smoking is glamorous.

    (E) it satisfies an id impulse.

177. The area of the brain where the sense of smell is processed is the

    (A) olfactory bulbs.   (B) frontal lobe.

    (C) parietal lobe.   (D) pineal gland.

    (E) medulla oblongata.

178. Whether or not a neuron will fire is determined by the

    (A) ratio of potassium to sodium within the neuron.

    (B) the summation of all the excitatory and inhibitory synapse inputs present.

    (C)   amplitude of the incoming neural impulse.

    (D)   amount of calcium within the neuron.

    (E)   type of neurotransmitter the cell uses.

179. Psychology is the study of

    (A)   the mind.   (B)   overt behavior.

    (C)   social norms.   (D)   human behavior.

    (E)   behavior and mental processes.

180. The psychologist that convinced the world that children could feel true complex passions was

    (A)   Jean Piaget.   (B)   James Olds.

    (C)   B.F. Skinner.   (D)   Sigmund Freud.

    (E)   Erik Erikson.

181. The fact that most people act differently at a funeral relative to the way they behave at a party is an example of

    (A)   a reactionary cognitive state.

    (B)   social acclimation.

    (C)   a stereotype.

    (D)   the halo effect.

    (E)   situational inducement.

182. An experimental procedure used to assess the cognitive abilities of animals is called

    (A)   discrimination training.   (B)   second order conditioning.

    (C)   escape-avoidance training. (D)   matching-to-sample.

    (E)   chaining.

183. Destruction of this part of the brain results in obesity in rats.

    (A)   Ventromedial hypothalamus (B) Amygdala

    (C)   Vas deferens   (D) Posterior hippocampus

    (E)   Medial thalamus

184. The validity of a test refers to

(A)   how well the subjects do.

(B)   whether the results can be reproduced with other subjects.

(C)   whether the test measures what it claims to assess.

(D)   whether the test is reliable.

(E)   if it can be completed in the time allowed.

185. The tendency to hold people totally responsible for their behavior and discount environmental factors (fat people have no self-control) is known as

(A)   cognitive dissonance.

(B)   the fundamental attribution error.

(C)   the reference group misjudgment.

(D)   an altruistic excuse.

(E)   situational inducement.

186. The James-Lange theory of emotion claims that

(A)   we run because we are afraid.

(B)   we are afraid because we are running.

(C)   we simultaneously run and are afraid.

(D)   running and being afraid are not necessarily related.

(E)   this theory really does not exist.

187. The area of the brain that controls whether we are awake or asleep is the

(A)   hypothalamus.   (B)   parasympathetic nervous system.

(C)   lateral ventricles.   (D)   substantia nigra.

(E)   reticular activating system.

188. The sense that humans depend on more than the other four combined is

(A)   vision.   (B)   audition.

(C)   taste.   (D)   olfaction.

(E)   touch.

189. A test that produces consistent results each time it is administered is

(A)   valid.   (B)   valid, but may not be reliable.

(C)   reliable and valid.

(D)   reliable, but may not be valid.

(E)   neither valid nor reliable.

190.   We most prefer people that are

(A)   attractive.

(B)   familiar.

(C)   similar to us.

(D)   frequently in proximity to us.

(E)   all of the above

191.   Children are often observed playing in proximity to each other, but oblivious to one another. This is an example of

(A)   severe autism.

(B)   space conservation.

(C)   social indifference.

(D)   parallel play.

(E)   the visual cliff effect.

192.   Intramodal interference refers to the fact that

(A)   we cannot think and speak simultaneously.

(B)   our expectations distort what we perceive.

(C)   we cannot simultaneously listen to two people and then totally remember both of their statements.

(D)   a headache disrupts our ability to concentrate.

(E)   all of the above

193.   Sensory deprivation experiments place a person in an isolated environment where their senses are provided little or no inputs, i.e., they can't see, hear, smell, or taste, and their sense of touch is severely limited. After a short time, the typical reaction of most people is

(A)   elation.

(B)   sleep.

(C)   boredom.

(D)   hallucinations.

(E)   a restive content state.

194.   Modern psychology started during the last century in

(A)   Germany.

(B)   Britain.

(C)   the United States.

(D)   Russia.

(E)   Japan.

195. A social norm is

    (A) the unwritten rules of a community.

    (B) the best way to act under the circumstances.

    (C) the laws of the region.

    (D) a rule for success that is taught to children.

    (E) all of the above

196. The eight basic emotional responses that an infant is capable of include

    (A) fear and envy.   (B) joy and revenge.

    (C) anger and distress.   (D) interest and guilt.

    (E) guilt and joy.

197. Other than albinos, most humans said to be color blind are not. They actually

    (A) see all the colors but mis-name them.

    (B) see two of the three major color groups.

    (C) see colors intermittently instead of constantly.

    (D) see all the colors but not as vividly as others see them.

    (E) see only black and white and shades of gray.

198. Broca's area and Wernicke's area of the brain are involved in the _____ and ____ of speech, respectively.

    (A) production, comprehension

    (B) understanding, production

    (C) comprehension, formulation

    (D) important, unimportant aspects

    (E) organization, production

199. If a twelve year old scored 100 on the Stanford-Binet I.Q. test, her mental age would be

    (A) 8.   (B) 10.

    (C) 12.   (D) 16.

    (E) 20.

200. One of the reflexes found in infants is the rooting reflex. This refers to

    (A) attempts by the babies to burrow into their blankets.

    (B) the fact that stimulation of the cheek will cause the infant to turn towards the source of stimulation and suck.

    (C) the tendency of infants to spread out their limbs when they are tossed into the air.

    (D) the fact that if something is placed in the palm of the hand, the infant will close its hand tightly.

    (E) the spreading of the toes when the sole of the foot is rubbed.

201. A rat is trained to pick up a marble, carry it to a hole, and drop it in. This response turns on a light over a chain suspended from the ceiling of the Skinner box. Pulling the chain now causes a light to turn on over a lever mounted in the corner of the box. The rat now presses the lever and receives a food pellet. The rat's behavior is under the control of

    (A) second order conditioning.

    (B) backward classical conditioning.

    (C) a behavioral chain.

    (D) a fixed ratio 3 schedule.

    (E) a concurrent schedule.

202. The attempts by the body to maintain a certain internal environment in terms of oxygen, sugar levels, temperature, etc., is referred to as

    (A) encephalic balance.

    (B) bio-inertia.

    (C) psychological consistency.

    (D) the James-Lange theory.

    (E) homeostasis.

203. The reason why Freud's theories are not called Freud's laws is because

    (A) not enough people believe in them.

    (B) they have not been proven.

    (C) they have been totally discredited.

    (D) a theory must stand for a century before it is considered a law.

    (E) of political reasons.

204. The psychologist who is considered one of the pioneers in the humanistic approach claimed that a person's personality developed in order to allow them to satisfy a hierarchy of needs. This hierarchy was frequently depicted as a pyramid with physical needs at the bottom and self-actualization at the top. The psychologist was

    (A)   Sigmund Freud.   (B)   Neal Miller.

    (C)   Carl Rogers.   (D)   Rollo May.

    (E)   Abraham Maslow.

205. A child born with ambiguous sexual organs is referred to as a(n)

    (A)   eunuch.   (B)   Siamese twin.

    (C)   hermaphrodite.   (D)   victim of the corsican syndrome.

    (E)   neuteroid.

206. The fact that a swinging door is still perceived as a rectangle instead of a trapezoid is an example of _____ constancy.

    (A)   size   (B)   location

    (C)   brightness   (D)   angle

    (E)   shape

207. A condition where a person suddenly falls asleep at inappropriate times (while giving a lecture for example) is called

    (A)   sleep apnea.   (B)   narcolepsy.

    (C)   catatonic stupor.   (D)   cataplexy.

    (E)   hypnogogic reactions.

208. Long term use of I.Q. tests have demonstrated that

    (A)   blacks have a lower I.Q. than whites.

    (B)   women have lower I.Q.s than men.

    (C)   no racial or ethnic group has been shown to be superior to the others.

    (D)   immigrants are less intelligent than native Americans.

    (E)   there is a correlation between I.Q. and occupation.

209. Piaget noted that some children will mimic a behavior or repeat a phrase that they heard a day or so earlier. He called this phenomena

    (A)   modelling.   (B)   delayed flattery.

(C)   deferred imitation.   (D)   spatial regression.

(E)   retrograde play.

210. The last stage in Erikson's theory of psychosocial development wherein a person reflects on their life is

(A)   integrity vs. despair.   (B)   productivity vs. stagnation.

(C)   competence vs. inferiority.   (D)   pride vs. regret.

(E)   peace vs. resignation.

211. Smoking cigarettes _____ a true physical addiction because _____ .

(A)   is not, people can quit

(B)   is, people think that they need them

(C)   is not, cigarettes only affect the lungs and not the brain

(D)   is, people develop a tolerance for them and there are withdrawal symptoms

(E)   is not, they are legal

212. The three functions of long-term memory are

(A)   storage, remembering, and retrieval.

(B)   encoding, storage, and retrieval.

(C)   meaning, emotions, and recall.

(D)   recognition, recall, and regression.

(E)   consolidation, organization, and retrieval.

213. The Stanford-Binet I.Q. test actually measures

(A)   knowledge of school subjects.

(B)   intelligence.

(C)   creativity.

(D)   cooperativeness.

(E)   all of the above

214. According to _____, the Oedipus complex occurs between the _____ and _____ stages.

(A)   Maslow, sensorimotor, self actualization

(B)   Freud, phallic, latency

(C)   Skinner, classical, operant

(D)   Jung, preconscious, postconscious

(E)   Freud, anal, genital

215. By definition, an ego defense mechanism must accomplish all the following EXCEPT

(A)   distort reality.   (B)   occur unconsciously.

(C)   make us feel better.   (D)   potentially lead to neurosis.

(E)   be an effective coping strategy.

216. One rat (the master) is placed in an operant chamber with a running wheel. Occasionally a buzzer sounds for ten seconds and is followed by an electric shock. If the rat runs in the wheel during the buzzer warning period, the buzzer turns off, and the shock is cancelled. The rat learns to avoid most but not all of the shocks. A second rat (the slave or yoked subject), is in an identical box except it has no control over shocks. Whenever the master rat does not respond to the buzzer, both rats receive a shock. Which rat(s) develop ulcers, if any?

(A)   the slave   (B)   the master

(C)   both   (D)   neither

(E)   the results are inconsistent

217. Which correlation coefficient below has the most statistical significance?

(A)   +.27   (B)   0.0

(C)   −.34   (D)   +.82

(E)   −.96

TEST 6

ANSWER KEY

1.	(A)	26.	(D)	51.	(E)	76.	(B)
2.	(C)	27.	(D)	52.	(E)	77.	(C)
3.	(C)	28.	(C)	53.	(D)	78.	(A)
4.	(B)	29.	(E)	54.	(C)	79.	(A)
5.	(B)	30.	(A)	55.	(E)	80.	(D)
6.	(E)	31.	(D)	56.	(C)	81.	(B)
7.	(B)	32.	(A)	57.	(A)	82.	(E)
8.	(D)	33.	(E)	58.	(B)	83.	(B)
9.	(A)	34.	(C)	59.	(D)	84.	(C)
10.	(D)	35.	(A)	60.	(B)	85.	(D)
11.	(E)	36.	(C)	61.	(E)	86.	(B)
12.	(A)	37.	(B)	62.	(C)	87.	(C)
13.	(D)	38.	(A)	63.	(B)	88.	(A)
14.	(B)	39.	(B)	64.	(A)	89.	(E)
15.	(D)	40.	(B)	65.	(E)	90.	(E)
16.	(B)	41.	(D)	66.	(D)	91.	(E)
17.	(B)	42.	(D)	67.	(E)	92.	(E)
18.	(C)	43.	(C)	68.	(A)	93.	(B)
19.	(E)	44.	(D)	69.	(D)	94.	(A)
20.	(A)	45.	(B)	70.	(B)	95.	(B)
21.	(B)	46.	(D)	71.	(C)	96.	(C)
22.	(C)	47.	(E)	72.	(E)	97.	(A)
23.	(C)	48.	(A)	73.	(C)	98.	(A)
24.	(E)	49.	(D)	74.	(D)	99.	(D)
25.	(A)	50.	(B)	75.	(A)	100.	(E)

101.	(B)	131.	(E)	161.	(E)	191.	(D)
102.	(A)	132.	(E)	162.	(E)	192.	(C)
103.	(E)	133.	(A)	163.	(D)	193.	(D)
104.	(C)	134.	(E)	164.	(A)	194.	(A)
105.	(D)	135.	(D)	165.	(E)	195.	(A)
106.	(D)	136.	(C)	166.	(B)	196.	(C)
107.	(B)	137.	(D)	167.	(D)	197.	(B)
108.	(C)	138.	(E)	168.	(C)	198.	(A)
109.	(D)	139.	(C)	169.	(B)	199.	(C)
110.	(C)	140.	(D)	170.	(A)	200.	(B)
111.	(D)	141.	(D)	171.	(C)	201.	(C)
112.	(D)	142.	(C)	172.	(D)	202.	(E)
113.	(A)	143.	(A)	173.	(A)	203.	(B)
114.	(A)	144.	(B)	174.	(E)	204.	(E)
115.	(C)	145.	(E)	175.	(D)	205.	(C)
116.	(B)	146.	(A)	176.	(B)	206.	(E)
117.	(B)	147.	(A)	177.	(A)	207.	(B)
118.	(B)	148.	(E)	178.	(B)	208.	(C)
119.	(D)	149.	(A)	179.	(E)	209.	(C)
120.	(B)	150.	(C)	180.	(D)	210.	(A)
121.	(D)	151.	(B)	181.	(E)	211.	(D)
122.	(D)	152.	(E)	182.	(D)	212.	(B)
123.	(D)	153.	(D)	183.	(A)	213.	(A)
124.	(D)	154.	(D)	184.	(C)	214.	(B)
125.	(C)	155.	(A)	185.	(B)	215.	(E)
126.	(B)	156.	(C)	186.	(B)	216.	(A)
127.	(E)	157.	(C)	187.	(E)	217.	(E)
128.	(C)	158.	(B)	188.	(A)		
129.	(E)	159.	(B)	189.	(D)		
130.	(B)	160.	(C)	190.	(E)		

DETAILED EXPLANATIONS OF ANSWERS

GRE PSYCHOLOGY TEST 6

1. **(A)** Rods and cones convert light into neural impulses that the brain can understand. Bipolar cells and neurons are involved in vision but these cells do not respond directly to light. Olfactory receptors are involved in our sense of smell while chromocells and phototrons do not exist. Finally, efferent neurons convey signals from the brain to muscle groups.

2. **(C)** Pavlov discovered that organisms can learn to associate neutral stimuli with natural reflexes. In his famous experiment, a dog learns to salivate to the sound of the bell because the bell (a neutral stimulus that does not usually produce salivation) has been consistently paired with food, a stimulus that does produce a natural salivation response. Pavlov's work has relevance to the establishment of phobias and manias in humans. B.F. Skinner discovered the principles of operant conditioning. No Russian cosmonaut has walked on the moon. Pavlov studied neither language nor aggression. The bulk of these studies came over forty years after Pavlov.

3. **(C)** Interviews with homosexuals reveal that many have had unsatisfactory heterosexual experiences. There is no evidence to indicate that it is caused by hormone imbalances. Human sexual behavior is not controlled by hormones as it is in lower species. Giving testosterone to a male homosexual produces a more muscular and aggressive homosexual, not a heterosexual. Throughout history, homosexuals have existed in all climates.

4. **(B)** The Freudians believe that much of our behavior is motivated by subconscious sexual and aggressive drives. It is the humanists that believe that we strive towards self-actualization. Choices (C), (D), and (E), represent the behavioral, cognitive, and medical approaches to personality, respectively.

5. **(B)** Chomsky believes that humans are innately endowed with some rules for language acquisition. B.F. Skinner's position is that language acquisition is shaped by the environment through the use of rewards and punishments. Chomsky never questioned the value of animal research. They have never publically argued about the difference between phonemes and morphemes, dyslexia in infants, or whether chimps can acquire language.

6. **(E)** Proactive inhibition refers to the situation where old learning (i.e., a well known phone number) interferes with new learning. Conduct aphasia refers

to difficulty understanding speech while dyslexia is a tendency to reverse letters while reading. Broca's syndrome does not exist. Retrograde inhibition is a case where new learning interferes with the recall of old material.

7. **(B)** Dissociative reactions refer to maladies that enable us to break away from some aspect of our reality. The category includes multiple personality, fugue, and amnesia.

8. **(D)** Research such as the Ashe studies indicate that people will alter their views under the influence of peer pressure. This fact has serious implications for people serving on jury duty who may vote along with the majority rather than vote their conscience. Further, they will change their views to justify their decision.

9. **(A)** Behaviorism is based on the functional approach. Study only observables and do not invent mentalistic structures that may not exist, i.e., id, self-actualization as a motivating force.

10. **(D)** A physical addiction is present when the person needs greater quantities to get the drug effects, and suffers withdrawal symptoms when deprived of the drug. Hallucinogenic drugs (marijuana, PCP, peyote, LSD) do not produce these tolerance and withdrawal effects. Alcohol is a depressant and not a separate drug class.

11. **(E)** Projective personality tests are unstructured. That is, they do not provide a series of questions to answer, as the MMPI test does. They provide ambiguous stimuli to describe. The theory is that some people will begin to project some aspects of their own personality into the way they interpret the inkblots or pictures.

12. **(A)** The behavioral approach treats the symptoms as the problem, and does not consider them as representing some subconscious conflict. Systematic desensitization is a behavioral treatment for phobias.

13. **(D)** The fovea is densely packed with cones. Staring focuses the image on the fovea. In dim light, the fovea is much less responsive than the periphery of the retina which is packed with rods. Rods are more sensitive to light than cones. Night blindness is caused by a lack of vitamin A.

14. **(B)** Lorenz, an ethologist, demonstrated that an animal would follow (imprint on) the first moving object that it saw within hours after hatching. Mead, Milgram, Erikson, and Piaget all worked with human subjects.

15. **(D)** Drinking large quantities of alcohol during pregnancy can cause enormous damage to the developing fetus, including severe brain damage. Through the umbilical cord, the fetus receives whatever its mother ingests. Be-

cause of its much smaller size, the fetus frequently gets more than twenty times the concentration of substances that can be found in the mother's blood stream.

16. **(B)** Psychosomatic disorders refer to real physical illnesses produced by psychological factors. Ulcers, high blood pressure, and migraine headaches are psychosomatic illnesses. Choices (A), (C), and (D) are all examples of conversion reactions (hysteria), i.e., physical ailments with no organic base.

17. **(B)** The correlation between weight and height is less than 1.00 because underweight and overweight people exist. The question is not beyond statistical measurement because statistics can be performed on any variables that allow precise measurements. Although it is true that weight and height vary with age, that does not exclude the possibility that the ratio of one to the other cannot remain constant. For example, a person could, during their entire life, weigh two pounds for each inch of height.

18. **(C)** No casino would program a slot machine on any schedule other than a variable ratio. Choice (A) is a fixed interval 50 minute schedule, while choice (B) is a variable interval 50 schedule. Ratio schedules require work to be done and have no time limit. Choice (D) is continuous reinforcement followed by extinction; (E) is the reverse — extinction followed by continuous reinforcement.

19. **(E)** The occipital lobes are located in the back of the head. Temporal lobes are located on the sides behind the temples. The parietal and frontal lobes are located on top and in front, respectively. There is a brain structure known as the hippocampus but there are no such things as hippocampal lobes.

20. **(A)** Maturation refers to the sequence of skills all humans are genetically preprogrammed to develop. These activities include language acquisition, walking, manual dexterity, and puberty.

21. **(B)** Choice (A) is incorrect because chimps do not sign long-worded statements like a human deaf person frequently does. The animals have no language of their own and their reasoning and symbolic powers are very limited compared to humans.

22. **(C)** Electric shock therapy has been successful in alleviating the symptoms of severe depression. Unfortunately, it has recently been linked to brain damage. Lithium is a metal that all of us have in minute quantities in our bodies. Some people who suffer from manic-depression (extreme mood swings) have a lithium deficiency. Lithium carbonate capsules are prescribed for them, and it alleviates the problem. Thorazine is one of the anti-psychotic drugs, and is not prescribed for depression alone.

23. **(C)** Freud's psychosexual theory of personality development was the

first formal personality theory. It stressed the importance of childhood experiences on adult personality. It also depicted children as being sensual creatures rather than simple innocents.

24. **(E)** Edward Thorndike is the author of the law of effect. His experiments with cats are classics. He demonstrated the usefulness of the experimental approach and the fact that results obtained with animals might have relevance for humans.

25. **(A)** Myelination refers to tissue attached to the walls of the neuron's cell body. It enables neural signals to travel through the neuron faster relative to a signal passing through an unmyelinated neuron. Dull and sharp pain are believed to be controlled by these differential speed factors. Axons and dendrites are part of every neuron. Soma cells do not exist. The term dopaminergic refers to neurons that use the neurotransmitter dopamine. Sensory and motor neurons convey messages to and from the brain, respectively.

26. **(D)** Choices (C), and (D) come from the work of Jean Piaget who studied children most of his life. Object permanence refers to the ability of children who, after about 11 months, learn objects exist when not in view. The game "Peek-a-Boo" is not as much fun for them. Conservation of matter and objects (A) and (E) do not exist. Conventional morality refers to part of Kohlberg's theory on moral development. Conservation of number means a child knows that spreading objects around or bunching them together in a small group does not change the number of objects that you have.

27. **(D)** Milgram was interested in how people can be induced to perform acts that are morally reprehensible to them, or in contradiction to their dominant personality traits. His research indicates that a person will commit acts, including murder, if a legitimate authority orders it, and more importantly, if that authority figure accepts the responsibility and consequences of these acts. Hence, it is possible to turn a boy into a killing soldier within a few weeks of basic training.

28. **(C)** Long term study of several individuals indicates that the personality characteristics that we develop during the first decade of our lives remain fairly constant. Only extraordinary experiences radically alter our behavior patterns. There is little evidence for genetic inheritance of specific personality traits that will show up regardless of environmental experiences.

29. **(E)** The cilia, or auditory hair cells, vibrate and convert the auditory information into neural impulses. The stapes, cochlea, and tympanic membrane (the eardrum) convert sound into mechanical vibrations. Papilla are structures found on the tongue.

30. **(A)** A person who lacks a conscience is known as a sociopath. Sociopaths are not psychotic. Instead, they are frequently good-looking, intelligent, and ruthless.

31. **(D)** Anton Mesmer set up a business in Paris during the last century. He "cured" people of various mental ills by having them sit in tubs of blue water. Wearing robes and waving a wand, Mesmer serviced their "animal spirits." He probably hypnotized some of his subjects and suggested that they felt better. For some, it worked.

32. **(A)** Diffusion of responsibility refers to the fact that the larger the group of people, the less any member of the group feels personally responsible for the events that are occurring. Members of lynch mobs, gangs, and crowds at sports events often act as spectators to events that they do not condone.

33. **(E)** Systematic desensitization is a successful behavioral treatment program for phobias. First, a list is composed ranking the fear provoking stimuli from the least feared to the most. Next, the client is taught relaxation exercises. Finally, the client is taught to remain relaxed in the presence of stimuli that used to elicit a fear reaction.

34. **(C)** Classical conditioning refers to glandular and emotional responses. Choices (A), (B), and (D) refer to muscular activity which is within the domain of operant conditioning, or instrumental learning.

35. **(A)** Primacy and recency effects refer to better recall of the beginning and the end of an event. The other terms are all relevant to the topic of memory but are incorrect choices for this question.

36. **(C)** Delusions are thought disorders while hallucinations are sensory disorders. There are several types of delusions, including hypochondria, persecution, nihilism, and influence. Someone with a delusion of grandeur believes that he is someone famous or powerful. Being God, a political figure, or a millionaire are common delusions.

37. **(B)** The mother always donates an X chromosome for the sex of the child. If her egg is fertilized by an X bearing sperm, she will have a daughter. If a Y bearing sperm fertilizes the egg, she will have a son. Hence, the father determines the sex of the child.

38. **(A)** Neural signals travel at a speed between 3 and 200 miles an hour depending on the number of excitatory and inhibitory connections involved. The speed of light is 186,000 miles a second. Six hundred miles an hour is close to the speed of sound.

39. **(B)** Premack's principle states that organisms will engage in less preferred behavior in order to get the opportunity to engage in preferred behavior. Examples include: Eat your spinach and you can have ice cream; finish your homework and you can go to a movie. The law of latency states that rewarded behavior will occur more and more frequently. Choices (C) and (D) do not exist.

Classically conditioned responses are glandular and involuntary.

40. **(B)**   Mental illness was considered a curse from God or demonic posses-sion. Treatment included floggings, starvation, exorcism rituals, prayer, herbs, and death (for witches). The purpose of these treatments was to drive the demons out of the person.

41. **(D)**   Children tend to believe that the world and all that exists within it serves no purpose other than to serve and amuse them. This phenomena is re-ferred to as egocentricism.

42. **(D)**   Discrimination refers to responding differentially to different stim-uli, e.g., stop at red lights and go on green ones. Matching-to-sample is a research technique used to assess cognitive abilities in animals. Secondary reinforcers are positive stimuli such as money, praise, and medals. Generalization refers to situa-tions in which we respond to stimuli that are similar to the stimuli we were originally exposed to.

43. **(C)**   Visual information is first stored in iconic memory. It is then trans-ferred to short-term memory and finally long-term memory. Echoic memory is involved in the processing of auditory information. Episodic and semantic mem-ory are not specific parts of memory processing system.

44. **(D)**   The social psychologists have demonstrated that the larger a group of people is, the less likely any of them will perceive a serious situation as an emergency. This tendency towards pluralistic ignorance has been tragically dem-onstrated during fires, earthquakes, and other tragic events.

45. **(B)**   Research indicates that people who have satisfactory relationships with others report that they come from homes where physical contact was en-couraged (kissing, wrestling, hugging, etc.). People who have sexual problems, or are incapable of feeling true love frequently report the opposite childhood experiences. That is, they were raised by people that discouraged physical con-tact. Harlow's monkey experiments demonstrate similar results on an animal's ability to function socially.

46. **(D)**   Cones enable us to see colors. They do not work in dim light. All the cars look grey because the rods only allow us to perceive shades of grey, black and white. You "see" your yellow car because you remember its color, and the brain fills in the color that the eyes are not transmitting. Color constancy refers to our perceiving the colors of familiar objects regardless of poor lighting conditions.

47. **(E)**   Intelligence tests measure knowledge of school subjects, and famil-iarity with one's culture. The early tests had questions on them such as "_____ is the name of the Chicago baseball team." Questions like these would be difficult

for a recent immigrant to answer. They have been accused of being culturally biased because the vocabulary section is geared towards students in suburban schools. Some claim that the state has no right to assess your intelligence, and teachers have been known to treat students differently depending on their I.Q. test score.

48. **(A)** Zimbardo's original experiment had to be terminated in less than a week because of the dangerous environment that developed in his mock prison. Depersonalizing people by giving them numbers instead of names, and giving the guards total authority created an environment of rebellion among the prisoners that the guards began to handle with cruel punishments.

49. **(D)** Auditory hallucinations are the most common form. The hallucination usually takes the form of a voice or voices, of God, dead relatives, or famous people. The voices advise and sometimes order the person to do certain acts.

50. **(B)** Tolerance, or the ability to consume greater quantities of the drug is one sign of a physical drug addiction. Withdrawal symptoms, ranging from fever to convulsions and death, is the other condition. Not all drug addicts have criminal records, ill health, poor hygiene or suffer bouts of insomnia.

51. **(E)** A sense must have a physical sense organ, a brain area associated with it, and it must be qualitatively different from the other senses, i.e., vision is a different experience than hearing or smell, etc. The sense of balance is a function of the fluid in the middle ear, and there are brain centers associated with this ability. Similarly, kinesthesis, the ability to know where your limbs are without looking at them also satisfies the above three criteria for a true sense. The other choices are all forms of ESP which have no identifiable sense organ, or brain centers associated with them.

52. **(E)** Research indicates that, more often than not, people who use excessive levels of corporal punishment were themselves beaten as children. The lessons that our parents taught us as children, via modelling, were learned by us, whether or not we liked or disliked their behavior. Excessive use of physical punishment is not recommended by psychologists because the side effects include aggression, distrust, rebelliousness, and blunted initiative in children exposed to it.

53. **(D)** "State dependent learning" refers to the fact that we will recall information better if we are again in the same drug state in which we first learned the material. Studying for exams under the influence of stimulants may result in poorer recall the next day when you take the exam sober. The other choices represent techniques designed to facilitate recall.

54. **(C)** The premise in Freudian psychoanalysis is that all adult psychological problems stem from unresolved psychic conflicts originating in childhood.

The role of the therapist is to get the client to relive childhood traumas (abreaction). This experience leads to gaining insight into the problem. What remains is for the client to then convince themselves that these childhood experiences should not exercise so much influence over them. This last step is referred to as "working through."

55. **(E)** Freud believed the mind consisted of three components: the id, which consists of our sexual and aggressive motivating forces; the ego, which is our consciousness; and the superego, which is our sense of morals and conscience. The ego has to constantly try to satisfy the demands of the id while operating within the limits set by the superego.

56. **(C)** Myopia is caused by an elongation of the eyeball. The result is that the lens focuses the image beyond the retina. Cataracts are a cloudy cornea. The other choices would produce major vision problems regardless of the distance of the object.

57. **(A)** Sleep research indicates that there are five stages of sleep—levels one through four and REM. Dreams most often occur during REM sleep but nightmares occur during deep (phase 4) sleep.

58. **(B)** The experimental group in any experiment is exposed to the principle variables the experiment is investigating.

59. **(D)** According to Freud, a very strong love-hate relationship develops between a boy and his mother. He loves her because she has nurtured him throughout his existence. He resents his dependency on her, and her ability to make him feel good or bad. Around six years of age, the boy comes to see his father as a rival for his mother's affection. The boy wishes his father were eliminated so he could continue to be the center of his mother's life. This is the Oedipus complex, named after the Greek tragedy in which a man unknowingly kills his father and marries his mother. Daughters experience the Electra complex, a desire to eliminate their mother and have their father's full devotion.

60. **(B)** Monkeys that are raised with "doll mothers" have had no model to demonstrate nurturing techniques. They have also been deprived of physical contact with their own species. As adults, they show little interest in sex. After they are artificially impregnated and give birth, they reject their young. The research suggests that there is no mothering instinct in primates, and humans. Our parenting techniques are based on our own childhood experiences.

61. **(E)** Insight learning refers to the sudden solution to a problem without having to rely on trial and error. It is frequently referred to as the "Aha!" experience where we suddenly know exactly what to do without systematically trying several solutions until one works.

62. **(C)**   Rain can be an aversive stimulus. The reinforcement for running indoors is the termination of getting wet. Responses that are reinforced because they eliminate unpleasant stimuli are known as escape responses. Choices (A), (D), and (E), refer to positive reinforcement situations where rewards are earned. Punishment is defined as a situation where a response produces, rather than eliminates, an unpleasant stimulus.

63. **(B)**   Identification is an ego-defense mechanism wherein we model our behavior after someone we admire. By acting like our heroes, we feel that we are more like them, and therefore more admirable. Advertising takes advantage of this by having famous people hawk products in commercials. Even children want to eat the same breakfast cereal as a TV persona that they love. The other choices are all ego-defense mechanisms.

64. **(A)**   All infants regardless of race or nationality attempt to develop communication skills in the same sequence: crying, cooing, babbling, then patterned speech.

65. **(E)**   Retrograde amnesia refers to a trauma to the brain, produced by an accident, that frequently erases the memory traces of recent experiences before they become part of long-term memory. Anterograde amnesia refers to difficulty remembering new experiences.

66. **(D)**   As the term suggests, applied psychologists apply principles discovered in basic research to real world situations. They would engage in all of the activities listed in this question, except basic research with birds.

67. **(E)**   Although it has been tried on a variety of mental illnesses, electroconvulsive therapy has only had reliable success in the treatment of depression. No one knows for sure how it affects the brain. The dominant theory is that it alters brain chemistry.

68. **(A)**   Piaget studied the cognitive development of children, and described four different phases that represent the evolution of the mind's capacity to go from simple analysis to abstract thought. Choice (B) consists of some of the phases contained in Erikson's theory of psychosocial development. Choice (C) provides the main components of Kohlberg's theory of moral development.

69. **(D)**   Morphemes are the smallest units of speech that carry meaning. Most prefixes and suffixes are morphemes. Phonemes refer to simple sounds that humans are capable of making. They have no meaning until they are emitted as groups of sounds.

70. **(B)** The unconditioned (unlearned) response to food is salivation. The dog learns to salivate to the bell that signals that food is about to be presented. The other choices are incorrect because each contains at least one stimulus (the bell, the food, the dog) and the question is asking for you to identify two responses.

71. **(C)** The Thematic Apperception Test (TAT) is used as a tool for assessing personality. The theory is that a person will inject their own fears, desires, and world view into their interpretation of the pictures. The Rorschach test is based on the same theory but it uses inkblots instead of recognizable pictures.

72. **(E)** Sex role development refers to the fact that parents, primarily due to their own upbringing, believe that there are appropriate ways for a child to act, depending on their sex. Boys are expected to be aggressive, dominant, and mechanically inclined. Girls are expected to be more submissive and gentle. Some parents reinforce their children for behaving in accordance with the sex stereotypes.

73. **(C)** A conditioned reinforcer is a stimulus that we have been taught has value. For example, young children are taught the value of money. Paper money is not a natural reinforcer for them. The other choices are all primary reinforcers, stimuli that naturally work as reinforcers.

74. **(D)** Damage to the hippocampus results in mild to severe difficulty in learning new material, i.e., transferring experiences to long-term memory. The medulla monitors automatic functions such as heart rate. The hypothalmus controls basic drives such as hunger and thirst. The amygdala is involved in emotional responses.

75. **(A)** The survey research method is one of the most economical techniques available. Copies of the survey can be made on a photocopy or mimeograph machine for a penny apiece. Subjects are often available in introductory college courses. The problems with surveys include experimenter bias, the fact that people tell you what they think you want to hear, and the validity of accepting a person's answer on a survey as representing how they would really act in a given situation.

76. **(B)** Young children frequently imitate what they see and hear. They assimilate the habits, good or bad, of peers, parents, and others around them. Both boys and girls who see an adult abusing a doll tend to imitate the behavior when given the opportunity.

77. **(C)** The humanistic approach is based on the premise that the client knows what is best for them. The therapist acts as a sounding board and lets the

client decide the direction that therapy should take. Hence, it is referred to as client-centered therapy.

78. **(A)** Infants have difficulty acquiring concepts. Hence, verbal labels are often overgeneralized to objects that do not belong in the class. A child will call all things with wheels a car, including a bicycle or a wagon.

79. **(A)** Neural signals can only travel in one direction. That is, across a synapse to the dendrites of a neuron, through the cell, and out the axon terminals to the synapse, where the signal causes the axon terminals to release a neuro-transmitter into the synapse to other cells.

80. **(D)** People can be motivated to perform slower (social loafing) or faster (social facilitation) depending on the nature of the influencing agent, and the response of those people around them.

81. **(B)** Moving the chalk up to your face would increase the size of the chalk focused on the retina many fold. The brain perceives this change in size as an object approaching, rather than growing. This size constancy perception is learned. Humans living in rain forests have had limited experience with objects approaching from a great distance. Consequently, they frequently report that insects grow into cattle as you approach them.

82. **(E)** People have a need for acceptance and approval from their peers. Social loafing refers to the fact that people will regulate their performance to coincide with the group mean performance.

83. **(B)** According to Piaget, formal operations is the highest level of cogni-tive development. At this level, we can reason abstractly enough to realize that changing the shape of an object (rolling a ball of clay into a cigar shape, for example) doesn't change the amount of material we have to work with.

84. **(C)** The limbic system, which includes the amygdala, has been shown to control emotions. Electrical stimulation of this area produces rage reactions in animals. The sympathetic and parasympathetic systems are located in the spinal cord, not the brain.

85. **(D)** Syntax refers to the grammatical rules of speech. The animals fre-quently act as if the word order does not matter. The chimp may sign "Give Lana apple," or "Lana give apple," "Apple Lana give" or other combinations of the three words.

86. **(B)** Independent variables are directly under the control of the re-searcher. Examples include the nature of the task, time of day, selection of subjects. The dependent variable is what the subject does.

87. **(C)** Carl Jung, an early disciple of Freud did not believe that sex and aggression were as influential as Freud theorized. Part of his personality theory included the collective unconscious, racial memories of symbols and myths common to all humans.

88. **(A)** Kohlberg's theory of moral development states that human morality evolves in a certain order. During the preconventional phase, children accept and obey rules not because they believe in them but because of the different consequences associated with obeying or disobeying them. He considered the ability to resist natural impulses to explore and manipulate the environment (playing with the dials on a TV for example) in order to conform to rules, as the first step in moral development.

89. **(E)** Trace classical conditioning refers to a situation where the CS is presented and then removed. After a delay, the US is presented. The CR occurs towards the end of the delay between CS and US.

90. **(E)** Neurons fire on an all-or-none basis. They can be either on or off like a light bulb. The action potential (neural impulse) is always the same voltage. Increasing the intensity of a stimulus can only make the neuron fire more frequently.

91. **(E)** The behavioral therapy approach known as assertive training is designed for people who have difficulty exercising authority due to an inferiority complex. Through the use of models and positive reinforcement, a client is taught to assert themselves with co-workers, spouses, and other family members.

92. **(E)** Algorithms are rules that always result in the successful solution to a problem. However, they are time consuming. For example, if you had to fill in the missing letters to the word IN–––T, you could systematically try every combination of the letters of the alphabet and arrive at INSERT. Heuristics are strategies that improve chances of success, but do not guarantee success every time. Various chess strategies are examples of heuristics.

93. **(B)** An I.Q. of 120 is slightly above one standard deviation of the mean and would indicate above average intelligence. Genius would be three standard deviations above the mean, or an I.Q. beyond 150.

94. **(A)** The Oedipus and Electra complexes cause children a lot of anxiety. The boy fears that his father will discover that he sees him as a rival for his mother's affections, and suffers castration anxiety. The boy reduces his anxiety by consciously identifying with, and copying the behavior of the father. Daughters engage in similar identification with their mothers.

95. **(B)** According to Freud, dreams have two components. The manifest

content of a dream is what you actually dream. The latent content refers to the hidden meaning of the dream. The id tries to produce sexual and aggressive fantasies in dreams. The superego edits the dream by changing the symbols for objects. Choices (A), (C), and (D) could all be the latent content of the dream described.

96. **(C)** Endorphins are the brain's natural form of painkiller. Adrenaline, dopamine, and serotonin are all neurotransmitters that enable neurons to pass along messages to and from the brain.

97. **(A)** The brain of the dolphin has more convolutions (folds) than does the human brain. Hence the interest in their intelligence. Gorillas and chimps have brains similar to humans but their frontal lobes are not as developed.

98. **(A)** Psychosurgery refers to an irreversible operation on the brain. The frontal lobes of the brain are surgically cut and therefore functionally separated from the rest of the brain. The typical results include emotional blunting, inability to reason at an abstract level, and decrements in motivation. From the 1930s to the 1970s, over forty thousand lobotomies were performed. Today, they are seldom done.

99. **(D)** Projection is an ego defense mechanism wherein we blame other people or things for our failures. "The coach had it in for me," "It was in my stars," are two other examples. The other four choices are also ego defense mechanisms. Fantasy refers to daydreaming. Rationalization is providing socially acceptable reasons for inappropriate behavior. Denial is a case where we refuse to accept the truth. For example, a neighbor denies that her son has a drinking problem although he frequently comes home drunk. Displacement is taking out our frustrations on substitute objects or people. The boss says "You're an idiot" and you say nothing. When you get home, your spouse asks how your day went. "Can't a person ever find a hot meal waiting when they get home?" is your reply. The spouse turns to the son and says "Why aren't you doing your homework?" The boy kicks the dog on his way to his room.

100. **(E)** Psycho (mind) kinesis (movement) refers to the ability to move objects with mental energy. This ability has never been conclusively demonstrated under laboratory conditions. Psychokinesis is not a form of extrasensory perception (ESP).

101. **(B)** Humans spend their lives classifying objects by function and resist visualizing the use of an object in a novel way (fixedness). For example, a person could place a glass against a wall, place their ear against the glass, and hear a conversation going on in the adjacent room. Most people can only visualize a glass as a receptacle for liquids, and not as a microphone, so they would not think to try the alternate use.

102. **(A)**   Reliability of a test refers to the fact that the results are reproducible. Getting the same results does not prove that the test is valid or fair.

103. **(E)**   Pluralistic ignorance refers to the fact that the larger the group, the less likely the members of the group will perceive a true emergency as such. Further, each member of the group will feel less personally responsible for correcting the situation. Hence, the result is group indifference to social issues such as pollution, nuclear weapons, and poverty.

104. **(C)**   The neural wiring in the brain changes with experience. The brain is genetically "prewired" to develop certain skills such as language acquisition. However, the environment must provide the necessary stimulation for these skills to develop, or these brain areas will not respond as well later. The time limit for these developments is referred to as the critical period.

105. **(D)**   Drive-reduction theory states that all behavior is motivated by a physiological need. Every choice except (D) involves a physiological need: thirst, hunger or cold. Drive reduction theory cannot explain why a human would ride a roller coaster, an experience that increases arousal and can produce (not reduce) fear or nausea.

106. **(D)**   Absolute threshold refers to the minimum amount of stimulation required to trigger a sensory system. Below the absolute threshold, the light is too dim for the rods of the retina to fire, or the sound is not loud enough to cause the eardrum to vibrate.

107. **(B)**   Impotence, the inability to produce or maintain an erection, is the only choice that is not illegal. It is considered a medical problem. Pedophilia refers to people who get sexually aroused by children. Necrophilia is sexual behavior with a corpse. Voyeurs achieve sexual arousal by secretly watching people undress, and exhibitionists achieve arousal by exposing their genitals to unsuspecting strangers.

108. **(C)**   Few therapists are purely Freudian, humanistic, or behavioral in their approach. Most use elements from each approach that they feel will benefit the client.

109. **(D)**   The formal experiment enables total control over all relevant independent variables. The other choices are more vulnerable to situational variables that may influence the outcome.

110. **(C)**   The visual cliff experiments demonstrate that an infant has depth perception. Since the infant's environmental experiences are few because of young age, the dominant view is that depth perception is innate in humans, as it is in simians.

111. **(D)**   Inductive reasoning refers to situations in which we take known facts and use them in novel ways. Creativity involves inductive reasoning. Deductive reasoning is the opposite. We take a variety of facts and eliminate all but the relevant ones. Every choice but (D) is a case of deductive reasoning.

112. **(D)**   When our actions contradict our self perceptions of what we believe we are capable of, dissonance results. Cognitive dissonance refers to this feeling of discomfort. Since we cannot undue what we have done, we alter our beliefs to justify our behavior.

113. **(A)**   During the 19th century, Lombroso wrote a popular book that attempted to correlate physical characteristics with criminal activity. Having a tattoo was one sign of the criminal mind. Research has not supported this view. Criminals come in all shapes and sizes and are represented in every racial and ethnic group.

114. **(A)**   The hippocampus is the brain site believed to be the location where short-term memories are translated into long-term memory storage. Damage to this area does not affect old memories already stored in long-term memory. However, there is a deficit in the ability to transfer new experiences into long-term memory. This condition is known as anterograde amnesia.

115. **(C)**   Neither the APA nor any other reputable organization considers astrology to be anything more than a pseudoscience aimed at the gullible.

116. **(B)**   A compulsion refers to the irresistible need to engage in ritualistic acts such as constantly rearranging furniture and hand washing. An obsession is a thought disorder which may or may not be accompanied by compulsive behavior.

117. **(B)**   A conjunction fallacy refers to the superstitious connection that people make between two consecutive events. Primitives used to throw virgins into volcanoes because they concluded that sacrificing women appeased the volcano god who would then keep the volcanoes from erupting. A belief in Indian rain dances and astrology is based on the same fallacy.

118. **(B)**   Chimps have been taught to "communicate" by forming the hand signals of the American sign language used by the deaf. They have also been taught to use differently shaped plastic discs and computer panels to make statements. Attempts to teach them to speak have failed primarily because they lack the brain centers necessary to control vocalizations.

119. **(D)**   The nativist view states that much of human behavior is innate. The fact that a blind infant could not be imitating a smile that it had seen supports the nativist view that smiling is an innate predisposition in humans.

120. **(B)**   Eidetic, or photographic, memory is the ability to recall memories in great detail. This ability is predominantly a childhood phenomenon and is typically lost during puberty.

121. **(D)**   A catatonic schizophrenic often engages in "statue poses" for hours at a time. This behavior may require the patient to be force fed. Although bizarre, this form of schizophrenia comes on suddenly and has one of the best chances of being cured.

122. **(D)**   In order to prescribe drugs, a person has to have completed medical school. A psychiatrist is an MD who has had additional training in psychology.

123. **(D)**   Double-blind research controls for experimenter bias and the placebo effect. Some researchers may unconsciously treat the experimental subjects differently than the controls if they know who they are. Some subjects will show results if they expect to, even if they have not been given the drug. This placebo effect is reduced if the subject does not know if he or she is in the experimental or control group.

124. **(D)**   A discrimination is present when an organism responds differently to different stimuli. We say hello to friends but not strangers. We discriminate between different businesses (for example, a bowling alley, funeral parlor, and a grocery) and act differently within them. The rat differentially responds to the lever depending on the state of the light. Hence, its behavior is described as a discrimination.

125. **(C)**   The medical approach sees abnormal behavior as symptomatic of some underlying biological problem. The solution, therefore, is biological intervention including drugs. The other choices pair therapy techniques with an approach that does not use it. For example, the behavioral approach does not endorse the use of electric shock therapy.

126. **(B)**   Phrenology was very popular at the beginning of the 20th century. People believed that the head shape and the bumps and valleys of the skull could be read and would provide insight into the person's personality. The idea was discounted but is still with us. People expect brilliant individuals to have dome-shaped heads, although the head and brain of known geniuses such as Einstein and Mozart were no bigger than that of an illiterate laborer.

127. **(E)**   Flashbulb memories refer to detailed recall of very important events. Your senior prom, winning a prize, and receiving an acceptance letter from graduate school are events that are recalled in better detail than everyday experiences. Repressed memories are inaccessible to the conscious mind, and eidetic memory refers to photographic memory which recalls all experiences in great detail. Answers (A) and (B) do not exist.

128. **(C)**   The brain uses the contrast between figure and background to decide how an object should be perceived. When it makes an error that is called an illusion. The phi phenomenon refers to situations where lights strobed in sequence are perceived as a moving light. A delusion is a thought disorder and does not involve the senses.

129. **(E)**   The ego is constantly bombarded by contradictory impulses from the id and superego. Consciousness is therefore a series of frustrations. Only death can relieve us of this burden. The death wish is credited with motivating us to engage in suicidal behavior such as drugs, overeating, and dangerous thrill seeking.

130. **(B)**   Psycho (mind) metrics (measure) refers to attempts to quantify human potential.

131. **(E)**   Computer programs currently have to be programmed for every eventuality they may encounter. When they are given an input for which they have no instructions, they stop working. The goal of artificial intelligence is to teach machines to "think" for themselves, and to alter their decision-making process in light of new information. Most of the computers in science fiction films such as Star Wars (C3PO and R2D2) have artificial intelligence.

132. **(E)**   Insulin is an enzyme used to metabolize sugar. It is not manufactured in the brain. Diabetics do not produce enough of it so they must inject supplementary doses into themselves. The other four choices are all neurotransmitters that are involved in neural function.

133. **(A)**   Many of the people in a lynch mob, as well as looters, have never engaged in criminal behavior before. They report that they were caught up in the moment. A group often takes on a personality very different from the members that make it up.

134. **(E)**   Most cults do not use aversive methods to indoctrinate new members. Novices pay lip service to the cult leader (compliance) in order to be accepted by the other members. Over time, the novice begins to identify with the group, and comes to internalize the beliefs of the cult.

135. **(D)**   Watson wrote one of the most influential books in psychology. Called *Behaviorism*, it laid the foundation of the behavioral approach.

136. **(C)**   Ethologists study animals in their natural habitats. Experimental psychologists study animals and humans under laboratory conditions. Applied psychologists apply the results of research to therapy while a psychoanalytic psychologist is trained in Freudian techniques.

137. **(D)**   Telegraphic speech refers to the two or three word statements that make up most of the verbalizations of very young children. They frequently leave out verbs and articles in their remarks.

138. **(E)**   Anorexics are obsessed with their appearance, wanting to be thin but not recognizing when they actually are. They typically lose weight by not eating and by being highly physically active. Bulimia is a related eating disorder that involves binging followed by purging in order to prevent weight gain.

139. **(C)**   The nativist position is that many human faculties, intelligence, perceptual abilities, and temperament for example, are wired in the human. The empiricist approach believes that experience molds us. The other choices are empirical explanations for the observed behavior.

140. **(D)**   A free recall experiment asks the subjects to repeat information that they have been given recently. It is called "free" because they can repeat the information in any order. If they had to repeat the words in the order in which they saw them, that would be a serial learning task. A recognition task would present them with words and ask them if they recognize the words as belonging to the group they originally saw.

141. **(D)**   Surveys indicate that adolescents are most frequently introduced to alcohol and other drugs by their friends.

142. **(C)**   There are no Nobel Prizes given in psychology. Pavlov received his in medicine, as did Huble and Wiesel (for the discovery of receptor fields in the visual field) and Sperry for his split-brain research.

143. **(A)**   Habituation refers to the cases in which a stimulus that initially drew our attention no longer registers in our conscious mind. City dwellers are usually oblivious to the odor of air pollution around them, but a tourist will immediately notice the smell and be aware of it for several minutes.

144. **(B)**   Even at a rock concert, we can tune out the sound of the musicians, screaming fans, and other sounds to focus on the statements of our companions. This form of selective attention is called the cocktail party effect. The other choices are all true but not related to the question.

145. **(E)**   Research by environmental psychologists indicates that excessive noise levels interfere with our ability to concentrate. Reducing noise levels in factories has been shown to decrease the number of accidents that occur.

146. **(A)**   Level six is the highest stage of moral development a human can attain. At this level, we have our own philosophy, and practice it even if it makes us unpopular with our peers.

147. **(A)** Since they predominantly measure past school performance, I.Q. tests can be used to predict future school performance. I.Q. tests do not measure personality traits, and there is no strong correlation between I.Q. and financial success.

148. **(E)** The use of language requires the organism to have the capability of symbolically representing the world in verbal or written symbols. Concept ability is essential in order to do this. Additionally, one must have brain areas capable of comprehending speech, fine control over the muscles needed to produce intelligible sounds, and a brain area (Broca's) necessary to coordinate it all.

149. **(A)** Lorenz (a Nobel Prize winner) spent many years studying aggression in animals. The members of other species seldom hurt each other. They engage in mock fights in order to establish dominance in the group or herd. This ensures that the strongest have their choice of mates thereby strengthening the gene pool of the group. Tinbergen, another ethologist, studied the mating behavior of fish. The other three choices are all well known psychologists.

150. **(C)** Infants require contact comfort in order to thrive. Just the act of giving them attention increases their rate of development. Infants that are frequently interacted with walk and talk sooner than children left alone much of the time.

151. **(B)** Humans have a tremendous need for acceptance. Peer pressure refers to the fact that many people will engage in activities they would never initiate if they were alone, solely because their peers are pressuring them to join in.

152. **(E)** Long term abuse of alcohol causes brain damage. One type is Korsakoff's syndrome, named after the Russian who first described it. The other choices can all cause memory problems but Korsakoff's syndrome only refers to alcohol-induced memory losses.

153. **(D)** The skin, which is several square feet in size and senses temperature, pressure, and pain, is by far the largest sense organ of the body.

154. **(D)** The APA reclassified homosexuality as an alternate lifestyle in the early 1970s because the majority of gay people live healthy, productive lives.

155. **(A)** Transsexuals are people who would prefer to live their lives as members of the opposite sex. They must undergo extensive psychotherapy before the transformation is permitted. Surgery and hormones are used to alter their appearance.

156. **(C)** Several well-documented cases such as "The Wild Boy of Aveyron"

suggest that there is a critical period after which the acquisition of language is severely limited. Puberty, or about twelve years of age seems to be the limit. Films like *Tarzan, the Legend of Greystoke* are impossible. Having lived in the jungle among apes until he was an adult would have made Tarzan a functional moron, incapable of acquiring spoken language.

157. **(C)** For the Freudians, all behavior is motivated by sexual and aggressive drives. Therefore, all behavior is sexual, aggressive, or a socially acceptable substitute for them. Sublimation refers to these substitutes for overt sexual and aggressive acts.

158. **(B)** Anna Freud, the daughter of Sigmund, became famous in her own right for her research on ego defense mechanisms.

159. **(B)** Animals do not have the developed brain centers necessary for them to experience hatred the way a human can. In humans, language is a key component of emotional experience. Try remembering an emotional experience without using words to think about it. Most animal displays of aggression to other members of their group are sham performances.

160. **(C)** Some attempts to shape certain behaviors in animals have failed because of their instincts. It is impossible to punish a rat for standing on its hind legs. Raccoons "wash" tokens they have been taught to handle in order to obtain food. It is easier to teach a pigeon to peck a disc then to teach it to press a lever for food because pecking is more natural for birds.

161. **(E)** For the behaviorists, personality is a label for the collected habits we develop during our lifetimes. These habits are shaped by rewards, punishments, and learning by observing others.

162. **(E)** A person must have a Ph.D. or M.D. degree, and do an internship in order to obtain a license and call him or herself a psychologist or psychiatrist. However, anyone can call themselves a therapist and offer counselling services.

163. **(D)** Mean (or average score), mode (the most frequently occurring score), and range (the difference between the highest and lowest score) all indicate what the majority or centermost results were.

164. **(A)** Shaping refers to reinforcing successive approximations of a desired behavior. At first, we will accept any attempt at writing that a child does. Later, we demand more precise control of the pencil. A tennis instructor reinforces successive approximations to a perfect serve. He raises his criteria for what is an acceptable serve until a perfect serve is well established.

165. **(E)** The lower a species is on the phylogenetic scale, the more its behav-

ior is controlled by hormones and instinct. In humans and apes, sexual behavior is influenced by hormones but experience dictates sexual receptivity.

166. **(B)** Denial is an egodefense mechanism wherein we literally refuse to accept the truth about some aspect of reality because to do so is painful for us.

167. **(D)** The humanistic approach states that each of us strives to be the best that we can be at something. The process is called self-actualization. If our goals are blocked, deviant behavior may result. For example, the student who ruins his or her life with drugs because he or she could not get into medical school.

168. **(C)** Huble and Wiesel (both Nobel Prize winners) demonstrated that the visual system of chimps (and presumably humans) is innately wired to respond to particular shapes. Further, these receptor fields must be stimulated in order to develop to their fullest.

169. **(B)** Auditory information first enters into echoic memory which is part of the sensory apparatus for hearing. The information lasts less than a second before it is discarded or sent along to short-term memory.

170. **(A)** Freud believed that the death wish in humans was stronger than the life force. Most religions (represented in our superegos) forbid suicide. So some individuals choose socially acceptable ways of dying by getting into dangerous professions.

171. **(C)** A stereotype refers to the tendency in humans to catalog all people in an occupation, race, religion, or ethnic group based on the behavior of a small sample from that group.

172. **(D)** Apparent motion of a string of stationary lights is known as the phi phenomenon. Location constancy refers to our perceiving objects as stationary as we move about them. Binocular disparity allows us to have depth perception. It is the slight difference in the image sent by each eye to the brain that we use as a cue to depth. The remus effect does not exist.

173. **(A)** Twin studies indicate that the environment can influence I.Q. by over 15 points, The probability of inheriting your parents' I.Q. is 50%. When environmental factors are equated for, the case for innate I.Q. becomes weak.

174. **(E)** Drugs are classified according to how they affect the brain, not how they make you act. Alcohol is a depressant although you may act less inhibited. Cocaine increases the activity of certain areas of the brain, and is therefore a stimulant.

175. **(D)** Via the mechanism of generalization, we expect people who excel

at one attribute to be superior at others. It is common for people to believe that a well-known movie star who appears on a talk show and discusses politics knows more than the average person about the subject.

176. **(B)** For the behaviorists, there must be a reward factor, or the behavior would not occur. Since they prefer to deal only with observable data, (B) is the correct choice. The other choices may be relevant, but each (physiological need, thoughts, perceptions, etc.) is not directly observable.

177. **(A)** The olfactory bulbs are located directly beneath the brain above the nasal passages. The frontal and parietal lobes are located at the front and top of the brain, respectively. Neither they, the pineal gland, nor the medulla oblongata is involved in our sense of smell.

178. **(B)** A neuron can have hundreds or thousands of other neurons synapsing with it. Some of these adjacent neurons release neurotransmitters that encourage the neuron to fire (+). Others release neurotransmitters that inhibit the neuron (–). If the +'s out-influence the -'s, the neuron will fire.

179. **(E)** The study of behavior and mental processes is the domain of psychology. The other choices are too narrow or vague.

180. **(D)** Freud was the first psychologist to depict children as sexually aggressive creatures capable of strong feelings of jealousy, anger, love, and other passions usually attributed only to adults.

181. **(E)** Through the socialization process, we are taught to act certain ways in particular social circumstances. Teachers reward students for appropriate classroom behavior, etc.

182. **(D)** Cognitive, or concept learning, ability in animals requires the animal to use old training to solve new problems without relying on trial and error. The matching-to-sample procedure presents the animal with a sample color (say red) projected on a disc. After the animal presses the disc, two other discs light up. One of these discs presents the same red color as the sample disc. The other shows a non-matching color (blue or green). The animal gets food if it presses the disc showing the choice that matches the sample. If the animal has learned a concept, i.e., picks the one that matches the sample, then it should perform above chance when novel colors are introduced.

183. **(A)** The ventromedial hypothalamus is the "stop" center for eating. It is active when the stomach is full or blood sugar levels are up. Destruction of this area causes overeating in animals. A normal 350-gram rat grows to 1200 grams after this surgery.

184. **(C)** Validity refers to the fact that the test actually measures what it was intended to measure. For this test to be valid, each question must be in psychology, since this practice exam is claiming to test your preparedness to take the GRE.

185. **(B)** People tend to blame environmental factors for their own mistakes. but do not extend this courtesy to others. They hold people totally responsible for their behavior. Attributing behavior solely to dispositional factors, and discounting environmental influences, is the fundamental attribution error.

186. **(B)** The James-Lange theory states that environmental stimuli trigger physiological changes, i.e., hormone and glandular activity. When these changes register in the brain, we feel an emotion. Hence when threatened, we may begin running and then sense the fear afterwards.

187. **(E)** The recticular activating system, located in the base of the brain, controls consciousness. It releases chemicals that put the brain to sleep. Malfunction can cause narcolepsy and possibly crib death.

188. **(A)** Unlike most other mammals, humans rely on vision for over 80% of their interactions with their environments. This is why most humans rank blindness as their number one fear.

189. **(D)** Reliability means that the test results are reproducible. Even so, that does not prove that the test is valid.

190. **(E)** Research shows that we prefer attractive people that we can relate to. Over time, people who work in the same office often come to like each other.

191. **(D)** Children are often absorbed in their own games and do not require (in fact, they resent) the participation of other children. Autism refers to a serious problem where the child never makes contact with other people.

192. **(C)** Our auditory processing systems are single channel. We cannot simultaneously process two sources of input. If we try, we remember part of each, but not all of either.

193. **(D)** Sensory deprivation experiments indicate that if the brain is not provided with sensory input, it manufactures its own, i.e., hallucinations. Delusions and terror have also occurred during test conditions.

194. **(A)** It is generally agreed that the first modern psychology lab was established in Germany, by Gustav Fechner. His research area was psychophysics.

195. **(A)**   Social norms can vary by town. They are the subtle rules dictating what is acceptable behavior within the community. They are not always laws and they are not always acceptable to other communities, i.e., racism.

196. **(C)**   According to Carroll Izard, the eight basic emotions an infant is capable of include joy, anger, surprise, distress, interest, disgust, sadness, and fear. Envy, revenge, and guilt require cognitive abilities beyond the infant's capabilities.

197. **(B)**   Humans normally are sensitive to three color areas and are called trichromats. A dichromat (a color-blind person) is insensitive to one of these three regions, usually red-green discriminations.

198. **(A)**   Broca's area of the brain is involved with speech production. Damage causes difficulty in making statements. Damage to Wernicke's area produces problems in comprehending what is said.

199. **(C)**   The formula for the I.Q. score is obtained by dividing the mental age by the physical age and multiplying the answer by 100. Hence if a person's mental and physical age are the same, the equation always comes out to be 100.

200. **(B)**   The rooting reflex refers to the baby's readiness to nurse whenever the cheek is stimulated. Choice (D) is referred to as the grasping reflex.

201. **(C)**   A behavioral chain is a situation in which two or more responses must be emitted in a certain sequence to produce a reinforcer. Getting dressed in the morning is an example. You must put on your clothes in a certain order, underwear, shirt, sweater, pants, coat. Typing a report also requires that you push certain keys in a certain sequence.

202. **(E)**   The body requires optimum levels of various substances in order for it to function. Oxygen levels must be maintained beyond a minimum value. Liquid must be ingested to prevent dehydration. Homeostasis is the general term that refers to the body's attempt to maintain stability.

203. **(B)**   Theories are a system for explaining phenomena. A theory becomes a law after it is proven that the theory holds up in every case it can apply to.

204. **(E)**   Abraham Maslow, one of the champions of the humanistic approach, has written several influential books. He believed that if society provided all the basic needs for the population, people would be free to strive for perfection in their chosen fields.

205. **(C)**   A hermaphrodite is a person born with both sex organs. Although, strictly speaking, their sex depends on the twenty-third chromosome (XX

is a girl, XY is a boy). However, a medical decision, whether surgery should be performed, is usually made based on their physiology. A eunuch is a castrated male.

206 **(E)** Size constancy refers to the fact that things appear to stay the same size regardless of their distance to us. Location and brightness constancies refer to the fact that we perceive objects as being stationary as we navigate around them, and colors appear to be the same regardless of changes in lighting, respectively. The fact that objects appear to keep their shape regardless of the angle we view them at is an example of shape constancy.

207. **(B)** Narcolepsy, the tendency to fall asleep when we get excited, is believed to be a malfunction of the reticular activating system. Sleep apnea refers to people who stop breathing while asleep. The other choices are sleep disorders that occur while we are already asleep.

208. **(C)** Although the claims made in the other choices have been popular at different times in history, they were supported by fraudulent data.

209. **(C)** Whether they appear to pay attention or not, children are constantly absorbing information from the environment. There can be a several day delay between their observations and their emitting the behavior themselves.

210. **(A)** Erikson proposed that there are eight stages of development. Within each stage, a person undergoes a psychosocial crisis. The last phase, integrity vs. despair, refers to a person reviewing their life with a sense of accomplishment and pride, or with despair for a life misspent.

211. **(D)** A physical drug addiction requires tolerance and withdrawal symptoms, both of which are present in smokers. Physical drug addiction is defined biologically and has nothing to do with whether or not the drug is legal. Absence of tolerance and withdrawal symptoms, but the person believes that they need the drug, is an example of a psychological drug addiction.

212. **(B)** Experiences are temporally stored in the sensory memory (encoding), then translated into neural impulses that through the hippocampus alter the brain memory areas (storage). To recall memory, we must scan the brain's memory areas and reconstruct the original experience (retrieval).

213. **(A)** No one has ever defined intelligence in a way that satisfies everyone. The standard I.Q. test is based predominantly on general information and school subjects.

214. **(B)** The Oedipus complex is a key concept in Freud's theories. It occurs between the phallic and latency phases of personality development. It refers to a boy's erotic desire for his mother, and a desire to eliminate his father.

215. **(E)**   By the nature of the fact that they distort reality, ego defense mechanisms are not effective coping mechanisms. Rationalizing inappropriate behavior, blaming others for our failures, and denying unpleasant truths do not serve the best interests of the person.

216. **(A)**   Exposure to stress provoking situations is not a sufficient condition to cause ulcers. Research indicates that lack of control over the onset, duration, or frequency of contact with aversive situations, causes ulcers. The slave rat cannot control any of these factors, and therefore gets the ulcers.

217. **(E)**   A correllation coefficient can vary from −1 (a perfect negative correlation) to +1 (a perfect positive correlation. −.96 represents a more significant negative correlation than +.82 (a strong positive correlation). 0.0 signifies no relationship at all.

GLOSSARY

This glossary has been provided to better assist you in preparing for the GRE Psychology Test. It features more than 2,000 terms—all of them extensively defined—which should be familiar to those studying psychology. In conjunction with taking REA's practice tests, studying our glossary will prove useful in preparing for the GRE Psychology Test.

A-B variable – A variable that describes the effectiveness of therapists with schizophrenic or neurotic patients. "A" therapists work best with schizophrenics, and "B" therapists work best with neurotics.

Ability – Possessing the necessary skills to perform a specific act at the present time, as opposed to aptitude (having the potential to perform with additional training).

Ability tests – Subdivided into tests of aptitude and achievement, ability tests are designed to measure individual differences in knowledge and skills to determine what a person can do.

Ablation – Removal of a body part for the purpose of studying it.

Abnormal behavior – Behavior which creates a problem for the individual and/or for society. Abnormal behavior is often maladaptive to the individual's functioning in society.

Abortion – A spontaneous or induced expulsion of the fetus usually prior to the twentieth week of pregnancy.

Abreaction – A term used by Breuer and Freud to describe a patient's, sometimes violent, expression of a repressed emotion during hypnosis. This release of strangulated affect is synonymous with catharsis.

Abscissa – The x-axis, or horizontal axis of a graph. The independent variable is plotted on the abscissa.

Absolute refractory period – A brief period toward the end of neural stimulation during which the nerve cannot be restimulated.

Absolute threshold – The lowest level of intensity of a stimulus at which its presence or absence can be correctly detected 50 percent of the time.

Abstract intelligence – The ability to deal effectively with ideas expressed in symbols such as words, numbers, pictures, or diagrams.

Accommodation – In vision, the changes of lens shape or curvature that produce sharpened retinal images of objects at varying distance from the eye.

Accommodation – In Piaget's system, the adaptive modification of the child's cognitive structures in order to deal with new objects or experiences. (See Assimilation.)

Acculturation – The learning of behaviors and attitudes one is expected to adopt as a member of a particular culture.

Acetylcholine – An acid that acts as an excitatory substance to facilitate neural transmission at many synapses and neuromuscular junctions.

Achievement motivation – The need, or drive, to perform a task successfully as judged against standards of excellence. The concept predominates in the expectancy value theory of motivation.

Achievement test – The part of an ability test designed to assess what an individual has already learned through prior training.

Achromatic – Without hue or saturation, varying only on the brightness dimension. For example, the black, gray, and white series.

Achromatism – Total color blindness due to congenital absence of cone cells.

Acoustic stimulus – A sound wave arising from the vibrations around an object in the air. Sound waves are generally referred to as acoustic stimuli only when they are audible.

Acquisition – The gradual strengthening of a response through learning as it is incorporated into the behavioral repertoire.

Acquisition curve – The graphic representation of the acquisition process in which response strength is displayed on the vertical axis and amount of practice on the horizontal.

Acrophobia – A neurotic fear of heights.

Act – A single unit in the continuous stream of behavior.

ACTH (adrenocorticotrophic hormone) – A hormone secreted by the pituitary gland in response to stress, causing the adrenal cortex to secrete corticosterone.

Acting out – 1. The performance in a new setting of behavior learned from and appropriate to another social situation. 2. In psychoanalysis, the carrying out of repressed impulses; the manifest behavior that is often symbolic of earlier stages of the individual's life.

Action decrement – The tendency of an organism not to repeat the action just completed.

Action potential – The nerve impulse; the changes in electrical potential along a nerve fiber that constitute the nerve impulse as it travels through the axon.

Action-specific energies – (Lorenz) Motivating energies that impel only very specific sequences of behavior; motivating energy for instinctual behaviors.

Active analytic psychotherapy – The form of psychoanalysis developed by Wilhelm Stekel in which the therapist takes a directive role as educator.

Active avoidance learning – A learning task in which the subject must make a prescribed response in order to avoid an aversive stimulus.

Active learning – Learning procedures that stress recitation and performance as opposed to simple reading of materials.

Actualization – The desire to realize one's own potential; in Maslow's theory of motivation, the highest level in the human need hierarchy.

Acuity – Sharpness of perception. Usually visual acuity, the ability of the eye to see spatial detail.

Adaptation – 1. A reduction in the sensitivity of a sense organ due to continued stimulation from the same source. 2. Behavioral or anatomical changes which enhance the possibility of survival. 3. In Piaget's system, the process of cognitive growth which modifies psychological structures to suit the environment.

Adaptation level – The level of stimulation to which an individual has already adapted and against which new stimulus conditions are judged.

Addiction – A state of dependence upon a drug or chemical in which discontinued use of the substance results in extreme psychological and/or physiological reactions.

Adipsia – A condition resulting from the destruction of the lateral hypothalamus that causes the victim to stop drinking.

Adjective checklist – A technique, used in the assessment of adult emotions, in which the subject is presented with a list of emotion words and is then instructed to check off those that are most appropriate to his feelings.

Adler, Alfred – A personality theorist who emphasized social factors in personality development. Founder of the school of Individual Psychology, he broke away from Freud in 1911.

Adolescence – The period from the onset of puberty to adulthood (11 to 19 years of age).

Adrenal cortex – The outer layer of the adrenal gland that secretes several hormones, including corticosterone, in response to emotional arousal.

Adrenal gland – A gland of the endocrine system that produces many hormones; especially important in regulating bodily responses to stress.

Adrenal medulla – The inner core of the adrenal gland that secretes the hormones epinephrine and norepinephrine into the bloodstream.

Adrenal steroids – Hormones secreted into the circulatory system by the adrenal cortex during emotional arousal.

Adrenaline – Also called epinephrine; a substance produced by the adrenal gland which is related to increases in general arousal.

Affect – A synonym for emotion; sometimes employed as a quantitative term to express a person's emotional capacity and degree of reaction to given situations.

Affective component – The emotional or feeling aspect of an attitude.

Affective feedback – The feelings of pleasantness or unpleasantness following an organism's responses.

Affective psychosis – Psychotic behavior characterized by extremes of mood. The most common include depressive reactions or manic-depressive reactions.

Affective state – The emotion of an individual at a specified point in time; can include negative, positive, or neutral feelings.

Afferent nerves – Nerves carried by the dorsal root which relay sensory impulses (information about the environment) to the central nervous system; sometimes used synonymously with sensory nerves.

Afferent neuron – A neuron carrying information to the central nervous system.

Affiliation – The need to associate with others; also, the quantity and quality of group memberships and friendship bonds.

Affirmation rule – In concept learning, a rule specifying that all items with a particular attribute are instances of the concept.

Afterbirth – The placenta and other membranes that are expelled from a woman's body following the birth of a child.

Aftersensation – Most often in vision (afterimages), the continuation of a sensation even after the removal of the stimulus.

Age equivalent – 1. In testing, a score conversion in which a test score is assigned the age value for which that score is the average score. 2. In development, the average age at which a child reaches a particular developmental stage.

Age norms – Norms based upon large samples of children at each age.

Aggression – Hostile action or feelings, especially those caused by frustration, which may result in harm or injury to another person.

Aggressive drive – One of the inherited instincts proposed by Freud and thought to give rise to the destructive components of human behavior.

Agoraphobia – A strong fear of open places; often referred to as a form of neurosis.

Albinism – The congenital absence of hair, eye, and skin pigmentation. An albino is color-blind.

Alcoholism – A substance-use disorder marked by compulsive drinking and inability to control drinking behavior.

Alexia – A form of aphasia, usually caused by brain damage, in which one has an inability to read or understand written or printed language.

Algorithm – A method for attacking a problem which is assured of success; often involves repetitive operations which survey the possibilities at each step.

Alienation – The state of feeling separated or withdrawn from one's culture and/or social and personal relationships; the central theme of existential philosophy.

Allele – One of a pair of genes located at corresponding positions on a pair of chromosomes. Each pair contains the genetic code for a particular trait, with one allele often dominant (i.e., the determinant of the trait).

All-or-none law – The principle that the axon of a neuron fires either with full strength or not at all to a stimulus, regardless of its intensity, provided the stimulus is at least at the threshold value.

Allport, Gordon – American psychologist who studied the development of personality. He favored a dynamic trait model.

Alpha rhythm – A wave pattern, found in the EEG during periods of relaxed alertness, which has a frequency of 8 to 12 cycles per second.

Alpha waves – A particular brain wave pattern that occurs when the subject is in a state of "relaxed wakefulness." People can be taught to control the presence of alpha waves through biofeedback training.

Altered state of consciousness – State that occurs when the overall functioning of the mind takes on a pattern that is qualitatively different from normal.

Alternation – Experimental method used in the study of thinking in which the subject is required to alternate responses in a pattern (such as left-right-left-right or left-left-right-right).

Altruistic behavior – Behavior that benefits others and is not directly rewarding to the self.

Amacrine cells – Retinal cells believed to be of importance in summation effects. They interconnect bipolar or second order neurons.

Ambiguity – The possibility that a given stimulus can elicit more than one definition response.

Ambivalence – The bipolarity of feeling; the state of being drawn to or away from two mutually antagonistic goals at the same time.

American Psychiatric Association (APA) – The major and official professional organization for psychologists in the United States.

American Sign Language – The gestural language used by the deaf in North America.

Amnesia – The inability to recall events in one's past, sometimes including one's identity, often as a result of physical or psychological trauma. In the absence of physical trauma, amnesia is often attributed to neurotic dissociation of threatening aspects of one's past sometimes restricted to one severely traumatic event.

Amniocentesis – The removal of fetal cells from the fluid of the amniotic sac to test for the presence of abnormal chromosomes.

Amniotic fluid – A dark, watery fluid that fills the amniotic sac during pregnancy. The sac lines the uterus and contains the developing child.

Amphetamine – A class of drugs that stimulates the central nervous system. Chemically all amphetamines contain $C_9H_{13}N$. Use can become addictive.

Amplitude – The intensity or loudness of sound, measured in decibels.

Amygdala – A part of the limbic system, the system where emotion is organized, located between the hypothalamus and pituitary gland which becomes active whenever we encounter anything new or unexpected.

Anal character – In psychoanalytic personality, one characterized by stinginess, orderliness, and compulsive behavior because of an infantile fixation on the anal region.

Anal stage – The second of Freud's stages in which libidinal interest and conflicts center on excretory functions and toilet training. This stage usually occurs between the ages of 8 and 18 months.

Analog computer – A computer that operates on continuous signals of varying voltages.

Analysis of variance – A statistical test appropriate for analyzing reliability from experiments with any number of levels on one or more independent variables.

Analytical psychology – The term applied to the form of psychoanalysis developed by Carl Jung.

Anaphrodisiac – Having to do with a lack of sexual feeling.

Anchorage effect – Resistance to attitude change because of particularly strong beliefs or group support.

Androgens – Substances associated with male sex hormone activity in vertebrates, produced mainly by the testes and to a small extent by ovaries and the adrenal cortex.

Androgyny – Having psychological characteristics expected of members of both sexes.

Anecdotal record – A written report describing an incident of an individual's behavior. Theoretical conclusions based solely on anecdotal reports are often suspect. They do, however, often serve as the basis for actual research.

Anechoic chamber – An enclosure, the walls of which are especially absorbing of sounds.

Angell, James – One of the founders of Functionalism.

Anger – An acute emotional reaction characterized by strong impulses in the autonomic nervous system which may occur when the attainment of a goal is blocked. Often induced by frustration.

Anima – According to Jung, an archetype representing the feminine characteristics as opposed to the animus, or male archetype.

Animism – The belief held by young children to the effect that nonliving objects have some of the characteristics of living beings, such as will and intention.

Anisocoria – A pathological condition in which the pupils of the two eyes are of unequal diameter.

Anomalous color defect – Anomalous dichromatism and trichromatism. In dichromatism only two colors are seen (most often blue and yellow). In trichromatism weakness in the red-green region is observed.

Anomy – A term employed by Bull to describe the earliest stage in the development of mortality. Refers to the absence of a moral orientation.

Anorexia – (nervosa: self-starvation) Extreme loss of appetite accompanied by pathological and dangerous weight loss.

Anosmia – Complete absence or serious deficiency in the sense of smell.

Anoxemia – An oxygen deficiency which interferes with normal metabolism.

Anoxia – A condition in which the brain does not receive enough oxygen to allow it to develop or function properly.

Antabuse – Drug that causes intense nausea if a person drinks alcohol while the chemical is in his bloodstream. Used as a method of controlling the pathological drinking behavior of alcoholics.

Antecedent-consequent research – Research strategy that studies subjects of the same age to determine how different environmental conditions affect performance.

Anthropomorphism – The attribution of human characteristics to subhuman species. Anthropomorphic explanations often attribute conscious thought, etc., to animals or to inanimate objects (most common in children).

Anticipation – A technique for testing learning and memory that requires the subject to indicate the learned material in a determined order.

Anticipation learning – A form of rote-learning procedure in which the subject tries to give the next item in the list during each trial. Affords a running account of the subject's progress.

Antidepressant – A drug which elevates the mood and relieves depression. Most antidepressants are "set-point" drugs which, like aspirin, have no effect on an individual unless he or she is in an abnormal state (e.g., has a headache). People who are not depressed do not feel better after taking antidepressants (just as aspirin will not change the temperature of someone who already has a temperature of 98.6°F.)

Antipsychotics – These drugs are used with major psychotic disorders such as schizophrenia. The drugs have a calming effect and seem to alleviate schizophrenic symptoms such as delusions and hallucinations. Some examples are chlorpromazine and reserpine (also known as "major tranquilizers").

Antisocial behavior – Behavior characterized by a failure to act according to societal standards and the absence of anxiety about such behavior; also called psychopathic or sociopathic behavior.

Anvil – A small bone in the middle ear located between the hammer and stirrup (synonym: incus).

Anxiety – Feeling of dread and apprehension without a specific and realistic fear of some threatening object.

Anxiety reaction – A form of neurosis characterized by vague feelings of anxiety. Often called free-floating anxiety because it is not attached to any specific stimulus. Physiological symptoms of anxiety reactions include heart palpitations, tremors, nausea, and shortness of breath.

Apathy – Extreme indifference to situations that normally arouse a response. In extreme cases (depression), complete and total indifference to one's surroundings.

Aphagia – Condition in which an animal refuses to eat, ignores food, and starves to death unless treated. Aphagia has been produced experimentally by surgical removal of the lateral hypothalamic nucleus.

Aphasia – Loss or impairment of the ability to express or receive linguistic communications, resulting from cerebral damage to the parietotemporal cortex.

Aphonia – Loss of speech resulting from emotional or laryngeal disorders.

Apoplexy – A cerebral hemorrhage or blocked blood vessel causing a loss of consciousness and motor control.

Apparent motion – An illusion in which objects either appear to move but, in fact do not, or appear to move in directions contrary to their actual movement.

Appetitive behavior – Behavior directed toward some positive goal (from the Latin, *petere*: to seek).

Applied psychology – Any branch of psychology that employs psychological principles for solution of practical problems.

Approach-approach conflict – The conflict in which a person or organism is motivated toward two gratifying goals or stimuli that are incompatible.

Approach-avoidance conflict – A conflict situation in which one is both attracted to and repelled by the same goal. For example, one may want to go to college, but be fearful of the work that would be involved.

Approach-withdrawal systems – The organization of behavior patterns according to whether the response is toward or away from objects and events.

Aptitude test – An ability test designed to appraise, to predict, what the individual can learn to do if he receives appropriate education or job training.

Aquaphobia – Fear of water.

Aqueous humor – A fluid behind the cornea of the eye.

Arachnoid – The middle protective tissue layer of the central nervous system between the piamater and duramater.

Archetype – According to Jung, a symbolic representation of a universally meaningful concept based on the experiences of all one's ancestors in the inherited "collective unconscious."

Arithmetic mean – The common average, obtained by adding together all of the scores in a set and dividing by the number of scores.

Arousal – Increased alertness and attention accompanied by changes in the central and autonomic nervous systems and increased muscle tension.

Arousal jag – An increase in arousal, followed by a decrease in arousal; the decrease and its anticipation are reinforcing.

Arousal potential – The capacity of stimuli, or of their characteristics to cause or raise arousal.

Arousal theory – A motivational theory that assumes man needs to maintain arousal at an optimal level for specific behavior. Arousal theory explains behavior involved in risk-taking, gambling, curiosity, and learning.

Artificial insemination – An artificial breeding procedure often employed in animal husbandry and sometimes with humans. This procedure obviates the necessity for a physical union between a pair of opposite-sexed individuals.

Asch situation – A test of the effectiveness of a group on an individual's judgment in which the subject is falsely led to believe that his perceptions are different from those of the majority.

Assertion-structured therapy – The term applied to the system of psychotherapy developed by E. Lakin Phillips in which the behavioristic therapist models assertive behavior patterns for the client.

Assertiveness training – Teaching someone to express emotions, feelings, and beliefs in an "open" or forthright way.

Assessment – The evaluation of a person with respect to some psychologically meaningful characteristic, trait, or disposition.

Assimilation – In Piaget's theory, the taking in of new information. Assimilation ultimately results in the accommodation of a schema to the new information.

Association – The functional relationship between two psychological phenomena or concepts based on prior learning.

Association cortex – Largest portion of the cerebral hemispheres, most highly developed in man. The more complex functions like perception, language, and thought are centered here.

Association, Laws of – Principles formulated to account for functional relationships between ideas: similarly, contiguity, contrast, coexistence, succession, and causality.

Association theory – Asserts that all behaviors are the result of accumulations of stimulus and response associations.

Associationism – In psychophysics and cognition the theoretical approach that complex ideas are the result of associations between simple elements. In learning theories synonymous with the S-R connection (stimulus with response).

Associative attribute – In Underwood's theory of memory, one of the attributes of a memory. It consists of items to which that memory is linked associatively. For example, returning to one's hometown may facilitate the recall of memories long "forgotten."

Associative cortex – Areas of the cortex outside the primary sensory and motor areas.

Associative thinking – Uncontrolled thinking which is not directed to any goal, e.g., daydreaming. Also a train of thoughts, each one leading to another.

Asthma – A disorder characterized by increased airways resistance caused by constriction in the bronchioles, often aggravated or precipitated by psychological stress.

Asymptote – In a learning curve, the point at which performance has approached near maximum and begins to level off. The value of the dependent variable at which no further effects of the independent variable occur.

Atavism – A genetic carryover from an older phylogenetic ancestor.

Atmosphere effect – Refers to errors made in reasoning or behavior that are the result of the atmosphere surrounding the problem, namely, the subject's attitude or the way the problem is presented. Affirmative premises tend to create an affirmative atmosphere and, thus, imply an affirmative conclusion.

Attachment – The normal relationship of a child to parents and other significant individuals; usually develops during the first six months of postnatal development.

Attention – The selective focusing upon certain aspects of the environment to the neglect of others.

Attention-rejection – A way of classifying emotions according to the degree of orientation to the event the emotion produces.

Attention span – The number of elements or amount of material that can be perceived in a single brief exposure; the length of time a person focuses on a given object or task.

Attenuation – Weakening of the relationship between two measures because of the unreliability of either or both. Also the reduction in amount or degree of the stimulus.

Attitude – A fairly stable and lasting predisposition to behave or react in a characteristic way (positive or negative) toward individuals, objects, events, or institutions. Attitudes include feeling, thinking and behavioral components.

Attitude scale – Devices employed to measure the degree or strength of attitudes or opinions.

Attitude system – A cluster of attitudes which share common or similar concepts, beliefs, motives, and habits.

Attribute – A perceived characteristic of some object or person. As a verb, it means to infer that an individual has certain characteristics. Also a fundamental or characteristic property of anything.

Attribute identification – Learning to identify the relevant attributes is a component task of concept learning.

Attribution – Ways of assigning causality to the behaviors or cognitions of other people or oneself.

Audition – The sense of hearing.

Auditory canal – Sometimes referred to as the external auditory meatus. The tubular passage which connects the external ear with the middle ear.

Auditory localization – Identifying positions from which sounds emanate; often a function of the slight discrepancy between the times at which the signal reaches each ear.

Augmented sensory feedback – Synonymous with biofeedback. The control through conditioning of internal processes.

Authoritarian personality – Personality type characterized by, among other traits, high ethnocentrism, conservatism, antidemocratism, and prejudice.

Authoritarians – Those people who score high on the California F-Scale. Normally, such people exhibit certain antidemocratic personality characteristics and are often prejudiced against minorities; they consistently exhibit their need to establish authority.

Autism – A nearly total withdrawal from reality and escape into fantasy perceiving the world in terms of wishes.

Autistic – A term referring to psychological processes that do not correspond to reality and are strongly determined by a person's needs. Also refers to a severe mental illness of early childhood, involving extreme withdrawal and isolation, absorption in fantasy, and profound defects in thought and language.

Autogenic – Originating within the self.

Autokinetic effect – Apparent movement of a small spot of light seen against a dark background in a completely dark room.

Automatic action – A well-practiced response that occurs "automatically" when its appropriate stimulus is presented.

Autonomic conditioning – The eliciting of responses of the autonomic nervous system, including salivation, galvanic skin response, gastric motility, etc.

Autonomic nervous system (ANS) – The peripheral nervous system that controls the function of many glands and smooth-muscle organs. It is divided into the sympathetic and parasympathetic systems.

Autonomy – Self-determination, a need to be self-determining.

Average – The arithmetic mean, the median, and the mode are all measures of central tendency referred to as "the average."

Aversions – Stimuli that give rise to avoidance behavior.

Aversive behavior – Behavior aimed at avoiding unpleasant consequences.

Aversive conditioning – Instrumental conditioning in which an aversive stimulus can be prevented by making an appropriate response.

Aversive stimulus – Any stimulus the organism judges to be noxious or unpleasant.

Aversive therapy – A technique that pairs unpleasant aversive) stimuli with inappropriate behavior.

Avoidance-avoidance conflict – A conflict between two unattractive alternatives, for example, a child given the alternative to eat his spinach or go to bed without supper.

Avoidance conditioning – A form of learning in which the behavior change is motivated by the threat of punishment.

Avoidance response – Any response an organism makes in order to keep from experiencing an anticipated aversive stimulus.

Axillary hair – Armpit hair.

Axon – The elongated part of a nerve cell body which carries the nerve impulse away from the cell body toward another nerve fiber or neural structure.

Babbling – The relatively meaningless speech patterns comprising repetitive sequences of alternating consonants and vowels that infants repeat in the first six months of life.

Babinski reflex – A reflex present in the newborn child, but disappearing later in life. It involves fanning the toes as a result of being tickled in the center of the soles of the feet. Normal adults curl their toes inward rather than fanning them outward.

Backward conditioning – In classical conditioning, a trial in which the onset of the USC occurs before the onset of the CS. The procedure is often unreliable.

Balance theory – The theory which argues that people prefer and seek consistency with respect to their belief systems and avoid inconsistent and incompatible belief systems.

Balanced Latin square – An experimental design in which each subject is exposed to each experimental condition and employs a counterbalancing scheme in which each condition is preceded and followed equally often by every other condition.

Bales analysis – A technique for describing social groups by making functional analyses of the types of communications between the group members, with the aid of a computer which is programmed to score 164 different categories.

Band wagon – A propaganda technique in which the propagandist's view is made to appear the majority view which causes more and more people to associate themselves with the "majority opinion."

Barbiturate – A class of drugs that depress the central nervous system inducing drowsiness and muscular relaxation. Barbiturates are highly addictive substances (e.g., nembutal, seconal, and phenobarbital).

Barrier – Any environmental or psychological obstacle which interferes with one's needs.

Basal age – The highest year level at which a subject passes all the subtests of an intelligence test, used in conjunction with intelligence tests to compute mental age.

Baseline – A measurement of frequency of a certain variable prior to experimental treatment.

Basic anxiety – In Horney's theory, the anxiety that arises out of the helplessness and insecurity of childhood. The child may feel helpless and alone in a hostile world.

Basic research – Research performed solely to acquire knowledge which is often not "theory guided."

Basilar membrane – The cochlear membrane at the base of the cochlear canal on which is found the Organ of Corti. The basilar membrane is important in pitch perception.

Behavior – The term is usually employed to refer to anything a human being does: that is, any act or succession of acts which are objectively observable. Some psychologists would also include conscious phenomena such as cognitions, perceptions and judgments.

Behavior chain – Learning related behaviors in sequence in which each response serves as a stimulus for the next response.

Behavior control – The ability one person has to control another's inputs.

Behavior disorder – A general term referring to one of the various categories of psychopathology. Any behavior which is not socially acceptable.

Behavior modification – The application of scientifically derived principles (usually from learning) to the control of human behavior. Both classical and operant conditioning may be employed.

Behavior rating scales – Scales that are used to measure certain classes of observed behavior from which emotions or cognitions may be inferred.

Behavior therapy – The application of learning theory in treating behavioral disorders.

Behavioral arrest – Immobility resulting from severe conflict.

Behavioral genetics – The study of the influence of heredity on behavior.

Behavioral model – Model of psychopathology in which all behavior, normal or otherwise, is a product of learning about the environment.

Behavioral sink – When severely overcrowded conditions lead to pathological responding, despite environmental conditions that are otherwise normal.

Behavioral vacillation – Repeated cycles of movement toward and then away from a goal, characteristic of approach-avoidance conflicts.

Behaviorism – A system of psychology, founded by John B. Watson, which studied observable, measurable stimuli and responses only, without reference to consciousness or mental constructs which the system argues have no real utility. The objective is to predict the response evoked by certain stimuli.

Behavioristic theory – A general term for those theories of learning concerned primarily with the observable components of behavior (stimuli and responses). Such theories are labeled S-R learning theories and are exemplified in classical and operant conditioning.

Bel, decibel – A bel is a unit of auditory intensity relative to the auditory threshold; a decibel is one tenth of a bel. The decibel scale is often used as a scale of auditory loudness. Sounds of different pitch, but of the same decibel level often appear not to be equally as loud.

Belief prejudice – Beliefs which involve stereotyping: over-generalization and classification based upon rigid and biased perceptions of an object, group, class or individual.

Belonging – Thorndike's assumption that connections between items in learning are more readily formed if they are related in some way a priori.

Beta – A statistic in signal detection theory related to the criterion adopted by the observer. Beta is a measure of response bias and is independent of the observer's actual ability to detect a signal's presence.

Beta – In weight, the weights of multiple correlation predictors which yield the best prediction in multiple regression equations.

Beta rhythm – An EEG rhythm with a frequency from 13 to 25 hertz and a low amplitude that occurs during states of alertness.

Beta waves – Relatively low amplitude brain waves.

Between group variance – A measure of the dispersion among groups in an experiment.

Between-subject design – An experimental design in which each subject is tested under only one level of each independent variable.

Bias – In research, a factor that distorts data. In attitude, an internalized predisposition of affect because of the environment.

Biconditional rule – In concept learning, a rule that states that a given item is an instance of the concept if it possesses a given attribute, but only if it also possesses a second attribute.

Bilingualism – The ability to speak and understand two languages.

Binary – A term referring to a system with only two possible states. Binary numbers usually have only two values 0 and 1.

Binocular depth cues – Cues to depth perception based upon the simultaneous functioning of two eyes.

Binocular disparity – The minor difference between the two retinal images when viewing a solid (3-dimensional) object. It is caused by the separation of the two eyes with a consequent difference in the visual angle. Binocular disparity is important in depth perception.

Biofeedback – The use of a device to reveal physiological responses that are usually unobservable. Biofeedback experiments typically inform the subject about his heart rate, respiration rate, EEG activity, or similar responses in order to enable him to achieve some degree of control over the responses.

Biofeedback is now often used in psychotherapy in teaching individuals to control their own physiological states (e.g., to reduce anxiety and its symptoms).

Biological rhythms – Regular, repeating patterns of activity of various lengths or cycles.

Bipolar cell – Neuron in the retina connecting rods or cones to ganglion cells.

Bipolar disorder – A mood disorder in which there are recurrent and severe fluctuations of affective state between elation and depression. Formerly called "manic-depression."

Birth order – The position that a child occupies in the family (for example, first, second, or third born).

Birth-order effects – Various consistencies in personality that seem to be tied to whether a person was the first-born child in his family, the second-born, etc.

Birth trauma – The damaging effect on the psyche of the transition from uterine to extrauterine environment. In the Rankian literature, the birth trauma is treated as the fundamental anxiety experience out of which most subsequent neurotic conditions of the individual grow. The term is also used to refer to physical damage occurring at birth.

Black box – A term used by psychologists when referring to the organism's processing information (the stimulus) before acting (the behavior). The black box thus encompasses all cognitive processes including emotion, preference, and thoughts which are thought to mediate between stimulus and subsequent response.

Blind spot – The area in the retina where the optic nerve exits to the brain; no vision is possible here because there are no receptors.

Bloch's law – The inverse, linear relation between the duration of a visual target and threshold.

Block design – Dividing experimental subjects into homogeneous categories on a predetermined variable so that the categories can be treated as one unit.

Block sampling – 1. Sampling by geographic area. 2. The grouping of people or elements to be sampled into categories representative of the population.

Body language – A term referring to nonverbal and often unconscious communication by means of gestures, postures, expressions, etc.

Body-type theory – An attempt to predict personality by identifying the shape of the body and the characteristics that supposedly accompany that shape. Now thought to have little value as such systems are extreme oversimplifications at best.

Brain bisection – A longitudinal division of the brain between the two hemispheres. The procedure may be used to alleviate epileptic seizures and to study brain functions.

Brain lesions – Structural or functional alterations of the brain caused by injury; lesions can be produced by electrical coagulation of an area, by chemical means, by surgical removal of tissue, or by disease.

Brain stem – A part of the brain which regulates incoming and outgoing signals; it contains an area which influences the degree of general activity of an animal.

Brain waves – Rhythmic and spontaneous electrical discharges by the brain.

Brightness – That aspect of color perception that has reference to the black-white dimension correlated chiefly with wave amplitude.

Brightness constancy – Observation that objects maintain their brightness even though the amount of light reflected from them changes.

Broca's area – One of the areas of the cerebral cortex, located in the frontal lobe, which is important for the motor aspects of speech. Located in the inferior frontal gyrus in the left cerebral hemisphere of righthanded individuals and in the right hemisphere for left-handed people.

C factor – A variable, in some factor analyses of intelligence tests, which includes cleverness and quickness in thinking.

California F-Scale – The California Fascism Test, a test designed to measure authoritarianism, which isolates a personality type whose main characteristics are a rigid adherence to middle-class morality, deference to authority, and a dominating attitude.

Cannon-Bard theory – A theory of emotion that holds that bodily reaction and emotional experience occur simultaneously because they are both controlled from the same place in the mid-brain. It challenged the James-Lange theory of emotion (see James-Lange).

Cannula – A small tube inserted into some area of the brain in order to chemically stimulate that area or to extract some substance from that area.

Card stacking – A propaganda technique that involves the selective use of evidence in making an argument. Also designing an argument or experiment procedure such that it is almost certain, or at least "unfairly" likely, that any conclusion except the desired one will ensue.

Cardiac arrhythmias – Disorders involving heart rate.

Cardiograph – A device used for recording the rate and amplitude of the heartbeat.

Cardiovascular – Pertaining to the heart and blood vessels.

Case study (case history method) – It is an intensive investigation of a particular instance, or case, of some behavior which does not infer any cause and effect relationship but uses a combination of objective descriptive methods such as biographical data, psychological testing, and personal interviewing.

Castration anxiety – In Freudian theory, the fear experienced by a male child that he will be castrated by his father in reprisal for his sexual attraction to his mother. In the female child, the thought that she once possessed a penis but lost it by castration.

Catatonia – Generally, any reaction in which there is a complete withdrawal characterized by an inhibition of movement, speech, and responsiveness to the environment. (See catatonic schizophrenia.)

Categorization – The act of placing stimulus input in categories. According to Bruner, recognizing an object means placing it into an appropriate category.

Categorized list – Words used in memory experiments that are related in some taxonomic, associationistic, or other meaningful way.

Catharsis – Synonymous with abreaction.

Cattell, James – Personality theorist interested in trait measurement; developed the "factorial theory of personality."

Causation – The relation in which a given event produces the effect.

Ceiling – The maximum score set by the items in a test. A test that had items practically all of which could be answered by the average fifth grader would have a ceiling at the fifth grade level.

Ceiling age – The year level at which a subject fails to pass any subtests of an intelligence test.

Cell body – The mass, composed of cytoplasm, surrounding the nucleus of a cell not including any projecting fibers, which is responsible for the life processes of the entire cell; especially the cytoplasm around the nucleus of a neuron exclusive of the axons and dendrites (also called soma).

Centile – A method of ranking scores by computing the percentages of scores in a distribution that lie above and below a certain point in the distribution on a scale of – 1 to 100.

Centile rank – A measure of relative position in a group indicating what percentage of the norm group had poorer performance than the individual being measured.

Central nervous system (CNS) – The brain and spinal cord.

Central tendency – A typical measure summarizing a set of scores that reveals a middle representative value such as the mean, median, and mode.

Centralist position – The theory that behavior is explained best by reference to processes in the brain, as opposed to the peripheral structures.

Centrality of an attitude – The degree to which an attitude affects a person's thinking and behavior; the relevancy of an attitude.

Centration – The tendency to center attention on a single feature of an object or situation.

Cephalocaudal – Refers to the sequence of body growth in which development occurs first at the head and then moves downward through the rest of the body, part by part. Also, pertaining to the dimension of the body between the head and tail.

Cerebellum – The cerebellum or "little brain" lying at the rear of the medulla which is responsible for the control of coordination and posture. It receives fibers from the kinesthetic and vestibular pathways and also has interconnections with the cerebrum.

Cerebral cortex – The outermost half-inch layer of the cerebral hemispheres, it contains motor, sensory, and intellectual processes. It is made up of gray tinted cells and thus is sometimes called gray matter. (Also known as the neocortex of the new brain.)

Cerebral hemispheres – The largest parts of

the brain in man and other higher mammals, they are the seat of the more complex functions like language, numerical ability, and abstract thought, in addition to being responsible for sensation, some aspects of bodily movement, and many other functions.

Cerebral palsy – A type of paralysis caused by a lesion in the brain; frequently it is a congenital defect.

Cerebrotonia – In Sheldon's personality typology, one of the three primary temperamental states characterized by fast reactions, social inhibition, rigid bearing, sensitivity, hypersensitivity to pain, resistance to alcohol and the tendency to be a "loner." It is associated with the ectomorphic body build.

Cerebrum – The largest and most highly developed part of the nervous system in higher animals. It is divided into the right and left cerebral hemispheres which are connected to each other by the corpus callosum. It occupies the entire upper area of the cranium and is involved in the regulation of sensory processes, thought formation, and motor activity.

Cervix – The small circular opening to the womb (uterus) that dilates considerably during birth.

Cesarean birth – Delivery through a surgical incision into the mother's abdomen and uterus.

CFF (critical flicker frequency) – The frequency at which a flickering stimulus, e.g., light, when going on and off rapidly, appears to be steadily on.

Chaining – Type of instrumental conditioning whereby one learns to exhibit a series of behaviors in order to obtain reinforcement in which each response serves as a stimulus for the next response.

Chemical senses – Those classifications of experiences, such as taste and smell, whose stimuli are chemical and which react with receptors in such a manner as to produce nervous impulses.

Chemotherapy – A medical therapy involving the use of drugs to try to treat abnormal behavior or personality patterns.

Chi (square) – Chi refers to the Greek letter χ which is employed in the chi square, a statistical test. The chi square determines whether a distribution is significantly different from the expected or theoretical distribution.

Childhood – In humans, by convention, from two to eleven years of age.

Choleric – A temperament characterized by Hippocrates as prone to anger and outrage.

Chromatic color – A color having hue (wavelength) and saturation.

Chromosomes – Structures within the nucleus of a cell which contain the genes. Human cells contain 23 pairs of genes for a total of 46.

Chronological age (CA) – Length of life distinguished from "mental age."

Chronoscope – An instrument which measures speed of reaction.

CIE chromaticity diagram – A three-dimension model that reflects the main principles of additive color mixture.

Ciliary muscles – The circular mass of smooth muscles within the eye that are responsible for accommodation of the lens.

Circadian rhythms – Cyclical patterns of change in physiological functions such as hunger, sleep, or body temperature occurring at approximately 24 hour intervals.

Circular reaction – A type of behavior pattern observed in early infancy that involves repetitive behaviors that are self-stimulating, e.g., thumb-sucking.

Clairvoyance – A form of extrasensory perception in which one is aware of the past, present, or future without the use of sense organs.

Class – 1. A grouping of objects or people according to an a priori scheme. 2. In biology, a taxonomic category between Phylum (or Subphylum) and Order (or Subclass). 3. In statistics, a grouping of values into a single category.

Class interval – The arbitrarily selected range of scores within a given division of a measurement scale or frequency distribution.

Classical analysis (or psychoanalysis) – 1. Psychoanalytic theories and practices based on the earlier Freudian period with emphasis on unraveling the unconscious blockings of the libido. 2. Also used to refer to the hypotheses and techniques of Freud and his followers as opposed to all others.

Classical conditioning – (also known as Pavlovian or Respondent or Type S conditioning) A form of learning in which an originally neutral stimulus repeatedly paired with a reinforcer elicits a response. The neutral stimulus is the conditioning stimulus (CS), the reinforcer is the unconditioned stimulus (UCS), the unlearned response is the unconditioned response (UR), and the learned response is the conditioned response (CR).

Claustrophobia – A fear of closed spaces.

Client-centered therapy – Treatment of mental illness in which the patient is responsible for working out his problems; nondirective therapy. Generally associated with Carl Rogers.

Clinical case history – Records or data from therapy situations; used to identify behaviors and to suggest problems that need to be studied.

Clinical investigation – An experimental technique involving the use of a laboratory or clinic, usually in order to administer tests or provide experiences that require elaborate or non-portable equipment.

Clinical psychiatrist – A physician (M.D. degree) whose training emphasizes the treatment of mental disorders using both psychotherapeutic and medicinal treatments.

Clinical psychologist – A psychologist (either M.A. or Ph.D. degree) whose training emphasizes the assessment, treatment, research, and prevention of mental disorders.

Clinical psychology – A branch of psychology concerned with assessment and treatment of mental illness and with practical research into its causes.

Cloning – The process of reproducing identical individuals from selected cells of the body. Cloning ordinarily involves replacing the nucleus of one egg cell with a cell from the body of the individual who is being cloned (reproduced).

Closure (Gestalt Law) – The tendency to perceive gaps as being filled in, usually completing a figure.

Cloze technique – A procedure in which words are deleted from verbal passages, and subjects are required to identify the missing words.

Cochlea – The bony, coiled structure in the ear containing the receptor organ for hearing. The cochlea contains three tubes: the scala vestibular, scala media, and scala tympani.

Cochlear microphonic – Electrical activity recorded from the cochlea of the ear that, up to relatively high frequencies, closely matches the frequency and amplitude of the stimulus.

Codability – Ease with which a stimulus can be assigned a language label.

Coding – The transformation of data from one form into another so that it can be communicated over some channel. In information theory, the transformation of messages into signals.

Coding system (Bruner) – A concept referring to a hierarchical arrangement of related categories.

Coefficient of contingency – A correlational measure used when the distributions are on nominal scales.

Coefficient of correlation – A numerical index of the degree of relationship between two variables.

Cognition – A concept including all forms of knowing, perceiving, imagining, reasoning, judging, and thinking.

Cognitive component – The part of an attitude revealing the beliefs a person has about a stimulus.

Cognitive consistency – Attitude formation and change that stresses the motive to attain consistency between one's various beliefs, emotions, and behaviors. Also, such a state of consistency or congruity.

Cognitive development – Changes in sensory, perceptual, and intellectual performances with age.

Cognitive dissonance (Festinger) – An uncomfortable psychological conflict between beliefs and behavior. Also the motivational position that the individual will take to reduce the dissonance.

Cognitive psychology – An approach to psychological phenomena that focuses upon hypothetical cognitive structures (representations of experience) rather than upon responses.

Cognitive style – One's individual approach to perceiving and thinking about events or the world.

Cognitive theory – Approach to personality that emphasizes the cognitive processes such as thinking and judging and is thus highly rational in its outlook. Such theories have been developed by George Kelly and Edward Tolman.

Coherence – The quality of systematic and predictable connection; consistency.

Cohesiveness – The overall attractiveness of a group for its members. The quality of "hanging together," as applied to social groups perceptual phenomena, traits, or items learned.

Colic – A syndrome characterized by a distention of the abdomen, apparently resulting in severe pain and causing a baby to cry violently and continuously; also, used loosely to describe the symptoms of infants who have regular or prolonged bouts of paroxysmal crying during their first few months.

Collative variables – Employed by Berlyne to describe those properties of stimuli most likely to increase arousal in an organism. Such characteristics of stimulus objects as novelty, surprise, complexity, and ambiguity are collative variables.

Collective unconscious – In Jungian psychoanalytic theory, one of the two parts of one's unconscious mind which is inherited and common to all members of the species. It houses the archetypes and contains racial memories and psychic material.

Color – The quality dimension of light. The hue of a visual stimulus, determined by the wavelength of the light.

Color blindness – Inability to experience the colors of the spectrum in the same fashion as would a normal member of the same species.

Color circle – A circular arrangement of hues in which sectors of complementary colors are opposite and in which saturation of color is represented by the radial distance from the center.

Color constancy – The tendency to perceive an object as of the same hue under wide variations of illumination.

Color solid – A geometric 3-dimensional representation of the hue, brightness, and saturation of color.

Combinativity (compensation) – A term which refers to changes compensating each other.

Common fate (factor of uniform density) – A Gestalt principle that elements in perception which function, change, or move in the same direction will be apprehended together.

Communication – 1. The transmission of messages. 2. The transfer of energy from one place to another in an organism or system. 3. Any message or signal which does not always require language. 4. A psychotherapist's information as given by a patient.

Communication net – The channels of communication in a group; the number of channels compared to the number of potential channels is the conductivity of the communication net.

Communication network – The pattern of open and closed channels of communications among the members of a group.

Community mental health – Approach to mental health that emphasizes the prevention of mental illness and the need for broader and more effective mental health services based within communities including community support systems.

Comparative psychology – The branch of psychology which compares behavioral differences among the species on the phylogenetic scale to discover development trends.

Comparison level – In social exchange theory, the standard by which one evaluates what he deserves which is usually based on the average of past experiences.

Comparison level for alternatives – The experience level below which the individual will attempt to seek alternate interactions. An individual engaged in a social interaction or relationship above his comparison level for alternatives will continue the interaction.

Compensation – Emphasizing a behavior or trait to account for or cover up some perceived deficiency in other areas. Also a defense mechanism in which one behavioral act is substituted for another behavioral act in an attempt to alleviate anxiety.

Competence – 1. Appropriateness. 2. The view that a person is responsible for his actions.

Competence motivation – The motive to develop those skills necessary to effectively manipulate the environment.

Competition – Trying to get the best in a situation, a mutual striving between individuals or groups for the same objective.

Complementarity – The tendency for people to be attracted to each other because they possess opposite qualities, and thus fulfill each other's needs.

Complementary colors – Two hues that when mixed in proper proportion yield an achromatic additive mixture, i.e., gray.

Complex concept – A concept that represents more than one stimulus property simultaneously.

Compliance – Performance of an act at another's request, regardless of one's own attitudes.

Compound schedules – Partial reinforcement schedules in which a response is reinforced according to the requirements of two or more schedules that operate at the same time.

Compromise formation – In psychoanalysis, behavior representing a fusion or accommodation between a repressed force or impulse and the repressive forces of the psyche, such that the behavior may become manifest without censorship of the ego.

Compulsion – 1. An irrational and unwanted repetition of an activity which arises when one can no longer control an anxiety or attempts to satisfy an obsession. 2. The forcing of an individual to act against his own wishes.

Computer-assisted instruction (CAI) – The use of a computer to store and select material to be presented in a learning program.

Computer program – A set of directions, or algorithm, telling a computer exactly what to do.

Computer simulation – Programming a computer to "behave" in exactly the way specified by a theory. More generally, programming a computer to do something an organism or system does.

Conative component – The part of an attitude revealed by the actions a person takes in response to a stimulus.

Concentrative meditation – Meditation that involves "one-pointedness" of the mind limiting one's attention on a specific object for some period of time.

Concept – 1. A general idea or meaning. 2. An idea which combines several elements to form a notion, abstract properties, or relationships.

Concept formation – The process of finding the common element in a set of events or objects. Abstracting a quality or property of an object or event and then generalizing that quality or property to appropriate objects or events.

Conception – The beginning of human life which occurs with the union of a sperm cell with an egg cell.

Conceptual problems – Problems that can be solved by recognizing or learning the concept the solution is based on, by the use of systematic strategies.

Conceptual replication – An attempt to demonstrate an experimental phenomenon with an entirely new paradigm or set of experimental conditions. Typically new independent and dependent variables are selected which are thought to have the same underlying meaning (concept) in the experimental situation.

Concordance – In genetics, having the same trait(s) as a relative under study, usually an identical or fraternal twin.

Concordance rate – Probability that one of a pair of twins will show a given characteristic, given that the other twin has the characteristic.

Concrete operational period – The third of Jean Piaget's stages of cognitive development (from seven to eleven years of age). The child's thoughts become organized, with understanding of time, space, and logic, but he can apply them only to concrete situations.

Concurrent schedules – Partial reinforcement schedules in which two or more responses are made to satisfy two or more schedules at the same time.

Concurrent validity – A measure of how well a test measures what it was designed to measure by comparing the test results of the experimental group with test results of those people who are already in the field for which the test was designed.

Condensation – A dream process that disguises material by having one aspect of a dream, such as a person, actually represent or be a composite of several things in real life.

Conditional rule – In concept formation, if an item has one specified property, then it must also have another property in order to be an instance of the concept.

Conditioned emotional responses – Emotional reactions which result from being classically conditioned to stimuli in the environment.

Conditioned inhibition – The suppression of a conditioned response by pairing it with a neutral stimulus without any reinforcement so that the neutral stimulus becomes a signal for no reinforcement and the conditioned response is suppressed.

Conditioned reflex – A learned response elicited by a conditioned stimulus. Also called conditioned response.

Conditioned reflex therapy – The term applied to the system of psychotherapy developed by Andrew Salter in which clients learn to be assertive to overcome inhibitions. The six basic techniques used are feeling-talk, facial talk, contradiction and attack, using "1," express agreement and improvisation.

Conditioned reinforcer – Something that, through association with the primary reinforcer, becomes a reinforcer itself.

Conditioned response (CR) – In classical conditioning, the response elicited by the conditioned stimulus. It usually resembles its corresponding unconditioned response.

Conditioned stimulus (CS) – An originally neutral stimulus that, through repeated pairings with an unconditioned stimulus becomes effective in eliciting the conditioned response.

Conditioning – The process of evoking a specific response other than one that would have been produced naturally by presenting a particular stimulus.

Conditioning, classical – (See Classical conditioning.)

Conditioning, instrumental – (See Operant conditioning.)

Conduct disorder – A disorder of childhood or adolescence involving a pattern of violating age-appropriate social norms or the basic rights of others through aggressions, theft, deceitfulness, and violating rules.

Conduction —1. Pertaining to the transmission of sound waves. 2. The transmission of a nervous impulse from one area in the nervous system to another.

Cones – The cone shaped photoreceptor cells located in the retina particularly the fovea, which are responsible for color and high acuity vision.

Confabulation – The act of filling in memory gaps with statements that make sense but that are untrue. The person believes his statements to be true.

Confederates – In research, collaborators of the experimenter who pose as subjects. Their true identity is unknown to the other subjects.

Confidence interval – A statistic which specifies at some known probability level, the range within which the population mean must lie given a known sample measure.

Conflict – A term referring specifically to behavioral indecision as a result of the positive or negative qualities of goal situations. Conflicts may be approach-approach involving equal temptation to strive for two incompatible goals; avoidance-avoidance, involving the struggle to avoid unpleasant consequences although doing so will incur other unpleasant consequences; or approach-avoidance, in which a single behavior has both pleasant and unpleasant consequences.

Conflict frustration – Frustration of a motive because it is in conflict with some other motive.

Confluence – 1. In perception, the fusing of perceptual elements. 2. The flowing together of motives or responses. 3. As developed by Adler, the merging of several instincts into one.

Conformity – The tendency to change or develop attitudes and behavior in accordance with peer group pressure; to acquiesce to group norms.

Confounding – Simultaneous variation of a second variable with an independent variable of interest so that any effect on the dependent variable cannot be attributed with certainty to the independent variable; inherent in correlational research.

Confusion error – A classification error in which an instance of one category is thought to be an instance of another; it is often assumed that these errors are not random but depend on the degree to which the two categories have similar characteristics.

Congenital – A characteristic acquired during development in the uterus and not through heredity; existing at or dating from the time of birth.

Congruence (Rogers) – Term meaning that what is experienced inside and what is expressed outwardly are consistent.

Conjunctive concepts – A concept which is defined by several attributes, usually all of which must be present.

Conjunctive rule – In concept formation, the rule that all examples of a concept must have one or more attributes in common.

Connectionism – The doctrine that the activity of the central nervous system is to connect stimuli and responses. Intelligence may also be viewed as a neural bond, dependent upon the number and availability of connections.

Connector cells – Cells in the brain and spinal cord that transmit nerve impulses from the afferent cells to the efferent cells.

Connotation – That aspect of the meaning of a word which refers to its associations and emotional implications.

Conscience – 1. The sense of right and wrong in conduct; that is, an individual's system of moral values. 2. As developed by Freud, the part of the superego that contains the moral values, attitudes, and rules which one acquires from parents. The conscience is internalized to govern behavior.

Conscious – 1. Awareness. 2. That which is attainable through introspection. 3. In Freudian theory, the images, thoughts, and ideas of which one is aware. The portion of the mind which is aware of the immediate environment.

Consciousness – The sum total of a person's mental experiences; one's complete awareness.

Consensual validation (Sullivan) – The process whereby a person reaches a more realistic point of view by comparing his thoughts and feelings with those of his associates. The corrective experience for an individual's parataxic distortions.

Conservation – 1. Piaget's term implying that certain quantitative attributes of objects remain unchanged unless something is added to or taken away from them. Such characteristics of objects as mass, number, area, volume, and so on, are capable of being conserved. For example, at a certain level of development one realizes that the amount of water is not changed by pouring it into glasses of different shapes. 2. Concerning memory or retention.

Conservative focusing – A systematic approach to solving conceptual problems in which the subject uses a positive instance of the concept as focus and then compares it with other single instances, each differing in one and only one dimension from his or her focus. By this method, irrelevant dimensions are eliminated (one at a time) until only the relevant dimension remains.

Consistency principle – The underlying view of cognitive dissonance and balance theories. The basic premise is that people strive to be consistent in their behavior. In this connection, attitudes held by a particular individual are mutually supportive and do not conflict with each other. Also, it is a tendency to segregate liked objects from disliked objects and to structure thoughts in simple black-and-white terms.

Consolidation theory – The postulate that short-term memories are converted into long-term memories. Consists of two stages – reverberating circuits and structural changes. In order for any experience to be permanently stored, it must be strengthened because of retroactive inhibition and retrograde amnesia.

Consonance – 1. Harmonious tone combinations. 2. In cognitive dissonance theory, when one idea or belief implies another in some psychological sense.

Conspecific recognition – Recognizing members of one's own species; discrimination of members of one's own species from members of other species.

Constancy – The tendency to perceive the properties of objects as unchanging in spite of changes in the retinal image; accomplished by integration of information from several sensory mechanisms.

Constancy hypothesis – As developed by the structuralists and behaviorists, the view that there is a one-to-one correspondence between stimulus and response, regardless of surrounding conditions.

Constancy of internal environment – As developed by Cannon, the tendency for metabolic processes (such as, levels of heat, blood sugar, and blood pressure) to remain constant.

Constant error – A continuous one-directional error, such as always underestimating.

Constellation – 1. In psychoanalysis, a group of emotionally charged ideas. 2. Any complex.

Constitutional factors of aggression – Relatively enduring dispositions and physiological traits, whose foundations are organic or hereditary, that are related to aggressive behavior; distinguished from environmental and learning factors.

Constriction – 1. In perception, a decrease in the diameter of the pupil of the eye. 2. Being overly determined by external factors. 3. In testing, poor form responses (F responses) on the Rorschach Test. 4. Any contraction or shrinking.

Construct – 1. A concept, trait, or dimension which represents relationships between variables in the formulation of theories. Empirical constructs are based on observed facts or data and represent measurable variables. Hypothetical constructs are verified indirectly. These constructs are inferred to have real existence. 2. A scientific model. 3. A piece of apparatus.

Construct validity – The extent to which a particular item in a test is a true measure of some abstract trait or concept that can only be verified indirectly.

Contact analog display – An integrated visual display that is arranged so that the information one receives is analogous to what one would get from direct visual contact.

Contact comfort – The satisfaction in many young organisms from having something warm and soft to cling to.

Contact desensitization – A technique of behavior therapy which involves physical contact during systematic desensitization.

Content – 1. As developed by Guilford, the raw material of intellectual activity such as thoughts and feelings. 2. As developed by Piaget, the term for uninterpreted, behavioral data relating to one's behavior. 3. The material in a test, the material in consciousness, or the material expressed by a patient in an analytic session.

Content validity – The extent to which a particular instrument samples the behavior it is supposed to measure or predict.

Context – 1. Conditions which surround a mental process and thus alter its meaning. 2. The related verbal or perceptual material which clarifies the meaning of a word, phrase, or statement.

Contextual learning – The derivation and assimilation of meaning for a new item from the surrounding context.

Contextual stimuli – In adaptation level theory of motivation. The background simulation against which the individual makes his judgments.

Contingency – 1. In instrumental conditioning, a situation in which reinforcement is not delivered unless certain responses are made. 2. An expression which indicates a meaningful relationship between two variables.

Continuation – The perceptual tendency to see objects in the form of some continuous pattern, e.g., a line or curve.

Continuity – A law of perceptual organization that states that incomplete contours tend to become closed.

Continuity theory – The theory that learning occurs by incremental increases in the strength of S-R bonds.

Continuous culture – A culture that does not clearly demarcate passage from one period of life to another. Contemporary Western societies are usually continuous.

Continuous reinforcement – A schedule of reinforcement in which every correct response is followed by reinforcement.

Contour – In perception, the boundary of a perceptual figure.

Contrast – 1. The perceptual effect of a specific visual area, caused by the difference between the area and its surroundings. 2. The stressing of a difference between two sensations by the immediate successive juxtaposition of two stimuli. 3. The intensified perception of differences between any stimuli by bringing them into juxtaposition.

Control – An experimental condition identical to other conditions in the experiment, but lacking the independent variable, (the experimental treatment), thus allowing results in the other conditions to be attributed solely to the independent variable.

Control group – The group of subjects in an experiment which is statistically equivalent in all respects to the experimental group, except that it does not receive the treatment of the independent variable (the experimental treatment). Thus the control group can be used as a comparison to the experimental group to ascertain whether subjects were affected by the experimental procedure.

Control variable – A potential independent variable that is held constant in an experiment.

Convergent hierarchy – According to mediational theory, a hierarchy of different external stimuli, all of which can elicit the same response. Seen as the basis for forming concepts.

Convergent thinking – As termed by Guilford, thinking which results in a unique correct solution to a problem.

Converging operations – A set of related lines of investigation that all support a common conclusion.

Conversion reaction – A neurotic reaction which reduces anxiety by inactivation of part of the body; the psychological problem is converted into a physical one which prevents anxiety-provoking behavior. The underlying psychological conflict is transformed into a sensory or motor symptom, such as blindness or paralysis.

Converted score – A score expressed in some type of derived unit, such as an age equivalent, grade equivalent, percentile, or standard score.

Convulsion – An involuntary seizure involving rapid spasmodic contraction of the voluntary muscles.

Cooperation – Working with or assisting someone else in an attempt to reach a mutual satisfying goal.

Cornea – The transparent outer coating of the eye that allows light to pass through to the interior.

Corneal-reflection technique – A technique for studying eye movement which involves photographing light reflected from the cornea.

Corpus callosum – The structure consisting of a large group of nerve fibers that connect the left and right hemispheres of the cerebrum, allowing the hemispheres to communicate with each other.

Correlation – A statistical term that describes the relationship between two variables in such a way that change in one is associated with change in the other positive–in the same direction, negative–in the opposite direction.

Correlation coefficient – A statistical index expressing the degree of relationship between two variables. The range of possible values is from +1.00 to –1.00. The numerical size of the correlation is an expression of the strength of the relationship. The sign of the correlation coefficient is an indication of the direction of the relationship. A positive correlation indicates that a change in one variable is associated with a change in the other variable in the same direction. A negative correlation indicates an inverse relationship between the two variables. A correlation of .00 represents no relationship between the variables.

Correlational approach – Research method used to discover the degree of relationship between two or more variables by analyzing how well one variable helps predict the value of another. Testing, interviewing, surveying are often combined under the general heading of correlational approach.

Cortex – The outer layer of any organ.

Cortical lobes – The four somewhat arbitrarily designated divisions of the cortex: frontal parietal, occipital, and temporal.

Corticosteroid – A group of chemicals produced by the metabolism of cortisone and other chemical secretions of the adrenal cortex. These chemicals have been shown to increase during acquisition of a conditioned emotional response. Also known as adrenal steroids.

Cortisone – A hormone secreted by the adrenal cortex in response to stress, serving to reduce inflammation.

Cotwin control method – The use of twins in an experiment. One twin serves in the control condition and the other twin serves in the experimental condition.

Counseling psychology – The branch of psychology dealing with personality, marital and vocational problems.

Counterbalancing – An experimental procedure used to eliminate the effect of irrelevant variables, confounding, by systematically varying the order of conditions in an experiment. For example, the effect of practice on variable X may be eliminated by presenting X at the beginning, middle, and end of a series.

Counterconditioning – The weakening or elimination of a conditioned response by the learning of a new response that is incompatible with, and stronger than, the one to be extinguished. It is used in therapy to replace unacceptable responses with acceptable ones.

Countermovement – An attempt to resist social change.

Cranial nerves – The twelve pairs of nerves which have their origin or termination within the ventral surface of the brain.

Creativity – A process of thought resulting in

new and original ideas that are useful solutions to problems.

Crespi effect – A disproportionate increase or decrease in performance of a learned response as compared to the increase or decrease of the reinforcement.

Cretinism – A physiologically caused form of mental retardation and other abnormalities resulting from a prenatal thyroid insufficiency.

Crisis – 1. A point in a person's life which has great psychological significance for the individual. 2. A turning point characterized by a marked improvement or a marked deterioration.

Crisis intervention – A major feature of the primary prevention approach to mental health, whereby someone is always on call to help people handle a crisis in effective ways.

Criterion – 1. An absolute standard of performance used to evaluate a subject's performance on a test. 2. An outside measure against which a test can be validated.

Criterion of mastery in learning – The level of performance at which practice is terminated.

Critical period – As developed by Binet, the period early in life during which imprinting is possible. Any limited period in development in which the organism is especially susceptible to a given developmental process.

Cross-cultural studies – The observance of the effect of the same environmental conditions on behavior in different cultures.

Cross-sectional research – A research strategy that tests at a given period of time a sample of persons or variables that are representative on several dimensions of the population as a whole. Age and ability level are two frequently used variables.

Cross-validation – A technique for determining the validity of a procedure by testing it for a second time on another sample after its validity has been demonstrated on a first sample. Cross-validation is important when items or test weights have been chosen from a large number of possible alternatives, and when the original sample was small.

Crossing-over – A process in which genes that were previously linked become unlinked or linked with a different set of genes due to the detachment of a chromosome part and possible reattachment to a new chromosome during cell division.

Crossover interaction – When the effect of one independent variable on a dependent variable reverses at different levels of a second independent variable.

Crystallized intelligence – Intelligence used in the application of already-learned materials which is usually considered to be rigid or unchanging.

Cue – In motivational theory, any distinctive property of a stimulus that can serve to determine the direction or nature of a response; an obscure secondary stimulus.

Cue-dependent forgetting – Inability to remember learned information due to retrieval failure. Cues present during learning are not present during recall.

Cultural relativity – The belief that the behavior and the personality of an individual can only be understood and evaluated within the context of the culture in which he or she originated.

Culturally biased – An adjective expressing the relative dependence of a concept or a test on cultural influence.

Culture – The total set of values, expectations, attitudes, beliefs, and customs shared by the members of one group which characterize them as a group and distinguish them from other groups.

Culture-fair tests – Tests that try to eliminate bias by using items that should be equally well-known to all subjects taking the test, regardless of their cultural or subcultural background.

Culture-free test – A test for which the solutions do not depend on any specific culture. All items which depend upon cultural factors have been eliminated.

Cumulative frequency – A sum of all the cases falling below a specified score, achieved when each new case up to a specified criterion is added to the preceding total. The cumulative percent is the accumulated percent of cases falling below a specified score.

Cumulative record – A continuous and complete tally or record of appropriate or satisfactory instrumental responses made in a given time period.

Cumulative recorder – An instrument for recording and displaying the complete sequence of responses over time.

Curiosity – The motivation to seek out and respond to novel stimuli, sometimes regarded as one of the primary drives.

Curve of forgetting – The graph plotting the percentage of learned materials retained as a function of time since the absolute amount forgotten for each subsequent time interval decreases over time, which means most loss of retention occurs soon after acquisition.

Cutaneous senses – The senses whose receptors are located in the skin. These are usually classified as cold, hot, pain, and pressure.

Cybernetics – The science of communication and control theory that is especially concerned with the comparative study of automatic control systems.

Cycle of motivation – A proposal explaining many motive situations as a sequence of need, instrumental response, goal, and relief; the cycle often repeats itself.

Cytoplasm – The protoplasmic material surrounding the nucleus of a cell, exclusive of the material in the nucleus.

d' – A statistic in signal detection theory related to the sensitivity of the observer.

d reaction test – A reaction time test in which a subject must not make a response until he has identified which of two stimuli has been presented. For example, a subject is asked to push a lever when the green light appears and not when the red light appears.

Dark adaptation – A process of increasing sensitivity to light whereby the retina becomes over a million times more sensitive resulting from the reduction or complete absence of light energy reaching the eye, attributable to a resynthesis of a rod stimulating substance which is broken down under bright light. The DA curve has two segments, one for rod and one for cone vision.

Data – A collection of statistics, facts, or information obtained by observation, experimentation, or computation on a dependent variable.

Day-residues – Apparently trivial but unconsciously important events of the day that play a part in dream content.

Death instinct (thanatos) – In psychoanalytic theory the instinct for destruction and death and when fused with pleasure, inward and outward directed drives for pain. Like the life instinct, Eros, it originates from the libido, which is the source of all energy in the individual.

Decay theory of STM – A view that holds that without rehearsal or re-presentation, the traces of an experience fade with time until the experience is forgotten completely.

Decentration – Jean Piaget's term for the ability to shift the center of one's attention.

Decerebrate – An animal whose cerebral cortex has been removed.

Decibel (db) – A logarithmic unit for measuring physical sound intensity.

Decile – In a ranked distribution, a division containing one-tenth of the cases. The first decile is the score value below which one tenth of the cases fall. The fifth decile is the same as the median, or the 50th percentile.

Deduction – The logical process of reasoning from the general to the particular.

Deep structure – The meaning transmitted by words used in a language.

Defense mechanism – As termed by Freud, the unconscious process by which an individual protects himself from anxiety. Defense mechanisms discussed by Freud include repression, rationalization, reaction formation, projection, isolation, introjection, regression, and thought dissociation. These mechanisms are often termed ego defenses.

Deferred imitation – As espoused by Piaget, the ability of a child to imitate behaviors long after the child has seen them. This occurs in the pre-operational stage after representation has been attained.

Degrees of freedom (df) – The number of values free to vary if the total number of values and their sum are fixed.

Deindividuation – Relative anonymity of individual characteristics and identifications in certain social situations such as mobs and crowds.

Deiter's cells – Elongated cells found in the outer portion of the organ of Corti which anchor the hair cells.

Déjà vu – An illusion of familiarity in a strange place or experience. For example, some features in a new city may be similar to those features which have already been experienced. From the French "already seen."

Delay of reinforcement – A period of time between the response and reinforcement in a contingency situation.

Delayed conditioning – In classical conditioning a trial in which the onset of the conditioned stimulus precedes the unconditioned stimulus, with the conditioned stimulus staying on at least until the unconditioned stimulus has occurred.

Delayed instinct – An instinct which does not manifest itself immediately after birth.

Delinquency – Antisocial acts committed by persons who are legal minors, usually in a repetitive fashion.

Delta waves – A wave of 1–3 Hz of high voltage found in the EEG which is characteristic of low arousal and deep sleep.

Delusion – A belief or thought that a person maintains as true despite irrefutable evidence that it is false, e.g., believing that one is being persecuted; this is characteristic of psychotic reactions.

Delusions of grandeur – The false belief that one is a great or powerful person.

Demand characteristics – Those cues available to subjects in an experiment that may enable them to determine the purpose of the experiment, or what is expected by the experimenter.

Dementia – The deterioration of intellectual and emotional processes; usually associated with senility and psychoses.

Demographic – Pertaining to characteristics of populations; used loosely to refer to such characteristics as sex, age, social class, ethnic background, and so on.

Dendrite – A neural fiber that transmits electrical impulses toward the cell body of a neuron.

Denial – A defense mechanism in which there is minimization of the importance of a situation or event or of unacceptable impulses or feelings.

Denotation – That aspect of the meaning of a word which refers to what the word indicates.

Denotative meaning – That aspect of meaning that has reference to the describable characteristics of an object.

Deoxyribonucleic acid (DNA) – An extremely complex molecule, assumed to be the basis of all life, composed of phosphates, bases, and sugars.

Dependence – 1. A relationship of causality between two occurrences such that a change in one produces a change in the other. 2. A reliance on others for ideas, emotions, and opinions.

Dependent influence – A change in a person's attitudes or behaviors that occurs because of the social characteristics of a model or group.

Dependent variable – That factor which the experimenter wants to measure, which may be affected by the independent variable.

Depersonalization – 1. In psychopathology, a condition in which one experiences a loss of personal identity. 2. In existentialism, the feeling attributed to man as being insignificant in a vast world.

Depolarization – The process by which the electrical charge of a neuron reverses and becomes positive during the passage of an action potential.

Depression – A state of extreme sadness and dejection. As a psychological disorder it is accompanied by lowered sensitivity to certain stimuli, reduction of physical and mental activity, and difficulty in thinking.

Depressive reactions – A state in which the person responds to life's disappointments with excessive emotionality and withdrawal, usually precipitated by an event such as the loss of a loved one.

Deprivation – The loss or removal of something desired or loved. In developmental psychology, a significant reduction of stimulation or opportunity.

Depth-oriented therapy – Any form of psychotherapy which professes to treat the unconscious sources of an individual's problems. The Freudian and Jungian systems of psychoanalysis exemplify depth psychology.

Depth perception – The ability to perceive three dimensionality and the awareness of distance between an observer and an object.

Derived lists – Learning materials arranged so that subsequent lists are systematically related to original lists by taking every other item in order, every third item, every fourth item, etc.

Descartes, René – Seventeenth-century French philosopher and mathematician. He is important in the history of psychology for his views on the interaction of mind and body.

Descriptive research – Research involving the collection and objective reporting of data about a particular characteristic of the subjects under study without any attempt at identifying causal relationships. Techniques include introspection, observation, surveys and clinical investigation.

Descriptive statistics – Measures or techniques that allow a summary portrayal of collected data including measurements of central tendency, variability, and correlation.

Desensitization – A form of behavior therapy in which the individual is reconditioned so that previously aversive stimuli no longer elicit anxiety responses.

Desurgency – As developed by R. B. Cattell, a factor analysis personality trait which is characterized by anxiety, agitation and isolation.

Detached affect – An idea separated from its emotional counterpart.

Detachment – 1. According to Horney, a neurotic characteristic involving a lack of feeling for others and a tendency to view one's problems in an objective fashion without any emotional attachment. 2. The development of independent behavior which often occurs when an adult of high attachment status is close by.

Detection theory – A theory which accurately assesses the subject's sensory capacities. It is a psychophysical method of studying the process of motivation, stimulus probability, and extraneous stimuli on the decision regarding the presence or absence of a given stimulus or a change in stimulus value. It employs such factors as hits, misses, correct rejections, and false alarms. Also known as: signal detectability theory, theory of signal detection and decision theory.

Deterioration index – As measured by the Wechsler-Bellevue tests, an approximation of the amount of loss of mental abilities due to age. The mental abilities tested are digit span, digit symbol, block design, and similarities.

Determinism – In general, the philosophical doctrine that for every effect there is a cause. As applied to psychology, the view that all behavior is related to an antecedent event, and all of man's motivation is subject to forces over which he has no volitional control.

Detour problem – A problem solving situation

in which one has to learn to take a roundabout route to a goal instead of trying to approach it directly.

Deuteranope – A color-vision defective individual who sees shades of gray instead of red and green, possibly because of insensitivity to blue-green light.

Development – The total progressive and continuous change whereby an individual adapts to his environment via the processes of growth, maturation, and learning; qualitative growth.

Developmental age – A measure of the degree of a person's physiological or cognitive maturity. This includes such factors as dental maturity and skeletal maturity, and the ability to think or behave in a particular manner, contrasted with chronological age.

Developmental psychology – The area within psychology that is concerned with discovering the principles of behavioral change in the individual from conception to death. All the topics in psychology such as personality, learning, and cognition as they relate to the dimensions of growth and maturation. In its broadest sense, developmental psychology includes the periods of infancy, childhood, adolescence, and adulthood.

Developmental scale – Reports of average or typical behavior for a particular age group based upon data collected from large groups of individuals for the purpose of measuring the level of development a child has attained.

Deviance – Departure from what is considered to be correct, normal and proper. In statistics, the departure from the norm or mean.

Deviant case analysis – Investigation of similar cases that differ in outcome in an attempt to specify the reasons for the different outcomes.

Deviation – 1. In statistics, the difference between a score and a reference point such as the mean or median. If the mean is 40 and a score is 25, the deviation of that score from the mean is -15. 2. A departure from what is considered normal, correct, or proper. 3. In optics, the bending of light rays from a straight line.

Deviation IQ – A standard score on an intelligence test in which the mean is set at 100 and the standard deviation at 15 or 16. It expresses the extent to which the individual deviates from the average score obtained by his peers. The meaning of the deviation IQ is similar to that of the conventional IQ, namely, the value obtained on the Stanford-Binet.

Dewey, John – Dewey was one of the founders of the functionalistic movement in psychology and education. He wrote one of the first textbooks in the field.

Diagnosis – The process of determining the nature of an abnormality or disease using information gained from tests, interviews, and other observations.

Diagnostic test – A test that is utilized to determine the nature and source of an individual's difficulties or skills, in contrast with survey tests, which give a general appraisal of an area of achievement.

Diastolic blood pressure – The lowest pressure recorded from an individual during a cardiac cycle which is the period of ventricular dilation during which the ventricle fills with blood (contrasted with systolic blood pressure).

Diathesis – Genetic predisposition to a particular psychotic disorder or disease.

Diathesis-stress theory – Theory of what causes schizophrenia; states that schizophrenia develops when there is a genetic predisposition (diathesis) present and there are environmental factors (stress) that trigger the disorder.

Dichotic listening – A test of attention in which two separate messages are delivered simultaneously, one to each ear.

Dichromat – A color-defective individual whose full range of color experience can be produced by the mixture of two (rather than the normal three) primary colors. Most common is red-green blindness; blue-yellow blindness is rarer.

Difference threshold (or **just-noticeable difference**) – Given an initial level of stimulation, the DL is the minimally effective stimulus difference which is correctly reported by the subject as being different. By convention a 75 per cent judgment rate has been adopted.

Difference tone – A sound heard when two tones are sounded simultaneously. The pitch of the difference tone is the difference in frequency between the two original sounds.

Differential extinction – The selective gradual diminishing of one response while another is being maintained.

Differential psychology – The field of psychology which concerns itself with individual differences in reference to their consequences, causation, and magnitude among groups.

Differentiation – 1. In development, the process of cells developing into specialized tissues. 2. The change in a psychological field from homogeneity to heterogeneity. 3. In conditioning, the process by which an organism is trained to respond to only certain stimuli, that is, to discriminate between stimuli. 4. In mathematical psychology, the process of obtaining a differential.

Difficulty index – A numerical value used to express the difficulty of a test item. In the United States, the difficulty index, also called the facility index, is usually the percent getting the item correct.

Diffraction – The bending of light waves as they pass over the edge of an object.

Digit-span test – A test of short term recall in which the subject repeats a random series of digits following a single presentation.

Digital computer – A computer that operates on two-valued signals, typically +1 and 0, as contrasted with an analog computer.

Dilation – An increase in the diameter of the pupil of the eye.

Dimming effect – The intensification of an afterimage by reducing the intensity of the field upon which it is projected.

Dioptric power – The ability of a lens to bend, or refract, light.

Dipsomania – A continuous craving for alcohol.

Direct aggression – An attack or aggressive behavior which is projected upon the source of frustration.

Direct analysis – The term applied to the system of psychotherapy developed by John Rosen. Rosen contends that the therapist must identify with the unhappy patient.

Direct replication – Repeating an experiment as closely as possible to determine whether or not the same results will be obtained.

Directed thinking – Thinking that is governed by a goal or thinking that occurs for a purpose, such as problem solving.

Directional hypothesis – A prediction that a specific change in the conditions of an experiment will result in a particular change in the outcome of the experiment.

Directive counseling – The treatment of mental illness in which the patient is given positive advice and direct suggestions as to what activities and attitudes he should adopt. Also the counselor suggests the area of personality to be explored.

Directive psychotherapy – As developed by Frederick Thorne, a system of therapy in which the therapist assumes an active role for the purpose of breaking down resistance.

Discontinuous culture – A culture with clear demarcations between various states or stages. For example, discontinuous cultures often mark the passage from childhood to adulthood by elaborate ritual and ceremony.

Discriminated operant – An instrumentally learned response that is reinforced only if made in the presence of a particular stimulus.

Discrimination – 1. The ability to recognize the distinctive features of similar but nonidentical things. 2. The process of distinguishing differences between stimuli. 3. In learning, differentiation, the ability to withhold a behavioral response except in the presence of a specific stimulus.

Discrimination index – A graphic or numerical expression of the extent to which a test or test item differentiates between subjects having or not having the trait being tested.

Discrimination learning – Learning to distinguish between two or more different stimuli, or between the presence and absence of a stimulus. In general, any learning in which the task is to make choices between alternatives.

Discriminative stimulus (S_D) – A signal presented only when reinforcement is present or is to follow, thereby controlling the occurrence of the response.

Disinhibition – 1. The temporary restoration of an extinguished response that is manifested when the conditioned stimulus is presented in a novel way. 2. A loss of self-control upon overindulgence in alcohol or while under the influence of drugs. 3. In modeling, observing a response and learning that the response is appropriate to a given situation.

Disinhibition of aggression – A reduction in the self-control or inhibition of aggressive behaviors in response to environmental stimulation or aggression eliciting events.

Disjunctive concept – A complex concept based upon the simultaneous consideration of two or more stimulus properties, but in which the presence of any one stimulus property is adequate to qualify the stimulus as an instance of the concept.

Disjunctive rule – In concept formation, a rule which specifies that any object having a particular attribute is an example of a given concept.

Disowning – The process developed by Carl Rogers, whereby an individual avoids being aware of experiences and needs which have not been symbolized and which are inconsistent with the self. Disowning is similar to repression and dissociation in the Freudian and Sullivanian theories, respectively.

Dispersion – A measure that shows the scatter of a group of scores in a distribution. The common measures of dispersion are the range, average deviation, standard deviation, variance, and the semi-interquartile range.

Displaced aggression – Aggressive behavior oriented away from the source of frustration to other "safer" targets.

Displacement – The process or result of shifting an idea, activity, or emotional attachment from its proper object to another object. It may be a rechanneling of instinctual energy from an unacceptable object to one that is of neutral value to society (Freudian defense mechanism). It is also a dream process by which material is disguised. It involves changing the affective emphasis of something in a dream so that if it is very important in real life, it is seemingly unimportant in the dream or vice versa.

Displacement activity – In ethology, seemingly irrelevant behavior made in the presence of two simultaneous but incompatible releaser stimuli; vacuum activity.

Displacement theory – The view that forgetting from short-term memory is due to a distortion of items from a temporary store by the occurrence of new items.

Display design – The study of effective presentation of information in a man-machine system.

Dissociation – 1. A defense mechanism in which there is a separation of activities and psychological processes which may then function independently. An extreme form would be the multiple personality. It is also present in amnesia, fugue, and schizophrenia. 2. In Sullivanian theory the process by which one excludes from awareness certain aspects of his experience which lead to acute anxiety. It is similar to Freudian repression and Rogerian disowning.

Dissociative disorders – A group of disorders involving the abandonment of the sense of self-consistency characteristic of normal functioning. Dissociative behavior is evident in sleepwalking (somnambulism), amnesia, fugue, and multiple-personality (dissociative identity disorder).

Dissonance – 1. In cognitive dissonance theory, when one idea or belief a person holds contradicts another cognition he or she also holds. 2. The unpleasant effect produced by two notes which are sounded simultaneously and do not blend into a mellifluous sound.

Distal effect – A response which changes the environment in some way.

Distal receptors – Sense receptors that allow man to apprehend sensation that emanates from a distance. Vision and hearing are the two most important distal receptors, or distance senses.

Distal stimulus – A stimulus as it emanates from environmental objects such as a doorbell.

Distal variable – A variable which originated as a stimulus in the environment which is mediated via a proximal stimulus (a stimulus acting on our sense organs).

Distinctiveness – The tendency of some items to "stand out" from the context in which they occur. Distinctiveness is one factor determining how well material can be learned.

Distorting lenses – Lenses utilized to present an illusory set of stimuli to the retina by the bending of an image achieved by changing orientation, line formation, or color.

Distortion – 1. In psychoanalysis, the cognitive alteration or disguising of unacceptable impulses so that they can escape the dream censor. 2. In perception, the changing in orientation of a stimulus to the retina.

Distortion theory – A theory of forgetting that maintains information is not entirely forgotten but becomes distorted with the passage of time.

Distracting task – A task that is assigned to the subject of a memory experiment between the time of presentation of the material to be learned and the time of recall or recognition, thus interfering with the rehearsal and processing of that material into memory.

Distractor – A term sometimes used to designate the incorrect response options provided in a multiple-choice item.

Distributed learning – The spacing of learning trials into several time periods instead of one long learning session.

Distribution – An array of the instances of a variable arranged so that different classes of the variable are ordered in some manner and the frequency of each class is indicated.

Distributive analysis and synthesis – The phrase applied to the characteristic procedures of psychobiologic therapy. This view emphasizes the importance of obtaining a clear and full understanding of the patient's own views of his or her problems.

Disuse theory – The theory of forgetting that states that memory lapses are due to lack of use of what has been learned.

Divergent hierarchy – According to mediational theory, a hierarchy of responses all of which can be elicited by a single stimulus. Seen as the basis for problem solving in most situations.

Divergent thinking – Guilford's term for the type of thinking that produces several different solutions for a problem. Divergent thinking is assumed to be closely related to creativity, and the term is often used interchangeably with it.

Dizygotic – Developing from two different fertilized eggs.

Dizygotic (or fraternal) twins – Twins which develop from two separate eggs.

Dogmatism scale – A questionnaire designed to measure rigidity and inflexibility in thinking.

Dominance – A term used to refer to the fact that in many animal groups there is a "pecking order," usually related to strength. Animals high in the "pecking order" usually have first access to food and mates.

Dominant gene – The gene that takes precedence over other related genes in determining genetic traits. The presence of a dominant gene means that the characteristic which is controlled by that gene will be present in the individual.

Dominator module theory – In perception, the view that brightness vision is communicated through a special dominant receptor and that color vision is mediated by receptors which control the response of the dominant receptor.

Double approach-avoidance conflicts – A conflict in which there are two goals, with each goal having an attraction and a repulsion.

Double-bind theory – In the etiology of schizophrenia, the hypothesis that traces the origins of schizophrenia to situations in which a parent gives conflicting messages to an offspring. Thus, the child is "damned if he does and damned if he doesn't."

Double blind – An experimental technique in which neither the experimenter nor the subject knows who is in the experimental and control groups. The double blind technique is used to control for demand characteristics and other extraneous variables.

Down's syndrome – A congenital form of mental retardation which is caused by the failure of the 21st pair of chromosomes to separate properly when an egg or sperm is formed. Characteristics of the disease are a limited intelligence, a flat face, a skin fold at the corner of the eyes, a broad nose, and a protruding tongue.

Dream – An experience that occurs during the sleeping state, drugged state, or hypnotic state that involves a more or less coherent awareness of imagery, scenes and events.

Dream analysis – The process, originally used by Freud, of deciphering the meaning of a dream. Based on the idea that dreams are symbolic representations of our impulses and conflicts, and that by understanding the symbols, we can learn about ourselves.

Dream processes – Various methods used to disguise material so that when it is presented in a dream, it is not too emotionally threatening.

Drive – A goal-directed tendency of an organism based on a change in organic processes; any strong stimulus that impels an organism to action. For example, the hunger drive results from the need for food.

Dualism – 1. A philosophical position, as developed by Plato, which holds that mind and matter are two fundamentally different substances. 2. In psychology, the idea that the mind and the body are separate entities.

Ductless glands Endocrine glands that release their hormones directly into the bloodstream.

Dura (dura mater) – The outer protective tissue layer of the central nervous system.

Dyad – Two persons interacting with each other.

Dynamic culturalists – The term applied to the psychoanalytic theories and practices of those who deviate from the teachings of Freud by placing less emphasis on the instinctive and more emphasis on the changing social sources of human behavior.

Dynamic lattice – As developed by R. B. Cattell, a graphic representation of the interrelations between goal seeking and motives.

Dynamic model – Model of psychopathology in which abnormal behavior reflects a "dynamic" battle or conflict between parts or aspects of a person's personality rather than any physical or organic deficiencies.

Dynamism – A relatively enduring and consistent mode of behavior used in interpersonal relations, drive satisfaction, and alleviation from psychological stress.

Dynamometer – An instrument utilized for measuring the strength of muscular response, such as a hand-grip.

Dyscontrol – A personality dimension, scored on the Emotions Profile Index, which measures tendencies to act impulsively.

Dyslexia – An inability to read which is usually characterized by a specific reading impairment, such as reversing similar letters or numbers.

Dyssocial character – Individual who has no personality disorganization, but rather has values that conflict with the usual mores of the society; cultural deviant.

Eardrum (tympanic membrane) – The beginning of the middle ear separating the outer ear and auditory canal. The sound reaching the eardrum sets in motion the three bones of the middle ear.

Early childhood – The second period of postnatal development; from approximately age two to age six.

Early training project – A preschool project developed by Gray and Klaus emphasizing enriched and distinctive stimulation for children from impoverished backgrounds.

Ebbinghaus, Hermann – A pioneer psychologist in the field of learning. He devised the nonsense syllable and the completion test.

Ebbinghaus curve of retention – As developed by Ebbinghaus, a curve which displays the retention of nonsense material.

Echoic memory – Information stored briefly as an auditory image of a stimulus.

Echolalia – A perfunctory repetition of words or phrases by mental patients.

Echopraxia – An automatic imitation of movements by another. This reaction is sometimes found in catatonics.

Eclectic – A psychologist who uses the theories and techniques of several approaches or models, rather than specializing in one.

Eclecticism – In general, the selection and organization of a variety of approaches from many sources. In psychotherapy, an approach which uses various methods depending upon the patient and other circumstances.

Ecological – Pertaining to the study of biological forms, both among species and between species and their environment. According to Lewin, pertaining to those aspects of an individual's environment which are important parts of his or her life space.

Ectomorph – One of Sheldon's somatotyping classifications; ectomorphs are frail and are inclined to a long, stringy, and skinny body. They are associated with cerebrotonia; that is, they are assumed to be restrained in movement, concerned with privacy, sensitive, and socially inhibited.

Edging – In reference to the Rorschach test, a tendency of an individual to turn the cards edgewise.

Educable mentally retarded – (EMR, IQ score 52-70) This group of individuals is considered capable of being educated. The intellectual level as adults is comparable to that of the average 8- to 11-year old child. Socially, EMRs approximate the adolescent, however, they lack imagination, inventiveness, and judgment. Many, with proper guidance, can function in society and support themselves. Also called mildly retarded.

Educational psychology – A science that is concerned primarily with the application of psychological knowledge to problems of education.

Educational quotient – The ratio of educational age to chronological age, multiplied by a factor of 100.

$$EQ = \frac{EA}{CA} \times 100$$

Edwards personal preference schedule (EPPS) – A test, employing a forced choice technique, which is designed to measure the needs proposed by Murray's theory of personality.

E – F scale – A subscale of the Minnesota Multiphasic Inventory of Personality which measures authoritarianism and ethnocentrism.

Effect, law of – As developed by Thorndike, the view that, all other things being equal, an animal will learn those habits which lead to satisfaction and will not learn those habits which lead to annoyance.

Effectance motivation – The concept of competence (that is, effectively interacting with the environment).

Effective-habit strength – As developed by Hull, the strength of a learned reaction as a function of the number of reinforcements.

Effectors – Neural cells that are directly involved in glandular or muscular behavior.

Efferent nerves – Nerves that transmit impulses from the central nervous system to the end organs.

Effort syndrome – An anxiety neurosis characterized by palpitations and circulatory disorders.

Ego – In the structural model of psychoanalytic theory as proposed by Freud, the largely conscious mental institution which mediates between the demands of the id and demands of the environment. The ego is sometimes called the executive agency of the personality because it controls action, selects the features of the environment to which a person will respond, and decides how the person's needs can be satisfied.

Ego-analysis – A form of psychoanalysis which emphasizes the strengths and weaknesses of the ego. There is little concentration on deeply repressed processes, and it is shorter than conventional psychotherapy.

Ego ideal – In Freudian theory, the image of the self that a person consciously and unconsciously strives to become, and against which the person judges him- or herself.

Ego-involvement – Perception of a situation in terms of its potential effect on one's self-concept.

Egocentric speech – Piaget's term for speech that does not take into account the point of view of the listener. The three basic manifestations of egocentric speech are repetition, monologue, and collective monologue.

Egocentrism – Lack of differentiation between one's own point of view and that of others. As used by Piaget, it refers to the early adolescent's failure to differentiate between what he and others are thinking about. Young children's thinking is heavily egocentric.

Eidetic imagery Ability to retain an image of a picture or a scene with great clarity for a fairly long period of time. Sometimes called "photographic memory."

Eigenwelt – In existential psychology, the term which refers to man's relationship with himself.

Einstellung – A set; an attitude. Learned habits and preparatory outlooks toward a problem or direction which may be geared by preceding events which often are factors in thinking.

Electra complex – A Freudian stage occurring around the age of 4 or 5 years, during the phallic stage, when a girl's awareness of her genital area leads her to desire her father and to become jealous of her mother. This corresponds to the Oedipus complex in the male.

Electroconvulsive shock (ECS) – A form of psychotherapy used in the treatment of manic depressive psychosis and schizophrenia. An electrical current is passed through the brain resulting in convulsions and a short period of unconsciousness. Also called electroshock therapy.

Electrode – A small insulated wire that is surgically implanted into an area of the brain in order to artificially stimulate that area.

Electroencephalogram (EEG) – An instrument used to measure the electrical activity of the brain.

Electromagnetic spectrum – The variety of changes occurring in electrical and magnetic fields measured in terms of wavelength or frequency of vibrations.

Electromyogram (EMG) – A record of the electrical activity of a muscle usually recorded from the surface of the skin.

Elicited response – A response brought about by a stimulus. The expression is synonymous with respondent.

Eliciting effect – That type of imitative behavior in which the observer does not copy the model's responses but simply behaves in a related manner.

Ellipsis – The omission of ideas in free association.

Embryo – The second stage of prenatal development, beginning around the first week after conception and terminating at the end of the sixth week.

Embryonic period – The second of the three stages of gestation, from the third to the sixth week, at the end of which many body systems are in operation and the embryo begins to resemble the human form.

Emergency reaction – As developed by Walter Cannon, a term describing the reactions of fight or flight of an animal to dangerous situations. These reactions include increased heart rate, increased blood flow to the muscles, inhibition of digestion and expansion of the air sacs in the lungs.

Emitted response – A response not elicited by a known stimulus, but simply emitted by the organism. An emitted response is an operant.

Emmert's law – The principle that the perceived size of an image on the retina varies directly with the perceived distance of the object that presumably is projecting the image.

Emotion – A complex state of the organism, usually marked by a heightened state of arousal and the feelings accompanying that condition. Includes such human feelings as fear, rage, love, or desire.

Emotional meaning – Connotative meaning as opposed to denotative meaning. Meaning suggested by a term or symbol beyond its explicit or referential meaning.

Empathic understanding – Rogerian concept referring to the importance that a therapist actively understand the immediate feelings of his client.

Empathy – 1. The acceptance and understanding of the feelings of another person, but with sufficient detachment to avoid becoming directly involved in those feelings. 2. In Sullivanian theory, a kind of vague, biologically derived process whereby the infant senses the emotions of the mothering one through "contagion and communion."

Empirical – That which is based on the observation of events occurring in an experiment or in nature, as distinguished from that founded on opinion, beliefs, or reasoning.

Empirical key – A scoring key, typically for a measure of personality. The items to be weighted and the manner in which they are weighted are based on data showing the extent to which the items do, in fact, differentiate different groups of individuals.

Empirical study – An arrangement of conditions such that observations can be made systematically.

Empirical testing – Testing that relies on observation or experimentation for its answers.

Empiricism – 1. The philosophical view that experience is the source of knowledge. John Locke, George Berkeley, David Hume, David Hartley, and James Mill were empiricists. 2. The psychological view that behavior depends upon learning, experience, and objective observations. There is a strong emphasis on operational definitions and on relating theories to experimental findings.

Empty nest syndrome – Restlessness, anxiety, and depression in middle-aged parents whose children have left home; formerly said to be due to a woman's menopause and the loss of ability to bear children.

Enactive mode – The most primitive (or basic) way that humans convert immediate experiences into a mental model, as proposed by Bruner. It is based upon action or movement and is nonverbal.

Encephalitis – Any type of infection of the brain that causes inflammation.

Encounter group – A form of group psychotherapy focused on personal growth, more effective interpersonal communication, and open expression of feelings. The aim is a more direct encounter with one's own feelings toward others, and vice versa. Openness, honesty, emotional expression, and sensitivity is encouraged.

Enculturation – The process of adapting to a new culture.

Endocrine glands – A group of ductless glands which secrete hormones directly into the bloodstream.

Endocrine system – The functioning order of glands which produce hormones, it is central in the control and regulation of behavior and interacts closely with the nervous system.

Endogenous control – Control that comes from within the body.

Endomorph – One of Sheldon's somatotyping classifications. Endomorphs are described as soft and rotund. They are viscerotonic and are believed to love comfort and eating, be relaxed and slow in movement, and social.

Engineering psychology – A branch of psychology which concentrates on the relationships between people and machines.

Engram – A hypothetical physiological change corresponding to something learned; also called a memory trace.

Entropy – 1. In psychoanalysis, the extent to which psychic energy cannot be transferred once it has been invested in an object. 2. The number of possible outcomes an event may have. 3. In social psychology, the tendency for social progress to diminish, because each new change uses up energy which is not available for the succeeding change.

Environment – The totality of significant aspects of an individual's surroundings. Includes all experiences and events that influence an individual's development. The three basic subcategories of environment are postnatal, prenatal, and cellular.

Environmental factors – Those factors that act as stimulating forces on the organism.

Environmental-mold trait – A personality trait, developed by R. B. Cattell, which has been evolutionized through environmental influences.

Environmentalism – The belief that emphasizes environmental differences as the cause for individual differences. Holds that heredity has only a minor role in behavior.

Enzyme – A complex protein substance that acts as a catalyst in regulating chemical reactions in the body.

Epigenesis – The hypothesis that new traits emerge during embryonic development. These are traits not contained in the original fertilized cell. Rather, they develop out of prenatal environmental and intracellular influences.

Epilepsy – Epilepsy refers to a general condition characterized by convulsions. The various convulsions associated with epilepsy are: petit mal, grand mal, and psychomotor.

Epileptoid personality – A compilation of personality traits which are believed to be associated with epilepsy, including stubbornness, irritability, and uncooperativeness.

Epinephrine – (See adrenaline.)

Episiotomy – A small cut made in the perineum to facilitate the birth of a child. An episiotomy prevents the tearing of membranes and ensures that once the cut has been sutured, healing will be rapid and complete.

Episodic memory – Retention of specific events which we have ourselves experienced, like dates, names, events.

Epistemic behavior – A label employed by Berlyne to describe behavior designed to gather information.

Epistemology – That branch of philosophy concerned with the acquisition and validity of people's knowledge about the world.

Equilibration – 1. The balance between what is taken in, assimilated, and what is changed, accommodated. Equilibration is the mechanism for cognitive growth and development. 2. The achievement of balance between two opposing forces.

Equilibrium – As developed by Piaget, a term referring to a balance between assimilation and accommodation. The concept of equilibration is of primary importance to Piaget's explanation of motivation. He assumed that an individual constantly interacts with his or her environment through assimilation and accommodation to achieve a state of equilibrium.

Equity norm – The rule of social exchange which says that a person's outcomes should be proportionate to his or her inputs to the group.

Equivalent form – One of two or more forms of a test that have been built to the same specifications to measure the same attribute or attributes, and that consequently have approximately the same statistical characteristics.

Erg – As developed by R. B. Cattell, an innate predisposition of certain response activities to certain stimuli.

Erikson, Erik – A noted child psychoanalytic psychologist. He coined the term "identity crisis."

Erikson, Ego psychology of – Erikson's theory of personality development which emphasizes ego development. Ego psychology is an eight-stage theory requiring a successful coping at each stage for proper development.

Erogenous zone – An area of the body, when stimulated, which gives rise to sexual feeling.

Eros – A Greek word meaning love, employed by Freud to describe the life instinct present at birth that includes all drives for self-preservation. Early in his career, Freud classified 'Eros' as the sex instinct.

Error of measurement – 1. The amount by which any specific measurement differs from the individual's hypothetical "true" score in the quality being measured. Since no measurement procedure is perfectly exact, each has included in it some component of error. 2. An error due to the unreliability of an instrument.

Erythrolabe – A pigment in retinal cones that absorbs light mostly in the red region of the spectrum.

ESP – (See extrasensory perception.)

Escape conditioning – A form of learning in which the proper response ends noxious stimulation.

Escape response – Any response made by an organism in order to get away from an already-present aversive stimulus.

Essential hypertension – A disorder characterized by high blood pressure of unknown origin.

Este's statistical model of learning – In learning theory, the view that all stimuli are composed of a large number of elements and that only a small percentage can be effective at any given time.

Estrogen – A female sex hormone secreted by the ovaries, which maintains sexual characteristics and the reproductive functions.

Ethical model – Model of psychopathology in which psychopathology comes from guilt over immoral behavior; assumes that individual has responsibility for his or her behavior.

Ethology – The study of organisms and their behavior in their natural habitats.

Eugenics – A form of genetic engineering that selects specific individuals for reproduction. The term was coined by Galton and is really an expression of the belief that individuals should be selected for breeding purposes in order to enhance racial characteristics.

Eunuch – A castrated male.

Euphoria – A psychological state of well-being and heightened motor activity. When pathological it may be characteristic of manic states.

Eustachian tube – The valved tube connecting

the middle ear and mouth which provides an equilibrium of atmospheric pressure between the outside and middle ear.

Evaluation – The complete process of comparison and determination of the relative importance of a phenomenon and the appraising of the extent to which certain objectives have been achieved.

Evoked potential – A very small change in voltage recorded from the cerebral cortex of the brain following stimulation of one of the sense modalities.

Evolution – 1. In general, the orderly development of a theory, system or body. 2. The process of orderly changes in the phylogenetic species which have been brought about by environmental and genetic changes with survival of the best-adapted mutants. Evolutionary processes are assumed to be responsible for the present variety and distribution of life forms.

Evolutionary biology – Study of living organisms stressing the importance of understanding the similarities and differences between animals.

Ex post facto – Literally, "after the fact"; refers to conditions in an experiment that are not determined prior to the experiment, but only after some manipulation has occurred naturally.

Excitation – General level of arousal or a state of activity stemming from arousal; stimulation resulting from the firing of nerve cells; agitated emotional state; generalized in Salter's theory to refer to a state in the individual in which he or she is ready for vigorous action.

Excitatory postsynaptic potential (EPSP) – Depolarizing effects of synaptic transmission on the postsynaptic neuron.

Excitatory potential – As developed by Hull, the strength of a tendency to respond.

Excitatory tendency – The ability of a stimulus to evoke a response.

Exhibitionism – A sexual variant form of behavior which involves the intentional exposure of the genitals to unsuspecting people under inappropriate conditions.

Existential analysis – The term applied to the system of psychotherapy which combines some of the teachings of existential philosophy with some of the theories and practices of psychoanalysis. The goal is to restore to the individual a sense of freedom and responsibility for his or her own choices.

Existential model – An explanation of abnormal personality patterns that stresses the influence of present events rather than past experiences.

Existential neurosis – Feeling a loss of meaning in life even though one is a successful member of society.

Existential therapy – A type of psychotherapy developed by Rollo May and other existentialists, it emphasizes the here-and-now, or human's present being, and the uniqueness and separateness of each individual.

Existentialism – A philosophical-psychological movement characterized by a preoccupation with existence. Existential philosophers describe the human condition in such terms as abandonment, loneliness, despair, and alienation. These feelings are purported to result from the individual's lack of knowledge about his or her origin and eventual end. Hence the term existentialism, since the only knowable reality is existence. A philosophy which adheres to the idea that at any moment in time humans are in a state of growth toward whatever they will to become.

Exocrine glands – Glands, having ducts, which secrete fluids onto the body's surface or into its cavities.

Exogenous control – Control that comes from outside the body.

Exorcism – Ritual used to drive out evil spirits.

Expansion gradient – The less dense part of a visual path (texture gradient) which appears to be closer.

Expectancy – 1. The probability of an occurrence. 2. A learned anticipation by an organism that a certain response to a stimulus will result in the occurrence of a specific situation. 3. An attitude characterized by attentiveness and heightened muscular tension.

Expectancy table – A table showing, for each level of a predictor test, the frequency of different levels of success in some outcome variable.

Experience – Learning, or the effects of the environment on development.

Experiential therapy – The term applied to the system of psychotherapy developed by Carl

Whitaker and Thomas Malone. The emphasis is placed on matters of maturity. The goal is to increase the ease in the exchange of energies within an individual.

Experiment – A scientific investigation carried out under controlled conditions for the purpose of observing a specific variable.

Experimental control – Holding constant extraneous variables in an experiment so that any effect on the dependent variable can be attributed to manipulation of the independent variable.

Experimental group – In a scientific experiment, those subjects who respond to an independent variable that is "specially" manipulated by the experimenter; the responses of the experimental group can then be compared with the responses of the control group.

Experimental method – Research procedure in which the psychologist manipulates one variable and tests to see what effects the manipulation has on a second variable. Controls are used to eliminate the effects of all extraneous variables. This procedure can establish a cause and effect relationship between manipulated and unmanipulated variables.

Experimental neurosis – The result of an experimentally induced conflict in which an animal in a difficult discrimination situation is unable to respond. At a critical point the animal finally "breaks down," exhibiting indiscriminate, restless behavior.

Experimental psychology – A field of psychology that studies behavior by performing experimental research. Problem areas investigated are learning, perception and sensation, memory, motivation, and the underlying physiology of behavior.

Experimenter bias – The effect that an experimenter may unknowingly exert on results of an experiment, usually in a direction favoring the experimenter's hypothesis.

Experimenter effect – The effect on subjects' behavior that is attributable to the experimenter's expectations about how the subjects should perform. Also called the Rosenthal effect.

Exploratory behavior – A global term describing behavior that has no specific goal object, but rather seems to be directed solely toward the examination or the discovery of the environment. The term frequently denotes curiosity-based activities.

External auditory meatus - The canal leading

from the outside of the ear to the tympanic membrane.

External inhibition – The temporary suppression of a conditioned response that is manifested when the CS is accompanied by a novel stimulus.

Externalization – 1. The arousal, via learning, by external stimuli, of a drive which previously was aroused by internal stimuli. 2. In development, the process of differentiating between self and not self. 3. The projection of one's own psychological processes to the environment, characteristic of paranoid or hallucinatory states.

Extinction – In classical conditioning, the gradual disappearance of the conditioned response. This occurs with repeated presentation of the conditioned stimulus in the absence of the unconditioned stimulus. In instrumental conditioning, the elimination of a learned behavior resulting from withholding all reinforcement of that behavior.

Extirpation – Removal of some part of the nervous system to determine the effect on behavior.

Extraneous variable – A condition that may affect the outcome of an experiment but is irrelevant to the experiment.

Extrasensory perception – Alleged ability to get information about ideas or objects through some means other than the usual sensory channels. This phenomenon includes telepathy, clairvoyance, and precognition.

Extra-specific aggression (inter-specific aggression) – Fighting or other aggression directed at a member of a different species; i.e., aggression between organisms from different species.

Extraversion – One of the types of personality proposed by Jung in which the predominant interest is in social interaction and the external world.

Extrinsic motivation – Motivation based on material rewards, not inherently internalized.

Extrinsic rewards – Candy, money, and similar objects that can be given to organisms with the effect of increasing the frequency of behaviors that precede them.

Extrovert – A person characterized by more attention to external stimuli than to his internal thoughts and feelings; he is more spontaneous, distractible, and changeable in mood than the introvert. Introversion-extroversion is one of the major dimensions in Eysenck's theory of personality.

F - minus - K index – A measuring of a subject's attempt to fake a socially desirable score on the Minnesota Multiphasic Inventory of Personality.

Face validity – From an intuitive standpoint, the test items should look as if they are related to what is supposedly being measured. That is, there should be a reasonableness or plausibility of test tasks in terms of measuring what the test is supposed to be measuring.

Facial talk – A method used by Salter in his system of conditioned-reflex therapy to help a patient to overcome inhibitions by learning to show emotions on his or her face.

Factitious disorders – Disorders in which an individual deliberately produces psychological or physical symptoms in an attempt to be seen by others as sick and be able to assume the role of "patient." Sometimes actual physical symptoms are exaggerated or self-inflicted, but often physical or psychological symptoms are made up.

Factor – An element in a causal explanation.

Factor analysis – This refers to a variety of statistical techniques whose common objective is to represent a set of variables in terms of a smaller number of hypothetical variables, called factors. In psychology, these factors represent intellectual or personality traits. For example, one could account for the intercorrelations among tests of multiplication, division, and subtraction with a factor called number.

Factor analytic approach – Trait theory approach used by Cattell that seeks to understand personality by summarizing the dimensions of personality.

Factor rotation – A process usually associated with factor analysis which involves the manipulation of the axes in a centroid analysis so that they will pass through the maximum number of correlations.

Factorial design – An experimental design in which each level of every independent variable occurs with all levels of the other independent variable.

Fading – An instrumental conditioning technique that gradually introduces or removes a stimulus so that ongoing behavior is not disrupted.

Fading theory – A theory of forgetting that maintains items of information can no longer be remembered when the "memory trace" associated with them has disappeared.

Fallopian tubes – Tubes linking the ovaries and the uterus. Fertilization ordinarily occurs during the egg's passage through the fallopian tubes.

False alarm – In signal detection theory, the trial in which the signal is not present, but the subject says he sees the signal. Also called a false positive report.

False negative report – A report that a signal or event was not present when in fact a signal was actually presented, usually associated with signal-detection theory. Also called a miss.

Family therapy – Psychotherapy with members of a family meeting together with the therapist.

Fantasy – Creative imagination of a complex object or event, existent or non-existent, in concrete symbols or images, usually in the pleasant sense of a wish-fulfillment.

Fate control – The ability a person has to control one's own or another's outcomes.

Fear – A primary emotional response to a specific object or situation perceived as dangerous, and which the individual believes he or she cannot control.

Feature extraction – Identification of the most important aspects of a total stimulus configuration.

Fechner's law – A rule that relates any level of intensity of stimulation with a level of experience by the law $S = K \log I$, where S is physical stimulation, K is Weber's constant, and I is the stimulus. This states that physical stimulation increases logarithmically as experience increases arithmetically.

Feedback – 1. Information received by an individual on the effects of some previous action which is to be used by the individual to regulate further output. 2. In neuropsychology, the afferent impulses from proprioceptive receptors which give rise to motor movements. 3. In a man-made system, a means of controlling input by connecting the system to output, such as, a thermostat.

Feral children – Children raised in social isolation with only animal contact and raised by animals.

Ferry-Porter law – The relation between the apparent brightness of a flickering light, with a frequency greater than the critical flicker-fusion frequency, and the duration and intensity of the "on" portion of the light-dark cycle.

Fertilization – The union of sperm and ovum.

Fertilized ovum stage – The first stage of prenatal development beginning at fertilization and ending at approximately the second week; also called the zygote stage.

Fetal growth – The development of the fetus in the uterus.

Fetal stage – The third period in prenatal development, from approximately the seventh week until delivery; in a full-term pregnancy of thirty-eight weeks, the last thirty-two weeks.

Fetish – Maladaptive preference for an object or nonsexual part of the body rather than a person, as a source of sexual satisfaction.

Fetus – The term for the embryo during the final stage of prenatal development which begins approximately 6 weeks after conception and lasts until birth.

Fiber tract – A group of axons located within the central nervous system.

Field dependent – Type of personality involving dependency on external reference points for the formation of perceptions.

Field independent – Type of personality involving an emphasis on internal reference points for the formation of perceptions.

Field research – Observation of behavior in its natural setting where subjects typically do not know that they are in an experiment.

Figural aftereffect – A change in the apparent shape or location of a visual figure following inspection of another figure, because there is a tendency to maintain constancy in the figure-ground relationship.

Figure-ground – A principle of Gestalt psychology that holds that we organize our perceptions into figure and background. The figure gives the appearance of solidity or three dimensionality and the background is not clearly shaped or patterned.

Filtering – A hypothetical perceptual process involving selective attention that prevents unimportant signals from reaching awareness. New, unusual, or important signals, however, are processed into consciousness, implying that the stimulus meaning can be discriminated by this process.

Fissure – A major indentation in the cerebral cortex. Smaller indentations are called sulci.

Fixation – 1. In psychoanalytic theory, the failure of psychosexual development to proceed normally from one stage to the next, so that an individual's libidinal energy must in part be expended to satisfy motives appropriate to an earlier stage. 2. In perception, the point at which the eyes are directed. 3. In behavior, an inability to reject an incorrect stimulus or extinguish an incorrect response for a correct response. 4. In personality, a relatively strong and enduring emotional attachment for another person.

Fixed-action pattern (FAP) – Unvarying sequences of movement, keyed by a releaser, sign, or stimulus which are species-specific.

Fixed alternative – In a test or questionnaire, when a person must choose an answer from among a few specified alternatives.

Fixed-interval schedule – A reinforcement schedule in which a reinforcement is delivered after every response that follows a specified and constant time period since the previous reinforcement.

Fixed ratio schedule – A plan of partial reinforcement in which the subject is rewarded each time a set number of correct responses have occurred.

Fixed schedule – An intermittent schedule of reinforcement in which the reinforcement occurs at fixed intervals of time, an interval schedule, or after a specified number of trials, a ratio schedule.

Flesch index – A gauge of the reading difficulty of a passage.

Fluid intelligence – Intelligence that can adjust to new situations; usually considered as flexible or adaptive thinking.

Focal stimuli – Stimuli which are the focus of attention; in adaptation-level theory of motivation, they represent one factor determining the adaptation level.

Focus gambling – An approach to solving conceptual problems in which the subject varies two or more attributes in each comparison with the focus; it sometimes produces quicker solutions but it can also backfire, causing slower problem solving.

Focused attention – Attending to one aspect of a stimulus while ignoring all other parts.

Fontanelles – The soft areas of connective tissue on the skull of the newborn. They allow some flexibility in the skull during labor and growth.

Forced-choice (item) – A pattern, used in rating scales, in which the individual is required to select one of a set of statements as most descriptive and perhaps another as least descriptive. In preparing the sets of statements, the attempt is usually made to have all the statements in a set approximately balanced for acceptability or desirability, but quite different in what they signify about the person.

Forebrain – The frontmost division of the brain, encompassing the thalamus, hypothalamus, and cerebral hemispheres. This part of the brain is responsible for higher processes in man.

Forgetting – The loss of retention or the inability to retrieve a stored memory.

Formal group – A gathering of people in which formal titles, rules, hierarchy, and other designations are significant.

Formal operational period – The fourth stage of cognitive development as proposed by Piaget, it occurs during early adolescence, as the teenager learns to conceive of events beyond the present, imagine hypothetical situations, and develop a complex system of logic.

Fourier analysis – A mathematical procedure for breaking down complex waves into simple sine waves.

Fovea – A small indentation in the center of the retina into which most of the cone cells are packed. Form and color vision are centered here.

Frames – Systems of rules, understandings, and expectancies operative in repetitive social situations, such as waiting rooms.

Fraternal twins – See dizygotic twins.

Free association – 1. In psychoanalytic therapy, the reporting of whatever comes to the mind of the individual being analyzed. 2. In testing, a word-association test where no restrictions are put on the nature of the subject's response.

Free-floating anxiety – Anxiety reactions that have no referent in the environment.

Free recall – A technique for testing memory that requires the subject to reproduce learned items, but not in any specific order.

Free-response rate – Rate at which an organism responds in an operant situation.

Free-running rhythm – A rhythm that does not derive its regularity from an entraining stimulus.

Free will – The philosophical view that behavior is ultimately directed by volition. Man is capable of independent choice and action.

Frequency – The number of times something occurs within a given length of time. The number of vibrations or cycles per second reaching a given point in space; often refers to a dimension of sound.

Frequency distribution – Classifying data in a graphical format for a group of individuals in which the possible score values are arranged in order from high to low, and the number of persons receiving each score is indicated.

Frequency of usage – A count of how often a particular event occurs in some block of time or sequence of behavior, most commonly how often a particular word occurs in a text.

Frequency polygon – A graphic representation of a frequency distribution, in which the number of cases in each score category is plotted, and the successive points are connected with straight lines.

Frequency principle – A physiological law stating that a neuron will fire more rapidly to stronger stimuli than weaker ones, generating more action potentials per given period of time.

Frequency theory – A theory of pitch discrimination that assumes that pitch is dependent upon the rate at which the whole basilar membrane vibrates.

Freud, Sigmund – Founder of psychoanalytic theory.

Freudian slip – An error in speaking or writing which unintentionally reveals the speaker's or writer's true meaning.

Frigidity – Lack of any enjoyment from sexual intercourse with a partner; also termed arousal insufficiency.

Frontal area of the brain – The part of the cerebral cortex lying in front of the central sulcus.

Frontal lobe – The area of the cortex in front of the central sulcus and above the lateral fissure.

Frontal lobotomy – Surgical severing of the connections between the frontal lobe and the rest of the brain. Usually restricted to the prefrontal region, it is done only to treat severely psychotic patients.

Frustration – An unpleasant state of tension engendered by being blocked from attaining a goal or gratification; also, the process of blocking motivated behavior; also, the emotional response to blocking the goal.

Frustration-aggression hypothesis – A theory proposed by Dollard and Miller, according to which the only cause of aggression is frustration. Further, that frustration always leads to some kind of aggressive reaction, whether explicit or implicit.

Frustration tolerance – The general resistance of an individual to anxiety in frustrating situations without undue psychological harm.

Fugue state – A defense by actual flight; that is, a neurotic dissociative reaction in which a person has amnesia for the past, but avoids the anxiety associated with such loss of identity. This is accomplished by developing a new identity and fleeing from the intolerable situation. An individual's activities during the fugue could range from spending a great deal of time in movie theaters to starting a completely new life.

Functional autonomy – As developed by Allport, a situation in which a response which was made originally to satisfy some motive becomes intrinsically motivating.

Functional disorder – A malfunction or pathological condition without a known organic cause.

Functional fixedness – In problem-solving, a tendency or mental set in which one considers only the common uses of objects, rather than the possibilities for novel or unusual functions.

Functional invariant – As termed by Piaget, those aspects of human interaction with the environment that are unchanging as the individual develops. The functional invariants of adaptation are assimilation and accommodation, since the processes of assimilating and accommodating remain constant as the child develops.

Functional psychoses – Psychotic reactions that are provoked by psychological or experiential influences and have no demonstrable bodily origin.

Functionalism – Early school of psychological thought which emphasized how conscious behavior helps one adapt to the environment and the role learning plays in this adaptive process. This school of thought held that the mind should be studied in terms of its usefulness to the organism in adapting to its environment.

Functioning – As termed by Piaget, the processes by which an organism adapts to its environment. These processes are known as assimilation and accommodation.

Fundamental – 1. In audition, the lowest frequency in a compound tone. 2. In perception, hues that make up the primaries for any given theory of color vision. 3. In industrial psychology, a skill needed before further skills can be learned.

"G" factor – Spearman's construct for a hypothetical factor, presumably measured by a test of general intelligence, which affects performance on a variety of different tasks (as opposed to specific aptitudes).

Galvanic skin response (GSR) – A change in the electrical resistance of the skin as detected by a sensitive galvanometer. The GSR has been correlated with emotional states, strain, and tension.

Gamete – The mature reproductive cell; specifically, the sperm or the egg.

Ganglion – A cluster of nerve cell bodies that can be located outside of the central nervous system or in the subcortical regions of the brain.

Ganglion cells – Neurons in the retina connecting bipolar cells to relay areas in the brain; axons of ganglion cells form the optic nerve.

Ganzfeld – A homogeneous visual field.

Gastrointestinal system (g.i.) – Extends from the lips to the anus, including the stomach and intestines.

Gene – An area within a chromosome composed of deoxyribonucleic acid that determines hereditary traits.

General adaptation syndrome (GAS) – A pattern of physiological responses to extreme stress including increased autonomic activity and longer-term endocrine activity.

General habit – The learned tendency which results in a person's maintaining the same relationship between corresponding stimuli and responses in a class of situations.

General intelligence – A trait postulated to account for the positive relation found between many different kinds of tests of abilities and achievement.

General motive – Motives, that have in common an abstract goal, which involve diverse activities and situations.

Generality of results – The issue of whether or not a particular experimental result will be obtained under different circumstances, such as with a different subject population or in a different experimental setting.

Generalization – 1. The application of a response to a whole class or group after having been conditioned to respond in that way to a limited portion of the class or group. 2. Of or relating to forming an idea or judgment which is applicable to an entire class of objects, people, or events.

Generalized reinforcement – A form of secondary reinforcement that is not specifically related to any single need state, such as praise, smiling, and thanks.

Generative grammar – As developed by Noam Chomsky, the concept that linguistic utterances are learned through general rules which allow for great variety and originality in linguistic production.

Generativity – In E. Erikson's personality theory, the positive outcome of one of the stages of adult personality development, specifically, the ability to do creative work or to contribute to the raising of one's children. It is the opposite of stagnation.

Genetic model – The point of view that present behavior and development is to be understood in terms of heredity and developmental history.

Genetic opportunity – The likelihood of having an experience which influences a given trait as a function of the expression of another genetic trait not related to the first. For example, the genetic trait of skin color influences the opportunity to have experiences which may influence IQ test performance.

Genetic transmission – The processes involved in passing genetic material from one generation to the next.

Genetics – The study of the transmission of hereditary characteristics as it relates to evolutionary theory.

Genital period – In Freudian psychoanalytic theory, the final psychosexual stage beginning with puberty at approximately the age of 11, during which sexual interest is shifted from autoeroticism to heterosexuality by involvement with normal adult modes of sexual gratification.

Genitalia – A term referring generally to sex organs.

Genotype – A person's genetic makeup composed of both dominant and recessive genes.

Geriatric – A specialization in the treatment of diseases of old age.

Germ cells – Reproductive cells during any stage of their development. In the female, the egg; in the male, the sperm.

Germinal period – The first two weeks of the prenatal period, during which the blastula forms.

Gerontology – The science of old age, including geriatrics, psychology, sociology, and anthropology.

Gestalt – The term has no exact equivalent in English. The approximate English equivalents are configuration, meaningful organized whole, structural relationship, and theme.

Gestalt psychology – Founded by Max Wertheimer, the basic premise is that "the whole is greater than the sum of its parts." Gestalt psychology not only contends that stimuli are perceived as whole images rather than as parts built into images, but also maintains that the whole determines the parts instead of the parts determining the whole. The theory originally focused on perception, however, is applicable to a broad range of areas.

Gestalt therapy – A distinctive formal theory of personality in which therapeutic techniques are based on existential philosophy and emphasizes the here and now awareness of personal sensations and feelings. The goal is to enable a person to form meaningful configurations of personality.

Gestation – The prenatal phase of life lasting an average of 266 days in humans.

Gland – A bodily structure whose function is to manufacture chemicals, called hormones, that are secreted into the bloodstream and regulate bodily activities. The two general types are endocrine glands and exocrine glands.

Goal – In motivation, the satisfier of a motive condition.

Goal gradient – The tendency for motivation

to increase or decrease as the organism approaches the goal.

Goal specificity – The desire to satisfy a motive condition with a particular reinforcement rather than with any satisfying reinforcement.

Gonad – The primary sex gland, ovaries in the female and testes in the male.

Good form – A Gestalt principle of organization which asserts that figures or patterns are perceived in such a way as to be as uniform as possible.

Goodenough Draw-a-Man Test – A test of intelligence in which one is asked to draw the best possible picture of a man; primarily used with children up to age 11.

Grade equivalent – A score conversion in which a test score is assigned the grade value for which it is average.

Grade norm – A standard of performance which represents the average performance of a given population.

Graded potential – The sum of the excitation and inhibition at a given synapse; generator potential; receptor potential.

Gradient of stimulus generalization – Mathematical curve that illustrates the degree of generalization between various stimuli. Generally, the closer the stimuli to the conditioned stimulus, the greater the response.

Graphic rating scale – A rating scale in which the rater indicates his rating by making a mark at some point along a line. Selected points on the line are characterized by evaluative adjectives or descriptions of the quality of behavior represented.

Gray matter – A general term for the neural tissue found in the brain, spinal cord, and ganglia, comprised of cell bodies.

Group-centered therapy – The term applied to the system of group therapy developed by Carl Rogers and associates in which the individuals in the group rather than the therapist has the primary role in the therapeutic relationship.

Group factors – 1. Psychological factors postulated to account for interrelations of groups of tests; typically numerical, clerical, verbal, spatial, etc. 2. In factor analysis, any factor that is manifested in at least two tests that constitute the correlation matrix.

Group pressure – The effect that the opinions, feelings, exhortations, or behavior of groups has on a single individual.

Growth therapies – Therapies aimed at helping an individual achieve maximum self-actualization.

Group therapy – Any therapy in which more than one patient is present in the therapy setting at the same time.

Grouping – The tendency to perceive objects in groups, rather than as isolated elements; is determined by proximity, similarity, good form, and continuity.

Growth – Ordinarily refers to such physical changes as increasing height or weight; quantitative growth.

Growth curve – A statistical curve derived from plotting weight and height against chronological age for comparison of an individual child's growth pattern with the average rate of growth.

GSR – See Galvanic Skin Response.

Habit – An acquired response that becomes fixed and relatively automatic through constant repetition.

Habituation – Decreased response to a stimulus because it has become familiar. It is often a condition resulting from repeated use of a drug and characterized by a desire for the drug; little or no tendency to increase the dose; and psychological, but not physical, dependence.

Hair cells – Receptor cells possessing cilia (tiny hairs) such as the auditory receptor cells located in a membrane in the cochlea that are stimulated by vibrations in the cochlear fluid.

Hallucination – Perception of an external object, often bizarre in nature, in the absence of stimulation.

Hallucinogenic drugs – A group of drugs also known as psychedelic drugs and psychotogenic drugs, that produce hallucinations and often provoke highly imaginative thought patterns and/or unusual and mixed perceptions.

Halo effect – The tendency, when rating an individual on one characteristic, to be influenced by another characteristic of his personality, e.g. physically attractive people are more likely to be judged as intelligent than unattractive people.

Haptic system – The perceptual system whereby object properties are perceived through active touch. It includes the tactile sense as well as proprioception.

Hawthorne effect – Generally, the effect on subjects' performance attributable to their knowledge that they are serving as experimental subjects or being treated in a special manner. Sometimes, the tendency for people to work harder when experiencing a sense of participation in something new and special.

Head turning reflex – A reflex elicited in the infant by stroking his cheek or the corner of his mouth. The infant turns his head toward the side being stimulated.

Hedonic – The motivation to seek pleasure and avoid pain.

Hedonic tone – The affective quality of an emotion; degree of pleasantness or unpleasantness of an emotion; a basic dimension of all emotions.

Hedonic value – The value of a stimulus or an experience on a scale from pleasant to unpleasant.

Hereditary factors – Those inherited biological factors that are involved in the development of the structure and function of the body.

Heredity – The biological transmission of genetic traits from parent to offspring.

Hering theory – Theory of color vision postulating six primaries, black-white, red-green, and blue-yellow in three opponent process pairs.

Heritability – A statistical concept which reflects the percentage of variability in a trait that is associated with differences in the genetic composition of the individuals in the group. The capability of being inherited.

Hermaphrodite – An animal or plant having both male and female reproductive organs.

Hertz (Hz) – A frequency measurement of cycles per second. One Hz equals one cycle per second, etc.

Heterogeneous – Dissimilar, characteristic of groups, sets of data, or individuals who show differences or dissimilarities.

Heteronomy – An intermediate stage in Bull's scheme of moral development in which the individual responds to situations primarily by their effect on him- or herself. Also, pertaining to activities originating outside the self or

the guidance of one individual by another (e.g., hypnosis).

Heterophemy – Speaking or writing the opposite of what is intended.

Heteroscedasticity – The quality or condition of a matrix in which the arrays show significantly different standard deviations.

Heterosexuality – An attraction toward members of the opposite gender.

Heterozygous – Refers to an individual who has both one dominant and one recessive gene for a given trait.

Heuristic – A principle or strategy used in problem solving which serves as a device for shortening the solution process; often used when there are many different ways to solve a problem; a solution is not guaranteed.

Hierarchical model of intelligence – The view that intelligence is hierarchically structured with general intelligence, group factors, specific factors, and, finally, specific information in an interdependent system.

Hierarchization – A term used in linguistics to suggest that in the course of development, the child's linguistic abilities build upon and elaborate upon constructions made at earlier phases of development.

Hierarchy of needs – A proposal (Abraham Maslow) that arranges motives in an order of importance; those lower in the hierarchy must be satisfied before the higher ones can be satisfied. The lower motives being food, shelter, etc. progressing to "self-actualization" as the motive highest in the hierarchy.

Hierarchy of skill – A task that displays several levels of organization or structure. Performance curves often show interesting evidence of such structure.

Higher-order conditioning – A form of classical conditioning in which the previously trained conditioned stimulus now functions as an unconditioned stimulus to train a new conditioned stimulus.

Higher order interaction – Interaction effects involving more than two independent variables in multifactor experiments, often making interpretation difficult.

Hindbrain – Phylogenetically, the oldest portion of the brain. It contains the medulla, cerebellum, pons, and base of the reticular formation. Also known as the rhombencephalon.

Histogram – A graphic representation of a frequency distribution in which the cases falling in each score category are represented by a bar whose size is proportional to the number of cases. Since each bar is the full width of the score category, the bars make a continuous "pile" showing the form of the frequency distribution.

Hit – The correct detection of a signal that has been presented; usually associated with signal-detection.

Holophrases – A term used in linguistics to describe the phenomena wherein a young child will use a single word in the sense of a phrase or sentence. "Johnny" can mean "Pick Johnny up" or "Give Johnny some water," and so on.

Homeostasis – A state of optimal organismic balance, brought about by internal regulatory mechanisms.

Homeostatic mechanisms – Mechanisms for achieving homeostasis.

Homogeneous – Highly similar; coming from the same background. For example, a homogeneous culture is one in which all members have had highly similar experiences.

Homosexuality – An attraction toward members of the same gender.

Homosexual panic – In a heterosexual individual, the fear arising from homosexual thoughts or the suggestion that one might have such thoughts.

Homozygous – Refers to an individual whose two genes for a given trait are both either dominant or recessive.

Hope of failure – A desire for failure; not as well investigated as hope of success or fear of failure or success.

Horizontal decalage – A term introduced by Piaget to describe the fact that conservation of different quantities occurs at different times, even though all conservations require the same mental operations for their attainment. For example, number conservation is routinely observed to appear before length conservation.

Hormone – A chemical manufactured and secreted into the bloodstream by an endocrine gland, which may then activate another gland or help to regulate bodily functioning and behavior.

Hospitalism – A medical name for the syndrome (configuration of symptoms) associated with the inability of infants to survive in children's homes or hospitals. Symptoms of hospitalism include listlessness, inability to gain weight, unresponsiveness, and eventual death.

Hostility – Angry, hateful, or destructive behavior against another. Also, the motive behind this behavior.

Hue – That aspect of color experience referred to by color names, e.g., blue or yellow. Hue is the psychological correlate of wavelength.

Human engineering – The applied field of psychological specialization concerned with the design of equipment and the tasks performed in the operation of equipment.

Humanism – In psychology, a recent movement in personality and clinical psychology that focuses uniquely upon human experience, rather than abstract conceptions of human nature. There is an emphasis on positive, constructive human capacities.

Humanistic psychology – Psychology based on humanistic principles (see Humanism).

Humanitarianism – Concern with the welfare of man.

Hunger – A drive state or tissue need based on the deprivation of food; also, the feelings associated with such deprivation.

Huntington's chorea – A disorder characterized by progressive mental and physical deterioration and death, usually after the age of 20 or 30. Huntington's chorea is caused by a dominant gene and is always fatal.

Hydraulic drive model of motivation – A belief that motives or tensions behave like fluid under pressure that must break out or find release when the pressure builds up and becomes too great.

Hypermania – A manic-depressive state of excitement characterized by ravings, continuous movement, and disorientation as to time and place.

Hyperopia – Farsightedness. The inability to see near objects clearly because the image is focused behind the retina instead of on it.

Hyperphagia – Condition in which an animal eats abnormally large amounts of food and shows no satiation of hunger, produced experimentally by destruction of the ventromedial hypothalamic nucleus.

Hypertension – A condition of abnormally high blood pressure.

Hypnagogic imagery – Imagery that occurs as one is dropping off to sleep. It may be visual, auditory, or somesthetic, and is more vivid in some people than in others.

Hypnagogic state – State of consciousness experienced when passing from wakefulness to sleep.

Hypnoanalysis – Psychoanalysis carried on while the patient is under hypnosis.

Hypnosis – A technique (or group of techniques) for inducing an altered state of consciousness. It is characterized by increased suggestibility, relaxation or alertness, and possible distortion of reality.

Hypochondriasis – A neurotic reaction in which a person is excessively concerned with his or her physical health or welfare.

Hypomania – A manic-depressive state of excitement that is characterized by great enthusiasm and grandiose planning without any reality orientation.

Hypothalamus – A group of nuclei in the forebrain that controls the involuntary functions through the autonomic nervous system. It helps to control many basic drives and emotional processes, including sleep, thirst, temperature, sex, and hunger. It also controls much of the endocrine system's activities through connections with the pituitary gland.

Hypothesis – A testable statement that offers a predicted relationship between dependent and independent variables.

Hypothesis theory – Describes problem solving as a matter of formulating, selecting, and testing hypotheses about possible solutions until the correct one is found.

Hysteria – A form of neurosis in which patients manifest variable sensory, motor, vasomotor, visceral, and mental symptoms. These symptoms include paralyzed limbs, deafness, blindness, and other pathological conditions for which no anatomical or physiological causes could be found.

Iconic memory – A transient visual memory of a stimulus lasting about .5 seconds.

Iconic mode – As developed by Bruner, a method of converting immediate experience into mental models by using images in the form of sensory information.

Id – According to Freud, the id is the most fundamental component of personality, comprised of drives, needs, and instinctual impulses. It is unable to tolerate tension, is obedient only to the pleasure principle, and is in constant conflict with the super-ego.

Ideal self – The way a person would like to be, which may not match the way one actually is.

Idealism – A philosophical doctrine which affirms the pursuit of ideas and ideals rather than actuality or reality.

Idealized self-image – As developed by Horney, a pattern of perfectionistic strivings and godlike fantasies which constitute the core of a neurosis. The idealized image is a false and exaggerated estimate of one's true potentialities and abilities, and it is derived more from fantasy than from reality.

Identical twins – Two individuals that have developed as a result of the splitting of an already fertilized egg; thus, both individuals have identical chromosomal patterns. Also called monozygotic twins.

Identification – 1. In psychoanalytic theory, the internalization of a conscience through contact with one's parent of the same sex, creating a superego; also, a defense mechanism in which one incorporates the image of an object or individual into the psyche, taking the demands of an object or individual into the psyche and acting as if they were one's own. This is also called introjection. 2. In social psychology, the process through which someone is persuaded to a particular attitude because one has internalized the persuader's attitude. Also, the process by which people acquire a sense of personal definition from their reference group memberships. 3. According to E. Erikson, it is the process through which the infant learns a conviction of his or her self. This process is dependent on the mother's predictability and consistency in her relationship with the infant.

Identity – 1. A logical rule specifying that certain activities leave objects or situations unchanged. 2. The individual self.

Identity crisis – As proposed by Erikson, a period when one's sense of self and direction in life becomes clearer. It is marked by much confusion, experimentation, and emotionality. It generally occurs first during adolescence and may reoccur once or more often during adulthood.

Idiographic – The approach to personality study that emphasized those aspects of personality unique to each person.

Idiosyncratic – Unique to a particular person or situation.

Idiot-savant – A person with marked skill or talent in some specific activity, such as art, music or calculations, although his or her general intellectual level is low.

Illumination – In problem solving, one stage in which the answer seems to come in a flash of insight. The elements of the problem suddenly appear in a new relationship to each other. Since an emotional feeling often accompanies this experience, it is also called the Aha experience or insight.

Illusion – A distorted or false perception of an object, or an object or event that induces a false perception. One can experience illusions with respect to movement or perspective.

Image – 1. A mental representation of an object or event. 2. As developed by Titchener, one of three elements of consciousness; the other two are affective states and sensations. 3. The component of dreams.

Imagery – A characteristic of verbal material that tends to evoke images or internal symbolic representations; the representations themselves.

Imagination – The creation of objects which have only a mental existence without the aid of sensory date.

Imaginative play – Play activities that include make-believe games. These are particularly prevalent during the pre-school years.

Imitation – The modelling of one's actions on those of another; one of the fundamental ways a child learns.

Immature birth – A miscarriage occurring sometime between the twentieth and the twenty-eighth week of pregnancy, and resulting in the birth of a fetus weighing between 1 and 2 pounds.

Immediate memory – Continuation of the stimulus image for about a second after the stimulus has disappeared; sensory memory.

Implicit behavior – The convert movement of muscles which cannot be detected without the aid of instrumentation. Some examples are glandular secretions or the movements of the larynx at the time of speech. Some believe that thinking could be reduced to implicit subvocal behavior.

Implosive therapy – As developed by Stampfl

and Levis, a type of behavior therapy in which anxiety-arousing stimuli are presented in imagination while the patient is encouraged to experience as intense anxiety as possible. The therapist deliberately attempts to elicit a massive flood or implosion of anxiety. With repeated exposure in a safe setting, no objective danger is apparent, the stimulus loses its power to elicit anxiety, and the maladaptive behavior is extinguished.

Imprinting – In ethology, a social learning mechanism akin to learning, whereby animals of certain species, especially fowl, become "emotionally attached" to whatever stimulus they are first exposed to shortly after hatching or birth. The attachment is manifested by the animal's persistent following after the imprinted object. Imprinting occurs very early in life and is somewhat resistant to later modification.

Impulsive – A personality characteristic manifested in a greater concern with the rapid solution of problems than with their correct solution. There is an underlying need for immediate gratification rather than a need for a best possible solution.

Incentive motivation – An explanation for human behavior, referring to the belief that it is the reinforcing property of the outcome of behavior that determines whether or not the individual will behave. It is the incentive value of a behavioral outcome that determines its occurrence or nonoccurrence.

Incidence – The frequency with which any condition or event occurs.

Incidental learning – Learning which takes place without the set or instruction to learn, as opposed to intentional learning.

Incongruence – As developed by Carl Rogers, the state of behaving in ways that are different from the way we see ourselves or the way we feel. The disharmony experienced can result in anxiety or psychopathology.

Incremental theory – Any theory that regards development as an additive series of qualitatively similar steps.

Incubation – A phase of problem solving during which the person puts aside the problem and engages in irrelevant activity, yet unconscious processes seem to be working on the solution.

Independence – 1. An attitude characterized by a reliance upon one's own perceptions and past experience to guide behavior. 2. In statistics, no causal or correlational relationship exists between the variables under study.

Independent influence – A change in a person's attitudes or behaviors that occurs because a perceived message itself, rather than the sender of the message, is persuasive.

Independent variable – In psychological research, the condition which the psychologist manipulates. By convention, it is plotted on the Y axis.

Individual differences – Refers to the fact that all individuals vary and are different from other individuals, even though they may have some things in common.

Individual psychology – The term applied to the system of psychotherapy developed by Alfred Adler. Its emphasis is on the uniqueness of individual personality. Once the particular lifestyle of the individual is fully understood, the job of the therapist is to re-educate the patient toward healthier experiences and goals.

Individual test – Psychological tests given to only one subject at a time.

Induced movement – Apparent movement of a stationary object that is induced by movement of a surrounding frame.

Induction – 1. Discipline that is based on reasons. Most effective if tailored to the child's cognitive level. 2. In logic, reasoning from the particular to the general. 3. In physiology, the arousal of activity in one area as a result of the spread of activity from an adjoining area.

Industrial psychology – A branch of psychology that studies ways of improving efficiency in industry, both in terms of human beings and machinery. This area devises methods of selection, training, counseling of personnel, and psychological engineering.

Infancy – The period from birth to two years of age.

Infantile autism – Psychotic patterns of behavior shown by children under age ten, characterized by poor communication, no desire for personal contact, and a desire for status quo.

Inference – A guess about unobservable processes that is based on data.

Inferential statistics – Measures or techniques that allow for the analysis or evaluation of relationships that exist within a sample of data or between samples of data. Such analy-

sis is useful in making predictions.

Inferiority complex – As developed by Adler, the concept that a person may experience feelings of deficiency that are reinforced in such a belief by others in society.

Inflection – A method of communication involving raising and lowering the voice and placing accents in certain spots during a verbal exchange.

Influence – A change in a person's attitude or behavior that is induced by another person or group.

Informal group – A gathering of people in which there are no formal rules or titles; however, unwritten guidelines may exist.

Information – A set of facts or ideas that are obtained through learning; in information theory, a quantitative property of items that enable the items to be categorized in some meaningful manner. The bit is the unit of information.

Information-processing theory – Theory of problem solving which refers to the way a person receives information from the environment, operates on it, integrates it with other information available in memory, and uses it as a basis for deciding how to act.

Informational feedback – The stimuli which follow an organism's responses and show it the effect of its responses.

Infrared rays – An invisible part of the electromagnetic spectrum with wavelengths that are longer than visible red; experienced as heat.

Ingratiation – Behaving in a friendly, positive manner toward another with the aim of manipulating that person in order to serve one's own purpose.

Inheritance – The genetic composition of an organism.

Inhibition – 1. In general, a reduction of response due to suppression or restraint. 2. In physiology, a decrease in the firing of a neuron. 3. In psychoanalytic theory, the process by which the superego intervenes with the instinctual impulses of the id, thus preventing those impulses from reaching consciousness.

Inhibitory-disinhibitory effect – Imitative behavior that results in either the suppression (inhibition) or appearance (disinhibition) of previously acquired deviant behavior.

Inhibitory postsynaptic potential (IPSP) –

Hyperpolarization of the membrane of a postsynaptic neuron which decreases the probability of neural firing.

Innate – Present at birth; inborn; due to heredity; not learned.

Innate releasing mechanism – An internal mechanism of an organism's nervous system triggering a fixed action pattern (instinctive pattern) when a releasing stimulus is presented.

Inner ear – The part of the ear that contains the cochlea (hearing), semicircular canals, utricule, and the saccule (balance).

Inner speech – Internal representations of verbal stimuli, thought to be a process in memory and thinking.

Innervation – The supply of neurons to a muscle or gland.

Inoculation effect – When first exposure to mild arguments creates a set for a person so that later, stronger arguments can be resisted.

Insanity – A legal but not psychological term denoting the inability to distinguish between right and wrong or to know what one is doing.

Insight-oriented therapy – Type of psychotherapy that emphasizes change in motivation and knowledge. It focuses on increasing self-knowledge or insight of which the subject was unaware.

Instinct – An invariant sequence of complex behaviors that is observed in all members of a species and that is released by specific stimuli in the apparent absence of learning. Innate behaviors that are unaffected by practice.

Instrumental behavior – Activity that usually achieves some goal or satisfies a need.

Instrumental conditioning – (See Operant conditioning.)

Instrumental response Behavior leading toward a goal.

Insulin – A hormone secreted by the islands of Langerhans in the pancreas. It is involved in the utilization of sugar and carbohydrates in the body. Also used in insulin shock therapy.

Insulin shock therapy – An early form of shock therapy that utilizes insulin induced comas to treat mental disorders.

Integration – 1. The process by which parts are unified into a whole, as in the coordination of several neural impulses into a unified whole. 2. In personality, the state in which the traits of an organism work smoothly together in a coordinated whole.

Intellectualization – A Freudian defense mechanism whereby the individual emphasizes the intellectual or rational content of his or her behavior in order to exclude any of the emotional connotations of that behavior.

Intelligence – Intelligence is a difficult term to define with any precision. Generally, it is a trait postulated to underlie abilities to make judgments, solve abstract problems, succeed in academic activities, etc. Operationally, it is that which is measured by intelligence tests.

Intelligence quotient (IQ) – An index for expressing the results of an intelligence test. The intelligence quotient is an indicator of the individual's standing in relation to his own age group. Originally, quotients were computed by the ratio

$$100 \left(\frac{\text{Mental age}}{\text{Chronological age}} \right)$$

Currently, practically all intelligence quotients are standard scores, designed so that the average individual receives an intelligence quotient of 100, and the standard deviation in the group is 15 or 16.

Intelligence tests – Tests designed to measure intelligence; usually consisting of a series of aptitude tests that predict academic ability.

Intensity – Strength or amount of energy in a stimulus or response.

Interaction – 1. An experimental result that occurs when the levels of one independent variable are differentially affected by the levels of other independent variables. 2. A relationship between systems such that events taking place in one system influence events taking place in the other.

Interaction-oriented group – A group whose primary goal is to provide opportunity for social interaction.

Interest tests – Tests which focus on occupational and educational interests and assess an individual's selection of activities that he or she would like to engage in.

Interference – 1. The obstruction of learning something new caused by previously or subsequently learned material; a theory of forgetting, invoking the above process. 2. In cognition, a decrease in the amplitude of a sound or light wave because two waves occurring simultaneously are out of phase.

Intermittent reinforcement – Any pattern of reinforcement which is not continuous. It may vary according to ratio or interval.

Internal clock – A hypothetical physiological mechanism that regulates the cyclic variations recorded from many physiological systems.

Internal consistency – Degree of relationship among the items of a test, that is, the extent to which the same examinees tend to get each item right. Measures of reliability based upon a single testing are really measures of internal consistency.

Internal inhibition – A hypothetical process postulated by Pavlov to account for extinction. The special term given to the type of extinction in which the CS does not simply lose its effectiveness in eliciting the CR, rather it actively inhibits the CR.

Internalization – The process by which the individual's moral behaviors become independent of external reward and punishment.

Interpersonal attraction – Issue of friendship and romantic involvement, and attitudes of liking; subject of social psychological research.

Interpersonal relations – The often reciprocal interactions between two or more persons, or the characteristic pattern of such interactions. Most commonly employed in Sullivan's writings.

Interpolated task – A task used to fill the interval between the study of material and its recall in memory experiments.

Interposition – A monocular depth cue in which one object appears closer to the viewer because it partly blocks the view of another object.

Interquartile range – The middle 50 percent of the distribution of values. It falls between the first and the fourth quartiles.

Inter-role conflict – When an individual is confronted with expectations based upon at least two different roles that cannot be fulfilled simultaneously.

Inter-stimulus interval (ISI) – The time between two successive stimuli measured from the onset of the first to the onset of the second, usually the time between the onset of the CS and the onset of the UCS.

Intertrial interval – The delay after the feedback and before the start of the next stimulus presentation.

Interval scale – Numbers arranged to order a variable in such a way that equal changes in the variable are represented by equal differences in the numbers.

Interval schedules – A reinforcement schedule in which reinforcement is delivered after a response that has been made at the end of a given time period.

Intervening variable – Factor that stands between and provides a relationship between some stimulus in the environment and some response on the part of an organism.

Intervention programs – A global term referring to educational programs, which are typically remedial in nature. Many intervention programs have been organized at the preschool level to supplement the backgrounds of culturally deprived children.

Interview – A conversation between investigator and subject for the purpose of obtaining factual information, for evaluating one's personality, or for therapeutic purposes.

Intra-role conflict – When an individual is confronted with two or more expectations, which arise from only one role but cannot be fulfilled simultaneously.

Intraverbal responses – Verbal responses that are related to other verbal responses; word associations; facts known through verbal chains.

Intrinsic rewards – A form of reward that results from the activity itself because the activity is interesting, pleasurable, and rewarding.

Introjection – A defense mechanism in which the ego protects itself against an impulse from the id that is anxiety-producing by identifying itself with another person.

Introspection – The attempt of describing one's own private, internal state of being, including one's thoughts and feelings.

Introversion – As developed by Jung, the personality dimension describing an orientation inward toward the self. An introvert is self-directed and concerned with his own thoughts, avoids social contact, and tends to turn away from reality. At the two extremes are the extroverts and introverts.

Intuitive judgment – A decision based upon statistical data and other information, and the feelings of the psychologist giving the test.

Intuitive thought – One of the substages of the preoperational period, beginning around age 4 and lasting until age 7 or 8. Intuitive thought is marked by the child's natural ability to solve many problems and also by his or her inability to respond correctly in the face of misleading perceptual features of problems.

Invariance – 1. The degree to which given relationships among properties of objects, events, or individuals are unaffected by specified changes in the conditions under which those things are observed. 2. The characteristic of an afterimage retaining its size, despite changes in the distance to which it is projected.

Inverse relationship – The relationship indicated when an increase in one variable is paralleled by a decrease in another variable; a negative correlation.

Iodopsin – A photosensitive pigment found in cone cells that apparently is involved in color vision.

Ipsative test – A test yielding multiple scores, in which the sum of scores for all individuals is the same. Thus, an individual who is high on some scales of the test must be low on others. A test in which the individual's profile is expressed in relation to his own overall average, rather than in relation to some outside group.

Ipsilateral – On the same side, often used in describing brain-to-body relationships; the opposite of contralateral.

IQ – (See Intelligence quotient.)

Iris – The colored part of the eye containing the pupil (a group of muscles that regulates the amount of light entering the eye).

Irradiation – An increase in the number of muscles coming into play in a localized reflex, due to an increase in the strength of stimulation.

Irrelevant dimensions – The stimulus dimensions that do not provide defining information about the concept.

Irregular verbs – Verbs that take idiosyncratic modification, rather than regular endings, to show change of tense: eat-ate, run-ran, etc.

Isolation – The defense mechanism whereby the affect connected with a painful past event is dissociated from the memory or thought of the event.

Isomorphism – The Gestalt hypothesis that there is a point-for-point correspondence between a stimulus and its representation in the cerebral cortex.

Item analysis – Study of the statistical properties of test items. The typical qualities of interest are the difficulty of the item and its ability to differentiate between more capable and less capable examinees. Difficulty is usually expressed as the percent getting the item right, and discrimination is exposed as some index comparing success by the more capable and the less capable students.

James-Lange theory of emotion – A theory proposing that emotion-producing stimuli generate physical reactions, which in turn are perceived as felt emotions.

Jensen hypothesis – The controversial argument advanced by Jensen on the basis of some evidence regarding heredity and environment. With respect to intelligence, the most influential environmental factors are prenatal, and racial and social class differences in intelligence test scores cannot be accounted for by differences in environment alone. Hence, genetic factors are assumed to be responsible for some of the observed differences in intelligence among different racial groups.

jnd (just noticeable difference) – The smallest difference between two stimuli that can be detected reliably (by convention, 50% of the time).

Jump stand – An experimental device developed by K.S. Lashley to test visual discrimination and discrimination testing. The subject, usually a rat, must choose which of several doors to jump through to obtain a reward.

Jung, Carl Gustav – (pronounced yung) Swiss psychoanalyst who broke with Freud (1913) and founded the school of Analytical Psychology. Jung rejected the central importance of libido as a sexual energy and emphasized the meaning of art, religion, history, mythology, anthropology, and literature in his complex theory of personality.

Just noticeable difference – (See jnd.)

Justification – The use of rationalizations to achieve a feeling of equity; real equity is not achieved.

Juvenile era – (Harry Stack Sullivan) The stage in a child's development which begins when he or she shows a need for playmates and lasts until the emergence of a need for an intimate relationship with another person of comparable status at preadolescence.

Karyotyping – The process of photographing chromosomes and analyzing them into the pairs that are characteristic of the species.

Kinesthesis – The sense of movement and bodily position, as mediated by receptors in the muscles, tendons, and joints.

Kinship (anthropology) – Relationship between two or more persons based upon common descent and genetic similarity.

Knowledge of results (Kb) – Any information about the effect of a response; also called feedback.

Koffka, Kurt – One of the founders of Gestalt psychology.

Köhler, Wolfgang – One of the founders of Gestalt psychology.

Korsakoff's psychosis – A mental disorder brought on by alcoholism and characterized by a memory disturbance in which there is an inability to form new associations.

Krause end bulb – An encapsulated neural ending located at the junction of mucus membranes and dry skin, thought to be a receptor for cold.

Kuder-Richardson reliability – Reliability estimated from data available from a single test administration, using the average score on the test, its standard deviation, and difficulty indices for the separate items.

Kymograph – A device, now rarely used, for recording the strength of a response on a moving drum.

Labor – The process during which the fetus, the placenta, and other membranes are separated from the woman's body and expelled. The normal termination of labor is birth.

Labyrinth – The area in the head containing the organs of the middle and inner ear.

Laguno – Downy, soft hair that covers the fetus. Laguno grows over most of the child's body some time after the fifth month of pregnancy and is usually shed during the seventh month. However, some laguno is often present at birth, especially on the infant's back.

Landolt ring – A figure in the shape of a C, or a ring with a small gap, used in the laboratory assessment of visual acuity.

Language – No universally acceptable defini-

tion is available. Used loosely, it can mean anything from simply "a communication system" to "a learned arbitrary set of symbols passed along from one generation to the next in a culture."

Language acquisition device (LAD) – Innate biological mechanism common to all humans which operates on language data provided by parents and other speaking organisms, and produces a given language structure. The basic mechanism for language acquisition.

Lashley jumping stand – Device used to study discrimination learning. (See Jump stand.)

Latency – The length of time between stimulation and response.

Latency stage – In psychoanalytic theory, a stage of personality development in which sexual expression is repressed and channeled into other activities; about ages 6 to 12.

Latent content (of dreams) – Unconscious wishes or impulses that seek expression through dreams; the symbolic meaning of a dream.

Latent learning – Learning that appears to occur in the absence of reinforcement, facilitating performance in later trials when reinforcement is introduced.

Later childhood – The third period of postnatal development; from approximately age six until age twelve (the onset of puberty).

Law of effect – A proposal by Thorndike which suggests that behavior which is satisfying or pleasing is "stamped in," while behavior that leads to annoyance or unpleasantness is "stamped out." In general, the principle that reinforcement is necessary for, or facilitates, learning.

Law of least effort – The tendency to choose an act which accomplishes the goals of the organism and which requires the least expenditure of energy.

Law of similarity – One of the laws of organization which states that things similar to each other tend to be grouped as part of the same entity.

Laws of association – Classic treatment of knowing and thinking which held that associations arose from three sources: similarity, contrast, and contiguity in space or time.

Laws of organization – Rules by which perceptions are integrated and made coherent. Gestaltists believed that these rules reflected brain functioning.

Learned helplessness – (Seligman) The acceptance of what seem to be the unalterable consequences of a situation on the basis of previous experience or information, even if change may now be possible.

Learned motives – Conditions that result from experience and initiate, guide, and maintain behaviors; often called social motives.

Learning – The acquisition of any relatively permanent change in behavior traceable to experience and practice.

Learning curve – A graphic representation of the change in performance as a function of time or number of trials.

Learning set – An acquired ability to learn more rapidly in new learning situations because of previously learned responses.

Learning strategies – Methods for forming concepts and generally for acquiring and using information about the environment. Children gradually develop more sophisticated and efficient strategies.

Learning to learn – A gradual improvement, via positive transfer, in learning to solve problems of the same type as previously solved. Thought by some to account for "insight learning."

Lens – Transparent structure in the eye changes shape to focus the optic array the retina at the back of the eye.

Lesbianism – Homosexuality among women.

Lesion – Damaged or destroyed part of the body. Lesions are often made in the nervous system by cutting out or electrically burning tissue in order to study the physical and psychological effects that occur.

Level of aspiration – A self-imposed standard against which a person judges his or her own performance.

Level of confidence (level of significance) – In statistics, the confidence that the null hypothesis can be rejected. It is the probability that the desired result could occur by chance.

Level of tension – As a dimension of emotion, the level of activity to which the individual is impelled in his or her anticipation of affective change.

Leveling – Cognitive style whereby one ignores differences and emphasizes similarities in perceiving the world.

Lewin, Kurt – Founder of Field Theory in social psychology.

Libidinal gratification – The gratification of sexual impulses. Within the context of Freud's theory, these need not necessarily involve what the layman considers to be the sexual regions of the body.

Libido – The name given in Freudian theory to the instinctual or id energy that is the source of all psychological energy. Sometimes used to refer specifically to sexual motivation.

Life cycle – Regularly occurring episodes and events throughout the life period from conception to death which have impact upon the total development of the person.

Life space – A term employed by Lewin to describe the individual's interpretation of his or her environment. The life space includes the individual, personal goals and aspirations, the alternatives necessary to obtain those goals, and the barriers that obstruct his or her action.

Life style – In Adler's writings, an individual's characteristic and pervasive pattern of behavior for gaining status and dealing with feelings of inferiority.

Light adaptation – A decrease in sensitivity to light resulting from an increase in light energy reaching the eye.

Limbic system – A group of anatomical structures surrounding the brain stem; thought to be involved with motivated behavior and emotion.

Linear program – Any programmed learning situation that progresses in the same way for each subject.

Linguistic-relativity theory – A theory of thinking that states that the form and structure of a language are the determinants of the ways of thought. (See Worfi hypothesis.)

Live modeling – One organism copying a behavior of another organism that is physically present and observed.

Lobotomy – Type of psychosurgery that involves severing the connections between the frontal lobes and the rest of the brain. It has been used to treat extremely hyperemotional mental patients but is infrequently used today.

Locus of control – (Rotter) A personality construct which is dependent upon whether the individual perceives rewards as being contingent upon his or her own behavior.

Logarithmic scale – A scale in which the intervals are based on logarithms instead of on the original numbers.

Logical positivism – The position in philosophy that in science, meaningful statements must be operationally defined. The consequence of this position is to deny mentalistic concepts.

Logical syllogism – Three-step argument which consists of two premises, assumed to be true, and a conclusion that may or may not follow from these premises.

Long-term memory – Memory for learned material over a relatively long retention interval (generally an hour or more). A hypothetical memory system for permanent storage of learning.

Longitudinal study – An investigation conducted over a fairly long period of time, using the same subjects throughout; the study may be used to determine how age, the independent variable, affects behavior.

Looming – A perceptual phenomenon occurring when an object appears to be directly approaching the observer because of a symmetrical increase in size.

Loudness – The psychological attribute corresponding to amplitude of a sound wave.

Love-withdrawal – Discipline based on threatened loss of love (showing anger or hurt, isolating, or threatening to leave the child.) Excessive use may lead to anxiety, dependency, and inhibitedness.

LTM – (See Long-term memory.)

Lucid dream – Special type of dream during which the dreamer is aware that he or she is dreaming and possesses his or her normal ability to think and reason.

Luminosity – The effective brightness of light, with intensity constant, a result of the varying sensitivity of the visual system to different wavelengths of light.

Mach bands – Visual contours that appear where there is no corresponding physical discontinuity in light intensity.

Machiavellianism – A personality characteristic, measured by the Mach scale, in which one tends to manipulate other people for one's own ends.

Macula – Generally, an anatomical structure shaped like a spot; the central region of the retina; a receptor organ in the inner ear that responds to gravitational pull.

Magazine training – The establishment of conditioned reinforcers by periodically providing reinforcement no matter what the subject is doing.

Magnitude estimation – A psychophysical method in which the observer judges the intensity of the stimulus in some numerical ratio to a standard stimulus.

Main effect – When the effect of one independent variable is the same at all levels of another independent variable.

Major gene determination – A hereditary process whose outcome is determined by the presence or absence of a single dominant or recessive gene.

Malleus – The outer of the three bones in the middle ear that transmit vibrations from the eardrum to the cochlea. Sometimes referred to as the hammer.

Mand – A verbal utterance under the control of the state of deprivation of the speaker. A basic form of verbal behavior in Skinner's system.

Mandala – 1. A model of the cosmos, based on concentric shapes; often includes images of deities. 2. In Jung's theory, a magical circle that represents self-unification efforts.

Mania – Psychotic affective reaction involving speeding up of thought processes and motor behavior and exaggerated feelings of optimism.

Manic depression – A mood disorder in which there are recurrent and severe fluctuations of affective state between elation and depression. Currently called "bipolar disorder."

Manifest Anxiety Scale – The most widely used paper-and-pencil test to measure anxiety.

Manifest content (of dreams) – In psychoanalysis, dream materials that are recalled by the dreamer; concrete objects and events of the dream.

Manipulative drive – A tendency to explore and utilize new objects in the environment independent of their immediate utility.

Mantra – A word or phrase to be recited, contemplated, or sung, especially as a part of meditation.

Marasmus (also called anaclitic depression) –

The label given to the condition brought about by maternal deprivation. Results of marasmus include retarded development, depression, and occasionally death. The progressive atrophy of tissue because of nutritional disease is also common.

Marathon – In psychotherapy, a group session of exceptionally long, uninterrupted duration, usually eight or more hours.

Marbe's law – The generalization that the latency of a response in word association increases as the popularity or commonness of the response decreases.

Marijuana – A psychoactive substance prepared from the flowers or leaves of the Indian hemp plant Cannabis sativa, the active ingredient being THC.

Masochism – The turning of any sort of destructive tendencies inward upon oneself.

Massed practice – Bunching learning trials close together without rest periods. Adversely affects performance and sometimes retention.

Mastery test – A test that is being used to determine whether a pupil or pupils have mastery of some unit that has been taught. In a mastery test, one is not really concerned about differences between individuals.

Matched groups design – An experimental design in which subjects are matched on some variable assumed to be correlated with the dependent variable and then randomly assigned to conditions.

Matched sampling – A technique for selecting subjects in which an experimenter makes sure that each group in the experiment contains the same number of subjects who possess a certain characteristic that might influence the outcome.

Maternal behavior – Behavior concerned with giving birth to young and providing postnatal care.

Maturation – A developmental process defined by changes that are relatively independent of a child's environment. While the nature and timing of maturational changes are assumed to result from genetic predispositions, their manifestation is at least partly a function of the environment.

Mature birth – The birth of an infant between the thirty-seventh and forty-second week of pregnancy.

Maze-bright – An adjective describing those rats able to learn to run through mazes very easily.

Maze-dull – An adjective describing the rat who has a great deal of difficulty in learning how to run a maze.

Mean – A measurement of central tendency that is computed by dividing the sum of a set of scores by the number of scores in the set, otherwise known as the arithmetic mean or average.

Meaningfulness – In verbal learning, the number of associations evoked by material that is being learned.

Means-end analysis – Problem solving process in which one tests for difference between the present situation and a solution situation and continues to perform operations until no difference is detected. Applicable whenever there is a clearly specifiable problem situation and a clearly specifiable solution.

Measurement – The assignment of numbers to events on the basis of rules.

Mechanical problem – Lowest level of problems studied by psychologists. All mechanical problems have specific, known solutions which can be found relatively automatically by following a simple series of steps. They may emphasize perceptual or verbal factors.

Mechanistic – A theoretical point of view which holds that all things in the universe, including living organisms, may be best understood as machines.

Median – A measure of central tendency; the middle score of a distribution, or the one that divides a distribution in half.

Mediated association – Association between two items via another item. Thus, if A is associated with B and B is associated to C, A is mediately associated with C.

Mediation – A term used to describe the processes assumed to intervene between the presentation of a stimulus and the appearance of a response. Mediation is often assumed to be largely verbal.

Mediational response – According to mediational theory, an internalized version of an external response which is formed during the learning process and manipulated in the thinking process. May be located in the nervous system, muscles, and glands, or may be thought of as purely a theoretical construct.

Mediational theory of thinking – Holds that as a consequence of external stimulus-response associations, the individual may form internal miniaturized versions of these stimuli (mediational stimuli) and responses (mediational responses) which serve as the connecting link between the environment and the way one responds to it.

Medical model – A model of psychopathology in which pathological behaviors are viewed as symptoms of a disease.

Medical therapies – Therapies that involve the use of physical procedures to try to treat abnormal personality problems.

Meditation – Concentration technique used to purify the ordinary state of consciousness by removing illusions and to facilitate the production of states of consciousness in which truth is more directly perceived.

Meditational process – A hypothetical process that bridges the gap between stimuli and responses.

Medulla (medulla oblongata) – The lowest and most posterior part of the brain, which is connected to the spinal cord. It contains several kinds of nuclei, especially those concerned with breathing, heartbeat, and blood pressure.

Meiosis – The division of a single sex cell into two separate cells, each consisting of 23 chromosomes rather than 23 pairs of chromosomes. Meiosis, therefore, results in cells that are completely different.

Melancholia – A mental state of extreme depression often accompanied by bodily complaints, hallucinations, and delusions.

Memory – The term designating the mental function of recalling what has been learned or experienced; the physical retention of information.

Memory drum – An electromechanical device used to present materials for verbal learning experiments.

Memory trace – A hypothetical physiological change in the nervous system during learning. Also called engram. Gestaltists hold that the trace undergoes systematic change and reorganization.

Memory trace change theory – The theory that forgetting is due to qualitative changes in the memory trace over time.

Menarche – The girl's first menstrual period. An event which transpires during pubescence.

Menses – A monthly discharge of blood and tissue from the womb of a mature female. The term refers to menstruation.

Mental age (MA) – A term applied to both items and scores on intelligence tests. For an item, the age level is that age at which 50-70 percent of children pass the item. For an individual it is the age group of children who would pass the same items he or she has passed.

Mental chronometry – The attempt to measure mental functions by subtracting simpler tasks from more complex ones.

Mental health – A state of personality that shows self-actualization, ability to withstand stress, and high productivity; the absence of symptoms of mental illness. (Freud: The ability to love and work.)

Mental illness – A state of personality in which behavior is statistically infrequent, violates societal norms, or impairs functioning.

Mental retardation – A designation for exceptional subjects whose IQ scores are below the -2 standard deviations from the mean of a normal probability distribution of intelligence test scores, generally a score below 68.

Mental set – The tendency to respond in a given way regardless of the requirements of the situation. Sets sometimes facilitate performance and sometimes impair it. (Impairment is referred to as "functional fixedness.")

Mentalistic – Subscribing to the principle that mental processes are distinct from physiological processes and that conscious processes can be exposed by introspection; explanations of psychological processes in terms of the operation of the mind.

Mentally gifted – Persons with IQ scores substantially above average.

Mescaline – A hallucinogenic drug obtained from the peyote cactus.

Mesomorph – A body type in Sheldon's system characterized by muscular build. A mesomorph has the personality characteristics of somatotonia: assertiveness, love of adventure and risk, physical courage, etc.

Metabolism – A general term referring to chemical and physical processes in the body cells including the assimilation of food, the storage and utilization of energy, the repairing of tissues, and the disposal of cellular wastes.

Methadone – A drug used in treatment of heroin addiction, which prevents withdrawal symptoms and blocks the heroin "high" but still is addictive.

Method of adjustment – A psychophysical method in which the observer sets the stimulus to some predetermined limit, e.g., just detectable.

Method of constant stimuli – A psychophysical method in which the stimuli are presented relative to a standard, the observer judging between them, e.g., larger than.

Method of limits – A psychophysical method in which stimuli presented in ascending and descending series, the observer reporting when he or she can detect stimulation.

Method of locations – A method of facilitating memory by associating new items to be recalled with specific familiar locations or places. Also called the method of loci.

Method of successive approximations – Shaping by reinforcing behavior that successively approximates a desired behavior.

Midbrain – One of the parts of the cerebrum lying beneath the forebrain situated between the forebrain and the hindbrain. Also known as the mesencephalon, it is the primary location of the reticular formation.

Middle childhood – An arbitrary division in the sequence of development beginning somewhere near the age of 6 and ending at approximately 12.

Milieu therapy – A type of therapy that tries to incorporate the social standards of a culture or community into the hospital or treatment setting.

Minimal social situation – A laboratory game which simulates social exchange.

Minimum age of viability – The youngest age at which the fetus can survive outside the womb. Currently this age is about 6 months.

Minimum principle – In perceptual organization, the organization that is perceived in an ambiguous stimulus is the one which keeps changes, discontinuities, and differences to a minimum; simplicity of organization is a determinant of what will be seen.

Minnesota Multiphasic Personality Inventory (MMPI) – A widely used empirically derived paper-and-pencil personality test designed to provide a measure of a subject's similarity to various psychopathological groups.

Minority group – Describes a cultural, social, ethnic, or religious group existing within a larger cultural group.

Mitosis – The process of cell division by which the body produces new cells in order to maintain growth and good health, each cell being nearly identical to the original.

Mixed-motive game – A laboratory game in which the distinction can be made between players who cooperate to achieve profits and players who compete to achieve profits.

Mixed-motive group – A group in which members share some common goals but also have some opposing goals.

Mnemonics – Memory aids or systems for learning materials.

Modality effect – Different effects on retention often produced by visual and auditory presentation; auditory presentation usually produces better memory for the last few items in a series than does visual presentation.

Mode – The score value that occurs most frequently in a given set of scores.

Model – A physical, mathematical or heuristic representation of a process, an object, or an event.

Model status – The standing or position accorded the model by the observer.

Modeling – In social learning theory, a form of learning in which the subject imitates the actions or reactions of another person. In behavior modification therapy, a technique based on imitation and perceptual learning.

Mongolism (Down's syndrome) – A form of mental retardation, often characterized by somewhat Mongoloid facial features. Caused by an extra chromosome (47 instead of the normal 46).

Monitoring task – A form of dichotic listening where observers are not required to verbalize a message as it is presented.

Monochromator – An instrument for producing light of a very narrow wavelength band.

Monocular cues for depth – Cues for depth perception derived from information in the optic array that is available to either eye alone; interposition, size perspective linear perspective, shading, aerial perspective, texture gradients.

Monotonic relationship – Relationship between two variables in which an increase on one variable is accompanied by a consistent increase or decrease on the other variable.

Monozygotic – Developing from the same fertilized egg. Identical twins resulting from the division of a single fertilized egg.

Moods – Transient states, sometimes called affects; they refer to the perception by an individual of internal feelings associated with emotions.

Moral anxiety – Feelings of guilt.

Moral realism – The immature orientation in all the areas of moral judgment studied by Piaget. An attitude that the morality of an act is inherent in that act and can be perceived immediately by an observer as an objective fact.

Moral relativism – The mature orientation in all the areas of moral judgment studied by Piaget. Morality and rules are seen as something that is flexible and subject to consensus, rather than fixed.

Moro reflex – An automatic response shown by most normal infants to a startling stimulus, it involves throwing the arms to the side, extending the fingers, and then curving the hands back to the midline.

Morpheme – The smallest part of a word that conveys meaning and cannot be further subdivided without destroying the meaning; the units into which phonemes are arranged to make a language.

Mosaic hypothesis – The postulation of a simple one-to-one correspondence between perceptual experience and physical stimulation; the basic weakness, according to Gestalt theorists, in the system of Structuralism.

Motion parallax (Relative motion) – The apparent movement of stationary objects occurring when the observer changes position.

Motivated forgetting theory – The theory that holds that forgetting is due to a person's motivation, e.g., a desire to avoid certain memories, which are therefore repressed. Freud argued for this theory of forgetting.

Motive – A condition or tension that initiates, guides, and maintains behavior.

Motor – Refers to information being carried out from the central nervous system. Efferent is a synonym.

Motor area – An area of cerebral cortex around the central fissure controlling voluntary movements of the skeletal muscles.

Motor learning – Learning in which the primary elements are the control of bodily movements through various cue systems; e.g., visual, auditory, and kinesthetic cues.

Motor nerves – The bundles of neurons that conduct impulses from the central nervous system to muscles and glands.

Motor sequence – The series of events involving the development of posture, crawling and walking in infants. These events tend to occur in a set order and at approximately the same age in most infants of a particular culture.

Motor theory – An early stimulus-response theory of thinking espoused by behaviorists and proposing that thinking always involves muscular or glandular activity of some kind. According to this theory, most human thought is basically subvocal speech activity.

Motor units – Groups of motor neurons, many of which comprise a muscle or glandular terminal.

Movement parallax – The difference in the rate of motion over the retinal surface of images projected by objects at different distances from a moving observer; motion parallax.

Multiple approach-avoidance conflict – A situation in which a subject must choose between two (or more) stimulus situations, each of which has both positive and negative values (double bind).

Multiple personality – An extremely rare form of dissociation in which a person displays two or more relatively distinct personalities, each with its own set of memories. The second personality often exhibits traits repressed in the first.

Multiple schedules – Partial reinforcement schedules that require the subject to satisfy two or more independent schedules that are presented successively, each cued.

Multiple therapy – Any form of psychotherapy in which two or more therapists simultaneously participate.

Muscle spindle – Receptors in muscles that signal muscular stretching.

Mutation – A change in, or deformation of, a gene, causing a modification in the character that the gene determines.

Mutual satisfaction – A leadership style in which policies are made by the group, with the leader simply acting as a focal point for carrying out their wishes.

Myelin – A white fatty substance which covers many axons, usually surrounding the axon in a bead-like arrangement.

Myelin sheath – The fatty, or lipid, substance that surrounds the axons of some neurons. The greater the degree of myelinization, the greater the speed of transmission of neural impulses. The sheath is whitish in color.

Myoneural junction – The meeting point between neural axons and muscle fibers. Also called the neuromuscular junction.

Myopia Nearsightedness; deficient acuity for distant objects.

Mysticism – A belief in a spiritual meaning or reality that is neither apparent to the senses nor rationally obvious.

N – Symbol used to represent the number of cases in the group being studied.

Naive realism – The philosophy that perceptual experience is a mirror of the objective world.

Name calling – The propaganda technique giving an object a name with either pleasant or unpleasant connotations.

Narcissistic – Self-centered, egotistical gratification-oriented; characteristic of the infant and of persons whose personalities retain infantile features.

Narcotherapy – The treatment of mental illness, particularly personality disorders, by giving sleep inducing drugs, e.g., sodium amytal. The patient is encouraged to discuss his difficulties, and interpretations are given afterwards.

Narcotic drugs – Drugs that can be used as painkillers, opiates, such as heroin or morphene.

Nativism – Encompasses the notion that there are innate ideas, such as space and time perception, as well as the notion that the capacity for intelligence is inherited.

Nativist – One who emphasizes the role of heredity in the behavior of mature individuals rather than to the specific experiences in the course of development.

Nature – That side of the nature-nurture issue which represents the influence of heredity.

Nature-nurture controversy – The question of determining the relative contribution of heredity and environment to the development of the individual.

Natural childbirth – Refers to the birth of a child in which a mother employs no anesthetics (or very little) to relieve pain. Physical exercises, exercises in relaxation, and mental preparation are advocated for the mother prior to the birth of the child.

Natural selection – The theory Darwin posed to explain evolution by which traits that aid the organism to survive and propagate their own kind recur in future generations, while those that are unsuitable do not; "survival of the fittest."

Naturalistic observation – A method for research in which subjects are observed in their natural setting, rather than in the laboratory. The researcher attempts to be as unobtrusive as possible.

Need – Any deficiency which an organism feels is necessary for its welfare. It may be learned or innate; an animal drive or physiological motive.

Need achievement (McClelland) – An indicator of motivation; concern with improvement of performance; aggressive and ambitious people possess a higher need for achievement than more passive and less ambitious people.

Need for affiliation – Concern for establishing, maintaining, and cultivating relationships with people, often assessed by means of the content analysis of TAT stories.

Need for power – Concern with having or attaining status, reputation, and influence, often assessed by means of analyzing the content of TAT productions.

Need-reduction theory – The theory that reinforcement is based on reduction of primary physiological drives through consummatory behavior.

Negative acceleration – A decrease in the rate of growth or change in a function with time or practice; a curve of diminishing returns, characteristic of learning and forgetting.

Negative afterimage – After staring at a colored stimulus for a period of time, a person sees the same stimulus in complementary colors against a neutral background.

Negative instances – All stimuli in a population which do not have those characteristics that illustrate a given concept. For example, if mammal is the concept, then reptiles are negative instances.

Negative reinforcement – In operant conditioning, where reinforcement is paired with or contingent upon the termination of an aversive stimulus. Thus the absence of the stimulus condition strengthens or maintains a response.

Negative skew – When most of the scores of a distribution are found at the upper end of the measurement scale and the tail of the distribution is predominantly on the left; skewed to the left.

Negative transfer – The inhibitory effect of prior learning upon new learning.

Negative transfer of training – When the learning of one task increases the difficulty of learning a second task.

Neobehavioristic theories – A division in learning theory that includes those theoretical positions that, although they are still concerned with stimuli and responses as the fundamental data of psychology, they do take into account the events that intervene between stimuli and responses.

Neocortex – The outer, highly developed, convoluted covering of the brain. It is the most recently evolved neural tissue.

Neo-Freudian – Refers to a large number of psychologists who agree with some of Freud's ideas but have amended his theory to develop their own, more modern theories. Also called "neoanalytic," the category includes Horney, Erikson, and Fromm.

Neo-Freudian analysis – The psychoanalytic theories and practices of therapists who claim to have revised, rather than to have rejected, the teachings of Freud. These practices emphasize social factors, insecurity, and interpersonal relationships in the causation of neuroses.

Neonate – The newborn infant.

Nerve – A bundle of axons from many neurons. Outside of the central nervous system, it runs from one point in the body to another and carries nerve impulses; used synonymously with neuron.

Nerve impulse – A change in polarity in the membrane of a nerve fiber that is propagated along the length of the fiber when its initial segment is stimulated above threshold; an ac-

tion potential.

Nervous breakdown – Popular term usually used to describe a person whose emotional problems are so severe that he can no longer cope with home or work responsibilities and requires hospitalization; not a description of a physical nervous condition.

Nervous system – The brain and spinal cord, plus all of the neurons traveling throughout the rest of the body. It is a communication system, carrying information throughout the body.

Neurasthenia – A neurotic reaction in which the person is constantly tired and feels vaguely unwell. It is no longer included in the standard psychiatric nomenclature.

Neurilemma – A thin covering of Schwann cells over the myelin sheath in neurons of the peripheral nervous system necessary for the regeneration of injured fibers.

Neurohumor – A chemical substance emitted at the tips (terminal button) of neural fibers that participates in transmission of impulses across the synaptic junction; transmitter substance; neurotransmitter.

Neuron – The basic structural unit of the nervous system, composed of a cell body, an axon, and one or more dendrites; its function is to send and receive messages.

Neurosis – Any of several less severe personality disturbances instigated and maintained for the purpose of contending with stress and avoiding anxiety, characterized by anxiety and rigid and unsuccessful attempts to reduce it.

Neurotic – Person who is experiencing a neurosis. (See Neurosis.)

Neurotic anxiety – In Freud's theory the fear that the impulses of the id will get out of control; in learning theory, conditioned fear.

Neurotic depression – A mild depressive reaction, usually in response to some environmental stress. The patient is quite dejected and inactive physically and mentally.

Neurotic need – (Horney) A strategy employed by an anxious person to find a solution to the problems of disturbed human relationships and to cope with his or her feelings of isolation and helplessness; it takes the form of a compulsive demand for certain behavior on the part of others.

Neurotic paradox – Refers to the fact that the

neurotic person persists in his maladaptive behavior despite its self-defeating nature and the resulting unpleasant consequences.

Neurotic reactions – Behavior patterns produced by high levels of conflict and frustration that are repetitious and maladaptive.

Neutral transfer – Lack of transfer of any training effects from prior learning to present learning.

Noise – In detection theory, the term used to describe any extraneous stimuli; the background of stimulation in which the signal is embedded.

Nominal realism – The belief held by young children that names are identical with the properties or objects that they name; by naming an object it is made real.

Nominal scaling – The assignment of numbers to groups as names, used to distinguish between logically separated groups, e.g., Team Numbers, 1, 2, 8, 20.

Nomothetic – Approach to personality study that involves looking for traits common to all persons.

Nonconformity – When a person responds in a manner contrary to a group's opinions or expectations.

Noncontingent reinforcement – Reinforcement that is not dependent on a response made by the organism.

Noncontinuity theory – The theory that learning occurs on one trial or not at all.

Nondirective therapy – A form of therapy originated by Carl Rogers in which the therapist serves mainly to reflect the feelings expressed by the patient, accepting them without evaluation; client-centered therapy.

Nonintellective behaviors – Behaviors which are not specifically cognitive or intellectual in nature, but rather involve such things as social, emotional, and physically oriented actions.

Nonreactive – Term to describe observations that are not influenced by the presence of the investigator; unobtrusive methods.

Nonreversal shift – A type of discrimination learning in which the subject, who has been reinforced for selecting one value of a dimension, is now reinforced for selecting stimuli on the basis of another dimension. For example, the subject who has been taught to select black animal figures and reinforced for doing so is now reinforced for selecting animal figures regardless of their color.

Nonsense syllable – A syllable, usually with three letters, constructed to be as devoid of meaning as possible, used often in verbal learning experiments. There are two varieties: consonant-vowel-consonant syllables and consonant trigram syllables.

Nonverbal communication – Communication by means other than words. Often termed body language.

Norepinephrine – An excitatory neurotransmitter substance found in the brain and in the sympathetic division of the autonomic nervous system.

Norm – A representative standard for performance or behavior; an established rule for identifying desirable behavior.

Normal curve – A mathematically defined curve that is bell-shaped and in which the mean, median, and mode are all in the same interval; it is the graphic representation of the normal probability distribution.

Normal distribution – The distribution is bell-shaped, that is, symmetrical with a piling up of cases in the middle, steep shoulders, and flat tails. It is thought to approximate the distribution of many biological and psychological characteristics. Its mathematical formula is derived from the laws of probability.

Norm group – The group with which an individual is being compared.

Normative developmental research – Research strategy that compares the behavior of children at different ages in a particular situation. It tends to be used by psychologists who stress the role of maturation in development and aims to chart behavioral norms for different ages.

Normative test – A test in which the individual's performance is expressed in relation to that of some norm or reference group, as contrasted with an ipsative test.

Nuclear family – A family consisting of a mother, a father, and their offspring.

Nucleus – Structure containing genetic material found in the center of most cells. Also, a cluster of cell bodies of neurons in the central nervous system.

Null hypothesis – States that the independent variable will have no effect on the dependent variable.

Null result – An experimental outcome where the dependent variable was not influenced by the independent variable.

Nursery school – A preschool institution that accepts children at an early age and that emphasizes child care, and emotional and social development.

Nurture – That side of the nature-nurture issue which reflects the influence of the environment, socialization, education, and training on the development of an organism.

Nystagmic eye movements – Rapid involuntary movements of the eye followed by a slow return to normal fixation, as in the following of a moving target.

Obesity – Corpulence; fatness. The condition of being 20% or more overweight.

Object – A relatively stable aspect of the environment with relatively consistent meanings. It can also mean a goal.

Object concept – Piaget's expression for the child's understanding that the world is composed of objects that continue to exist quite apart from his or her perception of them.

Object conservation – The discovery by the infant, towards the end of the first year of life, that objects continue to exist even when they are outside the range of the infant's sense perceptions. Also the child's ability to ignore irrelevant transformations (e.g., the child knows that when water is poured from a wide-short glass, into a tall glass the volume is the same; is conserved).

Object permanence – A term in Piaget's theory of development which refers to a child's belief that an object continues to exist even though it is no longer visible.

Objective – Having an existence independent of the observer, existing in fact or physical reality; unbiased.

Objective psychotherapy – The term applied to the system of psychotherapy developed by Benjamin Karpman in which the patient receives a memorandum based on his or her answers to autobiographical questions.

Objective test – A test made of up structured response items which provide both a specific problem and a limited set of choices from which the student must select his or her answer.

Objectivity – When judgments made are free from bias or the influence of personal feeling.

Observational methods – Research techniques based on simply observing behavior without trying to manipulate it experimentally; field or natural setting research.

Obsession – An idea, often irrational or unwanted, usually associated with anxiety, that persists or frequently recurs and cannot be dismissed by the individual.

Obsessive-compulsive reactions – Neurotic reactions in which undesirable thought and activity patterns are repeated in a ritualistic way.

Obstetrics – The medical art and science of assisting women who are pregnant, both during their pregnancy and at birth; midwifery.

Occipital area (or lobe) of the brain – The part of the cerebral cortex lying at the back of the head involved in vision.

Oddity problem – A problem in which the solution lies in choosing the stimulus item which is unlike the others. If two circles and one square are presented, the square is correct.

Oedipal conflict (complex) – Proposed by Freud, this is the attraction a boy has for his mother and its accompanying anxiety and guilt. In the female Electra conflict, it is her attraction for her father and the resulting anxiety and guilt.

Ogive – A curve that is loosely described as S-shaped.

One-tailed test – Test that places the rejection area at one end of a distribution. Events falling in the other end of the distribution are ignored as being spurious.

Ontogenetic (genetic) – Pertaining to development within the members of a species.

Opening-up meditation – An attempt to produce continuous attention to all aspects of the stimulus environment.

Operant – The label employed by Skinner to describe a response not elicited by any known or obvious stimulus. Most significant human behaviors appear to be operant. Such behaviors as writing a letter or going for a walk are operants, if no known specific stimulus elicits them. ("Operating" on the environment so as to produce a result.)

Operant conditioning – A type of learning involving an increase in the probability of a response occurring as a result of reinforcement. Much of the experimental work of B. F. Skinner investigates the principles of operant conditioning. (See "classical conditioning.") Also referred to as Instrumental Conditioning.

Operant conditioning chamber – An apparatus used for experimental testing of instrumental conditioning; several varieties exist, the best known being the "Skinner box."

Operant level – The rate at which a response is emitted prior to the introduction of a reinforcement schedule.

Operation – According to Jean Piaget, a process that changes its object.

Operational definition – A definition of a concept in terms of the operations that must be performed to demonstrate the concept a definition by concrete example.

Opinion – The verbal expressions of a belief, often still open to modification.

Opponent process theory – A theory of color vision holding that there are three kinds of visual receptors, one for brightness and two for color (red-green and blue-yellow), and that any color experience results from a combination of excitation and/or inhibition of these color receptors.

Optic array – A pattern of observable light energy, reflected from the surface of an object, that enters the eye.

Optic chiasm – A structure on the base of the brain that transmits the impulses from the receptors in the eye to the brain. In man, half of the optic fibers cross to the opposite hemisphere at the optic chiasm thus providing information from both eyes to each hemisphere.

Optic disc – The area of the retina where all the nerve impulses leave the eye to form the optic nerve and where there are no rods or cones, creating a "blind spot" on the retina.

Optical resolving power – The ability of the lens in the eye to focus the optic array sharply on the retina and not in front of or behind it.

Oral stage – In the genetic model of psychoanalytic theory, the first stage of psychosexual development, in which libidinal interest and conflicts center on the mouth — on sucking, eating, biting, and so on.

Order effect – An effect on behavior attributable to the specific sequence of experimental conditions to which subjects are exposed.

Ordinal scale – Numbers arranged to correspond to the increase or decrease in the variable being measured. A set of ranks. The relative distances between the elements need not be, and usually are not, equal.

Ordinate – The y-axis, or vertical axis, of a graph. By convention the dependent variable is plotted on the ordinate.

Organ of Corti – The lining on the basilar membrane of the inner ear that contains the hair cells which are the receptors for hearing.

Organic disorder – An emotional problem resulting from biological causes, usually from impairment of brain functioning.

Organic psychoses – Psychotic reactions having a demonstrable bodily origin, e.g., brain injury or neurological disease.

Organism – A form of life exhibiting integration and coordination of function, which has the capacity for self-maintenance. In psychology the term is often used to refer to the higher animals including human beings.

Organization – The process of cognitive growth which, according to Jean Piaget, integrates one psychological structure with another.

Orientation reaction (response) – The initial response of humans and other animals to novel stimulation. Also called the orienting reflex or orienting response. Components of the orientation reaction include changes in EEG patterns, in respiration rate, in heart rate, and in galvanic skin response.

Orthogenetic – Refers to Heinz Werner's theory of the sequence of development which takes place in the same direction and through the same stages in every organism despite differing external conditions. Also, pertaining to that which encourages desirable development.

Orthogenetic principle – The generalization that the psychological development of individuals is characterized by increasing differentiation among the subparts of their personalities and by increasingly complex organizational structures among those parts.

Orthographic attribute – In Underwood's theory of memory, the attribute of a memory relating to the physical shape of the remembered item.

Oscilloscope – An electronic device for displaying waveforms on a cathode ray tube screen. It is widely used in studying nervous impulses.

Osgood's transfer surface – A three-dimensional representation, first formulated by Charles Osgood, representing positive and negative transfer as a function of stimulus and response similarity.

Osmotic pressure – A difference in the concentration of fluids on either side of a semipermeable membrane.

Ossicles – Three tiny bones in the middle ear which transmit the sound vibrations from the eardrum to the cochlea.

Ossification – The process of bone formation, starting from a few locations and spreading outward from those locations.

Otolith organs – Sense organs in the inner ear that are sensitive to changes in the tilt of the head, involved in maintaining equilibrium.

Out-of-body experience (OOBE) – An experience during which a person feels that he or she is located at a point other than where the physical body is, and still feels a normal state of consciousness.

Ovaries – The reproductive organs in females: they are also endocrine glands that secrete hormones (including estrogens), regulating sexual cycles and behavior, and supporting pregnancy.

Overlearning – The amount of practice occurring after a performance criterion has been reached, resulting in no mistakes in a given number of trials.

Overloading – The presentation of material to one sense modality at such a high rate that the person cannot absorb it; stimulus overload.

Overt – Outward or external. Capable of being observed. Not concealed physically or psychologically.

Overtones (Partials) (Harmonics) – Components of a complex periodic sound wave which are multiples of the fundamental, or lowest, frequency. The pattern of overtones determines the timbre of a musical instrument.

Ovum (plural ova) – The sex cell produced by a mature female approximately once every 28 days. When mature it consists of 23 chromosomes as opposed to all other human body cells (somatoplasm), which consist of 23 pairs of chromosomes. It is often referred to as an egg cell.

Pacinian corpuscle – A tactile receptor found below the skin, in the joints, and in other deep tissues. It consists of a nerve fiber inside of a capsule; the capsule moves under pressure activating the fiber.

Pain – The drive aroused by noxious stimulation, especially at high intensity levels. The actual mechanism for pain detection remains a mystery.

Paired-associate learning – Learning a list of paired items such that one member of the pair can be recalled given the other member as a stimulus.

Paleocortex – Parts of the cerebral cortex considered to be old, with respect to evolution.

Palmar reflex – The grasping reflex that a newborn infant exhibits when an object is placed in his or her hand.

Pancreas – Produces the hormone insulin and thus regulates the use of sugar in the body. Below-normal production of insulin by this gland leads to diabetes mellitus, or too much sugar in the blood.

Paper-and-pencil tests – Psychological tests that use written or check-type answers only.

Papilla – A small, nipple-shaped protuberance. Papillae are located on the skin, the tongue, and the nasal mucosa, and contain receptors for touch, taste, and smell.

Paradigm – A pattern or model. In psychology, the term is often used to apply to an accepted procedure for investigating some phenomenon, such as the paradigm for studying transfer of training.

Paradigm clash – Conflict between two radically different views of the nature of the physical or psychological world.

Parallel attention – Sensory processing when several stimuli are attended to simultaneously.

Parallel forms – Two alternative forms of a test that yield equivalent results.

Parameters – Measurements describing a population. Parameters are usually inferred from statistics, which are measurements describing a sample.

Paranoia – A psychotic reaction in which there are delusions of persecution or grandeur, with no withdrawal or impairment of other intellectual functioning.

Paranoid schizophrenia – Subtype of schizophrenia in which paranoid tendencies predominate, characterized by delusions of persecution, suspicion of others, and delusions of grandeur.

Parapraxis – A minor error in behavior, such as a slip of the tongue or pen, memory blockings, small accidents, misplacing articles, etc.

Paraprofessional – The designation of a person with relatively little training who works to help individual's confront personal problems.

Parapsychology – Study of topics that are related to psychology (such as ESP, clairvoyance, telepathy, and psychokinesis) but are not fully accepted as belonging under the heading of psychology.

Parasympathetic nervous system – A division of the autonomic nervous system which functions to maintain and conserve bodily resources.

Parataxic distortion (Sullivan) – Any attitude toward another person based on fantasy or identification of that person with other figures. The Freudians call this transference.

Parathyroid – A gland of the endocrine system that controls nervous tissue excitability by regulation of calcium and phosphorus levels in the body.

Paresis – A mental disorder caused by syphilitic infection of the brain.

Parietal lobe – The area of the cortex from the rear of the central fissure to the central back of the brain.

Part learning – Learning by dividing the materials into subsections or units, learning each unit separately, then combining at the end. Distinguished from whole learning.

Partial reinforcement – A reinforcement schedule in which less than 100 percent of all correct responses are rewarded.

Partial reinforcement effect – The finding that responses conditioned under partial reinforcement are more resistant to extinction than are those conditioned under continuous reinforcement.

Passive avoidance learning – A learning task in which the subject must refrain from making a prepotent response in order to avoid an aversive stimulus.

Passiveness – A personality trait characterized by overdependency, lack of assertiveness, and lack of autonomy.

Pathology – The science of diseases and disorders; the abnormality of structure and function characteristic of a disease.

Pavlovian conditioning (classical conditioning) – Process in which an originally neutral stimulus repeatedly paired with a reinforcer comes to elicit a response.

Peck(ing) order – A dominance hierarchy established in a group of fowl, such as chickens; sometimes refers to any dominance hierarchy.

Peak experience – According to Maslow, the most important experiences humans have. They may involve much tension and excitement or deep peace and relaxation. They generally are marked by total involvement in the present.

Pedophilia – Characterized by an individual who is sexually aroused by children.

Peer group – Those who are members of one's social group, especially in cultures in which membership is determined by age or status, and by whom one is treated as an equal.

Peer-group influence – The attachment to and the effects of age mates; increasingly important as a child grows older.

Penetrance – A characteristic of a gene, which refers to the extent to which the traits it is responsible for will be expressed in the face of environmental variations.

Penis envy – A Freudian concept referring to the repressed envy that a young girl is assumed to have for males, since they have a penis.

Percentile – The score value below which a specified percent of cases falls. Thus, the 50th percentile on an examination is the raw score below which 50 percent of examinees fall.

Percentile band – A range of percentile values within which the true percentile for an individual may be expected to lie. Usually the band extends one standard error of measurement above and below the percentile rank corresponding to the obtained score.

Percentile norms – A system of norms based on percentiles within a specific reference group.

Perceived locus of causality – A judgment as to whether the source of another's behavior lies in one's own motivations (internal locus) or in the nature of the situation in which one is placed (external locus).

Perception – The reception of information through sensory receptors and interpretation of that information so as to construct meaningfulness about one's world.

Perceptual constancies – The tendency for our experience of objects to remain relatively constant in spite of changing stimulus conditions.

Perceptual defense – Failure to recognize stimuli that are threatening because of their relation to unconscious conflicts.

Perceptual displacement – Perceiving an event as having occurred at some other time or place than its actual occurrence, usually as a consequence of the structure of its context.

Perceptual deprivation or isolation – A condition in which patterned stimulation is reduced; sensory deprivation.

Perceptual learning – The effects of past experience on current perception, usually as a result of sensorimotor changes.

Perceptual segregation – The tendency to organize one's perception into figure and ground, or focus and margin.

Perceptual selection – The tendency to focus upon only part of the potentially available stimuli.

Perceptual vigilance – Heightened sensitivity to stimuli that are threatening because of their relation to unconscious conflicts; related to perceptual defense.

Performance – The responses or behavior exhibited by an organism, which may or may not reveal what the organism has learned.

Performance test – A test, most often an intelligence test, in which ability is primarily evaluated in terms of motor skills.

Perilymph – The fluid filling the inner ear that responds to bone displacements from the ossicles.

Period – The time required for any oscillation to make a complete cycle.

Period of the embryo – The second of the three principal stages of gestation, during which the blastocyst is implanted in the uterus wall. From the second to the eighth week of gestation.

Period of the fetus – The third of the three principal stages of gestation beginning in the eighth week until birth, during which body systems advance and the fetus grows rapidly.

Peripheral nervous system (PNS) – Those nerves outside the central nervous system; it has two subdivisions, the somatic and autonomic systems. It contains all the neurons connecting to muscles, glands and sensory receptors.

Peripheral skin temperature – The skin temperature of the hands and feet.

Peripheralist position – The theory that thinking is explained best by reference to speech or other muscular movements, as opposed to central (cortical) processes.

Persona (Jung) – The mask of conscious intentions and fulfillments of social requirements of the individual behind which one hides (from oneself as well as others); the more deeply rooted components of personality; the role which a person plays.

Personal construct – In Kelly's personality theory, a hypothetical learned process that determines how one construes a particular set of events.

Personal equation – The correction of an observation for the observer's time error.

Personal responsibility – Seeing an outcome as due to one's own efforts or skills (or lack of), rather than due to luck, chance, fate, or the actions of others.

Personal space – The physical distance surrounding a person; often considered by the person as his or her "own." The invasion of this space by another who is not on special terms can make the person feel uncomfortable.

Personal unconscious – In Jung's theory of personality, the part of personality that holds memories and repressed desires.

Personality – The unique organization of relatively enduring characteristics possessed by an individual as revealed by his or her interaction with this environment.

Personality assessment – Administering and evaluating a variety of tests (and perhaps interviews) in order to develop an understanding of an individual's personality.

Personality disorders – A classification of abnormal personality patterns characterized by the person's inability to act in accordance with societal standards, although not to the extent of neurosis or psychosis.

Personality impression – A characterization by one person of the invariant affects, intents, and abilities that are peculiar to another individual.

Personality inventories – Personality assessment procedures that use many statements or questions by which the person may evaluate himself.

Personality test – Tests of personality undertaken to appraise the individual's typical or habitual way of acting and thinking, as distinct from his ability to perform.

Personality trait – A combination of perceptual, conceptual, motivational, and acting tendencies which gives rise to relatively stable, consistent behavioral dispositions in a class of situations.

Personification – A type of projection in which an individual attributes favorable or unfavorable qualities to another person as a result of his own unconscious conflicts.

Perspective – A monocular depth cue in which perception of distance is based upon previous knowledge of size-distance and shape-slant relationships.

Perspective theory – Explanation of how physically equal stimuli are perceived as unequal by proposing that one uses perspective clues to judge depth and then uses this depth information in perceiving size.

Perversion – Sexual conduct that deviates from normally accepted sexual behavior.

Phallic stage – In psychoanalytic theory, the third stage of psychosexual development, lasting from age $1^1/_2$ to 6, in which primary gratification is obtained through stimulating the genitalia.

Phallic symbol – A symbol representing some aspect of sexual experience and generally having an elongated, pointed or upright shape.

Phantom limb – Term applied to sensory experiences seeming to arise in a limb, or part of a limb, that has been amputated.

Phase – A point in a wave-form that recurs in a cyclic manner.

Phenomenal field – Everything experienced by an individual at any moment, including awareness of the self. Objects physically present but not perceived are not part of the phenomenal field, and objects not physically present but thought about are.

Phenomenalistic causality – Belief held by young children that events that occur together cause one another. For example, a little boy may scratch his head and win a game; thereafter he may believe that scratching his head will always help him to win games.

Phenomenological point of view – The hypothesis that an individual's behavior may be entirely understood and explained in terms of his or her phenomenal field (all that he or she experiences at a given moment).

Phenomenological report – A subject's description of his or her own behavior or state of mind; also called subjective report.

Phenomenology – The study of the experience of objects and events, in contrast with the study of the objects and events themselves. Sometimes contrasted with behavioristic approaches to psychology.

Phenomenon – An event, occurrence, or happening.

Phenotype – The observable properties or characteristics of organisms resulting from the influence of the genotype and the environment.

Pheromone – A chemical, secreted by one member of an animal species that communicates usually through the sense of smell, with another member of the species; often used as trail or territory markers or in sexual signaling.

Phi phenomenon – The apparent movement that occurs when two or more visual figures are successively illuminated as in stroboscopic motion.

Phlegmatic – A temperamental characteristic in Hippocrates's system. The phlegmatic person is apathetic and sluggish.

Phobia – An intense, compelling, and irrational fear of something; according to analytic theory it involves displacement of anxiety onto a situation that is not dangerous or only mildly dangerous.

Phobic reaction – A neurotic reaction characterized by fear of situations, e.g., crowds or high places.

Phone – In the science of phonology, the actual sound made by a speaker on any particular occasion.

Phoneme – The smallest unit of sound that has meaning in the language, generally consisting of a single sound such as a vowel.

Phonology – The study of the system of speech sounds within and across languages.

Photographic memory – Uncommonly vivid imagery as though the subject were actually perceiving; common in childhood but usually disappears during adolescence; eidetic imagery.

Photon – A quantum of radiant energy. It is the stimulus that excites photoreceptive cells, rods being able to detect the presence of only one photon.

Photopic – Pertaining to visual functioning under conditions of relatively high-intensity illumination; cone vision.

Phrase – In grammar, a group of words that can function as a unit in grammatical structure.

Phrenology – An obsolete system developed by Franz-Joseph Gall for identifying types of people by examining their physical features, especially the configuration of "bumps" on their skulls.

Phylogenetic development – The evolutionary development of the species from its origins to its present state. Phylogeny is contrasted to ontogeny, in the sense that it refers to the development of a species rather than to the development of an individual.

Physiological psychology – A branch of psychology which studies the physiological, or bodily, foundations of behavior.

Physiological responses – Any bodily changes, e.g., heart rate, occurring in response to stimuli.

Piaget's theory – A theory of cognitive development that describes changes in the cognitive abilities of children. The four stages described by Piaget are sensorimotor, pre-operational thinking, concrete operations, and formal operations.

Pigment – A substance that absorbs certain wavelengths of light and reflects others. The light reflected accounts for the color of the pigment. Visual pigments, contained in the rods and cones, absorb the light that ultimately results in visual experience.

Pilomotor response – The response of hair cells to stimulation in which they stand up, producing the effect called goose pimples; also termed piloerection.

Pineal gland – A gland located in the center of the brain whose functions are obscure.

Pitch – The psychological attribute of sounds that corresponds approximately to the fundamental frequency of the waveform.

Pituitary – An endocrine gland located at the base of the brain consisting of an anterior portion that controls other glands and growth and a posterior portion that is involved in metabolism. Because it regulates other glands it is sometimes referred to as the "master gland."

Pivot grammar – A form of grammar found among young children—usually consists of a single, "pivot" word and a class of "open" words that can be joined with the pivot—e.g., "Bobby go."

Place theory – A theory of pitch discrimination that holds that specific places on the basilar membrane respond to different frequencies.

Placebo – A chemically inert material that has the same appearance as an active drug; allows psychologists to test the effects of the expectations of subjects who believe they are actually taking a drug; by analogy, the "placebo effect" is any situation in which subjects believe they are experiencing a manipulation by the experimenter when in fact they are not.

Placenta – The disk-shaped mass of tissue that serves as a two-way filter between the bloodstreams of the mother and the embryo.

Placental stage – The third and final stage of labor, during which the placenta and the attached membranes and cord (the afterbirth) are expelled from the uterus.

Plateau – In a learning curve, a period of little or no change in performance preceded and followed by periods of performance improvement.

Plato – Greek philosopher and early proponent of dualism who first divided the mind into rational and irrational elements.

Play therapy – A technique for the treatment of mental illness in children in which they are given an opportunity to express their otherwise forbidden feelings and desires in a permissive playroom situation.

Pleasure centers – Areas in the brain which, when electrically stimulated, produce very strong, pleasurable sensations. May be involved in determining what is rewarding for animals in everyday life.

Pleasure principle – A concept originated by Freud, it is the idea that humans strive to avoid pain and seek pleasure. It is on this principle that the id operates, seeking immediate gratification.

Polar adjectives – Adjectives having opposite meanings; used in the semantic differential procedure.

Polygenetic determination – The determination of a trait through the interaction of a number of genes, rather than through major gene determination.

Polygraph – An instrument used to record various physiological measures such as galvanic skin response, heart rate, etc. The lie detector is a common form of a polygraph.

Pons – A part of the hindbrain containing large bands of nerve fibers connecting the lobes of the cerebellum, pathways going to and from higher centers, and many vital nuclei.

Population – The entire group from which samples may be chosen.

Population genetics – The application of genetic principles to the study of the pattern and frequency of traits throughout an entire population or species.

Positive acceleration – A value that changes by larger and larger steps as a function of time or trials. In learning curves, a curve of increasing returns.

Positive instances – All stimuli in a population which have the characteristics that illustrate a given concept. For example, if flying animals is the concept, birds are positive images.

Positive regard – In Roger's theory of personality, the concept of acceptance by others; may be unconditional (unrestricted) or conditional (restricted).

Positive reinforcement – A type of event in which the presence of a stimulus condition strengthens or maintains a response.

Positive skew – When most of the scores of a distribution are found at the lower end of the measurement scale used.

Positive transfer – The facilitory effect of prior learning on present learning.

Possession state – State in which the subject feels as if his own personality or soul has been taken over or displaced by some non-physical entity.

Posthypnotic effects – Behavior caused by suggestions given to the subject while he or she is hypnotized but which occur after the subject has been brought back to a normal state of consciousness.

Postmature birth – The birth of an infant after the forty-second week of pregnancy.

Postnatal – Following birth.

Postpubescent stage – The third stage of puberty, at which time the sex organs are capable of adult functioning.

Postsynaptic neuron – A neuron that receives the information (transmitter substance) from the axon of a presynaptic neuron.

Post-traumatic stress disorder – Inability to successfully cope with stress, brought on by a single traumatic incident or by prolonged, intense stress from which there is no escape, such as battle stress in war.

Postural reflexes – Those reflexes involved in keeping the body upright without conscious control.

Power – In modeling, potential influence. In social relations, the ability to influence others.

Power-assertion – Discipline based on the physical or material superiority of the parents.

Power law – The principle that sensation increases as some power of the physical stimulus. $S = aI^K$ where S is sensation, I is intensity of the physical stimulus and a and K are empirically derived constants.

Power (of a statistical test) – The probability of rejecting the null hypothesis in a statistical test when it is in fact false.

Power test – A test given with ample time, and designed to appraise how well the individual can perform, rather than how fast he or she can work.

P-O-X model (Heider) – Descriptive model used to diagram relationships according to balance theory; P (person) has an orientation toward O (another person); P also has an orientation toward X (usually an object); and P perceives O as having an orientation toward X. The nature of the orientations determines whether a balanced state exists.

Practice effect – The systematic change in scores on a test, ordinarily a gain, resulting from previous practice with the test.

Preadolescence – The period in the development of the individual, which follows upon the juvenile period and ends with the beginning of genital sexuality.

Precipitating factors – Stimuli that actually initiate or trigger behavioral patterns.

Precognition – An alleged ability to predict events in the future, without the benefit of sensory information.

Preconceptual thought – The first substage of the period of preoperational thought, beginning around age 2 and lasting until 4. It is so called because a child has not yet developed the ability to classify and therefore has an incomplete understanding of concepts.

Preconscious – In Freudian theory, the ideas, thoughts, and images which a person is not aware of at a given moment but which can be brought into awareness with little or no difficulty. Any thought which happens to be conscious at a given moment is preconscious both before and after that particular moment.

Predicaments – Regularly occurring events during the life cycle, such as birth, entering school, or marriage, which may have a possibility of producing a crisis or disorder.

Prediction (actuarial) – Prediction of a trend or average tendency of a group of subjects, as opposed to prediction of the behavior of an individual.

Prediction (clinical) – Prediction of the behavior of an individual.

Predictive validity – The degree to which a test measures what it is supposed to measure.

Predispositions – The background characteristics of a person that serve to influence personality patterns, particularly hereditary characteristics which favor the development of a particular trait.

Prefrontal lobotomy – A form of psychosurgery in which the connections between the prefrontal areas of the cerebral cortex and the thalamus are cut. This once popular procedure results in permanent brain damage, an inability to inhibit impulses and an unnatural tranquility and shallowness.

Pregenital stages – In psychoanalysis, the stages of the infantile period which precede the phallic phase during which the libido seeks satisfaction from the anal and oral regions.

Prehension – A term denoting the ability to grasp.

Preimplantation period – The first of the three stages of gestation, during which all cells are exact replicas of the zygote and are not attached to the wall of the uterus.

Prejudice – Attitude held toward members of another group that is emotionally, rigidly or inflexibly felt and acted on, and negative.

Premack principle – In operant conditioning, the principle that given two behaviors which differ in their likelihood of occurrence, the less likely behavior can be reinforced by using the more likely behavior as a reward.

Premature birth – Refers to the delivery of a fetus before the normal gestation period has been completed; between the 29th and 36th week of pregnancy.

Prenatal development – The period of development beginning at conception and ending at birth during which the zygote differentiates and grows.

Preoperational period – The second of Jean Piaget's stages of cognitive development (from two to seven years of age), characterized by the child's development of symbolic representation. During this time children are still confused in their use of language and explanations of causality.

Preparedness – An evolutionary concept regarding the organism's readiness to learn; used to try to explain why some learning occurs easily while other learning may be quite difficult.

Prepubescent stage – The first stage of puberty, during which the secondary sex characteristics begin to develop, but the reproductive organs do not yet function.

Presbyopia – Deficient visual acuity in old age, attributable to loss of flexibility of the tissues of the lens, resulting in decreased ability to accommodate.

Presumptive symptoms – The initial, highly probabilistic signs of pregnancy frequently noted by prospective mothers. These include cessation of menses, morning sickness, changes in the breasts, and occasionally an increase in the frequency of urination.

Presynaptic neuron – The neuron whose axon releases transmitter substance into the synaptic cleft thereby transmitting information across the synapse to the postsynaptic neuron.

Prevention services – Community-based services that are designed to identify and reduce stress factors in the community.

Primacy effect – In verbal learning, the tendency to recall items at the beginning of the list better than items in the middle. There is little proactive interference at this point.

Primal therapy – A "pop" therapy technique emphasizing the release of "frozen" pain often through the primal scream.

Primary circular reaction – An expression employed by Piaget to describe a simple reflex activity such as thumb sucking.

Primary drives – The behaviorally activating concomitants of physiological need states; in some motivational models, the innate motives on which all others are based.

Primary emotions – Emotions directly involved in goal-oriented behavior, related to gratification or frustration of our motives; joy, anger, fear.

Primary gain – For neurotic behavior, the immediate reduction of anxiety.

Primary group – A reference group with which a person spends a great deal of time, which exerts a major influence on his behavior beliefs, and standards.

Primary mental abilities – Major components of intelligence. Group factors posited by the Thurstones as a result of factor analyses.

Primary prevention – Programs and services designed to change the behavior of persons and organizations in order to reduce rates of occurrence of disorder and promote psychological well being.

Primary process – The characteristic functioning of the id, whereby there is immediate and direct satisfaction of an instinct. Primary process thinking is the dominant mode for the young child and persists in the unconscious in adult life and manifests itself chiefly through dreams, humor, and pathology.

Primary receptive area – An area of the cerebral cortex that receives afferent information from a sense organ by relatively direct routes.

Primary reinforcement – A stimulus that is reinforcing in the absence of any learning. Such stimuli as food and drink are primary reinforcers, since presumably an organism does not have to learn that they are pleasurable.

Primary stimulus generalization – The generalization of responses exhibited toward a primary stimulus to similar stimuli.

Principle of least interest – In a dyadic relationship, when the person with the least involvement establishes the conditions, and the other accepts them in order to maintain the relationship.

Prismatic lenses – Lenses made in the shape of a prism that distort color and line in a perceptual field.

Proactive interference – In learning, the negative influence of previously learned material on the recall of new material. When the influence is on the learning of the new material, it is called negative transfer.

Probability – An estimate of the likelihood that a particular event will occur.

Probability matching – In a discrimination task where each stimulus alternative has a finite probability of being correct, the tendency of subjects to respond to each stimulus with a probability that approximates the probability that the stimulus is correct.

Process schizophrenia – A form of schizophrenia for which the symptoms are slow in onset, beginning at a relatively early age, and for which the prognosis is relatively poor.

Product-moment correlation(r) – A correlational measure used when the distributions are on either interval or ratio scales.

Proficiency test – A measure of current level of skill in some aspect of a job or of an educational program. The term is used with almost the same meaning as achievement test, but with somewhat more implication of a job-oriented skill.

Profile – Graphic representation of a set of scores for an individual, organized so that the high and low scores can be identified. In order for scores to be meaningfully displayed in a profile, they must be converted to some common score scale, such as standard scores or age or grade equivalents.

Prognosis – The probability of recovery.

Prognostic test – A test designed to predict progress in achieving skill or knowledge in some area.

Program – A compilation of statements used in a teaching machine for automated instruction; the statements that control the operation of a computer.

Programmatic reasoning – Reasoning using already-existing systems of thought.

Programmed learning – A learning method based on operant conditioning, it involves taking the student through a set of learning materials in small steps and requiring mastery of each step before proceeding to the next. Reinforcement is immediate and usually positive.

Projection – A Freudian defense mechanism whereby the individual protects his ego from the recognition of an undesirable id impulse by relocating the impulse in another person.

Projective technique – A method of investigation or observation in which the subject is encouraged to respond in his own way to relatively nebulous stimuli, and the investigator then interprets the subject's response. The assumption is that the subject will project his true feelings, thoughts, or beliefs.

Projective test – A relatively unstructured test designed so as to enhance the likelihood that the test-taker's motives and conflicts, and his style of dealing with them, will be revealed in his responses.

Prolactin – A hormone secreted by the pituitary gland that stimulates the production of milk in female mammals and brooding in birds.

Propaganda – An organized attempt to change attitudes in a desired direction.

Proposition – In psychological jargon it refers to a statement that can be either true or false.

Proprioceptors – Receptors that sense position and movement of the limbs and the body in space. The principal proprioceptors are Pacinian corpuscles, muscle spindles, Golgi tendon organs, semicircular canals, utricles, and saccules.

Pro-social aggression – Aggressive behaviors which may be harmful to the target person but which are generally sanctioned in the society as contributing to social order.

Prosody – Modes of expression, intonations, accents, and pauses peculiar to a particular language.

Protanope – A dichromat with a red-green deficiency (colorblindness) due to a relative insensitivity to red light.

Protocol – The original notes or records of an experiment from which scientific data may be extracted.

Proximity – A Gestalt law of organization which asserts that elements which are close to one another will tend to be perceptually organized together.

Proximo-distal trend – The tendency for the central portions of the body to develop before

and more quickly than the peripheral portions.

Pseudoconditioning – A temporary elevation in the amplitude of the conditioned response following a conditioning series that is not due to association between the conditioned stimulus and unconditioned stimulus. Apparently the conditioning series sensitizes the subject to respond.

Psilocybin – A hallucinogenic drug found in a certain type of mushroom.

Psyche – The mind or the organized totality of all mental processes or psychological activities.

Psychedelic – In reference to drugs, it denotes any drug whose primary effect is to induce an altered state of consciousness characterized by intensified sensory experience, distorted perceptions, hallucinations, and mood changes.

Psychiatrist – A physician (M.D.) with specialized training in the treatment of mental illness.

Psychiatry – A specialty of medicine that is concerned with the diagnosis and treatment and prevention of abnormal personality patterns.

Psychic determinism – The assumption that there is either a conscious or unconscious cause behind every mental process, including errors, dreams, and slips of the tongue.

Psychic energy – In Freud's system, the energy, like physiological energy, which is involved in psychological processes. It is organized into instincts, or motives.

Psychoactive drugs – Any of a number of drugs that can cause subjective or psychological effects for a person.

Psychoanalysis – A method of treatment of mental illness developed by Freud stressing motivational processes in behavior and the importance of early experience in the development of the adult personality. It attempts to uncover repressed material from the unconscious mind by free association and dream analysis.

Psychoanalyst – Any therapist who treats mental illness according to psychoanalytic theories.

Psychoanalytic theory – The complex personality theory developed by Freud and his followers which emphasizes unconscious ideas, motives, and conflicts and which stresses the biological-sexual basis of personality development.

Psychobiologic therapy – The term applied to the system of psychotherapy developed by Adolf Meyer which emphasizes environmental manipulative and supportive approaches.

Psychodrama – A method of therapy originated by Moreno, in which patients act out plays about their conflicts in which the roles are those of significant people in their lives.

Psychodynamic – A term referring to processes that motivate behavior, particularly unconscious processes.

Psychokinesis – Making physical events happen in a desired manner with no physical intervention, such as moving objects by using only thought processes.

Psycholinguistics – The study of the learning, use, and understanding of language.

Psychological abnormality – A failure to meet one or more of the criteria of adjustment.

Psychological hedonism – The belief that people act to obtain pleasure and avoid pain.

Psychological testing – The use of some measurement technique to try to assess a behavioral characteristic.

Psychology – The scientific study of behavior and the systematic application of behavior principles.

Psycholytic therapy – A type of psychotherapy that uses small doses of LSD or other psychedelics during regular therapeutic work.

Psychometric test – Any device designed to obtain a quantitative assessment of an individual's psychological attributes.

Psychopath – A very general term for an individual who is not deterred from committing immoral or antisocial acts by the anxiety that normally accompanies such behavior; attributable to inadequate socialization.

Psychopathology – The branch of psychology concerned with the investigation of mental disorders.

Psychopharmacology – The study of the psychological effects of drugs.

Psychophysics – The study of the relationship between physical stimulation and the conscious sensations it provokes in a person.

Psychophysiology – The study of the relationship between behavior and bodily changes, usually in humans; psychobiology, physiological psychology.

Psychosexual stages of development – A Freudian term describing child development as a series of stages based on the focus of libidinal energy. The sequence of the stages is: oral, anal, phallic, latent, and genital.

Psychosis – A severe psychological disorder characterized by gross distortion of reality or by loss of reality testing, inability to distinguish between reality and fantasy, hallucinations, and/or delusions.

Psychosocial crises – In Erikson's theory of personality development, a series of stages at which critical choices must be made in regard to one's relationship to other people and to society in general.

Psychosomatic disorder – A physical disorder that has a psychological cause.

Psychosurgery – A medical therapy involving the surgical destruction of brain tissue with the aim of reducing or eliminating psychological symptoms or maladaptive behavior.

Psychotherapy – Any of several techniques employing psychological, rather than physiological, methods for treating personality disturbances.

Psychotherapy by reciprocal inhibition – The system of psychotherapy developed by Joseph Wolpe which employs conditioning to overcome a maladaptive habit by forming a new and antagonistic habit in the same stimulus situation.

Psychotic – A person who is experiencing a psychosis.

Psychotic episode – A sudden experience, generally triggered by some specific stimuli in the environment, during which a person develops a psychosis.

Psychotomimetic drug – Any drug that produces a state of being similar to a psychosis.

Puberty – The period of adolescence during which an individual reaches sexual maturity and acquires secondary sexual characteristics.

Pubescence – The period in late childhood or early adolescence during which secondary sexual characteristics begin to develop.

Public opinion poll – A technique in which a

sample from a population is asked a few questions regarding attitudes toward a particular topic.

Punishment – The presentation of an unpleasant stimulus or removal of a pleasant stimulus for the purpose of eliminating undesirable behavior.

Pupil – The aperture in the eye, surrounded by the iris, through which light passes.

Pupillary reflex – An involuntary change in the size of the pupil as a function of brightness or darkness. The pupillary reflex is present in the neonate.

Pure line – A breeding line of animals that are relatively homogenous genetically.

Pure tone – A sinusoidal sound wave composed of only one frequency.

Purity – A psychological sensation corresponding to the degree of mixing of different wavelengths in one light stimulus; increasing the degree of mixing reduces the purity of a color experience; saturation.

Purkinje shift – A change in the perception of color brightness as levels of illumination change. As illumination decreases the subjective brightness of the extremes of the visible spectrum (particularly the red) also decreases.

Q-sort – A personality questionnaire in which the subject or rater sorts a large number of statements into piles which range from "highly typical" to "highly atypical."

Quartile – A score value that separates one quarter of a group from the next. There are three quartiles. The first or lower quartile separates the lowest quarter of the group from the upper three-fourths. The second quartile is the same as the median. The third or upper quartile separates the top quarter of the group from the rest.

Quickening – The name given to the first movements of the fetus in utero that the mother can feel; does not occur until after the fifth month of pregnancy.

Race – A large subdivision of a species; in humans, these divisions are based on common ancestry and visible or somatic characteristics but they still contain a deeply arbitrary nature.

Random – Occurring by chance; in a haphazard manner.

Random error – Chance errors. Such errors form a normal distribution about the mean of the measurements.

Random groups design – When subjects are randomly assigned to conditions in a between subjects design.

Random sample – A sample of cases drawn from some larger population in such a way that every member of the population has an equal chance of being drawn for the sample.

Random schedule (variable schedule) – An intermittent schedule of reinforcement. It may be either interval or ratio, and is characterized by the presentation of reward at random intervals or on random trials.

Range – The range of a set of scores is the difference between the highest and the lowest score in a set of scores. The distance between the highest and lowest data points.

Rank-difference correlation – A correlation measure used when the distributions are on ordinal scales. Also called the rank order correlation.

Rapid eye movement (REM) – One component of paradoxical sleep, characterized by rapid eye movements, an EEG like that of light sleep, and difficulty in waking. Dreams are thought to occur in this stage of sleep.

Rapport – A reciprocally comfortable and unconstrained relationship between two or more persons, especially between therapist and patient or between tester and testee.

Rating scale – A pencil-and-paper measuring device by which a person rates the personality traits, performance, and any number of characteristics of another person.

Ratio scale – An interval scale beginning with a true zero point. Only on such a scale are ratios meaningful.

Ratio schedules – Partial reinforcement schedules in which the reinforcement delivered is based upon the number of correct responses made.

Rationalization – A defense mechanism whereby one interprets and defends his or her behavior in terms of some motive other than the one actually responsible for the behavior; an intellectualized explanation or excuse.

Raw score – A score expressed in the units in which it was originally obtained, that is, pounds, inches, or points earned on a test. Raw scores are often transformed into "normal form" for ease of interpretation and comparison.

Reactance – The tendency to resist being manipulated by other people. As a theory, the position that if opportunity to choose an object is limited, its attractiveness will be increased (Jack Brehm).

Reaction formation – A Freudian defense mechanism whereby the individual behaves in a manner opposite to his or her inclinations. Reaction formation is illustrated by an individual who intensely desires someone but is unable to obtain that person, and consequently, shows evidence of disliking that person. Results from unconscious or repressed desires or traits.

Reaction time (RT) – The minimum time between a stimulus and a response.

Reaction type – A psychiatric diagnostic classification in terms of the preponderating symptom.

Reactive – Term to describe observations that are influenced by, contaminated by (or may be, in part, a reaction to) the detected presence of the investigator. More generally, phenomena (including neurosis and psychosis) precipitated by adverse conditions or occurrences in the environment.

Reactive schizophrenias – Schizophrenic reactions in which the onset of symptoms is relatively sudden; sometimes called acute schizophrenias.

Readiness – A concept in development referring to one's state of being ready to learn a particular skill.

Real self – The concept of I, me, or myself as one really is; one's own awareness of his or her existence.

Realistic-group-conflict theory – Theory of prejudice stating that if two groups are in conflict with each other, members of each group will tend to develop prejudice against members of the other group.

Reality anxiety – In Freud's theory, reality anxiety is anxiety for which there is a realistic cause, i.e., fear; objective anxiety.

Reality principle – The process by which the ego becomes aware of the demands of the environment and works out an adjustment between these demands and the basic needs of the id, in a socially and psychologically accepted manner. The reality principle utilizes the secondary process.

Reappearance hypothesis – The notion that copies of images are stored in memory and that remembering consists of making these copies reappear.

Recall – A method for measuring retention of material previously learned, The material must be reproduced, verbally or in writing, either exactly in the order in which it was given (serial recall), or in any order desired by the subject (free recall).

Recency effect – The tendency to recall or incorporate into cognitive schemes material that was recently learned rather than earlier material; such a tendency as depleted by a serial position curve.

Reception paradigm – A procedure in concept learning; the experimenter presents the subject with stimuli which the subject must learn to categorize without error.

Receptive field – Area of the retina corresponding to a single cell in the visual cortex.

Receptive language – What is understood from words that are used.

Receptor – A specialized structure for transducing particular stimulus energy into a form processable by the nervous system.

Recessive gene – The gene in a pair of dissimilar genes that does not usually affect the process of development (the phenotype), but does affect the genotype of the individual and may be transmitted genetically to the next generation.

Reciprocal inhibition – Learning to decrease the presence of a response like anxiety by increasing the presence of an incompatible response like relaxation while the original anxiety-producing stimulus occurs.

Reciprocal innervation – The relaxation of a muscle when the one antagonistic to it is excited.

Reciprocity norm – The rule of social exchange that people should help and not hurt those who have helped them. (Piaget) The child's acquired belief that punishment should be logically related to an offense.

Recognition – A test of memory in which the subject must indicate which one of a set of items was previously experienced, or is the correct answer. In contrast to recall, the spontaneous generation of the correct answer is not necessary.

Recollection redintegration – The reinstatement of a memory upon the appearance of an element, a part, of the entire memory.

Reconnaissance – From the French "to know"; that part of therapy characterized by the collection of biographical information about the patient through intensive interrogation (Sullivan).

Reconstruction – The notion that memory consists of an abstraction and coding process and that recall involves decoding and elaboration and not simply the recovery of, for example, "photographs" of the memory from a storage space.

Reconstructive therapy – Any psychotherapy which professes to effect major changes in the personality of a patient.

Redintegration – Remembering the whole event on the basis of partial cues; recollection.

Redirection – An organism's inappropriate responding in the presence of a single releaser stimulus.

Reductionism – The point of view that the explanation of events at one level (for example, psychological) is best accomplished by reference to processes at a "lower" or more basic level (for example, physiological).

Redundancy – The extent to which stimuli are predictable and repetitious. In assertion structured therapy, circular and self-defeating behavior, developed as a result of the individual's persisting in assertions which meet with disconfirmation.

Re-educative therapy – Systems of psychotherapy which are believed to help the individual to handle problems more effectively rather than to reconstruct his or her personality. Contrasted with reconstructive therapies.

Reference group – A group to which a person belongs, or identifies with, that influences his or her attitudes, standards, proper conduct, etc.

Referent – The object or thing to which a word refers.

Reflective – A personality predisposition exhibiting a tendency to evaluate alternatives and to delay decisions in order to avoid errors.

Reflex – An automatic response to a stimulus dependent on unlearned neural connections; exhibiting reflexive behavior.

Refraction – The bending of light rays when they pass from one medium to another, as through a lens.

Refractory period (phase) – Time interval, usually following a response, during which almost no stimulus will produce another response.

Regression – A defense mechanism of neurotic behavior, symbolic of returning to earlier period of development.

Regression to the mean – The tendency for extreme measures on some variable to be closer to the group mean when remeasured, due to unreliability of measurement.

Regularization – The tendency of young children to learn the rules of grammar before they learn the exceptions and to deal with the exceptions as if they followed the rule; some examples are "feets," "runned," "bringed." Often taken as evidence of innate language ability.

Rehearsal – The repetition of a verbal input.

Reinforcement – A stimulus occurring after a response that increases the probability of the response.

Reinforcement schedule – A rule specifying the occasions on which reinforcements will be delivered.

Relational concept – A complex concept based upon the relation between two features of a stimulus situation rather than having any absolute basis.

Relearning – A measure of retention in which the time or trials necessary for the second learning of a task are compared to the time or trials necessary for original learning.

Releaser – A concept in ethology, referring to highly specific stimuli that release fixed action patterns, or complex sequences of instinctive species-specific behavior.

Relevant attributes – Characteristics of a stimulus which make the stimulus a positive instance of a given concept. Also, characteristics of a stimulus or environment of interest to the researcher.

Relevant dimension – Stimulus dimension along which a concept is defined. For example, color is a relevant dimension along which the concept red is defined; size is not a relevant dimension for the concept red.

Reliability – The degree to which a test score remains stable over repeated measurements.

Reliability coefficient – The correlation coefficient between two equivalent measurements.

The measurements may be two applications of the same test at different points in time, or the application of two equivalent forms of a test.

REM sleep – A stage of sleep in which brain waves are recorded that look very much like those recorded when the subject is awake and in which rapid eye movements occur. Dreaming accompanies this stage.

Reminiscence – A rise in performance of learned behavior beyond the level at which it was learned, which follows a rest after learning. It is thought to be due to a loss of work inhibition.

Repeatability – The attribute of observations that appear regularly under the same experimental conditions.

Repeated learning – Relearning material previously learned back to the point of mastery. Normally reduces subsequent forgetting.

Replication – Repeating an experiment precisely as it was conducted before; replication is usually necessary before any empirical findings are scientifically acceptable.

Representational thinking – Characteristic of the second stage in Piaget's system. The child develops representations for things that one can do. One-and-a-half to four years.

Repressed emotions – According to the psychoanalytic tradition, a person who has an emotion without being conscious of it–the existence of such unconscious emotions can only be inferred through indirect means; for example, gestures, facial expressions, tone of voice and dreams.

Repression – A defense mechanism in which painful memories or frustration are prevented from reaching the conscious level.

Research – A systematic attempt to discover by means of experimental investigation.

Residual stimuli – Stimulation carried over from recent experience that influences adaptation level.

Resistance – Opposition by a patient to the orders, actions, recommendations, or suggestions of the therapist.

Resistance to extinction – A measure of learning in which the number of unreinforced responses, before the response disappears in extinction, is used as the index of response strength in acquisition.

Respondent (Skinner) – A response elicited by a known specific stimulus. Unconditioned responses of the type referred to in classical conditioning are examples of respondents.

Response – Any measurable behavior. Sometimes specific to behavior elicited by a stimulus.

Response amplitude – A measure of the magnitude or intensity of a response as measured on a predetermined dimension.

Response chaining – Putting several responses together into one integrated behavior.

Response competition – The association of two (or more) responses to the same stimulus, which will only evoke the more strongly associated of the two.

Response discrimination – Learning to give only one particular response in a given situation.

Response generalization – Responding to the original stimulus not only with the original response, but with other similar responses.

Response integration – Unitizing or knitting together a complex response to be learned.

Response probability – The frequency with which a response occurs relative to the number of opportunities for its occurrence.

Response-produced cues – Cues that result from a response and that act as stimuli for the next response in a chain.

Response specificity – Change in one response system that is not seen in another.

Response strength (See Response amplitude.)

Resting potential – The nonactivated state of a neuron, in which the inside of the cell is slightly negative in potential when compared to the outside.

Retarded – A general term describing abnormally slow development, or those people who have not developed either physically or intellectually as rapidly as normal.

Retention – Memory for material previously learned. The persistence of a learned behavior or experience after a temporal interval.

Retention interval – The period of time between acquisition of a response and the correct retrieval of that response from storage.

Reticular activating system (RAS) – A network of nerve fibers spread through the brain that acts as a general activating system responsive to sensory stimulation.

Retina – The layer of photosensitive cells at the back of the eye containing the receptors and other neural structures responsible for vision.

Retinal disparity – The slight difference in stimulus patterns produced on the two retinas of the eyes from one object; an important depth cue, also referred to as "binocular disparity."

Retinal receptive field – The small areas on the retina which, when stimulated, give rise to electrical activity in a single neuron in the visual cortex.

Retrieval – The process of bringing materials from storage.

Retrieval cue – Information presented at the time of a memory test to aid recall.

Retrieval failure – A theory of forgetting which suggests that forgetting is caused by failure in the retrieval process and not in "loss" of the stored material itself.

Retroactive inhibition (interference) – Difficulty in recalling learned information because of something learned after the information one is trying to recall.

Retrograde amnesia Forgetting of past events (i.e., before the amnesia) caused by physiological or psychological trauma.

Retrospective study – An investigation involving recollected data reported by people who were significant in a person's life. Errors in recollection often result in unintentional "retrospective errors."

Reverberating circuit – The first stage posited by consolidation theory; consists of short-lived electrical events occurring in the brain. These circuits are capable of maintaining activity after the initial impulse has died out.

Reversal (ABA) design – Small n design in which a subject's behavior is measured under a baseline (A) condition, then an experimental treatment is applied during the B phase and any changes in behavior are observed; finally, the original baseline (A) conditions are reinstituted to ensure that the experimental treatment was responsible for any observed change during the B phase.

Reversal learning – A discrimination-learning procedure in which the roles of the "correct" and "incorrect" stimuli are switched after the

subject has reached a criterion performance level.

Reversal shift – A solution shift where all stimuli are reassigned to their opposite response category.

Reversibility – (Piaget) A property of mental operations such that an operation proceeding in one direction may also proceed in the opposite direction. It is responsible for the development of conservation of various quantities.

Reward – An object, stimulus, event, or outcome that increases the probability of a learned behavior; reinforcement.

Rewrite rules – Set of rules in a transformational grammar specifying what a sentence consists of and how it can be rewritten; a way of describing a language. Rewrite rules specify structure but not meaning.

Rh factor – A substance present in the red blood cells of most people and causing antigenic reactions when the mother's blood is Rh negative and the fetus' blood is Rh positive.

Rhodopsin – The photosensitive pigment found in the rod cells of the retina of the eye involved in dark adaptation.

Ribonucleic acid (RNA) – Large molecules concerned with protein synthesis, possibly implicated in memory storage.

Ricco's law – The inverse linear relation between the area of a visual target and its threshold.

Rigidity – The characteristic of continuing to perform a task in a stereotyped fashion even after better methods become possible. A personality trait characterized by inability to change one's attitudes, opinions, or manner of adjustment.

Risky shift – A group decision that is more venturesome than what could have been predicted from the responses of any one individual in the group or the mean response of the group.

Rites of passage – The procedures whereby a child becomes an adult member of his culture. Also called puberty rites. Often ritualistic and ceremonial in more primitive cultures.

RNA (See ribonucleic acid.)

Rods – The visual receptors which function primarily in dim or dark conditions; they are located toward the periphery of the eye and operate only in a black-and-white dimension.

Role – A person's function in a group; the set of behaviors expected of a person serving a particular function in a group.

Role consistent or role appropriate – Behavior that is consistent with what is expected on the basis of a role; the individual may or may not be comfortable with the behavior.

Role playing – Technique involving the acting out of specific roles in order to work through problems.

Rorschach Ink Blot Test – A projective personality test consisting of 10 cards, each containing a bilaterally symmetrical ink blot. The subject is instructed to tell what the blot reminds him or her of.

Rote learning – Learning verbatim; learning "by heart"; sometimes, learning without understanding.

Saccadic eye movement (saccade) – An abrupt point to point dart of the eye as it moves from its original fixation point to a new one.

Sadism – The compulsive tendency to vent aggression and destructiveness on another person; overt sexual satisfaction may or may not be derived from this behavior.

Safety needs (Maslow) – A term to describe the individual's need to maintain an orderly and predictable environment — an environment not threatening in either a physical or psychological sense.

Saliency – An inherent quality of some properties of stimuli that makes those properties more noticeable than others. The relative prominence or distinctiveness of some parts of the cognitive field over others.

Sample – A set of elements drawn from a population; the attempt should be made to make the sample as representative as possible of the population when the sample is to be used as the data base for research.

Sample bias – Any procedural variable which can cause a sample to be nonrepresentative of its population.

Sample error – The error caused by sample bias which occurs when a sample is non-representative.

Sampling – Selection of subjects from a population; in general, the experimenter attempts to make the sample as representative of the population as possible.

Sampling techniques – Procedures for selecting a small number of cases from a large population such that the sample that results is representative of the larger population.

Sanguine – One of the four temperaments in Hippocrates's system of personality types. A sanguine person is warm and confident. Once thought to be due to the predominance of healthy blood.

Sanity – The condition of "normalcy" with respect to behavior as defined by society.

Saturation – One of the three attributes of color experience, saturation is the psychological correlate of purity, or number of different wavelengths in the color mixture. More wavelengths result in less saturation.

Savings – The measure of retention (or forgetting) by measuring the time or number of trials needed to relearn something as opposed to the time originally taken to learn the material.

Scale – Any series of values, objects or magnitudes according to which a phenomenon can be quantified. In science there are nominal, ordinal, interval, and ratio scales.

Scale attenuation effects – Difficulties in interpreting results when performance on the dependent variable is either nearly perfect (a ceiling effect) or nearly lacking altogether (a floor effect).

Scanning – Strategy for solving conceptual problems which uses a hypothesis testing approach. Successive scanning involves testing possible solutions one at a time. Simultaneous scanning involves testing more than one hypothesis at a time.

Scapegoat theory – Theory that prejudice is a displacement of aggression and thereby serves as an outlet for personal feelings of hostility and aggression.

Scattergram (scatterplot) – A pictorial way of displaying the correlation between two variables by plotting on a graph.

Schachter-Singer theory (1962) – A theory of emotionality that holds that emotions are differentiated by their cognitive content, rather than by physiological responses.

Schedules of reinforcement – Ways of arranging partial reinforcement according to either a time interval or the number of responses made by the subject.

Schemes (also schema or schemata action) –

Systems that allow the child to test out the characteristics and properties of things in the physical world.

Schizoid personality – A type of personality characterized by withdrawal, avoidance of others, and often eccentricity.

Schizophrenia – Group of psychotic disorders in which there are severe disturbances in thought processes as well as emotions and a marked distortion of reality; often characterized by emotional blunting, disturbances in interpersonal relationships, depersonalization, and preoccupation with inner fantasies.

Scholastic tests – Aptitude tests used to predict future performance in academic pursuits.

School psychology – A branch of psychology which specializes in testing, counseling, and guiding students.

Scoring profile – The presentation of a summary of the results collected from the administration of a test battery, as in a personality profile.

Secondary appraisal – A reinterpretation of the causes of an emotion; may change the explanation from the one that was first proposed.

Secondary circular reaction – Infant responses that are circular in the sense that the response serves as a stimulus for its own repetition, and secondary since the responses do not center on the child's body, as do primary circular reactions.

Secondary drives – Drives acquired through the contiguity of previously neutral stimuli and primary drives; drug addiction, for example.

Secondary elaboration – Process of forming manifest dream content into a more cohesive unit through combining or creating elements.

Secondary gain – For neurotic behavior, other positive consequences in addition to the relief from tension or anxiety; as when being ill results in attention or relief from work.

Secondary group – A reference group with which a person has less contact than a primary group but which influences his or her behavior in some situations.

Secondary process – The characteristic functioning of the ego in which it fulfills id impulses by indirect routes while at the same time meeting the demands of the external environment; the reality principle.

Secondary reinforcers – Originally neutral stimuli that come to function as reinforcers as the result of their learned association with primary reinforcers or through exchange for a reward, as in token economy therapy.

Secondary sexual characteristics – Physical features — such as growth of beard in males and enlarging of breasts in females — that appear during puberty as indicators of sexual maturity.

Secondary stimulus generalization – Stimulus generalization based upon the subject's knowledge of language or some other type of symbol.

Sector therapy – The system of psychotherapy developed by Felix Deutsch to change defensive attitudes and to discriminate present realities from past experiences. The therapist focuses on symptoms and conflicts revealed by the patient's own words.

Security – In Sullivanian terminology, a state of belonging, of being accepted and of being nonapprehensive about future satisfaction of one's needs.

Sedative – Drug that reduces anxiety by inducing muscle relaxation, sleep, and inhibition of the cognitive centers of the brain.

Segmentation – In speech perception, the process of dividing the acoustic wave into meaningful units. Pauses are perceived between segments, although they may not necessarily be present in the wave itself.

Selection paradigm – A procedure in concept learning; subjects select the stimuli which are classified by the experimenter until the subject can define the concept.

Selective attention – A sensory state in which an organism attends to certain aspects of the environment while ignoring others.

Selective breeding – Planned matings between individuals having certain genetic backgrounds, with the aim of getting offspring of a particular genotype.

Selective inattention – Not being guided in behavior by an aspect of the situation that is perceived. Doing so avoids the anxiety of unpleasant or discrepant information.

Selective learning – Selection of a dominant response in response competition by means of selective reinforcement.

Self – That which is perceived as one's own conscious being; the individual revealed through introspection as the persistent center of psychological processes; the ego or I.

Self-actualization (Maslow) – The process or act of developing one's potentiality, achieving an awareness of one's identity and fulfilling oneself; the highest level of need.

Self-arousal – In modeling, a motive condition that arises out of the observation and retention of the behaviors of others and brings the individual closer to some action or cognition.

Self-concept – The definition of oneself including the person's mental image of his or her physical self, expectations about his or her behavior, and the attitudes and other cognitions that define the person's meaning.

Self-dynamism (Sullivan) – Pattern of the enduring motivations toward satisfaction and toward security that form the self-system.

Self-esteem needs – Maslow's term used to describe the individual's desire for others to hold him in high regard and for the individual himself to maintain a high opinion of his behavior and his person.

Self-fulfilling prophecy – When an expectation appears to lead to or cause the anticipated behavior. In research, an experimenter's expectations may inadvertently get his subjects to act in a particular way, ensuring that the prediction comes true.

Self-image – The personality as viewed by the self; self-concept.

Self-reinforcement – In modeling, the satisfaction of standards that have been established by observing others' behaviors.

Self-stimulation – Generally, stimulation of oneself; also a procedure whereby a human or animal may administer electrical stimuli to areas of his or her own brain (intra-cranial self-stimulation).

Self theory – Approach to personality that focuses on the individual as a whole, unified self. It takes a fairly positive view of humans and is a part of the humanistic approach to psychology.

Semantic differential – A rating-scale approach to connotative meaning developed by Osgood. Each adjectival concept is rated on a series of bipolar scales like good-bad.

Semantic generalization – Transfer of a response from one word as it was initially learned to another word that is meaningfully related to the first.

Semantic memory – Retention of rules, knowledge of our language, and other material not specifically related to particular places, times, or events.

Semantics – The study of the relation of words, signs and symbols to what they mean or denote.

Semicircular canals – Three fluid filled canals in the inner ear, which contain receptors responsive to acceleration resulting from body rotation. They are partly responsible for maintaining equilibrium and posture.

Semi-interquartile range (Q) – One half of the difference between the upper and lower quartiles. The semi-interquartile range provides an index of the variability of a set of scores.

Sensation – The simplest form of experience resulting from stimulation of a sense organ; a feeling.

Sense modality – A category of perceptual experience which depends on a particular kind of energy affecting a particular type of receptor.

Sensitivity – The range over which a test measures differences.

Sensitivity training – Group experience aimed at improving human relations, skills, and honesty and understanding of oneself and others; also called T-group.

Sensitization – An outcome of repeated stimulation whereby a particular response temporarily becomes easier than usual to elicit; an increase in sensitivity to some stimulus.

Sensorimotor – The knowledge possessed by a child during Piaget's first stage of development which extends until age two. A child acquires object constancies, the independent existence of objects and representations of the world during this period.

Sensorimotor period (or stage) – The first stage of development in Piaget's classification. It lasts from birth to approximately age 2 and is so called because the child understands his world primarily through his contact and physical manipulation of it.

Sensorimotor play – Play activity involving the manipulation of objects or execution of activities simply for the sensations that are produced.

Sensory – Refers to information being brought into the central nervous system; pertaining to the sense organs. Afferent is a synonym.

Sensory adaptation – The process of adjustment to unusual levels of stimulation by either an increase or decrease in sensitivity in that receptor.

Sensory cortex – Areas of the cerebral cortex that are the highest level receiving stations for sensory information.

Sensory deprivation – A situation in which an experimental subject is placed in a condition of reduced stimulation, either in intensity or variety. Subjects in prolonged conditions of sensory deprivation experience restlessness, impaired perceptual and cognitive functioning and hallucinations.

Sensory gating – A brain process that reduces the input into certain sensory systems while allowing other systems to remain fully functioning.

Sensory memory – One of several hypothesized memory stores. In sensory memory the input is stored in relatively raw form and for brief periods of time.

Sensory nerves – The bundles of neurons that conduct impulses from the receptors to the central nervous system; also termed afferent nerves.

Sensory overload – Excess stimulation; extremely high levels of a stimulus that may result in pain, improper assimilation of information, and temporary or permanent impairment.

Sensory storage – The very brief retention of a signal in its unprocessed sensory form; also termed very short-term memory.

Septal region – A portion of the limbic system of the forebrain that is thought to be involved in the inhibition of emotional behavior.

Sequential attention – Sensory processing in which single units of information are treated in succession as opposed to simultaneous attention.

Serendipity – The experience of finding one thing while looking for another. Not an infrequent occurrence in science.

Serial act – A group of acts which occur in sequence in such a way that the stimuli produced by each act serve as cues for the successive act.

Serial anticipation – A learning method in which the subject is given a series of items to memorize in order and is asked to predict, as each item in the list comes up, what the next item will be.

Serial learning – Learning in which materials or operations are presented in a particular order that must be followed.

Serial position curve – A graphic representation of retention as a function of the input position of the information; usually memory is better for the first items (primacy effect) and the last items (recency effect) than for those in the middle.

Seriation – The ordering of objects according to one or more empirical properties.

Serotonin – An inhibitory neurotransmitter found in the brain and believed to play a role in sleep and emotion.

Servo system – A closed-loop system in which behavior of one part affects, through feedback, all other parts of the system.

Set – A predisposition to respond in a particular way; in problem solving, a tendency to persist in solving a problem according to a particular procedure.

Sex chromosomes – Chromosomes contained in sperm cells and ova responsible for determining the sex of the offspring. Sex chromosomes produced by the female are of one variety (X); those produced by the male may be either X or Y.

Sex definition – Definition of an individual as male or female by physical criteria.

Sex differentiation – Increasing differences in physical development of males and females before or after birth; differential treatment of individuals on the basis of sex.

Sex-linked characteristic – A hereditary characteristic determined by a gene carried on the X or the Y chromosome, which also determines sex; red-green colorblindness is an example of such a characteristic.

Sex role – A set of expectations for behavior and characteristics held for a person on the basis of sex.

Sex-typed behavior – A behavior in which males and females do differ or are expected to differ; actual differences are not necessarily the same as expected differences.

Sexual deviation – Sexual behavior which is in violation of accepted norms regarding method or target.

Sexual dimorphism – When the males and females of a species are of dissimilar size, shape or coloration.

Sexual impotence – Inability of the male to engage in sexual intercourse.

Sexual instinct – Refers to sexual craving or erotic desire.

Shadowing – A procedure used in studies of attention, in which the subject must repeat word for word a message as it is being presented.

Sham rage – Ferocious, undirected rage behavior provoked by very mild stimulation; experimental condition produced by surgical removal of the cerebral cortex.

Shape constancy – The tendency to perceive an object as of constant form in spite of change in the contours of the retinal image.

Shaping – In operant conditioning, the procedure whereby the desired behavior is gradually "put together" by reinforcing the series of successive steps which culminate in the final response.

Shaping behavior — Modifying behavior by reinforcing only those responses that tend toward the direction desired by the experimenter.

Sharpening – The cognitive process of accentuating certain details and dropping others in memory, so that objects and events become more clearly defined in the recall than they were in the original experience.

Shock therapy – The treatment of mental illness by the administration of some agent causing convulsions and coma. Such agents include insulin, metrazol, and electric current (electroconvulsive therapy, ECT) applied to the brain.

Short-term memory (STM) – One of several hypothetical memory stores. STM has a persistence on the order of 30 seconds but can be prolonged by rehearsal. It is of limited capacity, about 7 items (bits).

Shuttle box – Device with two compartments separated by a door, used to study learning and motivation.

Sibling rivalry – Jealousy or competition between brothers and/or sisters (siblings), which often develops in a child upon the birth of a new brother or sister due to competition for parental attention.

Sign stimulus – A stimulus which triggers one phase of an instinct.

Signal – A stimulus pattern which serves as a basis for a particular response; stimuli that can be used for communication.

Signal detection theory – A psychophysical method in which the observer is placed in varying conditions, e.g., variation in frequency of stimulus presentation, and asked to state if a particular stimulus is present.

Significance level – Probability that an experimental finding is due to chance, or random fluctuation, operating in the data; the p value.

Significant difference – A difference between two statistics which is so great that it is quite unlikely that it could have occurred by chance. The cutoff point is usually at the .05 or .01 level of confidence.

Similarity – Gestalt law of organization, which says that elements that are similar to one another will tend to be grouped together.

Simple schizophrenia – Subtype of schizophrenia characterized by withdrawal, indifference and apathy, but seldom any delusions or hallucinations.

Simulation – In psychology, the attempt to use a computer program to duplicate the processing (thinking) stage in problem-solving.

Simultaneous conditioning – A classical conditioning procedure where the conditioned stimulus and the unconditioned stimulus occur at the same time.

Simultaneous contrast – The effect on brightness or color produced by presenting in close proximity, and at the same time, complementary visual stimuli, usually resulting in the detection of a greater contrast.

Sine wave – A sound pressure wave with regular cyclical properties; any complex waveform may, through Fourier analysis, be analyzed into a series of sine waves.

Single-blind control – An experimental situation in which the subjects are unaware of how or when the variables are manipulated by the experimenter, but the conditions are known to the experimenter.

Situational attribution – The judgment that situational constraints rather than an actor's typical motivations have shaped his or her behavior in a particular situation.

Situational instigators of aggression – Stimuli or events in the environment that increase the probability that aggressive behavior will occur.

Situational test – A test for studying behavior or personality based upon the simulation of a natural life situation, as opposed to artificial laboratory situations.

Size constancy – The tendency to perceive an object as of the same size in spite of variations in retinal image size, which occur when we move away from an object.

Skeletal muscles – Striated muscles under voluntary control that move the trunk and limbs.

Skew – When the scores of a distribution occur with greater frequency at one end of the distribution.

Skewed distributions – Nonsymmetrical frequency distributions. A distribution is skewed in the direction of the longer tail.

Skin resistance (GSR, PGR) – Sometimes called the galvanic skin response or psychogalvanic response, it reflects a sudden decrease in the electrical resistance of the skin, usually due to increased sweating.

Skinner box – Experimental apparatus employed by Skinner in much of his research with rats and pigeons. It is a cagelike structure, equipped, usually with a lever, to allow the animal to make a response and the experimenter to reinforce or punish it for the response.

Small n design – Research design utilizing a small number of subjects.

Smell – Sense that deals with the reception of chemical stimuli in the olfactory organs.

Smooth muscles – Muscle tissue innervated by the autonomic nervous system which shows no striations and is not under voluntary control; found in the blood vessels and the gastrointestinal system. (Synonym: involuntary muscles.)

Snellen chart – A series of letters varying in size, used for the clinical assessment visual acuity.

Social attitude – Combination of feelings beliefs, and action tendencies toward classes of persons or objects that are directly or indirectly social in nature.

Social change – A significant alteration of social structure.

Social class – A group of people, differentiated from other members of society in terms of income, housing, values, privileges, and prestige, who associate with other members of the group socially and are perceived by themselves and others as belonging to a distinctive social level.

Social comparison – The process of determining one's own standards or standing on the basis of the behavior of others or using the behavior of others for purposes of evaluating one's own behavior, particularly in situations of uncertainty.

Social development – The development of a child's ability to interact with others. A consideration of social development frequently includes such topics as games, morality, the learning of language, and the learning of socially appropriate and inappropriate behaviors.

Social exchange theory – Interpersonal attraction can be analyzed in terms of rewards and costs of each event or type of interaction.

Social facilitation – Phenomenon in which the mere presence of other persons, as an audience or as coworkers, without any verbal exchange, increases individual performance.

Social interaction – Communication among individuals who both send and receive messages, verbally or by gestures.

Social interference – When the presence of others appears to hinder performance of a particular response.

Social learning – Acquiring patterns of behavior that conform to social expectations. Learning what is acceptable and what is not acceptable in a given culture.

Social learning theory – Attempt to explain personality in terms of learning, based on the assumption that much of what we call personality is learned behavior involving imitation. Social learning therapy tries to restructure maladaptive behavior using this theory.

Social motive – A motive whose satisfaction requires the presence of at least one other person and often involves status or companionship.

Social movement – An attempt by a large group of people to cause social change.

Social psychology – A psychology that draws upon the social sciences; a study of the effect on individual behavior of the real or implied, immediate or past, presence of others.

Social responsiveness – The extent to which a person responds to subtle social pressures and the presence of other people.

Social stimulus value – The effect of the external aspects of personality (appearance and behavior patterns) and other situational variables on the behavior and attitudes of others.

Social structure – A description of the ways in which the persons in a given society are ranked and related to one another.

Social system – A group of participants united through stable patterns of interaction and interdependent organizational structures.

Socialization – The complex process of learning those behaviors that are appropriate within a given culture as well as those that are less appropriate.

Society – A group of people living in one area who have developed patterns of interaction for getting along with one another.

Sociogram – A pictorial or graphic representation of the social structure of a group.

Sociometry – Technique for describing the structure of social groups by showing the patterns of preferences and aversions among the members.

Socionomy – An intermediate stage in Bull's scheme of moral development in which the individual begins to accept external social rules and incorporates them into an internal system for determining morality.

Somatic – Refers to the body.

Somatic nervous system – The part of the peripheral nervous system that innervates the skeletal muscles and peripheral sense organs.

Somatic therapy – Any of several forms of therapy for mental illness involving physical treatment, including drugs, shock therapy, etc.

Somatoform disorders – A group of disorders that involve real motor or sensory deficits that nevertheless have no neurological or medical basis.

Somatotonia (Sheldon) – A temperamental characteristic associated with mesomorphy. The somatotonic individual is restless, aggressive, noisy, competitive, and active.

Somatotype – W. H. Sheldon's system of grouping body types into the categories of endomorph (soft and rounded), mesomorph (well-muscled), and ectomorph (thin and frail), each of these somatotypes correlating with certain personality types.

Somesthesis – Perceiving stimulation of the body surface.

Sone scale – A scale of auditory loudness based on direct loudness judgments. It is a logarithmic scale because the auditory system is forced to compress the broad range of intensities it can perceive.

Sound localization – The capacity to determine where a sound is coming from. It is dependent upon time of arrival, intensity, and phase differences between the signals perceived by the two ears.

Source traits (Cattell) – The personality traits that are the basic causes of one's overt, or surface, behavior.

Space perception – The ability to see depth.

Spaced practice – Practice in which trials are separated by sufficient amounts of time to dissipate fatigue.

Specific factors – Reliable component of a test score specific to the test itself, that is, not correlating with other tests.

Spectral – Pertaining to the visible band of wavelengths within the range of electromagnetic radiation.

Spectral sensitivity curve – The curve representing the perceived brightness of equal intensities of light of various wavelengths.

Speed-accuracy tradeoff – In reaction time experiments, the ability of the responder to substitute changes in the percentage of correct responses for changes in speed of responding.

Speed tests – Psychological tests in which the time limit for completion is considered a crucial variable.

Sperm cell – The sex cell produced by a mature male. It is haploid, like the egg cell (ovum) consisting of 23 chromosomes rather than 23 pairs of chromosomes.

Spermatogenesis – Development of sperm, the male reproductive cell.

Spike potential – The large amplitude change in electrical potential that constitutes the "neural impulse"; the magnitude of the spike follows the all-or-none law.

Spinal cord – That portion of the central nervous system located in the vertebral column. It is the main neural pathway for somatic information traveling to and from the brain and capable of reflex action interchanges.

Split-brain experiments – Research conducted when the corpus callosum has been severed, creating two entirely separate hemispheres which function independently.

Split-half reliability – Determining the reliability of a test by dividing the test items into two arbitrary groups and correlating the scores obtained on the two halves of the test.

Spontaneous recovery – In classic conditioning, the reoccurrence of an extinguished response following a rest period between extinction and retesting, and with no retraining.

Spontaneous remission – Recovery from abnormal personality patterns without any therapy. This phenomenon has always confounded attempts to assess the effectiveness of therapy.

Spreading depression – Procedure that involves chemically preventing part of the brain from functioning.

Stages of development – Periods in the development of a child when his or her mental operations can be characterized in a particular way and certain phenomena can be observed.

Stages of sexuality (Freudian theory) – The developmental periods through which the individual is pushed by the libido toward the achievement of mature sexuality. The first period is the oral stage. The second is the anal stage. The third period is the phallic stage, during which interest is first focused on the penis or clitoris, but soon fastens upon the parents.

Standard deviation – A measure of the variability or spread of scores in a group. The standard deviation is the square root of the average of the squared deviations from the arithmetic mean of the group.

Standard error of the mean – An estimate of the amount that an obtained mean may be expected to differ from the true mean due to chance; σ (for populations), s (for samples).

Standard error of measurement – A measure of the size of errors that are likely to result from the application of a particular measurement procedure. It is the standard deviation of the distribution of errors.

Standard score – A relative score that indicates the score's relation to the norm in terms of the number of standard deviations from the mean.

Standardization – The establishment of norms or standards for administering, scoring, and interpreting a psychological test. It usually involves administering the test to a large group of people representative of those for whom the test is intended.

Standardization group – Persons chosen to be tested with a new test; their scores determine the norms for the test when it is given to other persons drawn from the same population.

Standardized test – A test that has been published for general use. The most distinctive feature is a set of norms established on the basis of preliminary tryout and analysis of the test on a general reference population.

Stanford-Binet test – A revision of the Binet intelligence test made by psychologists at Stanford University, it is an individual test using age level subtests. It is the most widely used children's intelligence test.

Stapes – The third of the three tiny bones in the middle ear that conduct the sound vibrations from the eardrum to the cochlea.

Startle pattern – A primitive pattern of emotional responses to any sudden, unexpected stimulus which produces reflexive responses of the head, neck, face and arms as well as the visceral system.

State anxiety – Momentary, consciously perceived feelings of apprehension and tension.

State dependent learning – Ability of the learner's internal physiological state to affect learning; the more similar this state is during learning and recall, the better recall will be.

Statistical judgment – Decisions based solely on statistical (or numerical or data-based) information.

Statistics – The discipline that deals with the collection analysis interpretation, and presentation of numerical data.

Status – A position in a social structure that is defined by the privileges and responsibilities of the persons having that position.

Status envy – Hypothesis that a person will identify with the person who is a rival for resources which he covets but cannot control.

Stereogram – A set of two pictures taken from two different points of regard so that retinal disparity is simulated. Viewing a stereogram in a stereoscope results in stereoscopic vision.

Stereoscope – An instrument for presenting one visual stimulus to the right eye and a different stimulus to the left eye; used in the laboratory for investigating the perception of depth.

Stereotype – A set of relatively rigid, oversimplified or overgeneralized beliefs about a group of people.

Stereotyped behavior – Making the same response(s) over and over, regardless of environmental change; occurs in situations involving high frustration levels.

Stimulant – A substance that increases physiological activity and alertness.

Stimulation needs – A class of motives in which a person seems to require certain levels of sensory or perceptual stimulation, as shown by stimulation deprivation studies.

Stimulus – Any event in the physical environment capable of affecting an organism; specifically, anything that can activate a sensory neuron.

Stimulus control – State of learning in which the organism is responding only to the discriminative stimulus in an operant situation.

Stimulus discrimination – Learning to respond differently to various stimuli that may have some similarities.

Stimulus generalization – The elicitation of a learned response by a stimulus similar to, but not identical with, the conditioned stimulus.

Stimulus satiation – Loss of interest in a stimulus after continued exposure to it, as measured by a reduction in exploration, inspection or choice of that stimulus in competition with a fresh alternative.

Stimulus-seeking – Tendency of isolated subjects to provide self-stimulation and to value and be rewarded by external stimuli introduced into the situation.

STM – (See short-term memory.)

Stranger anxiety – A development in the third quarter of the infant's first year in which unfamiliar people are frightening and separation from familiar people is distressing.

Stratified sampling – A technique for selecting subjects in such a way that nonoverlapping subgroups are sampled in proportion to each group's representation in the total population.

Stress – Psychological state of an organism when there is a disparity between its ability to cope comfortably with demands of the environment and the level of such demands.

Stroboscopic – Illusion or effect; apparent motion produced by presentation of stimuli at successive intervals, too short for the visual system to record as separate events; e.g., motion pictures.

Stroop effect – Difficulty in attending to or responding to a given stimulus due to an inability to block responses to irrelevant features in the stimulus situation; a response competition phenomenon.

Structural change – The second stage of learning posited by consolidation theory; consists of a relatively permanent change in neurophysiological activities.

Structural hypothesis – The third and last theory of the psyche proposed by Freud, in which he distinguished three functionally related structures of the psyche: the id, the ego, and the superego.

Structuralism – Early school of psychological thought originated by Wundt which held that psychology should attempt to analyze psychological phenomena into its components and determine how the components are synthesized; the primary method was introspection.

Structure – Term employed by Piaget to describe the organization of an individual's capabilities, whether they be motor or cognitive.

Structured test – A test that permits the selection of only particular given response alternatives.

Subject representativeness – Determination that samples are considered true or valid indices of the characteristics of the entire population.

Subject variable – Characteristics of people that can be measured or described, but cannot be varied experimentally (e.g., height, weight, sex, I.Q., etc.).

Subjective – Accessible only to private experience and unverifiable by others; dependent upon individual interpretation; nonstructured; used in contrast with objective.

Subjective orientation – Moral judgment of an act based on the intentions of the person who committed the act.

Subjective report or test – One in which the responses or answers are nonstructured or creative resulting from open-ended questions.

Subjectivity – When judgments are affected by bias, prejudice, or personal feeling.

Sublimation – A defense mechanism in which an acceptable activity is substituted for an unacceptable activity or motive.

Subliminal perception – The supposed understanding or interpretation of stimuli that occur at a level slightly below the threshold value.

Subliminal stimulation – Stimulation that falls below some psychophysical threshold but that still has a measurable behavioral effect.

Subtractive method – Donder's technique to estimate the amount of time required for various mental operations by subtracting one component from another.

Subvocal activity – Behavior of speaking to oneself (moving the muscles of the voice apparatus at very low levels without speaking overtly). According to the motor theory of thinking, subvocal activity is the basic behavioral component of thinking.

Sucking reflex – The automatic sucking response of a newborn child when the oral regions are stimulated. Nipples are particularly appropriate for eliciting the sucking reflex.

Suicide – The deliberate taking of one's own life.

Superego – In Freudian theory, the part of the personality developing out of the ego during childhood. It contains values, morals and basic attitudes as learned from parents and society.

Superstitious behavior – Responses made by an organism in an operant situation that are not necessary for reinforcement but that have become associated with it nonetheless, due to reinforcement following an arbitrary movement.

Suppression – In psychoanalysis, the conscious act of keeping an impulse or memory just below the level of awareness, in the preconscious, because it is likely to provoke anxiety or other negative consequences.

Supraoptimal motivation – Motivation at such a high level that performance is impaired.

Surface structure – In linguistics, the arrangement of words in a language at the level of interpersonal communication.

Surface traits – In Cattell's approach to personality, the typical behaviors of an individual, as opposed to the underlying source traits that are the basic causes of the behavior; postulated to account for the correlations observed among tests of personality.

Surrogate mother – Term used by Harry Harlow to describe a wire or a terry cloth covered figure that he used as a substitute, or surrogate, for a monkey's real mother.

Survey research – Technique of obtaining a limited amount of information from a large number of people, usually through random sampling by asking a fixed set of questions to all of n.

Surveys – Opinion-polling; usually done with a sample taken from some predetermined population.

Sutures – The places where the skull bones become fused together.

Syllables – Sound uttered at a single effort of voice. The smallest speech units to which the receiver usually attends.

Syllogism (syllogistic reasoning) – A logical form that consists of two premises and a conclusion based on the two premises.

Symbol – Any specified stimulus which has become a commonly understood representation for some object, event, action, or idea.

Symbolic – The final stage in the development of a child's representation of his world. The term is employed by Bruner to describe a representation of the world through arbitrary symbols. Symbolic representation including language, as well as theoretical or hypothetical systems.

Symbolic learning – In modeling, learning a behavior without actually observing it; verbal descriptions are used to establish the modeled response.

Symbolic mode – The most sophisticated method for converting immediate experiences into mental models. As proposed by Bruner, it involves using words and sentences as symbols of objects, events, and states of affairs.

Symbolization – Dream process that disguises material in the dream so that something in the dream represents or stands for something else in real life.

Symmetry – A law of perceptual organization that states that balanced figures are usually perceived from exposure to ambiguous or complex stimuli. Balanced figures are aesthetically pleasing.

Sympathetic nervous system – A part of the autonomic nervous system, it prepares the organism for emergencies, making much bodily energy available for use.

Synapse – The space between the terminal button of an axon and the membrane, or dendrites of another neuron. Transmitter substance flows across this space completing the circuit.

Synaptic space – Small gap separating the ends of the axon and dendrite in a synapse.

Synaptic vesicles – Membranous packets found in the terminal buttons of neurons from which transmitter substance is discharged into the synaptic cleft.

Syncretic – Refers to a developing organism's behavior, its qualities being fused though striving toward being separate and distinct.

Syncretic reason – A type of semilogical reasoning characteristic of the classification behavior of the very young preschooler. It involves grouping objects according to egocentric criteria, which are subject to change from one object to the next. In other words, the child does not classify on the basis of a single dimension, but changes dimensions as he or she classifies.

Syndrome – A group of symptoms that go together and (usually) characterize a particular disease or condition.

Synesthesia – A condition in which stimulation in one sensory modality arouses imagery in a different modality.

Syntactic boundary – The edges of constituents of sentences.

Syntactics – The study of the rules of language, particularly of sentence production.

Syntax – The grammar of a language consisting of the rules that govern the arrangement of words as elements in a sentence showing their interrelationships and dependencies; sentence structure.

System of psychology – Any particular body of theories of psychology used in the organization or interpretation of all of behavior.

Systematic desensitization – Type of behavior therapy developed by Wolpe to help people overcome fears and anxiety. It involves step-by-step classical conditioning in which an anxiety-producing stimulus (CS) is paired with relaxation (UCS).

Systematic replication – Repeating an experiment while varying numerous factors considered to be irrelevant to the phenomenon to see if it will survive these changes.

2 + 2 phenomenon – Adoption of a prejudiced attitude from an erroneous conclusion about facts. Logical error based on unquestioned acceptance of an erroneous or deceiving premise.

Tabula rasa – In reference to the mental content of a newborn, the empiricist notion that the mind is initially a "blank tablet" to be inscribed upon by experience.

Tachistoscope (T-scope) – An apparatus for presenting visual stimuli for brief, controlled periods of time.

Tact – A verbal utterance under the control of events in the world rather than specific needs of the speaker. A basic form of verbal behavior in Skinner's system.

Task-oriented group – A group whose primary goal is to perform a specific task, such as producing something, solving a problem, providing ideas, or reaching a consensus. Such a group concentrates on performing the task rather than on factors unrelated to the group's goal, e.g., social relations within the group.

Taste – The sense that deals with the reception of dissolved chemical stimuli through the papillae on the tongue.

Taste buds – Receptors for taste; located on the surface of the tongue. They are not neurons but they synapse directly onto sensory neurons.

TAT (Thomatic Apperception Test) – A basic projective measurement technique in which the subject is asked to tell a story about each of several relatively ambiguous pictures; often used in the measurement of aspects of achievement motivation.

Teaching machines – Devices that present material to be learned in a series of single statements, to each of which the learner must respond for reinforcement.

Tectum – The upper portion (roof) of the midbrain, comprising the inferior and superior colliculi.

Tegmentum – The lower portion of the midbrain beneath the tectum.

Telepathy – An alleged phenomenon whereby one person can communicate with another without benefit of the known sensory channels or known forms of physical energy.

Temperament – A general term used to refer to an individual's disposition, energy level, and social orientation. An aspect of personality.

Template matching – A theory of pattern recognition which suggests that patterns are recognized by being matched to internally stored templates.

Temporal conditioning – A classical conditioning procedure in which the UCS occurs at regular intervals; these regular intervals are treated as the CS.

Temporal lobe – The area of the cortex in front of the occipital lobe and below the lateral fissure.

Temporal maze – An apparatus for studying temporal order rather than spatial sequences.

Temporal summation – The compounding of the effects of several subthreshold depolarizations that occur one right after another to produce an action potential.

Tension reduction – A view of reinforcement or reward which holds that reduction in stimulation from the attainment of a goal is the basic condition for reinforcement.

Teratogens – Environmental agents that produce abnormalities in the developing fetus.

Terminal buttons – The ends of an axon which form the synaptic knob and which release transmitter substance into the synaptic cleft.

Terminal response theory – The theory that reinforcement is based on response termination. Since the subject stops responding, what was done last is preserved until the next time the same stimulus is presented.

Terminal threshold – The maximum stimulus intensity which will still produce a sensation.

Territorial instinct – An organism's innate desire or drive for complete control of the physical area in which it lives.

Tertiary circular reaction – An infant's response that is circular in the sense that the response serves as the stimulus for its own repetition, but where the repeated response is not identical to the first response. This last characteristic, the altered response, distinguishes a tertiary circular reaction from a secondary circular reaction.

Test – Any form of measurement which yields quantitative data.

Test anxiety – An increase in anxiety brought on by a testing situation.

Test battery – The combination of several different psychological tests into a series presented to a subject.

Test norms – Data collected in the course of validating a test that enable a test user to compare a person's score with the scores for the population of which that person is a part.

Test-retest reliability – Reliability estimated by giving the same test on two occasions and finding the correlation between the scores for the two administrations. Since the test is unchanged, differences from test to retest reflect either change or inconsistency of the individual from one occasion to another.

Testes – Reproductive organs in males; endocrine glands that secrete many hormones which regulate sexual behaviors and characteristics.

Testimonials – A propaganda technique that uses statements from respected persons as to the worth of some person or thing.

Testosterone – A male sex hormone secreted by the testes, which is responsible for many male primary and secondary sexual characteristics.

Textual response – Reading; saying what one sees written. Also, a scoring category in the Rorschach Inkblot Test for responses based on the texture of the inkblot.

Texture gradient – The change in the appearance of texture based upon distance from the viewer; a monocular depth cue. The apparent increase in density and loss of separateness of the elements in a perceptual field, with increasing distance.

T-group – A sensitivity training encounter group.

Thalamus – One of the main structures of the diencephalon of the forebrain. It contains nuclei that relay information to the cerebral cortex.

Thanatos – A Greek word meaning death, employed by Freud in his later writings to describe what he calls the death wish or death instinct. It is used in contrast with the word Eros.

Thematic Apperception Test (TAT) – (See TAT.)

Theory – A set of general principles that explains existing related facts and permits the prediction of new facts.

Therapist – An individual who conducts treatment procedures; the agent who provides psychotherapy.

Theta – Relatively high amplitude brain waves; 4-7 Hz.

Thinking – The cognitive manipulation and reorganization of percepts, concepts, habits, motives, and rules.

Thirst – A postulated drive related to water deprivation; the sensations arising from water deprivation.

Threshold – A statistically determined point on a stimulus continuum at which there is a transition in a series of sensations or judgments.

Thymus – An endocrine gland located in the lower neck region involved with the lymphoid system and immunological reactions.

Thyroid – An endocrine gland located in the neck region that regulates metabolic rate and activity levels.

Timbre – The attribute of tonal sounds which is the correlate of waveform complexity. The characteristic tone quality of a voice or a musical instrument, their patterns of overtones (harmonics).

Time perspective – Organized concepts of past and future compared with the present.

Tip-of-the-tongue phenomenon (TOT) – When retrieval (usually verbal) from long-term storage seems almost possible, but cannot quite be accomplished.

Toddler – A nontechnical label sometimes used to describe the child between the ages of 18 months and $2^{1}/_{2}$ years.

Toilet training – Training the child to defecate and urinate in the proper place at appropriate times.

Token – A secondary reinforcer that can be exchanged for a primary reinforcer, e.g., as in a "token economy." Chips may serve as "money," for example, on a hospital ward or in a halfway house. Participants "earn" their tokens and exchange them for primary reinforcers (privileges, food, etc.) in the "economy" (e.g., the ward).

Trace – In theories of memory the hypothetical residual effect of stimulation, used to explain memory.

Trace conditioning – A classical conditioning procedure in which the onset and cessation of the CS occurs before the UCS is presented.

Trace-dependent forgetting – Loss of learned information due to the loss of a memory trace.

Tract – A bundle of neural fibers within the central nervous system, analogous to a nerve.

Trait – In respect to personality, a relatively persistent and consistent characteristic or attribute that serves to distinguish one person from another.

Trait anxiety – Anxiety proneness; the predisposition to respond with high state anxiety when under stress.

Trait cluster – Group of traits that tend to go together, so that a person who has one of the traits will probably have all of them.

Trait theory – An attempt to categorize personality using the presence or absence of several characteristics.

Tranquilizer – Any of several drugs that relieve anxiety without inducing sleep.

Transcendental meditation – One type of concentrative meditation, as taught by the Maharishi Mahesh Yogi. Its basis is the use of a mantra.

Transduction – The conversion of energy from one form to another, stimulus energy into action potentials as accomplished in a rod or cone cell, for example.

Transductive reasoning – Semilogical reasoning that proceeds from particular to particular, rather than from particular to general or from general to particular. One example of transductive reasoning is the following: Cows give milk. Goats give milk. Therefore goats are cows.

Transfer index – A measure of the ability to apply what one has learned previously to new situations. It is based upon performance in discrimination learning tasks but is presumably independent of overall learning ability.

Transfer of training – The effect of earlier learning on present learning; transfer is positive if the earlier learning makes present learning easier; negative if the earlier learning makes present learning more difficult.

Transference (psychoanalytic theory) – The stage of therapy in which the patient begins to respond to the analyst as though the analyst were some significant person (e.g., mother or father) in the patient's past.

Transformational grammar – Rules of grammar specifying how large units of language, such as sentences, can be modified to express different meanings.

Transmitter substance – A chemical, secreted by axon terminals, which excites or inhibits an adjacent neuron. Transmitters are responsible for synaptic action.

Transposition – The tendency to recognize common patterns in stimulus configurations made up of different elements.

Transverse presentation – A crosswise presentation of the fetus at birth, instead of the normal headfirst presentation.

Trauma – Damage or injury to the psyche; an experience or set of experiences that inflicts serious physical or psychological injury.

Tree diagram – A visual way of describing the phrase structure of a sentence.

Trephining – Cutting a hole in the skull; an operation used in ancient times to remove the evil spirits that supposedly caused mental illness.

Triad – Three persons interacting with one another.

Trial and error – A method of problem solving in which a sequence of acts is performed until one act produces the goal. This method involves a minimum understanding of the relationship between the factors involved.

Trichromatic theory – The Young-Helmholtz theory of color vision which posits the existence of three basic receptor types, each maximally sensitive to a limited region of the visible spectrum.

Tritanope – A dichromat with a blue-yellow deficiency. This form of color blindness is rare.

Trucking game (Deutsch and Krauss) – Decision making game used in research on cooperation and competition. Subject is asked to make a decision between cooperating for a steady reward or competing for a large but risky reward.

True prevalence – The presence of treated as well as untreated persons with mental disorders in a community.

True score – The hypothesized underlying ability of an individual on the attribute measured by a test. An obtained test score is considered to result from this true level of ability modified by an error of measurement that characterizes that particular test.

Truncated range – The amount of dispersion (or range) of scores on one variable may be small due to a small number of subjects, which may lead to low correlations.

Truth-table strategy – A systematic procedure for solving rule-learning problems.

T-score – A score on a test which is transformed to a score on a scale with a fixed mean and standard deviation.

T-test – The ratio of a statistic to its standard error. It is generally stated in terms of the probability or p value.

Two-phase movement – An act in which the initial movements are preparatory and perhaps opposite to the ultimately desired movement.

Two-tailed test – A test that places the rejection area at both ends of a distribution.

Tympanic membrane – The eardrum, separating the middle ear from the external auditory canal.

Type – In personality theory, a group of individuals having certain characteristics in common. Typologies are usually based upon a very limited set of categories and thus are not generally and completely accepted by most psychologists.

Type 1 error – The probability that the null hypothesis is rejected when it is in fact true; equals the significance level.

Type 2 error – Failure to reject the null hypothesis when it is in fact false.

Type R learning – A Skinnerian expression for operant conditioning. It is so called since both reinforcement and a response are involved in the learning.

Type S learning – A Skinnerian expression for classical conditioning. It is so called since stimuli are involved in classical conditioning.

Ultradian rhythms – Biological rhythms with cycles shorter than about 24 hours; may be as short as microseconds.

Ultrasonic – Referring to vibrations whose frequency is above the upper limit of human hearing, greater than approximately 20,000 Hz.

Ultraviolet – Electromagnetic radiation whose wavelength is below that of violet light, i.e., below about 380 nanometers.

Umbilical cord – A thick cord that runs from the fetus, at the point that will become the navel, to the placenta. It transmits nourishment and oxygen from the mother to the growing fetus and carries away the fetus' waste products.

Umweg learning – Detour learning. The subject must learn to move away from a goal in order to get around a barrier that prevents direct access to the goal.

Unconditioned positive regard (Rogers) – Concept involving the idea that a therapist must care about his client without any conditions put on the caring, even when the client reveals things that the therapist is uncomfortable about.

Unconditioned response (UCR) – In classical conditioning, the response elicited automatically, without any training, by the presentation of the unconditioned stimulus (UCS).

Unconditioned stimulus (UCS) – In classical conditioning, a stimulus that can elicit a response in the absence of conditioned learning.

Unconscious – A division of the psyche, the contents of which are at least temporarily (and usually permanently) unknown to the individual. According to Freud, this part of the psyche contains repressed material which is often the cause of human actions.

Unconscious motives – Information that is held in memory and continues to influence responding but is not recognized at a conscious level.

Undoing – Ego-defense mechanism whereby the individual engages in a ritual which is intended to abolish the effect of a previously committed act.

Unimodal – Having only one peak or mode, as opposed to bimodal or multimodal.

Unlearned motives – Innate conditions that initiate, guide and maintain behaviors.

Unlearning – The hypothesis that subsequent learning interferes with earlier learning by dissolving the earlier associations; a deliberate attempt to erase undesirable bad habits.

Unstructured test – A test that allows responses to vary widely to reveal personality.

Uterus – A relatively sophisticated term for what is frequently called the womb; the organ in the mother where fetal development takes place.

Utricle – A saclike structure within the inner ear, which contains receptors sensitive to gravitational pull.

Vacuum activity – Occurrence of behavior in the absence of appropriate stimuli and considered by ethologists to be the result of a high drive state; displacement activity.

Vagus nerve – The tenth cranial nerve, with fibers extending to the heart, lungs, thorax, abdominal viscera, external ear, larynx and pharynx.

Validity – The degree to which a test measures what it is supposed to measure as determined by a criterion.

Value – An abstract concept, often merely implicit, that defines what ends or means to an end are desirable; a general motive relating to one's behavior or goals.

Variability – The extent to which scores in a set of scores are spread out from the average score in the group; common measures are the range and the standard deviation.

Variable – A property, measurement, or characteristic which can take on two or more values; variables can be independent or dependent.

Variable interval schedule – A schedule of reinforcement in which the first response following a given interval of time is reinforced. The length of the time period, however, is changed from trial to trial.

Variable ratio schedule – A schedule of intermittent reinforcement in which every nth response is reinforced, with n varying from trial to trial.

Variable schedules – Partial reinforcement schedules that can change in ratio or interval, usually around some average value.

Variance – Measure of dispersion of scores around some measure of central tendency; the standard deviation squared.

Vasoconstriction – Reduction in the diameter of blood vessels by contraction of the smooth muscles surrounding these blood vessels.

Vasodilation – Increase in the diameter of blood vessels by relaxation of the smooth muscles surrounding these blood vessels.

Vasomotor activity – The activity in the smooth muscles of blood vessels which affects the degree of vasoconstriction and vasodilation of the small blood vessels.

Ventricles – The hollow spaces within the brain which form a continuous channel for the flow of cerebrospinal fluid; includes the lateral, third and fourth ventricles.

Verbal IQ – A special score given by the Wechsler IQ tests as a measure of the ability to deal effectively with words, based on the subtests of information, comprehension, digits forward and backward, arithmetic, similarities, and vocabulary.

Verbal learning – The learning of language, lists of words and wordlike material.

Veridical – Corresponding to objective reality or physical measurement.

Verifiability – The ability of a theory or group of results to be tested by observation or experimentation for veridicality; the ability of an experiment to be repeated yielding similar results.

Verification – The testing and application of hypothesis or theory as the solution to a problem.

Vertical decalage – Term used by Piaget to suggest developmental differences in cognitive ability; that different stages of child development reflect actual differences in cognitive functioning rather than arbitrary divisions along a continuum.

Very short-term memory – Memory for events presented for a very brief time (e.g., 50 milliseconds) which lasts only a second or so; sensory memory including iconic and echoic memory.

Vestibular sacs – Sense organs for perception of balance; enlargements at base of semicircular canals that respond to tilt, the utricle and saccule.

Vestibular sense – The perception of balance; the function of the three semicircular canals, the utricle and the saccule.

Vicarious learning – The experience of observing and understanding another's response and the consequences of that response.

Vicarious reinforcement – Reinforcement that results from observing someone else being reinforced.

Viennese School – The followers of Freud's teachings of psychoanalysis.

Viscerotonia (Sheldon) – A temperamental characteristic associated with the endomorphic body build; a cheerful person seeking a passive, accepting environment.

Visual acuity – Ability to discriminate fine detail in a patterned stimulus.

Visual cliff – An apparent but not actual drop-off designed to test depth perception in infants. It consists of a glass floor over a patterned surface which terminates and immediately continues, but at some distance below the glass. Through the glass a "cliff" is perceived.

Vocal tract – The entire assembly of the organs of speech including the larynx, pharynx, tongue, teeth, lips, nasal passages and mouth.

Vocational tests – Aptitude tests used to predict future performance in a job or career.

von Restorff effect – The tendency of items that are distinct in some way from the other items in a list to "stand out" and thus be more easily learned.

WAIS – Abbreviation for Wechsler Adult Intelligence Scale.

Warm-up – Any of a number of experiences that serve to prepare an organism for performance of a response.

Watson, John B. – Early twentieth-century American psychologist and founder of behaviorism.

Wavelength – The distance between successive peaks in a periodic waveform.

Weber fraction ($\Delta I/I$) – The ratio of the threshold increment to the baseline intensity. It is part of Weber's law that a JND increases with the magnitude of the baseline.

Wechsler Adult Intelligence Scale (WAIS) – An intelligence test, administered individually, and primarily concerned with the assessment of intelligence in adults.

Wechsler-Bellevue – Intelligence test battery, in adult and children's versions, composed of tests for different abilities. Divided into performance tests and verbal tests, it yields a point score which can be converted into an IQ.

Wernicke's area – An area within the temporal lobe of the brain that is involved in language perception. It has connections to memory areas of the brain and damage to the area results in Wernicke's aphasia where language has syntax but no meaning.

Wertheimer, Max – One of the founders of Gestalt psychology.

White matter – Neural tissue in the brain and

spinal cord consisting of axons that are whitish due to the light colored myelin sheath covering them.

White noise – Noise often used in experimentation consisting of a flat spectrum of energy at all frequency levels.

Whole learning – Learning the entire set of materials as a unit rather than by parts.

Whorfian hypothesis – The assumption that the form of expression in a language directs the form of thought processes that develop.

Will therapy – The term applied to the system of psychotherapy developed by Otto Rank in which the patient is encouraged to assert him- or herself and achieve independence, as in the birth trauma.

Within group variance – A measure of the dispersion among subjects in the same group in an experiment as contrasted with the variance which occurs as a result of different experimental conditions.

Within-sex variation – The dispersion of scores for subjects of only one sex.

Within-subject design – An experimental design in which each subject is tested under more than one level of the independent variable.

Word association – A projective technique for eliciting responses to single words. A word is presented and the subject is directed to respond with the first word it makes him think of.

Word-association norms – Tables of the frequency of occurrence of various responses to stimulus words for particular populations such as school children, college students, neurotics, etc.

Work inhibition – A buildup in fatigue due to continuous effort.

Wundt, Wilhelm – The founder of structuralism he also started the first experimental laboratory of psychology at Leipzig.

X chromosome – The chromosome responsible for sex determination. The XX chromosome combination in humans results in a female.

X-Axis – The abscissa or horizontal axis in a graph. By convention the independent variable is plotted on the abscissa.

XXY pattern (Klinefelter's syndrome) – A genetic abnormality once believed to be related to criminal or aggressive behavior.

Y chromosome – A chromosome responsible for sex determination. In humans, a Y chromosome paired with an X results in a male.

Yantra – A visual pattern that can be used in meditation.

Y-axis – The ordinate or vertical axis on a graph. By convention the dependent measure is plotted on the ordinate.

Yerkes-Dodson law – A statement that performance is a curvilinear function of arousal or motivation, showing first an increase and then a decrease as arousal or motivation is increased.

Young-Helmholtz theory – Theory of color vision, holding that there are three kinds of color receptors (cones), each for a different primary color, and that any color experience involves a combination of stimulation of the three types of receptors.

Ypsilanti project – A preschool project based heavily on instructional methodology derived from Piaget.

Z score – The difference between the obtained score and the mean, divided by the standard deviation.

Zeigarnik effect – Better recall of uncompleted than completed tasks, provided that the subject is concerned with the outcome of the task.

Zeitgeber – An event that is indicative of the passage of a particular period of time and that helps to maintain the periodicity of certain physiological functions. Daylight or a new moon are examples of such an event.

Zipf's law – The observation that the frequency of usage of a word in a text times its rank order equals a constant ($f \times r = C$).

Zygote – A fertilized egg cell.

INSTALLING REA's TEST*ware*®

SYSTEM REQUIREMENTS

Pentium 75 MHz (300 MHz recommended), or a higher or compatible processor; Microsoft Windows 98 or later; 64 MB RAM; Internet Explorer 5.5 or higher; minimum 100 MB available hard-disk space; VGA or higher-resolution monitor, 800x600 resolution setting; Microsoft Mouse, Microsoft Intellimouse, or compatible pointing device.

INSTALLATION

1. Insert the GRE Psychology TEST*ware*® CD-ROM into the CD-ROM drive.
2. Installation should start automatically. If this is not the case, choose the RUN command found in the Start Menu. When the RUN dialog box appears, type D:\SETUP (where D is the letter of your CD-ROM drive) at the prompt and click OK.
3. Windows Installer will begin the installation process for the GRE Psychology TEST*ware*®. A dialog box proposing the directory "Program Files\REA\TESTware" will appear. If the name and location are suitable, click OK. If you wish to specify a different name or location, type it in and click OK.
4. Start the GRE Psychology TEST*ware*® application by double-clicking on its icon.

REA's GRE Psychology TEST*ware*® is **EASY** to **LEARN AND USE**. To achieve maximum benefits, we recommend that you take a few minutes to go through the on-screen tutorial on your computer.

TECHNICAL SUPPORT

REA's TEST*ware*® is backed by customer and technical support. For questions about **installation or operation of your software**, contact us at:

> **Research & Education Association**
> **Phone: (732) 819-8880 (9 a.m. to 5 p.m. ET, Monday–Friday)**
> **Fax: (732) 819-8808**
> **Website: http://www.rea.com**
> **E-mail: info@rea.com**

Note to Windows XP Users: In order for the TEST*ware*® to function properly, please install and run the application under the same computer administrator-level user account. Installing the TEST*ware*® as one user and running it as another could cause file-access path conflicts.

580

GRE PSYCHOLOGY SCORE CONVERSION*

TOTAL SCORE

Raw Score	Scaled Score	%†	Raw Score	Scaled Score	%†
217	990	99	108–109	590	78
215–216	980	99	105–107	580	77
213–214	970	99	103–104	570	76
209–212	960	99	99–102	560	75
207–208	950	99	97–98	550	74
204–206	940	99	94–96	540	73
202–203	930	99	91–93	530	72
198–201	920	99	88–90	520	71
196–197	910	98	86–87	510	68
193–195	900	98	83–85	500	64
191–192	890	97	81–82	490	60
187–190	880	97	77–80	480	56
185–186	870	96	75–76	470	52
182–184	860	96	72–74	460	48
180–181	850	95	70–71	450	44
176–179	840	95	66–69	440	40
174–175	830	94	64–65	430	37
171–173	820	94	61–63	420	33
169–170	810	93	59–60	410	30
165–168	800	93	55–58	400	30
163–164	790	92	53–54	390	29
160–162	780	92	50–52	380	23
158–159	770	91	48–49	370	20
154–157	760	91	44–47	360	17
152–153	750	90	42–43	350	15
149–151	740	90	39–41	340	12
147–148	730	90	37–38	330	10
143–146	720	89	33–36	320	9
141–142	710	88	31–32	310	8
138–140	700	87	28–30	300	7
136–137	690	86	26–27	290	6
132–135	680	85	22–25	280	5
130–131	670	84	20–21	270	4
127–129	660	83	17–19	260	3
125–126	650	82	15–16	250	2
121–124	640	81	11–14	240	1
119–120	630	80	9–10	230	0
116–118	620	80	6–8	220	0
114–115	610	79	4–5	210	0
110–113	600	78	0–3	200	0

* Scoring for REA's GRE Psychology practice tests strongly approximates that for the actual test. The GRE itself, however, can change from one edition to the next. Readers should make allowances. For more information, please consult *www.gre.org*.

† Approximate percent of examinees scoring below the scaled score.

ABOUT RESEARCH & EDUCATION ASSOCIATION

Founded in 1959, Research & Education Association is dedicated to publishing the finest and most effective educational materials—including software, study guides, and test preps—for students in middle school, high school, college, graduate school, and beyond.

REA's Test Preparation series includes books and software for all academic levels in almost all disciplines. Research & Education Association publishes test preps for students who have not yet entered high school, as well as high school students preparing to enter college. Students from countries around the world seeking to attend college in the United States will find the assistance they need in REA's publications. For college students seeking advanced degrees, REA publishes test preps for many major graduate school admission examinations in a wide variety of disciplines, including engineering, law, and medicine. Students at every level, in every field, with every ambition can find what they are looking for among REA's publications.

REA's practice tests are always based upon the most recently administered exams, and include every type of question that you can expect on the actual exams.

REA's publications and educational materials are highly regarded and continually receive an unprecedented amount of praise from professionals, instructors, librarians, parents, and students. Our authors are as diverse as the fields represented in the books we publish. They are well-known in their respective disciplines and serve on the faculties of prestigious high schools, colleges, and universities throughout the United States and Canada.

We invite you to visit us at *www.rea.com* to find out how "REA is making the world smarter."

ACKNOWLEDGMENTS

In addition to our authors, we would like to thank Larry B. Kling, Vice President, Editorial, for his overall direction; Pam Weston, Vice President, Publishing, for setting the quality standards for production integrity and managing the publication to completion; John Paul Cording, Vice President, Technology, for coordinating the design and development of REA's TEST*ware*® software; Don Sharpsteen, Ph.D., associate professor of psychology, University of Missouri at Rolla, for ensuring our book's technical accuracy and its conformity with DSM-IV; Amy Jamison, Reena Shah, and Ben Kester for the development, design, and testing of REA's TEST*ware*® software; Rachel DiMatteo, Graphic Designer, for typesetting revisions; and Anne Winthrop Esposito, Senior Editor, for coordinating revisions.